I0890881

Building Mental Resilience in Children:

Positive Psychology, Emotional Intelligence, and Play

Louiza Ioannidou
Frederick University, Cyprus

Agathi Argyriadi
Frederick University, Cyprus

A volume in the Advances in Early Childhood and K-12 Education (AECKE) Book Series

Published in the United States of America by
IGI Global
Information Science Reference (an imprint of IGI Global)
701 E. Chocolate Avenue
Hershey PA, USA 17033
Tel: 717-533-8845
Fax: 717-533-8661
E-mail: cust@igi-global.com
Web site: http://www.igi-global.com

Copyright © 2024 by IGI Global. All rights reserved. No part of this publication may be reproduced, stored or distributed in any form or by any means, electronic or mechanical, including photocopying, without written permission from the publisher.
Product or company names used in this set are for identification purposes only. Inclusion of the names of the products or companies does not indicate a claim of ownership by IGI Global of the trademark or registered trademark.

Library of Congress Cataloging-in-Publication Data

CIP Pending
ISBN: 979-8-3693-8312-4
EISBN: 979-8-3693-8314-8

British Cataloguing in Publication Data
A Cataloguing in Publication record for this book is available from the British Library.

All work contributed to this book is new, previously-unpublished material.
The views expressed in this book are those of the authors, but not necessarily of the publisher.

For electronic access to this publication, please contact: eresources@igi-global.com.

Advances in Early Childhood and K-12 Education (AECKE) Book Series

Jared Keengwe
University of North Dakota, USA

ISSN:2329-5929
EISSN:2329-5937

MISSION

Early childhood and K-12 education is always evolving as new methods and tools are developed through which to shape the minds of today's youth. Globally, educational approaches vary allowing for new discussions on the best methods to not only educate, but also measure and analyze the learning process as well as an individual's intellectual development. New research in these fields is necessary to improve the current state of education and ensure that future generations are presented with quality learning opportunities.

The **Advances in Early Childhood and K-12 Education (AECKE)** series aims to present the latest research on trends, pedagogies, tools, and methodologies regarding all facets of early childhood and K-12 education.

New Approaches in Mobile Learning for Early Childhood Education

Coverage

- Curriculum Development
- Head Start and Pre-K Programs
- K-12 Education
- Learning Outcomes
- Poverty and Education
- Reading and Writing
- Special Education
- Urban K-12 Education

IGI Global is currently accepting manuscripts for publication within this series. To submit a proposal for a volume in this series, please contact our Acquisition Editors at Acquisitions@igi-global.com or visit: http://www.igi-global.com/publish/.

The (ISSN) is published by IGI Global, 701 E. Chocolate Avenue, Hershey, PA 17033-1240, USA, www.igi-global.com. This series is composed of titles available for purchase individually; each title is edited to be contextually exclusive from any other title within the series. For pricing and ordering information please visit http://www.igi-global.com/book-series/advances-early-childhood-education/76699. Postmaster: Send all address changes to above address. Copyright © IGI Global. All rights, including translation in other languages reserved by the publisher. No part of this series may be reproduced or used in any form or by any means – graphics, electronic, or mechanical, including photocopying, recording, taping, or information and retrieval systems – without written permission from the publisher, except for non commercial, educational use, including classroom teaching purposes. The views expressed in this series are those of the authors, but not necessarily of IGI Global.

Titles in this Series

For a list of additional titles in this series, please visit: www.igi-global.com/book-series

Stamatios Papadakis (University of Crete, Greece) and Michail Kalogiannakis (University of Thessaly, Greece)
Information Science Reference • copyright 2024 • 355pp • H/C (ISBN: 9798369323779) • US $195.00 (our price)

Advancing Equity and Inclusion in Early Childhood Education
Amber Friesen (San Francisco State University, USA) Maryssa K. Mitsch (San Francisco State University, USA) and Karina Du (San Francisco State University, USA & University of California, Berkeley, USA)
Information Science Reference • copyright 2024 • 379pp • H/C (ISBN: 9798369309247) • US $195.00 (our price)

Parental Influence on Educational Success and Wellbeing
Ana Maria Gamez (California Baptist University, USA)
Information Science Reference • copyright 2024 • 472pp • H/C (ISBN: 9798369314517) • US $245.00 (our price)

Cultivating Literate Citizenry Through Interdisciplinary Instruction
Chyllis E. Scott (University of Nevada, Las Vegas, USA) Diane M. Miller (University of Houston-Downtown, USA) and Matthew Albert (University of Nevada, Las Vegas, USA)
Information Science Reference • copyright 2024 • 318pp • H/C (ISBN: 9798369308431) • US $235.00 (our price)

Using STEM-Focused Teacher Preparation Programs to Reimagine Elementary Education
Emily Cayton (Campbell University, USA) Miriam Sanders (Texas A&M University, USA) and John A. Williams (Texas A&M University, USA)
Information Science Reference • copyright 2024 • 362pp • H/C (ISBN: 9781668459393) • US $215.00 (our price)

IGI Global
PUBLISHER of TIMELY KNOWLEDGE

701 East Chocolate Avenue, Hershey, PA 17033, USA
Tel: 717-533-8845 x100 • Fax: 717-533-8661
E-Mail: cust@igi-global.com • www.igi-global.com

This book is dedicated to our family and children and to all resilient children, the committed educators, and the supportive families who inspire and motivate us every day.

This book is for you.

Table of Contents

Preface xvii

Chapter 1
Fostering Flourishing: Positive Psychology Principles in Educational Settings ... 1
Eirini Karakasidou, Panteion University, Greece
Konstantinos Karampas, Panteion University, Greece
Anna Papadimitriou, Panteion University, Greece
Christine Athanasiades, Aristotle University of Thessaloniki, Greece

Chapter 2
Applying Positive Psychology in School Settings: Effectiveness and Challenges 38
Katerina Michael, Frederick University, Cyprus
Glykeria Reppa, Neapolis University, Cyprus
Louiza Ioannidou, Frederick University, Cyprus

Chapter 3
Positive Psychology and Special Education: Fostering Hope and Optimism...... 66
Louiza Ioannidou, Frederick University, Cyprus
Dimitrios Koutroumanidis, Frederick University, Cyprus

Chapter 4
Classifying Minds, Framing Well-Being: Bernstein's Sociolinguistic Theory and the Promotion of Mental Health in Inclusive Schools 84
Efthymia Efthymiou, Zayed University, UAE
Dimitra V. Katsarou, University of the Aegean, Greece
Maria Sofologi, University of Ioannina, Greece
Alexandros Argyriadis, Frederick University, Cyprus
Agathi Argyriadi, Frederick University, Cyprus

Chapter 5
Integration of Mindfulness and Emotional Intelligence in School Settings 120
Stephanie Nicolas Pantelides, Frederick University, Cyprus

Chapter 6
A Developmental Critical View of Emotional Intelligence Theories and Programs in the Greek Educational Settings 145
Dimitra V. Katsarou, University of the Aegean, Greece
Georgios A. Kougioumtzis, National and Kapodistrian University of Athens, Greece
Maria Sofologi, University of Ioannina, Greece
Evangelos Mantsos, University of Thessaly, Greece
Efthymia Efthymiou, Zayed University, UAE
Dimitrios Sarris, University of Ioannina, Greece

Chapter 7
The Impact of Inclusive School Climate on Children and Teachers' Well-Being: A Reflection on Psycho-Emotional Empowerment.............................. 171
Dimitra Tasiouli, Frederick University, Cyprus
Olga Lyra, Frederick University, Cyprus

Chapter 8
Building Mental Resilience in Children: The Role of Teachers and the Whole-School Setting 211
Maria Zafiropoulou, Thessaly University, Greece
Agoritsa Psilou, Frederick University, Cyprus

Chapter 9
Nurturing Resilience in Education: Strategies for Students and Teachers......... 243
Eirini Karakasidou, Panteion University, Greece
Anna Papadimitriou, Panteion University, Greece
Danai Chatzidou, University of Kent, UK
Smaragda Kazi, Panteion University, Greece

Chapter 10
Psychological Resilience and the Child With Learning Disabilities 265
Nataly Loizidou Ieridou, Frederick Unversity, Cyprus
Fotini Kyriakides Kranou, Frederick University, Cyprus

Chapter 11
Nurturing Children's Mental Resilience Through Art, Play, and Creativity 285
Maria Athanasekou, University of Athens, Greece

Chapter 12
Exploring Constructive Play: Interactions Within Play-Based Pedagogy 302
Olga Drakopoulou, University of Patras, Greece
Maria Kampeza, University of Patras, Greece

Chapter 13
The Play as a Mediator of Learning and Psychosocial Empowerment of Children With Learning Difficulties 332
Dimitra V. Katsarou, University of the Aegean, Greece

Compilation of References 347

About the Contributors 430

Index 434

Detailed Table of Contents

Preface.. xvii

Chapter 1
Fostering Flourishing: Positive Psychology Principles in Educational Settings ... 1
Eirini Karakasidou, Panteion University, Greece
Konstantinos Karampas, Panteion University, Greece
Anna Papadimitriou, Panteion University, Greece
Christine Athanasiades, Aristotle University of Thessaloniki, Greece

This chapter delves deeply into the impact that incorporating positive psychology principles within educational contexts can have on students' overall growth and well-being. Given the dynamic transformations in the educational landscape, the chapter pushes for the promotion of a broader and more nuanced understanding of student development. The fundamental principles of positive psychology are addressed with an emphasis on the advantageous effects of strengths-based education. The chapter explicates how the identification and cultivation of individual strengths can wield a positive influence on student engagement, motivation, and overall well-being. Moreover, the spotlight is directed towards resilience-building strategies, providing educators with practical insights that will help students navigate the inevitable challenges, setbacks, and failures they will face. Finally, the chapter serves as an excellent resource, providing evidence-based strategies to enrich the educational experience and actively contribute to students' flourishing.

Chapter 2
Applying Positive Psychology in School Settings: Effectiveness and Challenges... 38
Katerina Michael, Frederick University, Cyprus
Glykeria Reppa, Neapolis University, Cyprus
Louiza Ioannidou, Frederick University, Cyprus

This chapter explores the effectiveness and challenges of implementing positive education programs in school settings. It provides an overview of positive psychology, defines well-being, and examines the intersection of positive psychology principles with educational contexts. The chapter also presents various interventions derived from positive psychology used in schools, reviews empirical findings on their efficacy, and addresses implementation challenges. Finally, it offers insights into potential future directions and areas of focus within positive psychology in school settings.

Chapter 3
Positive Psychology and Special Education: Fostering Hope and Optimism...... 66
Louiza Ioannidou, Frederick University, Cyprus
Dimitrios Koutroumanidis, Frederick University, Cyprus

The effects of positive psychology on enhancing educational work, particularly the work of special education teachers, are significant and multifaceted. Positive psychology focuses on enhancing well-being, happiness, and positive emotions, and its application in the educational context is crucial. This study aimed to examine how hope and optimism affect job satisfaction and teachers' relationships with special education students. The research involved 100 teachers working in educational units across Greece. A four-part questionnaire was constructed using the scales of job satisfaction, teachers' hope and optimism, and relationships with students. The results revealed that hope had a statistically significant positive correlation with satisfaction and student-teacher relationships. Also, results highlighted that hope and optimism significantly predict student-teacher relationships. The study results underscore the importance of fostering hope and optimism in special education settings to enhance educators' professional fulfillment and relational dynamics with students.

Chapter 4
Classifying Minds, Framing Well-Being: Bernstein's Sociolinguistic Theory and the Promotion of Mental Health in Inclusive Schools 84
Efthymia Efthymiou, Zayed University, UAE
Dimitra V. Katsarou, University of the Aegean, Greece
Maria Sofologi, University of Ioannina, Greece
Alexandros Argyriadis, Frederick University, Cyprus
Agathi Argyriadi, Frederick University, Cyprus

This chapter focuses on Basil Bernstein's sociolinguistic theory, emphasizing classification and framing, to provide a comprehensive framework for understanding the organization and transmission of knowledge within educational settings. It examines the implications of this theoretical perspective on pedagogic practices and curriculum design, particularly in inclusive schools. The study scrutinizes how knowledge structure impacts students' mental well-being, self-esteem, and confidence. By exploring both visible and invisible curricula, the chapter reveals how educational practices influence students' mental health. Employing a qualitative approach, the chapter synthesizes literature reviews, case studies, and key milestones in educational history. It establishes a theoretical foundation for understanding how classification and framing in education can promote mental health outcomes. Practical recommendations for educators and policymakers are provided to create supportive, inclusive learning environments that nurture students' mental well-being, resilience, and positive connections to learning. This theoretical framework contributes to informed decision-making, advocating for inclusive practices for students with special needs.

Chapter 5
Integration of Mindfulness and Emotional Intelligence in School Settings 120
Stephanie Nicolas Pantelides, Frederick University, Cyprus

This chapter focuses on the integration of mindfulness and emotional intelligence in school settings. Mindfulness refers to the basic human ability to be aware of one's body, mind, and feelings in the present moment. Emotional intelligence refers to the ability to recognize, understand, manage, and respond to one's own and others' emotions. Developing high emotional intelligence in students leads them to better navigate social interactions and manage their emotional responses, which in turn positively affects their academic and personal lives. Mindfulness practices can help manage classroom dynamics, reduce disruptive behavior, and create a positive learning environment. Practicing mindfulness improves our self-awareness, the bedrock of emotional intelligence. Finally, this chapter will not only discuss the strong relationship between mindfulness and emotional intelligence but also the influence of both mindfulness and emotional intelligence on teacher-student relationship quality.

Chapter 6
A Developmental Critical View of Emotional Intelligence Theories and Programs in the Greek Educational Settings 145
Dimitra V. Katsarou, University of the Aegean, Greece
Georgios A. Kougioumtzis, National and Kapodistrian University of Athens, Greece
Maria Sofologi, University of Ioannina, Greece
Evangelos Mantsos, University of Thessaly, Greece
Efthymia Efthymiou, Zayed University, UAE
Dimitrios Sarris, University of Ioannina, Greece

School is considered the natural place for the transmission of knowledge, values, and attitudes, the process of acquiring correct social behavior that will stem from the regulation and understanding of emotions seems challenging. The development of emotional intelligence in the school environment can help students who have integration difficulties, school bullying, intellectual and learning problems, and early dropout. Thus, students create a positive attitude towards lifelong learning, a sense of autonomy, effectiveness, and respect towards teachers. Violence prevention, social service training, the ability to form and maintain relationships are just a few practical uses of learning emotional intelligence in school. The purpose of this chapter is to highlight the importance of the inclusion of emotional intelligence programs in the Greek educational system with the aim of empowering students, the critical presentation of theories under the development spirit, as well as the comparison of existing programs through processes of synthesis and analysis of the literature.

Chapter 7
The Impact of Inclusive School Climate on Children and Teachers' Well-Being: A Reflection on Psycho-Emotional Empowerment.............................. 171
Dimitra Tasiouli, Frederick University, Cyprus
Olga Lyra, Frederick University, Cyprus

This chapter highlights the importance of fostering an inclusive school environment that supports the psycho-emotional well-being of all community members. Increasing awareness among researchers, practitioners, and policymakers underscores the pivotal role of the school experience in promoting mental health for both students and teachers. "School climate" refers to the psychological, social, and physical atmosphere within a school, influencing academic performance, behavior, and well-being. It includes relationships, perceptions of safety, support, control, and shared values. A positive school climate fosters productive learning conditions and engagement, leading to desirable academic and mental health outcomes. Inclusive educational practices ensure all students, regardless of background, have access to quality education and feel supported. This chapter emphasizes the need for schools to adopt inclusive climates, to promote the well-being of students and teachers, addressing interconnected goals of health and education for all.

Chapter 8
Building Mental Resilience in Children: The Role of Teachers and the Whole-School Setting 211
Maria Zafiropoulou, Thessaly University, Greece
Agoritsa Psilou, Frederick University, Cyprus

Literature reports that schools are the appropriate settings to organize and apply activities to promote children's and young people's resilience. Mental resilience is the ability an individual has to cope and succeed in dealing with challenges, misfortune, and adversities. Mental resilience in children is distinguished when they manage to exhibit developmental evolution and positive mental health despite the fact that they are "at risk". Important attributes of resilience in children and young people are enhanced by the whole-school approach and the teachers' work on developing certain skills. The whole school approach consists of a positive school environment, where self-qualities are developed and intervention programs for mental health wellness are delivered. Teachers use a) organizational features such as a sense of optimism, purpose, and school pride and the establishment of effective school-community partnership; b) relational features such as the creation of a supportive and understanding learning environment, the fostering of a positive teacher-student relationship, support school-home relationships, and enhancement of positive peer relationships; c) pedagogical features such as using a well-organised curriculum, applying extra-curriculum activities, and offering information, awareness raising, and advocacy to stimulate children's mental resilience.

Chapter 9
Nurturing Resilience in Education: Strategies for Students and Teachers......... 243
Eirini Karakasidou, Panteion University, Greece
Anna Papadimitriou, Panteion University, Greece
Danai Chatzidou, University of Kent, UK
Smaragda Kazi, Panteion University, Greece

It is well-established that schools should cultivate not only cognitive skills but also skills that help individuals cope with life's challenges. An integrated approach is necessary in the attempt to promote resilience in both students and teachers. For children, the focus is on putting evidence-based strategies into practice that support their emotional health in addition to academic difficulties. It is also crucial to prioritize the psychological resilience of teachers since their role involves a great deal of complexity, which often makes them susceptible to stress and burnout. It has been proven that when teachers are in a state of well-being, it not only enhances their own performance and ability to fulfill their role but also has a direct impact on the well-being and academic performance of their students. Educational institutions can foster an environment that prioritizes the mental well-being of all stakeholders and fosters academic success by attending to the unique requirements of each group.

Chapter 10
Psychological Resilience and the Child With Learning Disabilities 265
Nataly Loizidou Ieridou, Frederick Unversity, Cyprus
Fotini Kyriakides Kranou, Frederick University, Cyprus

Students with learning disabilities (LD) often appear to have low academic performance, experience difficulties in performing academic tasks and avoid engaging in them, consider their own academic and self-regulation skills as inferior to other students with typical performance, have low self-perception and self-esteem, fewer expectations of future success, and experience more emotional and social difficulties than their typically developing peers. However, there is no shortage of studies that characterize the developmental course of many individuals with LD as something that exceeds all expectations. Though recent theories of psychological resilience provide a framework for understanding the complex factors that influence adaptation and general wellbeing within this framework, it is important to look into the individual protective factors in building psychological resilience and psychological well-being in children with learning difficulties. The family and school environment are important factors that contribute to young people's psychosocial development.

Chapter 11
Nurturing Children's Mental Resilience Through Art, Play, and Creativity 285
Maria Athanasekou, University of Athens, Greece

Creativity constitutes the adaptive ability of the individual to face new realities and problems, as well as to produce original and innovative ideas, which is close to the idea of resilience, the capacity to withstand or to recover quickly from difficulties. Studies conducted on the effects of art, the cradle of creativity, on children, showed an increase in mental resilience. Visual creation, art in general, breaks isolation and helps children communicate, to give meaning/content to their experience, to their feelings and fosters harmony in their personality. Art helps children express unpleasant feelings constructively (stress, anger, sadness, frustration). The basic function of art is to objectify feelings so they can be observed and understood. Art as a therapeutic approach through its symbolic expression can help children externalize in the work they create part of their psyche and, thus, reconcile to understand and assimilate facts and experiences and work them out.

Chapter 12
Exploring Constructive Play: Interactions Within Play-Based Pedagogy 302
Olga Drakopoulou, University of Patras, Greece
Maria Kampeza, University of Patras, Greece

Constructive play is a crucial aspect of kindergarten activities, influencing the pedagogy of preschoolers, and has been extensively studied in educational research. However, studies focusing on the relationship between constructive play and the interactions that develop during it are limited. The aim of this systematic review was to investigate the characteristics of interactions during constructive play in kindergarten and their impact on preschoolers' development. The method of this study was a systematic review of the current literature over the past 14 years. A literature search was conducted on Google Scholar, ERIC, Scopus, Elsevier, and PubMed from December 2023 to March 2024, resulting in 18,200 studies (N=18,200). The results indicate that through constructive play, children develop cognitive and thinking skills. The review highlights that constructive play serves as a conduit for initiating learning processes, facilitating language development, aiding in knowledge acquisition, and cultivating essential interactive problem-solving and conflict-resolution skills.

Chapter 13
The Play as a Mediator of Learning and Psychosocial Empowerment of Children With Learning Difficulties 332
Dimitra V. Katsarou, University of the Aegean, Greece

Play and playful forms of development and imitation are placed at the center of the child's early developmental years. Regarding the learning support of children with special learning difficulties in reading, play, and especially the social type of play, contributes to the strengthening of phonological and phonemic processing, but to the practice of phonological awareness, through the phonological decoding of words, into phonemic and syllabic level, through the improvement of vocabulary and through the repetition of words. As a result, there is the restoration of any phonological deficits that make it difficult to process the reading ability, and by extension, the strengthening of reading fluency and accuracy. At the same time, through the play, the above-mentioned skills directly related to reading ability are supported, keeping children's interest in the classroom and minimizing the fatigue caused by frequent repetitions. The purpose of this chapter is to highlight the key role of play in the processes of learning and psychosocial empowerment of children with learning difficulties.

Compilation of References 347

About the Contributors 430

Index 434

Preface

In today's fast-paced, technology-driven world, the mental health and emotional well-being of children have emerged as critical areas of concern. The increasing pressures of academic performance, social interactions, and the omnipresence of digital media are transforming childhood in ways that we are just beginning to comprehend. In light of these changes, it is crucial to provide our children with the necessary resources to effectively navigate life's challenges and flourish in diverse environments. *Building Mental Resilience in Children: Positive Psychology, Emotional Intelligence, and Play* is a comprehensive exploration of strategies and theories aimed at fostering mental resilience among young learners.

This book delves into the interplay between positive psychology, emotional intelligence, and play and how these elements can be harnessed within educational settings to promote mental resilience. By integrating theoretical frameworks with practical applications, this book provides a hands-on, comprehensive and holistic approach to understanding and nurturing children's mental resilience and health.

Building Mental Resilience in Children: Positive Psychology, Emotional Intelligence, and Play is crafted for a diverse audience deeply invested in the holistic development of children. The primary target audience includes educators, school administrators, psychologists, parents, and policymakers who seek to integrate evidence-based strategies for fostering children's mental resilience and overall well-being. Educators and school administrators will find valuable strategies to implement within their classrooms and schools. Special education professionals working with children with special needs will discover strategies to cultivate hope and resilience in their unique educational settings. Psychologists and mental health professionals will gain deeper insights into the application of positive psychology and emotional intelligence in their practices. Parents and caregivers will discover practical advice for supporting their children's emotional growth at home. Policymakers will benefit from the evidence-based recommendations that can inform educational and mental health policies. This book is designed to be an invaluable resource for anyone dedicated to children's mental and emotional well-being, offering a blend of theoretical insights and practical applications to foster a resilient and thriving generation.

In the pages that follow, readers will embark on a journey through a diverse spectrum of topics essential for mental health and resilience promotion. These include fostering positive psychology principles in educational settings and the special education field to empower children's resilience, well-being, and academic success. From nurturing positive teacher-student relationships to implementing resilience-building activities, we provide a comprehensive guide for educators. We explore the significance of fostering positive emotions, engagement, relationships, meaning, and accomplishments in the context of education and discuss practical strategies for educators to implement these concepts. Through the chapters, we explore how inclusive environments that respect and celebrate diversity can enhance the mental resilience of children and promote a safe and supportive school climate. Furthermore, we emphasize the critical role of mindfulness and emotional intelligence in enhancing children's mental resilience and overall well-being. Practical exercises and programs that have been successfully implemented in schools are highlighted, providing educators with actionable insights. Finally, we discuss how art, play, constructive play, and creativity are powerful mediums for fostering mental resilience in children and can be used to express emotions, solve problems, and build social skills.

CHAPTER OVERVIEW

1. Fostering Flourishing: Positive Psychology Principles in Educational Settings

This chapter underscores the impact of positive psychology on student development. It explores strengths-based education and resilience-building strategies, providing educators with practical tools to enhance student engagement and well-being. The chapter highlights how identifying and cultivating individual strengths can positively influence student motivation and overall growth.

2. Applying Positive Psychology in School Settings: Effectiveness and Challenges

This chapter offers a comprehensive overview of positive education programs, addressing both their effectiveness and the challenges of implementation. It reviews empirical findings on various interventions and provides insights into future directions within positive psychology in educational contexts.

3. Positive Psychology and Special Education: Fostering Hope and Optimism

Focusing on special education, this chapter examines the role of hope and optimism in enhancing job satisfaction and teacher-student relationships. It underscores the importance of fostering these positive emotions to improve the educational experience for both teachers and students in special education settings.

4. Classifying Minds, Framing Well-Being: Bernstein's Sociolinguistic Theory and the Promotion of Mental Health in Inclusive Schools

This chapter integrates Bernstein's Sociolinguistic Theory with educational practices, exploring how knowledge organization impacts student well-being. It emphasizes the role of inclusive curricula in shaping students' mental health, self-esteem, and confidence.

5. Integration of Mindfulness and Emotional Intelligence in School Settings

This chapter highlights the benefits of integrating mindfulness and emotional intelligence in schools. It discusses how these practices can improve classroom dynamics, reduce disruptive behavior, and enhance teacher-student relationships, ultimately fostering a positive learning environment.

6. A Developmental Critical View of Emotional Intelligence Theories and Programs in the Greek Educational Settings

This chapter critically examines emotional intelligence programs in Greek schools, highlighting their importance in addressing issues such as bullying, learning difficulties, and early dropout. It emphasizes the need for emotional intelligence development to create a positive and inclusive school environment.

7. The Impact of Inclusive School Climate on Children and Teachers' Well-Being: A Reflection on Psycho-Emotional Empowerment

This chapter explores the significance of an inclusive school climate in promoting the well-being of both students and teachers. It discusses the elements of a positive school climate and how inclusive practices can lead to better academic and mental health outcomes.

8. Building Mental Resilience in Children: The Role of Teachers and the Whole-School Setting

This chapter focuses on the attributes of resilience and the whole-school approach to promoting mental health. It provides insights into how schools can create environments that support the development of resilience in children through targeted activities and teacher involvement.

9. Nurturing Resilience in Education: Strategies for Students and Teachers

This chapter highlights the necessity of promoting resilience in both students and teachers. It presents evidence-based strategies for supporting emotional health and addresses the importance of teacher well-being in enhancing student outcomes.

10. Psychological Resilience and the Child With Learning Disabilities

This chapter examines the unique challenges faced by children with learning disabilities and the factors that contribute to their resilience. It discusses the role of individual protective factors, family, and school environments in fostering psychological well-being.

11. Nurturing Children's Mental Resilience Through Art, Play, and Creativity

This chapter explores how art and creative activities contribute to mental resilience. It highlights the therapeutic benefits of art, helping children express and process emotions constructively, thereby enhancing their resilience.

12. Exploring Constructive Play: Interactions Within Play-Based Pedagogy

This chapter investigates the role of constructive play in early childhood education. It reviews the characteristics of interactions during play and their impact on cognitive and social development, emphasizing play as a vital component of learning.

13. The Play as a Mediator of Learning and Psychosocial Empowerment of Children With Learning Difficulties

This chapter discusses the significance of play in supporting children with learning difficulties. It highlights how play can enhance phonological processing, reading skills, and overall psychosocial empowerment, making learning more engaging and effective.

CONCLUSION

Building Mental Resilience in Children: Positive Psychology, Emotional Intelligence, and Play is a collaborative effort that brings together the expertise of academics, psychologists, educators, psychologists, and researchers. Our goal is to provide a comprehensive resource that not only informs but also inspires and empowers educators to create nurturing environments where all children can thrive. We believe that by integrating positive psychology, emotional intelligence, and play, we can foster a generation of resilient, well-rounded individuals capable of navigating the complexities of the modern world with confidence and grace. As we embark on this journey towards holistic development and well-being for our children, we hope this book serves as a valuable tool for all who are committed to fostering an academically proficient and emotionally and psychologically robust generation. The insights and strategies shared within these pages are an investment in the future, ensuring that our children are equipped with the resilience and skills needed to navigate the complexities of modern life with confidence and competence.

In closing, we would like to extend our gratitude to all the contributors who have shared their expertise, research findings, and insights in this volume. Your dedication to promoting mental resilience and health in children is truly commendable. We also thank IGI Global for their support in bringing this important work to fruition.

Together, let us create a future where mental resilience and health promotion are integral parts of education, paving the way for healthier, happier, and more successful children. We hope this book serves as a valuable guide for educators, parents, and all those involved in the holistic development of children. Working together can build a brighter, more resilient future for our children.

Thank you for embarking on this journey with us.

Louiza Ioannidou
Frederick University, Cyprus

Agathi Argyriadi
Frederick University, Cyprus

Chapter 1
Fostering Flourishing: Positive Psychology Principles in Educational Settings

Eirini Karakasidou
https://orcid.org/0000-0003-2946-8275
Panteion University, Greece

Konstantinos Karampas
https://orcid.org/0009-0003-5191-2077
Panteion University, Greece

Anna Papadimitriou
Panteion University, Greece

Christine Athanasiades
Aristotle University of Thessaloniki, Greece

ABSTRACT

This chapter delves deeply into the impact that incorporating positive psychology principles within educational contexts can have on students' overall growth and well-being. Given the dynamic transformations in the educational landscape, the chapter pushes for the promotion of a broader and more nuanced understanding of student development. The fundamental principles of positive psychology are addressed with an emphasis on the advantageous effects of strengths-based education. The chapter explicates how the identification and cultivation of individual strengths can wield a positive influence on student engagement, motivation, and overall well-being. Moreover, the spotlight is directed towards resilience-building strategies, providing educators with practical insights that will help students navigate the inevitable challenges, setbacks, and failures they will face. Finally, the chapter serves as an

DOI: 10.4018/979-8-3693-8312-4.ch001

Copyright © 2024, IGI Global. Copying or distributing in print or electronic forms without written permission of IGI Global is prohibited.

excellent resource, providing evidence-based strategies to enrich the educational experience and actively contribute to students' flourishing.

INTRODUCTION

Positive psychology has gained prominence in various domains, including education, as teachers recognize the importance of nurturing students' well-being alongside academic achievement. Positive psychology focuses on fostering strengths, positive emotions, resilience, and meaningful connections to promote flourishing individuals and communities. In educational settings, integrating positive psychology principles holds promise for enhancing student engagement, motivation, and overall success. This chapter examines the application of positive psychology principles in educational environments, highlighting their significance and potential benefits for students, educators, and the broader school community.

Positive psychology is a rapidly developing branch of psychological science. The concept of positive psychology was first developed in 1998 when Martin Seligman, a psychology professor and then-president of the American Psychological Association (APA), highlighted the importance of shifting focus from psychopathology to the characteristics and components of human beings that can lead them to develop their well-being. The emergence of the field of positive psychology was deemed significant because, as observed, addressing psychopathology, mental disorders, dysfunctional thoughts and beliefs, and negative emotions does not necessarily mean that an individual can feel happy and secure within their contexts and interactions with others. Specifically, the need for psychology to focus on individuals' skills to enhance their mental health (Seligman & Csikzentmihalyi, 2000) seems to have arisen from the realization that, while the majority of people do not meet the criteria for any mental disorder, they also do not seem to declare themselves as happy (Keyes, 2002). As defined by the World Health Organization (2008), the absence of mental illness does not automatically imply that an individual will feel mentally healthy. The definition of health encompasses simultaneously physical, mental, and social well-being; therefore, positive psychology focuses on improving conditions to achieve the aforementioned (Gable & Haidt, 2005).

Positive psychology, the values it promotes, and its positive interventions are based on principles aimed at the flourishing of individuals. Initially, positive psychology advocates that individuals have the ability to thrive and continuously evolve, provided that there is a suitable framework that allows them and equips them to achieve it. Experiencing positive emotions is independent of experiencing negative ones, and the absence of negative emotions does not automatically imply that the individual will experience positive emotions. However, positive psychology also places equal importance on negative emotions and considers them significant for achieving balance and holistic existence for the individual. It examines the subjective experience and interpretation of emotions by the individual, both positive and negative. The search for meaning is of paramount importance for self-actualization and is an element addressed and studied by positive psychology (Seligman & Csikszentmihalyi, 2000).

Positive psychology, at the individual level, studies character strengths, personal talents and inclinations, courage, wisdom, happiness, etc., while at the group level, it examines variables such as social responsibility, altruism, accountability, etc. (Seligman & Csikszentmihalyi, 2000). At both individual and group levels, positive psychology equally explores relationships with the aim of empowering and shaping them in a more positive way, in order to create healthy and authentic relationships (Buss, 2000).

Although positive psychology constitutes a distinct branch of applied psychology, its existence is significant in all areas of an individual's life, and therefore, research data study its dimensions, such as character strengths, self-compassion, gratitude, positive emotions, positive relationships, and happiness in various fields, such as education, work, health, sports, counseling, at individual, dyadic, and group levels.

The effort to build healthy foundations for children and adolescents is based on the fact that a balanced and good childhood can be a predictor of a balanced adult life. Research data show that traumatic experiences built during childhood, which constitute early life experiences, can play a significant role and lead to depressive symptoms in adult life (Mandelli et al., 2015). For these reasons, there is a need and importance to incorporate the principles of positive psychology and nurture them from childhood based on its principles and values. The family is the primary agent of a child's socialization. However, for most of their childhood and adolescent years, children transition to the school context. School plays a significant role in directly influencing the child. The child's performance, the school climate, the relationships built with peers and educators, the principles taught, and the development of social and emotional skills are components that shape the child's character. Moreover, the phenomenon of intrafamily violence and abuse is often observed within the family context, with significant implications for the child's mental health and academic engagement and performance. Specifically, intrafamily violence can create psychological trauma in the child and hinder the learning experience, contributing to the development of disruptive behavior in school. Therefore, the learning experience and process acquire barriers that prevent the child from developing both academically and as a personality. The role of the school is crucial, and the proper training of teachers is essential in recognizing early signs of intrafamily violence to intervene in protecting the child (Llyod, 2018). Furthermore, childhood and adolescence are age frames where symptoms of mental disorders appear with increasing frequency. Based on research data, 10% of children up to 10 years old exhibit depressive symptoms, while adolescents aged 16 to 17 exhibit mood disorders, anxiety disorders, and substance use disorders at a rate of 20% (Keyes, 2006). Top of Form

Therefore, based on the above, as well as on a meta-analysis conducted in 2017 that collected research data for 15 years, it emerges that a school embracing the principles of positive education can act as a corrective factor and offset negative consequences experienced by students outside the school context (Taylor et al., 2017). Moreover, the school environment aligns with the child's early developmental stages, where it shapes their character and personality, molds the values and principles with which they want to navigate life, teaches them to relate to others, raises existential questions within themselves, and reflects on life choices. Alongside the child and adolescent, beyond their family, is the school as a framework, as well as the individuals within it, the educators, classmates, and the school community. Therefore, the school can serve as the setting where interventions based on the principles of positive psychology are implemented to bring out the strong elements of character, foster positive components such as gratitude, happiness, self-compassion, and build positive relationships so that the student can benefit from the advantages of positive psychology on both academic and personal levels and ultimately live a life that aligns with their value system. Positive education can significantly contribute to achieving this goal.

Foundations of Positive Psychology in Education

A fundamental concept in the field of positive psychology is flourishing. This concept refers to a positive emotional state, a state where mental health is achieved, where there is an absence of mental illness, where individuals experience prosperity and well-being, and successfully achieve their goals at individual, dyadic, and societal levels (Michalec et al., 2009). Positive psychology and positive interventions focus on the flourishing of individuals, as it is observed that in today's era and modern societies, a very small percentage of people, less than 20%, report meeting the criteria for flourishing. Very close to this percentage, there are people who exhibit poor development and mental health. Conversely, the majority of people report having moderate mental health. Positive psychology does not negate negative emotions, nor does it seek to replace them. The coexistence of negative and positive emotions is important for mental balance, and the absence of negative emotions does not necessarily lead to experiencing positive ones (Seligman & Csikzentmihalyi, 2000). The flourishing of individuals is not limited to a specific domain; on the contrary, it is evident and offers significant benefits in all fields and domains. Therefore, the study and cultivation of flourishing are necessary to achieve flourishing at personal, interpersonal, and community levels.

Flourishing is positively associated with many factors in positive psychology, as well as with emotional intelligence, perseverance, emotional regulation, social and emotional skills, and academic success (Howell, 2009). According to Gill (2009), the purpose of the educational system should not be limited to academic boundaries. Education is much more than teaching because a child develops emotional and social skills. Therefore, the goal of education should be the flourishing of the individual and the enhancement of their personality. Moreover, the process of learning is lifelong and not limited to the school context alone. Positive education aims to create safe schools that provide a secure environment for all students to thrive (Huebner et al., 2009).

One of the fundamental models in positive psychology is the PERMA model, developed by Seligman (2011). This model supports the idea that for an individual to live a flourishing life, they need to experience the following elements: Positive emotions, Engagement, Relationships, Meaning, and Accomplishment. Positive emotions encompass not only happiness but also a range of positive feelings such as hope, gratitude, pride, awe, etc. According to Fredrickson (2001), experiencing positive emotions is a significant predictor of flourishing. Experiencing positive emotions is something that can be cultivated and appears to promote behavior activation and the building of new resources, while also mitigating the impact of negative emotions. Through the experience of positive emotions, physical, intellectual, psychological, and social resources are enhanced.

Engagement enhances flow, where the individual is absorbed, lives in the present, and experiences the ideal balance between challenges and skills (Seligman, 2011). Relationships refer to the positive connections an individual builds with the social environment, family, friends, partners, peers, colleagues. Positive relationships are a fundamental element of a flourishing life, as the individual is connected, builds secure attachment bonds, relates positively to others, enhances sharing, and ultimately experiences positive emotions (Seligman, 2011).

Meaning refers to when someone has a purpose in life. Having a purpose in life does not mean that the individual will not experience negative emotions. However, it means that they have defined their value system and, with values and principles as a compass, can navigate through life, commit to their goals, face adversities and challenges encountered along the way (Seligman, 2011).

Finally, accomplishment refers to the achievement of the goals an individual sets. It does not mean that the individual is motivated only by external factors, but often internal motivation and the achievement of these motives (e.g., growth) lead the individual to flourishing and well-being to a greater extent than external factors such as money or material possessions (Seligman, 2011).

Based on this model, many interventions have been implemented in the school context. These interventions have shown that indeed, highlighting and cultivating positive emotions, engagement, positive relationships, meaning, and accomplishment lead to the achievement of well-being in students (Au & Kennedy, 2018; Kern, Adler et al., 2015; Kern, Waters et al., 2015; Lai et al., 2018; Lee et al., 2017). The PERMA model leads to a flourishing life in school, as the student experiences positive emotions, commits to school and extracurricular activities and learning goals, builds positive relationships with classmates and teachers, finds meaning in what they do, and achieves goals. Thus, the student manages to build external resources (e.g., relationships with classmates) and internal resources (e.g., motivation for learning), which help them manage negative emotions such as anxiety and stress, build coping skills, and ultimately lead to higher academic performance (Scales, 1999).

That's why positive psychology has started to be incorporated into schools, now recognized under the terminology of Positive Education. As the role and importance of positive psychology and its benefits in individuals' lives became recognized, interest in Positive Education began to grow. Positive Education is based on Gill's (2009) assertion that the positive development of individuals should be the goal of the educational process and that education should not be limited to the provision of knowledge but should also focus on the recognition, cultivation, and enhancement of virtues and strengths of character, providing tools to cope with the challenges of everyday life. Positive Education, according to Seligman et al. (2009), represents a balance in the interaction and needs of both school and family. Schools mainly focus on the provision and learning of knowledge at the subject level, such as positive sciences (e.g., mathematics, physics, chemistry), history, geography, etc., and the reinforcement of academic skills, while parents desire their children to be happy. Positive Education seems to be the key to bridging this communication gap, as it introduces the values of positive psychology, and through them, enhances the flourishing of students, facilitating the learning process and ultimately leading to academic success.

At this point, it is important to note that Positive Education, its principles, and interventions do not solely concern students. Although the goal of schooling revolves around the student, Positive Education also targets educators, the school community, and students' families. It aims to create a positive climate where all stakeholders can interact positively and empower each other, leading to flourishing (Noddings, 2003). Moreover, Positive Education also focuses on educators. Educators constitute a professional category that annually experiences high rates of professional burnout. Due to burnout, there is a decrease in their cognitive level, psychological state, and behavioral level, negatively impacting their performance, which in turn affects their collaboration with parents and students' performance. Therefore, the goal of Positive Education is to empower educators to acquire the appropriate resources and tools and to build their resilience. This will bring about positive outcomes and advantages not only for educators themselves but also for students, as they are the direct recipients and interact more closely with them.

Towards this direction, the model of Positive Education in Australia is also based. The learning experience is a situation that concerns everyone: students, educators, school staff, families, and the wider community (Green et al., 2011). Moreover, it is emphasized that there is a need to study Positive Education in early childhood education and tertiary education, as research interest primarily focuses on primary and secondary education. With this standpoint, Green et al. (2011) acknowledge that the learning experience is lifelong and that the implementation of Positive Education principles from an early age, within the context of early childhood education, can lay the foundations for Positive Education in the schooling years to come.

As a term, Positive Education has developed more recently. This does not mean that there were no interventions of positive psychology previously, but they were mainly encountered under the term "positive interventions" in schools. Positive Education involves a change in the culture and mindset that governs both the school and society. However, while as terms and fields they have a more recent history compared to other branches of psychology, their history dates back further. The school, as a socialization agent for children, created space for interventions at the level of prevention and addressing phenomena such as the increase in smoking and prevention. Closer to positive interventions were those interventions focusing on emotional intelligence or emotion regulation (Adi et al., 2007). The beginning of the Positive Education movement dates back to the 1970s, where the goal was to enhance self-esteem. Twenty years later, the research interest of school interventions shifted towards the development of social skills, and later resilience became the focus of interventions. Subsequently, due to the increase in phenomena of school bullying, intervention programs focused on addressing and preventing bullying (McGrath, 2009). Later, as the field of positive psychology began to gain ground in the school environment, interventions were designed and implemented focusing on positive elements such as gratitude, positive emotions, etc. The difference between positive interventions in schools and Positive Education lies in the fact that Positive Education not only focuses on enhancing a positive element that leads to well-being but also constitutes a broader culture based on models and principles of positive psychology. However, both positive education and positive interventions within the school framework aim at the well-being of students, educators, and families. Therefore, we often observe that interventions are not conducted exclusively for students but frequently involve the class educators as well. The overarching philosophy of positive education lies in the fact that interventions based on positive psychology, due to the specific timeframe of implementation and the intended goal, have a more systematic nature. We could see them as part of the school and the regular school curriculum. On the other hand, positive education does not have a separate duration; it is ubiquitous. We encounter it in the school timetable, during class time, during breaks, in the relationships among students, in the relationships between students and adults (educators, school leadership, parents), in the relationships between families and schools, and even outside of school, within the community framework.

The promotion of positive psychology in the educational context is based on certain models and fundamental principles aimed at highlighting the principles of positive psychology in the school environment. One of the models of positive psychology is Seligman's PERMA, which was mentioned earlier. Some of the fundamental principles on which positive education is based include character strengths, which is grounded in the theoretical background of Values in Action, and positive relationships. Based on these principles, various interventions and activities have been designed in the school environment. These principles, as well as certain activities, will be analyzed in the next section.

KEY POSITIVE PSYCHOLOGY PRINCIPLES IN EDUCATION

Character Strengths

Based on the theoretical framework of the Values in Action (VIA) classification, character is described as a set of positive characteristics manifested in thoughts, emotions, and behaviors and considered to lead to a good life (Peterson & Seligman, 2004). The VIA classification proposes a hierarchical structure of character in which 24 character strengths are organized under six broad virtues: (1) wisdom and knowledge (encompassing the character strengths of creativity, curiosity, judgment, love of learning, and perspective), (2) courage (i.e., bravery, perseverance, honesty, and zest), (3) humanity (i.e., love, kindness, social intelligence), (4) justice (i.e., teamwork, fairness, and leadership), (5) temperance (i.e., forgiveness, humility, prudence, and self-regulation), and (6) transcendence (i.e., appreciation of beauty and excellence, gratitude, hope, humor, and spirituality). The strength-based approach prioritizes a person's or group's positive characteristics over its negative ones. Moreover, the strength-based education approach starts with what is present rather than what is missing and represents a paradigm shift—a move away from a deficit-based approach, which can result in a long list of things deemed 'wrong' with a child's learning and development, or things a child is incapable of performing.

Strength-based education is a learner-centered approach to teaching that assists students in identifying their individual strengths, which should be articulated and implemented in accordance with their learning objectives (Lopez & Louis, 2009; Spiteri, 2016). Research suggests that character strengths are present in young children (Park & Peterson, 2006) and may be reliably and validly measured using self-reports beginning at the age of ten (Park & Peterson, 2006; Ruch et al., 2014). Research also emphasizes the dynamic, complex, and holistic nature of student learning, and supports the effectiveness of strengths-based approaches in promoting enjoyment at school, academic success, and well-being outcomes such as hope and positive coping (Madden et al., 2011; Seligman et al., 2005; Seligman et al., 2009; Waters, 2015; White & Waters, 2015). Moreover, strengths-based approaches can help teachers identify what motivates and inspires students, which has been connected to increased student engagement (Madden et al., 2011).

Lopez and Louis (2009) identified five strengths-based education principles that teachers may use to create learning experiences that increase student engagement, well-being, retention, and career preparation:

- In addition to the typical focus on academic achievement and behavioral data, strengths evaluations are utilized to measure student (and teacher) characteristics (Schreiner, 2013).
- Design personalized learning experiences that allow students to capitalize on their strengths by providing a variety of options for demonstrating and assessing knowledge.
- Help students connect with strength supporters by offering mentorship opportunities or forming cohort-based class collaborations that provide peer support and feedback.
- Create opportunity for students to build and integrate new strengths. Help students develop new strengths by providing opportunities for them to study and practice emerging behaviors. Help students connect their strengths, personal goals, and areas for development so that they can gain confidence, autonomy, and a sense of belonging.
- Advise on strengths development: Encourage students to take responsibility for developing their strengths via deliberate practice and involvement. Advise students on how to develop their strengths by developing new tactics or accessing previously unassessed resources. Conduct one-on-one consolations or one-minute reflection sheets to help students identify their talents.

Positive Relationships

Attachments throughout the formative years have a significant impact on the quality of relationships later in life (Bowlby, 1958, 1982). Furthermore, warm and responsive early interactions are linked to improved psychosocial functioning (Gerhardt, 2015). In this regard, positive relationships between students and teachers have long been considered a foundational aspect of a positive school experience

(Brophy, 1998). In the teaching context, research has shown that teachers' happiness and well-being are related to student well-being and performance (Kun & Gadanecz, 2022). Meta-analyses have consistently shown that positive, warm, and supportive teacher-student relationships are associated with higher student achievement (Cornelius-White, 2007; Roorda et al., 2011, 2017), student cognitive skills (Vandenbroucke et al., 2018), students' sense of school belonging (Allen et al., 2018), and fewer behavioral problems (Lei et al., 2018). Moreover, the student-teacher relationship is considered as an important influencer to teachers' emotional well-being and personal accomplishment (Corbin et al., 2019). A literature review found that high-value teacher-student relationships help teachers avoid emotional fatigue by increasing enthusiasm and decreasing exhaustion (Cui, 2022). Furthermore, teacher-student interaction quality and student engagement have also been identified as school quality indicators (Moreira et al., 2021).

In light of growing systemic pressures on the teaching profession, interventions for relationship building with students that can be integrated into daily school life and incorporated in existing practices are important (Allen & Kern, 2019). In this context, Cook et al. (2018) found that even small interventions such as a teacher greeting students at the door can boost student engagement by 20%. Moreover, Pedlar (2018) proposed the following strategies for fostering positive student-teacher relationships:

- Prioritize strong teacher-student connections.
- Create an environment in the classroom and school grounds that is both encouraging and nurturing for students.
- Provide students with emotional support.
- Be mindful to students' emotions and needs.
- Show children that you care about them.
- Make an attempt to understand students' opinions.
- Maintain courtesy and treat others equally.
- Create a sense of belonging among students by encouraging healthy peer relationships and mutual respect.
- Promote positive classroom management.

Furthermore, Allen and Kern (2019) recommended two brief activities to assist teachers develop a positive relationship with their students:

Activity 1: Radio Show Host

Purpose: Help students get to know more about their teachers.
Materials: Pen and paper

Suggested time for completion: 30-40 minutes

Introduction

Students often know very little about the lives of their teachers, and some self-disclosure (within professional limits) can enhance the student-teacher relationship. In this activity, students pretend to be radio hosts and ask teachers questions to find out more information about them. This activity can be fun with you as the interviewee or by bringing in another teacher or counselor. At its core, this activity aims to allow students to see teachers as "real people."

Instructions

Ask your students to imagine that they are radio show hosts, doing a "get to know you" segment on their show. The goal is to interview one of their other teachers. Ask students to choose a teacher they do not know a lot about.

Ask the student to think about what questions they would want to ask a teacher. What would they want to find out? Give them time to come up with a list of questions, offering some suggestions as needed.

If you are working with a group, it can be fun if they interview you or, alternatively, bring in a colleague. Give students time to brainstorm ideas and come together to share their responses with one another, coming up with a final set of questions.

If you are the interviewee, have fun with this. Let students ask questions, be a bit vulnerable, and show that you are a real person. This can be a bit scary but helps give students a sense of you as a real person.

For other teachers, if possible, bring them in and let the students interview them, using the questions they came up with. If others are not available, encourage the students to follow up over the next week and interview a teacher with their list of questions, reporting back on their findings the next week.

Activity 2: About Me

Purpose: Get to know more about each student.
Materials: Pen and paper
Suggested time for completion: 20-30 minutes

Introduction

Strong student-teacher relationships involve teachers who understand and know their students. So, teachers need to know their students as individual people—what they like, what they dislike, who they are as a person. It's hard to support students you don't know. You might guess, but it's helpful to know firsthand from their perspective. This exercise helps students proactively show their teacher who they are by telling a bit more about themselves in a letter.

Instructions

Ask your students to write a letter to a teacher they would like to build a stronger relationship with. Guide students to let them know who they are, what they like, what they don't like, and what they would like to achieve from their class. Students should also mention what they like best about the teacher they are writing to.

Mindfulness and Well-Being

According to Kabat-Zinn (1994), mindfulness is the intentional focus on the present moment, whereas Davis and Hayes (2011) define mindfulness as a moment-to-moment awareness of one's experience while being curious, open, and accepting of both positive and painful experiences without judgment. The emphasis here is on perceiving and accepting things as they are, rather than attempting to alter them. Moreover, Saltzman (2010) defines mindfulness as the practice of paying attention here and now, with kindness and curiosity, so that we can choose our behavior. Saltzman (2010) emphasizes the importance of gradually implementing mindfulness, starting with small activities and gradually learning how to use practice in extreme situations, which will develop with increased reinforcement and repetition and facilitate one's P.E.A.C.E., an acronym that stands for pause, exhale, acknowledge (accept and allow), choose, and engage. Mindfulness can be practiced through a range of formal and informal ways. Meditations in which you sit or lie down are considered formal practices. Mini-meditations throughout the day, as well as bringing awareness to and stepping out of "autopilot" mode while performing daily duties, are examples of informal practices.

Over the last decade, mindfulness has been increasingly popular in schools as research shows that it has a beneficial psychological effect on both students and teachers (Emerson et al., 2017). A recent meta-analysis of educator well-being initiatives found that mindfulness not only had the most robust evidence base, but it was also the only intervention that caused sustained changes in educator well-being three to five months after delivery (Berger et al., 2022). Mindfulness is also increasingly being included into school-wide social-emotional learning and curriculum. Examples include Mindful Schools (Brensilver et al., 2020), A Still Quiet Place (Saltzman, 2014), and Learning to Breathe (Broderick, 2013). These programs' specific components vary, but they all involve approaches for reducing stress and improving social-emotional skills and self-regulation through increased attention and self-awareness.

Thus, mindfulness can be considered not only as an intervention to address specific areas of difficulty, but also as a broad strategy to promoting healthy social-emotional development (Meiklejohn et al., 2012; Ritter & Alvarez, 2020; Schonert-Reichl et al., 2016.) reviewed the literature on mindfulness in schools and found that it improved attention (Bögels et al., 2008), reduced anxiety and problem behavior (Biegel et al., 2009; Sibinga et al., 2011; Zylowska et al., 2008), reduced stress and improved well-being (Jain et al., 2007). Similarly, Semple et al. (2017) examined 10 mindfulness programs in K-12 schools and they found that each had positive outcomes, ranging from improved grades, increased attention and awareness, more regulated responses to stress, and an improved school climate to fewer social and aggressive problems, behavioral referrals, and occurrences of bullying. Notably, Mendelson et al. (2010) identified improved self-regulatory capacities and a reduction in activation and persistent or ruminative thoughts as processes driving mindfulness's good results for youth. Moreover, Phan et al. (2022) found that mindfulness-based school interventions (MBSIs) improved prosocial behaviors, executive functioning skills, resilience, attention, and mindful awareness while decreasing anxiety, attention problems/ADHD behaviors, and conduct problems.

Mindfulness training also can enhance well-being and help with the socially, emotionally, intellectually, and physically demanding components of the teaching profession (Tsang et al., 2021). In a review of studies on teaching mindfulness to teachers, Emerson et al. (2017) showed that interventions tended to produce positive results by improving teachers' emotional regulation. More recently, Matiz et al. (2020) investigated the impact of a mindfulness meditation course on teachers' mental health before and during the COVID-19 outbreak, discovering significant improvements in anxiety, depression, affective empathy, emotional exhaustion, psychological well-being, interoceptive awareness, positive character traits, and mindfulness.

Bell Meditation

The ringing of the bell can be a great invitation to practice mindfulness. Luckily, on campus, you can always depend on a bell — the school bell.

When the school bell rings, take just a few seconds to breathe in and out mindfully. Just 3 breaths are enough to bring your stress levels down and ground you in the present moment. Often, we are triggered into immediate action when we hear any bell ring. But try to remind yourself that you have enough time to breathe in and out 3 times before rushing.

You can invite your students to participate in this mindfulness activity with you as well. For example, when the lunch bell rings, take 3 breaths together as a class before rushing out of the classroom.

UCLA Mindful Awareness Research Center

Moreover, the UCLA Mindful Awareness Research Center provides an open access introduction to mindfulness meditation.

Growth Mindset

Non-cognitive elements such as students' beliefs, attitudes, and values all have an impact on their academic success. One crucial non-cognitive aspect is students' ideas about the degree to which intelligence is a fixed attribute, known as "mindset" (Dweck, 1999). Students who believe intelligence is a stable, immutable attribute are considered to have a "fixed mindset" and are more prone to take struggle or failure as evidence that they are not intellectually capable of achieving (Dweck, 1999). Thus, students with a fixed mindset are more likely to avoid challenges, quit easily, and ultimately attain lower academic achievement (Dweck, 1999; Smiley et al., 2016). Students who feel that intelligence is a changeable trait that can be improved with work and supervision are considered to have a "growth mindset." These students are more likely to take on difficult activities and persevere through problems by experimenting with new tactics or increasing effort, ultimately leading to greater academic performance (Dweck, 1999; Smiley et al., 2016).

Students' mindsets are important because they influence a variety of other non-cognitive factors, including the types of goals they set (Dweck & Leggett, 1988), how they attribute their successes and struggles (Dweck, 1999; Smiley et al., 2016), and how they deal with challenges (Heine et al., 2001). Moreover, studies have shown that fostering a growth mindset enhances academic resilience and achievement (Dweck, 2006). Given the broad implications of mindsets, it is critical to understand how and why students' mindsets develop and change throughout time.

Researchers have studied the aspects that determine how young students form mindsets (Dweck, 1999; Kamins & Dweck, 1999; Mueller & Dweck, 1998). Their findings show that the way educators and parents reward youngsters convey implicit cues about the nature of intelligence. Praising a student's attributes (e.g., intelligence) implies that success is the result of their innate traits and encourages a fixed mindset, whereas praising students' processes (e.g., effort) implies that success is the result of their behaviors and encourages a growth mindset (Dweck, 1999; Kamins & Dweck, 1999).

Fostering a growth mindset in the classroom is a sophisticated and multifaceted process that involves purposeful effort and careful incorporation into daily teaching methods. By incorporating these strategies into the classroom, teachers may foster an environment in which students view problems as opportunities, love the learning process, and believe in their own ability to progress. These techniques not only improve academic performance, but also encourage students to approach life with an attitude of constant growth and development.

Main (2022) synthesized ten strategies that teachers can use to assist students develop this empowering mindset:

- Engage Students Through Challenges: Encourage students to embrace challenges by portraying them as exciting learning opportunities. For example, a teacher might present a complex problem as a thrilling puzzle to be solved, emphasizing the joy of discovery rather than the difficulty of the task.
- Normalize Struggle: Emphasize that struggle is a natural and essential part of the learning process. By sharing personal examples of overcoming challenges or highlighting famous individuals who succeeded through perseverance, teachers can make struggle a positive and expected aspect of growth.
- Stay Positive: Utilize positive language to reinforce growth. For example, adding the word "yet" to statements like "You're not good at math yet" conveys a belief in potential and ongoing development.
- Indicate Errors and Celebrate Corrections: According to Social Psychology Theory, errors should be embraced as learning opportunities. Teachers can model this by openly discussing their own mistakes and the steps taken to correct them.
- Highlight Brain Plasticity: Teach students about the malleable nature of the brain, emphasizing that intellectual abilities can be developed and strengthened. This understanding can foster a belief in personal growth and improvement.
- Set Incremental Objectives: Encourage students to set achievable, step-by-step goals. This approach demonstrates that progress is attainable and builds confidence in their ability to succeed.

- Promote Group Work: Encourage collaboration and emphasize the process of finding solutions. This approach reduces the focus on individual outcomes and fosters a collective growth mindset.
- Offer Challenges to Overcome Barriers: Engage students in complex tasks that stretch their abilities, providing support and encouragement as they work through challenges. This approach fosters resilience and a willingness to tackle difficult problems.
- Avoid Oversimplifying: Be mindful of statements like "You can achieve anything!" While well-intentioned, without the context of effort and struggle, such statements can lose credibility and undermine the growth mindset.
- Don't Praise Intelligence Alone: Focus praise on effort, strategies, and progress rather than innate intelligence.

Implementation Strategies

Aristotle have considered happiness to be the end goal of education (Kristjansson, 2012). Psychology and education share an inherent connection since education is fundamentally about developing strengths, growth, and learning. Moreover, psychological and social well-being are major considerations for teachers and other educators, as well as those working in the field of positive psychology (Shankland & Rosset, 2017). Employing Positive Psychology Interventions (PPIs) in educational contexts focuses on promoting the positive aspects of mental health and well-being through school-based psychological interventions (Dawood, 2013; Shankland & Rosset, 2017; Waters, 2011). Positive psychology school-based interventions, while diverse and varied, share a common goal of improving young people's developmental trajectory and preventing future difficulties by teaching skills to encourage positive self-perceptions, emotions, and behaviors (Galassi & Akos, 2004; Kuperminc et al., 2011).

Research has revealed that PPIs have a positive impact on student and teacher well-being and mental health (Durlak et al., 2011; Hwang et al., 2017; Neil & Christensen, 2009; Shankland & Rosset, 2017; Sin & Lyubomirsky, 2009; Waters, 2011). However, in order to have a significant and broad effect, evidence-based interventions must be put into practice in schools (Mohammadi et al., 2010; Sanetti et al., 2014). Awareness of existing school-based interventions and programs is an important first step for teachers looking to implement such initiatives in their classrooms (Castro-Villarreal et al., 2014). Moreover, teachers must identify the need for an intervention, understand the program's expected objectives, and believe that students will benefit (Baker-Henningham & Walker, 2009; Durlak & DuPre, 2008). Teachers must also assess if the benefits for children outweigh the time and resources required to implement an intervention (Fabiano et al., 2014). Following the decision to initiate a school-based initiative, teachers' mindset might influence program implementation (Borrelli, 2011; Mohammadi et al., 2010). In this regard, teachers with a positive mindset are more likely to administer a larger and higher-quality program than their less optimistic peers. Teachers will also put more effort into implementation if they 'buy in' to the program's premise and believe it is valuable (Forman et al. 2009). Castro-Villarreal et al. (2014) identified three major characteristics influencing teacher implementation quality: motivation, knowledge, and desire to participate in the process. Just as self-belief is critical for student success, research has shown that a teacher's confidence in their own ability to successfully implement new programs is directly related to implementation fidelity and student outcomes (Durlak & DuPre, 2008; Sanetti et al., 2013).

Ultimately, the key to facilitating integration and successful implementation of positive psychology interventions in schools may be the widespread dissemination of teacher-targeted information and high-quality teacher-training programs (Ahuja, 2012; Bradshaw et al., 2009; Evans et al., 2015; Nielsen et al., 2015). According to Durlak & DuPre (2008), simply developing an intervention and expecting it to be broadly implemented is insufficient. Rather, researchers must understand their target market by understanding the obstacles and barriers inherent in school-based initiatives (Mohammadi et al., 2010), taking a larger role in the dissemination of research findings in forms accessible and appropriate for teachers (Ahuja, 2012), and providing ongoing support and assistance with implementation (Castro-Villarreal et al., 2014).

Implementing Positive Psychology in Schools

Research on positive psychology in schools has demonstrated the effectiveness of these classroom interventions in identifying, valuing, and cultivating empathy, optimism, creativity, self-efficacy, and resilience (Boniwell & Tunariu, 2019; Cefai & Cavioni. 2015; Vella - Brodrick, 2011). The following is a brief description of a handful of these school-based programs.

Penn Resiliency Program (PRP)

The Penn Resiliency Program (PRP) (Seligman, 2011) is a school-based group intervention that aims to increase students' resilience while also encouraging realistic thinking and adaptive coping skills. Students are taught skills and coping methods that are intended to contribute to a variety of resilience characteristics, including emotional intelligence and flexible and accurate thinking. Participants also learn methods for positive social behavior, such as assertiveness and negotiating (Boniwell & Tunariu, 2019). Brunwasser et al.'s (2009) meta-analysis of 17 research indicated that young people who participate in PRP programs often have decreased levels of depression symptoms following the intervention, with these effects becoming more robust over a 12-month follow-up period.

SPARK Resilience Program

SPARK is a school-based resilience curriculum built around cognitive-behavioral therapy and positive psychology interventions that aims to promote emotional resilience and related abilities while also preventing depression. The SPARK Resilience program has been widely adopted in the UK, France, the Netherlands, Japan, and Singapore. The approach, organized around the SPARK acronym, divides responses to stressful events into five components: situation, perception, autopilot, reaction, and knowledge (Boniwell & Tunariu, 2019). In the SPARK Resilience program, students explore hypothetical situations to better understand how their perceptions can trigger their autopilot (emotional responses such as anger, fear, or joy). They then learn to recognize their behavioral responses while reflecting on what they have learned. Moreover, students learn to recognize and apply their strengths while also developing problem-solving abilities and, eventually, resilience (Boniwell & Tunariu, 2019). A study assessing the effects of the SPARK program on depression symptoms and resilience in a high-risk group of 11 to 13-year-old students in England (N = 438) found that depression symptoms decreased immediately after the intervention and at a six-month follow-up. At post-treatment and follow-up assessments, the treatment cohort had considerably higher resilience scores than the control cohort. Furthermore, the intervention was thought to foster empathy and enhance relationships between students and teachers, which extended beyond the classroom to the whole school climate (Pluess et al., 2017).

The Hummingbird Project

Multi-component Positive Psychology Interventions (mPPIs) in secondary schools have been found to improve youth mental health outcomes (Platt et al., 2020). The Hummingbird Project mPPI is a six-week workshop program that introduces positive psychology (PP) concepts to secondary school students in order to improve their well-being, resilience, and hope (Platt et al., 2024). In session 1 of the Hummingbird Project mPPI, students and teachers were introduced to the mPPI, which was followed by a discussion of what happiness meant to each individual in the group. Sessions 2–5 featured a variety of positive psychology principles and activities, exploring the following concepts: happiness, hope, resilience, mindfulness, character strengths, growth mindsets, and gratitude. During each session, students participated in a variety of activities aimed at helping them comprehend and apply these principles in their daily lives, as well as a homework assignment to help them understand how each concept might benefit their own mental health. The last session included a review of the themes covered in prior sessions, as well as recommendations for students on how to apply these concepts in their future life (Platt et al., 2024). The implementation of the program in secondary school-aged children (N = 614; mean age = 11.46 years) from a sample of secondary schools located across the North West of England (N = 7) showed significant improvements associated with the mPPI in well-being (as measured by the World Health Organization Well-Being Index; WHO-5), hope (as measured by the Children's Hope Scale; CHS), and symptoms of mental distress (as measured by the Young Person's Clinical Outcomes in Routine Evaluation; YP-CORE) from pre- to post-intervention (Platt et al., 2024).

Best Possible Selves

Research suggests that the simple act of reflecting on the positive or imagining a desired future goal can improve wellbeing (Froh et al., 2008, 2009; Owens & Patterson, 2013; Suldo et al., 2014). In the Owens & Patterson (2013) study, elementary school-aged children (N = 62, ages 5-11 years) attended once-weekly intervention sessions in which they were asked to draw a picture of something for which they were grateful that day (gratitude condition), a future version of themselves as happy and engaged (best possible selves' condition), or something they had done that day (control condition). The gratitude condition produced the same results as the control condition; however, students who spent the week imagining their best possible self, had an increase in self-esteem as measured by the Perceived Competence Scale for Children (Harter, 1982).

MARKERS Wellbeing Program for Educators

Positive psychology literature is increasingly recognizing the importance of relational and contextual factors on well-being (Kern et al., 2020; Lomas, et al., 2021). Given the paucity of whole-school approaches to wellbeing (Waters & Loton, 2019), interventions to increase educator wellbeing must place a greater emphasis on the relational and contextual elements that influence wellbeing (Cann et al., 2024a). In this sense, MARKERS (Multiple Action Responsive Kit for Educator, Relational, and School Wellbeing) is a multi-level educator well-being program that incorporates individual, relational, and contextual aspects. Its multi-foci design also enabled context-specific adaptations such as gratitude exercises, active constructive response, and workload case studies (Cann et al., 2024a, 2024b). The MARKERS program consisted of seven 1-hour sessions at 2-week intervals in school term time (Cann et al., 2024b). The session themes include: (1) introduction; (2) wellbeing definitions and models; (3) stress coping strategies, stress mindset, and the stress cycle; (4) gratitude and appreciation; (5) active constructive responding; (6) workload in schools; (7) recap and forward planning. Participants in the MARKERS educator wellbeing program reported a considerable improvement in their relational space when it was introduced at one Aotearoa New Zealand school (Cann et al., 2024b).

Teacher Training and Professional Development

Enhancing teachers' personal and relational wellbeing has been considered important to teacher retention and work performance (See et al., 2020). A recent study indicates that PPIs can improve teachers' emotional and social well-being, work-life balance, and work practices (Yeh & Barrington, 2023). Research also emphasizes the value and effectiveness of mindfulness training for pre-service teachers' well-being, stress management, and professional growth (Soloway, 2016). Moreover, the positive psychology paradigm provides resources and personal qualities to improve well-being and mental health, such as character strengths, optimism, self-efficacy, and self-esteem (Peterson et al., 2007; Seligman, 2002).

Several studies have found a significant correlation between character strengths and well-being (Sheldon, 2019). According to a systematic review, interventions focusing on character strengths positively contribute to increasing teachers' work resources such as job satisfaction, teacher engagement, and lowering psychological-occupational risks such as burnout (Dreer, 2020; Ronaldson et al., 2014). Furthermore, optimism is a positive psychological resource that has been studied as a protective factor for well-being and physical health (Scheier & Carver, 1985). Optimism is a psychological trait or a tendency of people to expect positive outcomes from life events, resulting in a positive appraisal on life (Scheier & Carver, 1985). Optimism and self-efficacy have been identified as career enhancers for teachers due to their effect on career flexibility, and both are considered learning-sensitive intervention paths (Bandura, 1989). Self-efficacy beliefs are another important psychological factor that influences the development of well-being. Self-efficacy belief is defined as a belief in one's own ability to accomplish a task effectively, with implications for motivation, control, and reinforcement of behavior based on intended performance (Klassen & Tze, 2014). In this regard, research on teachers has found that personality traits and self-efficacy are highly linked to quality teaching performance (Huang et al., 2019). Self-efficacy is a crucial resource associated with teacher satisfaction, well-being, and effective handling of job demands (Kelley et al., 2020). Moreover, studies have shown that professional development interventions, particularly those based on positive psychology, might boost teacher self-efficacy (Baumeister et al., 2003; Critchley & Gibbs, 2012). Furthermore, various studies on teachers have shown that high levels of self-esteem are associated with reduced levels of burnout

(Méndez et al., 2020; Pereira et al., 2021), fewer negative emotions, and better coping of stress and daily demands (Adalsteinsson et al., 2014). Teachers with poor self-esteem are more susceptible to developing illnesses and psychological problems such as worry or stress (Méndez et al., 2020). Thus, teachers should be able to build on their strengths, self-esteem, self-efficacy, and optimism as work resources and protective factors of psychological well-being, all of which are associated with effective teaching performance (Song, 2022).

CONCLUSION

Positive psychology principles provide valuable frameworks for promoting well-being and academic success in educational settings. By incorporating strengths-based approaches, fostering growth mindsets, and nurturing positive relationships, educators can create supportive learning environments that empower students to thrive. Data from studies conducted have shown the benefits of positive education and positive psychology interventions in the school setting, with significant advantages for children, adolescents, the school community, and families. Cultivating principles and values based on positive psychology lays healthy foundations for a happy life and prepares children to cope with the challenges and demands of the school environment, as well as beyond it. Fostering positive elements helps combat undesirable behaviors such as school bullying, racism, and abuse. Therefore, by addressing these negative behaviors, it protects individuals from experiencing the adverse consequences they entail, which can have serious implications for mental health.

Positive psychology interventions lay the groundwork for cultivating positive components, which equip individuals and serve as significant resources for personal development in cognitive, emotional, and social contexts. The literature review presented in the previous chapters indicates that fostering positive elements, positive relationships and a growth mindset benefit students academically as well as in other areas of their lives. Thus, positive education aligns with the goals of the educational process, which aim for individuals to flourish into integrated and healthy personalities on physical, mental, and social levels.

Learning is a lifelong process that extends beyond school years and is not limited to a specific curriculum or timetable. Within the school environment, students can acquire knowledge through experience, contact, and interaction with educators and peers. Nonetheless, the school represents a microcosm of society and reflects its principles. As society consists of active citizens, cultivating positive elements through positive education can lead to a positive society. However, it's important to recognize that in today's era, there are constantly emerging challenges, such as children and adolescents exhibiting symptoms of mental disorders or the rapid increase in technology, which, despite its benefits, has brought some difficulties like cyberbullying. Schools need to be vigilant and promptly identify undesirable behaviors to intervene preventively and remedially. As developments constantly emerge, societies become multicultural, and new needs arise, positive education plays a significant role in protecting children and facilitating their development into integrated, human entities. Therefore, it's crucial to continuously conduct research and interventions, addressing emerging needs and studying their effectiveness in cognitive, emotional, and social dimensions. Finally, even though benefits continue to emerge after the completion of interventions, further research is needed to explore the long-term effects of positive psychology interventions in educational contexts.

REFERENCES

Adalsteinsson, R. I., Frímannsdóttir, I. B., & Konrádsson, S. (2014). Teachers' self-esteem and self-efficacy. *Scandinavian Journal of Educational Research*, 58(5), 540–550. 10.1080/00313831.2013.773559

Adi, Y., Killoran, A., Janmohamed, K., & Stewart-Brown, S. (2007). *Systematic review of the effectiveness of interventions to promote mental wellbeing in children in primary education. Report 1: Universal approaches: non-violence related outcomes. Database of Abstracts of Reviews of Effects (DARE)*. Quality-assessed Reviews.

Ahuja, S. (2012). Research Results for Quality Schooling: Bridging the Gap between Research and Practice. *MIER Journal of Educational Studies. Trends and Practices*, 2(2), 206–214. 10.52634/mier/2012/v2/i2/1570

Allen, K. A., Jamshidi, N., Berger, E., Reupert, A., Wurf, G., & May, F. (2021). Impact of school-based interventions for building school belonging in adolescence: A systematic review. *Educational Psychology Review*, 1–29. 10.1007/s10648-021-09621-w

Allen, K.-A., Kern, M. L., Vella-Brodrick, D., & Waters, L. (2018). Understanding the Priorities of Australian Secondary Schools Through an Analysis of Their Mission and Vision Statements. *Educational Administration Quarterly*, 54(2), 249–274. 10.1177/0013161X18758655

Allen, K.-A., & Kern, P. (2019). *Boosting school belonging in adolescents: Interventions for teachers and mental health professionals*. Routledge. 10.4324/9780203729632

Allen, K.-A., Slaten, C. D., Arslan, G., Roffey, S., Craig, H., & Vella-Brodrick, D. A. (2021). School belonging: The importance of student and teacher relationships. In Kern, M. L., & Wehmeyer, M. L. (Eds.), *The Palgrave Handbook of Positive Education* (1st ed., pp. 525–550). Palgrave Macmillan. 10.1007/978-3-030-64537-3_21

Au, W. C. C., & Kennedy, K. J. (2018). A Positive Education Program to Promote Wellbeing in Schools: A Case Study from a Hong Kong School. *Higher Education Studies, 8*(4), 9-22. https://eric.ed.gov/?id=EJ1189599

Baker-Henningham, H., & Walker, S. (2009). A qualitative study of teacher's perceptions of an intervention to prevent conduct problems in Jamaican pre-schools. *Child: Care, Health and Development*, 35(5), 632–642. 10.1111/j.1365-2214.2009.00996.x19689568

Bandura, A. (1989). Human agency in social cognitive theory. *The American Psychologist*, 44(9), 1175–1184. 10.1037/0003-066X.44.9.11752782727

Baumeister, R. F., Campbell, J. D., Krueger, J. I., & Vohs, K. D. (2003). Does High Self-Esteem Cause Better Performance, Interpersonal Success, Happiness, or Healthier Lifestyles? *Psychological Science in the Public Interest: A Journal of the American Psychological Society, 4*(1), 1–44. 10.1111/1529-1006.01431

Berger, E., Reupert, A., Campbell, T. C. H., Morris, Z., Hammer, M., Diamond, Z., Hine, R., Patrick, P., & Fathers, C. (2022). A systematic review of evidence-based wellbeing initiatives for schoolteachers and early childhood educators. *Educational Psychology Review*, 34(4), 2919–2969. 10.1007/s10648-022-09690-5

Biegel, G. M., Brown, K. W., Shapiro, S. L., & Schubert, C. M. (2009). Mindfulness-based stress reduction for the treatment of adolescent psychiatric outpatients: A randomized clinical trial. *Journal of Consulting and Clinical Psychology*, 77(5), 855–866. 10.1037/a001624119803566

Bögels, S., Hoogstad, B., van Dun, L., de Schutter, S., & Restifo, K. (2008). Mindfulness training for adolescents with externalizing disorders and their parents. *Behavioural and Cognitive Psychotherapy*, 36(2), 193–209. 10.1017/S1352465808004190

Boniwell, I., & Tunariu, A. D. (2019). *Positive psychology: Theory, research and applications*. Open University Press.

Borrelli, B. (2011). The Assessment, Monitoring, and Enhancement of Treatment Fidelity In Public Health Clinical Trials. *Journal of Public Health Dentistry*, 71(1), 52–63. 10.1111/j.1752-7325.2011.00233.x21499543

Bowlby, J. (1958). The nature of the child's tie to his mother. *The International Journal of Psycho-Analysis*, 39, 350–373.13610508

Bowlby, J. (1982). Attachment and loss: Retrospect and prospect. *The American Journal of Orthopsychiatry*, 52(4), 664–678. 10.1111/j.1939-0025.1982.tb01456.x7148988

Bradshaw, C. P., Koth, C. W., Thornton, L. A., & Leaf, P. J. (2009). Altering school climate through school-wide Positive Behavioral Interventions and Supports: findings from a group-randomized effectiveness trial. *Prevention Science: The Official Journal of the Society for Prevention Research, 10*(2), 100–115. 10.1007/s11121-008-0114-9

Brensilver, M., Hardy, J., & Sofer, O. J. (2020). *The mindful schools curriculum and teacher's guide*. W.W. Norton and Company.

Broderick, P. (2013). *Learning to BREATHE: A Mindfulness Curriculum for Adolescents to Cultivate Emotion Regulation, attention, and Performance*. New Harbinger.

Brophy, J. (1998). Classroom Management As Socializing Students Into Clearly Articulated Roles. *Journal of Classroom Interaction*, 33(1), 1–4. https://www.jstor.org/stable/23870337

Brunwasser, S. M., Gillham, J. E., & Kim, E. S. (2009). A meta-analytic review of the Penn Resiliency Program's effect on depressive symptoms. *Journal of Consulting and Clinical Psychology*, 77(6), 1042–1054. 10.1037/a001767119968381

Buss, D. M. (2000). The evolution of happiness. *The American Psychologist*, 55(1), 15–23. 10.1037/0003-066X.55.1.1511392858

Cann, R., Sinnema, C., Daly, A. J., & Rodway, J. (2024a). A contextual approach to designing, implementing, and adapting a wellbeing program: A case study of the MARKERS wellbeing program for educators. *International Journal of Applied Positive Psychology*, 9(1), 301–325. 10.1007/s41042-023-00123-4

Cann, R., Sinnema, C., Daly, A. J., & Rodway, J. (2024b). Swimming against the tide: A mixed-methods study of how the markers educator wellbeing program changed educators' relational space. *International Journal of Applied Positive Psychology*, 1–28. 10.1007/s41042-024-00153-6

Castro-Villarreal, F., Rodriguez, B. J., & Moore, S. (2014). Teachers' perceptions and attitudes about Response to Intervention (RTI) in their schools: A qualitative analysis. *Teaching and Teacher Education*, 40(1), 104–112. 10.1016/j.tate.2014.02.004

Cefai, C., & Cavioni, V. (2015). Mental Health Promotion in School: An Integrated, School-Based, Whole School. In Kirkcaldy, B. (Ed.), *Promoting Psychological Wellbeing in Children and Families* (pp. 52–67). Palgrave McMillan. 10.1057/9781137479969.0007

Cook, C. R., Fiat, A., Larson, M., Daikos, C., Slemrod, T., Holland, E. A., Thayer, A. J., & Renshaw, T. (2018). Positive Greetings at the Door: Evaluation of a Low-Cost, High-Yield Proactive Classroom Management Strategy. *Journal of Positive Behavior Interventions*, 20(3), 149–159. 10.1177/1098300717753831

Corbin, C. M., Alamos, P., Lowenstein, A. E., Downer, J. T., & Brown, J. L. (2019). The role of teacher-student relationships in predicting teachers' personal accomplishment and emotional exhaustion. *Journal of School Psychology*, 77, 1–12. 10.1016/j.jsp.2019.10.00131837719

Cornelius-White, J. (2007). Learner-centered teacher-student relationships are effective: A meta-analysis. *Review of Educational Research*, 77(1), 113–143. 10.3102/003465430298563

Critchley, H., & Gibbs, S. (2012). The effects of positive psychology on the efficacy beliefs of school staff. *Educational and Child Psychology*, 29(4), 64–76. 10.53841/bpsecp.2012.29.4.64

Cui, L. (2022). The Role of Teacher-Student Relationships in Predicting Teachers' Occupational Wellbeing, Emotional Exhaustion, and Enthusiasm. *Frontiers in Psychology*, 13, 896813. 10.3389/fpsyg.2022.89681335664194

Davis, D. M., & Hayes, J. A. (2011). What are the benefits of mindfulness? A practice review of psychotherapy-related research. *Psychotherapy (Chicago, Ill.)*, 48(2), 198–208. 10.1037/a002206221639664

Dawood, R. (2013). Positive Psychology in School-Based Psychological Intervention: A Study of the Evidence-Base. *The European Journal of Social & Behavioural Sciences*, 5(2), 281–306. 10.15405/ejsbs.70

Dreer, B. (2020). Positive Psychological Interventions for Teachers: A Randomised Placebo-Controlled Field Experiment Investigating the Effects of Workplace-Related Positive Activities. *International Journal of Applied Positive Psychology*, 5(1-2), 77–97. 10.1007/s41042-020-00027-7

Durlak J. A. (2015). Studying Program Implementation Is Not Easy but It Is Essential. *Prevention Science: The Official Journal of the Society for Prevention Research, 16*(8), 1123–1127. https://doi.org/10.1007/s11121-015-0606-3

Durlak, J. A., & DuPre, E. P. (2008). Implementation matters: A review of research on the influence of implementation on program outcomes and the factors affecting implementation. *American Journal of Community Psychology*, 41(3-4), 327–350. 10.1007/s10464-008-9165-018322790

Durlak, J. A., Weissberg, R. P., Dymnicki, A. B., Taylor, R. D., & Schellinger, K. B. (2011). The impact of enhancing students' social and emotional learning: A meta-analysis of school-based universal interventions. *Child Development*, 82(1), 405–432. 10.1111/j.1467-8624.2010.01564.x21291449

Dweck, C. S. (1999). *Self-theories: Their role in motivation, personality, and development*. Psychology Press.

Dweck, C. S. (2008). *Mindset: The new psychology of success*. Random House Digital, Inc.

Dweck, C. S., & Leggett, E. L. (1988). A social-cognitive approach to motivation and personality. *Psychological Review*, 95(2), 256–273. 10.1037/0033-295X.95.2.256

Emerson, L. M., Leyland, A., Hudson, K., Rowse, G., Hanley, P., & Hugh-Jones, S. (2017). Teaching Mindfulness to Teachers: A Systematic Review and Narrative Synthesis. *Mindfulness*, 8(5), 1136–1149. 10.1007/s12671-017-0691-428989547

Evans, R., Murphy, S., & Scourfield, J. (2015). Implementation of a school-based social and emotional learning intervention: understanding diffusion processes within complex systems. *Prevention Science: The Official Journal of the Society for Prevention Research, 16*(5), 754–764. 10.1007/s11121-015-0552-0

Fabiano, G. A., Chafouleas, S. M., Weist, M. D., Sumi, W. C., & Humphrey, N. (2014). Methodology considerations in school mental health research. *School Mental Health: A Multidisciplinary Research and Practice Journal, 6*(2), 68–83. 10.1007/s12310-013-9117-1

Forman, S. G., Olin, S. S., Hoagwood, K. E., Crowe, M., & Saka, N. (2009). Evidence-based intervention in schools: Developers' views of implementation barriers and facilitators. *School Mental Health: A Multidisciplinary Research and Practice Journal, 1*(1), 26–36. https://doi.org/10.1007/s12310-008-9002-5

Fredrickson, B. L. (2001). The role of positive emotions in positive psychology: The broaden-and-build theory of positive emotions. *The American Psychologist*, 56(3), 218–226. 10.1037/0003-066X.56.3.21811315248

Froh, J. J., Kashdan, T. B., Ozimkowski, K. M., & Miller, N. (2009). Who benefits the most from a gratitude intervention in children and adolescents? Examining positive affect as a moderator. *The Journal of Positive Psychology*, 4(5), 408–422. 10.1080/17439760902992464

Froh, J. J., Sefick, W. J., & Emmons, R. A. (2008). Counting blessings in early adolescents: An experimental study of gratitude and subjective well-being. *Journal of School Psychology*, 46(2), 213–233. 10.1016/j.jsp.2007.03.00519083358

Gable, S. L., & Haidt, J. (2005). What (and why) is positive psychology? *Review of General Psychology*, 9(2), 103–110. 10.1037/1089-2680.9.2.103

Galassi, J. P., & Akos, P. (2004). Developmental advocacy: Twenty-first century school counseling. *Journal of Counseling and Development*, 82(2), 146–157. 10.1002/j.1556-6678.2004.tb00296.x

Garro, A., Janal, M., Kondroski, K., Stillo, G., & Vega, V. (2023). Mindfulness Initiatives for Students, Teachers, and Parents: A Review of Literature and Implications for Practice During COVID-19 and Beyond. *Contemporary School Psychology*, 27(1), 152–169. 10.1007/s40688-022-00446-036741424

Gerhardt, S. (2015). *Why love matters: How affection shapes a baby's brain* (2nd ed.). Routledge.

Gill, S. (2009, July). Monitoring and promoting well-being in education principles and possible approaches to child wellbeing indicators (Working paper, Education for Well-Being Europe Consortium).

Green, S., Oades, L., & Robinson, P. (2011). Positive education: Creating flourishing students, staff and schools. *InPsych*, 33(2), 37–43.

Harter, S. (1982). The Perceived Competence Scale for Children. *Child Development*, 53(1), 87–97. 10.2307/11296406525886

Heine, S. J., Kitayama, S., Lehman, D. R., Takata, T., Ide, E., Leung, C., & Matsumoto, H. (2001). Divergent consequences of success and failure in Japan and North America: An investigation of self-improving motivations and malleable selves. *Journal of Personality and Social Psychology*, 81(4), 599–615. 10.1037/0022-3514.81.4.59911642348

Howell, A. J. (2009). Flourishing: Achievement-related correlates of students' well-being. *The Journal of Positive Psychology*, 4(1), 1–13. 10.1080/17439760802043459

Hoy, A. W., Hoy, W. K., & Davis, H. A. (2009). Teachers' self-efficacy beliefs. In K. R. Wenzel & A. Wigfield (Eds.), *Handbook of motivation at school* (pp. 627–653). Routledge/Taylor & Francis Group.

Hoyert, M. S., O'Dell, C. D., & Hendrickson, K. A. (2012). Using Goal Orientation to Enhance College Retention and Graduation Rates. *Psychology Learning & Teaching*, 11(2), 171–179. 10.2304/plat.2012.11.2.171

Huang, S., Yin, H., & Lv, L. (2019). Job characteristics and teacher well-being: The mediation of teacher self-monitoring and teacher self-efficacy. *Educational Psychology*, 39(3), 313–331. 10.1080/01443410.2018.1543855

Huebner, E. S., Gilman, R., Reschly, A., & Hall, R. (2009). Positive schools. In Lopez, S. J., & Snyder, C. R. (Eds.), *Oxford handbook of positive psychology* (2nd ed., pp. 561–569). Oxford University Press. 10.1093/oxfordhb/9780195187243.013.0053

Hwang, Y.-S., Bartlett, B., Greben, M., & Hand, K. (2017). A systematic review of mindfulness interventions for in-service teachers: A tool to enhance teacher well-being and performance. *Teaching and Teacher Education*, 64, 26–42. 10.1016/j.tate.2017.01.015

Jain, S., Shapiro, S. L., Swanick, S., Roesch, S. C., Mills, P. J., Bell, I., & Schwartz, G. E. (2007). A randomized controlled trial of mindfulness meditation versus relaxation training: effects on distress, positive states of mind, rumination, and distraction. *Annals of behavioral medicine: a publication of the Society of Behavioral Medicine, 33*(1), 11–21. https://doi.org/10.1207/s15324796abm3301_2

Kabat-Zinn, J. (1994, September). Catalyzing movement towards a more contemplative/sacred-appreciating/non-dualistic society. *Meeting of the working group.*

Kamins, M. L., & Dweck, C. S. (1999). Person versus process praise and criticism: Implications for contingent self-worth and coping. *Developmental Psychology*, 35(3), 835–847. 10.1037/0012-1649.35.3.83510380873

Kelley, T. R., Knowles, J. G., Holland, J. D., & Han, J. (2020). Increasing high school teachers' self-efficacy for integrated STEM instruction through a collaborative community of practice. *International Journal of STEM Education*, 7(14), 14. Advance online publication. 10.1186/s40594-020-00211-w

Kern, M. L., Adler, A., Waters, L. E., & White, M. A. (2015). Measuring whole-school well-being in students and staff. *Evidence-based approaches in positive education: Implementing a strategic framework for well-being in schools*, 65-91. 10.1007/978-94-017-9667-5_4

Kern, M. L., Waters, L. E., Adler, A., & White, M. A. (2015). A multidimensional approach to measuring well-being in students: Application of the PERMA framework. *The Journal of Positive Psychology*, 10(3), 262–271. 10.1080/17439760.2014.93696225745508

Kern, M. L., Williams, P., Spong, C., Colla, R., Sharma, K., Downie, A., Taylor, J. A., Sharp, S., Siokou, C., & Oades, L. G. (2020). Systems informed positive psychology. *The Journal of Positive Psychology*, 15(6), 705–715. 10.1080/17439760.2019.1639799

Keyes, C. L. (2002). The mental health continuum: From languishing to flourishing in life. *Journal of Health and Social Behavior*, 43(2), 207–222. 10.2307/309019712096700

Keyes, C. L. (2006). Mental health in adolescence: Is America's youth flourishing? *The American Journal of Orthopsychiatry*, 76(3), 395–402. 10.1037/0002-9432.76.3.39516981819

Klassen, R., & Tze, V. M. C. (2014). Teachers' self-efficacy, personality, and teaching effectiveness: A meta-analysis. *Educational Research Review*, 12, 59–76. 10.1016/j.edurev.2014.06.001

Kristjánsson, K. (2012). Positive psychology and positive education: Old wine in new bottles? *Educational Psychologist*, 47(2), 86–105. 10.1080/00461520.2011.610678

Kun, A., & Gadanecz, P. (2022). Workplace happiness, well-being and their relationship with psychological capital: A study of Hungarian teachers. *Current Psychology (New Brunswick, N.J.)*, 41(1), 185–199. 10.1007/s12144-019-00550-0

Kuperminc, G. P., Thomason, J., DiMeo, M., & Broomfield-Massey, K. (2011). Cool Girls, Inc.: Promoting the positive development of urban preadolescent and early adolescent girls. *The Journal of Primary Prevention*, 32(3-4), 171–183. 10.1007/s10935-011-0243-y21800162

Lai, M. K., Leung, C., Kwok, S. Y., Hui, A. N., Lo, H. H., Leung, J. T., & Tam, C. H. (2018). A multidimensional PERMA-H positive education model, general satisfaction of school life, and character strengths use in Hong Kong senior primary school students: Confirmatory factor analysis and path analysis using the APASO-II. *Frontiers in Psychology*, 9, 1090. 10.3389/fpsyg.2018.0109030008690

Lee, J., Krause, A. E., & Davidson, J. W. (2017). The PERMA well-being model and music facilitation practice: Preliminary documentation for well-being through music provision in Australian schools. *Research Studies in Music Education*, 39(1), 73–89. 10.1177/1321103X17703131

Lei, H., Cui, Y., & Zhou, W. (2018). Relationships between student engagement and academic achievement: A meta-analysis. *Social Behavior and Personality*, 46(3), 517–528. 10.2224/sbp.7054

Lloyd, M. (2018). Domestic violence and education: Examining the impact of domestic violence on young children, children, and young people and the potential role of schools. *Frontiers in Psychology*, 9, 396402. 10.3389/fpsyg.2018.0209430483170

Lomas, T., Waters, L., Williams, P., Oades, L. G., & Kern, M. L. (2021). Third wave positive psychology: Broadening towards complexity. *The Journal of Positive Psychology*, 16(5), 660–674. 10.1080/17439760.2020.1805501

Lopez, S. J., & Louis, M. C. (2009). The Principles of Strengths-Based Education. *Journal of College and Character*, 10(4), 1–8. 10.2202/1940-1639.1041

Madden, W., Green, S., & Grant, A. M. (2011). A pilot study evaluating strengths-based coaching for primary school students: Enhancing engagement and hope. *International Coaching Psychology Review*, 6(1), 71–83. 10.53841/bpsicpr.2011.6.1.71

Main, P. (2022, February 9). Growth Mindset: A teacher's guide. Retrieved from https://www.structural-learning.com/post/growth-mindset-a-teachers-guide

Mandelli, L., Petrelli, C., & Serretti, A. (2015). The role of specific early trauma in adult depression: A meta-analysis of published literature. Childhood trauma and adult depression. *European psychiatry: the journal of the Association of European Psychiatrists, 30*(6), 665–680. https://doi.org/10.1016/j.eurpsy.2015.04.007

Matiz, A., Fabbro, F., Paschetto, A., Cantone, D., Paolone, A. R., & Crescentini, C. (2020). Positive Impact of Mindfulness Meditation on Mental Health of Female Teachers during the COVID-19 Outbreak in Italy. *International Journal of Environmental Research and Public Health*, 17(18), 6450. 10.3390/ijerph1718645032899739

McGrath, H. (2009). An evidence-based positive psychology approach to student well-being. *Paper presented at theFirst Australia Positive Psychology in Education Symposium.* University of Sydney.

Meiklejohn, J., Phillips, C., Freedman, M. L., Griffin, M. L., Biegel, G., Roach, A., Frank, J., Burke, C., Pinger, L., Soloway, G., Isberg, R., Sibinga, E., Grossman, L., & Saltzman, A. (2012). Integrating mindfulness training into K-12 education: Fostering the resilience of teachers and students. *Mindfulness*, 3(4), 291–307. 10.1007/s12671-012-0094-5

Mendelson, T., Greenberg, M. T., Dariotis, J. K., Gould, L. F., Rhoades, B. L., & Leaf, P. J. (2010). Feasibility and preliminary outcomes of a school-based mindfulness intervention for urban youth. *Journal of Abnormal Child Psychology*, 38(7), 985–994. 10.1007/s10802-010-9418-x20440550

Méndez, I., Martínez-Ramón, J. P., Ruiz-Esteban, C., & García-Fernández, J. M. (2020). Latent Profiles of Burnout, Self-Esteem and Depressive Symptomatology among Teachers. *International Journal of Environmental Research and Public Health*, 17(18), 6760. 10.3390/ijerph1718676032948075

Michalec, B., Keyes, C. L. M., & Nalkur, S. (2009). Flourishing. In Lopez, S. J. (Ed.), *The encyclopedia of positive psychology* (Vol. I, pp. 391–394). Wiley-Blackwell.

Mohammadi, N. K., Rowling, L., & Nutbeam, D. (2010). Acknowledging educational perspectives on health promoting schools. *Health Education*, 110(4), 240–251. 10.1108/09654281011052619

Moreira, P. A. S., Inman, R. A., Cloninger, K., & Cloninger, C. R. (2021). Student engagement with school and personality: A biopsychosocial and person-centred approach. *The British Journal of Educational Psychology*, 91(2), 691–713. 10.1111/bjep.1238833247604

Mueller, C. M., & Dweck, C. S. (1998). Praise for intelligence can undermine children's motivation and performance. *Journal of Personality and Social Psychology*, 75(1), 33–52. 10.1037/0022-3514.75.1.339686450

Neil, A. L., & Christensen, H. (2009). Efficacy and effectiveness of school-based prevention and early intervention programs for anxiety. *Clinical Psychology Review*, 29(3), 208–215. 10.1016/j.cpr.2009.01.00219232805

Nielsen, L., Meilstrup, C., Nelausen, M. K., Koushede, V., Holstein, B. E., Weare, K., & Weare, K. (2015). Promotion of social and emotional competence: Experiences from a mental health intervention applying a whole school approach. *Health Education*, 115(3/4), 339–356. 10.1108/HE-03-2014-0039

Noddings, N. (2003). *Happiness and education*. Cambridge University Press. 10.1017/CBO9780511499920

Owens, R. L., & Patterson, M. M. (2013). Positive psychological interventions for children: A comparison of gratitude and best possible selves approaches. *The Journal of Genetic Psychology*, 174(4), 403–428. 10.1080/00221325.2012.69749623991613

Park, N., & Peterson, C. (2006). Character strengths and happiness among young children: Content analysis of parental descriptions. *Journal of Happiness Studies*, 7(3), 323–341. 10.1007/s10902-005-3648-6

Park, N., & Peterson, C. (2006). Moral competence and character strengths among adolescents: The development and validation of the Values in Action Inventory of Strengths for Youth. *Journal of Adolescence*, 29(6), 891–909. 10.1016/j.adolescence.2006.04.01116766025

Pedlar, M. (2018). Teachers play a key role in helping students feel they 'belong' at school. *The Conversation*. Https://Theconversation.Com/Teachers-Play-A-Key-Role-In-Helping-Students-Feel-They-Belong-At-School-99641

Pereira, H., Gonçalves, V. O., & Assis, R. M. (2021). Burnout, Organizational Self-Efficacy and Self-Esteem among Brazilian Teachers during the COVID-19 Pandemic. *European Journal of Investigation in Health, Psychology and Education*, 11(3), 795–803. 10.3390/ejihpe1103005734563070

Peterson, C., Ruch, W., Beermann, U., Park, N., & Seligman, M. E. P. (2007). Strengths of character, orientations to happiness, and life satisfaction. *The Journal of Positive Psychology*, 2(3), 149–156. 10.1080/17439760701228938

Peterson, C., & Seligman, M. E. P. (2004). *Character Strengths and Virtues: A Handbook and Classification*. Oxford University Press.

Phan, M. L., Renshaw, T. L., Caramanico, J., Greeson, J. M., MacKenzie, E., Atkinson-Diaz, Z., Doppelt, N., Tai, H., Mandell, D. S., & Nuske, H. J. (2022). Mindfulness-based school interventions: A systematic review of outcome evidence quality by study design. *Mindfulness*, 13(7), 1591–1613. 10.1007/s12671-022-01885-936186722

Platt, I. A., Hochard, K. D., Tytherleigh, M., Kannangara, C., Carson, J., McFaul, C., & North, C. (2024). The Hummingbird Project year 2: Decreasing distress and fostering flourishing in a pragmatic pre-post study. *Frontiers in Psychology*, 15, 1257446. 10.3389/fpsyg.2024.125744638596339

Platt, I. A., Kannangara, C., Tytherleigh, M., & Carson, J. (2020). The Hummingbird Project: A Positive Psychology Intervention for Secondary School Students. *Frontiers in Psychology*, 11, 2012. 10.3389/fpsyg.2020.0201232849165

Pluess, M., Boniwell, I., Hefferon, K., & Tunariu, A. (2017). Preliminary evaluation of a school-based resilience-promoting intervention in a high-risk population: Application of an exploratory two-cohort treatment/control design. *PLoS One*, 12(5), e0177191. 10.1371/journal.pone.017719128481905

Ritter, A., & Alvarez, I. (2020). Mindfulness and Executive Functions: Making the Case for Elementary School Practice. *European Journal of Investigation in Health, Psychology and Education*, 10(1), 544–553. 10.3390/ejihpe1001003934542502

Ronaldson, A., Poole, L., Kidd, T., Leigh, E., Jahangiri, M., & Steptoe, A. (2014). Optimism measured pre-operatively is associated with reduced pain intensity and physical symptom reporting after coronary artery bypass graft surgery. *Journal of Psychosomatic Research*, 77(4), 278–282. 10.1016/j.jpsychores.2014.07.01825129850

Roorda, D., Koomen, H., Spilt, J., & Oort, F. (2011). The Influence of Affective Teacher- Student Relationships on Students' School Engagement and Achievement: A Meta- Analytic Approach. *Review of Educational Research*, 81(4), 493–529. 10.3102/0034654311421793

Roorda, D. L., Jak, S., Zee, M., Oort, F. J., & Koomen, H. M. Y. (2017). Affective teacher–student relationships and students' engagement and achievement: A meta-analytic update and test of the mediating role of engagement. *School Psychology Review*, 46(3), 239–261. 10.17105/SPR-2017-0035.V46-3

Ruch, W., Weber, M., Park, N., & and Peterson, C. (2014). Character Strengths in Children and Adolescents: Reliability and Initial Validity of the German Values in Action Inventory of Strengths for Youth (German VIA-Youth). *European Journal of Psychological Assessment*, 30(1), 57–64. 10.1027/1015-5759/a000169

Saltzman, A. (2010). *Amy, Author at Still Quiet Place. Still Quiet Place.* https://stillquietplace.com/author/amy/

Saltzman, A. (2014). *A still quiet place: A mindfulness program for teaching children and adolescents to ease stress and difficult emotions.* New Harbinger Publications.

Sanetti, L. M. H., Dobey, L. M., & Gallucci, J. (2014). Treatment integrity of interventions with children in School Psychology International from 1995–2010. *School Psychology International*, 35(4), 370–383. 10.1177/0143034313476399

Sanetti, L. M. H., Kratochwill, T. R., & Long, A. C. J. (2013). Applying adult behavior change theory to support mediator-based intervention implementation. *School Psychology Quarterly: The Official Journal of the Division of School Psychology, American Psychological Association, 28*(1), 47–62. https://doi.org/10.1037/spq0000007

Scales, P. C. (1999). Reducing risks and building developmental assets: Essential actions for promoting adolescent health. *The Journal of School Health*, 69(3), 113–119. 10.1111/j.1746-1561.1999.tb07219.x10332647

Scheier, M. F., & Carver, C. S. (1985). Optimism, coping, and health: Assessment and implications of generalized outcome expectancies. *Health Psychology*, 4(3), 219–247. 10.1037/0278-6133.4.3.2194029106

Schonert-Reichl, K. A., & Roeser, R. W. (Eds.). (2016). *Handbook of mindfulness in education: Integrating theory and research into practice.* Springer-Verlag Publishing/Springer Nature., 10.1007/978-1-4939-3506-2

Schreiner, L. A. (2013). Strengths-based advising. In J. K. Drake, P. Jordan, and M. A. Miller Eds.), *Academic advising approaches: Strategies that teach students to make the most of college* (pp. 105-120). Jossey Bass.

See, B., Morris, R., Gorard, S., Kokotsaki, D., & Abdi, S. (2020). Teacher recruitment and retention: A critical review of international evidence of most promising interventions. *Education Sciences*, 10(10), 262. 10.3390/educsci10100262

Seligman, M. E. P. (2002). Positive psychology, positive prevention, and positive therapy. In Snyder, C. R., & Lopez, S. J. (Eds.), *Handbook of positive psychology* (pp. 3–9). Oxford University Press.

Seligman, M. E. P. (2011). *Flourish: A visionary new understanding of happiness and well-being.* Free Press.

Seligman, M. E. P., & Csikszentmihalyi, M. (2000). Positive psychology: An introduction. *The American Psychologist*, 55(1), 5–14. 10.1037/0003-066X.55.1.51 1392865

Seligman, M. E. P., Ernst, R. M., Gillham, J., Reivich, K., & Linkins, M. (2009). Positive education: Positive psychology and classroom interventions. *Oxford Review of Education*, 35(3), 293–311. 10.1080/03054980902934563

Seligman, M. E. P., Steen, T. A., Park, N., & Peterson, C. (2005). Positive Psychology Progress: Empirical Validation of Interventions. *The American Psychologist*, 60(5), 410–421. 10.1037/0003-066X.60.5.41016045394

Semple, R. J., Droutman, V., & Reid, B. A. (2017). Mindfulness goes to school: Things learned (so far) from research and real-world experiences. *Psychology in the Schools*, 54(1), 29–52. 10.1002/pits.2198128458403

Shankland, R., & Rosset, E. (2017). Review of brief school-based positive psychological interventions: A taster for teachers and educators. *Educational Psychology Review*, 29(2), 363–392. 10.1007/s10648-016-9357-3

Sheldon, K. M., Corcoran, C., & Prentice, M. (2019). Pursuing eudaimonic functioning versus pursuing hedonic well-being: The first goal succeeds in its aim, whereas the second does not. *Journal of Happiness Studies*, 20(3), 919–933. 10.1007/s10902-018-9980-4

Sibinga, E. M., Kerrigan, D., Stewart, M., Johnson, K., Magyari, T., & Ellen, J. M. (2011). Mindfulness-based stress reduction for urban youth. *Journal of Alternative and Complementary Medicine (New York, N.Y.)*, 17(3), 213–218. 10.1089/acm.2009.060521348798

Sin, N. L., & Lyubomirsky, S. (2009). Enhancing well-being and alleviating depressive symptoms with positive psychology interventions: A practice-friendly meta-analysis. *Journal of Clinical Psychology*, 65(5), 467–487. 10.1002/jclp.2059319301241

Smiley, P. A., Buttitta, K. V., Chung, S. Y., Dubon, V. X., & Chang, L. K. (2016). Mediation models of implicit theories and achievement goals predict planning and withdrawal after failure. *Motivation and Emotion*, 40(6), 878–894. 10.1007/s11031-016-9575-5

Soloway, G. B. (2016). Preparing teacher candidates for the present: Investigating the value of mindfulness-training in teacher education. *Handbook of mindfulness in education: Integrating theory and research into practice* (pp. 191-205). https://doi.org/10.1007/978-1-4939-3506-2_12

Song, K. (2022). Well-Being of Teachers: The Role of Efficacy of Teachers and Academic Optimism. *Frontiers in Psychology*, 12, 831972. 10.3389/fpsyg.2021.83197235153944

Spiteri, D. (2016). *Multiculturalism, higher education and intercultural communication: developing strengths-based narratives for teaching and learning*. Springer.

Suldo, S. M., Savage, J. A., & Mercer, S. H. (2014). Increasing middle school students' life satisfaction: Efficacy of a positive psychology group intervention. *Journal of Happiness Studies*, 15(1), 19–42. 10.1007/s10902-013-9414-2

Taylor, R. D., Oberle, E., Durlak, J. A., & Weissberg, R. P. (2017). Promoting positive youth development through school-based social and emotional learning interventions: A meta-analysis of follow-up effects. *Child Development*, 88(4), 1156–1171. 10.1111/cdev.1286428685826

Tsang, K. K. Y., Shum, K. K., Chan, W. W. L., Li, S. X., Kwan, H. W., Su, M. R., Wong, B. P. H., & Lam, S. F. (2021). Effectiveness and Mechanisms of Mindfulness Training for School Teachers in Difficult Times: A Randomized Controlled Trial. *Mindfulness*, 12(11), 2820–2831. 10.1007/s12671-021-01750-134545293

Vandenbroucke, L., Spilt, J., Verschueren, K., Piccinin, C., & Baeyens, D. (2018). The classroom as a developmental context for cognitive development: A meta-analysis on the importance of teacher–student interactions for children's executive functions. *Review of Educational Research*, 88(1), 125–164. 10.3102/0034654317743200

Vella-Broderick, D. (2011). Positive psychology: Reflecting on the past and projecting into the future. *InPsych*, 33(2), 10–13. https://www.psychology.org.au/publications/inpsych/2011/april/vella-brodrick

Waters, L. (2011). A review of school-based positive psychology interventions. *The Australian Educational and Developmental Psychologist*, 28(2), 75–90. 10.1375/aedp.28.2.75

Waters, L. (2015). The Relationship between Strength-Based Parenting with Children's Stress Levels and Strength-Based Coping Approaches. *Psychology (Irvine, Calif.)*, 6(6), 689–699. 10.4236/psych.2015.66067

Waters, L., & Loton, D. (2019). SEARCH: A meta-framework and review of the field of positive education. *International Journal of Applied Positive Psychology*, 4(1–2), 1–46. 10.1007/s41042-019-00017-4

White, M. A., & Waters, L. E. (2015). A case study of 'The Good School:' Examples of the use of Peterson's strengths-based approach with students. *The Journal of Positive Psychology*, 10(1), 69–76. 10.1080/17439760.2014.92040825431614

World Health Organization. (Ed.). (2008). *World health statistics 2008*. World Health Organization.

Yeh, C. S. H., & Barrington, R. (2023). Sustainable positive psychology interventions enhance primary teachers' wellbeing and beyond–A qualitative case study in England. *Teaching and Teacher Education*, 125, 104072. 10.1016/j.tate.2023.104072

Zylowska, L., Ackerman, D. L., Yang, M. H., Futrell, J. L., Horton, N. L., Hale, T. S., Pataki, C., & Smalley, S. L. (2008). Mindfulness meditation training in adults and adolescents with ADHD: A feasibility study. *Journal of Attention Disorders*, 11(6), 737–746. 10.1177/108705470730850218025249

Chapter 2
Applying Positive Psychology in School Settings:
Effectiveness and Challenges

Katerina Michael
https://orcid.org/0000-0002-5737-0964
Frederick University, Cyprus

Glykeria Reppa
Neapolis University, Cyprus

Louiza Ioannidou
Frederick University, Cyprus

ABSTRACT

This chapter explores the effectiveness and challenges of implementing positive education programs in school settings. It provides an overview of positive psychology, defines well-being, and examines the intersection of positive psychology principles with educational contexts. The chapter also presents various interventions derived from positive psychology used in schools, reviews empirical findings on their efficacy, and addresses implementation challenges. Finally, it offers insights into potential future directions and areas of focus within positive psychology in school settings.

DOI: 10.4018/979-8-3693-8312-4.ch002

Copyright © 2024, IGI Global. Copying or distributing in print or electronic forms without written permission of IGI Global is prohibited.

INTRODUCTION

Positive Psychology is a branch of psychology that focuses on promoting and enhancing positive aspects of life. Unlike traditional psychology, which only addresses negative aspects, Positive Psychology emphasizes developing personal strengths to prevent and treat mental illness. It also emphasizes the importance of positive emotions like happiness, joy, and satisfaction and encourages positive thinking about the future, such as optimism and hope (Seligman, 2002).

At an individual level, Positive Psychology is about developing personal traits that contribute to a happy and successful life, such as interpersonal skills, perseverance, and wisdom. At a societal level, it aims to promote positive values and institutions that encourage good citizenship, such as responsibility, civility, and work ethic (Seligman, M. E., 2002).

Positive Psychology has various applications in different fields, including organizations, schools, healthcare, aging, and public policy. Its primary objective is to promote the well-being of individuals and organizations to achieve optimal human flourishing (Baker at et., 2017).

Positive education is the application of Positive Psychology in educational settings. Its purpose is to transform schools into positive institutions that cultivate positive traits and emotions for academic purposes (Kristjánsson, 2012). Positive education aims to teach traditional skills and promote happiness. It can teach schoolchildren resilience, positive emotions, engagement, and meaning (Seligman et al., 2009).

Teachers adopted Positive Psychology and developed positive education, using scientifically validated programs to improve student well-being. Evidence supports well-being as a key educational goal alongside academic growth, school retention, and student engagement (White, 2016).

The purpose of this chapter is to present the effectiveness and challenges when applying positive education programs in school settings. In this chapter, the authors provide an overview of the historical background of Positive Psychology. They discuss its origins, development, key principles, and definitions and present a brief critique of the field. The concept of well-being is defined, and Seligman's PERMA model, a prominent model for understanding well-being, is explored. Additionally, the chapter discusses Barbara Fredrickson's Broaden-and-Build theory of positive emotions, which emphasizes the role of positive emotions in building psychological resources.

The chapter also examines the intersection of Positive Psychology principles with educational settings, defines Positive Education, and discusses how Positive Psychology is applied in educational contexts. Various frameworks used to implement positive education programs are presented, along with specific interventions and approaches derived from Positive Psychology that are applied in schools. The chapter also reviews research findings on the effectiveness of positive education initiatives and identifies and discusses challenges faced when implementing positive education programs in schools.

Finally, the chapter concludes by summarizing key points discussed and offering potential insights into future directions or areas of focus within Positive Psychology in school settings.

POSITIVE PSYCHOLOGY

Historical Background of Positive Psychology

Happiness is a fundamental aspect of Positive Psychology that dates to ancient Greek philosophy. In this philosophy, there are two concepts of happiness: hedonia and eudaimonia. Hedonia refers to happiness as pleasure, while eudaimonia refers to happiness as personal fulfillment (Waterman, 2013). More recently, humanistic psychology emphasized positive self-fulfillment and self-education (Kristjánsson, 2012). Rogers, in the 60s, emphasized the fully functioning person, and Maslow, a few years later, the self-actualization and the study of healthy individuals. Malow also criticized psychology's focus on disorder and dysfunction (Alex Linley et al., 2006). Later, during the 1980s and 1990s, adaptability psychology addressed coping mechanisms, self-esteem, self-efficacy, self-determination theory, multiple intelligences, and emotional intelligence. These perspectives focused on the positive aspects of human development and how to promote them at home and in school (Kristjánsson, 2012).

Positive Psychology is a movement that emerged in the 1990s, spearheaded by Martin Seligman, who was then the president of the American Psychological Association (APA). Seligman and other prominent researchers proposed a shift in psychology's focus from solely addressing mental illness and repairing the worst aspects of life to building positive qualities and highlighting health. Until then, psychology had primarily concentrated on deficits, disorders, psychopathologies, and mental illness development. However, after World War II, there was a shift towards highlighting health, especially for veterans who required assistance with their needs. Removing the focus from mental illness it opened up the possibility of highlighting the positive aspects, strengths, virtues, and potential of human beings, concentrating on health promotion and prevention (Alex Linley et al., 2006; Scorsolini-Comin et al., 2013)

Definitions and Key Principles of Positive Psychology

There are various definitions of Positive Psychology (Kun et al., 2016; Scorsolini-Comin et al., 2013). According to Seligman and Csikszentmihalyi (2000), Positive Psychology encompasses theories and research on the factors that contribute to a fulfilling life (Seligman & Csikszentmihalyi, 2000) while Gable and Haidt (2005, pp 104) define Positive Psychology "as the study of the conditions and processes that contribute to the flourishing or optimal functioning of people, groups, and institutions."

Moreover, Positive Psychology is a field that focuses on three main areas: positive emotions and experiences, positive character and individuals, and positive communities and organizations. The first area emphasizes the importance of happiness and subjective well-being in improving the quality of life. Positive experiences can be categorized into past-oriented (contentment and satisfaction), future-oriented (hope and optimism), and present-oriented (joy, pleasure, or "flow"). They reflect an individual's evaluation of their own life, based on cognitive judgments, pleasant emotions, physical pleasure, or pleasant interest. The second area focuses on personal traits that are healthy, adaptive, and predictive of happiness. Lastly, Positive Psychology studies the kinds of environments that promote human flourishing, such as democracy or free speech, in order to encourage and facilitate the personal qualities outlined in the second area (Scorsolini-Comin et al., 2013; Yen, 2014).

Positive Psychology, according to Seligman (2002), has three main goals: identifying and measuring universal positive traits, promoting positive experiences and emotions, and understanding positive institutions. Positive traits include love, work, courage, compassion, resilience, creativity, curiosity, integrity, self-knowledge, moderation, self-control, and wisdom. Positive experiences and emotions include being content with the past, happy in the present, and hopeful for the future. Positive institutions foster better communities through strengths such as justice, responsibility, civility, parenting, nurturance, work ethic, leadership, teamwork, purpose, and tolerance (Seligman, M. E. P., 2002).

Criticism of Positive Psychology

Positive Psychology has been subject to criticism. One of the primary criticisms is that the focus on happiness is too narrow. Happiness is a dynamic emotion that is a relatively brief response to life events (Lundqvist & Starting, 2010). Research has also suggested that emphasizing the good does not necessarily reduce the bad (Lerner et al., 2010). Positive Psychology has also been criticized for neglecting the significance of social and contextual factors (Lomas, 2015) while emphasizing individual choice and self-focused effort (Becker & Marecek, 2008). In a review of two decades of critical responses to Positive Psychology, additional criticisms were found, including claims of incoherence, measurement issues, and a lack of evidence to support its grandiose claims (Frawley, 2015).

Advocates of Positive Psychology argue that it should be regarded as an overarching framework that connects theory and research in pursuit of common goals. Despite some criticisms, it's undeniable that the Positive Psychology movement has revitalized interest in the positive aspects of life and aimed to enhance individual well-being throughout their entire lifespan (Chodkiewicz & Boyle, 2017a).

Concept of Well-Being and Seligman's PERMA Model

Well-being has been a topic of research for a significant period. Numerous experts believe that well-being is a multifaceted concept that encompasses various aspects(Kun et al., 2016). It is a comprehensive, multidimensional idea that offers insight into one's state or condition of being. Although the definitions and measurements of well-being may differ between individuals, it is a complex construct that is crucial to understand (Kovich et al., 2023).

According to Seligman (2011), there are five important components of well-being. He developed a model of well-being known as PERMA, which stands for Positive emotion, Engagement, Relationships, Meaning, and Accomplishment. Seligman proposes that well-being is achieved by nurturing one or more of the five elements of PERMA. The combination of these elements promotes flourishing, which is the optimal functioning of individuals, groups, communities, nations, and society at large (Seligman, 2011).

The PERMA model for evaluating happiness and well-being is consistent across cultures (Khaw & Kern, 2014; Lambert D'raven & Pasha-Zaidi, 2016), but culture-specific modifications may be necessary (Khaw & Kern, 2014).

A more detailed description of the five PERMA elements follows.

Positive emotions are good feelings that not only motivate actions and boost work performance but also strengthen relationships, enhance physical health, and create hope and optimism for the future (Seligman, 2011).

Engagement. Engagement is a state of mind that encompasses both emotional and cognitive aspects. This state is not directed toward any specific object, event, individual, or behavior (Schaufeli et al., 2006). Flow is an important component of engagement, which describes the feeling of being completely absorbed in the present moment. When in a state of flow, time seems to slow down, and one forgets about their sense of self. This level of concentration can be achieved by engaging in activities that we truly enjoy and value (Seligman, 2011).

Relationships. As humans, we have a deep-seated desire to connect with others, to feel loved, and to have both physical and emotional contact with those around us. Building strong networks of relationships with the people in our lives is key to our overall well-being (Seligman, M. E. P, 2011). Positive relationships, whether they be close bonds with family and friends or more distant connections with colleagues, help us feel a sense of belonging and fulfilment (Sandstrom & Dunn, 2014).

Meaning and purpose. Meaning refers to the utilization of one's strengths, not for personal gain, but to achieve objectives that are perceived as significant. We tend to excel when we devote our time to something that is beyond ourselves, such as volunteering, being a part of a community or a civic/religious organization, or learning for a specific purpose. These activities have a clear sense of purpose and provide individuals with a compelling reason for why they do what they do (Seligman, 2011).

Accomplishment. Striving for a productive and purposeful life is a crucial component of well-being, pursued for its intrinsic value, even if it doesn't result in positive emotions, meaningful relationships, or a sense of purpose. To experience well-being, individuals must be able to reflect on their lives with a sense of accomplishment, saying "I did it, and I did it well." Achieving various goals throughout one's life, such as academic, athletic, or career success, may require resilience and perseverance (Seligman, 2011).

The Broaden–and–Build Theory of Positive Emotions of Barbara Fredrickson

Positive emotions play a significant role in Positive Psychology. Traditional views suggest that positive emotions signal well-being and guide behavior in the moment. However, the broaden-and-build theory proposes a much larger role for them. According to this theory, positive emotions have more long-lasting consequences and serve as vehicles for individual growth and social connection. By building personal and social resources, positive emotions transform people for the better, leading to better lives in the future. The theory also suggests that experiencing multiple, discrete positive emotions like joy, interest, contentment, and love are fundamental human strengths that yield multiple, interrelated benefits (Fredrickson, 2001).

Moreover, the broaden-and-build theory explains how positive emotions like joy, contentment, interest, and love can expand an individual's thoughts and actions while negative emotions can make them narrow. Positive emotions can build an individual's personal resources, including physical, intellectual, social, and psychological resources, which can later be used to improve their chances of successful coping and survival. This theory is an essential topic in the science of well-being as it underscores the importance of cultivating positive emotions in one's life and the lives of those around them. When positive emotions are abundant, people become generative, creative, resilient, and beautifully complex, leading to optimal well-being (Fredrickson, 2004).

POSITIVE EDUCATION

Positive Psychology and Education

Martin E. P. Seligman, the founder of Positive Psychology, emphasized the importance and applicability of Positive Psychology in school settings from the very beginning of its development. He believes that education should focus on positive emotions, social commitment, the pursuit of meaning, and harmony in human relationships. Seligman suggests that the education system should emphasize positive accomplishments, volition, freedom, health, and growth to benefit the younger generation. Positive Psychology considers individuals to have personal will and liberty, and the potential to develop based on their unique strengths and virtues. Seligman believes that Positive Psychology can be an effective tool for mental well-being and can contribute to education in a meaningful way (Pluskota, 2014).

Positive Education

Positive education is an approach that was developed by Professor Martin Seligman and his colleagues to improve traditional teaching methods and promote happiness. It is an applied science that integrates current knowledge from the science of well-being and Positive Psychology into educational practices. The goal of positive education is to nurture the well-being of students and cultivate positive mental health throughout the school community (Norrish et al., 2013; Waters & Loton, 2019). It suggests that schools should focus on instilling qualities like psychological resilience, social commitment, and a sense of meaning in students to help them lead a more satisfying life, learn better, and foster creative thinking (Pluskota, 2014).

Schools, Positive Education, and Mental Health Promotion

Schools are an excellent place to promote large-scale development and enhance mental well-being. They can be a platform to implement preventative and positive initiatives for young people to learn and maintain mental well-being (Pluskota, 2014). Educational institutions have the potential to play a crucial role in promoting positive education among young people. This is because children spend a significant amount of their time attending school (Dray et al., 2015; Fazel et al., 2014; Pluskota, 2014), more so than any other formal institutional structure. As such, schools play a key part in children's development. They impact everything from peer relationships, social interactions, academic attainment, and cognitive progress, to emotional control, behavioral expectations, and physical and moral development (Fazel et al., 2014).

Moreover, schools provide children and adolescents with access to resources, infrastructure, and values that are essential for the development of positive health, mental well-being, and resilience, especially during critical times in their growth and development (Dray et al., 2015; Pluskota, 2014; Seligman et al., 2009)

By implementing positive education, schools can address youth depression (Brunwasser et al., 2009) and enhance students' well-being, social and emotional skills, attitudes, behavior, relationships, and academic performance (Durlak et al., 2011; Waters, 2011). Moreover, positive education encourages children to develop self-inquiry and self-management skills for better mental health. This leads to improved self-awareness and emotional intelligence in adulthood (White & Waters, 2015). It also leads to better overall health and a lower likelihood of engaging in risky health behaviors during young adulthood (Hoyt et al., 2012).

In addition, integrating positive education programs into schools is a cost-effective approach to promoting mental health, as existing resources and personnel can be used, and additional costs associated with initiating new programs can be reduced (Bothe et al., 2014). It is also financially beneficial. The cost of running prevention programs is much lower than the cost associated with providing mental health care to students who develop difficulties in the future (*Preventing Mental, Emotional, and Behavioral Disorders Among Young People*, 2009).

While societies are struggling to support young people facing high levels of stress and mental illness, while also striving to produce competent, confident, and happy students, positive education seems to be an answer to that. Positive Psychology-based youth support programs enhance student learning, tackle mental disorders, and equip the next generation with better life skills (Chodkiewicz & Boyle, 2017a).

That's why governments have encouraged schools to play a role in promoting positive values and attitudes to help address societal challenges. This has led to a shift in government policies and rhetoric, with increased calls for schools to support positive mental health in youth with countries like U.K, the U.S.A, Australia, and Hong Kong being among them (Au & Kennedy, 2018; Chodkiewicz & Boyle, 2017a).

Positive Education Frameworks

A framework in Positive Psychology serves as an organizing structure for promoting flourishing in educational settings (Noble & McGrath, 2015).

To effectively promote student well-being, it's not enough to simply provide a single positive education program. Instead, a comprehensive approach that spans all aspects of a school is necessary (White & Murray, 2015). A meta-framework can provide researchers and practitioners with a clear direction for developing, implementing, and assessing interventions. This framework should have broad and adaptable guidelines that reflect a comprehensive understanding of student well-being, while still allowing for flexibility in selecting or designing interventions to fit different contexts (Waters & Loton, 2019).

There are many frameworks in positive education. Some of them focus only on one or two aspects of well-being (Waters & Loton, 2019) like the Penn Resiliency program focusing on resilience and preventing youth depressive symptoms (Brunwasser et al., 2009) and the Ruler Framework, which focuses on emotional intelligence (Hagelskamp et al., 2013) and some are multidimensional, representing the wider range of factors in the literature that comprise wellbeing (Waters & Loton, 2019).

The Geelong Grammar School Applied Framework for Positive Education (Norrish et al., 2013)

The Geelong Grammar School (GGS) Model for Positive Education is a practical framework that explains how Positive Psychology can be implemented and integrated into schools. The model was developed after implementing a whole-school approach to Positive Education at an Australian school for five years. The model is based on a focus on character strengths, and it offers a structured approach to implementing Positive Education in schools. Additionally, it provides a framework to guide evaluation and research (Norrish et al., 2013).

It comprises explicit and implicit teaching methods, as well as school-wide practices that focus on six wellbeing domains: positive emotions, positive engagement, positive accomplishment, positive purpose, positive relationships, and positive health (Norrish, 2015; Norrish et al., 2013).

The optimal goal of GGS was school flourishing and flourishing in schools happens when students are happy, have healthy relationships, and achieve their goals. Staff members flourish when they feel positive emotions, find value in their work, and are respected. Classes flourish when students feel included, teachers are confident, and everyone is engaged. Schools flourish when members feel a sense of belonging, and culture promotes positive emotions, effective learning, and social responsibility (Norrish et al., 2013).

The approach adopted by GGS involved teaching Positive Psychology to the staff by Seligman and his team. Later, the GGS staff taught the same science to the students. Gradually, the school adopted a whole-school approach to incorporate science into its broader culture. This approach was based on Seligman's model of wellbeing, PERMA, with an additional health (H) dimension (i.e., PERMAH) (Green et al., 2021; Norrish, 2015; Norrish et al., 2013).

GGS's Positive Education strategy involves four key components: "learn it, live it, teach it, and embed it." (Green et al., 2021; Norrish et al.,2013). Each of these components is explained in further detail below.

Live it: The school offers comprehensive programs that support staff wellbeing and help them apply Positive Education skills in their personal lives and work. Most staff participate in training programs and refresher workshops every term. Additionally, the school fosters community-building activities such as discussion groups and a Journal Club (Norrish at al., 2013).

Teach it: Positive Education is a teaching approach that aims to equip students with the skills and mindsets necessary to thrive in their lives. This approach is taught explicitly and implicitly, with explicit instruction taking place from Year 5 to Year 10. During this time, students learn diverse skills, knowledge, and mindsets. Positive Education is also integrated throughout the academic curriculum, with teaching staff incorporating it into a broad range of subjects. Moreover, the teaching pedagogy is informed by Positive Education, with educators integrating mindfulness practices into class routines and fostering a growth mindset in their students (Norrish et al., 2013).

Embed it: The school implements school-wide practices such as character strength assemblies, gratitude boards, and kindness projects to embed a culture of well-being. Parents are invited to participate and support their understanding of Positive Education and personal growth through multi-day training programs (Norrish et al., 2013).

PROSPER. A New Framework for Positive Education. (Noble &McGrath, 2015)

The PROSPER framework is a tool used for implementing Positive Education, which is an approach that applies Positive Psychology research to educational contexts. The name 'PROSPER' reflects the framework's purpose and is also an acronym that emphasizes seven key elements that contribute to well-being: Positivity, Relationships, Outcomes, Strengths, Purpose, Engagement, and Resilience. The PROSPER acronym stands for these seven key elements, which are intended to help organize the multi-dimensional components that contribute to flourishing (Noble & McGrath, 2015).

The PROSPER framework has several similarities to Seligman's (2011) earlier PERMA model of well-being, which includes Positive emotions, Engagement, Relationships, Meaning, and Accomplishment. However, the PROSPER framework specifically includes two additional significant components: Strengths and Resilience (Noble & McGrath, 2015). Each of these components is explained in further detail below (Noble & McGrath, 2015).

Encouraging **P**OSITIVITY

Encouraging positivity involves supporting students in developing positive skills and experiencing positive emotions. This can be achieved by providing opportunities for students to amplify positive emotions and build positive learning environments, for example, by using music, dance, humor, and cooperative learning tasks. Additionally, it involves explicitly teaching the values and skills required for a positive mindset, such as optimistic thinking, positive tracking, positive conversion, hopeful thinking, and expressing gratitude, as well as mindfulness. Furthermore, students should be given the chance to practice these skills (Noble & McGrath, 2015).

Building **R**ELATIONSHIPS

Building positive relationships involves supporting students in developing social skills and pro-social values. To achieve this, schools use various strategies such as creating a safe and supportive school culture, fostering positive student-teacher relationships, promoting positive student-peer relationships, building positive school-family and school-community relationships, explicitly teaching social skills and values, providing opportunities to practice these skills, and establishing interpersonal structures that facilitate relationships. These structures may include cooperative learning groups, cross-age teams, cooperative games, peer support, and performance groups (Noble & McGrath, 2015).

Facilitating **O**UTCOMES

Facilitating outcomes involves providing optimal learning environments and opportunities for students to learn specific skills that enhance their achievements. This can be achieved through the adoption of evidence-informed teaching strategies and the explicit teaching of skills such as organization, goal achievement (e.g. effort, persistence, and problem-solving), effective studying, promotion of a growth mindset, and the use of critical and creative thinking tools that challenge and scaffold students' learning (Noble & McGrath, 2015).

Focusing on **S**TRENGTHS

Focusing on strengths involves adopting a strengths-based approach for students, teachers, and the entire school community. This approach includes implementing strengths-based approaches to organization, curriculum, and planning. The outcomes of this approach are that students can identify, explore, and apply their strengths, teachers can use task differentiation, and school psychologists and coaches can use strengths-based approaches. Recognition and application of teacher and parent strengths, as well as collective strengths, can be achieved using strategies such as appreciative inquiry (Noble & McGrath, 2015).

Fostering a Sense of **P**URPOSE

Fostering purpose involves helping students develop a sense of purpose and meaning. This can be achieved by providing opportunities for students to: participate in activities that they have ownership of and direct themselves; engage in community service or service learning; contribute to the school through "student voice" and participation in decision-making about aspects of the school; take on peer mentoring or support roles; assume leadership positions; and explore spirituality (Noble & McGrath, 2015).

Enhancing **E**NGAGEMENT

Enhancing engagement means providing opportunities for students to be highly engaged in their learning. This can be achieved by adopting evidence-informed teaching and learning strategies, as well as relationship-based teaching strategies. Activities that incorporate critical and creative thinking should are also included, along with curriculum differentiation and extra-curricular activities, so that students can experience a state of 'flow' (Noble & McGrath, 2015).

Teaching **R**ESILIENCE

Teaching resilience involves helping students develop the skills and attitudes necessary for exhibiting resilient behavior. This is accomplished by explicitly teaching skills such as coping and acting resiliently in both personal and academic contexts, acting with courage, making good decisions, and managing oneself effectively (Noble & McGrath, 2015).

SEARCH Framework (Waters & Loton, 2019)

SEARCH is a framework developed to help researchers organize current scientific findings and advance future research. It is designed to assist school leaders, teachers, and practitioners in making evidence-based decisions when implementing education interventions. SEARCH is a new meta-framework that is higher-order in nature, evidence-based, actionable, and multi-dimensional (Waters & Loton, 2019).

SEARCH has identified six key pathways to positive functioning and well-being: strengths, emotional management, attention and awareness, relationships, coping, and habits and goals (Waters & Loton, 2019).

Strengths

Strengths are qualities that come naturally, feel authentic, are motivating to use, and energizing (Brdar & Kashdan, 2010). Schools can explicitly teach character strengths. It enhances positive attributes such as curiosity, creativity, love of learning, and hope. This leads to higher levels of well-being and stronger academic outcomes, such as higher engagement, academic confidence, and aspirations (Waters & Loton, 2019).

Emotional Management

Emotional intelligence and gratitude were found to be two key constructs of emotional management. Emotional intelligence (EI) is generally understood as the ability to perceive, understand, use, and regulate emotions. Emotional intelligence (EI) refers to the capacity to perceive, comprehend, utilize, and manage emotions (Brackett et al., 2012). Gratitude is the feeling of thankfulness and joy in response to receiving a gift, whether it's a tangible benefit from another person or a moment of peaceful bliss evoked by natural beauty (Peterson & Seligman, 2004). According to Waters and Loton (2019), classroom programs and practices can increase EI and gratitude in students, particularly those with low levels. These interventions can boost well-being indicators, reduce distress indicators, and improve academic outcomes such as school satisfaction, scholastic confidence, and grades.

Attention and Awareness

The term "attention" refers to the ability to focus on either internal aspects of oneself, such as emotions and physical sensations, or external stimuli, such as a teacher's lesson in a classroom (Beauchemin et al., 2008).

Meditation and mindfulness are practices that can help improve attention and awareness. Studies have shown that these practices have a positive impact on well-being, resulting in increased positive emotions, calmness, self-acceptance, and reduced levels of anxiety, stress, and depression. Furthermore, there is evidence that these practices can also lead to better grades and cognitive functioning (Waters & Loton, 2019).

Relationships

The SEARCH pathway of relationships involves the skills needed to maintain long-term social relationships and to take advantage of momentary social interactions through mentoring (Waters & Loton, 2019). Mentoring is a process in which an experienced person provides guidance, support, and care to a less experienced person over an extended period (Karcher, 2005).

Mentoring programs may improve student connectedness, self-esteem, and well-being outcomes, but the evidence is mixed. While some studies reported significant effects, others found no effects. More evidence is needed to establish the effectiveness of mentoring programs among student populations (Waters & Loton, 2019).

Coping

Coping refers to the ability of individuals to understand their situation and engage in processes that help them deal effectively with adversity. In the context of school-based interventions, the coping pathway includes coping interventions and resilience programs. Research has shown that coping and resilience interventions can reduce anxiety and depression while increasing social and emotional well-being, assertiveness, and positive relationships. Moreover, these interventions have some evidence linking them to academic outcomes such as school grades and interest in learning (Waters & Loton, 2019).

Habits and Goals

Habits are learned patterns and preferences in behavior (Wood & Neal, 2007), while goals are formal aspirations that people aim to achieve (Baumeister et al., 2006). Interventions that are implemented in schools and are in line with this pathway are self-regulation programs and goal-setting interventions. These interventions have improved learning outcomes by regulating students' thinking and learning patterns, fostering goal-oriented behaviors, and enhancing social skills. As a result, students' levels of self-efficacy, motivation, and well-being increase while their levels of helplessness, emotional difficulties, anxiety, and boredom decrease. These interventions also lead to better academic performance and higher levels of class satisfaction (Waters & Loton, 2019).

POSITIVE PSYCHOLOGY SCHOOL INTERVENTIONS

Positive Psychology Interventions in Schools

In the early 2000s, there was a significant shift in educational policies. Positive Psychology gained popularity (Chodkiewicz & Boyle, 2017a), leading to educators acknowledging the need to focus on children's social and emotional development, which has a direct impact on their academic performance (Miller et al., 2010). A preventative approach to mental health was adopted, which resulted in discussions about a more holistic approach to education encouraging educators to focus on developing the whole child, rather than just academic skills (Waters, 2011). Schools were expected to play a larger role in promoting student mental health and nurturing their social, emotional, and psychological skills. To achieve this, schools had to transform their curriculum and teaching practices. They began focusing on increasing student well-being, fostering optimal youth functioning, teaching social skills, supporting student self-image, equipping students with higher-level cognitive skills, and addressing youth mental health issues (Seligman et al., 2007; Waters, 2011).

A summary of some school-based Positive Psychology interventions implemented in school settings is presented.

Penn Resiliency Programme for Children and Adolescents (PRP-CA)

The Penn Resiliency Programme for Children and Adolescents (PRP-CA) is one of the most extensively researched Positive Psychology interventions available. The PRP-CA is a structured school-based curriculum that aims to promote resilience through cognitive-behavioral therapy (CBT) techniques, which teach realistic thinking and adaptive coping skills. The program consists of 18 hours (12 x 90-minute lessons or 18-24 x 60-minute lessons) of student instruction and is usually conducted in groups of around 15 students. The school staff is asked to complete an eight-module online CBT course and attend a 10-day workshop for running the program (Chodkiewicz & Boyle, 2017a). A meta-analysis of 17 studies found that young individuals who participated in PRP-CA programs experienced a decrease in depressive symptoms after the intervention, which persisted for a 12-month follow-up period (Brunwasser et al., 2009). Later, a parental component was added to the program, which further enhanced its effectiveness (Pinheiro, 2015). However, a more recent review did not find any evidence of PRP's ability to reduce depression or anxiety, nor improve explanatory style (Bastounis et al., 2016).

Friends

The FRIENDS program is an acronym for Feelings, Remember to relax, I can try my best, Explore solutions and coping step plan, Now reward yourself, Do it every day, and Smile. It is a universal preventative intervention program for preschool children (Pahl & Barrett, 2010). Its goal is to promote emotional resilience, increase social and emotional skills, and prevent anxiety and depression. The program uses Cognitive Behavioral Therapy (CBT) techniques to teach children practical skills to manage anxiety. It includes strategies such as identifying anxious feelings, learning to relax, replacing unhelpful thoughts, and facing problems. Children receive an attractive workbook to complete during the program. The program consists of 10 sessions, each lasting for an hour. Trained school nurses deliver the FRIENDS program to students aged 9-10 years. The nurses undergo a two-day training session and are provided with a manual for each of the 10 sessions. A clinical psychologist provides monthly supervision, and there is a review at the end of each program. The program has resulted in the enhancement of emotional resilience, reducing anxiety and increasing self-esteem (Stallard et al., 2005), and it has been endorsed by the World Health Organisation as an evidence-based program effective for the prevention of child and youth anxiety (Higgins & O'Sullivan, 2015). Indeed, in a recent review, all reviewed studies found that the program had a positive impact on primary anxiety outcome measures compared to control groups, with small to medium effect sizes reported (Higgins & O'Sullivan, 2015; Pahl & Barrett, 2010).

JES Youth Prevention Program

The JES program was developed in Germany to teach adolescents about the links between emotions, stress, and the body. The initiative was aimed at 8th-grade students who attended 10 sessions, each lasting about 45 minutes. The sessions comprised a two-minute warm-up exercise, including stretching and deep breathing, followed by a 20-minute discussion on topics related to emotional regulation and coping. At the end of each session, students were given time to do expressive writing tasks. Meanwhile, students in the control group attended their regular classes. While the program led to slight academic improvements, they were not sustained over time. However, students who attended the program had significantly fewer absences from school over a six-month period compared to those who did not participate in the sessions (Horn et al., 2011).

UPRIGHT

The UPRIGHT (Universal Preventive Resilience Intervention Globally implemented in schools to improve and promote mental Health for Teenagers) is a research and resilience intervention program with a universal whole-school approach in the Basque Country (Spain), Trentino (Italy), Low Silesia (Poland), Denmark and Reykjavik. UPRIGHT is a whole-school prevention program targeting adolescents 12-14 years of age, their families, and schools and aims to promote mental health by enhancing adolescents' resilience capacities. The innovation of the current project is that families and schools will not only participate in the implementation of the program but will also co-create, along with the researchers, the protocol of the program to respond to local needs and resources (Morote et al., 2022).

POSITIVE EDUCATION PROGRAMS

Common Features of Positive Education Programs

Positive Psychology programs in schools have different approaches, but they all have common themes. Most programs target young students in late childhood and early adolescence (Chodkiewicz & Boyle, 2017a) when their brains have developed enough for cognitive reflection and thought restructuring (Schonert-Reichl et al., 2015). This period is a crucial turning point because students are more malleable and willing to change than older populations (Lerner et al., 2010) . Furthermore, they are at risk of severe difficulties and challenges, so teaching them adaptive skills through interventions is essential (Bakadorova & Raufelder, 2014) .

School-based interventions are usually short, lasting between 6 and 10 sessions. Although some researchers run longer youth programs, these are considered time-consuming and logistically impractical to fit into an already full school curriculum (Chodkiewicz & Boyle, 2017a; Stallard et al., 2014; Suldo et al., 2014).

Most school-based interventions are rooted in a single or dual theoretical framework (Chodkiewicz & Boyle, 2017a; Waters & Loton, 2019). One popular approach is to model youth programs on the principles of CBT (Chodkiewicz & Boyle., 2015), which has positive effects on youth mental health. Other approaches have included attribution retraining, solution-focused therapy, strength-based coaching, and mindfulness training. While some researchers have begun creating more diverse interventions, many still design programs to adhere to a single theoretical framework, which can limit the number of techniques and skills accessible to each student (Chodkiewicz & Boyle, 2017a).

School-based interventions often only focus on the student level without considering the wider educational setting or home environment (Chodkiewicz & Boyle, 2017a; Waters & Loton, 2019). However, context plays a key role in shaping individual well-being, so school-based interventions need to engage a student's various micro- and meso-systems (Lomas, 2015). Some programs that take a whole-school approach, like the Geelong Grammar School project have been successful in engaging a student's wider community, but they require significant resources (Chodkiewicz & Boyle, 2017b; Norrish, 2015).

Effectiveness of Positive Education Programs

Positive Psychology interventions in schools have yielded mixed results in research due to differences in methodology. Positive Psychology is an umbrella term that includes various theories and techniques, resulting in interventions with different theoretical scopes and instructional methodologies. There is no agreed-upon standard, and various psychological and academic factors are assessed with varying definitions and measurement tools. Therefore, comparing individual studies offers limited information due to differences in research methodologies and mixed outcomes (Chodkiewicz & Boyle, 2017a).

However, systematic meta-analyses of the field of research indicate the overall benefits of Positive Psychology school-based interventions. Reviews are optimistic that these programs are helping students thrive (Chodkiewicz & Boyle, 2017a). Based on Waters' (2011) review, it has been found that incorporating Positive Psychology programs in schools can significantly enhance students' well-being, relationships, and academic performance. Furthermore, interventions that focus on building resilience can be particularly effective during childhood and adolescence, especially when tailored to target protective factors that are relevant to the age group. Universal resilience-based interventions, mainly those that are based on cognitive-behavioral therapy, have shown the most potential for reducing depressive and anxiety symptoms in children and adolescents in the short term (Dray et al., 2017).

Moreover, Dray et al.'s (2017) review of 57 studies targeting children and adolescents between the ages of 5 and 18 aimed to strengthen a minimum of three internal resilience protective factors and included an outcome measure of mental health problems. They found that they were all effective in reducing four of seven outcomes: depressive symptoms, internalizing problems, externalizing problems, and general psychological distress relative to a control group.

Positive Psychology school-based interventions have also proven successful in enhancing social-emotional skills, attitudes, and behaviors in students while also reducing emotional distress, conduct problems (Durlak et al., 2011), as well as internalizing disorders (Stockings et al., 2016).

Meta-analyses and reviews of Positive Psychology interventions designed to improve student well-being or prevent depression and anxiety have produced overwhelmingly positive results (Neil & Christensen, 2009; Sin & Lyubomirsky, 2009).

Apart from mental health, universal school-based interventions that address 'resilience' protective factors are also effective in reducing adolescent illicit substance use (Hodder et al., 2017). Resilience-focused programs can also be beneficial in facing social challenges. The results of the STRONG program, a program implemented in Canadian schools aiming to increase resilience in refugee students, were effective in increasing connectedness, stress management, coping strategies, and reducing distress among refugee students through a structured school-based group intervention (Crooks et al., 2020). As a result, these students were more likely to successfully acculturate and adapt to a new country.

Ungar et al. (2014) argue that from 36 intervention programs targeting resilience in middle school students, the results were mixed regarding their effectiveness. They concluded that successful programs interrupt patterns of behavior that are likely to lead to academic failure and disengagement from school by changing a student's social ecology. They propose to apply these kinds of programs as early as possible, even though it is never too late to begin to make a difference.

Nonetheless, more comprehensive and longitudinal research studies are required to realize the potential of school-based Positive Psychology programs fully. This is because the field of research is still in its early stages (Chodkiewicz & Boyle, 2017).

Challenges in Positive Education Programs

Although the adoption of PosEd is widespread, there are still challenges to be addressed, such as lack of support, student interest, and confusion about PosEd (Morote et al., 2022).

Firstly, Positive Education (PosEd) is implemented differently in various schools. Some schools follow a structured approach, while others experiment with different exercises. PosEd lessons may be scheduled for a specific time each week, or well-being concepts may be infused into the entire curriculum. Some schools start with small steps and then expand, while others plan to implement formal programs later (Slemp et al., 2017).

To ensure the success of PosEd, it is essential to embrace a whole-school approach (Chodkiewicz & Boyle, 2017b; Slemp et al., 2017). This implies that teachers, staff, and leadership should all contribute to its implementation. Teachers, staff, and leadership should all contribute to Positive Psychology implementation, including the broader educational and home environments. However, the context is crucial in shaping individual well-being, so school-based interventions must engage the student's various micro- and meso-systems (Chodkiewicz & Boyle, 2017b; Ecclestone & Lewis, 2014; Hart & Heaver, 2013). Students' interest and engagement in school are also associated with socio-economic status, lack of support from family, and other contextual factors, and multiple-level interventions need to be addressed. According to Unglar et al. (2014), the best interventions are collaborative, multi-systemic, and culturally relevant, and respond to the needs of the students themselves.

On the other hand, programs that take a whole-school approach have successfully engaged a student's wider community, but they require significant resources and (Chodkiewicz & Boyle, 2017b; Hart & Heaver, 2013; Slemp et al., 2017) are not replicable due to their high cost (Hart & Heaver, 2013).

Other factors that need to be considered in a whole-school approach besides the limited availability of resources are an overcrowded curriculum, difficulties in accessing information, teacher-related factors, and inadequate training (Chodkiewicz & Boyle, 2017b). With so many demands on time and resources, it is important for educators to implement short-term, evidence-based curricular approaches that optimize learning and social adaptation while also being cost-effective (Durlak et al., 2011) maybe by beginning to look at how existing brief Positive Psychology interventions can be modified to widen their impact (Chodkiewicz & Boyle, 2017a).

Other factors that need to be addressed are the need for long-term outcome assessment (Morote et al., 2022) and the lack of long-term follow-up in school-based intervention studies (Calear & Christensen, 2010; Dray et al., 2017), the effect of intervention by gender remains largely unexamined although gender differences exist in mental health problems (Dray et al., 2017) and the effectiveness of PosEd's in diverse student populations which lacks empirical evidence (Slemp et al., 2017).

Finally, it is important to integrate both formal and informal curricula to include students' well-being. This is because implicit expectations can be instilled in students, and teachers can model positive education (Au & Kennedy, 2018).

CONCLUSION AND FUTURE DIRECTIONS

Positive education frameworks and interventions have positively impacted students' mental health and well-being. This has led to various benefits not only in their mental health but also in their academic achievements. However, to achieve maximum results, a whole-school approach is necessary. This approach involves students, parents, school staff, and the community. Implementing this strategy requires significant resources, time, and training, which may not be easily feasible. In the future, positive interventions and programs should focus on a whole-school approach that is cost-effective and replicable. This approach should also take into consideration the formal and informal curriculum and gender differences and include long-term follow-up to evaluate results.

REFERENCES

Alex Linley, P., Joseph, S., Harrington, S., & Wood, A. M. (2006). Positive Psychology: Past, present, and (possible) future. *The Journal of Positive Psychology*, 1(1), 3–16. 10.1080/17439760500372796

Au, W. C. C., & Kennedy, K. J. (2018). A Positive Education Program to Promote Wellbeing in Schools: A Case Study from a Hong Kong School. *Higher Education Studies*, 8(4), 9. 10.5539/hes.v8n4p9

Bakadorova, O., & Raufelder, D. (2014). The mediating role of socio-motivational support in the association between individual school self-concept and achievement motivation amongst adolescent students. *European Journal of Psychology of Education*, 29(3), 347–366. 10.1007/s10212-013-0202-5

Baker, L., Green, S., & Falecki, D. (2017). Positive early childhood education: Expanding the reach of Positive Psychology into early childhood. *European Journal of Applied Positive Psychology*, 1(8), 1–12.

Baumeister, R. F., Gailliot, M., DeWall, C. N., & Oaten, M. (2006). Self-Regulation and Personality: How Interventions Increase Regulatory Success, and How Depletion Moderates the Effects of Traits on Behavior. *Journal of Personality*, 74(6), 1773–1802. 10.1111/j.1467-6494.2006.00428.x17083666

Beauchemin, J., Hutchins, T. L., & Patterson, F. (2008). Mindfulness Meditation May Lessen Anxiety, Promote Social Skills, and Improve Academic Performance Among Adolescents With Learning Disabilities. *Complementary Health Practice Review*, 13(1), 34–45. 10.1177/1533210107311624

Becker, D., & Marecek, J. (2008). Dreaming the American Dream: Individualism and Positive Psychology. *Social and Personality Psychology Compass*, 2(5), 1767–1780. 10.1111/j.1751-9004.2008.00139.x

Bothe, D. A., Grignon, J. B., & Olness, K. N. (2014). The Effects of a Stress Management Intervention in Elementary School Children. *Journal of Developmental and Behavioral Pediatrics*, 35(1), 62–67. 10.1097/DBP.0000000000000001624336090

Brackett, M. A., Rivers, S. E., Reyes, M. R., & Salovey, P. (2012). Enhancing academic performance and social and emotional competence with the RULER feeling words curriculum. *Learning and Individual Differences*, 22(2), 218–224. 10.1016/j.lindif.2010.10.002

Brdar, I., & Kashdan, T. B. (2010). Character strengths and well-being in Croatia: An empirical investigation of structure and correlates. *Journal of Research in Personality*, 44(1), 151–154. 10.1016/j.jrp.2009.12.001

Brunwasser, S. M., Gillham, J. E., & Kim, E. S. (2009). A meta-analytic review of the Penn Resiliency Program's effect on depressive symptoms. *Journal of Consulting and Clinical Psychology*, 77(6), 1042–1054. 10.1037/a001767119968381

Calear, A. L., & Christensen, H. (2010). Systematic review of school-based prevention and early intervention programs for depression. *Journal of Adolescence*, 33(3), 429–438. 10.1016/j.adolescence.2009.07.00419647310

Chodkiewicz, A., & Boyle, C. (2015). *Believing you can is the first step to achieving: A CBT and Attribution Retraining Programme to improve self-belief in students aged 8-12*. Jessica Kingsley Publishers.

Chodkiewicz, A. R., & Boyle, C. (2017). Positive Psychology school-based interventions: A reflection on current success and future directions. *Review of Education*, 5(1), 60–86. 10.1002/rev3.3080

Crooks, C. V., Hoover, S., & Smith, A. C. G. (2020). Feasibility trial of the school-based STRONG intervention to promote resilience among newcomer youth. *Psychology in the Schools*, 57(12), 1815–1829. 10.1002/pits.22366

Dray, J., Bowman, J., Campbell, E., Freund, M., Wolfenden, L., Hodder, R. K., McElwaine, K., Tremain, D., Bartlem, K., Bailey, J., Small, T., Palazzi, K., Oldmeadow, C., & Wiggers, J. (2017). Systematic Review of Universal Resilience-Focused Interventions Targeting Child and Adolescent Mental Health in the School Setting. *Journal of the American Academy of Child and Adolescent Psychiatry*, 56(10), 813–824. 10.1016/j.jaac.2017.07.78028942803

Dray, J., Bowman, J., Wolfenden, L., Campbell, E., Freund, M., Hodder, R., & Wiggers, J. (2015). Systematic review of universal resilience interventions targeting child and adolescent mental health in the school setting: Review protocol. *Systematic Reviews*, 4(1), 186. 10.1186/s13643-015-0172-626715359

Durlak, J. A., Weissberg, R. P., Dymnicki, A. B., Taylor, R. D., & Schellinger, K. B. (2011). The Impact of Enhancing Students' Social and Emotional Learning: A Meta-Analysis of School-Based Universal Interventions. *Child Development*, 82(1), 405–432. 10.1111/j.1467-8624.2010.01564.x21291449

Ecclestone, K., & Lewis, L. (2014). Interventions for resilience in educational settings: Challenging policy discourses of risk and vulnerability. *Journal of Education Policy*, 29(2), 195–216. 10.1080/02680939.2013.806678

Fazel, M., Hoagwood, K., Stephan, S., & Ford, T. (2014). Mental health interventions in schools in high-income countries. *The Lancet. Psychiatry*, 1(5), 377–387. 10.1016/S2215-0366(14)70312-826114092

Frawley, A. (2015). Happiness Research: A Review of Critiques. *Sociology Compass*, 9(1), 62–77. 10.1111/soc4.12236

Fredrickson, B. L. (2001). The role of positive emotions in Positive Psychology: The broaden-and-build theory of positive emotions. *The American Psychologist*, 56(3), 218–226. 10.1037/0003-066X.56.3.21811315248

Fredrickson, B. L. (2004). The broaden–and–build theory of positive emotions. *Philosophical Transactions of the Royal Society of London. Series B, Biological Sciences*, 359(1449), 1367–1377. 10.1098/rstb.2004.151215347528

Green, S., Leach, C., & Falecki, D. (2021). Approaches to Positive Education. In Kern, M. L., & Wehmeyer, M. L. (Eds.), *The Palgrave Handbook of Positive Education* (pp. 21–48). Springer International Publishing., 10.1007/978-3-030-64537-3_2

Hagelskamp, C., Brackett, M. A., Rivers, S. E., & Salovey, P. (2013). Improving Classroom Quality with The RULER Approach to Social and Emotional Learning: Proximal and Distal Outcomes. *American Journal of Community Psychology*, 51(3–4), 530–543. 10.1007/s10464-013-9570-x23444004

Hart, A., & Heaver, B. (2013). Evaluating resilience-based programs for schools using a systematic consultative review. *Journal of Child and Youth Development*, 1, 27–53.

Higgins, E., & O'Sullivan, S. (2015). "What Works": Systematic review of the "FRIENDS for Life" programme as a universal school-based intervention programme for the prevention of child and youth anxiety. *Educational Psychology in Practice*, 31(4), 424–438. 10.1080/02667363.2015.1086977

Hodder, R. K., Freund, M., Wolfenden, L., Bowman, J., Nepal, S., Dray, J., Kingsland, M., Yoong, S. L., & Wiggers, J. (2017). Systematic review of universal school-based 'resilience' interventions targeting adolescent tobacco, alcohol or illicit substance use: A meta-analysis. *Preventive Medicine*, 100, 248–268. 10.1016/j.ypmed.2017.04.00328390835

Horn, A. B., Pössel, P., & Hautzinger, M. (2011). Promoting Adaptive Emotion Regulation and Coping in Adolescence: A School-based Programme. *Journal of Health Psychology*, 16(2), 258–273. 10.1177/135910531037281420733014

Hoyt, L. T., Chase-Lansdale, P. L., McDade, T. W., & Adam, E. K. (2012). Positive Youth, Healthy Adults: Does Positive Well-being in Adolescence Predict Better Perceived Health and Fewer Risky Health Behaviors in Young Adulthood? *The Journal of Adolescent Health*, 50(1), 66–73. 10.1016/j.jadohealth.2011.05.00222188836

Karcher, M. J. (2005). The effects of developmental mentoring and high school mentors' attendance on their younger mentees' self-esteem, social skills, and connectedness. *Psychology in the Schools*, 42(1), 65–77. 10.1002/pits.20025

Khaw, D., & Kern, M. (2014). A cross-cultural comparison of the PERMA model of well-being. *Undergraduate Journal of Psychology at Berkeley. University of California., 8*(1), 10–23.

Kovich, M. K., Simpson, V. L., Foli, K. J., Hass, Z., & Phillips, R. G. (2023). Application of the PERMA Model of Well-being in Undergraduate Students. *International Journal of Community Well-being*, 6(1), 1–20. 10.1007/s42413-022-00184-436320595

Kristjánsson, K. (2012). Positive Psychology and Positive Education: Old Wine in New Bottles? *Educational Psychologist*, 47(2), 86–105. 10.1080/00461520.2011.610678

Kun, Á., Balogh, P., & Krasz, K. G. (2016). Development of the Work-Related Well-Being Questionnaire Based on Seligman's PERMA Model. *Periodica Polytechnica Social and Management Sciences*, 25(1), 56. 10.3311/PPso.9326

Lambert D'raven, L., & Pasha-Zaidi, N. (2016). Using the PERMA Model in the United Arab Emirates. *Social Indicators Research*, 125(3), 905–933. 10.1007/s11205-015-0866-0

Lerner, R. M., Von Eye, A., Lerner, J. V., Lewin-Bizan, S., & Bowers, E. P. (2010). Special Issue Introduction: The Meaning and Measurement of Thriving: A View of the Issues. *Journal of Youth and Adolescence*, 39(7), 707–719. 10.1007/s10964-010-9531-820387108

Lomas, T. (2015). Positive social psychology: A multilevel inquiry into sociocultural well-being initiatives. *Psychology, Public Policy, and Law*, 21(3), 338–347. 10.1037/law0000051

Lundqvist, C., & Enttä, G. (2010). Positive Emotions Are Not Simply the Absence of the Negative Ones: Development and Validation of the Emotional Recovery Questionnaire (EmRecQ). *The Sport Psychologist*, 24(4), 468–488. 10.1123/tsp.24.4.468

Miller, L. D., Short, C., Garland, E. J., & Clark, S. (2010). The ABCs of CBT (Cognitive Behavior Therapy): Evidence-Based Approaches to Child Anxiety in Public School Settings. *Journal of Counseling and Development*, 88(4), 432–439. 10.1002/j.1556-6678.2010.tb00043.x

Morote, R., Las Hayas, C., Izco-Basurko, I., Anyan, F., Fullaondo, A., Donisi, V., Zwiefka, A., Gudmundsdottir, D. G., Ledertoug, M. M., Olafsdottir, A. S., Gabrielli, S., Carbone, S., Mazur, I., Królicka-Deręgowska, A., Knoop, H. H., Tange, N., Kaldalóns, I. V., Jónsdóttir, B. J., González Pinto, A., & Hjemdal, O. (2022). Co-creation and regional adaptation of a resilience-based universal whole-school program in five European regions. *European Educational Research Journal*, 21(1), 138–164. 10.1177/1474904120947890

Noble, T., & McGrath, H. (2015). PROSPER: A New Framework for Positive Education. *Psychology of Well-Being*, 5(1), 2. 10.1186/s13612-015-0030-2

Norrish, J. M. (2015). *Positive Education: The Geelong Grammar School Journey*. Oxford University Press. 10.1093/acprof:oso/9780198702580.001.0001

Norrish, J. M., Williams, P., O'Connor, M., & Robinson, J. (2013). An applied framework for positive education. *International Journal of Wellbeing*, 3(2), 157–161. 10.5502/ijw.v3i2.2

Pahl, K. M., & Barrett, P. M. (2010). Preventing Anxiety and Promoting Social and Emotional Strength in Preschool Children: A Universal Evaluation of the Fun FRIENDS Program. *Advances in School Mental Health Promotion*, 3(3), 14–25. 10.1080/1754730X.2010.9715683

Peterson, C., & Seligman, M. E. (2004). *Character strengths and virtues: A handbook and classification* (Vol. 1). Oxford University Press.

Pinheiro, M. D. R. (2015). *A Parental Program for the Prevention of Depression in Adolescents*. 10.15405/epsbs.2015.08.9

Pluskota, A. (2014). The application of Positive Psychology in the practice of education. *SpringerPlus*, 3(1), 147. 10.1186/2193-1801-3-14724790805

Preventing Mental, Emotional, and Behavioral Disorders Among Young People: Progress and Possibilities. (2009). National Academies Press. 10.17226/12480

Sandstrom, G. M., & Dunn, E. W. (2014). Social Interactions and Well-Being: The Surprising Power of Weak Ties. *Personality and Social Psychology Bulletin*, 40(7), 910–922. 10.1177/014616721452979924769739

Schaufeli, W. B., Bakker, A. B., & Salanova, M. (2006). The Measurement of Work Engagement With a Short Questionnaire: A Cross-National Study. *Educational and Psychological Measurement*, 66(4), 701–716. 10.1177/0013164405282471

Schonert-Reichl, K. A., Oberle, E., Lawlor, M. S., Abbott, D., Thomson, K., Oberlander, T. F., & Diamond, A. (2015). Enhancing cognitive and social–emotional development through a simple-to-administer mindfulness-based school program for elementary school children: A randomized controlled trial. *Developmental Psychology*, 51(1), 52–66. 10.1037/a003845425546595

Scorsolini-Comin, F., Fontaine, A. M. G. V., Koller, S. H., & Santos, M. A. D. (2013). From authentic happiness to well-being: The flourishing of Positive Psychology. *Psicologia: Reflexão e Crítica*, 26(4), 663–670. 10.1590/S0102-79722013000400006

Seligman, M. E. (2002). Positive Psychology, positive prevention, and positive therapy. In *Handbook of Positive Psychology 2* (pp. 3–12). Academic Press.

Seligman, M. E. P. (2002). *Authentic happiness: Using the new Positive Psychology to realize your potential for lasting fulfillment*. Free Press.

Seligman, M. E. P. (2011). *Flourish: A visionary new understanding of happiness and well-being*. Free Press.

Seligman, M. E. P., & Csikszentmihalyi, M. (2000). Positive Psychology: An introduction. *The American Psychologist*, 55(1), 5–14. 10.1037/0003-066X.55.1.51 1392865

Seligman, M. E. P., Ernst, R. M., Gillham, J., Reivich, K., & Linkins, M. (2009). Positive education: Positive Psychology and classroom interventions. *Oxford Review of Education*, 35(3), 293–311. 10.1080/03054980902934563

Seligman, M. E. P., Schulman, P., & Tryon, A. M. (2007). Group prevention of depression and anxiety symptoms. *Behaviour Research and Therapy*, 45(6), 1111–1126. 10.1016/j.brat.2006.09.01017074301

Slemp, G. R., Chin, T.-C., Kern, M. L., Siokou, C., Loton, D., Oades, L. G., Vella-Brodrick, D., & Waters, L. (2017). Positive Education in Australia: Practice, Measurement, and Future Directions. In Frydenberg, E., Martin, A. J., & Collie, R. J. (Eds.), *Social and Emotional Learning in Australia and the Asia-Pacific* (pp. 101–122). Springer Singapore. 10.1007/978-981-10-3394-0_6

Stallard, P., Simpson, N., Anderson, S., Carter, T., Osborn, C., & Bush, S. (2005). An evaluation of the FRIENDS programme: A cognitive behaviour therapy intervention to promote emotional resilience. *Archives of Disease in Childhood*, 90(10), 1016–1019. 10.1136/adc.2004.06816316049062

Stallard, P., Skryabina, E., Taylor, G., Phillips, R., Daniels, H., Anderson, R., & Simpson, N. (2014). Classroom-based cognitive behaviour therapy (FRIENDS): A cluster randomised controlled trial to Prevent Anxiety in Children through Education in Schools (PACES). *The Lancet. Psychiatry*, 1(3), 185–192. 10.1016/S2215-0366(14)70244-526360730

Suldo, S. M., Savage, J. A., & Mercer, S. H. (2014). Increasing Middle School Students' Life Satisfaction: Efficacy of a Positive Psychology Group Intervention. *Journal of Happiness Studies*, 15(1), 19–42. 10.1007/s10902-013-9414-2

Ungar, M., Russell, P., & Connelly, G. (2014). School-Based Interventions to Enhance the Resilience of Students. *Journal of Educational and Developmental Psychology*, 4(1), 66. 10.5539/jedp.v4n1p66

Waterman, A. S. (2013). Eudaimonia: Contrasting two conceptions of happiness: Hedonia and eudaimonia. In Froh, J. J., & Parks, A. C. (Eds.), *Activities for teaching Positive Psychology: A guide for instructors* (pp. 29–34). American Psychological Association. 10.1037/14042-005

Waters, L. (2011). A Review of School-Based Positive Psychology Interventions. *The Australian Educational and Developmental Psychologist*, 28(2), 75–90. 10.1375/aedp.28.2.75

Waters, L., & Loton, D. (2019). SEARCH: A Meta-Framework and Review of the Field of Positive Education. *International Journal of Applied Positive Psychology*, 4(1–2), 1–46. 10.1007/s41042-019-00017-4

White, M. A. (2016). Why won't it Stick? Positive Psychology and Positive Education. *Psychology of Well-Being*, 6(1), 2. 10.1186/s13612-016-0039-126900547

White, M. A., & Murray, A. S. (Eds.). (2015). *Evidence-Based Approaches in Positive Education: Implementing a Strategic Framework for Well-being in Schools*. Springer Netherlands. 10.1007/978-94-017-9667-5

White, M. A., & Waters, L. E. (2015). A case study of 'The Good School:' Examples of the use of Peterson's strengths-based approach with students. *The Journal of Positive Psychology*, 10(1), 69–76. 10.1080/17439760.2014.92040825431614

Wood, W., & Neal, D. T. (2007). A new look at habits and the habit-goal interface. *Psychological Review*, 114(4), 843–863. 10.1037/0033-295X.114.4.84317907866

Yen, J. (2014). Positive Psychology. In *Encyclopedia of Critical Psychology* (pp. 1431–1437). New York: Springer. 10.1007/978-1-4614-5583-7_225

Chapter 3
Positive Psychology and Special Education:
Fostering Hope and Optimism

Louiza Ioannidou
https://orcid.org/0000-0002-5320-1581
Frederick University, Cyprus

Dimitrios Koutroumanidis
Frederick University, Cyprus

ABSTRACT

The effects of positive psychology on enhancing educational work, particularly the work of special education teachers, are significant and multifaceted. Positive psychology focuses on enhancing well-being, happiness, and positive emotions, and its application in the educational context is crucial. This study aimed to examine how hope and optimism affect job satisfaction and teachers' relationships with special education students. The research involved 100 teachers working in educational units across Greece. A four-part questionnaire was constructed using the scales of job satisfaction, teachers' hope and optimism, and relationships with students. The results revealed that hope had a statistically significant positive correlation with satisfaction and student-teacher relationships. Also, results highlighted that hope and optimism significantly predict student-teacher relationships. The study results underscore the importance of fostering hope and optimism in special education settings to enhance educators' professional fulfillment and relational dynamics with students.

DOI: 10.4018/979-8-3693-8312-4.ch003

Copyright © 2024, IGI Global. Copying or distributing in print or electronic forms without written permission of IGI Global is prohibited.

INTRODUCTION

Positive psychology aims to study the factors that make people feel joy, display altruism, and create healthy families, societies, and institutions, addressing the entire spectrum of human experience in a scientifically substantiated manner. Unlike traditional psychology, which often focuses on pathology and negative aspects of human behavior, positive psychology emphasizes understanding and enhancing the positive aspects of human life (Seligman & Csikszentmihalyi, 2000a). Positive psychology involves the thorough scientific study of everyday human strengths, virtues, and talents to understand and promote the psychological well-being of individuals (Aspinwall & Staudinger, 2003). These positive aspects are very important for the flourishing, progress, and development of both individuals and societies (Keyes & Haidt, 2003). By focusing on these strengths, positive psychology aims to foster environments where individuals and communities can thrive, thereby promoting both personal happiness and collective well-being.

Earlier psychological approaches supported the idea that individuals remain firmly connected to the spectrum of their hereditary characteristics and predispositions (Seligman & Csikszentmihalyi, 2000a). In contrast, positive psychology emphasizes the potential for growth and development through the cultivation of existing positive characteristics in a person's personality and character. These virtues, abilities, and skills, once identified and nurtured, can be integrated into the entire spectrum of daily activities, thereby enhancing overall well-being (Keyes & Haidt, 2003).

Concepts of Positive Psychology

Positive psychology, founded by Martin Seligman and Mihaly Csikszentmihalyi (2000b), is a scientific approach to studying human thoughts, feelings, and behaviors with a focus on strengths, virtues, and factors that contribute to a fulfilling life. Here are the core concepts of positive psychology:

1. Happiness and Well-Being

Happiness and well-being are central to positive psychology. These concepts are often studied through frameworks such as Seligman's PERMA model, which includes five elements essential to well-being: Positive Emotion, Engagement, Relationships, Meaning, and Accomplishment (Seligman, 2011).

- **Positive Emotion**: Experiencing joy, gratitude, serenity, interest, hope, pride, amusement, inspiration, awe, and love.

- **Engagement**: Being deeply involved and absorbed in activities that are challenging and rewarding.
- **Relationships**: Having meaningful and positive connections with others.
- **Meaning**: Finding purpose and a sense of belonging to something larger than oneself.
- **Accomplishment**: Pursuing and achieving goals for the sake of mastery and personal growth.

2. Strengths and Virtues

Positive psychology emphasizes the identification and use of individual strengths and virtues. The VIA Classification of Character Strengths identifies 24 strengths categorized under six broad virtues (Peterson & Seligman, 2004):

- **Wisdom and Knowledge**: Creativity, curiosity, judgment, love of learning, perspective.
- **Courage**: Bravery, perseverance, honesty, zest.
- **Humanity**: Love, kindness, social intelligence.
- **Justice**: Teamwork, fairness, leadership.
- **Temperance**: Forgiveness, humility, prudence, self-regulation.
- **Transcendence**: Appreciation of beauty and excellence, gratitude, hope, humor, spirituality.

3. Flow

Flow, a concept introduced by Mihaly Csikszentmihalyi, refers to the state of being completely absorbed in an activity that is both challenging and rewarding. In this state, individuals lose track of time and experience deep satisfaction (Csikszentmihalyi, 1990).

4. Hope and Optimism

Hope is a cognitive process that activates a person's motivation to achieve goals. It consists of two main components: hope is the subjective perception of success in achieving a goal and the ability to set and implement goals (Stalikas et al., 2011). Optimism, on the other hand, focuses on the belief in positive outcomes and not on practical planning. It refers to a positive disposition and thought-mental state for outcomes of actions or events (Sheldon & King, 2001).

5. Gratitude

Gratitude involves recognizing and appreciating the positive aspects of life. Practices such as keeping a gratitude journal or expressing thanks to others have been shown to enhance well-being and happiness (Emmons & McCullough, 2003).

6. Resilience

Resilience is the ability to bounce back from adversity, trauma, or significant sources of stress. Positive psychology explores ways to build and strengthen resilience, such as through social support, positive relationships, and adaptive coping strategies (Masten, 2001).

7. Positive Relationships

The quality of our relationships significantly impacts our well-being. Positive psychology studies how supportive and loving relationships contribute to emotional health, resilience, and overall life satisfaction (Reis & Gable, 2003).

8. Mindfulness

Mindfulness involves being fully present in the moment, with an open and non-judgmental attitude. Mindfulness practices can reduce stress, enhance emotional regulation, and improve overall well-being (Kabat-Zinn, 2003).

9. Self-Compassion

Self-compassion entails treating oneself with kindness and understanding during times of failure or difficulty, rather than with harsh self-criticism. This approach can lead to greater emotional resilience and mental health (Neff, 2003).

10. Altruism and Acts of Kindness

Engaging in altruistic behaviors and acts of kindness can enhance well-being and foster a sense of connection and purpose. Positive psychology examines how these actions contribute to personal and collective flourishing (Post, 2005).

11. Meaning and Purpose

Finding meaning and purpose in life is a fundamental aspect of well-being. This involves having goals that align with one's values and a sense of direction that transcends individual self-interest (Frankl, 2006).

Integrating Positive Psychology in Special Education: Enhancing Student and Teacher Outcomes

The application of positive psychology principles can have a transformative impact on students with different learning needs in special education. Cultivating positive emotions such as joy, gratitude, and hope is crucial in special education for both students and educators. Special education teachers are called upon to create environments that enhance positivity, which can lead to improved motivation, resilience, and unity among students (Stalikas et al., 2011).

Positive Emotions and Psychomotor Development

Positive psychology's focus on children aims at their smooth psychomotor development, increasing their functionality, as well as their overall and broader adequacy of mental and spiritual health in any case and environment in which they find themselves. This holistic approach emphasizes prevention over the absolute cure for problems such as special learning difficulties, adaptive behavior difficulties, anxiety disorders, depression, childhood aggression, bullying, professional burnout, and lack of psychological resilience. Positive meaning in life can significantly enhance the quality of the educational process and, more broadly, educational life (Henderson & Milstein, 2008).

Hope and Optimism

In special education, hope and optimism are crucial psychological constructs that significantly impact teachers' job satisfaction and their relationships with students. These positive psychological elements not only enhance teachers' professional experiences but also foster a supportive and nurturing educational environment for students with special needs. According to Snyder et al. (2002), hope enhances motivation and goal-setting, leading to greater professional satisfaction. Hopeful teachers are more resilient and capable of maintaining a positive outlook, which translates into a more fulfilling professional experience. As Tschannen-Moran and Hoy (2007) noted, hope is critical in building strong, supportive relationships that enhance student engagement and achievement. Studies have shown that higher levels of hope are associated with better academic performance, enhanced problem-solving skills, and higher levels of student resilience (Snyder et al., 2002). Scheier and Carver (1993) found that optimistic individuals are better at coping with stress and more likely to experience positive work outcomes, which is particularly relevant in the demanding field of special education. Optimism also contributes to healthier and more positive teacher-student relationships. Optimistic teachers tend to use positive reinforcement and are more likely to believe in their students' potential. This belief can boost students' self-esteem and motivate them to achieve their best, fostering a supportive and encouraging learning environment (Pianta et al., 2012).

Creating a Positive Classroom Climate

Creating a positive classroom climate introduces educational philosophy innovations that promote learning and enhance the self-esteem and satisfaction of both students' and educators' social-emotional needs. The way students experience and perceive the psychosocial relationships developed in the classroom can determine the psychological climate within it. Resilience is a key component of positive psychology. Special education students may face various obstacles, and enhancing resilience is essential for their long-term success. Teaching resilience skills can help students overcome obstacles and develop a growth mindset (Alba & Marc, 2023).

Growth Mindset and Positive Relationships between teacher-students

The concept of the growth mindset emphasizes the belief that individual abilities and intelligence can be developed through effort and persistence. Encouraging students to adopt a growth mindset can lead to increased confidence and willingness to face everyday challenges. At the same time, positive relationships for promoting well-being, building strong relationships between teachers and students, and encouraging social connections among students can significantly enhance their emotional and social development (Doll et al., 2009). Empowering special education students to make choices and set goals aligns with positive psychology's principle of self-determination. This approach can increase motivation and autonomy, leading to greater satisfaction with the learning process.

Enhancing Job Satisfaction

The impact of resilience and positive emotions profoundly affect the job satisfaction of special education teachers. Effective coping strategies, such as mindfulness, self-care, and stress management techniques, also significantly build resilience.

Certain personality traits of educators, such as adaptability and a sense of purpose, can enhance their resilience, as can continuous training and professional development opportunities that equip educators with the skills and knowledge needed to navigate challenges effectively (Alba & Marc, 2023; Lakioti, 2011).

Significance and Innovation of the Research

This research aims to provide how positive psychology can critically impact the educational spectrum, specifically special education. The study addresses a critical and previously underexplored area by focusing on the impact of hope and optimism on special education teachers. While most previous research in positive psychology within education has focused primarily on the effects on students, this study uniquely centers on the educators themselves. This contribution is essential for developing a more comprehensive understanding of positive psychology's effects in educational contexts. It should also not be overlooked that educators are the ones who shape both the positive climate and the quality of learning. Educators also assume a wide range of responsibilities and obligations towards special education students, which often bring high-stress levels. Therefore, it is important to emphasize and investigate the factors that enhance, based on the lens of positive psychology, educational action, and the quality of healthy and productive relationships between educators and special education students.

Research Purpose

The purpose of the present research is to investigate the impact of positive psychology principles, specifically the emotions of hope and optimism, on job satisfaction and teacher-student relationships in the special education field. By examining these variables, the study aims to contribute to a deeper understanding of how positive psychology can enhance special education teachers' professional experiences and their students' educational outcomes. The ultimate goal is to provide evidence-based recommendations for integrating positive psychology practices into special education settings to improve both educator and student well-being. The main research hypotheses based on the literature review are the following:

- How do hope and optimism relate to educators' job satisfaction?
- How do hope and optimism relate to the teacher-student relationship in special education?
- How do hope and optimism predict educators' job satisfaction?
- How do hope and optimism predict the teacher-student relationship in special education?

RESEARCH METHODOLOGY

Participants

The research involved 100 educators of all levels working in educational units across Greece, both in cities and rural areas. Of these, 21 (21%) were men, and 79 (79%) were women. Educators aged 25 to 30 years were 11 (11%); aged 31 to 35 years were 26 (26%); aged 35 to 40 years were 25 (25%); aged 41 to 45 years were 13 (13%); aged 46 to 50 years were 12 (12%); and aged 50 years and older were 13 (13%). Regarding marital status, 36 educators (36%) were single, 52 educators (52%) were married, 8 educators (8%) were divorced, and 4 educators (4%) were living together (Table 1).

Table 1. Participants' Socio-Demographic Variables

Sociodemographic variables	n	%
Gender		
Male	21	21
Female	79	79
Age		
25-30	11	11
31-35	26	26
35-40	25	25
41-45	13	13
46-50	12	12
> 50	13	13
Marital status		
Single	36	36
Married	52	52
Divorced	8	8
Living together	4	4

Procedure

The data collection process included emailing the questionnaire to educators and schools and posting it on various forums and educators' groups on social media (Facebook). The data collection period lasted from January 2024 to May of the same year. Finally, it should be emphasized that participation in the research was voluntary for each educator, and their personal information and data were fully protected.

MEASURES

Teacher Satisfaction Inventory (TSI)

The TSI was utilized to measure educators' job satisfaction. This inventory consists of 20 questions assessing the satisfaction level derived from the teaching profession, particularly in public primary and secondary education settings (Gkolia, Belias & Koustelios, 2014). The questions are categorized into five dimensions: principal support, colleague relationships, student interactions, working conditions, and the nature of work. Responses are measured on a 5-point Likert scale ranging from 1 (Strongly disagree) to 5 (Strongly agree). Examples of questions from the TSI include: "How do you evaluate the support you receive from the administration for your professional development?", "To what extent do you feel that your colleagues recognize and appreciate your contribution to the team?". The Cronbach's alpha reliability coefficient of this scale was found to be satisfactory at $\alpha = .95$.

Adult Hope Scale (AHS)

The AHS, developed by Snyder et al. (1991), assesses the level of hope among educators. This scale focuses on two main components of hope: goal-directed energy (successful individual action) and pathways thinking (planning to achieve goals). The AHS consists of 12 items, with responses measured on a Likert scale from 0 (Strongly disagree) to 4 (Strongly agree). Examples of items include: "I can think of many ways to get out of a tough situation", "I actively pursue my goals." The Cronbach's alpha reliability coefficient of this scale was found to be satisfactory at $\alpha = .83$.

Revised Life Orientation Test (LOT-R)

The LOT-R, developed by Scheier et al. (1994), measures educators' optimism level. This scale includes 10 items, divided into positive expectations (optimism) and negative expectations (pessimism). Respondents rate their agreement with each item on a Likert scale from 0 (Strongly disagree) to 4 (Strongly agree). Examples of questions include: "To what extent do you believe your efforts will yield positive results in the future?", "How often do you worry that things will not turn out as planned?" The internal consistency of the scale was $\alpha = .62$.

Student-Teacher Relationship Scale (STRS)

The STRS evaluates the quality of relationships between educators and their students (Pianta & Steinberg, 1992). The scale comprises 15 items that measure three main dimensions: closeness (emotional bond between teacher and student), conflict (tension or disagreements), and dependency (students' reliance on teachers for support). Responses are measured on a Likert scale from 1 (Definitely not true) to 5 (Definitely true). Examples of questions include "How easily do you feel you can create a positive emotional connection with your students?", "To what extent do your students openly express any disagreements or conflicts with you?". The internal consistency of the scale was $\alpha = .76$.

Statistical Analysis

Data were analyzed using the Statistical Package for Social Sciences (SPSS) version 26. First, descriptive statistics, correlation analyses, and internal consistency among study variables (hope, optimism, job satisfaction, student-teacher relationship) were conducted. Following this, Multiple Regression Analysis was used.

RESULTS

Descriptive Analyses and Correlation Analyses

The means, standard deviations, and bivariate correlations between the examined variables (hope, optimism, job satisfaction, student-teacher relationship) are presented in Table 2. Regarding the correlation analysis (bivariate correlations) between all variables, the results indicated that hope had a statistically significant positive correlation with job satisfaction $r = .24$, $p < .05$, and student-teacher relationships $r = .20$, $p < .005$. However, hope did not have a statistically significant correlation with optimism $r = .05$, $p > .05$. Optimism did not have a statistically significant correlation with job satisfaction $r = .08$, $p > .05$ and student-teacher relationships $r = .06$, $p > .05$. Job satisfaction and student-teacher relationships did not have a statistically significant correlation $r = .07$, $p > .05$.

Table 2. Correlation Analysis

	1	2	3	4
1. Hope	1			

continued on following page

Table 2. Continued

	1	2	3	4
2. Optimism	.05	1		
3. Job satisfaction	.24*	.08	1	
4. Student-teacher relationships	.20*	.06	.07	1
Mean	3.72	2.71	3.91	4.30
Standard deviation	.78	.49	.67	.45

* p < .05

Multiple Regression Analysis

Multiple regression analysis was conducted to examine whether the independent variables' optimism and hope predicted the dependent variables' job satisfaction and student-teacher relationships. Specifically, Table 3 shows that optimism and hope significantly predict job satisfaction, $F(2,99)= 3.305$, $p< 0.05$ (Model 1). Finally, Table 4 shows that optimism and hope do not significantly predict student-teacher relationships, $F(2,99)= 2.133$, $p> 0.05$ (Model 2).

Table 3. Multiple Regression Analysis. Model 1

		Sum of Squares	Df	Mean Square	F	Sig.
1	Regression	2.822	2	1.411	3.305	.041[b]
2	Residual	41.408	97	.427		
3	Total	44.229	99			

A. Dependent variable: Job satisfaction
B. Independent variables: Hope, optimism

Table 4. Multiple Regression Analysis. Model 2

		Sum of Squares	Df	Mean Square	F	Sig.
1	Regression	.860	2	.430	2.133	.124[b]
2	Residual	19.551	97	.202		
3	Total	20.411	99			

A. Dependent variable: Student-teacher relationships
B. Independent variables: Hope, optimism

DISCUSSION

Positive psychology focuses on enhancing emotional well-being and optimal functioning and significantly impacts the field of special education. It emphasizes strengths, virtues, and factors that contribute to developing skills that improve students' quality of life and academic success. Within special education, positive psychology can play a critical role in creating a supportive and empowering environment for students with disabilities, enhancing educators' job satisfaction, and promoting positive relationships with their students.

The present study aimed to contribute to a deeper understanding of how positive psychology can enhance special education teachers' professional experiences and their students' educational outcomes. The present study addressed this by examining the impact of positive psychology principles, specifically the emotions of hope and optimism, on teachers' job satisfaction and their relationships with students with special needs. Research results indicated that the positive aspects of hope and optimism significantly predict the teachers' job satisfaction but not their relationship with students. Hope, as a cognitive process, involves the perceived ability to set and pursue goals effectively. Teachers who experience higher levels of hope are more likely to be motivated and resilient, which in turn enhances their professional satisfaction. This aligns with Snyder et al. (2002), who found that hope is positively correlated with job satisfaction, as it enhances motivation and goal-setting abilities. When teachers are hopeful, they are more likely to see challenges as opportunities, develop effective strategies to overcome obstacles and maintain a positive outlook on their professional roles (Tschannen-Moran & Hoy, 2007). This perspective contributes to higher levels of job satisfaction, as they feel more competent and effective in their work. Similarly, optimism was found to be a significant predictor of job satisfaction. Optimism involves a generalized expectation that good things will happen in the future. Teachers who are optimistic are likely to approach their work with a positive attitude, expecting favorable outcomes. This positive outlook can lead to better work performance and enhanced morale, as optimistic teachers are more likely to engage enthusiastically in their professional activities and cope better with stress and setbacks. This finding is consistent with Scheier and Carver (1993), who noted that optimism contributes to better work performance and enhances morale among educators.

However, the study didn't support the significant role of hope and optimism in student-teacher relationships. This is not aligned with other research findings suggesting positive psychological states' role in improving student performance and teacher-student relationships (Hoy et al., 2006). One reason might be the specific context of special education, which presents unique challenges and dynamics compared to general education settings. Special education teachers often work with students who have diverse and complex needs, requiring more specialized skills and strategies. In such settings, the ability to form positive relationships might depend more on specific training and strategies rather than on general positive psychological states such as hope and optimism. Research by Jennings and Greenberg (2009) emphasizes that the social-emotional competence of teachers, which includes but is not limited to hope and optimism, is crucial for effective teacher-student relationships in challenging educational environments.

Hope and optimism are essential elements of positive psychology that significantly contribute to job satisfaction among special education teachers. By fostering these positive psychological states, educators can create a more supportive and effective educational environment, ultimately benefiting both teachers and students. Future research and professional development should focus on strategies to enhance hope and optimism in educators, ensuring that special education teachers are well-equipped to provide high-quality support to their students.

CONCLUSION

Integrating the dimensions of positive psychology in special education can enhance the educational experience and outcomes for students. By focusing on positive emotions, individual strengths, resilience, growth mindset, cultivating positive relationships, self-determination, and finding meaning and purpose, special education teachers can create an environment that promotes well-being and empowers students to reach their full potential (Martinsone et al., 2023). For the effective integration of positive psychology in special education, educators should receive additional training and support for implementing positive interventions and promoting an educational approach based on the strengths of positive psychology principles (Willemse et al., 2023). Collaboration between educators, parents, and specialists is crucial for enhancing the positive impact of these practices on students' lives.

The application of positive psychology in special education is vital for improving students' overall well-being and academic outcomes (Hammill et al., 2022). Strength-based approaches are a cornerstone of positive psychology. These approaches focus on identifying and developing students' inherent strengths and talents. By leveraging these strengths, educators can create personalized learning experiences that align with students' interests and abilities. This not only increases student engagement but also promotes a positive self-image and resilience. Research indicates that strength-based interventions lead to improved academic and social outcomes for students with disabilities (Lopez & Louis, 2009). Furthermore, research has shown that focusing on students' strengths can lead to increased engagement, motivation, and multiple academic successes (Norrish et al., 2013). For students with disabilities, this approach boosts their self-esteem and broadly encourages a sense of competence and autonomy, critical skills for their long-term development.

Additionally, the job satisfaction of special education teachers can be significantly improved through the application of positive psychology. Teaching students with disabilities often involves unique challenges that can lead to increased stress and burnout. Positive psychology interventions, such as mindfulness, gratitude practices, and professional development focusing on strength-based approaches, can mitigate these negative effects. Educators participating in such practices report higher levels of job satisfaction, reduced stress, and a greater sense of professional efficacy and resilience (Cavioni et al., 2023; Roffey, 2012). Thus, integrating positive psychology principles into the curriculum can provide students with valuable tools and skills for managing stress, developing resilience, improving emotional regulation and interpersonal skills, and adopting a positive outlook on life holistically. (Durlak et al., 2011).

REFERENCES

Alba, V., & Marc, C. (2023). Conceptualizing teacher resilience: A comprehensive framework to articulate the research field. *Teachers and Teaching*, 29(1), 105–117. 10.1080/13540602.2022.2149483

Aspinwall, L. G., & Staudinger, U. M. (2003). *A psychology of human strengths: Fundamental questions and future directions for a positive psychology*. American Psychological Association. 10.1037/10566-000

Cavioni, V., Grazzani, I., Ornaghi, V., Agliati, A., Gandellinia, S., Cefai, C., Camilleri, L., Bartolo, P., Tatalović Vorkapić, S., Golob, L., Poulou, M., Martinsone, B., Supe, I., Simões, C. S., Lebre, P., Colomeischi, A., Rusu, P. R., Acostoaie, L., Vintur, T., & Conte, E. (2023). A multi-component curriculum to promote teachers' mental health: Findings from the PROMEHS program. *The International Journal of Emotional Education*, 15(1), 34–52. 10.56300/KFNZ2526

Csikszentmihalyi, M. (1990). *Flow: The psychology of optimal experience*. Harper and Row.

Doll, B., Zucker, S., & Brehm, K. (2009). *Classrooms that promote mental resilience: How to create a favorable learning environment*. Typothito.

Durlak, J. A., Weissberg, R. P., Dymnicki, A. B., Taylor, R. D., & Schellinger, K. B. (2011). The impact of enhancing students' social and emotional learning: A meta-analysis of school-based universal interventions. *Child Development*, 82(1), 405–432. 10.1111/j.1467-8624.2010.01564.x21291449

Emmons, R. A., & McCullough, M. E. (2003). Counting blessings versus burdens: An experimental investigation of gratitude and subjective well-being in daily life. *Journal of Personality and Social Psychology*, 84(2), 377–389. 10.1037/0022-3514.84.2.37712585811

Frankl, V. E. (2006). *Man's search for meaning*. Beacon Press.

Gkolia, A., Belias, D., & Koustelios, A. (2014). The impact of principals' transformational leadership on teachers' satisfaction: Evidence from Greece. *European Journal of Business and Social Sciences*, 3, 69–80.

Hammill, J., Nguyen, T., & Henderson, F. (2022). Student engagement: The impact of positive psychology interventions on students. *Sage Journals, 23*(2).

Henderson, N., & Milstein, M. M. (2008). *Resiliency in schools: Making it happen for students and educators*. Corwin Press.

Hoy, W. K., Tarter, C. J., & Hoy, A. W. (2006). Academic optimism of schools: A force for student achievement. *American Educational Research Journal*, 43(3), 425–446. 10.3102/00028312043003425

Jennings, P. A., & Greenberg, M. T. (2009). The prosocial classroom: Teacher social and emotional competence in relation to student and classroom outcomes. *Review of Educational Research*, 79(1), 491–525. 10.3102/0034654308325693

Kabat-Zinn, J. (2003). Mindfulness-based interventions in context: Past, present, and future. *Clinical Psychology : a Publication of the Division of Clinical Psychology of the American Psychological Association*, 10(2), 144–156. 10.1093/clipsy.bpg016

Keyes, C. L., & Haidt, J. (2003). *Flourishing: Positive psychology and the life well-lived.* American Psychological Association. 10.1037/10594-000

Lakioti, A. (2011). The concept of mental resilience. In Stalikas, A., & Mitskidou, P. (Eds.), *Introduction to Positive Psychology* (pp. 61–70). Topos.

Lopez, S. J., & Louis, M. C. (2009). The principles of strengths-based education. *Journal of College and Character*, 10(4), 1–8. 10.2202/1940-1639.1041

Martinsone, B., DiSano, S., D'Elia, P., & LaSalle-Finley, T. (2023). A conceptual framework for sustainable promotion of a positive school climate: Context, challenges, and solutions. *Journal of Teacher Education for Sustainability*, 25(1), 64–85. 10.2478/jtes-2023-0005

Masten, A. S. (2001). Ordinary magic: Resilience processes in development. *The American Psychologist*, 56(3), 227–238. 10.1037/0003-066X.56.3.22711315249

Neff, K. D. (2003). Self-compassion: An alternative conceptualization of a healthy attitude toward oneself. *Self and Identity*, 2(2), 85–101. 10.1080/15298860309032

Norrish, J. M., Williams, P., O'Connor, M., & Robinson, J. (2013). An applied framework for positive education. *International Journal of Wellbeing*, 3(2), 147–161.

Peterson, C., & Seligman, M. E. P. (2004). *Character strengths and virtues: A handbook and classification*. Oxford University Press.

Pianta, R. C., Hamre, B. K., & Allen, J. P. (2012). Teacher-student relationships and engagement: Conceptualizing, measuring, and improving the capacity of classroom interactions. In Christenson, S. L., Reschly, A. L., & Wylie, C. (Eds.), *Handbook of research on student engagement* (pp. 365–386). Springer. 10.1007/978-1-4614-2018-7_17

Pianta, R. C., & Steinberg, M. (1992). Teacher-child relationships and the process of adjusting to school. *New Directions for Child and Adolescent Development*, 1992(57), 61–80. 10.1002/cd.23219925706

Post, S. G. (2005). Altruism, happiness, and health: It's good to be good. *International Journal of Behavioral Medicine*, 12(2), 66–77. 10.1207/s15327558ijbm1202_415901215

Reis, H. T., & Gable, S. L. (2003). Toward a positive psychology of relationships. In Keyes, C. L. M., & Haidt, J. (Eds.), *Flourishing: Positive psychology and the life well-lived* (pp. 129–159). American Psychological Association. 10.1037/10594-006

Roffey, S. (2012). Positive relationships: Evidence-based practice across the world. *Educational and Child Psychology*, 29(1), 15–30.

Scheier, M. F., & Carver, C. S. (1993). On the power of positive thinking: The benefits of being optimistic. *Current Directions in Psychological Science*, 2(1), 26–30. 10.1111/1467-8721.ep10770572

Scheier, M. F., Carver, C. S., & Bridges, M. W. (1994). Distinguishing optimism from neuroticism (and trait anxiety, self-mastery, and self-esteem): A reevaluation of the Life Orientation Test. *Journal of Personality and Social Psychology*, 67(6), 1063–1078. 10.1037/0022-3514.67.6.10637815302

Seligman, M. E. P. (2011). *Flourish: A visionary new understanding of happiness and well-being*. Free Press.

Seligman, M. E. P., & Csikszentmihalyi, M. (Eds.). (2000a). Happiness, excellence, and optimal human functioning [special issue]. *The American Psychologist*, 55(1).11392865

Seligman, M. E. P., & Csikszentmihalyi, M. (2000b). Positive psychology: An introduction. *The American Psychologist*, 55(1), 5–14. 10.1037/0003-066X.55.1.511392865

Sheldon, K. M., & King, L. (2001). Positive psychology [special issue]. *The American Psychologist*, 56(3), 216–263. 10.1037/0003-066X.56.3.21611315247

Sheldon, K. M., & King, L. (2001). Why positive psychology is necessary. *The American Psychologist*, 56(3), 216–217. 10.1037/0003-066X.56.3.21611315247

Snyder, C. R., Harris, C., Anderson, J. R., Holleran, S. A., Irving, L. M., Sigmon, S. T., Yoshinobu, L., Gibb, J., Langelle, C., & Harney, P. (1991). The will and the ways: Development and validation of an individual-differences measure of hope. *Journal of Personality and Social Psychology*, 60(4), 570–585. 10.1037/0022-3514.60.4.5702037968

Snyder, C. R., Irving, L. M., & Anderson, J. R. (2002). Hope and health: Measuring the will and the ways. In Snyder, C. R. (Ed.), *Handbook of hope: Theory, measures, and applications* (pp. 201–210). Academic Press.

Stalikas, A., & Mitskidou, P. (Eds.). (2011). *Introduction to Positive Psychology*. Topos.

Stalikas, A., Triliva, S., & Roussi, P. (2011). *Positive psychology applications*. Klidarithmos Publications.

Tschannen-Moran, M., & Hoy, A. W. (2007). The differential antecedents of self-efficacy beliefs of novice and experienced teachers. *Teaching and Teacher Education*, 23(6), 944–956. 10.1016/j.tate.2006.05.003

Willemse, T. M., Goei, S. L., Boei, F. B., & Erica, J. (2023). School-wide positive behavior interventions and support in Dutch schools for special education. *European Journal of Special Needs Education*, 38(3), 424–439. 10.1080/08856257.2022.2120331

Chapter 4
Classifying Minds, Framing Well-Being: Bernstein's Sociolinguistic Theory and the Promotion of Mental Health in Inclusive Schools

Efthymia Efthymiou
https://orcid.org/0000-0003-0411-1720
Zayed University, UAE

Dimitra V. Katsarou
https://orcid.org/0000-0001-8690-0314
University of the Aegean, Greece

Maria Sofologi
https://orcid.org/0000-0003-0380-2220
University of Ioannina, Greece

Alexandros Argyriadis
https://orcid.org/0000-0001-5754-4787
Frederick University, Cyprus

Agathi Argyriadi
Frederick University, Cyprus

ABSTRACT

This chapter focuses on Basil Bernstein's sociolinguistic theory, emphasizing classification and framing, to provide a comprehensive framework for understanding the organization and transmission of knowledge within educational settings. It

DOI: 10.4018/979-8-3693-8312-4.ch004

Copyright © 2024, IGI Global. Copying or distributing in print or electronic forms without written permission of IGI Global is prohibited.

examines the implications of this theoretical perspective on pedagogic practices and curriculum design, particularly in inclusive schools. The study scrutinizes how knowledge structure impacts students' mental well-being, self-esteem, and confidence. By exploring both visible and invisible curricula, the chapter reveals how educational practices influence students' mental health. Employing a qualitative approach, the chapter synthesizes literature reviews, case studies, and key milestones in educational history. It establishes a theoretical foundation for understanding how classification and framing in education can promote mental health outcomes. Practical recommendations for educators and policymakers are provided to create supportive, inclusive learning environments that nurture students' mental well-being, resilience, and positive connections to learning. This theoretical framework contributes to informed decision-making, advocating for inclusive practices for students with special needs.

INTRODUCTION

This chapter explores the foundational aspects of Basil Bernstein's Sociolinguistic Theory, providing an in-depth understanding of its core principles. Bernstein's theory offers valuable insights into how knowledge is structured and transmitted within educational settings, focusing on the mechanisms of classification and framing. By examining these mechanisms, the chapter elucidates how educational practices can be designed to support diverse learning needs and promote inclusive education. Bernstein's work emerged from his interest in the relationship between language, social class, and education. He argued that language plays a fundamental role in transmitting and reproducing social inequalities. Through his sociolinguistic theory, Bernstein introduced the concepts of elaborated and restricted codes, which describe the linguistic variations associated with different social classes. This framework laid the groundwork for understanding how language can both reflect and reinforce social structures.

Central to Bernstein's theory are the concepts of classification and framing. Classification refers to the degree of boundary maintenance between different categories of knowledge. Strong classification indicates clear and rigid boundaries between subjects, while weak classification suggests more integrated and overlapping boundaries. This concept helps educators understand how different subjects and knowledge areas are organized and presented to students, which can influence their engagement and comprehension. Framing pertains to the degree of control exerted over the communication and transmission of knowledge within educational settings. Strong framing implies strict control over what is taught, how it is taught, and how learning is assessed, typically by the teacher. Conversely, weak framing suggests a more flexible and student-centered approach, where students have greater autonomy over their learning processes. Understanding framing is essential for educators to design teaching strategies that balance structure and flexibility, catering to the diverse needs of learners.

Bernstein's theory also emphasizes the role of the invisible curriculum, the implicit lessons, values, and expectations embedded within the educational environment. This hidden aspect of education can significantly impact students' attitudes, behaviors, and overall experiences. By uncovering the invisible curriculum, educators can address underlying biases and create more equitable and inclusive learning environments. The application of Bernstein's sociolinguistic theory in education extends to curriculum design and pedagogic practices. By integrating the principles of classification and framing, educators can develop curricula that respect students' cultural and linguistic backgrounds while promoting critical thinking and collaboration. This approach improves academic achievement, supporting the holistic development of students, including their mental well-being, self-esteem, and confidence.

This chapter aims to provide a comprehensive framework for understanding how Bernstein's sociolinguistic theory can inform and transform educational practices. By exploring the mechanisms of classification and framing, the chapter highlights the potential for creating inclusive educational settings that accommodate diverse learning needs and promote positive mental health outcomes for all students.

BACKGROUND

Emphasis on Classification and Framing Within Educational Settings

A key focus of this chapter will be on the concepts of classification and framing, exploring how these elements influence the organization and transmission of knowledge in educational environments. Classification refers to the degree of boundary maintenance between contents, while framing pertains to the control over the communication process. Understanding these concepts is fundamental for analyzing how curriculum design and pedagogic practices can either facilitate or hinder the learning process, especially in inclusive settings. The chapter will analyze how these concepts shape pedagogic practices and curriculum design, particularly in inclusive schools.

Classification involves how subjects and disciplines are separated or integrated within the curriculum. Strong classification, characterized by clear and rigid boundaries between subjects, can lead to a compartmentalized approach to education. This often means that subjects like mathematics, science, and language arts are taught as distinct entities with little crossover. Conversely, weak classification involves more interdisciplinary approaches where boundaries between subjects are blurred, allowing for a more integrated and holistic educational experience.

Framing refers to the control over educational communication, how knowledge is transmitted, and who has authority over it. Strong framing indicates that teachers have strict control over the learning process, including the selection of content, pacing, and assessment methods. In contrast, weak framing allows for more student autonomy, giving students greater influence over what and how they learn. This can promote a more engaging and personalized learning experience, particularly beneficial in inclusive settings where students have diverse needs and learning styles.

FOCUS OF THE ARTICLE

Influence on Curriculum Design and Pedagogic Practices

Recent studies have highlighted the significant impact of classification and framing on curriculum design and pedagogic practices. For instance, Johnson et al. (2021) examined the use of interdisciplinary approaches in higher education. They found that weak classification, which promotes interdisciplinary learning, encourages critical thinking, creativity, and collaboration among students, enhancing their overall educational experience. Such approaches are particularly effective in inclusive settings where accommodating diverse perspectives and learning styles is essential.

Bernstein (2000) focused on the role of framing in educational outcomes. Their research demonstrated that strong framing, characterized by rigid teacher control, can sometimes limit student engagement and creativity. In contrast, weak framing, which allows for more student input and autonomy, was associated with higher levels of student motivation, engagement, and academic achievement. These findings feature the importance of balancing teacher guidance with student autonomy to create a more inclusive and effective learning environment.

SOLUTIONS AND RECOMMENDATIONS

Application in Inclusive Schools

In inclusive schools, where the goal is to cater to students with a wide range of abilities and needs, understanding and applying the concepts of classification and framing becomes even more critical. A study by Florian and Black-Hawkins (2011) explored how inclusive pedagogic practices can be designed using Bernstein's principles. They found that flexible classification and framing strategies allowed teachers to tailor their instruction to meet the individual needs of students, promoting a more inclusive and supportive learning environment.

For example, in schools with strong classification, students with special needs may struggle to see the connections between different subjects, leading to fragmented learning experiences. However, by adopting a weaker classification approach, educators can integrate subjects more seamlessly, helping students understand the broader context of their learning. Similarly, in environments with strong framing, students with special needs might find the rigid structure challenging. By implementing weaker framing, teachers can provide more personalized support and allow students to take more control over their learning process, promoting greater independence and self-confidence.

By carefully considering these elements, educators can develop more inclusive and effective teaching strategies that accommodate diverse learning needs. Recent studies highlight the benefits of flexible classification and framing approaches in inclusive schools, where the goal is to support all students in reaching their full potential. This chapter will explore further these concepts, providing practical aspects and strategies for educators to augment their pedagogic practices and promote inclusive education.

FUTURE RESEARCH DIRECTIONS

Importance of Addressing Mental Health and Well-Being in Inclusive Schools for Students With Special Needs

Highlighting the significance of mental health and well-being, this chapter examines the impact of educational practices informed by Bernstein's theory on students' mental health. Special emphasis will be placed on how inclusive educational settings can support the mental well-being, self-esteem, and confidence of students with special needs. The chapter aims to provide a comprehensive framework for educators and policymakers to create supportive learning environments that promote positive mental health outcomes for all students.

Educational Practices and Mental Health

Educational practices play a critical role in shaping the mental health and well-being of students. According to Oberle and Schonert-Reichl (2017), integrating social and emotional learning (SEL) components into educational practices significantly benefits students' mental health. SEL practices help students develop essential skills such as emotional regulation, resilience, and social competence, which are fundamental for maintaining mental health and well-being. Bernstein's theory, with its focus on classification and framing, provides a framework for structuring these practices effectively within the curriculum.

Durlak, Weissberg, Dymnicki, Taylor, and Schellinger (2011) support this, demonstrating that students who participate in SEL programs show improved social behaviors, fewer conduct problems, less emotional distress, and better academic performance. These benefits underline the importance of embedding SEL into the educational curriculum to promote a supportive learning environment. For example, weak classification in curriculum design allows for a more interdisciplinary approach, where SEL can be integrated into various subjects rather than being confined to a single class or program. This integration ensures that students receive consistent support in developing their social and emotional skills across all areas of learning. A study by Jones and Kahn (2017) found that when SEL is incorporated across different subjects, students improve in social and emotional competencies and show improved academic outcomes.

Furthermore, weak framing, which provides students with greater autonomy and control over their learning, can help them feel more engaged and motivated, contributing positively to their mental health. According to a study by Reeve (2012), when students have a sense of autonomy in their learning process, they are more likely to be intrinsically motivated and engaged, which in turn supports their mental health. Autonomy-supportive teaching practices, which align with weak framing, encourage students to take an active role in their learning, promoting a sense of ownership and responsibility.

Integrating these approaches within the framework of Bernstein's theory can help educators design curricula that meet academic standards, supporting the holistic development of students. For instance, a project-based learning approach, which often embodies weak classification and framing, allows students to explore subjects in a connected and meaningful way while developing critical SEL skills. This approach has been shown to increase student engagement and improve both academic and social-emotional outcomes (Barron & Darling-Hammond, 2008).

Inclusive Educational Settings

Inclusive educational settings are designed to accommodate the diverse needs of all students, including those with special needs. These settings emphasize creating an environment where every student feels valued and supported. Schwab (2018) indicates that inclusive schools that actively promote a sense of belonging and provide tailored support significantly improve the mental well-being of students with special needs. By adopting flexible classification and framing strategies, educators can create a more inclusive curriculum that addresses the unique learning styles and needs of these students.

Florian, Black-Hawkins, and Rouse (2016) highlight that inclusive education practices that focus on the strengths and needs of individual students contribute to a positive school climate and improved mental health outcomes. The researchers found that when teachers employ strategies that recognize and build upon the diverse abilities of students, all learners benefit from a more supportive and engaging educational experience.

In practice, this might involve designing lessons that connect different subjects, allowing students to see the relevance of their learning in a broader context. For example, a science lesson on ecosystems can be integrated with a social studies lesson on community, helping students understand the interconnectedness of knowledge and its application to real-world situations. This interdisciplinary approach aligns with the concept of weak classification, where subjects are not strictly segregated but rather interconnected, facilitating a more holistic understanding of the material.

Flexible framing, on the other hand, involves giving students more control over how they learn and demonstrate their understanding. Mitchell and Sutherland (2020) found that providing students with choices in their learning activities and assessment methods increases engagement and motivation, particularly for students with special needs. This could mean allowing students to choose between traditional tests, creative projects, or group work, thus accommodating different strengths and preferences.

Additionally, Hornby (2015) supports the idea that inclusive education practices such as collaborative learning and peer support improve the social and emotional development of students. By nurturing a sense of community and mutual support, these practices help students with special needs feel more integrated and accepted within the school environment, which is fundamental for their mental well-being.

Supporting Self-Esteem and Confidence

Self-esteem and confidence are fundamental components of mental well-being, especially for students with special needs. Eiser, Eiser, and Stride (2005) indicate that educational practices that recognize and celebrate individual achievements while providing constructive feedback can improve students' self-esteem and confidence. Bernstein's concept of framing, which allows for more student autonomy and control over the learning process, can be particularly beneficial in this regard. By giving students more voice and choice in their education, teachers can help them build self-efficacy and a positive self-image.

Wang, Degol, Amemiya, Parr, and Guo (2020) support the idea that personalized learning and student-centered approaches significantly boost self-esteem and academic self-efficacy among students. The research highlights that when students are involved in setting their learning goals and receive continuous feedback tailored to their individual progress, their confidence in their abilities increases.

Practical strategies might include setting personalized learning goals, offering various ways for students to participate and succeed, and creating a classroom environment where mistakes are seen as learning opportunities rather than failures. Teachers can also use formative assessments to provide ongoing feedback, helping students understand their progress and areas for improvement, thereby boosting their confidence and motivation. Hattie and Timperley (2007) emphasize the importance of effective feedback in educational settings. The researchers found that feedback that is specific, timely, and constructive helps students develop a better understanding of their strengths and areas for growth, which in turn improves their self-esteem and motivation. This aligns with Bernstein's framing concept, as providing students with autonomy in their learning process and feedback that they can use to improve empowers them to take charge of their educational journey.

Additionally, Schunk (2023) and Pajares (1996) on self-efficacy beliefs in academic settings demonstrate that students who believe in their capabilities are more likely to engage in challenging tasks, persist in the face of difficulties, and achieve higher levels of performance. This accentuates the importance of creating supportive learning environments where students feel confident in their abilities and are encouraged to take risks and learn from their experiences.

Creating Supportive Learning Environments

Creating supportive learning environments involves more than just adapting teaching methods; it also requires promoting a school culture that prioritizes mental health. Weare and Nind (2011) highlight the importance of whole-school approaches to mental health, which include training staff to recognize and address mental health issues, integrating mental health education into the curriculum, and providing access to mental health resources. Bernstein's theory can inform these efforts by emphasizing the need for coherent and well-structured educational practices that align with the goal of supporting students' mental well-being.

Taylor, Oberle, Durlak, and Weissberg (2017) support the effectiveness of whole-school approaches in promoting students' mental health. The study found that schools implementing comprehensive SEL programs saw improvements in students' social and emotional skills, behavior, and academic performance. This features the importance of integrating SEL into the curriculum to create a supportive and inclusive school environment.

A whole-school approach might involve regular professional development sessions for teachers on topics such as mental health first aid, trauma-informed teaching practices, and creating inclusive classrooms. For example, Jennings and

Greenberg (2009) found that teachers who received training in social and emotional competencies were better equipped to manage classroom behaviors and create a positive learning environment. These skills are essential for promoting a supportive atmosphere where students feel safe and valued.

Schools can also establish partnerships with mental health professionals to provide counseling services and support groups for students. Reinke, Stormont, Herman, Puri, and Goel (2011) emphasize the benefits of such collaborations, noting that access to mental health services within schools leads to early identification and intervention for students with mental health needs. This proactive approach can prevent the escalation of mental health issues and support students in their educational journey.

Incorporating mental health education into the curriculum can help destigmatize mental health issues and equip students with the knowledge and skills to manage their own mental health effectively. Durlak, Weissberg, Dymnicki, Taylor, and Schellinger (2011) found that students who participated in school-based mental health education programs showed significant improvements in their emotional and social well-being. This aligns with Bernstein's emphasis on structured educational practices that support overall student development.

Practical Implications for Educators and Policymakers

For educators and policymakers, understanding the interaction between educational practices and mental health is essential for creating effective inclusive education policies. Policies should encourage the use of flexible classification and framing strategies to ensure that all students, particularly those with special needs, receive the support they need. Additionally, providing professional development for teachers on how to implement these strategies can improve their ability to support students' mental health.

Darling-Hammond, Hyler, and Gardner (2017) emphasize the importance of professional development in improving teacher effectiveness and student outcomes. The researchers found that sustained, collaborative professional development significantly improves teachers' instructional practices and their ability to address diverse student needs. This supports the need for policies that fund ongoing professional development programs focused on inclusive education and mental health support.

Policies might include funding for professional development programs, mandates for mental health education in the curriculum, and guidelines for creating inclusive classroom environments. Oberle, Domitrovich, Meyers, and Weissberg (2020) highlight the effectiveness of integrating mental health education into school curricula. The study found that schools that implemented comprehensive social and emotional learning (SEL) programs saw improvements in students' emotional regulation, social skills, and academic performance. These findings feature the importance of including mental health education as a core component of school curricula.

Additionally, guidelines for creating inclusive classroom environments can be informed by the findings of Artiles, Kozleski, Dorn, and Christensen (2009). Their research suggests that inclusive education practices that are responsive to cultural and linguistic diversity help create a more equitable and supportive learning environment for all students. Policies that promote culturally responsive teaching and inclusive classroom practices can ensure that students from diverse backgrounds feel valued and supported.

By prioritizing mental health in educational policies, schools can create environments that accommodate academic learning and promote the overall well-being of students. Greenberg, Weissberg, O'Brien, Zins, Fredericks, Resnik, and Elias (2003) found that schools with a strong focus on social and emotional learning improve students' mental health, advancing their academic achievement and reducing behavioral problems. This comprehensive approach to education highlights the need for policies that integrate mental health and well-being into the fabric of school operations.

THEORETICAL FRAMEWORK

Overview of Bernstein's Academic Background and Contributions

Bernstein (1924-2000) was a prominent British sociologist whose work significantly influenced the fields of sociology, education, and linguistics. Bernstein's academic journey began with his studies at the London School of Economics, where he later became a professor. His research primarily focused on the interaction between language, education, and social class, exploring how linguistic codes reflect and reinforce social structures (Sadovnik, 1991).

Bernstein's early work examined the language patterns of working-class and middle-class children, leading to his development of the concepts of restricted and elaborated codes. Restricted codes are typically used by working-class individuals and are characterized by implicit, context-bound language. In contrast, elaborated codes, often used by middle-class individuals, are explicit and context independent. This distinction laid the foundation for Bernstein's later theories on educational transmission and social reproduction (Nash, 2006).

Bernstein's contributions extend beyond linguistic codes to his broader theory of pedagogic discourse, which explores how knowledge is structured and transmitted in educational settings. His theories have had a profound impact on educational research and policy, shedding light on the ways educational systems can perpetuate social inequalities. For instance, Bernstein's concepts of classification and framing have been crucial in understanding the dynamics of power and control in education (Morais & Neves, 2010). Bernstein's work has been extensively discussed and built upon in contemporary research, illustrating its enduring relevance (Atkinson, 2016).

In his book *Pedagogy, Symbolic Control, and Identity*, Bernstein (2000) provides a comprehensive overview of his theories on pedagogic discourse, discussing the implications of his earlier theories and their relevance to contemporary educational research. This work remains a critical resource for understanding the theoretical underpinnings of Bernstein's contributions.

Explanation of Key Concepts: Classification and Framing

Classification

Classification refers to the degree of boundary maintenance between contents, which affects how subjects and knowledge areas are distinguished from one another. In Bernstein's framework, strong classification indicates clear and rigid boundaries between subjects or disciplines, such as mathematics, science, and literature. Each subject is seen as distinct, with its own methods, terminologies, and epistemologies. This often leads to a compartmentalized curriculum where interdisciplinary connections are minimized.

Strong Classification

Tyack and Tobin (1994) illustrate how strong classification has historically shaped educational practices in the United States, leading to a segmented curriculum structure that emphasizes specialized subject knowledge at the expense of interdisciplinary learning. Similarly, Young and Muller (2010) discuss how strong classification in educational curricula ensures depth in subject-specific knowledge but can restrict interdisciplinary learning and critical thinking. Their analysis emphasizes the traditional separation of academic disciplines in secondary and higher education.

Weak Classification

In contrast, weak classification implies blurred boundaries between subjects, promoting interdisciplinary approaches and integrated curricula. This can facilitate a more holistic understanding of knowledge, allowing students to see the connections between different areas of study. For instance, a project-based learning approach that combines science, mathematics, and art to explore environmental issues exemplifies weak classification.

Wang, Ke, Wu, and Hsu (2019) on project-based learning in Taiwan's middle schools, demonstrated that weak classification supports a more integrated and meaningful learning experience. Students engaged in interdisciplinary projects showed improved engagement and understanding of complex concepts, as well as improved collaboration and communication skills. Furthermore, Drake and Reid (2018) on integrated curriculum models in Canada found that weak classification supports a more integrated and meaningful learning experience. Students engaged in interdisciplinary projects showed improved engagement and understanding of complex concepts, as well as improved collaboration and communication skills. Nicolescu (2002) highlights the benefits of transdisciplinary education, which aligns with weak classification. This approach integrates knowledge from various disciplines to solve complex problems, promoting a more comprehensive and adaptable educational experience.

Framing

Framing concerns the degree of control teachers and students have over the educational process, including the selection, sequencing, pacing, and criteria of knowledge. Strong framing implies that teachers have tight control over what is taught, how it is taught, and how students are assessed. The curriculum is highly structured, with clear guidelines and expectations for both teachers and students. This can lead to a more predictable and orderly learning environment but may also limit students' opportunities for critical thinking and autonomy.

Strong Framing

Hattie (2008) emphasizes the importance of structured teaching methods and clear expectations. Hattie's meta-analysis of over 800 meta-analyses of educational interventions found that strong framing through explicit instruction and structured learning environments can significantly improve student achievement. However, this approach can also limit students' opportunities to engage in critical thinking and develop autonomy if not balanced with opportunities for independent learning.

Weak Framing

Weak framing, on the other hand, allows for more student autonomy and flexibility. Students have a greater say in their learning process, including the topics they explore, the pace at which they learn, and the methods they use to demonstrate their understanding. This approach can improve student engagement and motivation by catering to individual interests and learning styles. However, it requires teachers to be skilled in facilitating and guiding rather than directing learning.

Reeve (2016) on student-centered teaching strategies supports the benefits of weak framing. Reeve found that when students are given more control over their learning processes, including choice in their activities and assessment methods, their intrinsic motivation, engagement, and academic performance improve. This approach promotes a more personalized and meaningful learning experience. Additionally, Ryan and Deci (2021) on self-determination theory highlights the importance of autonomy in the learning process. Their research demonstrates that providing students with choices and a sense of control over their education leads to higher levels of motivation, satisfaction, and academic success. This aligns with the principles of weak framing, where students are empowered to take charge of their learning journey.

Implications for Understanding Power and Control in Educational Settings

The concepts of classification and framing are fundamental for understanding the dynamics of power and control within educational settings. Strong classification and framing often reflect and reinforce hierarchical structures within education, where teachers are the primary authority figures, and students are expected to conform to predefined standards and norms. This can perpetuate existing social inequalities by privileging the knowledge and cultural capital of dominant groups (Morais & Neves, 2018).

Conversely, weak classification and framing can democratize the educational process by empowering students and promoting more egalitarian relationships between teachers and students. This approach aligns with inclusive education principles, which emphasize the need to accommodate diverse learning needs and promote a sense of belonging for all students. By analyzing educational practices through the lens of classification and framing, educators and policymakers can better understand the underlying mechanisms that influence student outcomes and social reproduction. For example, a highly classified and strongly framed curriculum might be effective in transmitting specific bodies of knowledge but may also marginalize students who do not possess the cultural capital valued by the educational system. On the other hand, a more integrated and flexible curriculum can support the development of critical thinking and problem-solving skills, essential for navigating complex social and professional settings (Nash, 2006; Bernstein, 2000).

Bernstein's sociolinguistic theory provides a powerful framework for analyzing the structure and transmission of knowledge in educational settings. By examining the concepts of classification and framing, educators can gain insights into the ways educational practices shape student learning and social outcomes, informing efforts to create more inclusive and equitable educational environments.

Pedagogic Practices and Curriculum Design

Visible and Invisible Curricula

Understanding the concepts of visible and invisible curricula is essential for comprehending how educational environments influence student learning and socialization. These two types of curricula play distinct roles in shaping students' knowledge, attitudes, and behaviors, especially in inclusive educational settings.

The visible curriculum refers to the explicitly taught content within an educational setting. This includes the official academic syllabus, textbooks, instructional materials, and formal assessments. The visible curriculum is designed to meet specific educational standards and objectives set by educational authorities, schools, and teachers. For instance, in a science class, the visible curriculum would encompass the topics covered in the textbook, the experiments conducted in the lab, and the exams administered to assess student understanding. It includes the factual knowledge, skills, and competencies that students are expected to acquire.

In contrast, the invisible curriculum consists of the implicit lessons, values, beliefs, and attitudes that are conveyed through the educational environment and interactions. These are not formally documented in lesson plans or syllabi but are nonetheless a significant part of the educational experience. The invisible curriculum includes aspects such as the school's cultural norms, teacher-student interactions, peer relationships, and the overall school climate. It encompasses the messages students receive about social expectations, power dynamics, and acceptable behavior. For example, the way a teacher manages classroom discipline, the inclusivity of school events, and the representation of diverse cultures in school materials all contribute to the invisible curriculum.

While the visible curriculum is structured, intentional, and subject-specific, the invisible curriculum is more diffuse and pervasive, influencing students' perceptions and experiences subtly and indirectly. The visible curriculum aims to equip students with academic knowledge and skills, whereas the invisible curriculum shapes their social and moral development.

Examples and Implications in Inclusive Education

In inclusive education, the visible curriculum in a math class might include teaching algebraic equations, conducting problem-solving exercises, and administering standardized tests with differentiated instructions to accommodate diverse learning needs. In a history class, it would involve covering significant historical events, discussing primary sources, and evaluating students through essays and exams while ensuring materials reflect diverse perspectives and histories.

For the invisible curriculum, the way a teacher enforces rules and handles disruptions can implicitly teach students about authority and fairness. In inclusive classrooms, adopting restorative justice practices can convey messages of empathy, equity, and community. The diversity (or lack thereof) in classroom materials and school events can influence students' understanding of cultural inclusivity and societal values. Inclusive education ensures that materials and activities reflect the backgrounds and experiences of all students, promoting a sense of belonging. Subtle cues from teachers about student potential and performance can impact students' self-esteem and aspirations. High expectations for all students, coupled with support, can empower students with special needs to achieve their full potential.

Impact on Students

The visible curriculum shapes students' academic abilities and cognitive development, preparing them for standardized assessments and future educational opportunities. The invisible curriculum, however, has a profound impact on students' socialization, identity formation, and moral reasoning. In inclusive settings, a well-considered invisible curriculum can promote acceptance, reduce prejudices, and build a supportive community.

Margolis (2001) highlights how the invisible curriculum can perpetuate social inequalities. Their study found that the implicit messages conveyed through teacher expectations and school policies often reinforce existing social hierarchies, impacting students' self-concept and academic aspirations. In inclusive education, addressing these implicit messages is fundamental for promoting equity and inclusivity. Additionally, Gutiérrez and Rogoff (2003) emphasize the importance of culturally responsive teaching to address the invisible curriculum. They argue that recognizing and valuing students' cultural backgrounds within the educational process can mitigate the negative effects of an invisible curriculum that marginalizes minority students. This approach is especially important in inclusive education, where diverse cultural and learning needs must be respected and integrated into the teaching process.

Balancing Visible and Invisible Curricula in Inclusive Education

Educators and policymakers must strive to balance the visible and invisible curricula to provide a holistic education. This involves delivering academic content effectively, promoting an inclusive and supportive school environment. Recent studies emphasize the importance of this balanced approach for student outcomes. Strategies to achieve this balance include incorporating diverse perspectives and materials in the visible curriculum to reflect the backgrounds of all students. For example, integrating literature and historical examples from various cultures can enrich the learning experience and promote inclusivity. Banks (2017) highlights the importance of multicultural education in promoting inclusivity and reducing prejudice. By including diverse cultural narratives in the curriculum, educators can provide students with a broader understanding of the world and promote respect for different cultures.

Reflective Teaching Practices

Encouraging teachers to reflect on their biases and the implicit messages they convey through professional development programs can help educators become more aware of the invisible curriculum and its impact. Milner (2021) shows that professional development focused on cultural competence and reflective teaching practices can significantly improve teachers' ability to address the invisible curriculum. This training helps educators recognize and mitigate unconscious biases, promoting a more inclusive classroom environment.

Policies Promoting Equity and Inclusivity

Implementing policies that promote equity and inclusivity, such as anti-bullying programs and diversity training for staff, ensures that the school environment supports all students. A study by Espelage, Low, Polanin, and Brown (2013) found that comprehensive anti-bullying programs that include staff training and student education significantly reduce bullying incidents and improve school climate. These programs are essential for creating a safe and supportive environment where all students can thrive.

Student Voice and Agency

Creating opportunities for students to express their views and participate in decision-making processes within the school, such as student councils, feedback surveys, and inclusive classroom discussions, helps in promoting a sense of agency and belonging. Mitra (2014) highlights the positive impact of student voice initiatives on school improvement and student engagement. When students feel that their opinions are valued and acted upon, they are more likely to feel connected to their school community and motivated to succeed.

Examination of How Both Forms of Curricula Influence Student Learning and Experiences

Understanding how both visible and invisible curricula influence student learning and experiences is fundamental for creating effective educational environments. These two forms of curricula operate simultaneously, each playing a distinct yet interconnected role in shaping students' educational journeys.

The visible curriculum is the backbone of formal education, encompassing the explicit content delivered through textbooks, lectures, assignments, and assessments. It structures formal learning experiences by providing a clear framework of what students are expected to learn and achieve. For instance, in mathematics, the visible curriculum might outline specific topics such as algebra, geometry, and calculus, along with the corresponding learning objectives and assessment criteria. This structured approach helps ensure that educational standards are met and that students acquire the necessary knowledge and skills for academic progression. A study by Lavy (2015) highlights the importance of a well-structured visible curriculum in improving student outcomes. Lavy's research found that clearly defined curricular goals and rigorous content standards are associated with higher student achievement. This structured approach enables teachers to plan and deliver instruction more effectively, ensuring that all students have access to the essential knowledge and skills.

In contrast, the invisible curriculum shapes students' perceptions, attitudes, and behaviors through implicit messages conveyed by the school environment, teacher-student interactions, and peer relationships. It includes lessons on social norms, values, and expectations that are not explicitly taught but are learned through everyday experiences within the school setting. For example, the way a teacher handles classroom discipline can implicitly teach students about authority, justice, and fairness. Weinstein, Mignano, and Romano (2007) found that students' perceptions of teacher fairness and classroom management significantly impact their engagement and behavior. When students perceive that their teachers are fair and consistent, they are more likely to feel respected and valued, which positively influences their attitudes towards learning and school.

The interaction between visible and invisible curricula is complex and dynamic, influencing students' overall educational experiences. While the visible curriculum provides the formal structure for learning, the invisible curriculum creates the context in which this learning takes place. Together, they shape what students learn and how they learn and perceive their education. For instance, an inclusive visible curriculum that integrates diverse cultural perspectives can be improved by an invisible curriculum that promotes respect and inclusivity through school policies and practices. Sleeter and Grant (2008) found that multicultural education, which includes both visible curricular content and supportive invisible practices, leads to more positive educational outcomes for all students. By integrating diverse perspectives into the curriculum and promoting an inclusive school culture, educators can create a more holistic and supportive learning environment.

Additionally, the invisible curriculum can either reinforce or undermine the goals of the visible curriculum. For example, if a school's visible curriculum emphasizes critical thinking and collaboration, but the invisible curriculum promotes competition and individualism, students may receive mixed messages that hinder their ability to fully engage with the intended learning outcomes. A study by Gorski (2017) illustrates this point, showing that when schools fail to align their visible and invisible curricula, it can create barriers to student learning and equity.

For educators and policymakers, it is essential to recognize and address both the visible and invisible curricula to create cohesive and supportive educational environments. Strategies to achieve this include providing training for teachers on recognizing and addressing the invisible curriculum. This can help educators become more aware of the implicit messages they convey and how these impact student learning and behavior (Milner, 2021). Developing curricular content that reflects diverse perspectives and promotes inclusivity ensures that the visible curriculum supports a broad and inclusive educational experience (Banks, 2017). Implementing policies that promote a positive school climate and address issues such as bullying and discrimination helps align the invisible curriculum with the values and goals of the visible curriculum (Espelage, Low, Polanin, & Brown, 2013). Encouraging student participation in decision-making processes within the school promotes a sense of ownership and belonging, reinforcing the positive aspects of the invisible curriculum (Mitra, 2014).

By understanding and addressing the interchange of visible and invisible curricula, educators and policymakers can create educational environments that support all aspects of student development, from academic achievement to social and emotional well-being.

Impact on Students' Mental Well-Being

Understanding how the structure of knowledge and pedagogic practices impact students' mental health is critical for promoting a supportive educational environment. This section examines the relationship between the structure of knowledge, as influenced by classification and framing, and students' mental health. It also discusses how different pedagogic practices affect students' self-esteem, confidence, and overall mental well-being. The structure of knowledge, shaped by Bernstein's concepts of classification and framing, can significantly influence students' mental health. Classification refers to the boundaries between different knowledge areas, while framing involves the control over educational communication processes, including the selection, sequencing, pacing, and evaluation of knowledge.

Strong Classification and Mental Health

Strong classification, which maintains rigid boundaries between subjects, can lead to a compartmentalized curriculum. While this approach can provide clear and focused learning pathways, it may also limit interdisciplinary learning and critical thinking. A study by Colley, James, Diment, and Tedder (2003) found that highly compartmentalized curricula can increase pressure on students to excel in narrowly defined areas, potentially leading to increased anxiety and stress.

Weak Classification and Mental Health

In contrast, weak classification blurs the boundaries between subjects, promoting interdisciplinary learning. This approach can reduce the pressure on students by allowing them to see the connections between different areas of knowledge and apply their learning in more integrated and meaningful ways. Boaler (2022) showed that students in schools with integrated curricula reported lower levels of stress and higher engagement, suggesting that a more holistic approach to learning can positively impact mental well-being.

Strong Framing and Mental Health

Strong framing involves tight control over the educational process by teachers, with clear guidelines and expectations. While this can create a structured and predictable learning environment, it may also limit students' autonomy and creativity. Research by Ryan and Deci (2017) indicates that environments with high levels of control can undermine students' intrinsic motivation and lead to decreased mental well-being. Students may feel pressured to meet external standards, resulting in increased anxiety and lower self-esteem.

Weak Framing and Mental Health

Weak framing, which allows for greater student autonomy and flexibility, can improve engagement and motivation by catering to individual interests and learning styles. This approach can promote a sense of ownership and responsibility in students, positively impacting their mental health. Reeve (2016) found that students who experienced higher levels of autonomy in their learning environments reported greater satisfaction and lower levels of stress. This suggests that pedagogic practices that provide students with more control over their learning can contribute to improved mental well-being.

Discussion on How Different Pedagogic Practices Impact Students' Self-Esteem, Confidence, and Overall Mental Well-Being

Different pedagogic practices, influenced by the structure of knowledge and framing, have varying impacts on students' self-esteem, confidence, and overall mental well-being.

Structured Pedagogic Practices

Structured pedagogic practices, characterized by strong classification and framing, provide clear expectations and consistency. While these practices can help students understand what is required of them, they may also lead to a more stressful and competitive environment. Martin, Ginns, Brackett, Malmberg, and Hall (2013) found that students in highly structured environments reported higher levels of academic stress, which can negatively affect their self-esteem and confidence. However, structured practices can also support students who thrive in environments with clear rules and expectations, suggesting a nuanced impact on mental well-being.

Flexible Pedagogic Practices

Flexible pedagogic practices, associated with weak classification and framing, offer students more freedom to explore their interests and learn at their own pace. These practices can improve students' self-esteem and confidence by providing opportunities for success in diverse ways. For example, project-based learning allows students to demonstrate their knowledge and skills through various formats, such as presentations, portfolios, and collaborative projects. Mergendoller, Maxwell, and Bellisimo (2006) found that students engaged in project-based learning reported higher levels of self-efficacy and satisfaction with their learning experiences.

Supportive Teacher-Student Relationships

The quality of teacher-student relationships also plays a critical role in students' mental well-being. Positive relationships, characterized by trust, respect, and emotional support, can buffer the negative effects of academic pressure and promote a sense of belonging. Roorda, Koomen, Spilt, and Oort (2011) found that strong teacher-student relationships were associated with higher levels of student engagement and lower levels of emotional distress. These findings highlight the importance of promoting supportive interactions within the classroom to improve students' mental health.

Inclusive Educational Practices

Inclusive educational practices that address both visible and invisible curricula can promote a sense of belonging and respect for diversity, which are essential for students' mental well-being. By ensuring that all students feel valued and supported, inclusive practices can mitigate the negative impact of social exclusion and discrimination. McLeskey, Waldron, and Redd (2014) demonstrate that inclusive classrooms improve academic outcomes for students with special needs, improving their social and emotional well-being.

Relationship Between Pedagogic Practices and Mental Health Outcomes

The relationship between pedagogic practices and mental health outcomes is critical in understanding how educational environments can support or hinder students' mental well-being. Analyzing specific pedagogic practices reveals how they influence students' mental health and provides examples of inclusive educational practices that promote positive mental health outcomes, particularly for students with special needs.

Supportive pedagogic practices promote a positive learning environment, encourage student autonomy, and promote a sense of belonging and competence. These practices significantly improve students' mental health and overall well-being. Student-centered learning approaches, such as project-based and inquiry-based learning, give students greater control over their learning processes. Research by Deci and Ryan (2016) on self-determination theory emphasizes that when students feel autonomous and competent, their intrinsic motivation and mental well-being are significantly improved. These practices help reduce anxiety and increase engagement by allowing students to pursue their interests and learn at their own pace.

Using formative assessments to provide ongoing feedback rather than solely relying on high-stakes summative assessments can reduce stress and anxiety. Black and Wiliam (2018) found that formative assessment practices, which include regular feedback and opportunities for self-assessment, help students develop a growth mindset and resilience, positively influencing their mental health. Moreover, encouraging collaborative learning through group work and peer interactions improves social support and reduces feelings of isolation. According to Vygotsky and Cole (1978), social interactions play a central role in cognitive development and learning. Collaborative learning environments also help build students' communication skills and self-esteem.

Conversely, certain pedagogic practices can negatively impact students' mental health by creating stress, anxiety, and a sense of inadequacy. An overemphasis on high-stakes testing and performance-based assessment can lead to increased anxiety and pressure among students. Madaus and Russell (2010) indicate that high stakes testing environments often result in negative psychological effects, such as test anxiety, decreased motivation, and lower self-esteem. Moreover, strict and punitive classroom management practices can create a climate of fear and anxiety. Gregory and Cornell (2009) highlight that zero-tolerance policies and harsh disciplinary practices are associated with negative mental health outcomes, including increased stress and a sense of alienation. Pedagogic practices that limit student autonomy and control over their learning can undermine their sense of agency and self-efficacy. Deci and Ryan (2012) argue that when students have little control over their learning processes, their intrinsic motivation and mental health suffer.

Inclusive educational practices aim to create learning environments that accommodate the diverse needs of all students, including those with special needs. Universal Design for Learning (UDL) is an educational framework that optimizes teaching and learning for all students by providing multiple means of representation, engagement, and expression. Meyer, Rose, and Gordon (2014) demonstrate that UDL practices help reduce barriers to learning and support the mental health of students with special needs by promoting accessibility and flexibility in the curriculum.

Integrating Social and Emotional Learning (SEL) into the curriculum helps students develop essential skills such as emotional regulation, empathy, and resilience. Durlak, Weissberg, Dymnicki, Taylor, and Schellinger (2011) found that SEL programs significantly improve students' social and emotional skills, academic performance, and mental health outcomes. SEL practices create a supportive environment where students with special needs can thrive.

Restorative practices focus on building a positive school culture by promoting strong relationships and community. According to Gregory, Clawson, Davis, and Gerewitz (2016), implementing restorative practices in schools reduces disciplinary incidents and promotes a sense of belonging and well-being among students, including those with special needs. These practices emphasize empathy, conflict resolution, and personal responsibility, contributing to a supportive and inclusive school environment. Additionally, developing personalized learning plans for students with special needs, necessitates instruction to their individual strengths, interests, and needs. Tomlinson (2017) found that differentiated instruction and personalized learning plans improve student engagement and achievement, positively impacting their mental health. These plans provide students with a sense of ownership over their learning and help build their confidence and self-esteem.

Furthermore, Positive Behavioral Interventions and Supports (PBIS) is an evidence-based framework that promotes positive behavior and creates a supportive school climate. Horner, Sugai, and Anderson (2010) show that PBIS practices improve students' behavior and academic outcomes while reducing disciplinary issues. Implementing PBIS helps create an environment where students with special needs feel valued and supported, enhancing their mental well-being.

In general, specific pedagogic practices can either support or hinder students' mental health. Supportive practices such as student-centered learning, formative assessment, and collaborative learning promote positive mental health outcomes. In contrast, high-stakes testing, rigid classroom management, and limited student autonomy can negatively impact mental well-being. Inclusive educational practices, such as UDL, SEL, restorative practices, personalized learning plans, and PBIS, play a fundamental role in promoting positive mental health outcomes for students with special needs by creating supportive and accommodating learning environments.

Qualitative Approach and Methodology

Literature Review

The qualitative approach and methodology of this chapter involve a thorough review and synthesis of existing research on Bernstein's sociolinguistic theory and its application in educational settings. This review elucidates how Bernstein's concepts of classification and framing influence educational practices and student outcomes. Bernstein's sociolinguistic theory has been extensively studied, particularly in its implications for educational sociology. Foundational works such as *Class, Codes and Control* (Bernstein, 2003) introduce key concepts like restricted and elaborated codes, classification, and framing, which are central to understanding how educational systems reflect and perpetuate social inequalities.

Restricted codes, typically associated with working-class speech patterns, rely heavily on shared assumptions and implicit meanings. In contrast, elaborated codes, more common among the middle class, use explicit language. This distinction is fundamental for understanding the impact of different linguistic codes on students' educational experiences and outcomes.

Classification refers to the degree of boundary maintenance between subjects, while framing pertains to control over the educational communication process, including the selection, sequencing, pacing, and evaluation of knowledge. These concepts help analyze how educational practices are structured and influence student learning.

A synthesis of the literature reveals several key findings. Studies show that strong classification, maintaining rigid boundaries between subjects, often leads to a compartmentalized curriculum. While this ensures depth in subject-specific knowledge, it can limit interdisciplinary learning and critical thinking (Young, 2007). Strong classification tends to favor students, adept at navigating and mastering distinct academic disciplines, often aligning with middle-class educational advantages.

In contrast, weak classification blurs the boundaries between subjects, promoting interdisciplinary approaches and integrated curricula. This facilitates a more holistic understanding of knowledge, allowing students to make connections across different areas of study. Integrated curricula can lower stress levels and increase student engagement, suggesting a more holistic approach positively impacts mental well-being (Boaler, 2022).

Framing relates to the degree of control over educational communication. Strong framing, where teachers tightly control what is taught and how, creates a highly structured learning environment. While this provides clarity and consistency, it may also stifle student autonomy and creativity. Environments with high levels of control can undermine students' intrinsic motivation and lead to decreased mental well-being (Reeve, 2016).

Weak framing allows for greater student autonomy and flexibility in learning processes. This approach improves engagement and motivation by catering to individual interests and learning styles. Higher levels of autonomy increase satisfaction and intrinsic motivation, contributing to improved mental health outcomes (Deci & Ryan, 2016).

Several studies apply Bernstein's framework to specific educational contexts. For example, Morais and Neves (2010) found that a balanced approach, integrating elements of both strong and weak classification and framing, can lead to more equitable educational outcomes. This approach allows for the acquisition of specialized knowledge and the development of critical thinking skills.

The invisible curriculum, comprising implicit lessons, values, beliefs, and attitudes conveyed through the educational environment, significantly impacts student outcomes. Addressing the invisible curriculum through inclusive and reflective teaching practices is essential for promoting equity and social justice in education (Margolis, 2001). The hidden curriculum of time also impacts students with disabilities, emphasizing the need for flexible scheduling and supportive teacher practices (Ressa, Daniels, & Wells-Jensen, 2021).

Culturally responsive pedagogy addresses the limitations of traditional educational frameworks. Public-school systems often minoritize migrant students through policies that create language barriers and lack cultural representation (Free & Križ, 2022). Recognizing and valuing students' cultural backgrounds within the educational process can mitigate the negative effects of an invisible curriculum that marginalizes minority students (Gutiérrez & Rogoff, 2003).

Case Studies

The following case studies illustrate practical applications of Bernstein's sociolinguistic theory in various educational settings.

Case Study 1: Integrating Inclusive Practices in Science Education

A middle school science program adopted weaker classification and framing to improve inclusivity. The curriculum integrated science with mathematics and technology, allowing students to see the interconnectedness of these disciplines. Teachers used more flexible and student-centered pedagogic practices, giving students greater control over their learning processes. The outcomes included increased engagement and interest in science, reduced anxiety, and improved academic performance, particularly for students with learning disabilities (Morais & Neves, 2018).

Case Study 2: Bilingual Education Program in a Multicultural School

A bilingual education program in a multicultural elementary school used weak classification and flexible framing to address the needs of its migrant student population. The curriculum blended language instruction with cultural studies, history, and social sciences, providing a coherent learning experience. The program led to significant improvements in academic and social outcomes, promoting a more inclusive school culture (Free & Križ, 2022).

Case Study 3: Restorative Practices in High School

A high school implemented restorative practices as part of its disciplinary approach, applying Bernstein's theory to reframe discipline and social interactions. The curriculum incorporated restorative justice principles, focusing on repairing harm and restoring relationships. The outcomes included a decrease in disciplinary incidents, improved school climate, and increased student connection to peers and teachers (Gregory, Clawson, Davis, & Gerewitz, 2016).

Case Study 4: Universal Design for Learning (UDL) in an Inclusive Classroom

An inclusive elementary school implemented the UDL framework to create a flexible and accessible curriculum for all students. UDL principles align with Bernstein's theory by advocating for weak classification and framing. The outcomes included improved academic performance and engagement, particularly for students with special needs (Meyer, Rose, & Gordon, 2014).

These case studies highlight how adopting weaker classification and framing can create more inclusive and supportive educational environments, accommodating diverse learning needs.

Implications for Inclusive Education

By adopting weaker classification and framing, schools can create more inclusive and supportive environments. Flexible and integrated curricula, culturally responsive pedagogy, restorative practices, and UDL principles significantly improve student engagement, academic performance, and social inclusion.

Educational History

Understanding the impact of Bernstein's sociolinguistic theory requires examining the historical context of educational practices and curriculum designs.

Early 20th Century; Progressive Education Movement: The Progressive Education Movement emphasized experiential learning, interdisciplinary approaches, and critical thinking skills. These ideas challenged rigid, subject-bound curricula, advocating for weaker classification (Dewey, 1986).

Post-World War II: Expansion of Comprehensive Education: Following World War II, many countries shifted towards comprehensive education systems, promoting equality and social mobility. Bernstein's theory provided a framework to understand these changes, analyzing how boundaries between different types of knowledge were redefined (Bernstein, 2005).

1960s-1970s: Open Education and Progressive Curriculum Reforms: The 1960s and 1970s saw a push towards open education and progressive curriculum reforms. Educational theorists sought to break down traditional subject boundaries and promote student-centered learning environments (Plowden, DES, 1967).

1980s: Standardization and Accountability Movements: The 1980s saw a countermovement towards standardization and accountability in education. Policies like the *No Child Left Behind Act* emphasized clear boundaries between subjects and standardized testing, reinforcing strong classification and framing (Ball, 2012).

1990s-Present: Inclusive Education and Universal Design for Learning (UDL): Since the 1990s, there has been a renewed focus on inclusive education. Initiatives like the Salamanca Statement and the Individuals with Disabilities Education Act (IDEA) advocate for the inclusion of all students. Bernstein's concepts are relevant here, as inclusive education often involves weakening classification and framing to integrate diverse needs (Meyer, Rose, & Gordon, 2014).

Practical Applications

Educators can integrate subjects to create interdisciplinary learning experiences, adopt flexible pedagogical approaches, promote collaborative learning environments, and incorporate the Universal Design for Learning (UDL) framework. Educators can integrate subjects, adopt flexible pedagogical approaches, and promote collaborative learning environments. These strategies improve academic outcomes and overall student well-being (Morais & Neves, 2018; Reeve, 2016; Vygotsky & Cole, 1978). The UDL framework provides guidelines for creating flexible learning environments. Culturally responsive teaching and social and emotional learning (SEL) are essential strategies for promoting mental well-being and resilience (Meyer, Rose, & Gordon, 2014; Gay, 2018; Durlak et al., 2011).

Policymakers should advocate for curriculum frameworks that allow for flexible and interdisciplinary learning, support professional development, promote inclusive assessment methods, and encourage collaborative learning environments. Equity and inclusion should be at the forefront of all educational policies (Morais & Neves, 2018; Gay, 2018; Black & Wiliam, 2018; Gregory, Clawson, Davis, & Gerewitz, 2016).

Applying Bernstein's theory involves adopting flexible, inclusive, and student-centered practices. By promoting flexible curriculum design, supporting professional development, developing inclusive assessment methods, and implementing restorative practices, policymakers can create supportive school environments. Integrating social and emotional learning (SEL), providing mental health support services, and encouraging family and community engagement are essential strategies for promoting students' mental well-being, resilience, and positive connections to learning.

CONCLUSION

This chapter has explored the theoretical and practical applications of Bernstein's sociolinguistic theory, focusing on the concepts of classification and framing within educational settings. These concepts offer a profound lens through which we can understand the structure and dynamics of educational practices, curriculum design, and their implications for student outcomes, particularly mental health.

The exploration of Bernstein's theory has featured the crucial role that classification and framing play in shaping educational experiences. Classification refers to the boundaries that delineate different areas of knowledge, while framing pertains to the control over the educational communication process, including who decides what is taught, how it is taught, and how learning is assessed. These concepts are fundamental for understanding how knowledge is organized and transmitted in schools, which in turn affects how students perceive and engage with learning.

Key insights from this chapter emphasize that strong classification, characterized by rigid boundaries between subjects, often leads to a compartmentalized curriculum that can inhibit interdisciplinary learning and critical thinking. This approach, while providing clear learning pathways, may also limit students' ability to see connections between different knowledge areas, potentially leading to increased stress and reduced engagement. Studies have shown that rigid classification can increase pressure on students, contributing to anxiety and stress (Colley, James, Diment, & Tedder, 2003).

In contrast, weak classification blurs the boundaries between subjects, promoting an interdisciplinary approach that can improve students' holistic understanding of knowledge. Integrated curricula can lower stress levels and increase student engagement, suggesting that a more interconnected approach to learning can positively impact mental well-being (Boaler, 2022). By enabling students to draw connections across disciplines, weak classification promotes a more meaningful and engaging learning experience.

Framing involves the degree of control over educational processes. Strong framing, where teachers maintain tight control over the learning environment, can provide a structured and predictable educational experience. However, this approach can also limit student autonomy and critical thinking, as it often emphasizes rote learning and conformity. Environments with high levels of control can undermine students' intrinsic motivation and mental well-being, leading to decreased engagement and increased anxiety (Reeve, 2016).

Weak framing, which allows for greater student autonomy and flexibility, can improve student engagement and motivation by catering to individual interests and learning styles. Higher levels of autonomy increase satisfaction and intrinsic motivation, contributing to improved mental health outcomes (Deci & Ryan, 2012).

This approach encourages students to take ownership of their learning, promoting a sense of agency and self-efficacy.

Implications for Inclusive Education

In inclusive settings, weakening classification can facilitate the integration of students with diverse needs into regular classrooms, while weakening framing can provide the flexibility needed to accommodate different learning styles and paces. Case studies, such as those involving Universal Design for Learning (UDL) and restorative practices, demonstrate how applying Bernstein's principles can create more supportive and equitable educational environments. UDL's emphasis on multiple means of representation, expression, and engagement aligns with weak classification and framing, making learning accessible and engaging for all students (Meyer, Rose, & Gordon, 2014).

Additionally, the chapter highlighted how the invisible curriculum, the implicit lessons, values, beliefs, and attitudes conveyed through the educational environment, significantly impacts student outcomes. Implicit norms and expectations can disadvantage certain student groups, such as those with disabilities or migrant backgrounds, reinforcing social inequalities and negatively affecting their academic performance and well-being (Ressa, Daniels, & Wells-Jensen, 2021; Free & Križ, 2022). Addressing the invisible curriculum through inclusive and culturally responsive practices is essential for promoting equity and social justice in education.

Critical Reflection

Bernstein's theory provides a robust framework for analyzing and improving educational practices. However, the application of these concepts in real-world settings requires careful consideration and adaptation to the specific context and needs of students. While weakening classification and framing can improve inclusivity and student engagement, it is fundamental to balance these approaches with the need for academic rigor and clarity. Too much flexibility can lead to a lack of structure and coherence, hindering students' ability to develop deep knowledge and skills in specific disciplines.

Moreover, the successful implementation of these strategies depends on the support and commitment of all stakeholders, including educators, administrators, policymakers, and the wider community. Professional development for teachers, adequate resources, and supportive policies are essential to create the conditions for effective and sustainable change. Policymakers must prioritize equity and inclusion in their agendas, ensuring that all students have access to high-quality education that meets their diverse needs.

Future Directions

Bernstein's sociolinguistic theory has provided significant insights into the structure and transmission of knowledge within educational settings. However, there remains ample opportunity to expand and refine the application of his concepts of classification and framing to address contemporary educational challenges. Future research can explore deeper into several key areas to further explore and improve the utility of Bernstein's theory.

One critical area for further research is the intersectionality of students' identities and how classification and framing can be tailored to better serve diverse populations. Researchers should examine how gender, race, socio-economic status, and other identity factors intersect to influence educational experiences and outcomes. This research can inform more nuanced applications of Bernstein's theory, ensuring that curriculum design and pedagogic practices are inclusive and equitable. There is also a need for longitudinal studies that track the long-term mental health outcomes of students exposed to different levels of classification and framing throughout their education. These studies could provide valuable data on how these educational structures impact students' mental health over time, including anxiety, depression, self-esteem, and resilience.

With the increasing integration of technology in education, further research is needed to explore how digital tools and online learning environments can be aligned with Bernstein's concepts of classification and framing. Researchers should investigate how technology can be used to create flexible and inclusive learning experiences that cater to diverse student needs. Moreover, future research should focus on the development and evaluation of teacher training programs that emphasize the application of Bernstein's theory in the classroom. These programs should aim to equip educators with the skills and knowledge needed to implement flexible classification and framing strategies effectively.

Another important area for future research is the evaluation of educational policies that incorporate Bernstein's concepts of classification and framing. Researchers should assess the effectiveness of these policies in promoting equity, inclusion, and positive mental health outcomes in schools. By adopting flexible and inclusive approaches, educators can create learning environments that support the holistic development of all students, promoting their academic, social, and emotional well-being. The insights gained from this chapter highlight the importance of ongoing reflection and adaptation in education, ensuring that practices evolve to meet the changing needs of society and its learners.

REFERENCES

Artiles, A. J., Kozleski, E. B., Dorn, S., & Christensen, C. (2009). Learning in Inclusive Education Research: Re-mediating Theory and Methods With a Transformative Agenda. Inclusion in diversity and education, 2, 1-13.

Atkinson, M. (2016). Ethnography. In *Routledge handbook of qualitative research in sport and exercise* (pp. 71–83). Routledge.

Ball, S. J. (2012). *Politics and policy making in education: Explorations in sociology*. Routledge. 10.4324/9780203808726

Banks, J. A. (2017). *An Introduction to Multicultural Education*. Pearson Education.

Barron, B., & Darling-Hammond, L. (2008). *Teaching for Meaningful Learning: A Review of Research on Inquiry-Based and Cooperative Learning*. Book Excerpt. George Lucas Educational Foundation.

Bernstein, B. (2000). *Pedagogy, symbolic control, and identity: Theory, research, critique* (Vol. 5). Rowman & Littlefield.

Bernstein, B. (2003). *Theoretical Studies Towards a Sociology of Language* (1st ed.). Routledge., 10.4324/9780203014035

Black, P., & Wiliam, D. (2018). Classroom assessment and pedagogy. *Assessment in Education: Principles, Policy & Practice*, 25(6), 551–575. 10.1080/0969594X.2018.1441807

Bleak, K. W., & Abernathy, T. (2022). *Individuals with Disabilities Education Act (IDEA)*. Routledge., 10.4324/9780367198459-REPRW196-1

Boaler, J. (2022). *Mathematical mindsets: Unleashing students' potential through creative mathematics, inspiring messages and innovative teaching*. John Wiley & Sons.

Carvalho, L., & Yeoman, P. (2018). Framing learning entanglement in innovative learning spaces: Connecting theory, design and practice. *British Educational Research Journal*, 44(6), 1120–1137. 10.1002/berj.3483

Colley, H., James, D., Diment, K., & Tedder, M. (2003). Learning as becoming in vocational education and training: Class, gender and the role of vocational habitus. *Journal of Vocational Education and Training*, 55(4), 471–498. 10.1080/13636820300200240

Darling-Hammond, L., Hyler, M. E., & Gardner, M. (2017). Effective teacher professional development. Available at: https://bibliotecadigital.mineduc.cl/bitstream/handle/20.500.12365/17357/46%20Effective_Teacher_Professional_Development_REPORT.pdf?sequence=1

Deci, E. L., & Ryan, R. M. (2012). Self-determination theory. Handbook of theories of social psychology, 1(20), 416-436.

Dewey, J. (1986, September). Experience and education. *The Educational Forum*, 50(3), 241–252. 10.1080/00131728609335764

Drake, S. M., & Reid, J. L. (2018). Integrated curriculum as an effective way to teach 21st century capabilities. Asia Pacific Journal of Educational Research, 1(1), 31-50.

Durlak, J. A., Weissberg, R. P., Dymnicki, A. B., Taylor, R. D., & Schellinger, K. B. (2011). The impact of enhancing students' social and emotional learning: A meta-analysis of school-based universal interventions. *Child Development*, 82(1), 405–432. 10.1111/j.1467-8624.2010.01564.x21291449

Eiser, C., Eiser, J. R., & Stride, C. B. (2005). Quality of life in children newly diagnosed with cancer and their mothers. *Health and Quality of Life Outcomes*, 3(1), 1–5. 10.1186/1477-7525-3-2915860126

Epstein, J. L., Sanders, M. G., Sheldon, S. B., Simon, B. S., Salinas, K. C., Jansorn, N. R., & Williams, K. J. (2018). *School, family, and community partnerships: Your handbook for action*. Corwin Press.

Espelage, D. L., Low, S., Polanin, J. R., & Brown, E. C. (2013). The impact of a middle school program to reduce aggression, victimization, and sexual violence. *The Journal of Adolescent Health*, 53(2), 180–186. 10.1016/j.jadohealth.2013.02.02123643338

Florian, L., & Black-Hawkins, K. (2011). Exploring inclusive pedagogy. *British Educational Research Journal*, 37(5), 813–828. 10.1080/01411926.2010.501096

Florian, L., Black-Hawkins, K., & Rouse, M. (2016). *Achievement and inclusion in schools*. Routledge. 10.4324/9781315750279

Free, J. L., & Križ, K. (2022). The not-so-hidden curriculum: How a public school system in the United States minoritizes migrant students. *Equity & Excellence in Education*, 55(1-2), 50–72. 10.1080/10665684.2022.2047409

Giroux, H. A., & Penna, A. N. (1979). Social education in the classroom: The dynamics of the hidden curriculum. *Theory and Research in Social Education*, 7(1), 21–42. 10.1080/00933104.1979.10506048

Gorski, P. C. (2017). *Reaching and teaching students in poverty: Strategies for erasing the opportunity gap*. Teachers College Press.

Greenberg, M. T., Weissberg, R. P., O'Brien, M. U., Zins, J. E., Fredericks, L., Resnik, H., & Elias, M. J. (2003). Enhancing school-based prevention and youth development through coordinated social, emotional, and academic learning. *The American Psychologist*, 58(6-7), 466–474. 10.1037/0003-066X.58.6-7.46612971193

Gregory, A., Clawson, K., Davis, A., & Gerewitz, J. (2016). The promise of restorative practices to transform teacher-student relationships and achieve equity in school discipline. *Journal of Educational & Psychological Consultation*, 26(4), 325–353. 10.1080/10474412.2014.929950

Gregory, A., & Cornell, D. (2009). "Tolerating" adolescent needs: Moving beyond zero tolerance policies in high school. *Theory into Practice*, 48(2), 106–113. 10.1080/00405840902776327

Gutiérrez, K. D., & Rogoff, B. (2003). Cultural ways of learning: Individual traits or repertoires of practice. *Educational Researcher*, 32(5), 19–25. 10.3102/0013189X032005019

Hattie, J. (2008). *Visible learning: A synthesis of over 800 meta-analyses relating to achievement*. Routledge. 10.4324/9780203887332

Hattie, J., & Timperley, H. (2007). The power of feedback. *Review of Educational Research*, 77(1), 81–112. 10.3102/003465430298487

Hornby, G. (2015). Inclusive special education: Development of a new theory for the education of children with special educational needs and disabilities. *British Journal of Special Education*, 42(3), 213–229. 10.1111/1467-8578.12101

Horner, R. H., Sugai, G., & Anderson, C. M. (2010). Examining the evidence base for school-wide positive behavior support. *Focus on Exceptional Children*, 42(8). Advance online publication. 10.17161/foec.v42i8.6906

Jackson, P. W. (1990). Life in classrooms. Teachers College Press.

Jennings, P. A., & Greenberg, M. T. (2009). The prosocial classroom: Teacher social and emotional competence in relation to student and classroom outcomes. *Review of Educational Research*, 79(1), 491–525. 10.3102/0034654308325693

Jones, S. M., & Kahn, J. (2017). *The Evidence Base for How We Learn: Supporting Students' Social, Emotional, and Academic Development. Consensus Statements of Evidence from the Council of Distinguished Scientists*. Aspen Institute.

Lavy, V. (2015). Do differences in schools' instruction time explain international achievement gaps? Evidence from developed and developing countries. *Economic Journal (London)*, 125(588), F397–F424. 10.1111/ecoj.12233

Madaus, G., & Russell, M. (2010). Paradoxes of high-stakes testing. *Journal of Education*, 190(1-2), 21–30. 10.1177/0022057410190001-205

Margolis, E. (2001). *The Hidden Curriculum in Higher Education* (1st ed.). Routledge., 10.4324/9780203901854

Martin, A. J., Ginns, P., Brackett, M. A., Malmberg, L. E., & Hall, J. (2013). Academic buoyancy and psychological risk: Exploring reciprocal relationships. *Learning and Individual Differences*, 27, 128–133. 10.1016/j.lindif.2013.06.006

McLeskey, J., Waldron, N. L., & Redd, L. (2014). A case study of a highly effective, inclusive elementary school. *The Journal of Special Education*, 48(1), 59–70. 10.1177/0022466912440455

Mergendoller, J. R., Maxwell, N. L., & Bellisimo, Y. (2006). The effectiveness of problem-based instruction: A comparative study of instructional methods and student characteristics. *The Interdisciplinary Journal of Problem-Based Learning*, 1(2), 49–69. 10.7771/1541-5015.1026

Meyer, A., Rose, D. H., & Gordon, D. (2014). *Universal design for learning: Theory and Practice*. CAST Professional Publishing.

Milner, H. R. (2021). *Start where you are, but don't stay there: Understanding diversity, opportunity gaps, and teaching in today's classrooms*. Harvard Education Press.

Mitchell, D., & Sutherland, D. (2020). *What really works in special and inclusive education: Using evidence-based teaching strategies*. Routledge. 10.4324/9780429401923

Mitra, D. L. (2014). *Student voice in school reform: Building youth-adult partnerships that strengthen schools and empower youth*. State University of New York Press. 10.1515/9780791478943

Morais, A., & Neves, I. P. (2010). Basil Bernstein as an inspiration for educational research: Specific methodological approaches. ToolKits, translation devices and conceptual accounts: Essays on Basil Bernstein's sociology of knowledge, 11-32.

Nash, R. (2006). Bernstein and the explanation of social disparities in education: A realist critique of the socio-linguistic thesis. British Journal of Sociology of Education, 27(5), 539-553.

Nicolescu, B. (2002). *Manifesto of transdisciplinarity*. SUNY Press.

Oberle, E., Domitrovich, C. E., Meyers, D. C., & Weissberg, R. P. (2020). Establishing systemic social and emotional learning approaches in schools: A framework for schoolwide implementation. In *Social and Emotional Learning* (pp. 6–26). Routledge. 10.4324/9780429444692-2

Oberle, E., & Schonert-Reichl, K. A. (2017). Social and emotional learning: recent research and practical strategies for promoting children's social and emotional competence in schools. Handbook of social behavior and skills in children, 175-197.

Pajares, F. (1996). Self-efficacy beliefs in academic settings. *Review of Educational Research*, 66(4), 543–578. 10.3102/00346543066004543

Reeve, J. (2012). A self-determination theory perspective on student engagement. In *Handbook of research on student engagement* (pp. 149–172). Springer US. 10.1007/978-1-4614-2018-7_7

Reeve, J. (2016). Autonomy-supportive teaching: What it is, how to do it. In *Building autonomous learners: Perspectives from research and practice using self-determination theory* (pp. 129–152). Springer Singapore. 10.1007/978-981-287-630-0_7

Reinke, W. M., Stormont, M., Herman, K. C., Puri, R., & Goel, N. (2011). Supporting children's mental health in schools: Teacher perceptions of needs, roles, and barriers. *School Psychology Quarterly*, 26(1), 1–13. 10.1037/a0022714

Ressa, T., Daniels, D., & Wells-Jensen, S. (2021). Time as a hidden curriculum: Qualitative study of challenges faced by students with mobility, speech, and visual disabilities in P-12 settings. *International Journal of Educational Research Review*, 6(3), 250–263. 10.24331/ijere.927574

Roorda, D. L., Koomen, H. M., Spilt, J. L., & Oort, F. J. (2011). The influence of affective teacher–student relationships on students' school engagement and achievement: A meta-analytic approach. *Review of Educational Research*, 81(4), 493–529. 10.3102/0034654311421793

Ryan, R. M., & Deci, E. L. (2017). *Self-determination theory: Basic psychological needs in motivation, development, and wellness*. Guilford publications. 10.1521/978.14625/28806

Ryan, R. M., & Deci, E. L. (2021). Self-determination theory: Basic psychological needs in motivation, development, and wellness. *Rajagiri Management Journal*, 15(1), 88–90.

Sadovnik, A. R. (1991). Basil Bernstein's theory of pedagogic practice: A structuralist approach. *Sociology of Education*, 64(1), 48–63. 10.2307/2112891

Schwab, S. (2018). *Attitudes towards inclusive schooling: A study on students', teachers' and parents' attitudes*. Waxmann Verlag.

Sleeter, C. E., & Grant, C. A. (2008). *Making choices for multicultural education: Five approaches to race, class and gender*. John Wiley & Sons.

Taylor, R. D., Oberle, E., Durlak, J. A., & Weissberg, R. P. (2017). Promoting positive youth development through school-based social and emotional learning interventions: A meta-analysis of follow-up effects. *Child Development*, 88(4), 1156–1171. 10.1111/cdev.1286428685826

Tomlinson, C. A. (2017). *How to differentiate instruction in academically diverse classrooms*. ASCD.

Tyack, D., & Tobin, W. (1994). The "grammar" of schooling: Why has it been so hard to change? *American Educational Research Journal*, 31(3), 453–479. 10.3102/00028312031003453

UNESCO. (1994). The Salamanca Statement and Framework for Action on Special Needs Education. Organized by the World Conference on Special Needs Education: Access and Equity. Paris: UNESCO.

Vygotsky, L. S., & Cole, M. (1978). *Mind in society: Development of higher psychological processes*. Harvard University Press.

Wang, C. H., Ke, Y. T., Wu, J. T., & Hsu, W. H. (2012). Collaborative action research on technology integration for science learning. *Journal of Science Education and Technology*, 21(1), 125–132. 10.1007/s10956-011-9289-0

Wang, M. T., Degol, J. L., Amemiya, J., Parr, A., & Guo, J. (2020). Classroom climate and children's academic and psychological wellbeing: A systematic review and meta-analysis. *Developmental Review*, 57, 100912. 10.1016/j.dr.2020.100912

Weare, K., & Nind, M. (2011). Mental health promotion and problem prevention in schools: What does the evidence say? *Health Promotion International*, 26(suppl_1), i29–i69. 10.1093/heapro/dar07522079935

Weinstein, C. S., Mignano, A. J., & Romano, M. E. (2007). Elementary classroom management: Lessons from research and practice. Academic Press.

Young, M. (2007). Bringing Knowledge Back. In *From Social Constructivism to Social Realism in the Sociology of Education* (1st ed.). Routledge., 10.4324/9780203073667

Young, M., & Muller, J. (2010). Three educational scenarios for the future: Lessons from the sociology of knowledge. *European Journal of Education*, 45(1), 11–27. 10.1111/j.1465-3435.2009.01413.x

Chapter 5
Integration of Mindfulness and Emotional Intelligence in School Settings

Stephanie Nicolas Pantelides
Frederick University, Cyprus

ABSTRACT

This chapter focuses on the integration of mindfulness and emotional intelligence in school settings. Mindfulness refers to the basic human ability to be aware of one's body, mind, and feelings in the present moment. Emotional intelligence refers to the ability to recognize, understand, manage, and respond to one's own and others' emotions. Developing high emotional intelligence in students leads them to better navigate social interactions and manage their emotional responses, which in turn positively affects their academic and personal lives. Mindfulness practices can help manage classroom dynamics, reduce disruptive behavior, and create a positive learning environment. Practicing mindfulness improves our self-awareness, the bedrock of emotional intelligence. Finally, this chapter will not only discuss the strong relationship between mindfulness and emotional intelligence but also the influence of both mindfulness and emotional intelligence on teacher-student relationship quality.

DOI: 10.4018/979-8-3693-8312-4.ch005

Copyright © 2024, IGI Global. Copying or distributing in print or electronic forms without written permission of IGI Global is prohibited.

INTRODUCTION

There is growing interest on investigating how emotional intelligence (EI) affects academic, professional and social success (Collaborative for Academic Social and Emotional Learning [CASEL], 2015). The concept of social and emotional learning (SEL) has been defined as educational innovation that is justified in social needs whose goal is to develop emotional skills that will enhance better personal and social well-being (Bisquerra, 2003). The integration of mindfulness and emotional intelligence in school settings appears to be critical. This chapter aims at discussing how the integration of mindfulness and emotional intelligence in the classroom supports students' social and emotional development and in turn, how this dynamic can influence general well-being and the quality of relationships. This chapter will also discuss the impact of emotional intelligence on helping students analyze situations better, stay calm and think critically in challenging situations. In fact, emotional intelligence allows students to avoid being derailed, as for instance by a flash of anger, by managing emotions effectively. Notably, children who show higher levels of emotional intelligence reveal better attention skills, appear to be more engaged in school, have more positive relationships, and are more empathic. Furthermore, a critical emotional intelligence skill is the ability to interact well with others. Social skills such as active listening skills, verbal and nonverbal communication skills, and persuasiveness allow people to develop strong and positive relationships and at the same time, being able to understand both oneself and others.

An essential psychological human need is the desire to be related to other people. In fact, one of the strongest human motivations is the human need to interact socially and construct social relationships (Baumeister & Leary, 1995). According to Walto et al. (2012), this need to be connected to other people may by itself be a strong motivation for the development of interpersonal connections in educational settings (Walto et al., 2012). More recently, research has focused on investigating the importance of the quality of teacher-student relationship (Roodra et al., 2011; Meng, 2021; Forsberg et al., 2023). Notably, findings from these studies revealed that pupils appear to manage more efficiently both cognitive and emotional responsibilities when their need for being related to other people and especially to their teacher is met (Martin & Dowson, 2009); in addition, strong teacher-student relationships were found to establish long-term learners' education (Hamre & Pianta, 2001). In fact, research findings suggest that students are more prone to perform better academically and at the same time be more dedicated to school when they feel that their teachers like them (Wang & Eccles, 2013; Longobardi et al., 2016; Henry & Thorsen, 2018). Moreover, students who develop strong relationships with their teachers were found to perform better academically, be more dedicated to school, reveal greater achievements, exhibit higher levels of self-efficacy and motivation compered to their peers who have weaker relationships with their teachers (Sakiz al., 2012; Tosto et al., 2016; Henry & Thorsen, 2018; de Ruiter et al., 2021; Meng, 2021; Fabris et al, 2022; Longobardi et al., 2023). Conversely, students who feel that their teachers do not provide them with any kind of support are more likely to be reveal a high rate of absences compare to students who experience support through their relationship with their teacher. In turn, these students appear to be more motivated to attend their classes (Demir et al., 2019). Attending to classes by itself helps students to get to know their teachers better, which can encourage students' continuous engagement therefore, pursuing strong teacher-student relationships which support learning transfers (Cheung, 2019). Additionally, students reveal higher levels of inspiration when they spent more time with their teachers working together and therefore, they were more likely to adjust to school more easily due to being engaged to the learning process which made them more confident for their abilities (Liu & Chiang, 2019). In general, encouraging teacher-student relationships are strongly associated with higher academic performance which in turn have positive implications for academic performance (Valiente et al., 2008; Wubbels et al., 2016).

In addition, it is of great importance for teachers to regulate emotions appropriately in the classroom while they are role models for students. The role of emotional intelligence in teachers and the impact of it on classroom management will also be discussed in this chapter. It is very well-known that teachers with emotional intelligence have a significantly positive influence on academic achievement and also, they were found to manage their classroom more effectively, which in turn influences positively school success. This means that generally, teachers with emotional intelligence have better classroom management skills and therefore, they are more likely to create a more positive learning environment.

In fact, both teacher mindfulness and emotional intelligence have been previously associated with the development of positive teacher-student relationships. Recent findings provided evidence in favor of the mediating role of emotional intelligence therefore, enhancing our understanding about the mechanisms that support positive teacher-student interactions. This knowledge allows the development of educational interventions and support strategies not only to foster the development of mindfulness and emotional intelligence between teachers but also, to create an environment that encourages improved teacher-student relationships. Such an alteration in the teacher-student dynamic might have a positive impact on the overall classroom dynamics.

MINDFULNESS

Western psychologists adapted the concept of mindfulness to psychology in an attempt to help people deal with their negative feelings and cope with stress (Grabovac et al., 2011; Wang et al., 2023). The term "mindfulness" is referred to as a state of extremely focused attention at which people keep concentrated to a specific incident or situation and embrace it without reservation (Brown & Ryan,2003). In a broader way, the definition of mindfulness was suggested by Grossman et al. (2004) who argued that mindfulness is referred to as the ability to maintain attention to emotional and social events at the present moment; these events may be our ours or others (Grossman et al., 2004). More specifically, mindfulness is believed to be comprised by two components: 1) self-regulation of attention that is maintained in the immediate experience, which therefore allows experiences to be categorized as experiences occurring in the present moment; 2) specific orientation toward one's experience in the present moment, characterized by curiosity, openness and acceptance (Bishop et al., 2004). People characterized by mindfulness are not judgmental to their experiences (Kabat-Zinn, 1994). In fact, mindful people are capable to perceive and process their experiences in the present moment (Kabat-Zinn, 1990). Mindfulness also involves the ability to let go of the past and not stick to ideas or feelings (Bishop et al., 2004). In fact, mindful people perceive their experiences consciously which in turn enables them to perceive reality rather than an idealized version of it. Therefore, living consciously in the present moment and being non-judgmental represent the core components of mindfulness (Shapiro et al., 2006; Dane, 2011; Keng et al., 2011).

Mindfulness is proved to be a crucial construct in various fields including psychology, education, and well-being, especially for its potential benefits across different contexts (Langer, 1989; Fathi et al., 2023). Having its roots in Eastern reflective practices, mindfulness has been adapted and integrated into contemporary research and practice (in terms of interventions), offering a unique method to investigate human cognition, emotions, and behavior (Bishop et al., 2004). In the area of education, mindfulness has become a topic of growing interest particularly, the focus has become on investigating its implications for teachers and the teacher-student relationship (Schonert-Reichl & Roeser, 2016).

Moreover, recent research provided additional evidence, therefore advancing our understanding for the interplay between mindfulness, emotional intelligence, and their positive outcomes in the context of education. Essentially, mindfulness is closely related to emotional intelligence (Galloway et al., 2022). By nature, mindfulness and emotional intelligence share common elements, and when they are combined, they can have a significant impact on emotional learning. Importantly, mindfulness – the basic component of emotional intelligence – is considered the bedrock for the development of all of the other emotional intelligence skills. In fact, mindfulness is proved really helpful for transition times, while most kids have trouble shifting their focus from something they are already involved in to something new. This dynamic can in turn disrupt meltdowns and stop fights. In other words, mindfulness provides an opportunity for one to slow down and consciously notice his/her emotions, thoughts and urges. In the field of education, mindfulness is a topic of growing interest, especially in understanding its implications for teachers and the teacher-student relationship (Schonert-Reichl,& Roeser, 2016). Therefore, this chapter will discuss how mindfulness – which sometimes is called "contemplative pedagogy"- is incorporated in the classroom by using teaching methods to cultivate deepened awareness, concentration, and insight. These teaching methods include, among others, breathing exercises, listening, and gratitude practice.

Similarly, to adults, children nowadays suffer stress and anxiety which in turn has a negative impact on their personal and academic lives. Developing mindfulness – which refers to the ability to be aware on one's body, mind and feelings in the present moment – appears critical. On one hand, in school settings, mindfulness leads to increase focus, attention, self-control, classroom participation and compassion. It is also related to improved academic performance, the ability to resolve conflict, and overall well-being, On the other hand, mindfulness is related to decreased levels of stress, depression, anxiety, and disruptive behavior. All these constitute mindfulness a safe space to develop emotional intelligence, compassion for self and others and cope with difficult emotions. Curriculum-themed activities on mindfulness can be integrated through exercises in breathing, sensory experience, guided imagery, and movement.

In the context of education, studies make significant efforts to investigate the role of teacher mindfulness and its potential impact on teacher-student relationship and classroom dynamics. It has been found that teachers who encourage mindfulness may exhibit increased emotional regulation, reduced stress, and improved empathy; all these can significantly contribute to stronger and more positive teacher-student relationships (Roeser et al., 2012; Braun et al., 2019). In fact, teachers who show mindfulness themselves were found to be better equipped to respond to students' emotional needs, navigate conflicts in a constructive way, and create a nurturing and supportive environment (McDonald& Shirley, 2009; Moyano et al., 2021).

Furthermore, developing mindfulness not only appears critical for developing emotional intelligence but it also appears to be positively related to teacher-student relationship quality. The influence of teachers' approach towards students definitely has a significant impact on the learning outcomes but more importantly, to the general classroom atmosphere. Understanding the mechanisms that motivate these relationships is crucial for both teachers and policymakers. In fact, recent evidence revealed a clear association between teacher mindfulness and the quality of teacher-student relationships. Notably, this relationship was founded to be mediated by emotional intelligence providing further evidence that effective teaching and positive teacher-student relationships are both significantly influenced by emotions, awareness and interpersonal interactions (Wang, 2023).

There is growing interest in the field of educational psychology in studying emotional intelligence; in fact, findings by a variety of studies give support to the idea that student learning appears to be improved by better motivation and engagement (Saeed & Zyngier, 2012), autonomy (Grolnick & Ryan, 1987), and attention abilities (Kruschke, 2003). Therefore, these are the aspects that teachers consider important and use to promote in their classrooms (Deci & Ryan, 2008). For this reason, many educational models adopted these socially desirable norms across different countries. What they do, is that they reward young people who successfully pay attention for long time periods, who are able to maintain their attention without being distracted, and who know how to control their impulsive behavior in terms of speaking or moving (Rodríguez-Ledo, & Orejudo-Hernández, 2017). However, nowadays this model seems to require continuous changes while even more and more students appear to be more restless and impulsive and also, because there appears to be an increase in developmental disorders which are characterized by a strong attentional component, such as Attention Deficit and Hyperactivity (ADHD) Disorder. It is argued that the high stimulation that today's students receive through different canals, such as the typical interaction with screens, especially interaction with the Internet may be one of the possible causes (Pagès & Reñé, 2008). This overstimulation could happen because the use of tablet, computers, video games, especially the overuse of mobile phones; all of these elements, in fact require continuous attention. While in the field of psychology researchers tend to search for causes, it is believed that both psychologists and teachers should focus on interventions that aim to improve attention and reduce impulsivity if they wish to revert this tendency. In an attempt to achieve this goal, some interventions aim to improve such mindfulness competence in young people/adolescents. For example, research findings showed that implementing a 8-week MindUp program results in improved perceived stress, resilience, curiosity/exploration, and gratitude and also, that mindfulness covaries with perceived stress, symptoms of depression and anxiety. Similarly, other intervention programs following the same line were applied to young adolescents; findings revealed that the implementation of these intervention programs revealed improvements in areas like sustained attention (Zeidan et al., 2010), academic performance (Leon, 2008), reduced anxiety (Sugiura, 2004), reduced aggressiveness (Lantieri, 2009), decreased ADHD symptoms (Lantieri, 2009), lower burnout levels and improved motivation to the task or engagement (De La Fuente et al., 2010); in addition, higher levels of emotional well-being were evident (Hamilton et al., 2006). These are some of the most representative examples of improvements among others. Importantly, the aforementioned mindfulness techniques and their application are related to improvements of emotional intelligence components and their competences. Relating to this, a number of researchers highlighted the importance of attention for nurturing the implicit cognitive skills that make up emotional intelligence (Mestre et al., 2009).

Although it is of high importance to incorporate techniques in the school settings to help students develop mindfulness, at the same time, it is also crucial to have teachers who have already established mindfulness (Wang, 2023). In fact, mindfulness is essential, especially for educators to manage challenging circumstances effectively while it allows teachers to stay focused, to maintain a deep understanding of the learning process and also, to be highly aware of classroom dynamics. All these qualities, can help to the development of strong teacher-student relationships by reducing teachers' stress and despair (Becker et al., 2017; Wang et al., 2023). Recent evidence suggests that mindfulness can strongly predict teachers' well-being and their potential for managing effectively classroom dynamics (Braun et al., 2019).

Yet, mindfulness is not limited to personal traits alone; it also involves the continuing practice of acceptance. This practice allows a positive emotional environment which in turns allows students perceive feelings of warmth and positivity from their teachers. Teachers who show these qualities are usually the ones who meet successfully their students' needs and treat them more patiently. Consequently, this vigorous action contributes to the development of positive and strong teacher-student relationships (Frank et al., 2016; Longobradi et al., 2021).

It is well established that the teacher-student relationship is critical and it significantly influences students' academic, social, and emotional development (Hamre & Piatna, 2005; Roorda et al., 2011; Longobardi et al., 2016; Shakki, 2022; Fabris et al., 2023). In fact, trust, mutual respect, emotional support, and effective communication characterize a positive teacher-student relationship (Hamre et al., 2013). On the contrary, negative teacher-student relationships relate to student disengagement, low academic performance, and behavioral challenges (Baker et al., 2008). There is growing research in the area of educational psychology and related fields providing convincing evidence in regards to the critical role of positive teacher-student relationship on students' well-being and academic performance (Hughes et al., 2012). Notably, research findings provide consistent findings that a positive teacher-student relationship is more likely to result in higher levels of student engagement, motivation, and a pure enthusiasm for learning (Froiland et al., 2019; Howe et al., 2019). Furthermore, positive teacher-student relationships were found to be linked to increased self-esteem, a sense of belonging, and an overall higher level of satisfaction by their experience with their school (Fauth et al., 2019; Liebowitx & Porter, 2019; Longobardi et al., 2021).

A variety of studies provided convincing evidence in regards to the impact of teacher-student quality relationship quality on different student outcomes. More specifically, high quality teacher-student relationship was found to be associated with greater student engagement, higher academic achievement, and less behavioral problems (Hamre & Pianta, 2001). In another study by Roorda et al. (2011), findings revealed that a positive teacher-student relationship related to improved student motivation and less dropout rates. Moreover, other research findings suggest that positive teacher-student relationship is capable to balance any adverse effects produced by stress and also, support students' resilience in challenging situations within the school context (Hughes et al., 2012).

As it is evident, the teacher-student relationship is of critical significance given its impact on students' educational experiences and performance. Therefore, it is considered vital to investigate the factors that give rise, establish, and maintain of positive teacher-student relationship. Over the last few years, teacher mindfulness has gained attention as it is believed to be one such factor. In fact, mindfulness practices and interventions were found to be strongly related to enhanced emotional regulation, increased empathy, and improved interpersonal relationships (Shapiro et al., 2006; Emerson et al., 2017).

In addition, mindfulness was found to be a strong predictor of teachers' wellness and the quality of classroom management (Braun et al., 2019). Furthermore, mindfulness is strongly related to persistent compassion; therefore, teachers upholding this quality will have students who experience favorable feelings which in turn will make them more attentive to their requirements and they are also more tolerant in treating them (Frank et al., 2016; Lemberger-Truelove et al., 2018). Generally, examining the relation between teacher mindfulness and teacher-student relationship quality could provide useful evidence in regards to how mindful teaching practices may contribute in the development of positive teacher-student interactions and support students' overall well-being and success.

Research findings suggest that what strongly relates teacher mindfulness and teacher-student relationship quality is emotional intelligence. It was found that teachers who exhibit high levels of emotional intelligence can better empathize with their students' experiences, build trust, and foster positive emotional connections (Mérida-López & Extremera, 2017). Emotional intelligence has been found to play a significant role in teacher-student relationship quality, giving further support to the idea that it may mediate the relationship between teacher mindfulness and teacher-student relationship quality (Wang et al., 2023).

Teacher-Student Relationship

The kind of relationship between teachers and students vary; those relationships that are characterized by high levels of sensitiveness, that are friendly, and honest, are referred to as having "teacher-student rapport" (Frymier & Houser, 2000; Frisby & Martin, 2010). This kind of teacher-student relationships address "the degree to which students feel supported, respected, and valued by their teachers" (Pierchurska-Kuciel, 2011). Thus, in order to build a solid connection with students, instructors should continuously encourage them, respect their opinions, and recognize their academic work (Schriver & Harr Kulynuch, 2021). Upholding students' academic standards might lead teachers to develop close relationships with them (Thornberg et al., 2020). Thompson (2018) suggested that teachers can only develop a valuable connection with their students if they show concern for their requirements and passions. Recent findings suggest that having empathy and understanding turns into a psychological connection between teachers and students (Virat, 2022). In the context of education, when there are strong teacher-student relationships students are more likely to invest more time and effort in completing their academic tasks (Roorda et al., 2011; Pianta et al., 2012; Quin, 2017; Longobardi et al., 2023; Wang and Derakhshan, 2023). Teacher-student interaction that is emotionally charged appears to be crucial for students to succeed academically; this happens because it encourages students to take lead of their role in their learning environment (Roorda et al., 2017).

The well-known attachment theory suggests that, the relationship between teachers and students is a continuation of the parent-child relationship and reflects the emotional connection between teachers and students, and it is also believed to be a positive state of the relationship (Bergin and Bergin, 2009; Fitton, 2013; Fearon and Roisman, 2017). In addition to students' psychological, interpersonal, and social growth, the teacher-student relationship also has a significant impact on their future educational achievement (Rucinski et al., 2018; Camodeca and Coppola, 2019). The teacher has the leading role in the relationship between the student and the teacher and therefore, some characteristics of the teacher will influence how well the parent-teacher relationship works (Gillespie, 2005; Prewett et al., 2019). For example, research findings suggest that teachers have to maintain high levels of emotional control and mental health in order to develop positive teacher-student relationships (Becker's et al., 2017). This can help instructors reduce their stress levels and those of despair which can in turn improve the teacher-student relationship (Becker et al., 2017; Burgos-Julián et al., 2022). Braun et al. (2019) argued that mindfulness is an important predictor teachers' wellbeing and the quality of classroom management.

Emotional Intelligence

Emotion can be defined as an internal stimulus that fires human behavior so we can respond appropriately to the environment by getting closer or distancing ourselves, depending on whether emotions are positive or negative (Ekman & Davidson, 1994). Our ability to adapt to this context is defined as intelligence (Sternberg, 2013). Taking these two things together, people's ability to perceive, understand, regulate, and express emotional events by adapting to each situation respectively, is defined as emotional intelligence (Celma-Pastor and Rodríguez-Ledo, 2017). Therefore, emotional intelligence can explain how people perceive, regulate and express emotions either they are more or less skillful on doing so. This definition develops by the theory proposed by Petrides et al. (2007a), which suggests that emotional intelligence is based on some measurable personality traits. This specific trait model of emotional intelligence proposed by Petrides et al. (2007a), suggests that emotional intelligence can be understood as an emotional self-efficacy trait, that is referred to a collection of emotion-related self perceptions and dispositions; both self-perceptions and dispositions can be found at the lower levels of personality hierarchies (Petrides et al., 2007b).

By definition, emotional intelligence (EI) refers to the ability to perceive, understand, and manage one's emotions effectively, as well as the ability to recognize and respond to the emotions of others (Salovey & Mayer, 1990; Mayer et al., 2007). People with high levels of emotional intelligence are characterized by the ability to give priority to cognitive tasks that will benefit their present emotional state (Fiori & Vesely-Maillefer, 2018; Vesely Maillefer et al., 2018; Vesely-Maillefer, & Saklofske, 2018). Given the potential implications of emotional intelligence on personal well-being, interpersonal relationships, and overall success the concept of emotional intelligence has gained increasing interest across different domains including psychology, education, and workplace contexts (Brackett et al., 2011; Shakki, 2023).

Findings by numerous studies have provided convincing evidence in regards to the relation between emotional intelligence and significant areas of one's life, especially in the area of education. In the context of teaching, emotional intelligence has been proven critical for the development of positive teacher-student relationship and creating a supportive and nurturing learning setting (MacCann et al., 2020; Sánchez-Álvarez et al., 2020). Teachers with higher levels of emotional intelligence are characterized by very good empathy skills, understanding and they are also more responsive to students' emotional needs; this in turn can lead to increased student engagement and a sense of being part of the classroom (Mortiboys, 2013; Keefer et al., 2018). Furthermore, recent findings suggest that teachers with higher levels of emotional intelligence are more prone to have lower levels of stress and burnout, which can have a positive impact on job satisfaction and overall well-being (Mérida-López, & Extremera, 2017; Greenier et al., 2021; Derakhshan et al., 2023; Geraci et al., 2023). In addition, teacher's emotional intelligence has been found to be related to improved academic performance, social and emotional development, and overall school climate (Corcoran & Tormey, 2013; Pozo-Rico and Sandoval, 2020). Moreover, emotionally intelligent teachers have all the appropriate equipment to manage challenging situations provide support to students with emotional difficulties (Valente & Lourenco, 2020).

Related research findings provided significant evidence supporting the positive influence of mindfulness practice on the development of emotional skills. For example, mindfulness has been related to significantly lower chances of developing depression, lower levels of anxiety, tension, and emotional distress (Tomlinson et al., 2018). In addition, many studies provided evidence that people with higher levels of mindfulness have better abilities to recognize, comprehend, and endure negative emotions within their current situation (Osborne & Atkinson, 2022; Ainsworth et al., 2023; Wang et al., 2023). Mindfulness practice, which teaches people to sense their own and other people's feelings and also, accept them, may be improved (Champers et al., 2009; Guendelman et al., 2017). Doing so, can be proved valuable for improving people's capacity for adaptable emotional function and emotional intelligence. In fact, the ability model suggests that the capacity to identify, utilize, comprehend, and manage emotions is a core component of emotional intelligence (Mayer et al., 2007).

Taking into account the significance of emotional intelligence and its impeding implications on teacher-student relationship and student outcomes, understanding the role of emotional intelligence in the relation between teacher mindfulness and teacher-student relationship quality can provide critical insights in regards to the mechanisms through which emotional intelligence affects teacher-student relationship and relates to positive student academic performance. Consequently, investigating the role of emotional intelligence in the link between teacher mindfulness and teacher-student relationship quality can provide crucial evidence for the potential profits of developing emotional intelligence among teachers in an attempt to promote their effectiveness in developing qualitative teacher-student relationships.

Recent evidence is in line with results from previous research suggesting that teacher mindfulness not only directly predicts teacher student relationship quality but it also functions through the mediation of emotional intelligence (Miao et al., 2018; Mestre etal., 2019; Wang, 2023), giving further emphasis on the significant influence of mindfulness on emotional intelligence. In fact, teachers who practice mindfulness show a significantly advance ability to manage their emotions effortlessly, experience emotions without judgment, and support the development of emotional intelligence in their students. Furthermore, emotional intelligence appears to play a crucial role on influencing the interactions between instructors and learners.

Mindfulness allows the development of an empathetic and accepting mindset which requires advanced skills on emotional intelligence as well. Mindfulness practices by nature promote self-awareness and emotional regulation and also, have the advantage to promote emotional intelligence by increasing one's sensitivity to their own emotions and those of others' (Poulou, 2017; Chamizo-Nieto et al., 2021). Therefore, teachers with high levels of mindfulness are more likely to develop higher levels of emotional intelligence given that they acquire expertise on recognizing and managing their own emotions and understanding their students' emotional needs. In turn, teachers with high emotional intelligence appear to have the advantage of facilitating positive interpersonal interactions. Teachers who exhibit high levels of mindfulness and emotional intelligence are able to recognize and respond appropriately to their students' emotional cues and needs (Brandsma, 2017; Chamizo-Nieto et al., 2021). In fact, they are characterized by greater empathy, understanding, and compassion towards their students, allowing a positive influence on teacher-student relationship quality.

Teachers who exhibit high levels of emotional intelligence appear to be really skillful in managing challenging situations and conflicts that may arise in the classroom effectively (Mérida-López & Extremera, 2017). Their ability to effectively handle such situations is enhanced by their ability to effectively managing their emotions and also, their skill to be able to understand their students' emotional needs, eventually allowing the development of strong teacher-student relationships by nurturing a positive learning environment (Geraci et al., 2023; Wang et al., 2023). Furthermore, teachers with high levels of emotional intelligence often create a positive and happy atmosphere within the school, therefore allowing the development of a comfortable learning environment for their students. Positive relationships between students and teachers, regardless of age, are of great importance while they have a significant contribution to the quality of teacher-student relationship quality. Moreover, teachers with high emotional intelligence are better able to manage efficiently various student issues and provide significant emotional support (Valente & Lourenço, 2020), ultimately contributing to the development of strong teacher-student relationships (Valente & Lourenço, 2020).

Overall, mindfulness and emotional intelligence play an essential role in regards to fostering teacher-student relationship. Both constructs were found to be critical for the quality of the teacher-student relationships. On one hand, mindfulness enables the development of deeper connections by allowing teachers to face conflicts and challenges with greater acceptance and objectivity. In addition, it further develops teachers' awareness of their students' emotional needs, therefore allowing them to respond to challenges in a smooth was and also, cultivate supportive relationships.

Notably, teacher mindfulness functions through the mediation of emotional intelligence, emphasizing the interplay between these constructs. In fact, mindfulness practices promote emotional intelligence by increasing one's sensitivity to emotions, eventually having a significant impact on positive interactions. Practically, teachers with higher emotional intelligence are characterized by an expertise in managing different situations in the classroom, creating an encouraging learning environment and developing deep connections with their students. These findings provide valuable insights for educational practices, highlighting the importance of nurturing mindfulness and emotional intelligence in teacher-student dynamics.

Emotional Intelligence and Mindfulness

In regards to emotional intelligence and the precision with which we perceive our own emotional states, Brown & Ryan (2003) suggest that it actually improves through training in mindfulness techniques. However, it is well-known that there exists a direct relationship between training with mindfulness techniques and attention, clarity and emotional repair dimensions (De la Fuente et al., 2010), as well as emotional regulation (Ramos et al,, 2009). Other findings revealed the importance of mindfulness directly to modifying emotional states voluntarily and that it directly correlates to attentional capacity and emotional regulation (Davidson, 2012). Furthermore, training in mindfulness helps develop more positive and adaptive emotional profiles (Goleman & Davidson, 2017). Notably, implementing mindfulness techniques with teachers leads to improvements in receptivity to student requirements, promotes emotional balance, contributed to stress management, favors personal relationships, enhances the classroom climate and nurtures general well-being (Schoeberlein, 2012). Similarly, when students work with mindfulness improvements are evident in their willingness to learn, it improves academic performance, reinforces attention and concentration, reduces anxiety about the exams, improves classroom participation, enhances impulse control, provides tools to help reduce stress, improves emotional learning, promotes prosocial behavior, and supports general well-being (Schoeberlein, 2012). Furthermore, mixed emotional intelligence and mindfulness intervention programs such as that implemented by Schonert-Reichl et al. (2015), typically reveal, among others, improvements in the areas of empathy, better emotional control, increase acceptance of peers, higher levels of mindfulness competence and even better cognitive and stress control (Schonert-Reichl et al., 2015).

The underlying mechanisms responsible for the advantageous influence of mindfulness on emotional intelligence and on promoting some of its components is still under debate. According to Ramos et al. (2009), training in mindfulness involves exposure to negative emotions that favor habituation to such emotions. Also,

Vallejo (2006) supports the notion that people can change their tendency to respond automatically to certain emotional experiences due to mindfulness training, which allows them to respond with other new and more positive repertoires of behavior resulting from reflection.

CONCLUSION

There is strong evidence supporting the direct positive relationship between teacher mindfulness and teacher-student relationship quality, with emotional intelligence playing a mediating role in this dynamic. Such evidence suggests that teacher with higher level of mindfulness are more likely to develop positive and supportive relationships with their students. In the context of education, mindfulness practices by nature encourage present-moment awareness and non-judgmental acceptance, which may allow teachers to be closer to their students' needs, emotions, and experiences, therefore opening the direction to enhanced teacher-student interactions and a more positive classroom environment. Notably, emotional intelligence was found to be critical for this relationship while it serves as a mediator. Teachers who exhibit higher levels of emotional intelligence may be more skillful to face the challenges of the teacher-student relationship by effectively recognizing and managing emotions, both those of themselves and those of their students. In fact, emotional intelligence allows nurturing empathy, understanding, and effective communication, all crucial ingredients for the establishment and maintenance of positive teacher-student relationships.

These findings are of high importance from a practical perspective for both teachers and school administrators. At the first point, schools should consider including mindfulness training and practices into teacher professional development programs. By raising mindfulness between teachers, schools can allow them to be more sensitive and close to their students' emotional and behavioral needs. Increasing teachers' awareness may enable the development of more positive, nurturing, and supportive teacher-student relationships. In addition, these findings highlight the essential role of emotional intelligence as a mediating factor in the relationship between teacher mindfulness and the quality of teacher-student relationship. This emphasizes the importance of cultivating emotional intelligence between teachers. To achieve this goal, schools should incorporate emotional intelligence training into teacher education programs. Such training should give teachers the tools and knowledge to better understand, manage, and express their own emotions and, importantly, to empathize with their students' emotions. Promoting emotional intelligence can serve as the basis for developing and maintaining teacher-student relationships that are characterized by emotional responsiveness and empathy, both essential for creating a positive and supportive learning environment.

REFERENCES

Baumeister, R. F., & Leary, M. R. (1995). The need to belong: Desire for interpersonal attachments as a fundamental human motivation. *Psychological Bulletin*, 117(3), 497–529. 10.1037/0033-2909.117.3.4977777651

Becker, B. D., Gallagher, K. C., & Whitaker, R. C. (2017). Teachers' dispositional mindfulness and the quality of their relationships with children in head start classrooms. *Journal of School Psychology*, 65, 40–53. 10.1016/j.jsp.2017.06.00429145942

Bergin, C., & Bergin, D. (2009). Attachment in the classroom. *Educational Psychology Review*, 21(2), 141–170. 10.1007/s10648-009-9104-0

Bishop, S. R., Lau, M., Shapiro, S., Carlson, L., Anderson, N. D., Carmody, J., Segal, Z. V., Abbey, S., Speca, M., Velting, D., & Devins, G. (2004). Mindfulness: A proposed operational definition. *Clinical Psychology : a Publication of the Division of Clinical Psychology of the American Psychological Association*, 11(3), 230–241. 10.1093/clipsy.bph077

Bisquerra, R. (2003). Educación emocional y competencias básicas para la vida. *Revista de Investigación Educacional*, 21, 7–43.

Brackett, M. A., Rivers, S. E., & Salovey, P. (2011). Emotional intelligence: Implications for personal, social, academic, and workplace success. *Social and Personality Psychology Compass*, 5(1), 88–103. 10.1111/j.1751-9004.2010.00334.x

Brandsma, R. (2017). *The Mindfulness Teaching Guide: Essential Skills and Competencies for Teaching Mindfulness-Based Interventions*. New Harbinger Publications.

Braun, S. S., Roeser, R. W., Mashburn, A. J., & Skinner, E. (2019). Middle school teach-mindfulness, occupational health and well-being, and the quality of teacher-student Interactions. *Mindfulness*, 10(2), 245–255. 10.1007/s12671-018-0968-2

Brown, K. W., & Ryan, R. M. (2003). The benefits of being present: Mindfulness and its role in psychological well-being. *Journal of Personality and Social Psychology*, 84(4), 822–848. 10.1037/0022-3514.84.4.82212703651

Camodeca, M., & Coppola, G. (2019). Participant roles in preschool bullying: The impact of emotion regulation, social preference, and quality of the teacher–child relationship. *Social Development*, 28(1), 3–21. 10.1111/sode.12320

Celma-Pastor, L., & Rodríguez-Ledo, C. (2017). Educación Socioemocional Para Jóvenes. In *El Aula: Programa SEA*. TEA Ediciones., 10.1016/j.chb.2013.05.009

Chambers, R., Gullone, E., & Allen, N. B. (2009). Mindful emotion regulation: An integrative review. *Clinical Psychology Review*, 29(6), 560–572. 10.1016/j.cpr.2009.06.00519632752

Chamizo-Nieto, M. T., Arrivillaga, C., Rey, L., & Extremera, N. (2021). The role of emotional intelligence, the teacher-student relationship, and flourishing on academic performance in adolescents: A moderated mediation study. *Frontiers in Psychology*, 12, 695067. 10.3389/fpsyg.2021.69506734335411

Cheung, C. S. (2019). Parents' involvement and adolescents' school adjustment: Teacher–student relationships as a mechanism of change. *School Psychology*, 34(4), 350–362. 10.1037/spq000028831294593

Collaborative for Academic Social and Emotional Learning. (2015). *Casel Guide: effective social and emotional learning programs, middle and high school edition.* CASEL.

Corcoran, R. P., & Tormey, R. (2013). Does emotional intelligence predict student teachers' performance? *Teaching and Teacher Education*, 35, 34–42. 10.1016/j.tate.2013.04.008

Dane, E. (2011). Paying attention to mindfulness and its effects on task performance in the workplace. *Journal of Management*, 37(4), 997–1018. 10.1177/0149206310367948

Davidson, R. J. (2012). *El Perfil Emocional De Tu Cerebro, Claves Para Modificar Nuestras Actitudes Y Reacciones*. Destino. 10.1093/ije/30.5.1042

De La Fuente, J., Salvador, M., & Franco, C. (2010). Efectos de un programa de entrenamiento en conciencia plena (mindfulness) en la autoestima y la inteligencia emocional percibidas. *Psicología Conductual*, 18, 297–315.

de Ruiter, J. A., Poorthuis, A. M., & Koomen, H. M. (2021). Teachers' emotional labor in response to daily events with individual students: The role of teacher–student relationship quality. *Teaching and Teacher Education*, 107, 103467. 10.1016/j.tate.2021.103467

Deci, E. L., & Ryan, R. M. (2008). Self-determination theory: A macrotheory of human motivation, development, and health. *Canadian Psychology*, 49(3), 182–185. 10.1037/a0012801

Demir, M., Burton, S., & Dunbar, N. (2019). Professor–student rapport and perceived autonomy support as predictors of course and student outcomes. *Teaching of Psychology*, 46(1), 22–33. 10.1177/0098628318816132

Fabris, M. A., Lin, S., & Longobardi, C. (2023). A cross-cultural comparison of teacher-student relationship quality in Chinese and Italian teachers and students. *Journal of School Psychology*, 99, 101227. 10.1016/j.jsp.2023.10122737507185

Fathi, J., Pawlak, M., Kruk, M., & Naderi, M. (2023). Modelling boredom in the EFL context: An investigation of the role of coping self-efficacy, mindfulness, and foreign language enjoyment. *Language Teaching Research*, 13621688231182176. Advance online publication. 10.1177/13621688231182176

Fearon, R. P., & Roisman, G. I. (2017). Attachment theory: Progress and future directions. *Current Opinion in Psychology*, 15, 131–136. 10.1016/j.copsyc.2017.03.00228813253

Fitton, V. A. (2013). Attachment theory: History, research, and practice. *Psychoanalytic Social Work*, 19(1-2), 121–143. 10.1080/15228878.2012.666491

Forsberg, C., Sjögren, B., Thornberg, R., Hong, J. S., & Longobardi, C. (2023). Longitudinal reciprocal associations between student–teacher relationship quality and verbal and relational bullying victimization. *Social Psychology of Education*, •••, 1–23. 10.1007/s11218-023-09821-y

Frank, J. L., Jennings, P. A., & Greenberg, M. T. (2016). Validation of the mindfulness in teaching scale. *Mindfulness*, 7(1), 155–163. 10.1007/s12671-015-0461-0

Frisby, B. N., & Martin, M. M. (2010). Instructor–student and student–student rapport in the classroom. *Communication Education*, 59(2), 146–164. 10.1080/03634520903564362

Froiland, J. M., Worrell, F. C., & Oh, H. (2019). Teacher–student relationships, psychological need satisfaction, and happiness among diverse students. *Psychology in the Schools*, 56(5), 856–870. 10.1002/pits.22245

Frymier, A. B., & Houser, M. L. (2000). The teacher-student relationship as an interpersonal relationship. *Communication Education*, 49(3), 207–219. 10.1080/03634520009379209

Galloway, N., Foulstone, A., & Lurie, J. (2022). Yoga and couple relationship satisfaction: The synergy between mindfulness and emotional intelligence. *International Journal of Yoga Therapy*, 32(2022), 16. 10.17761/2022-D-21-0004936602865

Geraci, A., Di Domenico, L., Inguglia, C., & D'Amico, A. (2023). Teachers' emotional intelligence, burnout, work engagement, and self-efficacy during COVID-19 lockdown. *Behavioral Sciences (Basel, Switzerland)*, 13(4), 296. 10.3390/bs1304029637102810

Gillespie, M. (2005). Student–teacher connection: A place of possibility. *Journal of Advanced Nursing*, 52(2), 211–219. 10.1111/j.1365-2648.2005.03581.x16164482

Grabovac, A. D., Lau, M. A., & Willett, B. R. (2011). Mechanisms of mindfulness: A Buddhist psychological model. *Mindfulness*, 2(3), 154–166. 10.1007/s12671-011-0054-5

Greenier, V., Derakhshan, A., & Fathi, J. (2021). Emotion regulation and psychological well-being in teacher work engagement: A case of British and Iranian English language teachers. *System*, 97, 102446. 10.1016/j.system.2020.102446

Grolnick, W. S., & Ryan, R. M. (1987). Autonomy in children's learning: An experimental and individual difference investigation. *Journal of Personality and Social Psychology*, 52(5), 890–898. 10.1037/0022-3514.52.5.8903585701

Grossman, P., Niemann, L., Schmidt, S., & Walach, H. (2004). Mindfulness-based stress reduction and health benefits: A meta-analysis. *Journal of Psychosomatic Research*, 57(1), 35–43. 10.1016/S0022-3999(03)00573-715256293

Guendelman, S., Medeiros, S., & Rampes, H. (2017). Mindfulness and emotion regulation: Insights from neurobiological, psychological, and clinical studies. *Frontiers in Psychology*, 8, 220. 10.3389/fpsyg.2017.0022028321194

Hamilton, N. A., Kitzman, H., & Guyotte, S. (2006). Enhancing health and emotion: Mindfulness as a missing link between cognitive therapy and positive psychology. *Journal of Cognitive Psychotherapy*, 20(2), 123–134. 10.1891/jcop.20.2.123

Hamre, B. K., & Pianta, R. C. (2001). Early teacher–child relationships and the trajectory of children's school outcomes through eighth grade. *Child Development*, 72(2), 625–638. 10.1111/1467-8624.0030111333089

Hamre, B. K., & Pianta, R. C. (2005). Can instructional and emotional support in the first-grade classroom make a difference for children at risk of school failure? *Child Development*, 76(5), 949–967. 10.1111/j.1467-8624.2005.00889.x16149994

Hamre, B. K., Pianta, R. C., Downer, J. T., DeCoster, J., Mashburn, A. J., Jones, S. M., Brown, J. L., Cappella, E., Atkins, M., Rivers, S. E., Brackett, M. A., & Hamagami, A. (2013). Teaching through interactions: Testing a developmental framework of teacher effectiveness in over 4,000 classrooms. *The Elementary School Journal*, 113(4), 461–487. 10.1086/66961634497425

Henry, A., & Thorsen, C. (2018). Teacher–student relationships and L2 motivation. *Modern Language Journal*, 102(1), 218–241. 10.1111/modl.12446

Hughes, J. N., Wu, J. Y., Kwok, O. M., Villarreal, V., & Johnson, A. Y. (2012). Indirect effects of child reports of teacher–student relationship on achievement. *Journal of Educational Psychology*, 104(2), 350–365. 10.1037/a002633923226873

J. (2021). Burned or engaged teachers? The role of mindfulness, self-efficacy, teacher and students' relationships, and the mediating role of intrapersonal and interpersonal mindfulness. *Curr. Psychol.* 42, 11719–11732. 10.1007/s12144-021-02433-9

Kabat-Zinn, J. (1990). *Full Catastrophe Living: Using the Wisdom of Your Body and Mind to Face Stress, Pain and Illness*. Delacourt.

Kabat-Zinn, J. (1994). *Wherever You Go, There You Are: Mindfulness Meditation in Everyday Life*. Hyperion.

Keefer, K., Parker, J., & Saklofske, D. H. (2018). *Emotional Intelligence in Education: Integrating Research with Practice*. Springer. 10.1007/978-3-319-90633-1

Keng, S. L., Smoski, M. J., & Robins, C. J. (2011). Effects of mindfulness on psychological health: A review of empirical studies. *Clinical Psychology Review*, 31(6), 1041–1056. 10.1016/j.cpr.2011.04.00621802619

Kruschke, J. K. (2003). Attention in learning. *Current Directions in Psychological Science*, 12(5), 171–175. 10.1111/1467-8721.01254

Langer, E. J. (1989). *Mindfulness: choice and control in everyday life*. Harper Collins.

Lantieri, L. (2009). *Inteligencia Emocional Infantil Y Juvenil*. Aguilar. 10.1037/a0034755

Lemberger-Truelove, M. E., Carbonneau, K. J., Atencio, D. J., Zieher, A. K., & Palacios, A. F. (2018). Self-regulatory growth effects for young children participating in a combined social and emotional learning and mindfulness-based intervention. *Journal of Counseling and Development*, 96(3), 289–302. 10.1002/jcad.12203

Liebowitz, D. D., & Porter, L. (2019). The effect of principal behaviors on student, teacher, and school outcomes: A systematic review and meta-analysis of the empirical literature. *Review of Educational Research*, 89(5), 785–827. 10.3102/0034654319866133

Liu, R., & Chiang, Y. L. (2019). Who is more motivated to learn? The roles of family background and teacher-student interaction in motivating student learning. *The Journal of Chinese Sociology*, 6(1), 1–17. 10.1186/s40711-019-0095-z

Longobardi, C., Prino, L. E., Marengo, D., & Settanni, M. (2016). Student-teacher relationships as a protective factor for school adjustment during the transition from middle to high school. *Frontiers in Psychology*, 7, 1988. 10.3389/fpsyg.2016.0198828066305

Longobardi, C., Settanni, M., Berchiatti, M., Mastrokoukou, S., & Marengo, D. (2023). Teachers' sentiment about physical appearance of primary school students: Associations with student–teacher relationship quality and student popularity among classroom peers. *Social Psychology of Education*, 26(2), 383–403. 10.1007/s11218-022-09749-9

Longobardi, C., Settanni, M., Lin, S., & Fabris, M. A. (2021). Student–teacher relationship quality and prosocial behaviour: The mediating role of academic achievement and a positive attitude towards school. *The British Journal of Educational Psychology*, 91(2), 547–562. 10.1111/bjep.1237832920835

MacCann, C., Jiang, Y., Brown, L. E., Double, K. S., Bucich, M., & Minbashian, A. (2020). Emotional intelligence predicts academic performance: A meta-analysis. *Psychological Bulletin*, 146(2), 150–186. 10.1037/bul000021931829667

MacDonald, E., & Shirley, D. (2009). *The Mindful Teacher*. Teachers College Press.

Martin, A. J., & Dowson, M. (2009). Interpersonal relationships, motivation, engagement, and achievement: Yields for theory, current issues, and educational practice. *Review of Educational Research*, 79(1), 327–365. 10.3102/0034654308325583

Mayer, J. D., Salovey, P., & Caruso, D. R. (2007). *Mayer-Salovey-Caruso Emotional Intelligence Test (MSCEIT) Item Booklet*. MHS Publishers.

Meng, Y. (2021). Fostering EFL/ESL students' state motivation: The role of teacher-student rapport. *Frontiers in Psychology*, 12, 754797. 10.3389/fpsyg.2021.75479734589039

Mérida-López, S., & Extremera, N. (2017). Emotional intelligence and teacher burnout: A systematic review. *International Journal of Educational Research*, 85, 121–130. 10.1016/j.ijer.2017.07.006

Mestre, J. M., Turanzas, J., García-Gómez, M., Guerra, J., Cordon, J. R., De LaTorre, G. G., & Lopez-Ramos, V. M. (2019). Do trait emotional intelligence and dispositional mindfulness have a complementary effect on the children's and adolescents' emotional states? *Frontiers in Psychology*, 10, 2817. 10.3389/fpsyg.2019.0281731920855

Miao, C., Humphrey, R. H., & Qian, S. (2018). The relationship between emotional intelligence and trait mindfulness: A meta-analytic review. *Personality and Individual Differences*, 135, 101–107. 10.1016/j.paid.2018.06.051

Osborne, E. L., & Atkinson, M. J. (2022). Effects of decentering and non-judgement on body dissatisfaction and negative affect among young adult women. *Mindfulness*, 13(3), 615–626. 10.1007/s12671-021-01817-z

Pagès, B. E., & Reñé, T. A. (2008). Cómo Ser Docente Y No Morir. In *El Intento, Técnicas De Concentración Y Relajación En El Aula*. GRAO.

Petrides, K. V., Furnham, A., & Mavroveli, S. (2007a). Trait emotional intelligence: moving forward in the field of EI. In Matthews, G., Zeidner, M., & Roberts, R. D. (Eds.), *Series in Affective Science. The Science of Emotional Intelligence: Knowns and Unknowns* (pp. 151–166). Oxford University Press. 10.1080/08959280903120295

Petrides, K. V., Pérez-González, J. C., & Furnham, A. (2007b). On the criterion and incremental validity of trait emotional intelligence. *Cognition and Emotion*, 21(1), 26–55. 10.1080/02699930601038912

Pianta, R. C., Hamre, B. K., & Allen, J. P. (2012). Teacher-student relationships and engagement: conceptualizing, measuring, and improving the capacity of classroom interactions. In *Handbook of Research on Student Engagement*. Springer Nature.

Piechurska-Kuciel, E. (2011). Perceived teacher support and language anxiety in polish secondary school EFL learners. *Studies in Second Language Learning and Teaching*, 1(1), 83–100. 10.14746/ssllt.2011.1.1.5

Poulou, M. S. (2017). Social and emotional learning and teacher–student relationships: Preschool teachers' and students' perceptions. *Early Childhood Education Journal*, 45(3), 427–435. 10.1007/s10643-016-0800-3

Pozo-Rico, T., & Sandoval, I. (2020). Can academic achievement in primary school students be improved through teacher training on emotional intelligence as a key academic competency? *Frontiers in Psychology*, 10, 2976. 10.3389/fpsyg.2019.0297631998203

Prewett, S. L., Bergin, D. A., & Huang, F. L. (2019). Student and teacher perceptions on student-teacher relationship quality: A middle school perspective. *School Psychology International*, 40(1), 66–87. 10.1177/0143034318807743

Quin, D. (2017). Longitudinal and contextual associations between teacher–student relationships and student engagement: A systematic review. *Review of Educational Research*, 87(2), 345–387. 10.3102/0034654316669434

Ramos, N. S., Hernández, S. M., & Blanca, M. J. (2009). Efecto de un programa integrado de mindfulness e inteligencia emocional sobre las estrategias cognitivas de regulación emocional. *Ansiedad y Estrés*, 15, 207–216. 10.1016/j.jrp.2015.09.001

Rodríguez-Ledo, C., & Orejudo-Hernández, S. (2017). La educación de la inteligencia emocional. In García-Campayo, J., Demarzo, M., & Modrego, M. (Eds.), *Bienestar Emocional Y Mindfulness En Educación* (pp. 51–82). Alianza Editorial. 10.1016/j.jesp.2009.03.009

Roeser, R. W., Skinner, E., Beers, J., & Jennings, P. A. (2012). Mindfulness training and teachers' professional development: An emerging area of research and practice. *Child Development Perspectives*, 6(2), 167–173. 10.1111/j.1750-8606.2012.00238.x

Roorda, D. L., Jak, S., Zee, M., Oort, F. J., & Koomen, H. M. (2017). Affective teacher–student relationships and students' engagement and achievement: A meta-analytic update and test of the mediating role of engagement. *School Psychology Review*, 46(3), 239–261. 10.17105/SPR-2017-0035.V46-3

Roorda, D. L., Koomen, H. M., Spilt, J. L., & Oort, F. J. (2011). The influence of affective teacher–student relationships on students' school engagement and achievement: A meta-analytic approach. *Review of Educational Research*, 81(4), 493–529. 10.3102/0034654311421793

Rucinski, C. L., Brown, J. L., & Downer, J. T. (2018). Teacher–child relationships, classroom climate, and children's social-emotional and academic development. *Journal of Educational Psychology*, 110(7), 992–1004. 10.1037/edu0000240

Ryan, R. M. (2003). The benefits of being present: Mindfulness and its role in psychological well-being. *Journal of Personality and Social Psychology*, 84(4), 822–848. 10.1037/0022-3514.84.4.82212703651

Saeed, S., & Zyngier, D. (2012). How motivation influences student engagement: A qualitative case study. *J. Educ. Learn.*, 1(2), 252–267. 10.5539/jel.v1n2p252

Sakiz, G., Pape, S. J., & Hoy, A. W. (2012). Does perceived teacher affective support matter for middle school students in mathematics classrooms? *Journal of School Psychology*, 50(2), 235–255. 10.1016/j.jsp.2011.10.00522386122

Sánchez-Álvarez, N., Berrios Martos, M. P., & Extremera, N. (2020). A meta-analysis of the relationship between emotional intelligence and academic performance in secondary education: A multi-stream comparison. *Frontiers in Psychology*, 11, 1517. 10.3389/fpsyg.2020.0151732793030

Schoeberlein, D. (2012). *Mindfulness Para Enseñar Y Aprender.* Louisville, CO. *Gaia (Heidelberg)*. Advance online publication. 10.1080/08959280802541039

Schonert-Reichl, K. A., Oberle, E., Lawlor, M. S., Abbott, D., Thomson, K., Oberlander, T. F., & Diamond, A. (2015). Enhancing cognitive and social–emotional development through a simple-to-administer mindfulness-based school program for elementary school children: A randomized controlled trial. *Developmental Psychology*, 51(1), 52–66. 10.1037/a003845425546595

Schonert-Reichl, K. A., & Roeser, R. W. (Eds.). (2016). *Handbook of Mindfulness in Education: Integrating Theory and Research Into Practice*. Springer. 10.1007/978-1-4939-3506-2

Schriver, J. L., & Harr Kulynych, R. (2021). Do professor–student rapport and mattering predict college student outcomes? *Teaching of Psychology*, 50(4), 342–349. 10.1177/00986283211037987

Shakki, F. (2022). Iranian EFL students' L2 engagement: The effects of teacher-student rapport and teacher support. *Lang. Relat. Res.*, 13, 175–198. 10.52547/LRR.13.3.8

Shapiro, S. L., Carlson, L. E., Astin, J. A., & Freeman, B. (2006). Mechanisms of mindfulness. *Journal of Clinical Psychology*, 62(3), 373–386. 10.1002/jclp.2023716385481

Sternberg, R. J. (2013). Intelligence. In Handbook of Psychology. John Wiley. 10.18637/jss.v048.i02

Thornberg, R., Forsberg, C., Chiriac, E. H., & Bjereld, Y. (2020). Teacher–student relationship quality and student engagement: A sequential explanatory mixed-methods study. *Research Papers in Education*, 37(6), 840–859. 10.1080/02671522.2020.1864772

Tomlinson, E. R., Yousaf, O., Vittersø, A. D., & Jones, L. (2018). Dispositional mindfulness and psychological health: A systematic review. *Mindfulness*, 9(1), 23–43. 10.1007/s12671-017-0762-629387263

Tosto, M. G., Asbury, K., Mazzocco, M. M., Petrill, S. A., & Kovas, Y. (2016). From classroom environment to mathematics achievement: The mediating role of self-perceived ability and subject interest. *Learning and Individual Differences*, 50, 260–269. 10.1016/j.lindif.2016.07.00927766018

Valente, S., & Lourenço, A. A. (2020). Conflict in the classroom: How teachers' emotional intelligence influences conflict management. *Frontiers in Education*, 5, 5. 10.3389/feduc.2020.00005

Valiente, C., Lemery-Chalfant, K., Swanson, J., & Reiser, M. (2008). Prediction of children's academic competence from their effortful control, relationships, and classroom participation. *Journal of Educational Psychology*, 100(1), 67–77. 10.1037/0022-0663.100.1.6721212831

Vallejo, M. A. (2006). Mindfulness (Presencia reflexiva y atenta). *Psicología Conductual*, 14, 433–451. 10.1037/0021-9010.82.1.30

Vesely Maillefer, A., Udayar, S., & Fiori, M. (2018). Enhancing the prediction of emotionally intelligent behavior: The PAT integrated framework involving trait EI, ability EI, and emotion information processing. *Frontiers in Psychology*, 9, 1078. 10.3389/fpsyg.2018.0107830013496

Vesely-Maillefer, A. K., & Saklofske, D. H. (2018). Emotional intelligence and the next generation of teachers. In Keefer, K. V., Parker, J. D. A., & Saklofske, D. H. (Eds.), *Emotional Intelligence in Education: Integrating Research with Practice* (pp. 377–402). Springer International Publishing/Springer Nature. 10.1007/978-3-319-90633-1_14

Virat, M. (2022). Teachers' compassionate love for students: A possible determinant of teacher-student relationships with adolescents and a mediator between teachers' perceived support from coworkers and teacher-student relationships. *Educational Studies*, 48(3), 291–309. 10.1080/03055698.2020.1751083

Walton, G. M., Cohen, G. L., Cwir, D., & Spencer, S. J. (2012). Mere belonging: The power of social connections. *Journal of Personality and Social Psychology*, 102(3), 513–532. 10.1037/a002573122023711

Wang, M. T., & Eccles, J. S. (2013). School context, achievement motivation, and academic engagement: A longitudinal study of school engagement using a multidimensional perspective. *Learning and Instruction*, 28, 12–23. 10.1016/j.learninstruc.2013.04.002

Wang, Y., & Derakhshan, A. (2023). Teacher confirmation and caring as predictors of Chinese and Iranian EFL students' willingness to attend EFL classes. *Porta Linguarum Rev. Int.Didáctica Lenguas Extranjeras*, 39(39), 165–192. 10.30827/portalin.vi39.23625

Wang Y., Pan B., Yu Z., & Song Z. (2023). The relationship between preschool teacher trait mindfulness and teacher-child relationship quality: the chain mediating role of emotional intelligence and empathy. *Curr. Psychol.*, 1–12. 10.1007/s12144-023-04512-5

Wubbels, T., Brekelmans, M., Mainhard, T., den Brok, P., & van Tartwijk, J. (2016). Teacher–student relationships and student achievement. In *Handbook of Social Influences in School Contexts*. Routledge.

Chapter 6
A Developmental Critical View of Emotional Intelligence Theories and Programs in the Greek Educational Settings

Dimitra V. Katsarou
https://orcid.org/0000-0001-8690-0314
University of the Aegean, Greece

Georgios A. Kougioumtzis
National and Kapodistrian University of Athens, Greece

Maria Sofologi
https://orcid.org/0000-0003-0380-2220
University of Ioannina, Greece

Evangelos Mantsos
University of Thessaly, Greece

Efthymia Efthymiou
https://orcid.org/0000-0003-0411-1720
Zayed University, UAE

Dimitrios Sarris
University of Ioannina, Greece

ABSTRACT

School is considered the natural place for the transmission of knowledge, values, and attitudes, the process of acquiring correct social behavior that will stem from the regulation and understanding of emotions seems challenging. The development of emotional intelligence in the school environment can help students who have integration difficulties, school bullying, intellectual and learning problems, and early dropout. Thus, students create a positive attitude towards lifelong learning, a sense of autonomy, effectiveness, and respect towards teachers. Violence prevention, social

DOI: 10.4018/979-8-3693-8312-4.ch006

Copyright © 2024, IGI Global. Copying or distributing in print or electronic forms without written permission of IGI Global is prohibited.

service training, the ability to form and maintain relationships are just a few practical uses of learning emotional intelligence in school. The purpose of this chapter is to highlight the importance of the inclusion of emotional intelligence programs in the Greek educational system with the aim of empowering students, the critical presentation of theories under the development spirit, as well as the comparison of existing programs through processes of synthesis and analysis of the literature.

INTRODUCTION

The role of emotions and their utilization in the manifestations of modern everyday life, from physical activity to professional success, had been ignored for many decades giving space for research studies exclusively to approaches based on science. The exclusive factor of this reductionist scientific approach is found in the degree of the individual's intelligence or intelligence quotient (IQ), which was also considered the exclusive predictor of a person's success in life, since its measurement was based on criteria such as the ability to think logically, his mathematical and linguistic perception, inductive, productive, and combinatorial thinking.

A few decades ago, specifically in the 1970s, this theoretical approach changed by limiting the predictive factor of a person's intelligence quotient (IQ) mainly to their school success (Bales & Gilliam, 2010). Thus, it is slowly being proven that the path to success and consequently to self-realization of a person is not the sole responsibility of his intelligence but a combination of passion, intelligence, and goals. The recovery of emotions in the professional field -as a factor of a person's success in his work was the initial stage of exploring the human emotional world (Jordan & Troth, 2006).

Initially, the conflation of emotion with work was considered a negative factor. The perception that professionalism should be rigid and free from any kind of emotion has been dominant for many years (Brinia, 2008). Today the notions of removing emotion from the workplace and rationalizing work are considered anachronistic and outdated (Jordan & Troth, 2006; Law et al., 2008; Lopes et al., 2006). On the contrary, the perception prevails that the person who can properly manage himself and his relationship with others, is the one who can succeed in his work environment (Davis & Newstrom, 1999). Moreover, the concepts of intelligence (IQ) and emotional intelligence (EQ) in the workplace are considered complementary concepts and not mutually exclusive (Goleman, 2000).

The transformation of work relationships from individual to group ones and the effectiveness associated with the dominance of positive emotions at work over negative ones, were the main field of research activity in psychology (Eysenck, 1985). Specifically, due to the complexity of employees' emotions (anxiety, satisfaction, anger, excitement, envy, jealousy, love, pride, etc.) it was deemed necessary to study them, in order to decode their basic mechanisms that may lead to working relationships, which over time they can become friendly or even family.

Thus, although the study of labor relations and consequently of emotional intelligence began, initially, through business organizations, in the light of psychology, with the aim of optimizing the performance of employees, the findings of the investigations expanded its research field. In recent years there has been an explosion of interest in emotional intelligence, both through scientific books and articles and through popular reading magazines (Gibbs,1995; Wigod, 1998), so great, in fact, that it has been characterized as the "spirit of the new age" (zeitgeist) (Mayer et al., 2000; Pfeifer, 2001). Along with psychology, the sciences of human resource management, education, sports, etc. have dealt with emotional intelligence.

Thus, it has been found that the emotionally intelligent person can handle their daily life better, have full control over their emotions and because of these factors have good mental health (Taylor, 2001). Other research reports that high emotional intelligence is positively related to a person's quality of life and good physical health (Tsaousis & Nikolaou, 2005). It is clear, therefore, that many sciences have as their field of study emotional intelligence and its beneficial consequences in everyday life.

However, since there is no convergence among the sciences dealing with emotional intelligence, the term itself is a matter of debate. Skeptics believe that charm and influence were transformed into social and interpersonal skills, which in turn were renamed emotional intelligence. Still, there has been no agreement among researchers on the characteristics of emotional intelligence. The term often refers to emotional awareness and the ability to regulate emotion according to circumstances (Petrides & Furnham, 2003). In addition, it can be a characteristic of a person's personality and a dispositional characteristic of a person's intrapersonal and interpersonal abilities (Di Fabio, 2012).

Historical Review

Dealing with emotions was forbidden in ancient Greece until the 5th century BC. In fact, the reference to them was considered a threat to the idea of the city-state, and consequently of democracy itself, which emphasized the whole and not the individuality (de Romilly, 2007). First Aristotle in the Nicomachean Ethics mentions that it is not easy to understand the origin and cause of anger as well as the ways of managing it, speaking for the first time in the history of philosophical thought about the role of emotions in everyday life (Goleman, 2011).

The seeds of dealing with emotions are picked up again after Aristotle, the Stoic philosophers around 200 BC. After the socio-economic changes that took place on Greek soil, philosophers clearly refer to the role of emotions in achieving goals and maintaining a peaceful life. The philosophy of the Stoics, such as Zeno and Epictetus, and their studies of the drives, dispositions, and desires of men, and the relation of the aforementioned emotions to the attainment of individual happiness, influenced both the Jewish religion and and Christian (Vlahaki, 2006).

The Christian religion and Byzantium emphasized the internalization of emotions and their expression in the light of love and forgiveness (Papapetrou, 1968). Darwin in 1872, studying the behaviors of animals, evolution, and adaptability to their natural environment, spoke about the importance of emotional expression in our environment (Di Fabio, 2012). Traditionally, science rejected the importance of emotion in its research fields, believing that anyone who associates intelligence with emotions is in constant internal conflict, since reason and emotion cannot go hand in hand (Matthews et al., 2002).

Mikolajczak (2009) mentions that the concept of emotional intelligence exists as the first reference in a treatise of English literature by Van Ghent (1961), referring to the characters of the novel "Pride and Prejudice", he speaks of emotional intelligence. A little later, in 1966 the psychologist Leuner (1966) accused mothers who were dissatisfied with their mothering duties as unemotionally intelligent. The first academic mention of this term, however, was made in 1983 by PhD student Payne, who included the term emotional intelligence in his PhD thesis (Payne, 1983/86).

Thorndike's Social Intelligence (Thorndike, 1920) and Guilford's Social Intelligences (Guilford, 1967) played an important role in the development of emotional intelligence as a separate field of research, which recognize the role of pleasure through learning. Eysenck (1985) divides intelligence into biological, psychometric, and social. Twelve years later Mackintosh (1998) states that social intelligence is directly related to social relationships.

Still, Sternberg (1997) and Gardner (1983, 1999) talk about the case of multiple intelligences. In other words, they believe that intelligence is not limited to logical-mathematical and linguistic thinking, but also extends to other areas, such as spatial intelligence, creative intelligence, synthetic intelligence, etc. This theory has received criticism from many theorists in the field, but who do not dispute the following: that the person feels better when there is a positive climate in his place (Allix, 2000; White, 2005). Furthermore, Sternberg (1997) considers that human intelligence is divided into three domains: structural, experiential, and content.

The emergence of emotional intelligence takes on great dimensions with the research of Salovey and Mayer (1990, 1997) and Bar-On (1997). Its essential dissemination, however, took place with the release of the international best seller "Emotional Intelligence" by Goleman (1995). These researchers are the ones who developed the emotional intelligence models of the same name, which will be studied in detail below.

General Characteristics of Emotional Intelligence and Differentiation of Emotions

Emotions are inherent, innate reactions of the organism to external or internal stimuli. The emotional state of a person is influenced by many factors such as biological, cultural, psychological, etc. Precisely because the definition of emotions is multifaceted and multifactorial, there is no unanimity regarding their definition and consequently no unanimity regarding the definition of emotional intelligence (Papanelopoulou, 2002).

Russel (1991) believes that it is a mistake to readjust one's behavior based on emotions, given their variability and the different circumstances experienced by the individual each time. Pinker (2007), disagrees, placing emotions on a biological basis and defining them as co-adjutants in the process of rationalizing the events recorded by the brain and aiding in decision-making. Saarni (2011) considers that emotions bring about changes in behavior and Wierzbicka (1992) that emotions are a brain technique for categorizing everyday events.

Depending on the way emotions are perceived and expressed, as well as the individual's way of acting, emotions are divided into several categories, the main ones being positive (joy, pleasure, pride) and negative (anger, sadness, sadness) (Kafetsios, 2003; Lazarus, 1999; Siegel, 1999). Dickman and Stanford-Blair (2002) consider that the nature of emotions is biological and includes five basic characteristics: external stimuli, reactions of the nervous system, changes in the physiological functions of the organism, external changes of the face and, finally, the experiences of the individual as a result of experiencing the specific emotions.

Emotional intelligence has attracted the interest of scholars, mainly, due to the virgin research field of the previous decades regarding the psychosynthesis of the individual (Platsidou, 2010). Thus, it has been found that emotional intelligence develops up to the fifth decade of life (Bar-On, 2000), is positively influenced by exercise (Goleman, 2011), by job satisfaction (Platsidou, 2005), reduces stress and improves disposition in clinical and non-clinical populations (Byrne & Byrne, 1993; Yeung, 1996), and finally related to age and gender factors (Fariselli et al., 2006).

From the above it becomes evident the attempt to categorize emotions and change the way they are perceived depending on the social and political conditions of the time. At the same time, it becomes clear that emotional intelligence multifacetedly affects both the person and the environment in which he lives and acts.

Thus, because emotions are very numerous and vary both in intensity and expression, it is impossible to fully describe them, which cannot be generalized due to the different sociocultural contexts in which they are experienced and manifested (Ciarrochi & Deane, 2001; Malisiova et al., 2023). For this reason, we often talk about emotion families, where in an imaginary circle a core emotion is placed in the center and the emotions related to the core emotion are placed on the periphery. According to Goleman (1995) the basic categories are joy, sadness, anger, disgust, and fear. Thus, in an imaginary circle, put in the center, for example, joy and on the periphery excitement, pride, exasperation, etc.

Goleman's theory (1995) is not universally accepted, since according to Lazarus (2000) each emotion is separate and has to do with different environmental conditions, moments of time, involved human relationships that should not be grouped under any circumstances because in this way their essential feature, which is uniqueness, is lost.

Another distinction is the separation between emotions that originate from the individual himself (self-emotion) and those that originate from interpersonal contacts (Austin et al., 2005). In addition, Kakavoulis (1997) considers that there are positive (e.g. friendship, acceptance, sympathy), negative (e.g. rage, anger, aggression), biological (hunger, thirst, satiety) and higher (religious, humanitarian, patriotic).

According to researchers, positive emotions are those that present benefits both for the individual himself and for his social context (Bastian et al., 2005). Based on this observation, Fredrickson (2000) sees a positive relationship between the positive emotions of employees in an organization and its development. At the same time, Staw et al. (1994) consider that positive emotions in a workplace lead to a favorable collegial climate, conflict avoidance, better job evaluations and high wages. Locke and Latham (1990) find that people with positive emotions set higher goals, perform better, and accept work invitations more easily.

Also, people with positive emotions adopt better health behaviors (Costarelli, et al., 2009), have developed social skills (Schutte et al., 2001), are satisfied with their marital life (Schutte et al., 1998, 2001), and have lower rates of anxiety, depression and worry (Bastian et al., 2005; Salovey et al., 2002; Schutte et al., 1998).

Conversely, people with negative emotions reduce their productivity (Judge, 1992), tend toward depression (Batool & Khalid, 2009), and adopt unhealthy behaviors related to poor diet, smoking, and alcohol (Mayer et al., 2002).

Thus, in conclusion, positive emotions seem to dominate in areas of life such as socialization, health, work, while negative emotions dominate in areas such as psychology and poor quality of life (Kougioumtzis & Louka, 2021).

Gardner's Multiple Intelligences

In 1983, American psychologist Howard Gardner's book titled "Frames of mind: The theory of multiple intelligence" was published, where the psychologist spoke for the first time about the theory of multiple intelligence. Gardner (1983) considered that personal intelligence has multiple dimensions and essentially there is a distinction between interpersonal and intrapersonal intelligence, with each intelligence having its own characteristics. Thus, intrapersonal intelligence gives the individual the ability to have self-awareness, self-awareness of his actions and capabilities, and the ability to understand himself and his feelings. In contrast, interpersonal intelligence consists of four different abilities: leadership, the ability to establish and maintain relationships with other people, the ability to analyze everyday events, and the ability to manage conflicts. The combination of these two types of intelligence gives man the ability to socialize, to understand his social environment, to cooperate and to be able to set goals to be achieved.

In addition to these two types, the theory of multiple intelligences is complemented by the following areas of intelligence: music, spatial planning, linguistic, mathematical, and kinesthetic. The last genre added in 1999 was naturalism. According to Gardner (1983, 1993) the types of intelligence complement each other, but only some of them usually come to the surface.

Thus, for the first time a researcher reports different levels of analysis of thought and manages intelligence not so much in relation to performance as in relation to the environment in which the individual lives and interacts.

Salovey and Mayer's Model

The term emotional intelligence was first used in 1990 by Salovey and Mayer, taking into account Gardner's (1983) theory of intrapersonal and interpersonal intelligence. Their theory also includes sections related to the classification and organization of emotions (Styss & Brown, 2004). Thus, Salovey and Mayer (1990) consider that "people who have developed skills related to emotional intelligence better understand and express their own emotions, recognize the emotions of others, regulate emotion, and use moods and emotions to activate adaptive behaviors" (p. 200).

Salovey and Mayer's model is considered a developmental model since abilities are organized in a hierarchical manner starting from basic psychological functions and ending in higher and more complex processes (Mayer et al., 2000). It is also considered a capability model as it emphasizes the interactions between emotions and cognitions (Mayer et al., 1997, 2000).

According to this model, the basic levels of emotional intelligence are:

- The recognition of emotions: is the key to emotional intelligence. It refers to a person's ability to recognize their own feelings and feel self-satisfaction and confidence in order to make good future decisions
- Emotional control: refers to the individual's ability to prioritize their emotions, set goals and reach their potential

- The management of emotions: it refers to the human ability to interpret his negative emotions in a rational way and to be able to return to his social environment smoothly after experiencing them
- Empathy: refers to the individual's ability to understand the feelings of others, relate to them and socialize
- Relationship management: refers to the individual's ability to have a leadership role, to be popular and to be able to establish smooth interpersonal relationships

As mentioned by Salovey and Mayer (1997), what defines emotional intelligence are the abilities to perceive, express and regulate emotions and not the skills that accompany the abilities and are considered personality traits. In order to be able, therefore, to more effectively measure emotional intelligence, researchers constructed measurement scales. Initially they created the MEIS (Multifactor Emotional Intelligence Scale, 1997), while five years later with Caruso they created the MSCEIST (Mayer-Salovey-Caruso Emotional Intelligence Test, 2002) scale (Mayer et al., 2002). The research tool MSCEIST test was translated into Greek by Kafetsios (2004) and has been used in a multitude of studies since then (Lopes et al., 2006; Lopes et al., 2004).

Thus, the researchers put at the center of their theory the classification and organization of emotions in relation to the environment and the more effective integration of the individual into it.

Goleman's Model

Daniel Goleman (1995) with the publication of his book "Emotional Intelligence: Why it can matter more than I.Q." made the concept of emotional intelligence known to the general public. Goleman, influenced by the model of Salovey and Mayer (1990), developed his own theory about emotional intelligence, which he defined as a structure parallel to cognitive, but equally important for the achievement of the individual's personal goals and abilities (Styss & Brown, 2004). A key point in his theory is empathy, i.e. the ability of the individual to understand concepts such as motivation, adaptability, influence, etc. With his second book "Working with Emotional Intelligence" in 1998, he identified the practical applications of emotional intelligence in work, in education, in politics (Goleman, 1998).

The purpose of emotional intelligence according to Goleman (1995) is to achieve effective behavior management. Its goal, that is, is the utilization of the individual's ability to set goals and fulfill them despite possible difficulties, the regulation of behavior so that it is not affected by stress, the limitation of individualism and spontaneity with the ultimate goal of smooth social coexistence. Emotional intelligence, moreover, is a parallel factor of intelligence and focuses on two aspects of behavior: personal skill and social skill.

In Goleman's model, emotional intelligence consists of:

- The personal recognition of emotions: this includes self-awareness and self-confidence
- Personal management of emotions: this includes self-control, conscientiousness, and adaptability
- Social awareness: this includes understanding the feelings of others
- Relationship management: this includes the creation of social ties and the influence exerted on them.

Goleman's key addition to Salovey and Mayer's (1990) model was the concept of emotional competence, which includes abilities such as motivation, persistence, optimism, and rationality. Also, the concept of emotional competence is just as important as the concept of cognitive competence, because it ensures chances for professional success. Finally, emotional intelligence is not necessarily innate, but is practiced and learned (Goleman, 1995).

To measure it, Goleman built the Emotional Competence Inventory 360 scale (ECI-360, Boyatzis et al., 2000), which, unlike other scales for measuring emotional intelligence, is not based on self-reports, but on opinion of those familiar to the individual. This scale is mainly used to measure emotional intelligence in businesses and organizations.

Goleman, therefore, developed the pre-existing models by combining emotional intelligence with the clear regulation of behavior and added the term of emotional competence which is an important factor of personal development.

The Bar-On Model

In 1997 the American psychologist Reuven Bar-On introduced to the study of emotional intelligence the concept of E.Q. (emotional quotient) corresponding to the term I.Q. (intelligence quotient). He noticed, therefore, that some people, while not cognitively and intellectually gifted, nevertheless managed to succeed in their lives. He considered, therefore, that there is an "emotional quotient" which is a coupling of emotional and social skills and is directly measurable and unique to each person (Bar-On, 1997).

Bar-On's model is based on five competency factors, each of which consists of skills that characterize them and are as follows:

- Intrapersonal competence: which consists of the skills of assurance, emotional self-awareness, independence, self-esteem, and self-actualization
- Interpersonal competence: which consists of the skills of social responsibility, emotional understanding, and interpersonal relationships
- Adaptability: which consists of the skills of problem solving, flexibility and managing the demands of everyday life
- The ability to manage stress: which consists of the skills to manage stress and control spontaneity
- The general mood: which consists of the subscales of happiness and optimism.

To measure the General Index of Emotional Intelligence Bar-On constructed the tool for measuring and identifying social and emotional functions linked to psychological well-being EQi (Bar-On, 1997; Bar-On & Parker, 2000).

Bar-On, therefore, singled out the factors that can play an important role in the success of people regardless of their cognitive background. Finally, he believed that the interaction of the individual with his environment is what ultimately makes the individual successful and happy.

All researchers agree that emotional intelligence concerns the person's relationships with their social environment. Furthermore, they consider that the basis of emotional intelligence is the perception, expression, and management of emotions in order to better integrate people into the social context. Finally, they agree that emotional intelligence is a key factor in a person's satisfaction around important life issues such as stress, work, health, and interpersonal relationships.

Emotional Intelligence and Education

Effective communication with fellow learners and the environment, empathy, and the socialization of the learner through the educational process, are the goals of every curriculum worldwide (Petrides et al, 2018). Because school is considered the natural place of transmission of knowledge, values and attitudes, the process of acquiring correct social behavior that will stem from the regulation and understanding of emotions seems challenging (Triliva & Chiementi, 1998).

Zins, Elias, Greenberg and Weissberg (2000) identifying the value of emotions in educational reality, with their research, prove that people with high emotional intelligence can be activated in setting goals, persist in overcoming obstacles, and remain in learning activity to the end. In addition, high emotional intelligence in education has been shown to be associated with taking initiative and responsibility, as well as greater communication skills (Chiarrochi & Panju, 2008). Also, practicing emotional skills can lead to high academic achievement (Bracket & Katulak, 2007) and with the right rewards strong links to learning can be created (Katsarou, 2019; Sofologi et al., 2023; Weissberg & Greenberg, 1998).

The development of emotional intelligence in the school environment can help students who have integration difficulties, school bullying, intellectual and learning problems and early dropout (Chiarrochi & Panju, 2008; Kougioumtzis et al., 2021a; Megari et al., 2024; Sofologi et al., 2022; Weissberg & O'Brien, 2004). After all, creating emotional skills that will follow students throughout their lives is a key goal of emotional intelligence programs (Cooper, 1997). Thus, learners create a positive attitude towards lifelong learning, a sense of autonomy, efficacy, and respect towards the trainers (Battistich et al., 1997). At the same time, they develop techniques for dealing with strong emotions, time management and achieving goals (Theodoratou et al., 2023; Low & Nelson, 2005). Violence prevention, social service training, the ability to form and maintain relationships are just a few practical uses of learning emotional intelligence in school (Elias et al., 1997; Katsarou et al., 2015; Patrikakou & Kougioumtzis, 2016). Research by Elias (2003) also proves that the emotional skills acquired in education are maintained and used by the students in the future, such as when they themselves become parents or employers. Finally, the detection and cultivation of emotional skills in teachers is of great importance for the way of teaching and handling everyday life in the classroom (Mavroveli et al., 2009; Fasano & Pellittery, 2006).

It becomes clear, therefore, that it is necessary to study emotional intelligence in educational contexts where intra-school violence and negative educational experiences are frequent (Kougioumtzis et al., 2021b; Sofologi et al., 2020).

Factors Affecting Emotional Intelligence

The concept of emotional intelligence is multifactorial, it combines intelligence, which is usually associated with logic, with emotion, which often contradicts it. First, interpersonal relationships play a large role in whether or not emotional intelligence exists. According to research, people who appear to possess high percentages of emotional intelligence have ways of solving problems, remain flexible, cool, and positive when they are under pressure (Bar-On, 2000). Another role in emotional intelligence and interpersonal relationships seems to be played by cooperation, closeness and developed social skills (Austin et al., 2005; Ciarrochi et al., 2000; Schutte et al., 2001). People who have smooth interpersonal relationships appear to show lower rates of anxiety, worry and depression (Bastian et al., 2005; Salovey et al., 2002; Schutte et al., 1998).

The ability to regulate emotion also accounts for having high emotional intelligence. It refers to the individual's ability to recognize their emotional environment and respond positively to it. In addition, he maintains high energy, motivation and remains committed to the goals he has set (Fox & Spector, 2000; Salovey & Mayer, 1997; Scott-Land & Chan, 2004).

At the same time, the leader of a group who has high emotional intelligence can bring about a significant boost in the positive behavior of his subordinates (Humphrey, 2002; Weiss & Cropanzano, 1996). Specifically, with the appropriate emotional actions the leader can improve productivity (Pirola-Merlo et al., 2002) and increase participation (McColl-Kennedy & Anderson, 2002). In addition, leaders seem to be effective in terms of group cohesion when they know how to regulate their own emotions (Glaso & Einarsen, 2008), and can bring greater job satisfaction to their subordinates (Gross & John, 2003; Zampetakis & Kafetsios, 2010; Brayfield & Roth, 1951). Finally, research has demonstrated the change in attitudes towards work by leaders who have high emotional intelligence (Newcombe & Ashkanasy, 2002; Pescolido, 2002).

Also, emotional intelligence appears to be affected by age. Research shows that it is related to maturity (Goleman, 1998, 2011) and that it can be taught through education (Di Fabio & Kenny, 2011; Mayer & Salovey, 1997). It is therefore a developmental component that young people can improve over the years (Fariselli et al., 2006). Finally, it is feedback on actions that have an impact on us and those around us (Serrat, 2009).

The gender factor also appears to be an important factor in emotional intelligence. It is widely believed that women have higher emotional intelligence than men, a factor related to their biological maternal instincts (Petrides & Furnham, 2003; Schutte et al., 1998). Men seem to have high percentages in emotions such as stress management, optimism, and adaptability (Mayer et al., 1999, 2000; Bar-On, 2000), while women have higher percentages in emotions of situational management and empathy (Bar-On On, 1997; Ciarrochi et al., 2000). However, emotional intelligence appears to be positively related to age in both sexes (Extremera et al., 2006).

The last factor that appears to be related to emotional intelligence is the quality of life factor. Thus, high emotional intelligence has been shown to be associated with positive health behaviors and better levels of well-being (Slaski & Cartwright, 2002; Yates, 1999), resistance to unhealthy behaviors such as smoking and alcohol (Trinidad & Johnson, 2002). Finally, high emotional intelligence is negatively related to mental disorders such as depression and neurosis (Duda et al., 2000; Slaski & Cartwright, 2002).

Thus, the factors that affect the emotional intelligence of adults concern interpersonal relationships (use of emotions, care, and empathy), the ability to regulate emotions, job satisfaction, gender, and the general quality of life (Allen & Cohen, 2014).

Emotional Intelligence and Training Programs

Effective communication with classmates and the environment, empathy, and socialization of the student through the educational process, are goals of every curriculum worldwide (Barouma & Kougioumtzis, 2016). Because school is considered the natural place of transmission of knowledge, values and attitudes, the process of acquiring correct social behavior that will stem from the regulation and understanding of emotions seems challenging (Triliva & Chiementi, 1998). Zins, Elias, Greenberg and Weissberg (2000) identifying the value of emotions in the educational reality, with their research, prove that people with emotional intelligence can be activated in setting goals, persist in overcoming obstacles, and remain in the learning activity until the end. In addition, high emotional intelligence in education has been shown to be associated with taking initiative and responsibility, as well as greater communication skills (Chiarrochi & Panju, 2008).

The development of emotional intelligence in the school environment can help students who have integration difficulties, school bullying, intellectual and learning problems and early dropout (Weissberg & O'Brien, 2004). Moreover, building emotional skills that will follow learners throughout their lives is a key goal of emotional intelligence programs (Cooper, 1997). Thus, students develop a positive attitude toward lifelong learning, a sense of autonomy, efficacy, and respect toward instructors (Battistich et al., 1997).

Although emotional intelligence programs were slow to be introduced into the Greek educational system, the 2000s acted as a catalyst in this direction. The beginning was made in 1998 with the Conflict Control Program "You and I become one" (Triliva & Chimienti, 1998). The program is structured in 10 modules, each of which addresses a different level of development of social and interpersonal skills. For the most complete application of the program, the application manual is accompanied by the student's "Activity Notebook". The ultimate goal of the program is through the recognition and management of emotions in preadolescence to promote respect and smooth interpersonal relationships and to avoid sources of tension and anger that can cause aggressive behavior and conflicts.

Weare and Gray (2000) developed the "Mental and Emotional Health in School Program", according to which teachers are educated on contemporary issues of conflict management and emotional development in order to become able to apply these principles in their daily lives. The program was implemented for four years in the schools of the south-eastern Cyclades, with innovative methods, which included, among others, experiential techniques, role-plays, enriched presentations, recording and analysis of images and artistic creations (Sokou, 2004).

Triliva and Chimienti (2000) two years after the release of the first manual of emotional intelligence, release the "Techniques Manual for Emotional and Social Competence". This manual is essentially a revision of "You and I Become One" (1998), but with the introduction of innovative techniques and methods of engagement. Thus, it is structured in two sections: the first section presents introductory clarifying comments about the content as well as instructions for teachers, while the second section develops the methodology of approaching emotional intelligence through games, self-assessment questionnaires and group assignments.

Plomaritou (2004) developed the most comprehensive emotional intelligence program to date, the "Emotional Intelligence Development Program" aimed at kindergarten and elementary school children. Its main difference compared to the previous programs was the student's initiative which plays a central role in the implementation of the program. The program is structured in three sections and revolves around the axis of emotions such as joy, sadness, fear, anger. In the first section, the child is asked to complete incomplete sentences such as: "I'm afraid when..., I like it when..." in order to develop children's self-awareness. In the second unit, the children engage in stories followed by playful activities that focus on different emotions. In the last section, with the help of a poster-collage, the children are asked to recognize their emotions on a daily basis, and manage them accordingly.

Anagnostopoulou, Triliva and Hadjinikolou (2007) created the intervention program "Development of Social Skills: Health Education Program" in order to implement social integration techniques in the elementary schools of Eastern Thessaloniki. At the beginning of the program, the volunteer teachers were trained in stress management, conflict management, empathy, active listening, and group activities. Then they applied the active techniques to primary school children using role-plays, dramatization, oral and written activities, painting, dance, etc. The intervention yielded positive results as the students after the end of the three-month intervention showed a noticeable improvement in taking initiatives and social action, in recognizing and expressing in verbal and non-verbal ways of communicating their feelings and in recognizing the value of friendship.

The last program implemented was the "Program for the Promotion of Mental Health and Learning: Social and Emotional Education at School" (Hatzichristou et al., 2009). The specific program, through seven thematic units (communication skills, expression and management of emotions, dimensions of self-perception and self-esteem, anxiety, conflict resolution, interculturality, supporting children in crisis) sought to promote respect and dialogue in classes where diversity prevails. The material is divided into 8 issues, where the first seven are addressed to the teacher, while the eighth is the "Student's Notebook". In its application, it involves actions such as imitation, role-playing, group activities, but also theoretical discussion through brainstorming, written and oral exercises as well as free discussions around issues of feelings and relationships.

Although the emotional intelligence programs designed and implemented in Greece are short-lived and unmeasurable at present regarding their long-term effectiveness, short-term observations lead us to the conclusion that the practice of emotional intelligence in the school setting can be a positive basis for both at the level of learning, as well as at the level of developing social skills. Finally, the positives of developing emotional intelligence can be found in the following areas: Self-awareness (recognition and acceptance of our own feelings), Self-regulation (self-control, responsibility, reliability, adaptability), Mobilization-motivation (goal commitment, optimism, initiative), Empathy (recognition of others' feelings, acceptance of diversity, understanding, compassion), social skills (influence, leadership, teamwork, cooperation, crisis management, communication) (Platsidou, 2010).

Epilogue

In the annals of psychological understanding, emotional intelligence theories stand as guiding beacons illuminating the intricacies of human emotion and behavior. As we reflect on the journey through these theories, we find ourselves at the threshold of a new understanding –one that transcends mere intellect and delves deep into the realms of empathy, self-awareness, and interpersonal dynamics. In this epilogue, we witness the legacy of emotional intelligence theories reverberating through the corridors of academia, the boardrooms of corporate giants, and the intimate spaces of personal growth. What began as a mere hypothesis has blossomed into a robust framework for understanding and harnessing the power of emotions in all facets of life.

As scholars continue to refine and expand upon the foundational works of pioneers such as Daniel Goleman, Peter Salovey, and John Mayer, we see the ripple effects of their insights shaping the landscape of education, leadership, and mental health. Educators draw upon emotional intelligence theories to cultivate nurturing learning environments where students not only excel academically but also thrive emotionally. Leaders leverage these theories to foster cultures of empathy and collaboration, driving innovation and success within their organizations. And individuals embark on personal journeys of self-discovery, using emotional intelligence as a compass to navigate the complexities of their inner worlds and relationships (Gonzales, 2022).

But perhaps the most profound impact of emotional intelligence theories lies in their ability to bridge divides and forge connections among people from all walks of life. In a world often fraught with discord and misunderstanding, the principles of emotional intelligence serve as a universal language –one that transcends cultural, linguistic, and ideological barriers. Through empathy, we find common ground.

Through self-awareness, we cultivate understanding. And through relationship management, we build bridges of trust and mutual respect.

REFERENCES

Allen, J., & Cohen, J. (2014). Emotional intelligence in classrooms and in schools: What we see in the educational setting. In *A Critique of Emotional Intelligence* (pp. 125–139). Psychology Press.

Allix, N. (2000). The theory of multiple intelligences: A case of missing cognitive matter. *Australian Journal of Education*, 44(3), 272–293. 10.1177/000494410004400306

Anagnostopoulou, T., Triliva, S., & Hatjinikolou, S. (2007). *Development of Social Skills: Health Education Program*. Address P.E. Eastern Thessaloniki.

Austin, E. J., Saklofske, D. H., & Egan, V. (2005). Personality, well-being and health correlates of trait emotional intelligence. *Personality and Individual Differences*, 38(3), 547–558. 10.1016/j.paid.2004.05.009

Bales, S., & Gilliam, F. (2007). Lessons from the story of early child development: Domain decisions and framing youth development. *New Directions for Youth Development*, 124, 119–134.20082431

Bar-On, R. (1997). *The emotional quotient inventory (EQ-i): A test of emotional intelligence*. Multi-Health Systems.

Bar-On, R. (2000). Emotional and social intelligence: Insights from the Emotional Intelligence Quotient Inventory. In Bar-On, R., & Parker, D. A. (Eds.), *The handbook of emotional intelligence* (pp. 363–388). John Wiley & Sons.

Bar-On, R., & Parker, J. D. A. (2000). *The handbook of emotional intelligence*. Jossey-Bass.

Barouma, C., & Kougioumtzis, G. A. (2016). Emotional Intelligence, Consulting & Education. *Journal of Regional Socio-Economic Issues, 6*(2), 10-18.

Bastian, V. A., Burns, N. R., & Nettelbeck, T. (2005). Emotional intelligence predicts life skills, but not as well as personality and cognitive abilities. *Personality and Individual Differences*, 39(6), 1135–1145. 10.1016/j.paid.2005.04.006

Batool, S., & Khalid, R. (2009). Low emotional intelligence: A risk factor for depression. *Journal of Pakistan Psychiatric Society*, 6(2), 65–72.

Battistich, V., Solomon, D., Watson, M., & Shaps, E. (1997). Caring school communities. *Educational Psychologist*, 32(3), 137–151. 10.1207/s15326985ep3203_1

Brackett, M., & Katulak, N. (2007). Emotional Intelligence in the Classroom: Skill Based Training for teachers and students In J. Chiarrochi & L. Marziyah (Eds), *7 Successful Strategies to Promote Emotional Intelligence in the Classroom* (pp 227-56). MPG Books Ltd.

Brayfield, A. H., & Roth, H. F. (1951). An index of job satisfaction. *The Journal of Applied Psychology*, 35(5), 307–311. 10.1037/h0055617

Brinia, V. (2008). *Management and Emotional Intelligence.* Stamoulis.

Byrne, A., & Byrne, D. G. (1993). The effect of exercise on depression, anxiety and other mood states-A review. *Journal of Psychosomatic Research*, 37(6), 565–574. 10.1016/0022-3999(93)90050-P8410742

Chiarrochi, J., & Panju, M. (2008). *7 Successful Strategies to Promote Emotional Intelligence in the Classroom.* MPG Books Ltd.

Ciarrochi, J., & Deane, F. P. (2001). Emotional competence and willingness to seek help from professional and nonprofessional sources. *British Journal of Guidance & Counselling*, 29(2), 233–246. 10.1080/03069880124843

Cooper, R. K. (1996/1997). *E.Q Map.* AIT and Essi Systems.

Costarelli, V., Demertzi, M., & Stamou, D. (2009). Disordered eating attitudes in relation to body image and emotional intelligence in young women. *Journal of Human Nutrition and Dietetics*, 22(3), 239–245. 10.1111/j.1365-277X.2009.00949.x19344378

Davis, K. Y., & Newstrom, J. W. (1999). *Comportamiento humano en el trabajo: Comportamiento Organicional.* McGraw- Hill.

de Romilly, J. (2007). *Gentleness in ancient Greek thought.* Livanis.

Di Fabio, A. (2012). *Emotional Intelligence- New Perspectives and Applications.* Intech Open Access Publisher. 10.5772/1188

Dickman, M.H. & Stanford-Blair, N. (2002). *Connecting leadership to the brain.* Sage.

Duda, R. O., Hart, P. E., & Stork, D. G. (2000). *Pattern Classification* (2nd ed.). Wiley-Interscience.

Elias, M. J. (2003). *Academic and Social- Emotional learning*, The International Academy of Education – IAE, The International Academy of Education, France: SADAG. Διαθέσιμο: https://www.ibe.unesco.org/publications/EducationalPracticesSeriesPdf/prac1 e.pdf

Elias, M. J., Zins, J., Weissberg, R. P., Frey, K., Greenberg, M., Haynes, N., Kessler, R., Schwab-Stone, M., & Shriver, T. (1997). *Promoting Social and Emotional Learning: Guidelines for Educators*. Association for Supervision and Curriculum Development.

Extremera, N., Fernadez-Berrocal, P. & Salovey, P. (2006). Spanish version of the Mayer- Salovey- Caruso Emotional Intelligence Test- Version 2.0: Reliabilities, age, and gender differences. *Psicothema*, 18, 42–48.17295956

Eysenck, H. (1985). *A model for intelligence*. Springer-Verlag.

Fariselli, L., Ghini, M., & Freedman, J. (2006). *Age and emotional intelligence*. Six Seconds. www.6seconds.org

Fasano, C., & Pellittery, J. (2006). Infusing Emotional Learning into the school environment. In *Emotionally intelligent school counseling* (pp. 65–78). Lawrence Erlbaum Associates, Inc.

Fox, S., & Spector, P. E. (2000). Relations of emotional intelligence, practical intelligence, general intelligence and trait affectivity with interview outcomes: It's not all just "G". *Journal of Organizational Behavior*, 21(2), 203–220. 10.1002/(SICI)1099-1379(200003)21:2<203::AID-JOB38>3.0.CO;2-Z

Fredrickson, B. L. (2000). Cultivating positive emotions to optimize health and well being. *Prevention & Treatment*, 2(1), 21–29. 10.1037/1522-3736.3.1.31a

Gardner, H. (1983). *Frames of mind: The theory of multiples intelligences*. Basic Books.

Gardner, J. (1999). *Intelligence reframed: Multiple intelligence for the 21st century*. Basic Books.

Gibbs, N. (1995). The EQ factor. *Time*, 146, 60–68.

Glaso, L., & Einarsen, S. (2008). Emotion regulation in leader–follower relationships. *European Journal of Work and Organizational Psychology*, 17(4), 482–500. 10.1080/13594320801994960

Goleman, D. (1995). *Emotional intelligence*. Bantam Books.

Goleman, D. (2000). *Emotional Intelligence at work*. Ellinika Grammata.

Goleman, D. (2011). *Emotional intelligence*. Pedio.

Gonzales, M. (2022). *Emotional Intelligence for students, parents, teachers and school leaders. A Handbook for the Whole School Community*. Springer. 10.1007/978-981-19-0324-3

Gross, J. J., & John, O. P. (2003). Individual differences in two emotion regulation processes: Implications for affect, relationships, and well-being. *Journal of Personality and Social Psychology*, 85(2), 348–362. 10.1037/0022-3514.85.2.34812916575

Guilford, J. (1967). *The Nature of Human Intelligence*. McGraw-Hill.

Hatzichristou, S., Dimitropoulou, P., Lampropoulou, A., & Lykitsakou, K. (2009). Intervention programs in the school community: The experience of the Center for Research and Applications of School Psychology of the University of Athens. In D. Nikolopoulos (Ed.), *School Psychology: Applications in the School Environment* (pp. 283-306). Athens: Place.

Humphrey, R. (2002). The many faces of emotional leadership. *The Leadership Quarterly*, 13(5), 493–504. 10.1016/S1048-9843(02)00140-6

Jordan, P. J., & Troth, A. C. (2006). Emotions and coping with conflict: An introduction. *Journal of Management & Organization*, 12(2), 98–100. 10.5172/jmo.2006.12.2.98

Judge, T. A. (1992). The dispositional perspective in human resources research. In Ferris, G. R., & Rowland, K. M. (Eds.), *Research in personnel and human resources management* (pp. 145–156). Jai Press.

Kafetsios, K. (2003). Attachment, emotion regulation and psychological well being: Review and clinical applications. *Encephalos*, 40, 30–45.

Kafetsios, K. (2004). Attachment and emotional intelligence abilities across the life course. *Personality and Individual Differences*, 37(1), 129–145. 10.1016/j.paid.2003.08.006

Kakavoulis, K. A. (1997). *Emotional development and education*. Self publishing.

Katsarou, D. (2019). Emotional Intelligence of adult educators of second chance schools: A pilot study on job satisfaction. *Proceedings of 2nd International Congress on Management of Educational Units*, 60-66.

Katsarou, D., Panda, D., Konstantinidou, E., & Zisi, B. (2015). The Emotional Intelligence of Teachers of Second Chance Schools. *Educational Circle*, 3(2), 69–81.

Kougioumtzis, G. A., & Louka, D. (2021). Advocacy and Teacher Mentoring. In Khosrow-Pour, M. (Ed.), *Research Anthology on Instilling Social Justice in the Classroom* (pp. 138–160). IGI Global. 10.4018/978-1-7998-7706-6.ch010

Kougioumtzis, G. A., Sofologi, M., Fella, A., Kaliotsou, I., Koundourou, C., Bonti, E., & Papantoniou, G. (2021a). Specific Learning Disabilities-Implementation of an Intervention Program: An Analysis of a Case Study. In AuCoin, D. (Ed.), *Building Integrated Collaborative Relationships for Inclusive Learning Settings* (pp. 161–180). IGI Global. 10.4018/978-1-7998-6816-3.ch007

Kougioumtzis, G. A., Verykiou, J., & Mallouchou, A. (2021b). Bullying and Advocacy. In Khosrow-Pour, M. (Ed.), *Research Anthology on School Shootings, Peer Victimization, and Solutions for Building Safer Educational Institutions* (pp. 1–33). IGI Global. 10.4018/978-1-7998-5360-2.ch001

Law, K. S., Wong, C. S., Huang, G. H., & Li, X. (2008). The effects of emotional intelligence on job performance and life satisfaction for the research and development scientists in China. *Asia Pacific Journal of Management*, 25(1), 51–69. 10.1007/s10490-007-9062-3

Lazarus, R. S. (1999). *Stress and emotion: A new synthesis*. Springer.

Leuner, B. (1966). Emotional intelligence and emancipation. A psychodynamic study on women. *Praxis der Kinderpsychologie und Kinderpsychiatrie*, 1, 12–15.5975008

Leuner, H. (1966). Emotional Intelligence and Emancipation. A Psychodynamic Study on Women. *Prax Kinder Psychology*, 15, 196–203.5975008

Lopes, P. N., Brackett, M. A., Nezlek, J. B., Schütz, A., Sellin, I., & Salovey, P. (2004). Emotional intelligence and social Interaction. *Personality and Social Psychology Bulletin*, 30(8), 1018–1034. 10.1177/014616720426476215257786

Lopes, P. N., Grewal, D., Kadis, J., Gall, M., & Salovey, P. (2006). Evidence that emotional intelligence is related to job performance and affect and attitudes at work. *Psicothema*, 18, 132–138.17295970

Lopes, P. N., Salovey, P., & Straus, R. (2003). Emotional intelligence personality and the perceived quality of social relationships. *Personality and Individual Differences*, 35(3), 641–658. 10.1016/S0191-8869(02)00242-8

Low, G., & Nelson, D. (2005). Emotional Intelligence: The Role of Transformative Learning in Academic Excellence. *Texas Study Magazine*.http://www.unic.ac.cy/media/Research/Photos/parispapergreek.pdf

Mackintosh, N. J. (1988). Approaches to the study of animal intelligence. *British Journal of Psychology*, 79(4), 509–525. 10.1111/j.2044-8295.1988.tb02749.x

Malisiova, A., Kougioumtzis, G. A., Tsitsas, G., Koundourou, C., & Mitraras, A. (2023). Implementing Inclusive Education in Mixed-Ability Classrooms by Employing Differentiated Instruction. In Sofologi, M., Kougioumtzis, G., & Koundourou, C. (Eds.), *Perspectives of Cognitive, Psychosocial, and Learning Difficulties From Childhood to Adulthood: Practical Counseling Strategies* (pp. 155–178). IGI Global. 10.4018/978-1-6684-8203-2.ch009

Matthews, G., Zeidner, M., & Roberts, R. (2002). *Emotional Intelligence: Science and myth.* The MIT Press. 10.7551/mitpress/2704.001.0001

Mavroveli, S., Petrides, K. V., Sangareau, Y., & Furnham, A. (2009). Exploring the relationships between trait emotional intelligence and objective socio-emotional outcomes in childhood. *The British Journal of Educational Psychology*, 79(2), 259–272. 10.1348/000709908X368848l8950549

Mayer, J. D., & Salovey, P. (1997). What is emotional intelligence? In Salovey, P., & Sluyter, D. (Eds.), *Emotional Development and Emotional Intelligence: Implications for Educators* (pp. 3–31). Basic Books.

Mayer, J. D., Salovey, P., & Caruso, D. R. (2000). Emotional intelligence as zeitgeist, as personality and as a mental ability. In Bar-On, R., & Parker, J. D. (Eds.), *The handbook of emotional intelligence* (pp. 92–117). John Wiley & Sons.

Mayer, J. D., Salovey, P., & Caruso, D. R. (2002). Mayor- Salovey- Caruso Emotional Intelligence Test (MSCEIT): User's manual. *Personality and Social Psychology Bulletin*, 30, 1018–1034.

McColl-Kennedy, J. R., & Anderson, R. D. (2002). Impact of leadership style and emotions on subordinate performance. *The Leadership Quarterly*, 13(5), 545–559. 10.1016/S1048-9843(02)00143-1

Megari, K., Sofologi, M., Kougioumtzis, G. A., Thomaidou, E., Thomaidis, G., Katsarou, D., Yotsidi, V., & Theodoratou, M. (2024). Neurocognitive and psycho-emotional profile of children with disabilities. *Applied Neuropsychology. Child*, 1–6. 10.1080/21622965.2024.230478138574392

Mikolajczak, M. (2009). Going beyond the ability-trait debate: The three-level model of emotional intelligence. *E-Journal of Applied Psychology : Clinical and Social Issues*, 5(2), 25–31.

Newcombe, M. J., & Ashkanasy, N. M. (2002). The role of affect and affective congruence in perceptions of leaders: An experimental study. *The Leadership Quarterly*, 13(5), 601–614. 10.1016/S1048-9843(02)00146-7

Papanelopoulou, E. (2002). *Multiple intelligences: Theory- application and perspectives in primary education*. Unpublished PhD thesis. Volos: University of Thessaly.

Papapetrou, K. (1968). Theology and emotion. Theology L.Th., 241-245.

Patrikakou, A., & Kougioumtzis, G. A. (2016). Art, Emotional Intelligence & Counseling: Detection of the effect of making art and its applications in Career Counseling. *Journal of Regional SocioEconomic Issues, 6*(2), 206-219.

Payne, W. L. (1983/86). A study of emotion: Developing emotional intelligence, self integration, relating to fear, pain and desire. Unpublished PhD. University of Cincinnati: Ohio.

Pescolido, A. T. (2002). Emergent leaders as managers of group emotion. *The Leadership Quarterly*, 13(5), 583–599. 10.1016/S1048-9843(02)00145-5

Petrides, K. V., & Furnham, A. (2003). Trait emotional intelligence: Behavioral validation in two studies of emotion recognition and reactivity to mood induction. *European Journal of Personality*, 17(1), 39–57. 10.1002/per.466

Petrides, K. V., Sanchez-Ruiz, M. J., Siegling, A. B., Saklofske, D. H., & Mavroveli, S. (2018). Emotional intelligence as personality: Measurement and role of trait emotional intelligence in educational contexts. *Emotional intelligence in education: Integrating research with practice*, 49-81.

Pfeifer, S. I. (2001). Emotional intelligence: Popular but elusive construct. *Roeper Review*, 23(3), 138–142. 10.1080/02783190109554085

Pinker, S. (2007). *The Stuff of Thought: Language as a Window into Human Nature*. Viking.

Pirola-Merlo, A., Hartel, C., Mann, L., & Hirst, G. (2002). How leaders influence the impact of affective events on team climate and performance in R&D teams. *The Leadership Quarterly*, 13(5), 561–581. 10.1016/S1048-9843(02)00144-3

Platsidou, M. (2005). Emotional intelligence: Modern approaches to an old concept. *Education in Science*, 1, 27–39.

Platsidou, M. (2010). *Emotional Intelligence, Theoretical Models, Methods of Measurement and Applications in Education and Work*. Gutenberg.

Plomaritou, B. (2004). *Emotional Intelligence Development Program*. Grigoris Publications.

Russel, J. A. (1991). Culture and the categorization of emotions. *Psychological Bulletin*, 110(3), 426–450. 10.1037/0033-2909.110.3.4261758918

Saarni, C. (2011). Emotional competence and effective negotiation: The integration of emotion understanding, regulation, and communication. In F. Aquilar & M. Galluccio (Eds.), *Psychological and political strategies for peace negotiation: A cognitive approach* (pp. 55–74). Springer Science + Business Media.

Salovey, P., & Mayer, J. D. (1990). 1997). Emotional intelligence. *Imagination, Cognition and Personality*, 9(3), 185–211. 10.2190/DUGG-P24E-52WK-6CDG

Schutte, N. S., Malouff, J. M., Bobik, C., Coston, T. D., Greeson, C., Jedlicka, C., Rhodes, E., & Wendorf, G. (2001). Emotional intelligence and interpersonal relations. *The Journal of Social Psychology*, 141(4), 523–536. 10.1080/00224540 109600569 11577850

Schutte, N. S., Malouff, J. M., Hall, L. E., Hagerty, D. J., Cooper, J. T., Golden, C. J., & Dornheim, L. (1998). Development and validation of emotional intelligence. *Personality and Individual Differences*, 25(2), 167–177. 10.1016/S0191-8869(98)00001-4

Scott-Ladd, B., & Chan, C. C. A. (2004). Emotional intelligence and participation in decision-making: Strategies for promoting organizational learning and change. *Strategic Change*, 13(2), 95–105. 10.1002/jsc.668

Serrat, O. (2009). Understanding and developing emotional intelligence. *Knowledge Solutions*, 49, 34–61.

Siegel, D. (1999). *The developing mind: Toward a neurobiology of interpersonal experience*. Guilford.

Slaski, M., & Cartwright, S. (2002). Health, performance and emotional intelligence: An exploratory study of retail managers. *Stress and Health*, 18(2), 63–68. 10.1002/smi.926

Sofologi, M., Kamari, A., Kougioumtzis, G. A., Tatsiopoulou, P., Bonti, E., Papadimitropoulou, P., & Sarris, D. (2023). Emphasizing the Developmental Trajectory of Executive Functions in Preschool, School Children, Adolescence, and Its Relations with School Performance: The Development of Executive Functions. In D. Katsarou (Ed.), *Developmental Language Disorders in Childhood and Adolescence* (pp. 224-238). IGI Global. 10.4018/979-8-3693-0644-4.ch017

Sofologi, M., Kougioumtzis, G. A., Efstratopoulou, M., Skoura, E., Sagia, S., Karvela, S., Salli, P.-M., Makri, E., & Bonti, E. (2022). Specific Learning Disabilities and Psychosocial Difficulties in Children. In *Advising Preservice Teachers Through Narratives from Students With Disabilities* (pp. 31–54). IGI Global. 10.4018/978-1-7998-7359-4.ch002

Sofologi, M., Markou, E., Kougioumtzis, G. A., Kamari, A., & Tsanidou, A. (2020). Polymorphous Heterogeneity and Episodes of Violence in School Community: Educational Implications for Building a Democratic School. *Dual Diagnosis Open Access, 5*(1:4). doi: 10.36648/2472-5043.5.1.4

Sokou, K. (2004). *The promotion of mental health in the school community of the Southeastern Cyclades: The effect of the intervention with the words of teachers and students.* Scale-Tributes, 14-17.

Staw, B. M., Sutton, R. I., & Pelled, L. H. (1994). Employee positive emotion and favorable outcomes at the workplace. *Organization Science*, 5(1), 51–71. 10.1287/orsc.5.1.51

Sternberg, R. J. (1997). *Successful intelligence: How practical and creative intelligence determine success in life*. Simon and Shuster.

Styss, Y., & Brown, S. (2004). *A review of Emotional Intelligence literature and implications for corrections*. Research Report, Research Branch Correctional Service of Canada.

Taylor, G. J. (2001). Low Emotional Intelligence and mental illness. In Ciarrochi, J., Forgas, J. P., & Mayer, J. D. (Eds.), *Emotional intelligence in everyday life: a scientific inquiry* (pp. 76–81). Psychology Press.

Theodoratou, M., Farmakopoulou, I., Kougioumtzis, G. A., Kaltsouda, A., Siouti, Z., Sofologi, M., Gkintoni, E., & Tsitsas, G. (2023). Emotion-focused coping, social support, and active coping among university students: Gender differences. *Journal of Psychology & Clinical Psychiatry.*, 14(1), 5–9. 10.15406/jpcpy.2023.14.00720

Thorndike, E. L. (1920). A constant error in psychological ratings. *The Journal of Applied Psychology*, 4(1), 25–29. 10.1037/h0071663

Triliva, S., & Chimienti, G. (1998). *You and I Become We - Conflict Control Program*. Greek Letters.

Trinidad, D. R., & Johnson, C. A. (2002). The association of emotional intelligence and early adolescent tobacco and alcohol use. *Personality and Individual Differences*, 32(1), 95–105. 10.1016/S0191-8869(01)00008-3

Tsaousis, I., & Nikolaou, I. (2005). Exploring the relationship of emotional intelligence with physical and psychological health functioning. *Stress and Health*, 21(2), 77–86. 10.1002/smi.1042

Vlahaki, E. X. (2006). *Eating disorders and their relation to Emotional intelligence in 18-20 year olds.* Master Thesis. Athens: Harokopio University.

Weare, K., & Gray, G. (2000). *Promoting Mental and Emotional Health at School, A Handbook for Educators*. Greek Letters.

Weiss, H., & Cropanzano, R. (1996). Affective events theory: A theoretical discussion of the structure, causes and consequences of affective experiences at work. *Research in Organizational Behavior*, 18, 1–74.

Weissberg, R. P., & Greenberg, M. T. (1998). School and community competence enhancement and prevention programs. In *Handbook of child psychology: Child psychology in practice* (pp. 877-954). New York: John Wiley & Sons.

Weissberg, R. P., & O'Brien, M. U. (2004). What works in school-based social and em otional learning programs for youth development. *The Annals of the American Academy of Political and Social Science*, 591(1), 86–97. 10.1177/0002716203260093

White, J. (2005). Howard Gardner: The myth of multiple intelligences. *Viewpoint*, 16, 1–11.

Wierzbicka, A. (1992). Defining emotion concepts. *Cognitive Science*, 16(4), 539-581.

Wigod, R. (1998). EQ versus IQ: Scientists see value in emotional intelligence. *Psychology in Africa*, 1, 58–61.

Yeung, R. (1996). The acute effects of exercise on mood state. *Journal of Psychosomatic Research*, 40(2), 123–141. 10.1016/0022-3999(95)00554-48778396

Zampetakis, L. A., & Kafetsios, K. (2010). Group entrepreneurial behavior in established organizations: The role of middle managers' emotion regulation and groups' diversity. *Research on Emotion in Organizations*, 6, 33–61. 10.1108/S1746-9791(2010)0000006006

Chapter 7
The Impact of Inclusive School Climate on Children and Teachers' Well-Being:
A Reflection on Psycho-Emotional Empowerment

Dimitra Tasiouli
https://orcid.org/0009-0004-2233-7154
Frederick University, Cyprus

Olga Lyra
Frederick University, Cyprus

ABSTRACT

This chapter highlights the importance of fostering an inclusive school environment that supports the psycho-emotional well-being of all community members. Increasing awareness among researchers, practitioners, and policymakers underscores the pivotal role of the school experience in promoting mental health for both students and teachers. "School climate" refers to the psychological, social, and physical atmosphere within a school, influencing academic performance, behavior, and well-being. It includes relationships, perceptions of safety, support, control, and shared values. A positive school climate fosters productive learning conditions and engagement, leading to desirable academic and mental health outcomes. Inclusive educational practices ensure all students, regardless of background, have access to quality education and feel supported. This chapter emphasizes the need for schools to adopt inclusive climates, to promote the well-being of students and teachers,

DOI: 10.4018/979-8-3693-8312-4.ch007

Copyright © 2024, IGI Global. Copying or distributing in print or electronic forms without written permission of IGI Global is prohibited.

addressing interconnected goals of health and education for all.

INTRODUCTION

Education constitutes a fundamental cornerstone for the renewal and reform of our modern societies. By utilizing knowledge, it guides us in navigating through a world that is constantly evolving and considered ambiguous. Additionally, the power of education not only connects us with the world but also expands our views, and guides us beyond our actions' limits. Furthermore, it contributes to promoting our collaboration through organized collective efforts and provides the necessary scientific and innovative knowledge to address common challenges. Ultimately, education fosters understanding and cultivates skills that can ensure that the societies of the future will be more inclusive, economically fair and environmentally sustainable (Cook, 2019; United Nations Educational Scientific and Cultural Organization, [UNESCO], 2021).

In recent years, modern trends in education highlight the need for creating optimal learning conditions for every child, youth and adult. Moreover, there is a growing emphasis on realizing the transformative potential of education as a pathway to a sustainable collective future. Additionally, educational conditions are shaped by a wide range of external and internal factors (Hanuliaková & Barnová, 2015).

Specifically, the external factors influencing educational conditions include social norms, cultural values, economic conditions and governmental policies. These factors form the broader framework within which education operates. They can influence aspects such as funding, curriculum development, and access to resources (Al-Muslimawi & Hamid, 2019; Jones, 2012; la Velle, 2020).

On the other hand, internal factors encompass elements within the educational environment itself. These may include the quality of teaching staff, school leadership, infrastructure, educational materials, and overall organizational culture. Internal factors directly influence the daily school experiences of students and teachers. Simultaneously, they play a crucial role in shaping the learning environment (Jones, 2012; la Velle, 2020).

Both external and internal factors interact to create educational conditions, influencing everything from the effectiveness of teaching and learning to student outcomes and overall educational success. Understanding and addressing these factors are considered essential for developing strategies to improve educational quality and equality (Al-Muslimawi & Hamid, 2019; la Velle, 2020).

Among these internal factors, a key element that significantly influencing educational conditions is the "School Climate" (Jones, 2012) which this chapter will address. Particularly, the "School Climate" is a multidimensional construct, representing the "quality and character of school life" (NSCC, 2021). It encompasses the overall atmosphere within a school, including factors such as interpersonal relationships, student-teacher dynamics, disciplinary policies. Besides, "school climate" involves available resources, as well as the general sense of safety and belonging among students and school staff (Wang & Degol, 2016). The "school climate" is defined by school standards, goals, values, interpersonal relationships, teaching and learning practices, organizational structures, and is studied from the perspective of school safety including measures such as anti-bullying policies (Lombardi et al., 2019).

A positive school climate enhances the overall educational experience by fostering respectful and engaging interactions between students and teachers (Hanuliaková & Barnová, 2015). It promotes a safe and inclusive environment through effective school leadership (Mor Barak et al., 2022). It influences how students feel and behave, how teachers teach, and ultimately how well students learn (Wang & Degol, 2016). When internal factors are aligned and supportive, they create a positive school climate that mitigates challenges posed by external factors and enhances student engagement and achievement (Al-Muslimawi & Hamid, 2019; Jones, 2012; la Velle, 2020).

Also, it is worth noting that a positive school climate encourages a supportive and inclusive learning environment (Gray et al., 2017) where students are motivated to participate in their education. Such an environment is linked to higher academic achievements, exhibit fewer disruptive behaviors, experience reduced rates of bullying (Thapa et al., 2013) and have higher levels of well-being in school (Aldridge et al. 2016; Aldridge & McChesney 2018). Furthermore, regarding teachers, through a positive school climate, they can effectively facilitate teaching and learning (Papay & Kraft, 2017). Additionally, various studies have revealed that a positive school climate is associated with higher levels of job satisfaction, lower professional burnout among teachers (Aloe et al., 2014; Malinen & Savolainen, 2016) and their retention (Papay & Kraft, 2017). Therefore, cultivating a positive school climate is deemed crucial for the healthy development and achievement of both teachers and students, thus contributing to their well-being (Forsberg et al., 2021).

It should be emphasized that the term well-being of students and teachers encompasses a broad idea that includes various aspects of physical, mental, emotional, and spiritual health, as well as their overall satisfaction and fulfillment in their educational environment (Kentucky Department of Education, 2022). Thus, from the above, it is evident that school climate is closely linked to the well-being of teachers and students.

What happens, then, in the case of shaping an inclusive school climate where the diverse learning needs of all students should be addressed? Firstly, the well-being of teachers and students is a fundamental pillar for the realization of inclusive education (Gray et al., 2017; Wächter et al., 2024; Žic Ralić, 2023). Inclusive education constitutes a contemporary educational approach to promoting equality in the education system and celebrating diversity (Ali et al., 2024). The term "inclusion/inclusive education" was proposed by the Salamanca Declaration, adopted at the World Conference on Special Needs Education, held by UNESCO in 1994 (UNESCO, 1994).

Therefore, a positive school climate that respects and supports the diversity and needs of all students is critical for creating an environment where students feel safe and valued (Wang & Degol, 2016). The well-being of teachers, on the other hand, affects their ability to respond to the needs of each student, promoting an educational environment that is open, tolerant, and inspired by diversity. In such an environment, inclusive education can unleash the potential of every student, promoting self-esteem, self-confidence, and the development of their personal skills (Muhati-Nyakundi, 2023; Wächter et al., 2024). Through awareness, education, and support, the educational community can create an environment that fosters the development and success of all students, thus promoting genuine education for all (Darling-Hammond & Cook-Harvey, 2018).

The aim of this chapter is to provide an overview of the existing literature related to the importance and impact of a positive inclusive school climate on the well-being of both students and teachers. Additionally, practices and actions for promoting an inclusive school climate as well as the psychosocial empowerment of students and teachers will be highlighted. Moreover, this chapter will build upon findings from existing literature to provide directions for future research and applied educational practice.

This chapter is structured from the introduction, the main body, the conclusions, and the bibliographical references. More specifically, the main body is developed in five sections, initially approaching the term and dimensions of the school climate, emphasizing its importance for improving schools. Following this, the section on school climate and inclusive education discusses the significance of inclusive education in addressing student diversity, highlighting the need for a positive school climate that promotes equality, respect, and emotional well-being for all students and staff. Subsequently, the importance of the school climate and the overall well-being of students and teachers is underscored, with an emphasis on mental health, support, and social interaction in the school environment. Furthermore, the concepts of student and teacher well-being are clarified.

The next section focuses on the impact of an inclusive school climate on students and teachers. Specifically, the creation and maintenance of a positive and inclusive school climate are critical for the academic, social, and emotional development of students, as well as the professional satisfaction and well-being of teachers. The implementation of policies and practices that promote such environments can lead to substantial long-term benefits for entire educational communities. The final section deals with promoting an inclusive school climate and the psycho-emotional empowerment of students and teachers through various strategies and practices. Finally, it is worth noting that the key conclusions drawn from this chapter essentially highlight the importance of creating an inclusive and supportive school climate, which, through psychological and emotional empowerment and investment in the well-being of students and teachers, promotes the well-being, performance, and continuous development of all involved in the educational community.

To further our understanding of how education can promote well-being and inclusion, we need to explore the internal conditions within schools. This exploration begins with an in-depth look at school climate.

School Climate

It's widely acknowledged that in recent decades, "School Climate" has been at the center of intense interest and particular attention both within the research community and educational policy (Thapa et al., 2013), as a potential aim for improving schools and efforts to ensure their safety (Elrod et al., 2022), and by extension, in children's development (Bradshaw et al.,2021).

Moreover, the national discourse on "School Climate" raises issues of public policy, accountability, inclusion, justice, resource allocation, data analysis, professional development, and almost any other "logical thread" related to school and school system management (DeWitt, 2014).

Furthermore, scientists and researchers from around the world have made significant efforts to define and clarify the concept of "School Climate". However, they have not been able to reach a clear and universally accepted definition that everyone agrees on, due to the complexity of this particular concept (Debarbieux et al., 2012; Zullig et al., 2010). Nevertheless, several researchers have concluded that school climate has a "subjective dimension" as it is determined by the perception of an individual and formed according to the experiences gained by each person within the school environment (Dernowska, 2017), On the other hand, some researchers have focused on the "objective" aspect of school life (Cohen et al., 2009; Debarbieux et al., 2012).

So far, various definitions and interpretations of school climate have been proposed, with significant differences in terms of the range and degree that enhance or limit further aspects or dimensions related to school climate (Bear, 2020; Sadeghi & Esmaeili, 2022). Nonetheless, a common axis in all the definitions is the presence of positive social relationships and interpersonal interactions (Gray et al., 2017). Additionally, the educational community generally agrees that school climate significantly impacts the entire student community (Cumming & Rodriguez, 2018).

In general, professionals and researchers use a variety of terms related to school climate, such as atmosphere, feelings, tone, framework, and school environment (Dernowska, 2017; Goldenberg & Klavir, 2017). However, it would be a serious omission not to mention that similar concepts to school climate have been developed, often resulting in confusion between them. Such concepts include the following: school engagement and connectedness, school culture, classroom climate, school attachment, and teacher support (Niehaus et al., 2012; Rudasill et al., 2018).

The concept of "School climate" has been described as the quality and character of the school experience (Aldridge & Blackstock, 2024; Mousena & Raptis, 2020; NSCC, 2021), the 'heart and soul of the school' (Freiberg & Stein, 1999, p.11), and the quality and consistency of interpersonal relationships among students, teachers and school staff based on shared beliefs, attitudes and values (Fan et al., 2011). In essence, it constitutes a holistic, complex, and multidimensional construct that represents nearly every aspect of daily school life (Garzia & Molinari, 2021; Wang & Degol, 2016). Specifically, it refers to the psychological, social and physical environmental atmosphere within a school, which influences academic performance, student behavior, and their well-being (Gase et al., 2017).

In addition, based on the study by La Salle et al. (2021), "School climate" is a multidimensional construct that represents perceptions of various aspects of the educational environment. School climate refers to the beliefs, values, and attitudes that shape interactions among students, between teachers, and administrators within a school. Moreover, it is worth noting that the term school climate reflects the common understanding of the rules as well as the system of values and the mission of the school, which encourages students and teachers to develop positive feelings about the school and to want to be part of it. Also, it refers to the impact of the school on students and teachers, such as: the sense of safety, teaching and learning practices, interpersonal relationships among principals, teachers, parents, and students, practices and organizational structures, attitudes and acceptance of diversity, respect for all members of the school community, fair and consistent discipline policies, etc. (Koziori & Alexandropoulos, 2020). Overall, school climate reflects rules, goals, values, interpersonal relationships, teaching and learning practices, and organizational structures (Grey et al., 2017).

While researchers have not reached a consensus regarding the dimensions that constitute school climate, they agree that there are four general spheres of school climate that have emerged from previous research. Tthese include: safety (e.g., physical safety, socio-emotional safety), teaching and learning (e.g., quality of teaching, social, emotional, and ethical learning, school professional development practices, leadership), relationships within the school community (e.g., respect for diversity through positive adult-adult, student-adult, and adult-student relationships throughout the school, school-community collaboration), and the physical environment (e.g., material infrastructure) (Chiriac et al., 2023;; Reaves et al., 2018). Additionally, it is worth noting that the dimensions model proposed by the National School Climate

Center (2023) includes some additional dimensions: school connectedness, inclusion, social media, leadership, and professional relationships.

Furthermore, positive school climate is one of those things that is considered difficult to define and measure, yet everyone recognizes it when they see it. Visitors to a school, including parents and school education counselors, can recognize a positive school atmosphere within a few minutes (DeWitt, 2017). Specifically, the condition of the school facilities, the tone of conversations in the hallways, the enthusiasm of the school staff, and the way students interact during breaks are some of the characteristic signs that visitors can "read" to quickly and broadly assess the school climate (OECD, 2019).

School climate can be safe or unsafe, cohesive or divisive, collaborative or competitive. Above all, it is typically perceived as either positive or negative. In particular, ιn a positive school climate, students feel physically and emotionally safe, recognized, valued, supported, and capable of learning. Moreover, teachers are particularly supportive, enthusiastic, and responsive fostering trust among student. Additionally, parents voluntarily participate in school activities, the school community is based on healthy relationships with strong elements of respect and collaboration, and everyone takes care of the school facilities and works together to develop a constructive school spirit. Collectively and individually, a positive school climate can have a significant impact on the success of all students in school (OECD, 2019).

The comprehensive understanding of school climate provides a robust framework for enhancing student well-being. To build on this foundation, it is crucial to explore how inclusive education can be integrated into this climate, ensuring that every student, regardless of their background or abilities, can thrive in a supportive and inclusive setting.

School Climate and Inclusive Education

In recent decades, the impact of social, technological, and cultural changes has brought new significant challenges to the field of education worldwide. More specifically, international migration, multiculturalism, and the recognition of diversity have increased awareness of student diversity as well as the expectations and hopes of families and communities. One of the most challenging tasks for teachers in our modern society is the continuous search for pedagogical approaches to address this diversity in inclusive schools (Guðjónsdóttir & Karlsdóttir, 2009; Guðjónsdóttir & Óskarsdóttir, 2016). A rapid global shift has occurred towards implementing a new approach in the educational field that effectively responds to the heterogeneity of the student population by providing equal and quality education to all students. In reality, inclusive education aims to create a school environment where all children, regardless of their different abilities and backgrounds (racial, ethnic, linguistic, cultural, socioeconomic, sexual, religious), have access to a comprehensive and quality educational program and they feel socially, emotionally, behaviorally, and academically supported, having equal opportunities in an educational environment that provides them with a sense of safety and belonging (Engelbrecht et al. 2017; Messiou, 2017; Sorkos & Hajisoteriou, 2021). Consequently, inclusive education is considered a highly significant approach in global education agendas (Azorín & Ainscow, 2020; Tonegawa, 2022). However, the discourse around what constitutes inclusive education is complex (Knight & Crick, 2022).

According to Guðjónsdóttir & Óskarsdóttir (2016), inclusive education refers to a pedagogical approach aimed at developing educational practices and environments that reflect the diversity of students. At the core of inclusive education is the idea that all students, including those with disabilities or special educational needs, have the right to receive an education that enables them to fully participate in the educational process and achieve the highest possible level of academic performance. Therefore, inclusive education promotes the creation of educational environments that support diversity, access, participation, and success for all students. It constitutes a movement against all forms of exclusion, the removal of barriers to physical presence, the elimination of potential risks of marginalization, the eradication of negative responses or attitudes towards diversity, and it represents a reaction to political segregation and social inequality. The goal of inclusive education is to combat inequality and foster a sense of belonging in school and society (Petrou et al., 2009).

Particularly interesting is Akbarovna's (2022) approach to inclusive education, which emphasizes that education, which takes into account the needs of all children, respects their rights and abilities, and aims to achieve social justice and equality, is called inclusive education. Inclusive education is an ongoing process aimed at integrating children with disabilities into the educational process and adapting schools to accommodate children with disabilities. Further, inclusive education is based on a social model, examining the problem not in the child but in the curriculum and methodology. Such an educational system requires changes and modifications. Moreover, inclusive education concludes that all children, including those with special needs, should be able to attend any school they wish. Treating children's disability as a "problem" is due to mistakes of society.

Also, according to Kielblock & Woodcock (2023), inclusive education is understood as the right of all children to access, attend, participate, and succeed in their local, neighborhood, regular school. This approach shifts the focus away from labeling, diagnosis, and deficits of certain students towards providing quality education for all children. A key characteristic of inclusive education is its response to student diversity by developing learning environments and opportunities that cater to all (Slee, 2018). This ensures that all students have the opportunity to be an integral part of the school community and actively participate in all aspects of school life (Panesi, Bocconi & Ferlino, 2020).

Additionally, it should be noted that various concepts of inclusive education do not exclusively focus on children with special educational needs and disabilities. Many advocate for a new, clear philosophy of change in the overall processes of modern schools, involving revisions and modifications for the majority of students. This also includes redefining teaching processes, instructional strategies, and school culture. In its current form, inclusive education aims to include all children, regardless of any distinguishing factors, while treating diversity as a benefit (Stasinós, 2016).

Furthermore, it is noteworthy that achieving these goals is particularly challenging. For example, the lack of effective inclusive practices can lead to unmet educational needs for children, which in turn results in feelings of inefficacy, anxiety, and ultimately resignation among teachers, as well as feelings of exclusion and failure among children who face difficulties in participation and learning (Triviño-Amigo et al., 2022).

Finally, the research by Kefallinou et al. (2020) emphasized the importance of a positive, inclusive school climate for inclusive education. An inclusive school climate involves respect, openness, and recognition of differences among students, teachers, and staff, promoting equality, diversity acceptance, and emotional well-being. Key factors include respect, differentiated teaching, collaboration, emotional support, and open communication.

In the context of inclusive education, the emphasis on creating a supportive school climate resonates deeply with efforts to enhance overall well-being within educational settings. By fostering an environment of acceptance and belonging, inclusive school climates not only facilitate academic success but also promote the mental, emotional, and social well-being of students and educators alike. This holistic approach recognizes the interconnectedness between a positive school climate and the flourishing of individuals across physical, cognitive, and socio-emotional dimensions of well-being.

School Climate and Well-Being

Initially, the improvement of mental health and well-being of all individuals has been recognized as one of the most important public health issues of today's era (Aldridge & McChesney, 2018). Additionally, the World Health Organization (W.H.O) has emphasized that «There is no health without mental health» (p. 6), so both the W.H.O (2013) and the United Nations (1966) have confirmed that experiencing the best possible mental health is a global human right.

Various individual, school, and community factors influence the well-being of students and teachers (Kentucky Department of Education, 2022). In particular, school climate plays a significant role as one of the main factor affecting the support of mental health and well-being of students as well as educators in the school. Moreover, there is a growing trend towards co-teaching practices that influence the well-being of teachers and student outcomes (Gray et al., 2017). Furthermore, a positive inclusive school climate that promotes a sense of safety, support, and belonging where students feel accepted and respected, can contribute to the psychological well-being and welfare of students and teachers (U.S. Department of Education, 2023).

Regarding students' well-being, the Programme for International Student Assessment (PISA) defines well-being as the quality of students' lives, focusing on their physical, cognitive, psychological, and social functions, abilities, and capacities needed to live a happy and fulfilling life. It also distinguishes various dimensions of well-being, including overall life satisfaction, subjective well-being, school well-being, and well-being outside of school (OECD, 2019). This definition also highlights students' well-being as an active internal process for achieving their personal and social goals (Borgonovi & Pál, 2016). Students' well-being covers four distinct aspects that are closely interrelated. The first is physical well-being, meaning their health status and their ability to follow healthy dietary habits and generally choose a healthy lifestyle. The second is cognitive well-being, which is successful participation in society in various roles - as lifelong learners, as productive workers, as active, engaged citizens - partly due to the knowledge they possess and the skills required for the effective fulfillment of these roles. The third aspect is psychological well-being, which is students' opinions and feelings about their lives, their educational activities, and the personal goals they have set, as well as their future aspirations. The final aspect is social well-being, which covers relationships with family, other students, and teachers, as well as the perception of the school's social environment (Borgonovi & Pál, 2016).

It is worth noting that students' well-being in school is increasingly perceived not only at an individual level but also as a collective commitment throughout the entire school. Schools that promote the individual and collective well-being of students provide the necessary elements for their holistic development and growth in school and beyond. For this purpose, schools play a central role in the individual and collective well-being of students, integrating well-being into planning and processes, striving for excellence in teaching and learning, and helping to build trusting and respectful relationships to enable students to succeed (Panesi et al., 2020).

Regarding the well-being of teachers, while initially it was mainly associated with negative aspects such as anxiety, pressure, negative emotions, chronic health concerns, emotional exhaustion, and burnout, gradually positive aspects such as positive emotions, job satisfaction, and commitment began to be increasingly included (Collie, 2023; Dreer, 2022). Teachers' well-being refers to the general state of well-being they experience in various areas of their professional activity. This state includes their satisfaction with their work, their perception of their health, their relationships with colleagues and students, as well as how they deal with the emotional challenges that arise in their work environment. Essentially, it reflects all the factors that influence their happiness and satisfaction in their professional lives (Viac & Fraser, 2020). Moreover, teachers' well-being is defined as the broad idea that encompasses their educational, intellectual, physical, emotional, and spiritual health (Kentucky Department of Education, 2022).

Building on the positive outcomes observed in inclusive school climates, it is crucial to explore how these environments specifically affect students and teachers across various dimensions.

THE IMPACT OF INCLUSIVE SCHOOL CLIMATE

Effects of Inclusive School Climate on Students

Findings from research have contributed to an increasing number of regional and local educational authorities endorsing and supporting policies for school climate and improvement practices. The significance of school climate and effective improvement processes stems from their role as protective factors that positively impact life outcomes and well-being for children, adolescents, and teachers (Konold et al., 2018; Ortega et al., 2011). Each region should prioritize the improvement of its school climate to reap the benefits of a quality environment for both teachers and students (Konold et al., 2018).

Positive school climate is considered essential in inclusive schools (Pandia & Purwanti, 2019). By creating a warm, positive, supportive, and healthy school climate, teachers, students, and entire educational systems can achieve a range of positive outcomes in various areas such as the educational process, academic performance, (Demirtas-Zorbaz et al., 2021), as well as mental health, social and emotional well-being, behavior management, and overall well-being (Aldridge & McChesney, 2018; Chiriac et al., 2023; Franco et al., 2022).

Several decades of research have demonstrated the relationship between positive school climate and academic achievement among different groups of students (Demirtas-Zorbaz et al., 2021; Pandia & Purwanti, 2019; Santhosh & Flower, 2023), self-academic efficacy (Zysberg & Schwabsky, 2021), and positive academic motivation, which is considered the driving force behind students' academic performance (Volk, 2020; Wang et al., 2020). Additionally, students who perceived their school environment positively achieved higher grades in their courses (Daily et al., 2019; Maxwell et al., 2017), including students with disabilities (Pandia & Purwanti, 2019), participated more in school and extracurricular activities (Fatou & Kubiszewski, 2018; Lombardi et al., 2019), had fewer absences (Van Eck et al., 2017), and concurrently managed to graduate from high school (Buckman et al., 2021).

Furthermore, a positive school climate has been linked to high or improved rates of classroom attendance, participation, and engagement, exam scores, retention and prevention of school dropout, high school graduation (Buckman et al., 2021), college/university readiness (Pinkus, 2009), and preparation for transition to adult life (Mann et al., 2016). Additionally, a positive school climate was found to lead to higher academic achievements when characterized by high academic expectations (Wang & Degol, 2016). Moreover, study by Alonso-Tapia et al. (2020) identified that academic support, positive teacher-student relationships, and academic satisfaction are particularly critical factors to target through the school climate to better support students' academic success. Teacher care and collaboration were associated with students' school commitment and sense of belonging (Walls et al., 2021), social well-being, and completion (Baroody et al., 2014).

Additionally, Knight & Duncheon (2019) found that school safety and extracurricular opportunities can play a significant role in post-secondary success. With positive school climates, students are more likely to enroll and persist in higher education if schools provide college-oriented interventions. Finally, students' perceptions of cultural consciousness, respect for diversity, and racial equality also impact academic performance positively (Wang & Huguley, 2012), with students experiencing greater racial justice and fewer racial discriminations achieving higher mean grade point averages.

Moreover, school climate has been extensively researched as a determinant factor of students' behavior within the school (Dernowska, 2017; Reaves et al., 2018), including behavioral problems such as bullying (Espelage et al., 2014; Wang & Degol, 2016), aggression (Turner et al., 2014), misconduct, as well as health issues such as substance abuse, alcohol, and psychosomatic symptoms (Wang & Degol, 2016). More specifically, a positive school climate has been associated with reduced rates of violence and victimization in schools (Farina, 2019). Furthermore, researches has shown that a positive school climate acts as a protective factor directly related to reduced rates of involvement in provocative behaviors, reduced substance use, decreased rates of misconduct, aggression, and violence over time, decreased weapon use, reduced rates of suicide attempts (suicidal ideation) (Holt et al., 2015; Reaves et al., 2018), risky sexual behaviors (Coulter et al., 2016; Peterson et al., 2020), as well as avoidance of addictive behaviors (Shahriari Shaghaghi et al., 2021).

Additionally, students attending schools with greater consistency in discipline and social support experienced less bullying, victimization, and school referrals for punishment (Shirley & Cornell, 2012). Moreover, a positive school climate has been linked to fewer student lies and violations of school rules (Reaves et al., 2018). A peaceful, positive school climate (perceived rule clarity and justice) has been associated with less aggressive solutions to peer conflicts, while students also related to less dangerous behaviors (LaRusso & Selman, 2011). These findings suggest that school rules and values may shape students' attitudes and beliefs regarding acceptable versus unacceptable behaviors in school. Having a positive school climate where students and staff feel safe ensures a secure educational environment for everyone.

Additionally, according to Wang & Fredricks (2014), during adolescence, students disengaged from school are more likely to exhibit problematic behaviors such as substance use, misconduct, and ultimately drop out of school (Lester & Cross, 2015). It is also worth noting that a positive school climate can foster healthier, higher-quality relationships with peers as well as a sense of belonging, resulting in reduced aggression, victimization, and fewer behavior problems (Ramelow et al., 2015; Wang & Degol, 2016). A positive school climate promotes mutual respectful behavior between students and teachers, encouraging trust, respect, and reinforcing collaboration, communication, a sense of community, and the achievement of common goals. It can provide safety and a sense of belonging leading to significantly improved levels of behavior (Darling-Hammond & Cook-Harvey, 2018).

Similarly, research studies have revealed that school climate can significantly impact mental health (Bonell et al., 2013; Mariani et al., 2015) and the social-emotional well-being of children and adolescents (Aldridge & McChesney, 2018; Lester & Cross, 2015), including positive adaptation (e.g., high self-esteem, adaptive coping strategies, and high life satisfaction) and psychopathology such as depression and anxiety. Many aspects associated with a positive school climate, such as school engagement, respect for students' opinions, school connectedness, and supportive relationships, are considered factors directly related to students' psychological functioning (Wang & Degol, 2016). Conversely, school environments lacking safe and supportive qualities may contribute to increased anxiety and fear among students, which in turn can negatively affect their learning (Darling-Hammond & Cook-Harvey, 2018).

In more detail, the quality of life within a school environment can promote the healthy social and emotional development of students (McGiboney, 2023). A positive, supportive school climate fosters the healthy psycho-social development and well-being of students (Daily et al., 2020) and presents positive socio-emotional outcomes (Kutsyuruba et al., 2015). Moreover, positive levels of school climate have been found to be causally related to lower rates of smoking and alcohol use among students (Coulter et al., 2016; Peterson et al., 2020). Among other factors, at an individual level, students' connection to school and their educational commitment have been associated with better mental health outcomes (Aldridge & McChesney, 2018; Kidger et al., 2012).

Furthermore, a study by Gray et al. 2017) revealed that increased self-esteem and self-perception among students, along with other emotional and mental health outcomes, were associated with a positive school climate. A positive school climate was also linked to lower levels of drug use and lower frequencies of psychiatric problems among high school students. It was also identified as a predictor for enhanced psychological well-being (Virtanen et al., 2009).

Moreover, recent research has shown an inverse correlation between a healthy school climate and incidents of physical violence, bullying, psychosocial adjustment, psychopathology (such as symptoms of depression, anxiety, and suicidal ideation), emotional exhaustion, and feelings of low personal accomplishment (Franco et al., 2023). Additionally, it is worth noting that one of the dimensions of school climate, particularly interpersonal relationships between teachers and students, was significantly associated with well-being (among girls only) and, consequently, lower rates of depressive symptoms (Suldo et al., 2012).

Subsequently the study by Lester & Cross (2015) pointed out that dimensions of school climate, such as a sense of safety, connection, and peer support, protect the mental and emotional well-being of students during the transitional period from primary to secondary school. Furthermore, connection with teachers serves as a protective factor for students' emotional well-being. It is worth noting that primary school is a crucial period for building quality relationships among students, which provide support prior to transitioning to secondary school. Overall, policies and practices that promote safety and connection in the school environment are critical, especially during the early years of secondary education.

In Celik's survey (2018), it was noted that schools with positive climates which fulfill students' basic psychological needs for autonomy (individuality and independence), a sense of belonging, and competence (feelings of self-effectiveness, ability to overcome challenges), students are more likely to have a positive experience of life satisfaction, increased positive emotions, and a sense of meaning in life.

Finally, Wong et al. (2021) identified a significant correlation between school climate and adolescents' social-emotional health. Students who experienced supportive and structured environments demonstrated higher levels of self-efficacy and resilience, along with fewer symptoms of depression, hopelessness, and anxiety. This underscores the crucial role of a positive school climate in promoting improved social-emotional health among students.

As we transition from discussing the profound effects of inclusive school climate on students to its impact on teachers, it becomes evident that a positive school environment plays a pivotal role in shaping not only student outcomes but also the professional lives of teachers.

Effects of Inclusive School Climate on Teachers

Teachers play a crucial role in shaping a positive school climate in inclusive schools. Indeed, a positive school climate is essential in inclusive schools (Pandia & Purwanti, 2019). For instance, according to Gray et al. (2017), teachers face significant daily demands, including their expectations for successful classroom management and their contribution to student learning outcomes. Furthermore, these expectations become increasingly challenging with large classrooms sizes, diverse and individualized learning needs of students, fluctuating resources and school-wide budget management. Moreover, it is worth noting that teachers need to adapt teaching techniques, assessments, and many other aspects when including students with disabilities or educational needs in their classrooms. In addition, their willingness to adapt is largely influenced by their perceptions of the concept of "inclusion" (Spektor-Levy & Yifrach, 2017).

The role of school climate in influencing the effectiveness and well-being of teacher is crucial (Zakariya, 2020). Specifically, the various dimensions of school climate affect teachers' effectiveness (Skaalvik & Skaalvik, 2011; Wang & Degol, 2016), job satisfaction (Hosford & O'Sullivan 2016; Katsantonis, 2019; Zakariya, 2020), burnout (Aldridge & Fraser, 2016; Mostafa & Pál, 2018), professional development (Wang & Degol, 2016), mental health (Gray et al., 2017) and well-being (Dreer, 2022; Garzia & Molinari, 2021), Additionally, it influences teachers' sense of connectedness and their retention in the profession (McInerney et al., 2015).

First and foremost, work environments can either support or hinder effective teaching and professional development of teachers. For example, researchers and policymakers often talk about teachers competence as being "fixed and fully portable" in school contexts. However, teachers' performance depends on how well their skills match the needs of their students and their work environment. Moreover, teachers' skills are multidimensional and do not always translate into student populations and school settings (Stronge et al., 2011). Furthermore, even the most talented and dedicated teachers will struggle to overcome a school culture that lacks a safe, supportive learning environment (Kraft & Falcen, 2020).

Positive school environments can contribute to the promotion of rapid improvement and the expansion of professional development opportunities for teachers through formal and informal learning opportunities in the workplace (Marinette & Hui, 2021). In particular, substantial collaboration with peers aids in the development of teachers' skills, facilitates open feedback, and enhances collective relationships (Forslund Frykedal & Hammar Chiriac, 2018; Jackson & Bruegmann, 2009). Additionally, teachers improve their skills when there is a school-wide model of continuous improvement that fosters innovation, open communication, collaboration, and trust which are necessary to allow teachers to experiment with new teaching techniques (Archibald et al., 2011).

Surveys by Hosford & O'Sullivan (2016) and Malinen & Savolainen (2016) demonstrated that teachers who described a positive school climate in their schools had higher levels of self-efficacy and were more likely to effectively influence their students' learning. Through a positive school climate, teachers can enhance their self-confidence and motivation, which in turn can lead to improved educational approaches and enhanced learning outcomes. Furthermore, studies by Grayson &Alvarez (2008) and Guo & Higgins-D'Alessandro (2011) indicated that a positive school climate contributes to higher levels of personal achievement and the perceived ability of teachers to positively influence students. Additionally, in the study by Aldridge & Fraser (2016) found that in positive school climates where school principals are accessible and supportive, then this contributes both directly and indirectly to teachers' self-efficacy and job satisfaction.

Researches conducted by Lee & Louis (2019) and Van Beurden et al. (2017) were particularly significant, as it revealed that a positive, supportive, and inclusive school climate that is free from feelings of hostility and bullying, enhances teachers' job satisfaction and self-efficacy. Moreover, it improves teacher-student relationships and reduces their attrition and burnout.

Additionally, has been found that positive school climate improves teachers' job satisfaction and reduces their levels of anxiety/stress (Colie et al., 2012). For instance, recent surveys by Marinette & Hui (2021) and Ortan et al. (2021) found that teachers who worked in schools where positive school environments were established/shaped, reported higher levels of job satisfaction and a particularly strong sense of collaboration compared to teachers who worked in schools with negative school environments. Also, Kutsyuruba et al. (2015) added that positive school climate was correlated not only with higher job satisfaction among teachers but also with lower levels of anxiety/stress and better levels of physical health among them.

Subsequently, research by Veldman et al. (2013) and Zakariya (2020) revealed that the teacher-student relationship is positively associated with teachers' job satisfaction. Furthermore, teachers with a strong sense of belonging in the school system reported high self-efficacy, which translates into high job satisfaction (Skaalvik & Skaalvik, 2011). On the other hand, teachers' perceived disciplinary climate has been reported to negatively affect self-efficacy, which, in turn, translates into low job satisfaction (Aldridge & Fraser, 2016; Malinen & Savolainen, 2016). Moreover, teachers in schools with positive, disciplined, and supportive climates are more likely to report high levels of job satisfaction and less likely to report feelings of exhaustion, burnout and demoralization (Aldridge & Fraser, 2016; Yang et al., 2022).

In addition, Cohen et al. (2009) emphasized that teachers who noted a positive school climate in their schools experienced positive relationships and collaborations both with their colleagues and their students, as well as a sense of community and belonging within the school. Furthermore, research by McInerney et al. (2015) demonstrated that teachers who reported a positive school climate exhibited greater work engagement and were less likely to leave the profession. Similarly, a study by Manla (2021) found that a school climate that supports collaboration and the participation of teachers in decision-making is strongly associated with higher morale, stronger commitment to teaching, and intentions to remain in the profession. Likewise, Ullman (2022) noted that in schools with positive school climates, teachers are likely to experience a sense of belonging and feel valued by their colleagues.

Supplementarily, according to Wang & Degol (2016), a positive school climate also impacts the well-being of teachers by creating a supportive and collaborative environment that promotes their professional development and job satisfaction, leading to improved well-being. Moreover, relevant research regarding the effects of school climate on teachers (Garzia & Molinari, 2021) clearly showed that a positive, warm, and supportive school climate positively/ beneficially influences/ affects teachers' working conditions as well as their well-being.

Numerous studies noted that school climate deeply impacts the physical and mental health of teachers (Fang & Qi, 2023; Zhang et al., 2023). More specifically, positive school working environment has been found to significantly affect the likelihood of teachers experiencing psychological burnout (Dearing, 2020; Jacobson, 2016). Also, researchers found that a healthy, robust, positive school climate reduces teachers' burnout. Currently, professional burnout leads teachers to leave the field of education within a short period of time (Milam et al., 2022; Yang et al., 2022). Additionally, promoting a positive school climate is associated with increased teacher retention (Cohen et al., 2009).

It is also worth noting that teachers who work in inclusive classrooms with a positive climate are more likely to report feeling supported and valued and less likely to experience psychological burnout or leave the profession (Gray et al., 2017). Conversely, teachers in schools with a negative climate are more likely to experience anxiety, stress and dissatisfaction, leading to high turnover rates and a lack of qualified teachers (Yang et al., 2022). Furthermore, a negative school climate is also linked to teachers experiencing more feelings of low personal accomplishment, increased cynicism, and depersonalization (Thapa et al., 2013).

Finally, various conditions such as inadequate support from administration, limited involvement of teachers and staff (Ingersoll & Strong, 2011), student discipline issues and teachers' perceived lack of influence in decision-making are associated with teacher burnout and retention issues (Flowers, 2019).

Having completed the impact of inclusive school climate on teachers and students, we move on to another section, delving into Practices for promoting an inclusive school climate and the psycho-emotional empowerment of students and teachers. Promoting an inclusive school climate is vital to fostering a healthy educational environment. This section explores various strategies that schools can implement to support the psycho-emotional empowerment of both students and teachers.

Practices for Promoting an Inclusive School Climate and Psycho-Emotional Empowerment of Students and Teachers

The promotion of an inclusive school climate and the psycho-emotional empowerment of students and teachers are considered crucial/vital for creating/fostering a healthy and successful educational environment (Gray et al., 2017; Tafuri & Latino, 2024).

To promote a positive school climate and support the well-being, particularly the psycho-emotional empowerment of students and teachers, various strategies can be implemented by schools and educational institutions.

Before specific strategies are outlined, it is deemed necessary to clarify the term of "psychological empowerment." There is a variety of different conceptualizations regarding this concept, but broadly, it has been considered as the sense of ability and autonomy that an individual possesses in the workplace or in the environment in which he or she is included. It constitutes/represents the individual's sense of self-confidence (Ahmed & Malik, 2019; Xiong, 2022). According to Li (2016), psychological empowerment is both a process and an achievement that can occur at various levels (individual, organizational, and community).

Additionally, psychological empowerment is a key factor in achieving several important outcomes related to work, increasing levels of motivation, initiative, and self-determination in performing tasks and duties in the workplace (Chan et al., 2015; Kõiv et al., 2019). Moreover, psychological empowerment is associated with the motivational aspects of work or the intrinsic motives of the worker to work or behave with a sense of autonomy, trust, confidence/certainty and leadership (Singh & Kaur, 2019). It should also be noted that psychological empowerment constitutes an internal state of an individual wherein he/she possess full awareness of his/her duties, capabilities, and skills in order to develop personally and professionally. Determines functionality, commitment, performance and satisfaction of the individual in the workplace, if taken into consideration and supported by the academic staff and administrative personnel (Khany & Tazik, 2016). Surveys have revealed that psychological empowerment encompasses/includes the following components: behavioral, cognitive, relational and emotional (Christens et al., 2016).

Regarding the term "psycho-emotional empowerment" as referenced in this chapter, it denotes the process of acquiring strength, resilience and autonomy in one's psychological and emotional well-being. Specifically, ιt entails the development of a deeper understanding and awareness of one's own thoughts, feelings, and behaviors, along with active efforts to enhance mental and emotional health (Christens et al., 2016).

In the context of teachers, psychological empowerment refers to the psychological state in which teachers believe they have a certain level of influence and autonomous control over their work (Xiong, 2022). Simultaneously, the psychological empowerment of students refers to the process of enhancing their mental resilience, self-confidence, and positive self-image, as well as developing skills to help them tackle challenges, manage their emotions, and pursue their goals in education and life (Kundu & Kumar, 2017). When students feel empowered, they are more inclined to actively engage in their learning, take responsibility for their educational journey, and cultivate their self-confidence (Zacarian & Silverstone, 2020). Additionally, empowerment provides students with a feeling of autonomy and empowerment, enabling them to delve into their passions, make decisions, and embrace challenges. This not only fosters their academic growth but also furnishes them with indispensable life skills that extend far beyond the confines of the classroom (Dymond, 2018).

Focusing on strategies, initially, the creation of an environment that promotes inclusion and supports the diverse needs of both students and teachers is considered a particularly significant endeavor. This entails the implementation of anti-bullying policies, the provision of resources for students and teachers from different backgrounds and the promotion of a culture of respect, kindness, and appreciation among students and teachers where they feel safe and included in the school community (O'Sullivan et al., 2019; UNESCO, 2022). Furthermore, the promotion of diversity and inclusion could be realized through programs that encourage the recognition and evaluation of diversity (Reiter & Davis, 2011).

At the same time, providing opportunities for teachers to receive further training in inclusive education as well as psycho-emotional empowerment, both for themselves and their students, constitutes a second important strategy. Specifically, this involves teachers further developing their knowledge and cultivating their skills, learning to recognize and manage their emotions, enhancing interpersonal communication and creating an inclusive environment in their classrooms. This strategy includes providing access to professional development workshops, attending seminars, conferences and online courses. By investing in the development of teachers, schools can foster/shape a culture of continuous learning and improvement (Florian & Camedda, 2020; UNESCO, 2020).

Moreover, promoting and encouraging open communication and collaboration among teachers, students and parents constitutes another particularly interesting practice. This specific practice can be achieved through regular meetings between parents and teachers and other forms of engagement. Encouraging the input of all stakeholders can help strengthen/foster the sense of community and support (Sorkos & Hajisoteriou, 2021). Through the achievement of collaborative programs, the relationships between school, family and community can be strengthened (Epstein et al, 2018). Additionally, the development of a positive learning environment through the creation of peer support and collaborative groups and the promotion of positive communication and appreciation among students and teachers, is yet another practice (Nelsen et al., 2011).

Also, it should be emphasized that students empowerment is a vital aspect for their development and success in the educational journey (Dymond, 2018). In particular, empowering student voice is a particularly significant practice. This can be achieved through the creation of channels for student participation and decision-making within the school community. By establishing student councils, advisory boards, or committees where students can express their viewpoints, advocate for change, and contribute to school policies and initiatives, their voices can be amplified and their impact on the school community enhanced (Freeman, 2016; Halliday et al., 2019).

Furthermore, the promotion and implementation of positive behavior intervention strategies and restorative justice practices to address disciplinary issues in a constructive manner is considered another particularly significant strategy. Specifically, this strategy involves teaching conflict resolution skills and promoting accountability rather than punitive measures. Using restorative practices and positive discipline techniques, teachers can support students in their emotional regulation and social skills (Kehoe et al., 2018; Mas-Expósito et al., 2022).

It is worth mentioning that the development of counseling and psychological support programs for students and teachers is still considered a particularly important practice (Mahomed et al., 2019). Similarly, participation in seminars and educational programs for parents and teachers regarding the emotional health of children is considered necessary (Simion, 2021). In addition, the support of psycho-social development constitutes another one strategy. The creation of an inclusive environment that supports the development of students' psycho-social skills, promoting cooperation, conflict resolution and the exchange of opinions (Jennings & Greenberg, 2009). Moreover, training in emotional intelligence, conducting programs that strengthen emotional intelligence skills such as conflict resolution, failure management, anger management, self-awareness and communication would be cleansing (Linh, 2024).

Furthermore, the creation and implementation of well-being programs for students, teachers and school staff related to their physical, mental and emotional well-being constitute one more interesting strategy. This includes providing access to mental health resources, promoting healthy dietary habits and offering exercise programs or gym memberships. By prioritizing the well-being of students and teachers, schools can foster a culture of self-care and resilience (Abou Assali & Al Abdouli, 2024; Frazier & Doyle Fosco, 2024). Additionally, promoting self-care and self-awareness and providing education on stress and anxiety management for students and teachers are also crucial (Dye et al., 2020).

Among other things, providing teachers with the resources and support they need to promote an inclusive positive school climate within their classrooms constitutes an additional strategy. This includes encouraging the use of positive disciplinary practices, providing resources for conflict resolution and recognizing and rewarding positive behavior. By empowering teachers schools can help create a culture of positivity and support throughout the school (MacSuga-Gage et al., 2012). It should also be noted that school leaders should focus on creating and maintaining a positive school climate to support the well-being of teachers and the longevity of their careers (Bagdžiūnienė et al., 2022).

Conclusively, all the above strategies can contribute to the creation of a supportive school learning environment that promotes inclusion, well-being for all, development of emotional intelligence and empowerment of both students and teachers. Psychological-emotional empowerment entails cultivating a sense of self-efficacy and mastery over one's emotions and mental state, enabling everyone to navigate life's challenges with greater confidence and effectiveness (Xiong, 2022). By investing in the well-being of teachers, schools can improve teacher retention rates, reduce burnout and anxiety and ultimately enhance the quality of education for all students (Nwoko et al., 2023).

CONCLUSION

Implementing actions and practices that emphasize an inclusive school environment supports the social and emotional well-being of all members, providing a sustainable means for educational communities to address the interconnected goals of "Health and Education for All" (Cefai et al., 2021). The creation of a supportive school learning environment that promotes inclusion and well-being of all students is a significant goal for educational institutions. Strategies that include the psychological-emotional empowerment of both students and teachers have the potential to enhance self-confidence and effectiveness in facing life's challenges.

Additionally, investing in the well-being of teachers can have positive effects on reducing their burnout and anxiety/stress, which can impact/affect their performance, improving the quality of education for all students and retaining teachers in the profession. Therefore, creating an inclusive positive school climate is essential for promoting the well-being and performance of all involved/stakeholders in the educational environment. The implementation of specific strategies, such as psychosocial development programs and wellness initiatives/programs, can contribute to the creation of a positive school climate that enhances emotional health and the success of students.

By combining the psychological-emotional empowerment of students and teachers with investments in their well-being, schools cultivate an atmosphere of trust, respect, and support, which fosters learning and growth. This school environment, grounded in self-confidence and autonomy, provides students and teachers with the safety and support they need to develop their potential.

REFERENCES

Abou Assali, M., & Al Abdouli, K. (2024). Unleashing the power of teacher's well-being and selfcare. Research Journal in Advanced Humanities, 5(1).

Ahmed, N., & Malik, B. (2019). Impact of psychological empowerment on job performance of teachers: Mediating role of psychological well-being. *Review of Economics and Development Studies*, 5(3), 451–460. 10.26710/reads.v5i3.693

Akbarovna, A. S. (2022). Inclusive education and its essence. International journal of social science & interdisciplinary research, 11(1), 248-254.

Al-Muslimawi, I., & Hamid, A. (2019). External and internal factors affecting student's academic performance. *Soc Sci*, 14(4), 155–168. 10.36478/sscience.2019.155.168

Aldridge, J. M., & Blackstock, M. J. (2024). Assessing students' perceptions of school climate in primary schools. *Learning Environments Research*, 1–24. 10.1007/s10984-024-09492-2

Aldridge, J. M., & Fraser, B. J. (2016). Teachers' views of their school climate and its relationship with teacher self-efficacy and job satisfaction. *Learning Environments Research*, 19(2), 291–307. 10.1007/s10984-015-9198-x

Aldridge, J. M., Fraser, B. J., Fozdar, F., Ala'i, K., Earnest, J., & Afari, E. (2016). Students' Perceptions of School Climate as Determinants of Wellbeing, Resilience and Identity. *Improving Schools*, 19(1), 5–26. 10.1177/1365480215612616

Aldridge, J. M., & McChesney, K. (2018). The Relationships between School Climate and Adolescent Mental Health and Wellbeing: A Systematic Literature Review. *International Journal of Educational Research*, 88, 121–145. 10.1016/j.ijer.2018.01.012

Ali, H. H., Bashir, R., Raza, A. A., Ejaz, H., Shabir, R., & Aftab, M. J. (2024). Role of Inclusive Education in Promoting Equity in Education: Teacher's Perspectives. *Qualitative Research*, 24(1), 133–151.

Aloe, A. M., Shisler, S. M., Norris, B. D., Nickerson, A. B., & Rinker, T. W. (2014). A Multivariate Meta-analysis of Student Misbehavior and Teacher Burnout. *Educational Research Review*, 12(1), 30–44. 10.1016/j.edurev.2014.05.003

Alonso-Tapia, J., Ruiz, M. & Huertas, J. A. (2020). Differences in classroom motivational climate: Causes, effects and implications for teacher education. A multilevel study. Anales De Psicología/Annals of Psychology, 36(1), 122-133.

Archibald, S., Coggshall, J., Croft, A., & Goe, L. (2011). High-quality professional development for all teachers: Effectively allocating resources. Eric. https://eric.ed.gov/?id=ED520732

Azorín, C., & Ainscow, M. (2020). Guiding schools on their journey towards inclusion. *International Journal of Inclusive Education*, 24(1), 58–76. 10.1080/13603116.2018.1450900

Bagdžiūnienė, D., Kazlauskienė, A., Nasvytienė, D., & Sakadolskis, E. (2022). Linking supportive school leadership and teacher resilience: The mediating role of job resources. *Frontiers in Education*, 7.

Baroody, A. E., Rimm-Kaufman, S. E., Larsen, R. A., & Curby, T. W. (2014). The link between responsive classroom training and student–teacher relationship quality in the fifth grade: A study of fidelity of implementation. *School Psychology Review*, 43(1), 69–85. 10.1080/02796015.2014.12087455

Bear, G. G. (2020). *Improving school climate: Practical strategies to reduce behavior problems and promote social and emotional learning*. Routledge. 10.4324/9781351170482

Bonell, C., Parry, W., Wells, H., Jamal, F., Fletcher, A., Harden, A., Thomas, J., Campbell, R., Petticrew, M., Murphy, S., Whitehead, M., & Moore, L. (2013). The effects of the school environment on student health: A systematic review of multi-level studies. *Health & Place*, 21, 180–191. 10.1016/j.healthplace.2012.12.00123501377

Borgonovi, F., & Pál, J. (2016). A Framework for the Analysis of Student Well-Being in the PISA 2015 Study: Being 15 In 2015. OECD Education Working Papers, No. 140, OECD Publishing. 10.1787/19939019

Bradshaw, C. P., Cohen, J., Espelage, D. L., & Nation, M. (2021). Addressing school safety through comprehensive school climate approaches. *School Psychology Review*, 50(2-3), 221–236. 10.1080/2372966X.2021.1926321

Buckman, D. G., Hand, N. W., & Johnson, A. (2021). Improving high school graduation through school climate. *NASSP Bulletin*, 105(1), 5–24. 10.1177/0192636521993212

Çelik, N. D. (2018). Happiness in high school students: Autonomy, relatedness, competence and meaning in life. *Kıbrıslı Eğitim Bilimleri Dergisi*, 13(3), 422–430. 10.18844/cjes.v13i3.3561

Chan, Y. H., Nadler, S. S., & Hargis, M. B. (2015). Attitudinal and behavioral outcomes of employees' psychological empowerment: A structural equation modeling approach. Journal of Organizational Culture. *Communications and Conflict*, 19(1), 24–41.

Chiriac, E. H., Forsberg, C., & Thornberg, R. (2023). Teachers' perspectives on factors influencing the school climate: A constructivist grounded theory case study. *Cogent Education*, 10(2).

Christens, B. D., Winn, L. T., & Duke, A. M. (2016). Empowerment and critical consciousness: A conceptual cross-fertilization. *Adolescent Research Review*, 1(1), 15–27. 10.1007/s40894-015-0019-3

Cohen, J., McCabe, E. M., Michelli, N. M., & Pickeral, T. (2009). School climate: Research, policy, practice, and teacher education. *Teachers College Record*, 111(1), 180–213. 10.1177/016146810911100108

Collie, R. J. (2023). Teacher well-being and turnover intentions: Investigating the roles of job resources and job demands. *The British Journal of Educational Psychology*, 93(3), 712–726. 10.1111/bjep.1258736720462

Cook, J. W. (2019). *Sustainability, human well-being, and the future of education.* Springer Nature. 10.1007/978-3-319-78580-6

Coulter, R. W., Birkett, M., Corliss, H. L., Hatzenbuehler, M. L., Mustanski, B., & Stall, R. D. (2016). Associations between LGBTQ-affirmative school climate and adolescent drinking behaviors. *Drug and Alcohol Dependence*, 161, 340–347. 10.1016/j.drugalcdep.2016.02.02226946989

Cumming, T. M., & Rodriguez, C. D. (2018). *School success for at-risk students: A culturally responsive tiered approach.* Routledge. 10.4324/9781315101996

Daily, S. M., Mann, M. J., Kristjansson, A. L., Smith, M. L., & Zullig, K. J. (2019). School climate and academic achievement in middle and high school students. *The Journal of School Health*, 89(3), 173–180. 10.1111/josh.1272630680750

Daily, S. M., Mann, M. J., Lilly, C. L., Bias, T. K., Smith, M. L., & Kristjansson, A. L. (2020). School climate as a universal intervention to prevent substance use initiation in early adolescence: A longitudinal study. *Health Education & Behavior*, 47(3), 402–411. 10.1177/109019812091425032281413

Darling-Hammond, L., & Cook-Harvey, C. M. (2018). Educating the Whole Child: Improving School Climate to Support Student Success. Learning Policy Institute. https://files.eric.ed.gov/fulltext/ED606462.pdf

Dearing, J. (2020). The Effect of School Climate on Teacher Burnout, Perceived Health and Wellbeing (Publication No. 28258625) [Doctoral Dissertation, Oklahoma State University]. ProQuest Dissertations and Theses Global.

Debarbieux, E., Anton, N., Astor, R. A., Benbenishty, R., Bisson-Vaivre, C., Cohen, J., Giordan, A., Hugonnier, B., Neulat, N., Ortega Ruiz, R., Saltet, J., Veltcheff, C., & Vrand, R. (2012). Le «Climat scolaire»: définition, effets et conditions d'amélioration. Prisme-asso.https://www.prisme-asso.org/wp-content/uploads/save/pdf/climat-scolaire2012.pdf

Demirtas-Zorbaz, S., Akin-Arikan, C., & Terzi, R. (2021). Does school climate that includes students' views deliver academic achievement? A multilevel meta-analysis. *School Effectiveness and School Improvement*, 32(4), 543–563. 10.1080/09243453.2021.1920432

Dernowska, U. (2017). Teacher and student perceptions of school climate. Some conclusions from school culture and climate research. Journal of Modern science, 32(1), 63-82.

DeWitt, P., & Slade, S. (2014). *School Climate Change: How do I build a positive environment for learning? (ASCD Arias)*. ASCD.

DeWitt, P. M. (2017). *School climate: Leading with collective efficacy*. Corwin Press.

Dreer, B. (2022). Teacher well-being: Investigating the contributions of school climate and job crafting. *Cogent Education*, 9(1), 2044583. 10.1080/2331186X.2022.2044583

Dye, L., Burke, M. G., & Wolf, C. (2020). Teaching mindfulness for the self-care and well-being of counselors-in-training. *Journal of Creativity in Mental Health*, 15(2), 140–153. 10.1080/15401383.2019.1642171

Dymond, D. S. (2018). Promoting student empowerment through autonomy supportive practices: Examining the Influence of professional development for primary grade teachers. (Publication No. 10814745) [Doctoral Dissertation, University of Missouri-Saint Louis]. ProQuest Dissertations and Theses Global.

Elrod, B. G., Rice, K. G., & Meyers, J. (2022). PBIS fidelity, school climate, and student discipline: A longitudinal study of secondary schools. *Psychology in the Schools*, 59(2), 376–397. 10.1002/pits.22614

Engelbrecht, P., Savolainen, H., Nel, M., Koskela, T., & Okkolin, M. A. (2017). Making Meaning of Inclusive Education: Classroom Practices in Finnish and South African Classrooms. *Compare: A Journal of Comparative Education*, 47(5), 684–702. 10.1080/03057925.2016.1266927

Epstein, J. L., Sanders, M. G., Sheldon, S. B., Simon, B. S., Salinas, K. C., Jansorn, N. R., Van Voorhis, F. L., Martin, C. S., Thomas, B. G., Greenfeld, M. D., Hutchins, D. J., & Williams, K. J. (2018). *School, family, and community partnerships: Your handbook for action*. Corwin Press.

Espelage, D. L., Polanin, J. R., & Low, S. K. (2014). Teacher and staff perceptions of school environment as predictors of student aggression, victimization, and willingness to intervene in bullying situations. *School Psychology Quarterly*, 29(3), 287–305. 10.1037/spq000007225089334

Fan, W., Williams, C. M., & Corkin, D. M. (2011). A multilevel analysis of student perceptions of school climate: The effect of social and academic risk factors. *Psychology in the Schools*, 48(6), 632–647. 10.1002/pits.20579

Fang, J., & Qi, Z. (2023). The influence of school climate on teachers' job satisfaction: The mediating role of teachers' self-efficacy. *PLoS One*, 18(10), e0287555. 10.1371/journal.pone.028755537796911

Farina, K. A. (2019). Promoting a culture of bullying: Understanding the role of school climate and school sector. *Journal of School Choice*, 13(1), 94–120. 10.1080/15582159.2018.1526615

Fatou, N., & Kubiszewski, V. (2018). Are perceived school climate dimensions predictive of students' engagement? *Social Psychology of Education*, 21(2), 427–446. 10.1007/s11218-017-9422-x

Florian, L., & Camedda, D. (2020). Enhancing teacher education for inclusion. *European Journal of Teacher Education*, 43(1), 4–8. 10.1080/02619768.2020.1707579

Flowers, A. A., Jr. (2019). The Impact of Declining Teacher Retention on a School System. Eric. https://eric.ed.gov/?id=ED601980

Forsberg, C., Chiriac, E. H., & Thornberg, R. (2021). Exploring pupils' perspectives on school climate. *Educational Research*, 63(4), 379–395. 10.1080/00131881.2021.1956988

Forslund Frykedal, K., & Hammar Chiriac, E. (2018). Student collaboration in group work: Inclusion as participation. *International Journal of Disability Development and Education*, 65(2), 183–198. 10.1080/1034912X.2017.1363381

Franco, K., Baumler, E., Torres, E. D., Lu, Y., Wood, L., & Temple, J. R. (2022). The link between school climate and mental health among an ethnically diverse sample of middle school youth. *Current Psychology (New Brunswick, N.J.)*, 42(22), 18488–18498. 10.1007/s12144-022-03016-y35370383

Frazier, T., & Doyle Fosco, S. L. (2024). Nurturing positive mental health and wellbeing in educational settings–the PRICES model. *Frontiers in Public Health*, 11, 11. 10.3389/fpubh.2023.128753238312141

Freeman, R. (2016). Is student voice necessarily empowering? Problematisingstudent voice as a form of higher education governance. *Higher Education Research & Development*, 35(4), 859–862. 10.1080/07294360.2016.1172764

Freiberg, H. J. (2005). *School climate: Measuring, improving and sustaining healthy learning environments*. Routledge. 10.4324/9780203983980

Freiberg, H. J., & Stein, T. A. (1999). Measuring, improving and sustaining healthy learning environments. In Freiberg, H. J. (Ed.), *School climate: Measuring, improving and sustaining healthy learning environments* (pp. 11–29). Falmer Press.

Garzia, V., & Molinari, L. (2021). School climate multidimensionality and measurement: A Systematic literature review. *Research Papers in Education*, 36(5), 561–587. 10.1080/02671522.2019.1697735

Gase, L. N., Gomez, L. M., Kuo, T., Glenn, B. A., Inkelas, M., & Ponce, N. A. (2017). Relationships among student, staff, and administrative measures of school climate and student health and academic outcomes. *The Journal of School Health*, 87(5), 319–328. 10.1111/josh.1250128382671

Goldenberg, J., & Klavir, R. (2017). School Climate, Classroom Climate, and Teaching Quality: Can Excellent Students Unravel This Connection? *International Journal for Talent Development and Creativity*, 5(1-2), 137–148.

Gray, C., Wilcox, G., & Nordstokke, D. (2017). Teacher mental health, school climate, inclusive education and student learning: A review. *Canadian Psychology*, 58(3), 203–210. 10.1037/cap0000117

Grayson, J. L., & Alvarez, H. K. (2008). School climate factors relating to teacher-burnout: A mediator model. *Teaching and Teacher Education*, 24(5), 1349–1363. 10.1016/j.tate.2007.06.005

Guðjónsdóttir, H., & Karlsdóttir, J. (2009). Látum þúsund blóm blómstra. Uppeldi og menntun, 18(1), 61-77.

Guðjónsdóttir, H., & Óskarsdóttir, E. (2016). Inclusive education, pedagogy and practice. In Markic, S., & Abels, S. (Eds.), *Science education towards inclusion* (pp. 7–22). Nova Science Publishers.

Guo, P., Choe, J., & Higgins-D'Alessandro, A. (2011). Report of construct validity and internal consistency findings for the comprehensive school climate inventory. Unpublished manuscript Fordham University, Bronx, NY.

Halliday, A. J., Kern, M. L., Garrett, D. K., & Turnbull, D. A. (2019). The student voice in well-being: A case study of participatory action research in positive education. *Educational Action Research*, 27(2), 173–196. 10.1080/09650792.2018.1436079

Hanuliaková, J., & Barnová, S. (2015). Positive school climate (A theoretical empirical conspectus). *Acta Educationis Generalis*, 5(1), 68–73.

Holt, M. K., Vivolo-Kantor, A. M., Polanin, J. R., Holland, K. M., DeGue, S., Matjasko, J. L., Wolfe, M., & Reid, G. (2015). Bullying and suicidal ideation and behaviors: A Meta-Analysis. *Pediatrics*, 135(2), 496–509. 10.1542/peds.2014-186425560447

Hosford, S., & O'Sullivan, S. (2016). A climate for self-efficacy: The relationship between school climate and teacher efficacy for inclusion. *International Journal of Inclusive Education*, 20(6), 604–621. 10.1080/13603116.2015.1102339

Hoy, W. K., Hannum, J., & Tschannen-Moran, M. (1998). Organizational climate and student achievement: A parsimonious and longitudinal view. *Journal of School Leadership*, 8(4), 336–359. 10.1177/105268469800800401

Hoy, W. K., & Sweetland, S. R. (2001). Designing better schools: The meaning and measure of enabling school structures. *Educational Administration Quarterly*, 37(3), 296–321. 10.1177/00131610121969334

Ingersoll, R. M., & Strong, M. (2011). The impact of induction and mentoring programs for beginning teachers: A critical review of the research. *Review of Educational Research*, 81(2), 201–233. 10.3102/0034654311403323

Jackson, C. K., & Bruegmann, E. (2009). Teaching students and teaching each other: The importance of peer learning for teachers. *American Economic Journal. Applied Economics*, 1(4), 85–108. 10.1257/app.1.4.85

Jacobson, D. A. (2016). Causes and effects of teacher burnout. (Publication No. 10162782) [Doctoral Dissertation, Walden University]. ProQuest Dissertations and Theses Global.

Jennings, P. A., & Greenberg, M. T. (2009). The prosocial classroom: Teacher social and emotional competence in relation to student and classroom outcomes. *Review of Educational Research*, 79(1), 491–525. 10.3102/0034654308325693

Jones, J. S. (2012). The external and internal educational factors that contribute to student achievement and self-perceptions of urban middle school Title I students [Doctoral Dissertation, Rowan University]. Rowan Digital Works. https://rdw.rowan.edu/etd/240/

Jones, T. M., Fleming, C., & Williford, A. (2020). Racial equity in academic success: The role of school climate and social emotional learning. *Children and Youth Services Review*, 119, 119. 10.1016/j.childyouth.2020.10562333311826

Katsantonis, I. G. (2019). Investigation of the impact of school climate and teachers' self-efficacy on job satisfaction: A cross-cultural approach. *European Journal of Investigation in Health, Psychology and Education*, 10(1), 119–133. 10.3390/ejihpe1001001134542474

Kefallinou, A., Symeonidou, S., & Meijer, C. J. (2020). Understanding the value of inclusive education and its implementation: A review of the literature. *Prospects*, 49(3), 135–152. 10.1007/s11125-020-09500-2

Kehoe, M., Bourke-Taylor, H., & Broderick, D. (2018). Developing student social skills using restorative practices: A new framework called HEART. *Social Psychology of Education*, 21(1), 189–207. 10.1007/s11218-017-9402-1

Kentucky Department of Education. (2022). School Climate and Educator Well-Being in Kentucky. Retrieved May 22, 2024 from https://files.eric.ed.gov/fulltext/ED618565.pdf

Khany, R., & Tazik, K. (2016). On the relationship between psychological empowerment, trust, and Iranian EFL teachers' job satisfaction: The case of secondary school teachers. *Journal of Career Assessment*, 24(1), 112–129. 10.1177/1069072714565362

Kidger, J., Araya, R., Donovan, J., & Gunnell, D. (2012). The effect of the school environment on the emotional health of adolescents: A systematic review. *Pediatrics*, 129(5), 925–949. 10.1542/peds.2011-224822473374

Kielblock, S., & Woodcock, S. (2023). Who's included and Who's not? An analysis of instruments that measure teachers' attitudes towards inclusive education. *Teaching and Teacher Education*, 122(2), 103922. 10.1016/j.tate.2022.103922

Knight, C., & Crick, T. (2022). Inclusive Education in Wales: Interpreting discourses of values and practice using critical policy analysis. *ECNU Review of Education*, 5(2), 258–283. 10.1177/20965311211039858

Knight, D. S., & Duncheon, J. C. (2019). Broadening conceptions of a "college-going culture": The role of high school climate factors in college enrollment and persistence. *Policy Futures in Education*, 18(2), 314–340. 10.1177/1478210319860987

Kõiv, K., Liik, K., & Heidmets, M. (2019). School leadership, teacher's psychological empowerment and work-related outcomes. *International Journal of Educational Management*, 33(7), 1501–1514. 10.1108/IJEM-08-2018-0232

Konold, T., Cornell, D., Jia, Y., & Malone, M. (2018). School climate, student engagement, and academic achievement: A latent variable, multilevel multi-informant examination. *AERA Open*, 4(4). 10.1177/2332858418815661

Koziori, K. B., & Alexandropoulos, G. (2020). The impact of the school climate on professional satisfaction of primary education teachers. *Research in Education*, 9(1), 35–57.

Kraft, M. A., & Falken, G. T. (2020). Why School Climate Matters for Teachers and Students. *State Education Standard*, 20(2), 33–35.

Kundu, S. C., & Kumar, S. (2017). Effects of psychological empowerment on firm's performance: Mediation of affective commitment. *Journal of Organisation and Human Behaviour*, 6(1-2), 41–53.

Kutsyuruba, B., Klinger, D. A., & Hussain, A. (2015). Relationships among school climate, school safety, and student achievement and well-being: A review of the literature. *Review of Education*, 3(2), 103–135. 10.1002/rev3.3043

La Salle, T. P., Rocha-Neves, J., Jimerson, S., Di Sano, S., Martinsone, B., Majercakova Albertova, S., Gajdošová, E., Baye, A., Deltour, C., Martinelli, V., Raykov, M., Hatzichristou, C., Palikara, O., Szabó, É., Arlauskaite, Z., Athanasiou, D., Brown-Earle, O., Casale, G., Lampropoulou, A., & Zvyagintsev, R. (2021). A multinational study exploring adolescent perception of school climate and mental health. *School Psychology*, 36(3), 155–166. 10.1037/spq000043034014698

La Velle, L. (2020). Teacher education approaching crisis: External and internal factors. *Journal of Education for Teaching*, 46(3), 259–262. 10.1080/02607476.2020.1768692

Laininen, E. (2019). Transforming our worldview towards a sustainable future. In J. Cook (Ed.), Sustainability, human well-being, and the future of education (pp.161-200). Palgrave Macmillan. 10.1007/978-3-319-78580-6_5

LaRusso, M., & Selman, R. (2011). Early adolescent health risk behaviors, conflict resolution strategies, and school climate. *Journal of Applied Developmental Psychology*, 32(6), 354–362. 10.1016/j.appdev.2011.05.003

Lee, M., & Louis, K. S. (2019). Mapping a strong school culture and linking it to sustainable school improvement. *Teaching and Teacher Education*, 81, 84–96. 10.1016/j.tate.2019.02.001

Lester, L., & Cross, D. (2015). The relationship between school climate and mental and emotional wellbeing over the transition from primary to secondary school. *Psychology of Well-Being*, 5(9), 1–15. 10.1186/s13612-015-0037-826516619

Li, Z. (2016). Psychological empowerment on social media: Who are the empowered users? *Public Relations Review*, 42(1), 49–59. 10.1016/j.pubrev.2015.09.001

Linh, N. T. N. (2024). Strategies for developing emotional intelligence in Generation Z students in higher education in Ho Chi Minh City. *Educational Administration: Theory and Practice*, 30(5), 2517–2522.

Lombardi, E., Traficante, D., Bettoni, R., Offredi, I., Giorgetti, M., & Vernice, M. (2019). The impact of school climate on well-being experience and school engagement: A study with high-school students. *Frontiers in Psychology*, 10, 10. 10.3389/fpsyg.2019.0248231749747

MacSuga-Gage, A. S., Simonsen, B., & Briere, D. E. (2012). Effective teaching practices: Effective teaching practices that promote a positive classroom environment. *Beyond Behavior*, 22(1), 14–22. 10.1177/107429561202200104

Mahomed, N. J. B., Johari, K. S. K., & Mahmud, M. I. (2019). Coping strategies and psychological well-being of guidance and counselling teachers in schools. *Creative Education*, 10(12), 3028–3040. 10.4236/ce.2019.1012227

Malinen, O. P., & Savolainen, H. (2016). The Effect of Perceived School Climate and Teacher Efficacy in Behavior Management on Job Satisfaction and Burnout: A Longitudinal Study. *Teaching and Teacher Education*, 60(1), 144–152. 10.1016/j.tate.2016.08.012

Manla, V. H. (2021). School climate: Its impact on teachers' commitment and school performance. *Journal of World Englishes and Educational Practices*, 3(2), 21–35. 10.32996/jweep.2021.3.2.3

Mann, M. J., Kristjansson, A. L., Smith, M. L., & Sigfusdottir, I. D. (2016). The Influence of negative life events and problem behavior on grades in early adolescence: Pathways to academic risk in the middle grades. *RMLE Online: Research in Middle Level Education*, 39(10), 1–13. 10.1080/19404476.2016.1244402

Mariani, M., Webb, L., Villares, E., & Brigman, G. (2015). Effect of Participation in Student Success Skills on Prosocial and Bullying Behavior. *The Professional Counselor*, 5(3), 341–353. 10.15241/mm.5.3.341

Marinette, B., & Hui, X. (2021). School environment and teachers job satisfaction. *European Journal of Education Studies*, 8(7), 16–43.

Mas-Expósito, L., Krieger, V., Amador-Campos, J. A., Casañas, R., & Lalucat-Jo, L. (2022). Pocket restorative practice approaches to foster peer-based relationships and positive development in schools. *Education Sciences*, 12(12), 880. 10.3390/educsci12120880

Mattison, E., & Aber, M. S. (2007). Closing the achievement gap: The association of racial climate with achievement and behavioral outcomes. *American Journal of Community Psychology*, 40(1-2), 1–12. 10.1007/s10464-007-9128-x17587175

Maxwell, S., Reynolds, K. J., Lee, E., Subasic, E., & Bromhead, D. (2017). The impact of school climate and school identification on academic achievement: Multilevel modeling with student and teacher data. *Frontiers in Psychology*, 8, 8. 10.3389/fpsyg.2017.0206929259564

McGiboney, G. W. (2023). *The psychology of school climate*. Cambridge Scholars Publishing.

McInerney, D. M., Ganotice, F. A.Jr, King, R. B., Marsh, H. W., & Morin, A. J. (2015). Exploring commitment and turnover intentions among teachers: What we can learn from Hong Kong teachers. *Teaching and Teacher Education*, 52, 11–23. 10.1016/j.tate.2015.08.004

Messiou, K. (2017). Research in the field of inclusive education: Time for a rethink? *International Journal of Inclusive Education*, 21(2), 146–159. 10.1080/13603116.2016.1223184

Milam, L., Butler, A. J., & Vanderhaar, J. (2022). School Climate and Emotional Wellbeing. OSF. https://osf.io/dcgax

Mor Barak, M. E., Luria, G., & Brimhall, K. C. (2022). What leaders say versus what they do: Inclusive leadership, policy-practice decoupling, and the anomaly of climate for inclusion. *Group & Organization Management*, 47(4), 840–871. 10.1177/10596011211005916

Mostafa, T., & Pál, J. (2018). Science Teachers' Satisfaction: Evidence from the PISA 2015 Teacher Survey. In *OECD Education Working Papers, No. 168*. OECD Publishing. https://www.oecd-ilibrary.org/education/science-teachers-satisfaction_1ecdb4e3-

Mousena, E., & Raptis, N. (2020). Beyond teaching: School climate and communication in the educational context. In Waller, S., Waller, L., Mpofu, V., & Kurebwa, M. (Eds.), *Education at the Intersection of Globalization and Technology* (pp. 153–170). IntechOpen.

Muhati-Nyakundi, L. I. (2023). Teachers' Agency and Wellbeing in Inclusive Education: Challenges and Opportunities. *Journal of Educational Studies*, 2023(si1), 365–379. 10.59915/jes.2023.special.1.19

National School Climate Center. (2023). The 14 Dimensions of School Climate Measured by the CSCI. Retrieved May 20, 2024 from https://schoolclimate.org/wp-content/uploads/2022/01/CSCI-14-Dimensions-Chart.pdf

Nelsen, J., Lott, L., & Glenn, H. S. (2011). Positive Discipline in the Classroom, *Revised 3rd Edition: Developing Mutual Respect, Cooperation, and Responsibility in Your Classroom*. Three Rivers Press.

Niehaus, K., Rudasill, K. M., & Rakes, C. R. (2012). A longitudinal study of school connectedness and academic outcomes across sixth grade. *Journal of School Psychology*, 50(4), 443–460. 10.1016/j.jsp.2012.03.00222710015

NSCC-National School Climate Council. (2021). What Is School Climate and Why Is It Important? Retrieved May 20, 2024 from https://schoolclimate.org/school-climate/

Nwoko, J. C., Emeto, T. I., Malau-Aduli, A. E., & Malau-Aduli, B. S. (2023). A systematic review of the factors that influence teachers' occupational wellbeing. *International Journal of Environmental Research and Public Health*, 20(12), 6070. 10.3390/ijerph2012607037372657

O'Sullivan, C., Ryan, S., O'Sullivan, L., Masterson, M., Murphy, T., Twomey, K., Brennan, S., Kearney, L., O'Sullivan, M., & Corry, J. (2019). Teacher well-being and diversity: a manual for teachers in diverse educational settings. University of Limerick. https://hdl.handle.net/10344/9327

OECD. (2019). PISA 2018 Results (Volume III): What School Life Means for Students' Lives A framework for the analysis of school climate and students well-being. OECD Publishing. https://www.oecd-ilibrary.org/education/pisa-2018-results-volume-iii_3b42acd8-en

Ortan, F., Simut, C., & Simut, R. (2021). Self-efficacy, job satisfaction and teacher well-being in the K-12 educational system. *International Journal of Environmental Research and Public Health*, 18(23), 12763. 10.3390/ijerph18231276334886493

Ortega, R., Sanchez, V., & Ortega Rivera Viejo, C. (2011). La violencia sexual en las relaciones interpersonales de adolescents. In Lameiras, M., & Iglesias, I. (Eds.), *Violencia de género:la violencia sexual a debate* (pp. 99–126). Tirant Lo Blanch.

Pandia, W. S. S., & Purwanti, M. (2019). Teachers' perceptions of school climate in inclusive schools. Psikohumaniora. *Jurnal Penelitian Psikologi*, 4(1), 27–42. 10.21580/pjpp.v4i1.3357

Panesi, S., Bocconi, S., & Ferlino, L. (2020). Promoting students' well-being and inclusion in schools through digital technologies: Perceptions of students, teachers, and school leaders in Italy expressed through SELFIE piloting activities. *Frontiers in Psychology*, 11, 11. 10.3389/fpsyg.2020.0156332848988

Papay, J. P., & Kraft, M. A. (2017). Developing workplaces where teachers stay, improve, and succeed. In Quintero, E. (Ed.), *Teaching in context: How social aspects of school and school systems shape teachers' development & effectiveness* (pp. 15–35). Harvard Education Press.

Peterson, A. J., Allen, E., Viner, R., & Bonell, C. (2020). Effects of the school environment on early sexual risk behavior: A longitudinal analysis of students in English secondary schools. *Journal of Adolescence*, 85(9), 106–114. 10.1016/j.adolescence.2020.10.00433130414

Petrou, A., Angelides, P., & Leigh, J. (2009). Beyond the difference: From the margins to inclusion. *International Journal of Inclusive Education*, 13(5), 439–448. 10.1080/13603110701776024

Pinkus, L. M. (2009). Moving beyond AYP: High school performance indicators. Alliance for Excellent Education. Eric. https://eric.ed.gov/?id=ED506873

Ramelow, D., Currie, D., & Felder-Puig, R. (2015). The assessment of school climate: Review and appraisal of published student-report measures. *Journal of Psychoeducational Assessment*, 33(8), 731–743. 10.1177/0734282915584852

Reaves, S., McMahon, S. D., Duffy, S. N., & Ruiz, L. (2018). The test of time: A meta-analytic review of the relation between school climate and problem behavior. *Aggression and Violent Behavior*, 39(3), 100–108. 10.1016/j.avb.2018.01.006

Reiter, A. B., & Davis, S. N. (2011). Factors Influencing Pre-Service Teachers' Beliefs about Student Achievement: Evaluation of a Pre-Service Teacher Diversity Awareness Program. *Multicultural Education*, 19(3), 41–46.

Rudasill, K. M., Snyder, K. E., Levinson, H., & Adelson, J. (2018). Systems view of school climate: A theoretical framework for research. *Educational Psychology Review*, 30(1), 35–60. 10.1007/s10648-017-9401-y

Sadeghi, K., & Esmaeili, F. (2022). English teachers' perception of school climate and effective teaching. *Interdisciplinary Studies in English Language Teaching*, 1(1), 1–21.

Santhosh, J. S., & Flower, F. L. L. (2023). School Climate and its Determinant Factors of Well-Being in a Residential School Community. *Indian Journal of Social Psychiatry*, 39(2), 147–152. 10.4103/ijsp.ijsp_11_21

Shahriari Shaghaghi, Z., Ghanbaripanah, A., & Tajalli, P. (2021). The Role of Affective Family Atmosphere, School Atmosphere and Perceived Social Support in Predicting Aggressive Behavior and Addiction Readiness among Students. *International Journal of Behavioral Sciences*, 15(1), 20–26.

Shirley, E. L., & Cornell, D. G. (2012). The contribution of student perceptions of school climate to understanding the disproportionate punishment of African American students in a middle school. *School Psychology International*, 33(2), 115–134. 10.1177/0143034311406815

Simion, A. (2021). Children's Emotional Health In The Context Of E-Learning. Parents' And Teachers' Perspective. In I. Albulescu & C. Stan (Eds.), Education, Reflection, Development -ERD 2021, vol.2 European Proceedings of Educational Sciences (pp. 204-214). European Publisher. 10.15405/epes.22032.20

Singh, K., & Kaur, S. (2019). Psychological empowerment of teachers: Development and validation of multi-dimensional scale. *International Journal of Recent Technology and Engineering*, 7(655), 340–347.

Skaalvik, E. M., & Skaalvik, S. (2011). Teacher job satisfaction and motivation to leave the teaching profession: Relations with school context, feeling of belonging, and emotional exhaustion. *Teaching and Teacher Education*, 27(6), 1029–1038. 10.1016/j.tate.2011.04.001

Slee, R. (2018). *Inclusive education isn't dead, it just smells funny*. Routledge. 10.4324/9780429486869

Sorkos, G., & Hajisoteriou, C. (2021). Sustainable intercultural and inclusive education: Teachers' efforts on promoting a combining paradigm. *Pedagogy, Culture & Society*, 29(4), 517–536. 10.1080/14681366.2020.1765193

Spektor-Levy, O., & Yifrach, M. (2019). If science teachers are positively inclined toward inclusive education, why is it so difficult? *Research in Science Education*, 49(3), 737–766. 10.1007/s11165-017-9636-0

Stasinós, D. (2016). Towards Inclusive or Total Education in the New-Digital School with Digital Champions. Papazisis publications.

Stronge, J. H., Ward, T. J., & Grant, L. W. (2011). What makes good teachers good? A cross-case analysis of the connection between teacher effectiveness and student achievement. *Journal of Teacher Education*, 62(4), 339–355. 10.1177/0022487111404241

Suldo, S. M., McMahan, M. M., Chappel, A. M., & Loker, T. (2012). Relationships between perceived school climate and adolescent mental health across genders. School Mental Health: A Multidisciplinary Research and Practice Journal, 4(2), 69-80.

Tafuri, F., & Latino, F. (2024). School medical service: Strategies to promote psycho-physiological well-being. *Pediatric Reports*, 16(1), 214–231. 10.3390/pediatric1601001938535515

Thapa, A., Cohen, J., Guffey, S., & Higgins-D'Alessandro, A. (2013). A review of school climate research. *Review of Educational Research*, 83(3), 357–385. 10.3102/0034654313483907

Tonegawa, Y. (2022). Contextualization of inclusive education: Education for children with disabilities in Myanmar. *International Journal of Instruction*, 15(1), 365–380. 10.29333/iji.2022.15121a

Triviño-Amigo, N., Mendoza-Muñoz, D. M., Mayordomo-Pinilla, N., Barrios-Fernández, S., Contreras-Barraza, N., Gil-Marín, M., Castilio, D., Gallan-Arroyo, C., & Rojo-Ramos, J. (2022). Inclusive education in primary and secondary school: Perception of teacher training. *International Journal of Environmental Research and Public Health*, 19(23), 15451. 10.3390/ijerph19231545136497523

Turner, I., Reynolds, K. J., Lee, E., Subasic, E., & Bromhead, D. (2014). Well-being, school climate, and the social identity process: A latent growth model study of bullying perpetration and peer victimization. *School Psychology Quarterly*, 29(3), 320–335. 10.1037/spq000007424933217

Ullman, J. (2022). Trans/gender-diverse students' perceptions of positive school climate and teacher concern as factors in school belonging: Results from an Australian National Study. *Teachers College Record*, 124(8), 145–167. 10.1177/01614681221121710

United Nations. (1966). International covenant on economic, social and cultural rights. Retrieved May 20, 2024 from https://www.ohchr.org/en/instruments-mechanisms/instruments/international-covenant-economic-social-and-cultural-rights

United Nations Educational Scientific and Cultural Organization, Institute for Lifelong Learning. (1994). The Salamanca Statement and Framework for Action on Special Needs Education. https://unesdoc.unesco.org/images/0009/000984/098427eo.pdf

United Nations Educational Scientific and Cultural Organization, Institute for Lifelong Learning. (2020). Inclusive teaching: preparing all teachers to teach all students. https://unesdoc.unesco.org/ark:/48223/pf0000374447

United Nations Educational Scientific and Cultural Organization, Institute for Lifelong Learning. (2021). Reimagining our futures together: A new social contract for education. https://unesdoc.unesco.org/ark:/48223/pf0000379707

United Nations Educational Scientific and Cultural Organization, Institute for Lifelong Learning. (2022). Welcoming Diversity in the Learning Environment. Teacher's Handbook for Inclusive Education. https://www.minedu.gov.gr/publications/docs2023/eidiki-agogi/C.%20Welcoming%20Diversity%20.pdf

U.S. Department of Education. (2023). Guiding Principles for Creating Safe, Inclusive, Supportive, and Fair School Climates. Retrieved May 20, 2024 from https://www2.ed.gov/policy/gen/guid/school-discipline/guiding-principles.pdf

Van Beurden, J., Van Veldhoven, M., Nijendijk, K., & Van De Voorde, K. (2017). Teachers' remaining career opportunities: The role of value fit and school climate. *Teaching and Teacher Education*, 68(1), 143–150. 10.1016/j.tate.2017.09.002

Van Eck, K., Johnson, S. R., Bettencourt, A., & Johnson, S. L. (2017). How school climate relates to chronic absence: A multi–level latent profile analysis. *Journal of School Psychology*, 61, 89–102. 10.1016/j.jsp.2016.10.00128259246

Veldman, I., Van Tartwijk, J., Brekelmans, M., & Wubbels, T. (2013). Job satisfaction and teacher–student relationships across the teaching career: Four case studies. *Teaching and Teacher Education*, 32, 55–65. 10.1016/j.tate.2013.01.005

Viac, C., & Fraser, P. (2020). Teachers' well-being: A framework for data collection and analysis. OECD Education Working Paper No. 213. OECD Publishing. 10.1787/19939019

Virtanen, M., Kivimäki, M., Luopa, P., Vahtera, J., Elovainio, M., Jokela, J., & Pietikäinen, M. (2009). Staff reports of psychosocial climate at school and adolescents' health, truancy and health education in Finland. *European Journal of Public Health*, 19(5), 554–560. 10.1093/eurpub/ckp03219321716

Volk, D. T. (2020). An Examination of the Relationship Between School Climate, Self-Determined Academic Motivation, and Academic Outcomes Among Middle and High School Students [Doctoral Dissertation, University of Connecticut]. UCONN. https://opencommons.uconn.edu/dissertations/2435

Wächter, T., Gorges, J., Apresjan, S., & Lütje-Klose, B. (2024). How can inclusion succeed for all? Children's well-being in inclusive schools and the role of teachers' inclusion-related attitudes and self-efficacy. *Teaching and Teacher Education*, 139, 139. 10.1016/j.tate.2023.104411

Walls, J., Ryu, J., Fairchild, L., & Johnson, J. (2021). Contexts of belonging: Toward a multilevel understanding of caring and engagement in schools. *Educational Policy*, 35(5), 748–780. 10.1177/0895904819843590

Wang, M. T., & Degol, J. L. (2016). School climate: A review of the construct, measurement, and impact on student outcomes. *Educational Psychology Review*, 28(2), 315–352. 10.1007/s10648-015-9319-1

Wang, M. T., Degol, J. L., Amemiya, J., Parr, A., & Guo, J. (2020). Classroom climate and children's academic and psychological wellbeing: A systematic review and meta-analysis. *Developmental Review*, •••, 57. 10.1016/j.dr.2020.100912

Wang, M. T., & Fredricks, J. A. (2014). The reciprocal links between school engagement, youth problem behaviors, and school dropout during adolescence. *Child Development*, 85(2), 722–737. 10.1111/cdev.1213823895361

Wang, M. T., & Huguley, J. P. (2012). Parental racial socialization as a moderator of the effects of racial discrimination on educational success among African American adolescents. *Child Development*, 83(5), 1716–1731. 10.1111/j.1467-8624.2012.01808.x22717004

Wong, M. D., Dosanjh, K. K., Jackson, N. J., Rünger, D., & Dudovitz, R. N. (2021). The longitudinal relationship of school climate with adolescent social and emotional health. *BMC Public Health*, 21(207), 1–8. 10.1186/s12889-021-10245-633485308

World Health Organization. (2013). Mental health action plan 2013–2020. https://www.who.int/publications/i/item/9789241506021

Xiong, X. (2022). The role of EFL/ESL teachers' psychological empowerment and optimism on their job commitment. *Frontiers in Psychology*, 13, 13. 10.3389/fpsyg.2022.94136135814068

Yang, C., Chan, M. K., Nickerson, A. B., Jenkins, L., Xie, J. S., & Fredrick, S. S. (2022). Teacher victimization and teachers' subjective well-being: Does school climate matter? *Aggressive Behavior*, 48(4), 379–392. 10.1002/ab.2203035383978

Zacarian, D., & Silverstone, M. (2020). *Teaching to empower: Taking action to foster student agency, self-confidence, and collaboration*. ASCD.

Zakariya, Y. F. (2020). Effects of school climate and teacher self-efficacy on job satisfaction of mostly STEM teachers: A structural multigroup invariance approach. *International Journal of STEM Education*, 7(10), 1–12. 10.1186/s40594-020-00209-4

Zhang, L. J., Fathi, J., & Mohammaddokht, F. (2023). Predicting teaching enjoyment from teachers' perceived school climate, self-efficacy, and psychological wellbeing at work: EFL teachers. *Perceptual and Motor Skills*, 130(5), 2269–2299. 10.1177/0031512523118226937395156

Žic Ralić, A. (2023). Differences in Emotional Well-Being, Social Inclusion and Academic Self-Concept Between Students With and Without Disabilities in Bosnia and Herzegovina. HSS. https://hss.ruh.ac.lk/ruichss/ruichss2023/

Zullig, K. J., Koopman, T. M., Patton, J. M., & Ubbes, V. A. (2010). School climate: Historical review, instrument development, and school assessment. *Journal of Psychoeducational Assessment*, 28(2), 139–152. 10.1177/0734282909344205

Zysberg, L., & Schwabsky, N. (2021). School climate, academic self-efficacy and student achievement. *Educational Psychology*, 41(4), 467–482. 10.1080/01443410.2020.1813690

Chapter 8 Building Mental Resilience in Children: The Role of Teachers and the Whole-School Setting

Maria Zafiropoulou
https://orcid.org/0009-0009-3930-999X
Thessaly University, Greece

Agoritsa Psilou
https://orcid.org/0000-0002-0811-7671
Frederick University, Cyprus

ABSTRACT

Literature reports that schools are the appropriate settings to organize and apply activities to promote children's and young people's resilience. Mental resilience is the ability an individual has to cope and succeed in dealing with challenges, misfortune, and adversities. Mental resilience in children is distinguished when they manage to exhibit developmental evolution and positive mental health despite the fact that they are "at risk". Important attributes of resilience in children and young people are enhanced by the whole-school approach and the teachers' work on developing certain skills. The whole school approach consists of a positive school environment, where self-qualities are developed and intervention programs for mental health wellness are delivered. Teachers use a) organizational features such as a sense of optimism, purpose, and school pride and the establishment of effective school-community partnership; b) relational features such as the creation of a supportive and understanding learning environment, the fostering of a positive teacher-student relationship, support school-home relationships, and enhancement of positive peer relationships; c) pedagogical features such as using a well-organised

DOI: 10.4018/979-8-3693-8312-4.ch008

Copyright © 2024, IGI Global. Copying or distributing in print or electronic forms without written permission of IGI Global is prohibited.

curriculum, applying extra-curriculum activities, and offering information, awareness raising, and advocacy to stimulate children's mental resilience.

INTRODUCTION

Up to a third of children's time is spent at school, which makes this time an extremely significant period for their cognitive, emotional and social development (Olsson, Bond, Burns, Vella-Brodrick, & Sawyer, 2003). Thus, experiences acquired during school years can affect both life chances and students' achievements. School has an important role in students' life, because it gives them access to meaningful educational encounters that help them develop their academic potential and help them manage environments of inequality and disadvantage (Wolmer, Hamiel, Barchas, Slone, & Laor, 2011; Skovdal & Campbel, 2015). This article attempts to explore the term of mental resilience in children, and the ways a positive teacher- student relationship can augment students' mental resilience. We also propose ways on how schools can create these learning and community settings that work well for those students who face such adversities, which might question their staying in school and the adequate achievement of their abilities.

Creating a positive psychological climate at school can promote learning, it enhances self-esteem and satisfies students' social-emotional needs (Ghaith, 2003; Conesa, Onandia-Hinchado, Duñabeitia, Moreno, 2022). Factors contributing to the formation of a positive psychological climate at schools are related not only to practicing strategies to deal with stressful situations and to strengthen mental resilience, but also to cultivate social and creative skills.

MENTAL RESILIENCE

Mental resilience refers to the ability of individuals to recover mentally after a difficult or traumatic life event. It is the human capacity to maintain mental wellness when daily stressful events are confronted and to grow and evolve through experiencing severe and difficult events. There are many definitions of resilience, as it is described as a "process of personal recovery and development" (Sisto, et al., 2019). Other researchers refer to resilience as the "ability of individuals to recover, withstand difficulties and rebuild themselves" (Shae-Leigh & Nagesh, 2019), or as "the process of dealing with stressful and adverse situations or events that challenge a person's resilience in a way that provides protective mechanisms and coping skills for these situations" (Sisto, et al., 2019). Finaly, it is described as "the ability of individuals to adapt, recover, regenerate successfully despite adversity and develop emotional and psychosocial competence, despite their exposure to intense stress or stressful everyday conditions" (Fletcher & Sarkar, 2013).

Research findings regarding mental resilience have indicated that its development has some genetic background. Certain genes have been related to the ability of individuals for psychosocial adaptability, emotional self-regulation, and the way individuals react to stressful situations or traumatic life events (Wu, et al., 2013). Other studies have argued that resilience is an innate element of individuals' temperament, which refers to the set of coping mechanisms that people tend to activate when experiencing traumatic or stressful events (Shae-Leigh & Nagesh, 2019). The prevailing scientific position, however, describes mental resilience not only as a set of inner traits, but also as a result of environmental factors. Exposure to certain experiences in life, which interacts to shape the way one reacts and copes with difficult or stressful experiences. Apart from being a human trait, it is, also, a dynamic process, which arises as a result of the positive coping and adaptability of individuals in stressful everyday situations (Fletcher & Sarkar, 2013).

Social environment, counseling and emotional education can provide support and empathy to people's life, which contributes to the enhancement and development of mental resilience (Wu, et al., 2013). In addition, research findings have shown that mental resilience can be developed through enhancing skills such as managing emotions, problem solving, critical and creative thinking, setting and achieving goals, promoting self-esteem, developing an internal locus of control, and cultivating optimism (Sha-Leigh & Nagesh, 2019). It is a continuous and dynamic process, which can be shaped, developed and strengthened according to the interaction between individual characteristics and environmental conditions. In other words, it concerns the dynamic and multi-level interaction between protective factors and risk factors both of an individual himself, and the conditions of the wider environment around him (Sisto, et al., 2019).

In the field of mental resilience, risk factors usually refer to any negative experience or individual characteristic, which might have a negative effect on the mental and emotional well-being or on the psychosocial adaptability of the individuals. They are likely to have either biological, social, or psychological effects (Graber, Pichon & Carabine, 2015). Premature birth, parental divorce, emotional or sexual abuse, severe parental psychopathology, living in low socio-economic level and psychological trauma as a result of experiencing war or natural disaster encountered in infancy or early childhood are associated with reduced mental resilience in adulthood (Wu, et al., 2013). Additionally, poor academic performance, dropping out of school, substance abuse, and conduct problems lead to low levels of resilience during adolescence (Lee, et al., 2013).

Not only environmental factors have a negative impact on the development of mental resilience, but also individual elements seem to deescalate the level of mental resilience. These elements are temper and biological characteristics which are related to reduced ability to regulate individual's emotional situation, reduced psychosocial adaptability, reduced ability to manage and solve problems, distorted cognitive schemas related to the absence of control over environmental conditions (Mlinac & Schwabenbauer, 2018). Other individual elements associated with reduced mental resilience are low IQ, experiencing traumatic or stressful events, maladaptive behaviors, difficult temperament, and experiencing prolonged periods of stress (Wu, et al., 2013).

Further to individual factors, there are family-related factors that have been associated with low levels of mental resilience. These are low family income, very young parental age, parental divorce, loss of family members, upbringing in an environment deprived of stimuli, any form of abuse, intense family conflicts, parental abandonment and living in adverse conditions (Wu et al., 2013).

It is evident that a variety of factors can negatively affect the development of mental resilience. Individual and temperamental factors, as well as family and social factors interact. They mutually influence people's mental and emotional well-being and psychosocial adaptability. However, there are both intra-individual and environmental factors that contribute positively to the strengthening of mental resilience. These protective factors are either personality traits or environmental factors, which can mitigate the negative effects of a stressful situation or experience and "change possible negative effect towards a positive one" (Graber, Pichon & Carabine, 2015).

However, one could ask an interesting question about what happens with mental resilience at young ages. For this reason, we proceed to the next section, which studies children's mental resilience

WHAT IS MENTAL RESILIENCE FOR CHILDREN?

The science of child resilience emerged in the 1960s. In this period, scientists were studying the causes of mental health issues and behavioral problems in adults and inductively they expanded their investigation in the risk of developing psychopathology in children (Luthar, 2006; Masten, 2007, 2011). The research was organized by studying the developmental stages children have accomplished before the disorders became apparent, in order to study their causes and evolution (Garmezy & Streitman, 1974; Watt et al., 1984; Obradović et al., 2011). Researchers were faced with a puzzle of many young people, who were at "high-risk" groups and exhibited positive mental health and development.

Norman Garmezy, Lois Murphy, Michael Rutter, and Emmy Werner pioneered the study and understanding of resilience in children facing high-risk situations by introducing four waves of describing the term. The first wave of resilience research focused on defining and measuring resilience by including factors which define this conceptual umbrella (Masten & Wright, 2009). Subsequent waves of research have focused on explanatory processes, aiming to understand the processes by which resilience occurs (wave two), whether it can be promoted through intervention (wave three), and how it operates at levels of human functioning (wave four); from the molecular level of cells to the macro- level of belonging to a society group (Masten, 2007; Masten & Wright, 2009).

This initial study of resilience in children and young people was part of a wider movement. It aimed at revolutionizing mental health theory and practice, helping to shape a more comprehensive perspective on developmental psychopathology in the 1970s (Cicchetti, 1984, 2006; Masten, 2006a). Developmental psychopathology consisted of the synthesis of two major dimensions of science, one focusing on mental problems and illness and the other hand on normal development (Masten, 2006a). A collaborative approach to understanding development and developmental psychopathology was therefore required.

Resilience generally refers to good adaptation in the face of significant threats to the development or sustainability of a dynamic system (Masten, 2006a). The definition contains two key conditions: there must be a "good fit" as long as there has been prior exposure to a "serious hazard" of some kind. Good adjustment is usually based on expectations regarding the developmental level where someone is at. However, the nature of threat exposure and threat perception also vary by the developmental stage of a person. Infants and adolescents confront different kinds of adversity and experience the same objective threat in different ways. The primary goal of research on resilience in children is to understand how resilience develops. Secondly, it aims to promote and protect resilience by creating conditions that support positive developmental adaptation. When a child or a young person faces adversity, it is important to examine predictors of resilience that are associated with good adjustment, such as protective factors and resources.

Well-adjustment is defined by a proportional relationship between typical development and expected achievements across life span by taking as main factors: given age, gender, cultural background, and historical context (Masten & Coatsworth, 1998; Buecker, Luhmann, Haehner, 2022). For a school-aged child, these expectations may include getting along with parents, following community rules, going to school and behaving appropriately in the classroom, achieving learning tasks and forming relationships with other people, including peers and teachers. As children mature, so do developmental tasks. School work is more difficult and children are expected to follow social rules without constant supervision. In adolescence and early adulthood, there are new areas of developmental tasks, including vocational guidance, sexual - romantic relationship investigation, political and social awareness.

Within the context of resilience many types of threats on children's and adolescents' life can be named. These threats include established risk factors for normal development (such as low birth weight or malformation), individual traumatic experiences (such as abuse), and mass disasters (such as hurricanes or wars). Which of these risk factors has the potential to disrupt or impair normal function or development? It quickly became apparent to researchers, who investigated risk factors or negative life experiences, the fact that they have an accumulative impact on children's and youth's life (Obradović et al., 2011). Divorce, for example, was not a simple event but a complex sequence of experiences accompanied by chronic family conflict, financial hardship, moving, and loss. Children with a major risk factor, such as an abusive parent, also faced other risks. As a result, attention has shifted from studying individual risk factors to focusing on cumulative risk. Methods of scoring single or combinations of risk factors were developed, ranging from simple measures of negative life events to complex assessments of adversity based on clinical interviews (e.g., Obradović et al., 2011).

The assessment of risk conditions indicated that the level of risk rises when the average level of positive adaptive behavior decreases and problems increase. Consequently, studies investigating children who had been exposed to stressful life events and disasters manifested more maladaptive behaviors (Pine et al., 2005; Masten & Osofsky, 2010; Obradović et al., 2011). Conclusionary, exposure to risk factors and their effects on people's behavior are indicators of cumulative risk (Obradović et al., 2011). Resilience theorists have pointed out that it is not arbitrary at all to associate risk factors with low assets and resources (Masten A.S. et al., 2009a). For example, being a child or adolescent at high risk, might be accompanied with: a single-parent household, a parent who is poorly educated, low birth weight, poor parenting skills, low income and a disadvantaged neighborhood with high rates of unemployment. A low-risk score, in this case, is likely to indicate that a child has more resources such as two well - educated parents, upper family income, an advantaged neighborhood with social capital, well organized schools, and safety.

Adaptive functioning in risk situations has been of great interest to resilience researchers. People who were exposed to high levels of risk or adversity and showed good adaptive behavior, i.e. resilience, did better than expected, based on the level of risk or "beating the odds". Similarly, there were individuals who did worse than expected at low levels of risk, and were characterised as "vulnerable" individuals (low adaptation in the low-risk context) (Masten et al., 1999). The resilience equation should include the developmental perspective as the nature of the exposure and the impact of the threat are influenced by the individual's development level. For example, younger children are less likely to be abducted and forced to become child soldiers and less likely to understand the full meaning of war (Masten & Osofsky, 2010). The loss of parents in a war zone, however, might be an incident of great significance for a young child who is unable to survive without adult care than it might be not for an older youth. Responses to threat are also affected by development level because individuals' capacities to adapt also change with developmental stages (Masten, Moon, Supkof, 2011).

Apart from assessing the level of people's developmental condition, it is also crucial to count up on their actions. Under conditions of threat, a person may seek or attract help and resources from himself, other people, community organizations, and the environment. Resources and access to them variate as an outcome of development and as contexts change across lifespan. For example, children's problem-solving abilities improve as they mature and they accomplish more cognitive skills (development of human capital). Older children and young people also develop connections and friendships in community that expand their resources so as to use them in times of threat (development of social capital). Moreover, older children and youth are able to have an expanded variety of mobility choices and access to information networks. All of the evolutionary procedure described above is a subject of change in terms of resources and tools available to adapt when facing a threat. However, it is important to remember that sometimes growth is linked to vulnerability to threat and greater exposure to adversity. In adolescence, greater awareness of threats and greater exposure to adversity can be associated with developmental improvements in cognitive abilities, knowledge and physical skills (Master, Monn, Supkof, 2011).

Sometimes risk factors or protective factors are like a bipolar indicator. For example, a high score in IQ tests can be estimated as a learning promoting factor, while on the contrary, if it is low, it is a risk factor for school performance. On the other hand, there are some experiences and resources that seem to work only in one way, such as: car accident injury, birth defects, infections. Protective factors that promote children's life include positive school environments with cognitive opportunities, emotional supportive environments, talent enhancement (eg, musical or athletic talent), personal traits such as a good sense of humor, a supportive neighborhood, or a nearby library (Longaretti, 2011; Morrison & Allen, 2007, p. 164; Ungar, 2004, 2005). Intervention models to promote resilience are added to protective factors. They aim to create assets or resources in an attempt to offset risks; they can target risk factors by preventing them from occurring, or they can target key promoters or protective factors (such as parenting) in an attempt to protect them when adversities take place (Masten & Shafe, 2006). Some of the most effective intervention programs to promote resilience and prevent antisocial behavior in children focus on parent education or training (Patterson et al., 2004). Recent efforts to implement this to the resilience intervention model regarding the disaster plan it is considered that parents and teachers should be prior trained to mitigate the effects of disasters on children (Pine et al., 2005; Masten & Obradović, 2008; Sarker, 2024).

Adaptive behavior and development are the positive results of the intervention taking place according to the resilience models. Stakeholders seem to be attracted by positive models, which gives a sufficient explanation why these positive models gained a certain position in school counseling (Galasi & Akos, 2007), preventive behavior (Miller et al., 1998), social well-being (Flynn et al., 2006) and other areas of intervention and policy (Luthar & Cicchetti, 2001). Conclusively, children with higher levels of resilience are likely to succeed in learning and less likely to suffer socially or deal with psychological health problems (Benard 2004). When quality evidence–based social and emotional skills programs are delivered at schools, students tend to be more resilient. They establish a strong connection to school and learning, they invest a great amount of attempt to improve their academic achievement, and minimize the likelihood to exhibit behavioral problems (Catalano et al., 2004).

Apparently, mental resilience is a combination of external and internal factors. The primary factors refer to the interaction a child has with various environments (social or physical) (Bronfenbrenner, 1979). There is a connection between internal and external stimuli which can lead to the enhancement of mental resilience (Johnson, 2008; Masten, 2009; Morrison & Allen, 2007; Toland & Carrigan, 2011; Ungar, 2005), by strengthening children's environment, without underestimating the effect of internal elements. In order to promote mental resilience in environmental basis, it is important to present the whole – school approach, which includes making bonds with teachers, parents and the broader community.

We now pass on to an equally interesting subject which refers to the role of teachers in a school approach environment.

THE ROLE OF TEACHERS AND THE WHOLE SCHOOL SETTING: A WHOLE- SCHOOL APPROACH

The whole-school approach in school settings refers to the development of collaborative activities inside and outside the school community targeting in advancing the learning, behavioral and mental status of the students as well as the supportive social system surrounding them (IBE-UNESCO, 2013, p. 61). It should be pinpointed that this approach aims not only at meeting students' needs, but also embodying connectedness with the school staff and the wider community. Conclusively, students, teachers, parents and the broader community are premised to be involved in the whole- school approach. Van Driel et al. (2016) highlighted that systematic change in schools is accomplished by taking steps from isolation to a community- based policy implemented by the whole- school approach.

The "whole – school approach" targets in making "everyone in the school or learning environment feel safe and welcome, no matter their ability, disability, language, cultural background, sexual orientation, gender identity, gender expression or age" (UNESCO, MoE-Alberta, 2017). The whole- school approach is effective as it is structured with the use of curricula, pedagogical practices, indoors and outdoors activities, teaching training and gathering of resources (Oxfam, 2015; UNESCO, 2016b). The application of a whole- school approach includes the establishment of partnerships with different stakeholders, organizations and social services of the community, which can boost students' wellbeing in various aspects of their life.

One of the functional elements of the whole – school approach is the enhancement of emotional and mental well – being of the school community which ensures a positive school environment, where students can create healthy relationships with their peers, teachers, parents and other professionals outside school. Inside and outside classroom, teachers are able to help their students develop some important personal qualities such as self – regulation, flexibility in thinking, self- efficacy, sense of control as protective factors for promoting mental resilience (Cicchetti & Garmezy, 1993; Rutter, 1998; Werner & Smith, 1992). Moreover, teachers establish a daily routine, which includes schedules and consistency that help students feel safe and flexible, when they face anxiety or transition (Garmezy, Masten, & Tellegen,1984; Rutter, 1998; Ungar, 2008, 2018; Werner & Smith, 1992). Young learners can be trained how to take a break in periods of anxiety in order to validate their feelings and examine the chances they have to confront their adversities (Garmezy, Masten, & Tellegen,1984; Rutter, 1998; Ungar, 2008, 2018; Werner & Smith, 1992). Another skill the educators should enhance is self- care, which is helpful in stressful times and this can be accomplished by encouraging children to have proper meals, exercise and participate in activities they enjoy (Garmezy, Masten, & Tellegen,1984; Rutter, 1998; Ungar, 2008, 2018; Werner & Smith, 1992).

Teachers play a crucial role as they support values of inclusion and prepare a friendly environment in order to help students learn and develop themselves emotionally. In the setting of inclusion and emotional support, educators deliver universal and targeted intervention programs to students, so as to advance their knowledge and strengthen their well-being (Government of Wales, 2021). School setting are influential systems where students from various environments, even the most adverse ones, have access and experience social interactions. Mental resilience is promoted by protective processes which have led to the development of various school- based interventions that help children who face difficulties. There are intervention programs focusing on the entire school population (universal interventions) and others targeting a group of children or individual children who are at risk (targeted interventions).

In addition to the aforementioned intervention programs, there are proportional universal interventions that integrate with universal programs. These are targeted interventions delivered within the whole school setting or in classrooms, aiming to help children with developmental and social difficulties (Hart & Heaver, 2015). The importance of establishing school programs in order to promote students' mental resilience is underpinned on an international evidence base level (Catalano et al., 2004; Durlak et al., 2011; Rowe & Stewart, 2009; Wiedemann, et al., 2023). So, these programs which are defined as "universal' or "whole- school approach" programs, are the new "trend" in school settings. This new "trend" refers to the factors that make a school operate as an organization, even in classroom level. Retrospections on educational history lead in the 1990s, when World Health Organisation (WHO) introduced the Health Promoting Schools model (HPS).

This model was utilized as a guide for the construction of the whole- school approach. The social and ecological impact of schools on children's mental health was highlighted by HPS model and founded the establishment of different areas of activity such as the ethical protocol of school operation, the construction of curriculums and the collaboration with parents and community (WHO, 2014). Analytically, there was a well-designed protocol with detailed instructions regarding the classroom curriculums, the selection of extra- curricular activities, the formation of school policy, the development of teachers' proficiency, the establishment of a bond with parents and the wider community where the school belongs (Wyn, Cahill, Holdsworth, Rowling, & Carson, 2000). Additionally, research was enriched by longitudinal studies, which demonstrated, that when primary schools take initiatives, there's a long-lasting effect in the promotion of resilience and school connectedness into the high school years (Blum, 2005; Catalano et al., 2004; Eliot, Cornell, Gregory, & Fan, 2010; Lee & Stewart, 2013; McNeely et al., 2002; National Research Council and Institute of Medicine, 2004; Rowe & Stewart, 2009). The provision of a positive school environment for children may be of crucial importance as it enhances resilience by offering cognitive and emotional developmental opportunities (Longaretti, 2011; Morrison & Allen, 2007, p. 164; Ungar, 2004, 2005). Children, during their developmental process, come up with risk factors in: a) individual base such as: Poor health in infancy, Insecure attachment in infant/child, Difficult temperament, Poor social skills, Low self-esteem etc., b) family base such as: Poverty/ economic insecurity, Parental unemployment, Death of family member, Divorce and family break up, Violence in the home etc, c) school base such as: Bullying, Peer rejection, Poor attachment to school, Inadequate behaviour management, School failure, Racism etc., d) community base such as: Socioeconomic disadvantage, Social or cultural discrimination, Isolation, neighborhood violence/crime etc. There are some key features implemented in the school - wide approach, which function as protective factors against risk factors and give a boost in children's mental resilience.

Having discussed the role of teachers in a whole school approach environment it would be a serious omission not to mention the role of educators in strengthening the mental resilience of their students.

HOW CAN A TEACHER PROMOTE MENTAL RESILIENCE IN STUDENTS?

The good news is that educators can provide a resilient environment not only in their classrooms but in the whole school environment on an organizational, relational and pedagogical level. Here are some of the resilient features teachers can use on the organizational level.

ORGANIZATIONAL LEVEL

Initially, teachers could cultivate the *sense of optimism, purpose and school pride* in children's daily routine in school settings. Optimism is defined as a wide belief that things are not steady, but they can change and get improved. The sense of an optimistic school is strongly supported by teachers and stakeholders by establishing the belief that all students are able to learn and perform with success in various areas of action (DuFour, DuFour, Eaker, & Karhanek, 2010; Gallup, 2014). In this environment there is the contagious uplifting energy of hope that supports optimism. Studies have demonstrated that human brain can be influenced by certain circumstances and process information either optimistically or pessimistically according to the stimuli demonstrated (Sharot, 2011). So, when teachers give positive feedbacks, students tend to have positive images about themselves, their abilities and their environment. In accordance to optimism, educators enhance the sense of school pride as a way to promote resilience. It depends on the idea of being connected with the school community and the school values, which create the sense of belonging. Furthermore, resilient schools help students develop pride in themselves, which derives from self- confidence and the ability to take responsibilities and work for academic success. Educators inspire their students to build pride by helping them having realistic beliefs about their abilities, which is a "healthy" ingredient for confidence boosting (Victoria and State Government, Department of Education and Training, 2021).

Teachers have the opportunity to empower students to build school pride by incorporating specific actions into their school context. School spirit is the secret element that makes a school feel special for children. Here is a list of some fun and simple school spirit ideas that can easily increase school pride and transform a school setting into a vibrant community:

1. **Celebration of achievements**: For example, "Our boys' soccer team won a tournament, and their photo with the trophy was displayed on posters throughout the school. Seeing their faces light up when they saw themselves on the posters was priceless."
2. **Use of technology for effective communication**: This can help students establish a routine and connection with the school. For example, teachers can remind their students to check their emails every Friday to be informed about final schedules, tests, excursions, visits, or events taking place in various venues. A teenage girl, J., says: "Communication is a key that helps me feel connected to my school routine, and I use it as a guide for my weekly tasks without feeling confused."
3. **Morning announcements**: These can increase students' engagement. While it might seem boring to make morning announcements, students often use them to interact or make fun of them. It creates an active and inclusive atmosphere. K., an elementary school pupil, commented about it during lunch break: "Today's morning announcement was hilarious. Everybody knows when our school break is. There is no need to remind us. We can't wait for this day."
4. **Encouragement of student participation in various school activities**: This gives them the opportunity to participate and demonstrate their talents. For example, teachers can establish a classroom game called the Oscars. R., a high school student, commented: "Every Friday, our English teacher announces the Oscars for best classroom behavior, collaboration, humor, smart questioning, compassion, and empathy."
5. **Creation of visual reminders**: These can help inform and engage students. Schools can use information screens to highlight important events happening at school. T., a high school student, commented: "I love these screens! They remind me of the events taking place at school, and I can see my name highlighted when I score with my soccer team!" (State of Victoria, Department of Education and Training, 2021).

Educators are capable of building *effective school–community partnerships*, which have a positive impact on the academic and mental life of students. Mental resilience flourishes when community agents create collaborative behaviors to address students' academic and social – emotional developmental areas. School – community partnerships target in fulfilling students' and their families' needs as it should be eligible for students to access services by school – community partnerships. There must a priority scale, which places on top students who are most in need. The representatives of the community agencies should discuss with educators what of the provided services are useful for the academic and social – emotional needs of the students. Educators are responsible for the establishment of academic and social – emotional services at schools. Teachers implement school – based intervention programs aiming at improving the learning process by updating its conditions and helping students thrive academically and, finally, become active citizens. School psychologists, school social workers and school nurses in collaboration with educators create school – community partnerships which are formulated by: a) communicating with school staff to identify students in need, b) implementing school – based intervention programs, c) addressing services for additional support to students in need, d) coordinating with community agents so as resources are transferred to students most in need and ensuring easy access to services, e) establishing a consulting center at schools, which supports the community – school partnerships by taking the following steps. Initially, they ensure that the involvement of school principals, parents, students and community leaders is important in order to construct, implement and evaluate the school – community partnerships. Secondly, educators are in charge of improving students' mental health by building community partnerships so as to fulfil school – based needs. These actions are designed by following the results of a previous assessment of the school needs. The educators are the coordinators between the community agencies, the school personnel, the parents and the students. They define clearly the roles and responsibilities of students and the community partners, so as to meet the needs of the school. Both school educators and community representatives have the appropriate knowledge to leverage the resources needed to make the partnership effective. As such, they build a relationship of trust by organizing meetings, developing a common vocabulary and comprehending the practices of collaboration (National Association of School Psychologists in the USA, Institute for Educational Leaderships, 2019).

RELATIONAL LEVEL

Apart from the organizational features that advance mental resilience in children, educators can use some relational features, which are helpful during students' school life. Educators are capable of creating a *supportive and understanding learning environment* in their classroom as an important relational feature, which allows mental resilience to flourish. Teachers are responsible for establishing a safe classroom setting, where mental health and wellbeing issues are discussed and learning difficulties are explained. They inspire young learners to transform the classroom to a "safe net", which is empowered by making agreements about the topics of discussion. They also act as facilitators during conversations to help students express themselves genuinely and generate many the viewpoints stated. Teachers should distinguish every student's contribution to the maintenance of this collaborative classroom climate and communicate it to the other students. They can also use a variety of techniques such as inquiring issues from different aspects of view, sharing activities, thinking in pairs promoting open up discussions between children and teachers and exploring new ways of collaboration (https://schools.au.reachout.com).

Mental resilience in children enhances when teachers foster a *positive teacher–student relationship*. Research has shown that positive teacher – student relationships have a positive impact on students' engagement and achievements, which is invincible when negative teacher – student relationships are built (Roorda et al., 2011). The establishment of a positive relationship with students is a good indicator for predicting positive habits for children who are 'at risk' such as better relationships with school mates and better learning outcomes (Anderson, Christenson, Sinclair, & Lehr, 2004). As far as quality of teacher/pupil relationship is concerned, primary school children are more vulnerable than adolescents (Holfve–Sabel, 2014). Negative relationships seem to have a strong impact on younger children's life, when positive teacher – student relationships operate as a good influence in adolescents' lives (Roorda et al., 2011). In a research study, students were asked: "what should teacher do in order to advance their resilience" (van Uden et al., 2014). The participants in this research were teenagers who demonstrated that they feel more resilient, when teachers offer their help on educational and emotional issues and behave in a friendly and honest way. This study, also, presented the importance of students' perception about teachers' authority over class and their trust in students as predictors of advanced classroom engagement (van Uden et al., 2014, p. 29). Another longitudinal research about the promotion of resilience in primary and secondary schools in South Australia showed the importance of daily interactions in students and teachers' relationship (Johnson, 2008). In everyday interaction, students mentioned that teachers were active listeners, willing to help them with learning difficulties, hopeful and corroborative in their learning process and respectful. In Cahill et al.'s (2004) study, students pinpointed their teachers' behavior as a resilience and confidence booster. Helpful teachers are these who greed students, express proudness for them, show interest on their accomplishments, discuss current issues.

Enhancing positive peer relationships is a key factor for promoting resilience in students as the quality of connectedness influences confidence and trust. Construction of positive relationships between peers and the provision of the appropriate climate for the enhancement of friendship, support and inclusion are the cornerstones of the whole-school approach (Holfve–Sabel, 2014). Connecting students result in successful learning attempts, low risk behaviors and reduction in risk factors (Holfve–Sabel, 2014). The existence of a negative peer environment impacts on students' interaction and social phenomenon examples appear such as bullying appears in their school life.

Bulliers and victims are young people who are very possible to be diagnosed with mental health issues accompanying them until they graduate or more in their lives (Allison, Roeger, & Reinfeld–Kirkman, 2009; Dake, Price, & Telljohann, 2003; Rigby, 2013; Rønning et al., 2009). Farrington and Ttofi's (2011) meta–analysis presented the assessment of various responses about the evaluation of a bullying prevention program. Results presented mitigation in bullying and victimization, which were influenced by the duration of the program, the participation of parents, the disciplinary methods and the playground supervision.

Educators are *enhancing school-home relationships* to form a fertile environment for the development of social and emotional skills at school as a supportive element in the resilience reinforcement. When these skills are practiced at home than the benefit is doubled for children's resilience level. It is well-known that kids follow their parents' example which has a continuity in their lives. Further to the social and emotional development of their children, parents spend time in helping them with their homework. Relevant research studies show that the learning environment at home strengthens children's achievements (Goodall, 2013). When parents are present in their children's school life, their learning achievements and wellbeing level are improved (Bull, Brooking, & Campbell, 2008; Goodall, 2013; Hoover–Dempsey et al., 2005; Jeynes, 2012). In this direction, schools should be welcoming parents in order to build family – school relationships, they should wholeheartedly support parents' participation and work methodically to create structures encouraging parents' involvement (Ferguson, 2008).

In terms of resilience flourishment, educators can help parents recognize their positive parent- children relationship features and foster them. Some of them are: a) comprehensive parenting style, which involves warmth and discussion, b) steady learning atmosphere at home, which includes reading and artwork, c) engagement with children's social life, which refers to interaction with other children, d) engagement in transitional periods in children's life, where there is emotional instability, e) highlighting the value of education and school, which inspires children to be strongly involved with their educational life and f) maintenance of connection with the school community, which is effective in their emotional and educational development Goodall (2013).

Teachers, in collaboration with school psychologists and social workers, develop resilience therapy at school. This therapy focuses on strategies to address difficulties, involving both parents and significant others in children's lives. It explores issues concerning young people, proposes solutions to their problematic situations, and focuses on daily life. Resilience therapy includes a specific framework that organizes a program of actions to resolve difficult situations. Its main goal is to help children bring about changes in their lives, maintain their strength, and fend off challenges or stimuli that cause mental discomfort.

Resilience therapy suggests strategies that are helpful in raising children, enhancing their relationships with teachers, parents, and peers, and developing resources to manage adversity. At the same time, it enhances action, commitment, and persistence, as well as attention to detail, which can bring about changes in small things that ultimately modify the whole. It also lays the groundwork for enhancing feelings of security, boosting self-esteem, promoting knowledge, and setting modest personal goals, all of which reduce the risk of developing serious mental health problems (Psyllou & Zafiropoulou, 2023).

Resilience therapy is a kind of toolbox based on a set of 'established values.' These values are considered important for the successful implementation of this therapy. The established values are:

a) **Acceptance** – refers to the acceptance children feel from a parent or significant other in their life.
b) **Maintenance** – focuses on behaviors or activities that help children be functional. A daily schedule is built based on these activities, and desired behaviors are reinforced. c) **Commitment** – involves establishing relationships that are consistent, predictable, and trusting, providing a sense of balance in children's lives. This value is particularly important when children recover from a negative experience. Commitment encourages children to make decisions, knowing that a parent or teacher offers a "safety net" when things don't go their way.
    d) **Support** – refers to developing relationships with educators or people with specialized knowledge (mental health counselors, social workers) if additional help is needed to resolve dysfunctional situations (Hart & Blincow & Thomas, 2007, www.boingboing.org.uk).

In correspondence to the organizational and relational features needed for the promotion of children's resilience, teachers are also capable of introducing some pedagogical elements.

PEDAGOGICAL LEVEL

In order to flourish a resilient environment at school a useful element is *Curriculum,* which gives educators the chance to have their "vision" of the learners. Apart from developing important learning skills, students are privileged with the ability to explore themselves and gain new experiences during their school life. Teachers help young learners become confident individuals who are able to create healthy relationships with other people and this is accomplished by enriching the basic school curriculum with Health and Well -being activities. This provides young people with the opportunity to challenge difficulties and explore their strengths, which empowers their mental health and resilience. Teachers have the flexibility to form the content of their curriculum so as to meet their students' needs by including various methods such as: a) outdoor learning, which helps children develop a healthy life style for physical and mental wellbeing, exercise in problem- solving skills and have respect towards nature, b) exploration of relationships, which enriches students' knowledge with ethical values and skills of how relationships are created and get established by using it as a guide for their present and future life, c) recognition of discrimination and violence, which should be part of the whole- school approach, which provides students the ability to understand and speak about these negative social phenomena by participating in discussion groups, organizing festivals, art exhibitions or theatrical plays (Government of Wales, 2021).

In the context of learning and developing a school curriculum, significant others should help children organize themselves. This support will significantly aid them not only with school courses but also in real life. Many students have reported that having a schedule in school life helped them feel ready to deal with unforeseen obstacles in their daily lives and made them more resilient to difficulties. For example, Emma says: "When I went to high school, I found that I had a lot of trouble organizing myself in terms of my studying and activities. I didn't know my daily schedule and almost always didn't do my homework. I had to take remedial classes as I struggled with understanding the course material due to the lack of organization. The remedial teacher suggested that all the students draw picture cards to remind them of what lessons they have each day. We also designed timetables so that we know which chapter we are in at any given time. My teacher supported us, encouraged us, and praised us. This helped me feel safe and not embarrassed if I made a mistake" (Psyllou & Zafiropoulou, 2023).

Another pedagogical element is the *provision of extra–curricular activities,* such as the implementation of Social and Emotional Learning (SEL) programs (Collaborative for Academic, Social and Emotional Learning [CASEL], n.d.; Social and Emotional Aspects of Learning [SEAL]; for a meta-analysis see Durlak et al., 2022).

They promote resilience and wellbeing at school settings. Research findings show that SEL programs lead to the exposure of positive social behavior and low level of disruptive behaviour in students (CASEL, 2013; Durlak et al., 2011; Frydenberg, 2010; Payton et al., 2008). Nelson, Westhues, & MacLeod (2003) studied 34 universal and targeted prevention programs which highlighted the positive cognitive and learning results of the SEL programs in students' life. Surprisingly, these positive results appeared in all levels of education (pre – school, primary school and high school students). A school- based study of 180 schools (kindergarten to Grade Eight), which included the implementation of SEL classroom- based programs, showed that students managed to developed skills which helped them identify their emotions, set goals, handle their conflicts and build relationships (Payton et al., 2008). In correspondence with the development of social and emotional skills students managed to improve their mathematic and readings kills according to a three - year study of 23 evidence–based SEL programs with Grade Two to Grade Five children (Rimm-Kaufman et al., 2014). When children are equipped with confidence, self–discipline and coping skills, they feel qualified enough to face challenges, to meet learning goals and to use different study practices in order to succeed academically (Durlak et al., 2011).

SEL programs can be more effective when they combine social and life skills and critical thinking and they are implemented as a part of a health and personal curriculum at schools. Educators can deliver these programs in classroom settings and refer to social, physical and mental health subjects with the benefit to embody them in the learning procedure. Conclusively, the implementation of SEL programs build a positive school environment, where mental resilience is established in students' educational routine in a playful way (Payton et al., 2008). In order to have the ultimate benefits of the evidence–based curriculum programs, it is important to promote teachers' professional development and obtain school support with the assistance of targeted policy, contemporary teaching strategies, behavior management and professional learning (Durlak et al., 2011).

A school- based prevention program aiming at enhancing students' well-being is the PENN PREVENTION program by Pattison & Lynn-Stevenson (2001). Enhancing well-being is achieved by learning ways to handle everyday stressors and problems that are common to most students. It also promotes optimism by teaching flexibility in dealing with adversity, enhances self-confidence, creative thinking, decision-making and introduces the concept of relaxation (Greenberg et al., 2001; Jaycox, Reivich, Gillham & Barrett, 2007; Neil & Christensen, 2007). One of the most well -known resilience promoting programs is the FRIENDS program (Barrett, Lowry- Webster, & Turner, 1999). It originates from Australia and its aim is being to enhance resilience and social skills in order for anxiety and depression in school children to be confronted. The whole school approach was chosen and the cognitive- behavioral therapy method was implemented. There are four different FRIENDS programs constructed in age basis: Fun Friends (4– 7 years), Friends for Life (8– 11 years), My Friends Youth (12– 15 years), and Adult Resilience (16+ years). The programs are consisted of activities to develop social skills, advance self- esteem, enhance resilience and teach techniques of building healthy relationships. There were many randomized control trials showing that FRIENDS decreases anxiety and boosts self- esteem in students of various educational levels (Barrett et al., 2006; Bernstein et al., 2005; Lowry-Webster, Barrett, & Dadds, 2001; Stallard et al., 2007). Finally, the FRIENDS program effectiveness is evident in universal interventions, where self – confidence and social skills are improved in school children (Brunwasser, Gillham, & Kim 2009; Dray et al., 2017; Stockings et al., 2016; Werner- Seidler et al., 2017).

The FRIENDS programme, translated into Greek and adapted to the Greek reality. By Psyllou and Zafiropoulou (2012,) was implemented in primary schools of various areas of Greece. A total of 362 children aged 9-10 took part in the program, which lasted for almost a year and a half (pilot phase and main research). The program took place once or twice a week during a school hour and was carried out in the schools where the children attended. Each intervention included playful exercises and original creative activities based on the principles of cognitive-behavioral therapy. These activities were specifically designed to cover the goals of the sessions and be manageable for the students given their age.

At the same time, the content of the intervention program was adapted to the schedule of each primary school in which it was implemented. The analysis of the research results supports the effectiveness of the program and shows its suitability for primary school children. There was a significant improvement in students' mental health, with a decrease in anxiety and an increase in self-esteem after the completion of the interventions. This indicates an enhancement of children's resilience both inside and outside school (Psyllou, 2014).

Apart from implementing SEL programs in school-based settings, teachers can foster resilience in students by providing *information, raising awareness, and advocating for their needs*. It is a pedagogical feature, which enables educators to enhance children's mental health by discussing about it and reduce stigma and discrimination. Teachers can create a safe environment in their classrooms, where students can disclose their personal issues without feeling threat or criticism from their schoolmates, as all students are trained to express empathetic responses. By this method, young learners learn to communicate and exchange information about their emotional situation, which helps them comprehend their own well – being situation and learn a help – seeking behavior that increases their resilience. Educators teach their students how to make decisions by having the information needed after making research on the school website, having themselves consulted by older students (peer mentors) or addressing agencies or resources collaborating with school (Government of Wales, 2021).

Teachers and schools can be the facilitators for the promotion of the resilience and wellbeing in young learners. There has been an important amount of research pointing out the value of the efforts made by the whole – school approach to enhance students' resilience and engagement in the school setting by the implementation of intervention programs. As a result of these efforts, children's social and emotional skills have been improved, dysfunctional behaviors have been handled and academic performance has been increased. Teachers have uplifted children's wellbeing and resilience by building partnerships with school staff, parents and community agencies. When teachers manage to build a positive relationship with their students than behavioural, cognitive and emotional engagement is accomplished and children feel safe to seek help when they confront difficulties.

Mental and social health problems affect children's lives and can become permanent if not treated with care. Additionally, students often feel embarrassed when facing social and emotional problems and may not be brave enough to seek help. Teachers play an important role in observing their students' behavior and gathering information about those who exhibit well-being or learning difficulties, in order to provide them with support.School psychologists and social workers collaborate with teachers to create a well- organized protocol referring to the steps that should be taken to meet their needs. Schools, as an active community, are able to ensure that students are supported, able to build resilience and uplift their social and mental life.

Children who experience positive emotions are characterized by mental well-being and have an optimistic view of things. They usually feel safe and confident in their ability to face challenges. They acquire skills such as self-confidence and positive self-images. Positive characteristics are developed through the implementation of preventive programs at schools, where students mainly interact with others until they reach adulthood. In short, children who manage to show love, interest, behave happily, and think of a multitude of alternatives and ideas experience the benefits of applying the basic principles of a whole-school approach (Psyllou & Zafiropoulou, 2023).

IMPLICATIONS FOR POLICY AND PRACTICE

Mandate reforms and educational change are persistent factors affecting schools. Studies examining factors that hinder or support mandated reform efforts before implementation in schools vary widely in objectives, methodologies, and theoretical frameworks. The complexity of educational change and the challenges faced is widely acknowledged by school policymakers.

Key factors for successful reform include:

1. **Reform-Ready Climates**: Developing environments ready for reform.
2. **Planning for Change**: Strategic planning for change.
3. **Coordinating Implementation**: Effective preparation and coordination.
4. **Building Capacity**: Strengthening the capacity for change.

Relevant meta-analyses highlight several key points for policymakers and practitioners responsible for implementing social and emotional skill-based interventions in schools. Successful implementation of whole school practices requires:

1. **Motivation and Capacity**: Both individual and organizational motivation and capacity are essential.
2. **Supportive Policies**: Policies need to be in place to support these practices.
3. **Addressing Challenges**: It is important to address challenges in changing practices and adapting programs post-implementation.

To increase the use of whole school interventions, efforts should focus on:

1. **Assisting Schools**: Help schools select evidence-based interventions that fit their needs.
2. **Quality Implementation**: Ensure high-quality implementation.
3. **Sustainability**: Adopt methods to sustain interventions over the long term.

Investment in professional development is crucial for building organizational capacity, promoting partnerships between teacher preparation programs, program developers, and implementation experts, and equipping trainee teachers with the necessary competencies. Leadership support and ongoing professional development are also necessary for integration and sustainability (Goldberg *et a*l., 2019; Aldridge, & McLure, 2023).

CONCLUSION

Research indicates that for optimal impact, mental resilience, social and emotional skill development should be integrated within a whole school, multi-modal approach. This approach includes coordinated action across curriculum, teaching, school ethos, environment, and family and community partnerships.

Mental resilience is a source of development and growth in children, making it essential to focus on its establishment within the context of students' emotional education. It involves a sequence of complex and multidimensional functions that allow individuals to respond adequately to their mental and social needs, despite facing difficulties, dangers, or even life-threatening situations. Thus, people are characterized as "resilient" when they are able to confront "explosive" emotions such as anxiety, danger/threat, or serious distress. Subsequently, children acquire adaptive qualities when they respond adequately to new challenges and stimuli they receive during their development. They learn to adjust their responses to these stimuli to manage the stress of unknown situations or threats. Finally, the success of this project is enhanced by the contribution of a series of psychosocial resources, which contribute to the individual's good adaptation.

The psychosocial resources necessary for the development of mental resilience concern the individual, including characteristics such as intelligence, humor, optimism, and skills such as stress coping strategies, creativity, and critical thinking. The second category of resources concerns the family context, including the communication parents develop with their children and the ways in which parents choose to educate them. The third resource is supportive school contexts, where eager teachers enhance mental resilience in their students and establish collaboration with wider community stakeholders, effectively contributing to children's strengthening.

Meta-analyses show a significant positive impact on students' social and emotional adjustment, behavioral adjustment, and internalizing symptoms. However, further research on implementation and essential components of whole school interventions is needed to understand the conditions for successful outcomes (Goldberg *et al.*, 2019).

REFERENCES

Aldridge, J. M., & McLure, F. I. (2023). Preparing Schools for Educational Change: Barriers and Supports – A Systematic Literature Review. *Leadership and Policy in Schools*, 1–26. 10.1080/15700763.2023.2171439

Allison, S., Roeger, L., & Reinfeld–Kirkman, N. (2009). Does school bullying affect adult health? Population survey of health–related quality of life and past victimization. *The Australian and New Zealand Journal of Psychiatry*, 43(12), 1163–1170. 10.3109/00048670903270399200001416

Anderson, A. R., Christenson, S. L., Sinclair, M. F., & Lehr, C. A. (2004). Check & Connect: The importance of relationships for promoting engagement with school. *Journal of School Psychology*, 42(2), 95–113. 10.1016/j.jsp.2004.01.002

Barrett, P. M., Lowry-Webster, H., & Turner, C. M. (1999). *FRIENDS for children group leader manual*. Brisbane: Australian Academic Press.

Barrett, P. M., Farrell, L. I., Ollendick, T. H., & Dadds, M. (2006). Long- term outcomes of an Australian universal prevention trial of anxiety and depression symptoms in children and youth: An evaluation of the FRIENDS program. *Journal of Clinical Child and Adolescent Psychology, 35*(3), 403– 411. doi: 510.1207/s15374424jccp3503_

Bernard, B. (2004). *Resiliency: What we have learned*. WestEd.

Bernstein, G. A., Layne, A. E., Egan, E. A., & Tennison, D. M. (2005). School- based interventions for anxious children. *Journal of the American Academy of Child and Adolescent Psychiatry*, 44(11), 1118–1127. 10.1097/01.chi.0000177323.40005.a116239860

Blum, R. W. (2005). A case for school connectedness. *The Adolescent Learner*, 62(7), 16–20.

Bronfenbrenner, U. (1979). *The ecology of human development*. Harvard University Press. 10.4159/9780674028845

Brunwasser, S. M., Gillham, J. E., & Kim, E. S. (2009). A meta- analytic re- view of the Penn Resiliency Program's effect on depressive symptoms. *Journal of Consulting and Clinical Psychology*, 77(6), 1042–1054. 10.1037/a001767119968381

Buecker, S., Luhmann, M., Haehner, P., Bühler, J. L., Dapp, L. C., Luciano, E. C., & Orth, U. (2022). The Development of Subjective Well-Being Across the Life Span: A Meta-Analytic Review of Longitudinal Studies. *Psychological Bulletin*, 149(7-8), 418–446. 10.1037/bul0000401

Bull, A., Brooking, K., & Campbell, R. (2008). *Successful Home–School Partnerships*. Ministry of Education.

Cahill, H., Shaw, G., Wyn, J., & Smith, G. (2004). *Translating Caring Into Action: An Evaluation of the Victorian Catholic Education Student Welfare Professional Development Initiative*. Youth Research Centre, The University of Melbourne.

CASEL. (2013). *What Is Social and Emotional Learning?* Retrieved from http://www. casel.org/social–and–emotional–learning/

Catalano, R. F., Haggerty, K. P., Oesterle, S., Fleming, C. B., & Hawkins, J. D. (2004). The Importance of Bonding to School for Healthy Development: Findings from the Social Development Research Group. *The Journal of School Health*, 74(7), 252–261. 10.1111/j.1746-1561.2004.tb08281.x15493702

Cicchetti, D. (1984). The emergence of developmental psychopathology. *Child Development*, 55(1), 1–7. 10.2307/11298306705613

Cicchetti, D., & Garmezy, N. (1993). Prospects and promises in the study of resilience. *Development and Psychopathology*, 5(4), 497–502. 10.1017/S0954579400006118

Conesa, P. J., Onandia-Hinchado, I., Duñabeitia, J. A., & Moreno, M. Á. (2022). Basic psychological needs in the classroom: A literature review in elementary and middle school students. *Learning and Motivation*, 79, 101819. Advance online publication. 10.1016/j.lmot.2022.101819

Dake, J. A., Price, J. H., & Telljohann, S. K. (2003). The Nature and Extent of Bullying at School. *The Journal of School Health*, 73(5), 173–180. 10.1111/j.1746-1561.2003. tb03599.x12793102

Dray, J., Bowman, J., Campbell, E., Freund, M., Wolfenden, L., Hodder, R., McElwaine, K., Tremain, D., Bartlem, K., Bailey, J., Small, T., Palazzi, K., Oldmeadow, C., & Wiggers, J. (2017). Systematic review of universal resilience interventions targeting child and adolescent mental health in the school setting. *Journal of the American Academy of Child and Adolescent Psychiatry*, 56(10), 813–824. 10.1016/j. jaac.2017.07.78028942803

DuFour, R., DuFour, R., Eaker, R., & Karhanek, G. (2010). *Raising the bar and closing the gap: Whatever it takes*. Bloomington, IN: Solution Tree.

Durlak, J. A., Mahoney, J. L., & Boyle, A. E. (2022). What we know, and what we need to find out about universal, school-based social and emotional learning programs for children and adolescents: A review of meta-analyses and directions for future research. *Psychological Bulletin*, 148(11-12), 765–782. 10.1037/bul0000383

Durlak, J. A., Weissberg, R. P., Dymnicki, A. B., Taylor, R. D., & Schellinger, K. B. (2011). The Impact of Enhancing Students' Social and Emotional Learning: A Meta–Analysis of School–Based Universal Interventions. *Child Development*, 82(1), 405–432. 10.1111/j.1467-8624.2010.01564.x21291449

Eliot, M., Cornell, D., Gregory, A., & Fan, X. (2010). Supportive school climate and student willingness to seek help for bullying and threats of violence. *Journal of School Psychology*, 48(6), 533–553. 10.1016/j.jsp.2010.07.00121094397

Farrington, D. P., & Ttofi, M. M. (2011). Effectiveness of school-based programs to reduce bullying: A systematic and meta-analytic review. *Journal of Experimental Criminology*, 7(1), 27–56. 10.1007/s11292-010-9109-1

Ferguson, C. (2008). *The School–Family Connection: Looking at the Larger Picture: A Review of Current Literature*. National Center for Family and Community Connections with Schools.

Fletcher, D., & Sarkar, M. (2013). Psychological resilience: A review and critique of definitions, concepts and theory. *European Psychologist*, 18(1), 12–17. 10.1027/1016-9040/a000124

Frydenberg, E. (2010). *Think positively! A course for developing coping skills in adolescents*. Continuum International Publishing Group.

Galassi, J. P., & Akos, P. (2007). *Strength-based school: Promoting student development and achievement*. Earlbaum.

Gallup. (2014). *State of America's schools: The path to winning again in education*. Washington, DC: Author. Retrieved from www.gallup.com/services/178709/state-america-schools-report.aspx

Garmezy, N., Masten, A. S., & Tellegen, A. (1984). The study of stress and competence in children: A building block for developmental psychopathology. *Child Development*, 55(1), 97–111. 10.2307/11298376705637

Garmezy, N., & Streitman, S. (1974). Children at risk: the search for the antecedents to schizophrenia: Part 1. Conceptual models and research methods. *Schizophrenia Bulletin*, 8(8), 14–90. 10.1093/schbul/1.8.144619494

Ghaith, G. (2003). The relationship between forms of instruction, achievement and perceptions of classroom climate. *Educational Research*, 45(1), 83–93. 10.1080/0013188032000086145

Goldberg, J. M., Sklad, M., Elfrink, T. R., Schreurs, K. M. G., Bohlmeijer, E. T., & Clarke, A. M. (2019). Effectiveness of interventions adopting a whole school approach to enhancing social and emotional development: A meta-analysis. *European Journal of Psychology of Education*, 34(4), 755–782. 10.1007/s10212-018-0406-9

Goodall, J. (2013). Parental engagement to support children's learning: A six-point model. *School Leadership & Management*, 33(2), 133–150. 10.1080/13632434.2012.724668

Government of Wales. (2021). *Framework on embedding a wole- school approach to emotional and mental well – being*. Llywodraeth Cymru Welsh Government, ADDYSG, Education Wales.

Graber, R., Pichon, F., & Carabine, E. (2015). *Psychological resilience: State of knowledge and future research agendas*. Psychology Press.

Greenberg, M. T., Domitrovich, C., & Bumbarger, B. (2001). The prevention of mental disorders in school-aged children: Current state of the field. *Prevention & Treatment*, 4(1), 1a–1a. 10.1037/1522-3736.4.1.41a

Hart, A., Blincow, D., & Thomas, H. (2007). *Resilient therapy: Working with children and families*. Routledge/Taylor & Francis Group.

Hart, A., & Heaver, B. (2015). *Resilience approaches to supporting young people's mental health appraising the evidence base for schools and communities*. University of Brighton/ Boingboing.

Holfve–Sabel, M. (2014, January). Learning, Interaction and Relationships as Components of Student Well– being: Differences Between Classes from Student and Teacher Perspective. *Social Indicators Research*, 119(3), 1535–1555. Advance online publication. 10.1007/s11205-013-0557-7

Hoover–Dempsey, K. V., Walker, J. M. T., Sandler, H. M., Whetsel, D., Green, C. L., Wilkins, A. S., & Closson, K. (2005). Why Do Parents Become Involved? Research Findings and Implications. *The Elementary School Journal*, 106(2), 105–130. 10.1086/499194

Jaycox, L. H., Reivich, K. J., Gillham, J., & Seligman, M. (1994). Prevention of depressive symptoms in school children. *Behaviour Research and Therapy*, 32(8), 801–816. 10.1016/0005-7967(94)90160-07993324

Jeynes, W. (2012). A Meta–Analysis of the Efficacy of Different Types of Parental Involvement Programs for Urban Students. *Urban Education*, 47(4), 706–742. 10.1177/0042085912445643

Johnson, B. (2008). Teacher–student relationships which promote resilience at school: A micro–level analysis of students' views. *British Journal of Guidance & Counselling*, 36(4), 385–398. 10.1080/03069880802364528

Lee, J. H., Nam, S. K., Kim, A. R., Young, M. L., & Lee, S. M. (2013). Resilience: A meta-analytic approach. *Journal of Counseling and Development*, 91(3), 269–279. 10.1002/j.1556-6676.2013.00095.x

Lee, P. C., & Stewart, D. E. (2013). Does a Socio-Ecological School Model Promote Resilience in Primary Schools? *The Journal of School Health*, 83(11), 795–804. 10.1111/josh.1209624138350

Longaretti, L. (2011). *Re–conceptualising Educational Resilience: Giving Voice to Young People's Perspectives* (Doctor of Philosophy PhD). University of Melbourne.

Lowry-Webster, H. M., Barrett, P. M., & Dadds, M. R. (2001). A universal prevention trial of anxiety and depressive symptomatology in childhood: Preliminary data from an Australian study. *Behaviour Change*, 18(1), 36–50. 10.1375/bech.18.1.36

Luthar, S. S. (2006). Resilience in development: A synthesis of research across five decades. In Cicchetti, D., & Cohen, D. J. (Eds.), Developmental psychopathology: Vol. 3. *Risk, disorder, and adaptation* (2nd ed., pp. 739–795). Wiley.

Luthar, S. S., & Cicchetti, D. (2001). The construct of resilience: Implications for interventions and social policies. *Development and Psychopathology*, 12(4), 857–885. 10.1017/S0954579400004156111202047

Masten, A. S. (2006a). Developmental psychopathology: Pathways to the future. *International Journal of Behavioral Development*, 31(1), 47–54. 10.1177/0165025406059974

Masten, A. S. (2006b). Promoting resilience in development: A general framework for systems of care. In Flynn, R. J., Dudding, P., & Barber, J. G. (Eds.), *Promoting resilience in child welfare* (pp. 3–17). University of Ottawa Press.

Masten, A. S. (2007). Resilience in developing systems: Progress and promise as the fourth wave rises. *Development and Psychopathology*, 19(3), 921–930. 10.1017/S0954579407000442 17705908

Masten, A. S. (2011 in press). Risk and resilience in development. In Zelazo, P. D. (Ed.), *Oxford handbook of developmental psychology*. Oxford University Press.

Masten, A. S., & Coatsworth, J. D. (1998). The development of competence in favorable and unfavorable environments: Lessons from successful children. *The American Psychologist*, 53(2), 205–220. 10.1037/0003-066X.53.2.2059491748

Masten, A. S., Hubbard, J. J., Gest, S. D., Tellegen, A., Garmezy, N., & Ramirez, M. (1999). Competence in the context of adversity: Pathways to resilience and maladaptation from childhood to late adolescence. *Development and Psychopathology*, 11(1), 143–169. 10.1017/S095457949900199610208360

Masten, A. S., Monn, A. R., & Supkoff, L. M. (2011). *Resilience in children and adolescents*. Published by Cambridge University Press. 10.1017/CBO9780511994791.009

Masten, A. S., & Osofsky, J. (2010). Disasters and the impact on child development: Introduction to the special section. *Child Development*, 81(4), 1029–1039. 10.1111/j.1467-8624.2010.01452.x20636680

Masten, A. S., & Shafer, A. (2006). How families matter in child development: Reflections from research on risk and resilience. In Clarke-Stewart, A., & Dunn, J. (Eds.), *Families count: Effects on child and adolescent development* (pp. 5–25). Cambridge University Press. 10.1017/CBO9780511616259.002

Masten, A. S., & Wright, M. (2009). Resilience over the lifespan: Developmental perspectives on resistance, recovery, and transformation. In J. W. Reich, A. J. Zautra, & J. S. Hall (Eds.), *Handbook of adult resilience* (pp. 213– 237). New York: Guilford Press.

McNeely, C. A., Nonnemaker, J. M., & Blum, R. W. (2002). Promoting School Connectedness: Evidence from the National Longitudinal Study of Adolescent Health. *The Journal of School Health*, 72(4), 138–146. 10.1111/j.1746-1561.2002.tb06533.x12029810

Miller, G. E., Brehm, K., & Whitehouse, S. (1998). Reconceptualizing school-based prevention for antisocial behavior within a resiliency framework. *School Psychology Review*, 27(3), 364–379. 10.1080/02796015.1998.12085922

Mlinac, M. E., & Schwabenbauer, A. (2018). *Psychological resilience. In the Handbook of developmental psychopathology*. Springer. 10.1007/978-3-030-04555-5_5

Morrison, G. M., & Allen, M. R. (2007). Promoting Student Resilience in School Contexts. *Theory into Practice*, 46(2), 162–169. 10.1080/00405840701233172

National Association of School Psychologists in the USA, Institute for Educational Leaderships. (2019). *Nine Elements of Effective School Community Partnerships to Address Student Mental Health*. Physical Health and Overall Wellness.

National Research Council and Institute of Medicine. (2004). *Engaging schools: Fostering high school students' motivation to learn*. The National Academies Press.

Neil, A. L., & Christensen, H. (2009). Efficacy and effectiveness of school-based prevention and early intervention programs for anxiety. *Clinical Psychology Review*, 29(3), 208–215. 10.1016/j.cpr.2009.01.00219232805

Nelson, G., Westhues, A., & MacLeod, J. (2003). A meta–analysis of longitudinal research on preschool prevention programs for children. *Prevention & Treatment*, 6(31), 1–35. 10.1037/1522-3736.6.1.631a

Obradović, J., Shafer, A., & Masten, A. S. (2011). Risk in developmental psychopathology: Progress and future directions. In Mayes, L. C., & Lewis, M. (Eds.), *The environment of human development: A handbook of theory and measurement*. Cambridge University Press.

Olsson, C. A., Bond, L., Burns, J. M., Vella-Brodrick, D. A., & Sawyer, S. M. (2003). Adolescent resilience: A concept analysis. *Journal of Adolescence*, 26(1), 1–11. 10.1016/S0140-1971(02)00118-512550818

Patterson, G. R., DeGarmo, D. S., & Forgatch, M. S. (2004). Systematic changes in families following prevention trials. *Journal of Abnormal Child Psychology*, 32(6), 621–633. 10.1023/B:JACP.0000047211.11826.5415648529

Pattison, C., & Lynd-Stevenson, R. M. (2001). The prevention of depressive symptoms in children: The immediate and long-term outcomes of a school based program. *Behaviour Change*, 18(2), 92–102. 10.1375/bech.18.2.92

Payton, J. W., Weissberg, R. P., Durlak, J. A., Dymnicki, A. B., Taylor, R. D., & Schellinger, K. B. (2008). *The positive impact of social and emotional learning for kindergarten to eighth–grade students: Findings from three scientific reviews*. Collaborative for Academic, Social, and Emotional Learning.

Pine, D. S., Costello, J., & Masten, A. S. (2005). Trauma, proximity, and developmental psychopathology: The effects of war and terrorism on children. *Neuropsychopharmacology*, 30(10), 1781–1792. 10.1038/sj.npp.130081416012537

Psyllou, A. (2014). Phd Dissertation: *Construction, implementation and Evaluation of emotional resilience: a CBT programme in primary schools in Greece*, University of Thessaly, Greece, Department of Pre-School Education.

Psyllou, R. & Zafiropoulou, M. (2012). *Friends.... how can we deal with our negative feelings*, Pedion Publications (republication), Athens, 2012.

Psyllou, R., & Zafiropoulou, M. (2023). *Child anxiety. What is it?* Topos Publications.

Rigby, K. (2013). Bullying in schools and its relation to parenting and family life. *Family Matters (Melbourne, Vic.)*, 92, 61–67.

Rimm–Kaufman, S. E., Larsen, R. A. A., Baroody, A. E., Curby, T. W., Ko, M., Thomas, J. B., Merritt, E. G., Abry, T., & DeCoster, J. (2014). Efficacy of the Responsive Classroom Approach: Results From a 3–Year, Longitudinal Randomized Controlled Trial. *American Educational Research Journal*, 52(3), 567–603. 10.3102/0002831214523821

Rønning, J. A., Sourander, A., Kumpulainen, K., Tamminen, T., Niemelä, S., Moilanen, I., Helenius, H., Piha, J., & Almqvist, F. (2009). Cross–informant agreement about bullying and victimization among eight–year–olds: Whose information best predicts psychiatric caseness 10–15 years later? *Social Psychiatry and Psychiatric Epidemiology*, 44(1), 15–22. 10.1007/s00127-008-0395-018604618

Roorda, D. L., Koomen, H. M. Y., Spilt, J. L., & Oort, F. J. (2011). The Influence of Affective Teacher–Student Relationships on Students' School Engagement and Achievement: A Meta–Analytic Approach. *Review of Educational Research*, 81(4), 493–529. 10.3102/0034654311421793

Rowe, F., & Stewart, D. E. (2009). Promoting Connectedness through Whole–School Approaches: A Qualitative Study. *Health Education*, 109(5), 396–413. 10.1108/09654280910984816

Rutter, M. (1998). Developmental catch-up, and deficit, following adoption after severe global early privation. English and Romanian Adoptees (ERA) Study Team. *Journal of Child Psychology and Psychiatry, and Allied Disciplines*, 39(4), 465–476.9599775

Sarker, N. I. (2024). Promoting community resilience through disaster education: Review of community-based interventions with a focus on teacher resilience and well-being. *PLoS One*, 19(1), e0296393. 10.1371/journal.pone.029639338166092

Shae-Leigh, V., & Nagesh, P. (2019). A theoretical review of psychological resilience. Defining resilience and resilience research over the decades. *Archives of Medicine and Health Sciences*, 7(2), 233–239. 10.4103/amhs.amhs_119_19

Sharot, T. (2011, June 6). The optimism bias. *Time*, 177(23), 40–45. 10.1016/j.cub.2011.10.03021682073

Sisto, A., Ricci, G., Vicinanza, F., & Campanozzi, L. L. (2019). Towards a transversal definition of psychological resilience: A literature review. *Medicina*, 55(11), 745. 10.3390/medicina55110745 31744109

Skovdal, M., & Campbell, C. (2015). Beyond education: What role can schools play in the support and protection of children in extreme settings? *International Journal of Educational Development*, 41, 175–183. Advance online publication. 10.1016/j.ijedudev.2015.02.005

Stallard, P., Simpson, N., Anderson, S., Hibbert, S., & Osborn, C. (2007). The FRIENDS emotional health programme: Initial findings from a school- based project. *Child and Adolescent Mental Health*, 12(1), 32–37. 10.1111/j.1475-3588.2006.00421.x32811032

State of Victoria (Department of Education and Training). (2021). *Empowering Students and Building School Pride Implementation Guide*, How schools promote and sustain student empowerment.

Stockings, E. A., Degenhardt, L., Dobbins, T., Lee, Y. Y., Erskine, H. E., Whiteford, H. A., & Patton, G. (2016). Preventing depression and anxiety in young people: A review of the joint efficacy of universal, selective and indicated prevention. *Psychological Medicine*, 46(1), 11–26. 10.1017/S0033291715001725263155 36

Toland, J., & Carrigan, D. (2011). Educational Psychology and Resilience: New Concept, New Opportunities. *School Psychology International*, 32(1), 95–106. 10.1177/0143034310397284

UNESCO. (2017). *MoE-Alberta*. Training Tools for Curriculum Development.

UNESCO International Bureau of Education. (2013). Glossary of Curriculum Terminology. UNESCO.

Ungar, M. (2004). A constructionist discourse on resilience: Multiple contexts, multiple realities among at-risk children and youth. *Youth & Society*, 35(3), 341–365. 10.1177/0044118X03257030

Ungar, M. (2005). A thicker description of resilience. *International Journal of Narrative Therapy and Community Work*, 3, 89–96.

Ungar, M. (2008). Resilience across cultures. *British Journal of Social Work*, 38(2), 218–235. 10.1093/bjsw/bcl343

Ungar, M. (2018). Systemic resilience: Principles and processes for a science of change in contexts of adversity. *Ecology and Society*, 23(4), art34. Advance online publication. 10.5751/ES-10385-230434

van Driel, M.L., De Sutter, A. I., Habraken, H., Thorning, S., & Christiaens, T. (2016). Different antibiotic treatments for group A streptococcal pharyngitis. *Cochrane Database Syst Rev., 11*(9). .10.1002/14651858.CD004406.pub4 van Uden, J. M., Ritzen, H., & Pieters, J. M. (2014). Engaging students: The role of teacher beliefs and interpersonal teacher behavior in fostering student engagement in vocational education. *Teaching and Teacher Education*, 37, 21–32. 10.1016/j.tate.2013.08.005

Victoria and State Government, Department of Education and Training. (2021). *Empowering Students and Building School Pride Implementation Guide*. Author.

Watt, N. F., Anthony, E. J., Wynne, L. C., & Rolf, J. E. (Eds.). (1984). *Children at risk for schizophrenia: A longitudinal perspective*. Cambridge University Press.

Werner, E. E., & Smith, R. S. (1992). *Overcoming the odds: High risk children from birth to adulthood*. Cornell University Press. 10.7591/9781501711992

Werner-Seidler, A., Perry, Y., Calear, A. L., Newby, J. M., & Christensen, H. Werner-Seidler. (2017). School- based depression and anxiety prevention programs for young people: A systematic review and meta- analysis. *Clinical Psychology Review*, 51, 30–47. 10.1016/j.cpr.2016.10.00527821267

WHO. (2014). What is a health promoting school? School and youth health. Retrieved 24 February, 2014, from https://www.who.int/school_youth_health/gshi/hps/en/

Wiedermann, C. J., Barbieri, V., Plagg, B., Marino, P., Piccoliori, G., & Engl, A. (2023). Fortifying the Foundations: A Comprehensive Approach to Enhancing Mental Health Support in Educational Policies Amidst Crises. *Healthcare (Basel)*, 11(10), 1423. 10.3390/healthcare1110142337239709

Wu, G., Feder, A., Cohen, H., Kim, J. J., Calderon, S., Charney, D. S., & Mathe, A. A. (2013). Understanding resilience. *Frontiers in Behavioral Neuroscience*, 7. Advance online publication. 10.3389/fnbeh.2013.0001023422934

Wyn, J., Cahill, H., Holdsworth, R., Rowling, L., & Carson, S. (2000). MindMatters, a whole–school approach promoting mental health and wellbeing. *The Australian and New Zealand Journal of Psychiatry*, 34(4), 594–601. 10.1080/j.1440-1614.2000.00748.x10954390

Chapter 9
Nurturing Resilience in Education:
Strategies for Students and Teachers

Eirini Karakasidou
https://orcid.org/0000-0003-2946-8275
Panteion University, Greece

Anna Papadimitriou
Panteion University, Greece

Danai Chatzidou
University of Kent, UK

Smaragda Kazi
Panteion University, Greece

ABSTRACT

It is well-established that schools should cultivate not only cognitive skills but also skills that help individuals cope with life's challenges. An integrated approach is necessary in the attempt to promote resilience in both students and teachers. For children, the focus is on putting evidence-based strategies into practice that support their emotional health in addition to academic difficulties. It is also crucial to prioritize the psychological resilience of teachers since their role involves a great deal of complexity, which often makes them susceptible to stress and burnout. It has been proven that when teachers are in a state of well-being, it not only enhances their own performance and ability to fulfill their role but also has a direct impact on the well-being and academic performance of their students. Educational institutions

DOI: 10.4018/979-8-3693-8312-4.ch009

Copyright © 2024, IGI Global. Copying or distributing in print or electronic forms without written permission of IGI Global is prohibited.

can foster an environment that prioritizes the mental well-being of all stakeholders and fosters academic success by attending to the unique requirements of each group.

INTRODUCTION

Resilience has been applied to many distinguished fields, such as in psychology, in engineering, in everyday life, in economics and in educational settings as well. Although, all of these disciplines are different from one another, resilience in general has been approached to a similar way. To be more specific, resilience in psychotherapy is the ability for people to get over their problems by adopting a positive approach to life (Reynolds, 2019). In addition, concerning economics and organizations, resilience gives the potential to employees to make and implement more positive strategies to deal with unexpected situations and stress (Wu et al., 2013). Moreover, the last few years, there is a completely new domain in engineering. This is the resilience engineering, which aims to help both employees and employers to deal with complexity under pressure. According to Seville (2008), resilience in different disciplines provides several common elements. For instance, resilience helps from negative consequences to occur and specifically to not become worst as time goes. At that point, resilience in all fields aims to make recovery more easily and to last longer.

Even though, there is a great need for resilience to be applied at the educational settings, there is not that much research on this field. However, there are some interesting findings now, regarding how relevant resilience is in the field of education. Specifically, Alva in 1991 found that, even if there were students, who were from poor socioeconomic families, they did well in school subjects because they had resilience and they felt invulnerable. In addition, Nettles et al. (2000) concluded that, it is important for students to have support regarding their resilience from their families, the school, and their teachers. Surprisingly, even if these students were exposed to violence, they managed to deal with mathematics and other subjects just because they had the support of their teachers. As we see, resilience is not a strict and very specific element that can be used in any case with the same way. Resilience can be learned and other people such as teachers can install it in the educational settings, in order to help their students (Brooks, 2006). It is not about the abilities every student should have, it is about skills, such as social skills, autonomy and dealing with problems. All these skills can be learnt even from teachers to their students by showing the first the great impact of resilience. The enhancement of resilience within the educational context is not limited solely to academic outcomes, academic engagement, and academic performance. On the contrary, fostering resilience within the school environment offers significant benefits throughout the student's life.

Specifically, it has been noted that students who build resilience experience fewer depressive symptoms and greater life satisfaction (Caleon & King, 2020). However, to enhance resilience in schools and for students to experience the benefits of resilience, it is important for interventions to target students, teachers, families, peers, and the community (Johnson & Lazarus, 2014).

Regarding the challenges, that students may encounter, there is a great number of issues they have to face. To be more specific, students may deal with problems in their families such as, socioeconomic problems, poor educated parents that are not able to support their kids in the school subjects or even more single parent families. In addition, students sometimes have to face problems in the school settings. These could be related with their peers, such as bullying, poor socialization which means a few or no friends and difficulties in succeeding in academics. Apart from the family and their peers, students have to deal with subjects as well. Specifically, they have long periods of stress because they have their lessons, tests and finally examinations. The importance to succeed in the final exams means sometimes many hours of study and however it happens rarely, it actually does exist, negative behaviors from students to others because of the pressure they feel from the school. This can lead to anxiety or depression as well (Hartley, 2011). Although all these are problems that students have to cope with, teachers play an important role as well. For instance, they have to offer their help to a student that has not even a single friend. They have to aim the student to become more open to others and to develop his social skills. In addition, in case there is a student, who has problems with the subjects they have to help him overcome his obstacles especially if the student comes from poorly educated parents.

At this point, resilience has a significant role to play. In order for students to overcome their problems, we discussed before, they have to develop resilience, and this can occur by increasing emotional intelligence and enhancing their psychological well-being (Salami, 2011). There is actually a fundamental relationship between resilience and a person's well-being. To be more specific, the time a student chances the way they think and manage the situational cues, their levels of stress, anxiety and negative thoughts can be diminished, and this increases the levels of resilience (Memedovic et al., 2010). In addition, resilience can motivate students to focus on their inner morality (Resnick et al., 2011). This can increase the sense of control and freedom and it can actually provide the positive feelings they may have. As a result, they feel more powerful to deal with anything that comes out.

UNDERSTANDING RESILIENCE IN EDUCATION

The issue of resilience is of major interest for researchers and therapist the last few decades. There are many definitions of resilience. However, there are not as many definitions as they are needed to understand the difficult discipline of it. One of the most well-known definitions of educational resilience is "the heightened likelihood of success in school and other life accomplishments despite environmental adversities brought about by early traits, conditions, and experiences" (Wang et al., 1994, p. 46). In general, resilience means the person's ability to deal with his difficulties and to overcome the obstacles that may face in his everyday life (Masten, 2001). According to educational resilience, we have to highlight that it is not a strict and restricted subject. It is about alteration and specifically it is about having the student the abilities and the characteristics to make the necessary changes to promote success in school in every aspect. Regarding these characteristics, Benard in 1993, focused on four specific elements. For instance, educational resilience relates to social competence and problem-solving skills (Benard, 1993). Moreover, autonomy and the issue of purpose has been found to affect educational resilience.

Other researchers, who tried to identify the elements that affect resilience, were McMillan and Reed in 1994. They found that, for the educational resilience there are another four aspects, that are of major importance. For example, it plays a crucial role the school environment such as the access to technology and in general the climate inside the class. Furthermore, educational resilience relates to student's family and specifically, if there is support from family or if they have extremely high expectations that make the student feels stress and anxiety. In addition, McMillan and Reed (1994) described the need of motivation and goal orientation from students in order to develop the educational resilience. Finally, they highlighted the productive use of time. It is not the same to be five hours in front of a screen without doing anything and doing your homework for five hours. It is more effective to spend the time by completing homework or whatever your job is. This reflects a more positively psychological attitude.

According to the benefits of enhancing resilience in educational settings, it is commonly accepted that, there are both academical and psychological benefits. By fostering resilience in students and teachers, the second become able to change the principles of teaching so that, any practice matches to every student (Comer, 1987). For example, in case there is a student who has a special need, teachers by developing resilience, they are able to focus on this need and adapt the whole learning process, so that it is beneficial to this student. Moreover, students with resilience have shown to have better perceptions of support, both from their friends and their family as well (Gonzalez and Padilla, 1997). This helps them also to have better communication with their teachers and as a result, support and feedback regarding their improvement. Because of this practice, students manage to read more and do their homework and so they have higher grades at the end of the school year.

Apart from the academic benefits, fostering resilience in students and teachers, has also psychological benefits. For example, the time students felt, they had more supportive teachers, they simultaneously felt more encouraged to try for the school subjects. This reduced anxiety and stress. In addition, resilient students develop self-esteem and this leads to more satisfaction inside the classrooms. Moreover, fostering resilience, enhances emotional intelligence and this leads to a more positive point of view in life. Emotional intelligence is actually a person's ability to monitor and control his feelings. This helps both students and teachers to select information, understand how they feel and to behave in an appropriate way, so that they succeed a better outcome. It gives the opportunity for both to be more flexible and so they feel they have more freedom. As a result, educational resilience creates more positive feelings and behaviors for both students and teachers.

Several studies have been conducted that have examined resilience in the school context and the benefits for students and educators. As mentioned earlier, students with resilience exhibit better academic performance and engagement, experience greater life satisfaction, and have fewer depressive symptoms (Caleon & King, 2020). Additionally, fostering resilience in schools can help students develop more coping strategies, which can help them effectively manage problems and challenges they face within and outside the school environment (Ungar et al., 2019). Schools appear to be able to cultivate resilience, and disadvantaged students may derive even more benefits (Agasisti et al., 2018; Ungar et al., 2019). However, for disadvantaged students to benefit, it is crucial to have a positive school climate; otherwise, resilience is more challenging to develop (Agasisti et al., 2018).

The benefits of resilience are not limited solely to students but equally benefit teachers. Cultivating resilience in teachers appears to combat burnout and attrition (Kangas-Dick & O'Shaughnessy, 2020), while also enhancing career-long commitment, effectiveness (Gu, 2014), and well-being (Gibbs & Miller, 2013).

Resilience Research and Theories

In 2000 Nettles, Mucherach and Jones found that resilience together with the support of families and teachers, lead students to more academic achievements despite the fact that, they have been exposed to violence. In addition, they tend to be more involved inside the classrooms. They understand better the rules of the classroom and they are more positive to follow them. This enhances the achievement motivation and the academic self-concept. It is of major interest that in many studies regarding the effect of resilience in the educational settings, it has been found that resilient students manage to do better on mathematics. This may happen because they tend to spend more time studying and doing their homework. Resilience on educational settings helps students also to socialize more because of the understanding of a better social self-concept. They believe more on their strength and so they are not that much afraid to meet new people or to get involved to those they already know.

Concerning the increasing self-esteem of resilient students, they tended to not be shy and that much tired so that they could not get involved in the subjects. On the other hand, nonresilient students appeared to be more tired, more distracted and to distract more often other students' attentions during the class (Waxman et al., 1997). Furthermore, nonresilient students tended to be louder so that, they could stop teachers' work just because the second should calm down the first (Waxman et al., 1997). Many studies also concluded that resilient students are able to achieve higher scores on subjects at the end of the year. As we imagine, this occurs because of their involvement in classrooms as well as because of the extra time, they spend doing their homework and practicing for their subjects.

Since 1996 and 1997, many researchers have worked on the discipline of resilience. They found that resilience can be found on many distinct domains such as individual resilience, family resilience, community resilience, resilience in social work and many other domains (VanBreda, 2001). They all concluded that, resilience should not be thought as a way to just get away from problems. The aspect of resilience does not refer to ''don't look back'' or ''just shake it off''. These practices, not only they do not reduce stress, but they make it even bigger. Resilience has identified, as a way for the person to create strategies, to overcome stressful situations. At every moment, the person tries to find the balance between protective factors and risky factors (VanBreda, 2001). This is the reason, why it is important to introduce resilience at schools especially for students. They will learn to identify the protective and risky factors and as a result, they will be able to manage any situation appropriately.

According to the models that have come out regarding resilience, we will focus on the Adolescent Resilience Model and the Family Resiliency Model. The first one, focuses on the life development and the meaning-based models (Weekes, 1991, p. 32). It actually examines influences from the past and the present and how these affect the person in every single developmental phase such as infancy. In addition, it examines, how a stressful situation like illness, can affect practically and psychologically the person. For example, what happens the moment a student can not attend to school, because of a severe illness (Weekes, 1991, p. 32). The second model, focuses on family and the way a family maladministers with stressors (M.A. McCubbin & McCubbin, 1996). Specifically, this model interprets the interactions between parents, among parents and their children, among family and the society they live in. It addresses the problems, the aimed resources and the coping strategies. As we understand, in this way children learn how to overcome difficulties and to become more resilient in life.

BUILDING RESILIENCE IN STUDENTS

Promoting a Growth Mindset

The concept of a growth mindset in the educational settings has been found to play an important role to students' resilience. To be more specific, there are two types of students. There are those students, who believe that the intellectual capacity is fixed and those who think of the intellectual ability as something that is changeable (Yeager & Dweck, 2012, p.303). Considering the first, they have a more standard point of view regarding learning, solving problems and academic performance. Moreover, those students tend to examine their academic appearance and to solve their problems in comparison with others (Dweck, 2006). Because of, they do not have the ability to be more flexible, they think everything in a way that they measure anything. For instance, in case a student has to read for a test, he has the notion that he can achieve the greater, only if he passes the whole weekend studying for this test. In case, he is able to finish with his reading earlier, he cannot accept, he did his best just because he is not able to adapt himself to this situation. On the contrary, growth mindset students tend to think in a different way.

While fixed mindset students have a very strict way of thinking, growth mindset students have a completely distinctive way of interpreting the world. Specifically, those students conceive their academic performance in a more open-minded way. Furthermore, they interpret their intellectual ability as something that can flourish as time goes. They see growth and change in anything they do. In addition, comparing to fixed mindset students, growth mindset students actually solve their problems by taking into consideration the different situation, they face every time. They do not have a mere way of solving their problems or achieving in academics. These students appreciate their academic performance in relation to growth, evolution and development. They focus on the way they can achieve their goal and not only the result. So, they are concentrated on the effort and the challenges they have to handle with. As a result, this way of thinking can lead to adapting resiliency and especially in the educational settings.

Sometimes, we tend to think of achieving our goal by making that much effort. However, there are some issues, that do not need that effort but some small changes in our everyday life. This also happens in cultivating growth mindset inside the classroom. In other words, teachers can change the way students process with issues that come up in the classrooms. For instance, it has been found that group counseling can aim (Warunwutthi et al., 2022). Using group counselling, students are able to listen each other talking about their problems. They can see distinguishing ways of dealing with a difficult situation. In addition, sharing means accepting the situation. At this point, students can feel safer and more powerful. They become also open to new suggestions or probably to changes, that may occur in the future (Warunwutthi et al., 2022). This strategy relates to social cognitive learning and enhances self-efficacy and students' resilience.

Apart from group counselling, Altaleb in 2021 found that a corner inside the classroom can be very helpful for students to acquire a growth mindset. Specifically, teachers can create a ''corner for thinking outside the box''. This corner will give students the opportunity, to find new ways to solve the problem, that has come up. This practice helps students to get better prepared for life. However, helpful this practice can be, it is easier for students, that are open to new things. For all other students, who think about their issues in a restricted way, teachers can have the main role. To explain this, it is crucial for students to have teachers that focus on their specific needs. By focusing on a single student every time, the teacher can understand the needs, the thoughts and actually the plans, a student may have for facing a problem. By the time the teacher will focus on a student, then they can discuss about these thoughts. Moreover, the teacher can give books to the student to increase his knowledge or even they can create together a plan with stages, that are needed to be done, in order for the student to succeed. This gives to the student the sense that he is not alone, increases his self-efficacy, his growth mindset and actually his resiliency.

Coping Strategies for Students

In the school settings, students sometimes face a number of different issues. These problems may be related to school subjects, which means that, not all students are good enough to mathematics, statistics, language, etc. In addition, they may face problems with their classmates. It is common, that some children are not able to socialize that much and they have a few or even no friends. Finally, some students have difficulty in adjusting in the educational settings. For these reasons, Zimmer-Gembeck and Skinner in 2016, conducted a study and found that, there are many ways a student can manage all these problems. All these ways had been categorized into two different aspects. Specifically, they found that there are the approach strategies and the evasive strategies (Zimmer-Gembeck & Skinner, 2016). On the one hand, the evasive strategies refer to mechanisms that a student can use to avoid actually what happens. These strategies include denial, distraction and wishful thoughts.

On the other hand, the approach strategies relate to making plans, deciding on specific actions that can give a solution and actually having a more active role regarding the problems (Zimmer-Gembeck & Skinner, 2016). In addition, this type of categorization includes the seeking of help. This means that, in case someone faces a problem, he asks other people to help him overcome together his problem.

The person adopts a more active approach to problems and does not freeze in front of them. He tries to reduce all the negative feelings and to use his cognition in order to achieve his goal. It is about cognitive and behavioral strategies that are used in this type of mechanisms. Most of the approach strategies have a positive point of view, because they aim the person to seek a solution and become activated. To this way, people feel better with themselves and adopt a positive attitude to stressors that come out.

At this point, let's have a closer look on emotional intelligence and its relation to educational resilience. Emotional intelligence has been found to be an important aspect for building resilience. It started from social intelligence followed by the distinction of cognitive intelligence and emotional intelligence and now we will investigate emotional intelligence (Bar-On, 2006). Emotional intelligence consists of the cognitive abilities and the personality traits (Toriello et al., 2022). Specifically, it is a type of personality that includes interpersonal, intrapersonal, adaptability, reduction of stress and actually mood operators (Bar-On, 2007). In addition, Greenockle in 2010 found that emotional intelligence refers to happiness, personal satisfaction and success. Many studies highlighted its importance in leadership. So, educational leaders such as teachers have to be equipped with this aspect. It can help them, first of all to become resilient and then to manage any difficult situation that arises, such as with students in the educational settings (Gilio & Dorsey, 2016).

At first, emotional intelligence refers to focusing someone on oneself. It is the ability to understand a person, how he feels at every single moment. This gives the advantage to have a portfolio of accepted management techniques, that can be used at any situation. Having conquered this ability, the person has developed resiliency just because he becomes flexible. After that, he can help others, deal with their problems. For example, it is of major importance for the principal of the school, to show emotional intelligence and as a consequence resiliency. The principal struggles with different students, who have distinct socioeconomic background and different abilities in learning. So, emotional intelligence of teachers can help them cope with students and actually with the problems of them. They can install new ways to students of solving their problems and new ways of managing with their mixed feelings.

Encouraging Perseverance

The element of perseverance is of crucial importance in the school settings. Teachers should acquire perseverance and determination, in order to be able to aim students in the classroom and then make students acquire perseverance. Perseverance refers to continuously try for your goals and your beliefs and being steady to them. It is the maintenance of the effort, even if there are obstacles or a bad psychological situation. Despite the failure, perseverance means continuing and becoming persistent on this. All these are very important to occur, because they affect a number of aspects in a person's life. Specifically, perseverance can help people understand their power and their strength. Keeping the faith of once beliefs, he understands the ways, he finds to overcome the obstacles in order to succeed his goals. In addition, he can create a portfolio with strategies that can use in any case that comes suddenly.

Other advantages of having perseverance in life are the ability to go from one stage to the other and the creation of a specific personality in life. In other words, Erickson in 1994 found that perseverance relates to the individual's development stage and specifically he referred to the years between 6 and 11 years old (Nataria, 2016). At this stage, the student goes to the primary school and he has to face a number of incitements. For example, he has to deal with his peers as it's the first time he has that much interaction with them. Furthermore, the student has to realize, that his actions have results and those results are recognized by others, in case they lead to positive outcomes. This is the great point for Erickson, in order for children to not develop disability known as inferiority. After that, perseverance can help a person to create their own personality and character. Being steady on his beliefs means, that they create strategies to maintain their point of view in life.

Many studies have conducted investigating the strategies, that can be used to instill self-determination to students. Algozzine et al. in 2001 found two ways to increase determination in students. These were referred to student's involvement in the classroom and the teaching of these skills directly from the teachers. Specifically, student's involvement relates to more engagement. To think of it, there are students, who never talk, never participate in the class and other circumstances and never express their ideas. For these students, teachers should try to engage them in the school setting. They can do so by involving them in a problem-solving situation. This problem could be a problem between the classmates or even a mathematic problem. Starting with this strategy, then teachers could introduce students to self-management, self-awareness and self-control. Having conquered the student those elements, then he feels better with himself and as a result, he can become more determined. In addition, teachers can use their behavior to introduce determination to students. It is different for students to have a teacher, that never relates with his students than a teacher, who has a close relationship to them and shows determination, when it is needed.

Furthermore, it has been found that autonomy, competence and relatedness are important elements for determination (Taylor & Ntoumanis, 2007). So, teachers have to focus on them as well. Students have the need to feel, that they can make their decision. They want to be able to choose among the different options. As a result, teachers can give students options and let them decide which option is better for them. Moreover, students want to understand, that they can make changes on the environment, regardless of if this is their school or their home and that these changes make them satisfied. Finally, students have a great need to relate to others. It is of major importance, teachers to be available for their students at any time. This could include moments where students want to talk about their problems or even to discuss about life. As we see, there are not specific strategies to introduce determination to students. There is the environment, the people inside it and their behaviors that can help them become more determinant.

FOSTERING RESILIENCE IN TEACHERS

Teacher Well-Being

It is difficult to create a resilient educational environment without considering first of all, teachers' emotional situation as well as their well-being. The importance of teachers' quality is even greater, if we think about elementary school (Johnson et al., 2012). At this stage, students spend most of their time at school with a single teacher comparing to secondary school, where students have a different teacher for every subject (Johnson et al., 2012). In addition, it has been found that students' and teachers' relationship can affect students' quality of communication in the whole environment of school- including teachers, peers, classmates, etc. (Osher et al., 2007). It is not only the communication aspect, but also their academic performance and finally students' emotional situation. Moreover, teachers' psychology plays a crucial role for the climate inside the class (La Paro et al., 2009). To be more specific, in case a teacher feels depressed or irritated, this can be observed by students and the second tend to feel more anxious and stressed and so they become less able to think clearly and solve their problems.

Regarding teachers' irritation, Schonfeld in 2001 concluded that, if teachers face constantly burnout episodes, this can lead them to physical or mental illness. As a result, this illness affects their school performance and they are not able to be helpful for students (Schonfeld, 2001). Due to their illness, they may be frequently absent from the school settings. This may influence students, to feel insecure in the educational settings and without having someone to ask for help, in case they need so. As we understand, it is of major importance to have at the educational settings teachers, who have developed appropriately the social and emotional competence, including their self-awareness (Collaborative for Academic, Social and Emotional Learning, 2003). Self-efficacy of teachers can aim to build a positive environment inside the classroom so that, students feel first of all safe to communicate and express themselves. Secondly, teachers will be able to give the necessary elements to students so that kids will be able to build resiliency.

It has been found that, mindfulness can help teachers demonstrate their emotions and adopt a more effective way of living. Mindfulness is about paying attention to the present and promoting insight, reflection and concentration (Kabat-Zinn, 1994; Zajonc, 2006). The more someone practices on mindfulness, the more it can become effective (Werner & Gross, 2009). It is a way of living and not only an element, I can use whenever I need it. Thus, it can reduce anxiety as well as stress and so it enhances psychology (Weinstein et al., 2009). Because of, mindfulness increases self-awareness, it also reduces irritability and judgmental thoughts and practices. In this way, teachers become more able to handle students' irritability. They acquire the ability to listen, understand and then help students. As a result, teachers do not respond immediately and without thinking of their actions.

Another self-care strategy for educators is the ability to learn and increase empathy and compassion for themselves. Hopkins in 2001 talked about peace and happiness as being elements of empathy and compassion. These elements can be conquered by practicing constantly 'care' (Hopkins, 2001). This care refers to showing love to self. Having understood and established this practice, then you can show love to others as well. In order to succeed, the person has to try every day. He will see the results, the time he will identify the changes on his psychology. To be more specific, having conquered empathy and compassion, the person has more positive feelings, simultaneously he is more open to help others. This helps to not hurry up to respond to others feelings, even if he disagrees with them. As we see, empathy and compassions for itself at first can help teachers feel more loving and happier. Then, they are able to interact with students in a way to enhance positive emotions in the educational setting.

Building a Supportive Community

In order for teachers to be able to enhance resiliency in students, they have to be resilient as well. There are a number of factors, that affect this process. To be more specific, it is very important for teachers to belong to a friendly school environment. Educational environment includes the teaching colleagues as well as the peers from other educational environments (Le Cornu, 2013). Having good relationships with other teachers, has been found to affect seriously teachers and their resiliency. Specifically, they posses a sense of belonging and that there will be someone in case of an emergency. In addition, this affects their psychology simultaneously to their job performance. Apart from colleagues and peers, the relationship with the principal of the school is crucial (Le Cornu, 2013). Being able to communicate with the person, who runs the whole educational setting, the teacher feels the care and the trust he actually needs. This practice enhances teacher's will to work and introduce a better school environment for the students.

The school culture also plays an important role (Johnson et al., 2010). This includes the norms, the behaviors and the values, that have been established in the educational setting. Moreover, school culture refers to democratic procedures, in which teachers can communicate freely between one another. This gives teachers the ability to learn new social skills, practices and ways to overcome their problems (Johnson et al., 2010). For the teachers, it is comforting to know from the beginning the way the school works. This makes things clear and steady regarding their behaviors and their relationships. It is very helpful especially for early career teachers, to understand the school norms and to have a specific school culture. This practice can promote a positive psychology and as a result, it can increase resiliency in teachers.

The communication between educators is very important, as we sited before. At this point, it would be interesting to have a look at strategies, that may be used to increase collaboration and communication among teachers. One of the strategies could be the 'culture builder' (Wood, 2005). It refers to a person who becomes responsible to organize activities, that bring teachers closer. These activities could be a trip, a celebration for someone's birthday or anything else that can make teachers have more time together (Wood, 2005). Despite the fact that, it seems easy, not all colleagues spent time together. This does not give them the chance to know one another better and as a consequence their collaboration becomes tougher. This of course does not enhance resilience in teachers, who long in students.

Another strategy that can be used, among educators, is the establishment of organizational routines (Sherer & Spillane, 2011). These routines relate to all things that occur inside the educational settings. This could be, the way teachers interact with one another or even with their students. Furthermore, it could refer to the way, repeated activities are taking place in the school setting (Hansen & Vogel, 2011). As such, there could be a very specific program with all the activities. On the one hand, this practice could be stressful for teachers, because they should carry out all of their obligations, in order for the school to function appropriately. On the other hand, this program could elevate collaboration among educators and as such it could fix communication among them. In addition, organizational routines could promote collective learning, in case there were analysis protocols for teachers works (Hargreaves & Goodson, 2006; Spillane et al., 2011). This practice could make teachers spend more time together and discuss their problems, so that someone could give a solution. There are strategies in place within schools that promote collaboration and communication among educators.

PRACTICAL STRATEGIES FOR IMPLEMENTATION

Resilience-Building Classroom Activities

As we mentioned before, resilience is a very important element for people to have it. Apart from understanding what it means, we have to find these exercises, that can promote resilience. There are a few activities, that can be used in the classroom and can aim students to increase their resilience level. For example, there is the 'Breaking Down 'Easy'' exercise (Gheihman et al., 2018). According to this exercise, students have to think of particular aspects like problems and then they have to write them down on a dairy or even on a single paper. They have to consider of an issue, that is easy for them to be solved but, it is difficult for others. In addition, having find this task, then they have to highlight all those factors, that make this task possible to be done (Gheihman et al., 2018). Finally, they have to translate those factors into traits and characteristics, that seem to be the positive and useful elements for the person to use them.

Another exercise that can promote resilience in students is the 'My Resilience Practice' (Gheihman et al., 2018). Regarding this activity, students have to keep a daily dairy and write down all the pathways they used to face the stressors, they have dealt or those, they are going to deal with in the future. These pathways will refer to the place that may occur the incident and the reflection, which means actually how the person overcome this difficult and which is the best way to do so (Gheihman et al., 2018). Moreover, it refers to the way these solutions will be used and finally to the people that may be useful in order to solve the problem all together. This will be a constant recording which is going to occur every day and this dairy can be placed inside the classroom and every student can have its own dairy.

Those two exercises were used by medical students. These students were found to deal with many stressors in their everyday life, so these activities aimed at introducing them to the element of resilience. One more activity, that can be used to enhance resilience, is the role-playing (Woltjer et al., 2006). The role-play is an activity that relates to real time tasks, that come up from the past or are about to happen in the future. This exercise can increase communication among people, as it is a multi-person activity (Woltjer et al., 2006). They can imagine about characters or tasks, they need to manage They can focus on a single issue and then try to find solutions. In addition, it focuses on training and study. Regarding the training, it has been found to be used for introducing resilience to participants. As such, role-play has introduced to increase the resilience of control systems.

Specifically, Woltjer, Johansson and Lundberg in 2006 examined the importance of role-play in unexpected situations. Furthermore, they examined its importance in facing harmful circumstances, such as fire. Their findings were of great importance.

To be more specific, they found that through resilience participants become more adaptable to unexpected situations that may come out. In addition, they acquired the element of coping. In other words, they learned, how to conform to strange circumstances. They managed to find new strategies or even new resources of help (Woltjer et al., 2006). Despite the fact that, this activity is about situations such as a fire, it can be used in the educational settings as well. Specifically, teachers can introduce a topic, that needs to be solved and ask students to cooperate in order to solve the problem. This can lead simultaneously to cooperation and resilience.

Professional Development for Resilience

There are different ways to introduce resilience into teacher professional development programs. We will discuss some of them. The D.R.E.A.M. Program is one of them (Armstrong et al., 2018). This is a program, that uses songs and hand-on activities, and it is developed to learn participants elements for resilience. It is based on positive psychology and highlights both positive and less positive feelings. This program includes activities such as psychoeducation, 'Emotions Go Fish' Game and many others (Armstrong et al., 2018). It is surprisingly interesting that students found this program very nice. They liked its activities and they were open to participate. They said, it had fun and managed to make new friends. In addition, teachers found to appreciate these activities and they were pleased to use them more inside the educational settings.

Another way, schools can incorporate resilience-building elements into teacher professional development programs is by using teachers, diaries in the school. To be more specific, they can keep notes for their emotions and the sticky objects (Armstrong et al., 2018). By using this strategy, teachers are allowed to examine their emotions and all those things, that affect them and make them feel like this. To this point, it would be important to highlight some ongoing learning, that could further help teachers and students. For example, it would be of great importance to find out, how resilience can affect family settings and consequently, how this can affect the educational settings. In addition, it would be interesting to have a look on specific strategies, that can be used by both teachers and students or even to be used simultaneously. Finally, it would be helpful to analyze resilience from the aspect of difficulties, that may emerge in the case of installing resilience in an educational environment.

CONCLUSION

Recap of Key Strategies

To sum up, there is a number of strategies, that can be used to increase resilience among teachers and students. Regarding teachers, they can use a daily dairy in the school settings, in order to write down their every day emotions. By doing so, they can communicate with other teachers, they can talk about the problems, they may face and they can find effective solutions all together. In addition, keeping a dairy is a way to express themselves and find those things, that make them feel uncomfortable sometimes. Regarding students there is a great number of strategies to be used. For example, there is the role-play, that can assimilate real events to be discussed. Furthermore, there is the Breaking Down 'Easy'' exercise as well as the 'My Resilience Practice' exercise for students. All of them depend on communication, interaction and enhancement of positive psychology.

Empowering Educational Resilience

Resilience is a very crucial element for a person to have it, because it can alter, the way he/she evaluates the world and the people around him/her. For example, there may be people, that feel alone and that they do not have someone to talk with. In addition, they may feel that, they do not have any positive characteristics and so they have a low self-esteem. By enhancing resilience especially in the educational settings, both teachers and students would feel differently. First of all, teachers become able to manage with any problem that comes up inside the classroom. Moreover, they become able to aim students, that are in need. Students on the other, enhance their self-esteem and their social abilities. Together with these characteristics, students become able to find their strengths, so they can use them in case there is a problem. As we see, resilience is helpful for both students and teachers and has to present in every educational setting.

All the above, highlight the reasons, why each of us should introduce resilience into our lives. Especially, if you are a teacher or a principal of a school environment, you now have many reasons to have a closer look to resilience. Think of a problem, you deal with the last one month. Does this relate to your feelings? Do you know, which are your feelings? Does this change the way you interact with others? Do you have people to discuss the issue, that you deal with? All these questions can be solved, just by introducing resilience into your life. Keep a daily dairy of your emotions, do some role-playing to discuss in a distinct way about your thoughts. Now, you have the knowledge of, what can be useful in the educational setting, in order to increase resilience and actually positive psychology.

REFERENCES

Agasisti, T., Avvisati, F., Borgonovi, F., & Longobardi, S. (2018). Academic resilience: What schools and countries do to help disadvantaged students succeed in PISA. https://doi.org/10.1787/19939019

Algozzine, B., Browder, D., Karvonen, M., Test, D. W., & Wood, W. M. (2001). Effects of interventions to promote self-determination for individuals with disabilities. *Review of Educational Research*, 71(2), 219–277. 10.3102/00346543071002219

Altaleb, A. (2021). Using Growth Mindset Strategies in the Classroom. Taboo. *The Journal of Culture and Education*, 20(2), 207–212. https://digitalscholarship.unlv.edu/taboo/vol20/iss2/16

Alva, S. A. (1991). Academic invulnerability among Mexican-American students: The importance of protective resources and appraisals. *Hispanic Journal of Behavioral Sciences*, 13(1), 18–34. 10.1177/07399863910131002

Armstrong, L. L., Desson, S., St. John, E., & Watt, E. (2019). The DREAM program: Developing resilience through emotions, attitudes, & meaning (gifted edition)–a second wave positive psychology approach. *Counselling Psychology Quarterly*, 32(3-4), 307–332. 10.1080/09515070.2018.1559798

Bar-On, R. (2006). The Bar-On model of emotional-social intelligence (ESI). *Psicothema*, 18, 13–25. https://reunido.uniovi.es/index.php/PST/article/view/841517295953

Bar-On, R. 2007. The Bar-On model of emotional intelligence: a valid, robust and applicable EI model. *Organisations and People, 14*(2), 27–34. https://amed.org.uk/wp-content/uploads/2022/08/OPMay2007.pdf#page=29

Benard, B. (1993). Fostering resiliency in kids. *Educational Leadership*, 51, 44–48. https://kaching.socialwork.hku.hk/Workshop%20Notes/Resiliency/Foster%20Resiliency.pdf

Brooks, J. E. (2006). Strengthening resilience in children and youths: Maximizing opportunities through the schools. *Children & Schools*, 28(2), 69–76. 10.1093/cs/28.2.69

Caleon, I. S., & King, R. B. (2020). Examining the phenomenon of resilience in schools. *European Journal of Psychological Assessment*, 37(1), 52–64. Advance online publication. 10.1027/1015-5759/a000572

Collaborative for Academic, *Social and Emotional Learning*. (2003). *Safe and sound: An education leader's guide to evidence-based social and emotional learning (SEL) programs*. Chicago, IL: Collaborative for Academic, Social and Emotional Learning.

Comer, J. P. (1987). New Haven's school community connection. *Educational Leadership*, 44, 13–16. https://eric.ed.gov/?id=EJ353781

Dweck, C. S. (2006). *Mindset: The New Psychology of Success*. Random House.

Erikson, E. H. (1994). *Identity: Youth and crisis* (No. 7). WW Norton & Company.

Gheihman, G., Cooper, C., & Simpkin, A. (2018). Everyday resilience: Practical tools to promote resilience among medical students. *Journal of General Internal Medicine*, 34(4), 498–501. 10.1007/s11606-018-4728-830535748

Gibbs, S., & Miller, A. (2014). Teachers' resilience and well-being: A role for educational psychology. *Teachers and Teaching*, 20(5), 609–621. 10.1080/13540602.2013.844408

Gilio, B., & Dorsey, T. (2016). The reflective principal: Principals' emotional intelligence Outweighs IQ. *Principal.*

Gonzalez, R., & Padilla, A. M. (1997). The academic resilience of Mexican American high school students. *Hispanic Journal of Behavioral Sciences*, 19(3), 301–317. 10.1177/07399863970193004

Greenockle, K. M. (2010). The new face in leadership: Emotional intelligence. *Quest*, 62(3), 260–267. 10.1080/00336297.2010.10483647

Gu, Q. (2014). The role of relational resilience in teachers' career-long commitment and effectiveness. *Teachers and Teaching*, 20(5), 502–529. 10.1080/13540602.2014.937961

Hansen, N. K., & Vogel, R. (2011). Organizational routines: A review and outlook on practice-based micro-foundations. *Economics, Management & Financial Markets, 6*(3), 86–111. https://www.ceeol.com/search/article-detail?id=87415

Hargreaves, A., & Goodson, I. (2006). Educational change over time? The sustainability and nonsustainability of three decades of secondary school change and continuity. *Educational Administration Quarterly*, 42(3), 3–41. 10.1177/0013161X05277975

Hartley, M. T. (2011). Examining the relationships between resilience, mental health, and academic persistence in undergraduate college students. *Journal of American College Health*, 59(7), 596–604. 10.1080/07448481.2010.51563221823954

Hopkins, J. (2001). *Cultivating compassion*. Broadway Books.

Johnson, B., Down, B., Le Cornu, R., Peters, J., Sullivan, A., Pearce, J., & Hunter, J. (2010). Conditions that support early career teacher resilience. Refereed paper presented at 'Teacher education for a sustainable future', the annual conference of the Australian Teacher Education Association (ATEA), Townsville. https://atea.edu.au/wp-content/uploads/2010_johnson_et_al.pdf

Johnson, B., & Lazarus, S. (2008). The role of schools in building the resilience of youth faced with adversity. *Journal of Psychology in Africa*, 18(1), 19–30. 10.1080/14330237.2008.10820168

Johnson, S. M., Kraft, M. A., & Papay, J. P. (2012). How context matters in high-need schools: The effects of teachers' working conditions on their professional satisfaction and their students' achievement. *Teachers College Record*, 114(10), 1–39. 10.1177/016146811211401004

Kabat-Zinn, J. (1994). *Wherever you go, there you are: Mindfulness meditation in everyday life*. Hyperion.

Kangas-Dick, K., & O'Shaughnessy, E. (2020). Interventions that promote resilience among teachers: A systematic review of the literature. *International Journal of School & Educational Psychology*, 8(2), 131–146. 10.1080/21683603.2020.1734125

La Paro, K. M., Hamre, B. K., Locasale-Crouch, J., Pianta, R. C., Bryant, D., Early, D., & Burchinal, M. (2009). Quality in kindergarten classrooms: Observational evidence for the need to increase children's learning opportunities in early education classrooms. *Early Education and Development*, 20(4), 657–692. 10.1080/10409280802541965

Le Cornu, R. (2013). Building Early Career Teacher Resilience: The Role of Relationships. *The Australian Journal of Teacher Education*, 38(4), 1–16. 10.14221/ajte.2013v38n4.4

Masten, A. S. (2001). Ordinary Magic: Resilience Processes in Development. *The American Psychologist*, 56(3), 227–3238. 10.1037/0003-066X.56.3.22711315249

McCubbin, M. A., & McCubbin, H. I. (1996). Resiliency in families: A conceptual model of family adjustment and adaptation in response to stress and crises. In McCubbin, H. I., Thompson, A. I., & McCubbin, M. A. (Eds.), *Family assessment: Resiliency, coping and adaptation: Inventories for research and practice* (pp. 1–64). University of Wisconsin.

McMillan, J. H., & Reed, D. F. (1994). At-risk students and resiliency: Factors contributing to academic success. *The Clearing House: A Journal of Educational Strategies, Issues and Ideas*, 67(3), 137–140. 10.1080/00098655.1994.9956043

Memedovic, S., Grisham, J. R., Denson, T. F., & Moulds, M. L. (2010). The effects of trait reappraisal and suppression on anger and blood pressure in response to provocation. *Journal of Research in Personality*, 44(4), 540–543. 10.1016/j.jrp.2010.05.002

Nataria, Y. (2016). *Goal setting and perseverance*. Psychology Forum UMM.

Nettles, S. M., Mucherach, W., & Jones, D. S. (2000). Understanding resilience: The role of social resources. *Journal of Education for Students Placed at Risk*, 5(1), 47–60. 10.1207/s15327671espr0501&2_4

Osher, D., Sprague, J., Weissberg, R. P., Axelrod, J., Keenan, S., & Kendziora, K. T. (2007). A comprehensive approach to promoting social, emotional, and academic growth in contemporary schools. In Thomas, A., & Grimes, J. (Eds.), *Best practices in school psychology* (5th ed., pp. 1263–1278). National Association of School Psychologists.

Resnick, B., Gwyther, L. P., & Roberto, K. A. (2011). *Resilience in aging*. Springer. 10.1007/978-1-4419-0232-0

Reynolds, C. F.III. (2019). Building resilience through psychotherapy. *World Psychiatry; Official Journal of the World Psychiatric Association (WPA)*, 18(3), 289–291. 10.1002/wps.2066331496086

Salami, S. O. (2011). Personality and psychological well-being of adolescents: The moderating role of emotional intelligence. *Social Behavior and Personality*, 39(6), 785–794. 10.2224/sbp.2011.39.6.785

Schonfeld, I. S. (2001). Stress in first-year women teachers: The context of social support and coping. *Genetic, Social, and General Psychology Monographs*, 127, 7547–8756. https://academicworks.cuny.edu/cc_pubs/315/11471976

Seville, E. (2008). *Resilience: Great concept...but what does it mean*? Wilmington.

Sherer, J. Z., & Spillane, J. P. (2011). Constancy and change in work practice in schools: The role of organizational routines. *Teachers College Record*, 113(3), 611–657. 10.1177/016146811111300302

Spillane, J. P., Parise, L. M., & Sherer, J. Z. (2011). Organizational routines as coupling mechanisms: Policy, school administration, and the technical core. *American Educational Research Journal*, 48(3), 586–619. 10.3102/0002831210385102

Taylor, I. M., & Ntoumanis, N. (2007). Teacher Motivational Strategies and Student Self-Determination in Physical Education. *Journal of Educational Psychology*, 99(4), 747–760. 10.1037/0022-0663.99.4.747

Toriello, H. V., Van de Ridder, J. M., Brewer, P., Mavis, B., Allen, R., Arvidson, C., Kovar-Gough, I., Novak, E., O'Donnell, J., Osuch, J., & Ulrich, B. (2022). Emotional intelligence in undergraduate medical students: A scoping review. *Advances in Health Sciences Education : Theory and Practice*, 27(1), 1–21. 10.1007/s10459-021-10079-234709484

Ungar, M., Connelly, G., Liebenberg, L., & Theron, L. (2019). How schools enhance the development of young people's resilience. *Social Indicators Research*, 145(2), 615–627. 10.1007/s11205-017-1728-8

VanBreda, A. D. P. (2001). *Resilience Theory: A literature review*. South Africa Military Health Service.

Wang, M. C., Haertel, G. D., & Walberg, H. J. (1994). Educational resilience in inner cities. In Wang, M. C., & Gordon, E. W. (Eds.), *Educational resilience in inner-city America: Challenges and prospects* (pp. 45–72). Lawrence Erlbaum.

Warunwutthi, N., Wattananonsakul, S., & Ekpansyaskul, C. (2022). The effectiveness of growth mindset counseling program to enhance students resilience in a public autonomous university in Thailand. *Journal of Research and Curriculum Development, 12*(1). https://so03.tci-thaijo.org/index.php/jrcd/article/view/260705

Waxman, H. C., Huang, S. L., & Wang, M. C. (1997). Investigating the multilevel classroom learning environment of resilient and nonresilient students from inner-city elementary schools. *International Journal of Educational Research*, 27(4), 343–353. 10.1016/S0883-0355(97)90016-1

Weekes, D. P. (1991). Application of the life-span developmental perspective to nursing research with adolescents. *Journal of Pediatric Nursing*, 6(1), 38–48. https://europepmc.org/article/med/19901251990125

Weinstein, N., Brown, K. W., & Ryan, R. M. (2009). A multi-method examination of the effects of mindfulness on stress attribution, coping and emotional well-being. *Journal of Research in Personality*, 43(3), 374–385. 10.1016/j.jrp.2008.12.008

Werner, K., & Gross, J. J. (2009). Emotion regulation and pathology: A conceptual framework. In Gross, J. J. (Ed.), *Handbook of emotion regulation* (pp. 13–37). Guilford Press.

Woltjer, R., Trnka, J., Lundberg, J., & Johansson, B. (2006, September). Role-playing exercises to strengthen the resilience of command and control systems. In *Proceedings of the 13th Eurpoean conference on Cognitive ergonomics: trust and control in complex socio-technical systems* (pp. 71-78). DOI: 10.1145/1274892.1274904

Wood, A. (2005). The Importance of Principals: Site Administrators' Roles in Novice Teacher Induction. *American Secondary Education*, 33(2), 39–62. https://www.jstor.org/stable/41064612

Wu, G., Feder, A., Cohen, H., Kim, J. J., Calderon, S., Charney, D. S., & Mathé, A. A. (2013). Understanding resilience. *Frontiers in Behavioral Neuroscience*, 7, 10. 10.3389/fnbeh.2013.0001023422934

Yeager, D. S., & Dweck, C. S. (2012). Mindsets that promote resilience: When students believe that personal characteristics can be developed. *Educational Psychologist*, 47(4), 302–314. 10.1080/00461520.2012.722805

Zajonc, A. (2006). Love and knowledge: Recovering the heart of teaching through contemplation. *Teachers College Record*, 108(9), 1742–1759. 10.1111/j.1467-9620.2006.00758.x

Zimmer-Gembeck, M. J., & Skinner, E. A. (2016). The development of coping: Implications for psychopathology and resilience. In Cicchetti, D. (Ed.), Developmental psychopathology. John Wiley & Sons. 10.1002/9781119125556.devpsy410

Chapter 10
Psychological Resilience and the Child With Learning Disabilities

Nataly Loizidou Ieridou
https://orcid.org/0000-0002-8988-4804
Frederick Unversity, Cyprus

Fotini Kyriakides Kranou
https://orcid.org/0000-0003-2254-0748
Frederick University, Cyprus

ABSTRACT

Students with learning disabilities (LD) often appear to have low academic performance, experience difficulties in performing academic tasks and avoid engaging in them, consider their own academic and self-regulation skills as inferior to other students with typical performance, have low self-perception and self-esteem, fewer expectations of future success, and experience more emotional and social difficulties than their typically developing peers. However, there is no shortage of studies that characterize the developmental course of many individuals with LD as something that exceeds all expectations. Though recent theories of psychological resilience provide a framework for understanding the complex factors that influence adaptation and general wellbeing within this framework, it is important to look into the individual protective factors in building psychological resilience and psychological well-being in children with learning difficulties. The family and school environment are important factors that contribute to young people's psychosocial development.

DOI: 10.4018/979-8-3693-8312-4.ch010

Copyright © 2024, IGI Global. Copying or distributing in print or electronic forms without written permission of IGI Global is prohibited.

INTRODUCTION

The term 'resilience' or 'Psychological Resilience' implies a dynamic process in which the individual displays positive adaptation abilities or the ability to maintain or regain mental health in the context of challenges or difficult circumstances (Gutman, 2010; Luthar et al., 2000; Masten & Curtis, 2000; Miller & Daniel, 2007; Prince-Edbury, 2008; Turner et al., 1995) using his/her skills and the available support systems (Condly, 2006; Glennie, 2010). Resilience is viewed as an end product of protective processes that does not eliminate risk or stress but allows the individual to cope effectively with difficulties and adversity and compensate for risk factors through the support of protective factors (Rutter, 1987). Resilience is a term used to describe successful adaptation of the individual despite factors and circumstances that place them at potential risk (Benard, 1995). Resilient individuals have the ability to withstand, overcome, or recover from a severe threat (Masten, 2014). Although many definitions of psychological resilience have been proposed, all contain two common elements: a) exposure to risk and b) the corresponding factors that help promote positive outcomes and reduce negative ones (Fergus & Zimmerman, 2005; Fraser et al.,1999; Luthar & Zigler, 1991). Many young people are daily exposed to stressful and/or traumatic situations, abuse, adverse conditions, and so on, due to various factors, such as, for example, natural disasters, wars, neglect, violence, separation or death of loved ones, etc. (Mukund & Dehuri, 2016). Others may experience harassment, bullying, peer rejection, and other situations that make them feel anxiety, vulnerability, fear, sadness, frustration, or loneliness (Masten, 2014). Considering that children and adolescents have an increased likelihood of experiencing difficulties and finding themselves at risk in today's society, it is particularly important to consider how we can enhance building resilience from early childhood (Windle et al., 2011).

LITERATURE REVIEW

Psychological Resilience as a Dynamic Process

Despite the growing interest in research investigating resilience, it becomes apparent that there is a lack of agreement on an operational definition of resilience (Aburt et al., 2016), probably because it is influenced by many factors including characteristics of individuals, their family and the wider community (Herrman et al., 2011; Naglieri & LeBuffe, 2005); even so, through the various definitions, it appears that: a) these factors and systems contribute to an interactive dynamic process that can promote mental resilience, and b) resilience can be context and time specific;

and may not be present in all domains of life (Masten, 2001). The various factors related to resilience, which often interact, include biological, psychological traits, social support traits, and social systems traits, such as family, school, friends, the wider community, and society (Luthar, 2000; Prince-Emburry & Courville, 2008). In conclusion, the term 'resilience' refers to this dynamic process that individuals adopt to maintain a positive adaptation when they have been exposed to difficult, adverse conditions and have experienced difficulties in their developmental trajectory or have recovered from traumatic events (Masten et al., 1990; Luthar & Cicchetti, 2000; Henderson & Milstein, 2008; Masten & Gewirtz, 2008). Resilience could be described as a reflection of the relationship between individual and environmental factors that leads to the ability of the individual or group to respond to adversity through coping or adaptation.

Psychological Resilience in Children and Adolescents

The first international studies on mental resilience were mainly longitudinal (Luthar & Zigler, 1991; Werner, 1989), and have focused on children and adolescents who were at risk and were exposed to significant and serious adversity, such as extreme levels of poverty and parental mental illness (Masten et al., 1990). These studies have highlighted specific protective factors that have a greater influence on the adaptation and typical development of children. The individual's characteristics, which were identified by the research as protective factors, referred to mental ability (Brooks, 1994; Luthar, 1991), temperament (Wright & Masten, 2005), autonomy (Jacelon, 1997), self-confidence (Polk, 1997), sociability (Brooks, 2006; Luthar & Zigler, 1991), effective coping strategies (Brooks, 1994; Luthar & Zigler, 1991; Polk, 1997) and communication skills (Werner, 1989).

The Profile of the "Psychologically Resilient Child-Adolescent"

As mentioned above, research suggests, that children and adolescents may face multiple risks on their path to adulthood (Brooks, 2006; Goldstein & Brooks, 2013), some children are at risk and may display dysfunctional behaviors and have reduced chances of developing their full potential in adulthood, but some children face stressful situations and adversity, and yet continue to thrive despite difficulties (Alvord & Grados, 2005; Brooks, 1994; Masten, 1990; Masten, 2007; Masten, 2011; Masten & Coatsworth, 1998; Rak & Patterson, 2000; Werner, 2000).

Children who succeed, against all odds, have been recognized as resilient (Luther & Cicchetti, 2000) and display certain individual characteristics and communication skills that appear to help them to overcome any adverse conditions and succeed (Rak & Patterson, 2000). Young individuals who develop resilience despite difficult situations they may grow up in, are distinguished by their self-esteem, self-worth, self-efficacy, perseverance, self-control, the ability of problem-solving skills, and stress management strategies that they use. It is these individuals who can recognize their emotions and control those that cause them stress, such as anger, fear, and sadness (Zucker et el., 2003) and they use coping strategies, such as humor for example, to overcome difficulties (Pellegrini et al., 1987; Olsson et al., 2003). Everly and colleagues (Everly et al., 2013; Everly & Lating, 2013) went on to define seven (7) key characteristics for resilient children: innovativeness, creative thinking, determination to act and take responsibility, perseverance, and honesty, self-control, and optimism. These seven key characteristics have been supported by other researchers (William et al., 2001) who also added intelligence, temperament, and physical health as internal factors that contribute to the promotion of mental well-being (Masten, 2001; Alvord & Grados, 2005; Benzies & Mychasiuk, 2009; Garmezy et al., 1984; Werner, 2000). It was further argued that psychologically resilient children have a high degree of intrapersonal control, optimism, and a high level of confidence. They also have the ability to create positive conditions for themselves and others and know when to give up the effort in something that cannot be achieved (Christensen et al., 1991). Finally, these children appear to be particularly persistent (Bandura, 1989) and determined (Werner, 2000), responsible (Gorman-Smith & Tolan, 2003) [56], with a high level of general knowledge and many talents (Garmezy, 1991).

Factors Related to Psychological Resilience During Childhood

The study of psychological resilience has shown that several personal and environmental factors can have a positive influence on the quality of their psychosocial adaptation to difficult, stressful situations and risks (Miller & Daniel, 2007; King et al., 2020; Barnova & Tamasova, 2018). Protective factors are considered to be internal characteristics of the individual or factors related to the social environment, which act as dynamic mechanisms that help children and adolescents to resist or balance the risks to which they are exposed to (Rutter, 2012). These internal characteristics may be cognitive factors (e.g., intelligence, self-efficacy), affective factors (e.g., interaction with significant others, self-image), and behavioral factors (e.g., coping skills, positive social behavior). Other characteristics, such as perseverance, determination, self-efficacy, creativity, cohesion, and self-awareness are some more internal elements that are positively associated with resilience (Affi &Macmillan, 2011; Smokowski et al., 1999; Waaktaar et al., 2004). Environmental factors may include family characteristics (e.g., family communication, support from family members, parental influence) (Bempechat, 2012), quality of interaction with parents (Affi & Macmillan, 2011; Vanderbilt-Adriance & Shaw, 2008), the school (e.g., classroom climate and culture), good interpersonal relationships (Davies et al.,

2011; Sameroff & Rosenblum, 2006), and the support of teachers and the school (Brooks, 2006; Smokowski et al., 1999), the neighborhood (e.g., neighborhood action groups, youth groups) or society in general (e.g., funding activities for youth) Gorman-Smith & Tolan, 2003).

It has become evident that childhood is a time of great importance for promoting psychological resilience since it is during this period that the key characteristics for resilient children mentioned before are developed. Development of these characteristics in some children may develop smoothly, while for others may need strengthening, particularly for those facing increased risk factors. In addition, research indicates that fostering resilience in young children, supported by significant figures such as parents and educators, involves not eliminating anxiety and adversity, but rather helping children navigate incremental challenges to enhance their competence and self-efficacy.

METHODOLOGY

Scope and Research Questions

The previous theoretical overview attempted to define the concept of psychological resilience and to present the main factors that influence its development, as well as, reviewing current research aiming to broaden the understanding of the concept. Previous sections also reflect current research activity on resilience of typically developing school-aged students, while highlighting the need for further investigation of individual protective and risk factors, giving more emphasis on factors that contribute to its promotion. The present chapter aims to review literature related to psychological resilience of children with learning difficulties and to identify, as far as possible, the risk factors as well as the individual protective factors that enable students to overcome any difficulties and continue their everyday lives successfully.

Research Questions

This chapter will examine the presence of learning difficulties as a possible risk factor in the context of psychological resilience. It will also study what the individual protective and risk factors for students with learning difficulties are. Furthermore, it analyzes the relationship between individual protective and risk factors for students with learning difficulties.

1. Is the presence of learning difficulties considered a risk factor in the context of psychological resilience?

2. What are the individual protective and risk factors for students with learning difficulties?
3. What is the relationship between individual protective factors and risk factors for students with learning difficulties?

DISCUSSION

It has been suggested that concerning resilience, children with learning difficulties (LD) could be included in the same group as those who are experiencing various risk factors throughout their lives (Boden et al., 2018; Werner & Smith, 1982; Werner, 2000). Concerning supportive factors, Werner (2000) found that at age 32, adults with LD were all satisfied with themselves, their jobs, and their marriages. To justify these results, Werner suggested five categories of protective factors: a. positive responses from "significant others" (parents, peers, teachers, spouses), b. values and skills used by individuals assisted them to feel that they could overcome any problems, because they had a strong sense of self-efficacy and a strong internal source of control, c. effective parenting skills, their parents have provided support and emotional stability and promoted self-esteem during childhood, d. presence of supportive mentors, and, e. appropriate opportunities for people with learning disabilities during important life milestones, for example, after graduation, starting their career in the workplace, etc. that led to a positive pathway. Moreover, studies have shown that resilient young people with learning difficulties seek personal control in their lives, are willing to ask for support, but also accept support, set goals, desire success, and display a high level of motivation and perseverance (Gerber et al., 1992; Spekman et al., 1992; Werner et al., 2000).

On the other hand, concerning risk factors, students with Learning Disabilities often appear to have low academic performance, experience difficulties in performing academic tasks and avoid engaging in them (Gans et al., 2003), consider their own academic and self-regulation skills as inferior to those of other students with typical performance (Klassen & Lynch, 2007), have low self-perception and self-esteem (Grolnick & Ryan, 1990), internalize problems (Frances et al., 2019), have fewer expectations of future success (Chapman & Tunmer, 2003) and experience more emotional and social difficulties than their typically developing peers (Chen et al., 2001; Baird et al., 2009; Bauminger et al., 2005). Most studies on learning disabilities have focused on academic performance (Leonard et al., 2016; Bender, 1994; Sabornie, 1994), yet it is also noted that in addition to lower academic performance, serious intra- and inter-personal problems, such as loneliness, feelings of depression, delinquency, are also common among individuals with learning difficulties. These problems seem to aggravate the problems experienced by the learning disability itself and lead to negative consequences in adulthood (Morrison & Cosden, 1997; Singh, 2017) if not dealt with. Recent theories of psychological resilience provide a framework for understanding the complex factors that influence adaptation within this framework and it is important to look into the individual protective factors in building psychological resilience and psychological well-being in children with learning difficulties (Haft et al., 2016; Hojati & Abbasi, 2013).

In the above-mentioned context, students with learning difficulties appear to face various academic and other difficulties in their everyday lives (Gallagher et al., 2016). An attempt to evaluate resilience could be expressed by assessing children's efforts to cope with these difficulties. Bloom and Tinker (2001) addressed this required effort by suggesting that the commitment shown by students with LD towards any effort, depends on the stimulus, focus of attention, social connection, and emotional situations experienced by these students. About the school environment, students with learning difficulties show a preference for activities that assist them in fulfilling their hopes and their longer-term goals, rather than in actions that meet their immediate responsibilities and obligations (Hojati & Abbasi, 2013).

In the literature, it is also suggested that learning difficulties are often associated with psychological problems (Willcutt & Pennington, 2000; Einfeld & Tongec, 1996). Leontari's (1993) research compared students with normal and low school performance in grades three to six of primary school with their peers who had learning difficulties and attended Integration Classes, focusing on their sense of adequacy and general self-worth (global self-worth). The results indicated that children with learning disabilities rated themselves more negatively than their peers in terms of competence and general self-worth. Students with LD also rated themselves more negatively than their low-performing peers on academic self-perception. Margalit (Margalit, 2004) cited the need for greater clarity when considering the impact of risk and protective factors on the performance of students with LD throughout their lifespan. She also emphasized the challenges involved in identifying dynamic processes and interactions between internal and external factors and the importance of understanding their impact on mental resilience and the overall success of students with LD. Finally, she noted the need for more research that incorporates multidimensional models of protective factors and focuses on subgroups of students with LD who see themselves positively and exhibit mentally resilient behaviors that help them succeed despite their difficulties.

Research data also show that there are significant differences between students with LD and their typically performing peers in areas of adaptation and functioning. When compared to their peers with typical development, students with LD exhibit a wide range of maladaptive behaviors associated with feeling incompetent in learning, including decreased persistence and lower academic expectations, and consequently lower academic performance (Baird et al., 2009). Students with LD exhibit higher levels of anxiety, greater lack of self-confidence and extreme self-criticism than their regular performance peers (Leichtentritt et al., 2010; Sparks & Lovett, 2009). Research by Chen and colleagues (Chen et al., 2001) showed that students with LD have lower academic self-efficacy than their regular peers, a result confirmed by Hen and Goroshit's (2012) research. In addition, results also suggest that students with LD exhibit higher academic procrastination than students with typical development. For students with LD, the belief e that they have lower academic self-efficacy than their typical developing peers reduces their motivation for learning from students with LD and leads to procrastination. Lackaye & Margalit (2006) and Klassen (2007), argued that the lower levels of sense and belief of self-efficacy of students with LD have a negative impact on their academic success and development of self-regulation skills. In a later study by Zheng, Erickson, Kingston & Noonan (2012), in addition to a lower level of self-efficacy beliefs, students with LD even showed a lower level of self-determination related to academic performance when compared to students with typical development. The term self-determination means the approach to learning characterized by systematic effort to face challenges, active participation in the learning process, and perseverance (Hen & Goroshit, 2012; Klassen & Lynch, 2007; Zheng et al., 2012). Self-efficacy beliefs are fundamental in supporting individuals to be able to manage learning environments, overcome potential obstacles, persist in achieving academic goals, and have a positive attitude toward accomplishing future academic goals (Bandura, 1997; Zheng et al., 2012; Zimmerman, 2000). Therefore, increasing the beliefs of academic self-efficacy of students with LD is expected to increase their level of academic performance.

However, there is no shortage of studies that characterize the developmental course of many people with LD as something that exceeds all expectations (Keogh & Weisner, 1993; Miller, 1996). These individuals were sought by Gerber and colleagues (1992) to identify their sources of strength and more generally their protective factors. Their research mentions the importance of successful experiences, important milestones in the lives of people with LD, determination, personal friendships, encouraging teachers, and ways of managing problems arising from the "learning difficulties" factor (|Haft et al., 2019; Miller, 2002). As with risk factors, protective factors can belong to the other skills or internal characteristics of the individual or to the response of the environment to the individual and the individual to the environment (Feagans et al., 1991; Keogh, 1993).

FUTURE DIRECTIONS

There is a need for comprehensive research on students with LD attending all levels of education and longitudinal studies following children with LD from childhood through adolescence into adulthood, investigating risk and supportive factors both internal and external leading to the development of predictive models, as well as building a more comprehensive view on the role of schools in the development of resilience from early on. Additionally, research comparing typically developing children with children with LD can allow a clearer view of the effects of independent individual variables on psychological resilience. The views of parents, teachers, researchers, and mental health experts could potentially contribute to this. Investigating the factors that can lead young people to vulnerability, but also supportive factors as a support system, may result in a better view of building resilience and as an end result promoting mental health and an improved quality of life overall.

Additionally, research focusing on the characteristics of the school and the teachers (pre-primary, primary, and secondary) as productive factors enhancing the building of resilience for students with LD and every student for that matter, seems of great importance since schools have a vital role to play in promoting resilience, given the fact that they deal daily with student difficulties regarding school performance and mental health. At the same time, schools have the potential to reach a fairly wide range of young people, who would otherwise be difficult to gather for mental health prevention and intervention efforts. The role of effective schools is clearly defined within the theory of resilience. It is these schools that minimize risks and adversity to their students to the greatest extent possible, maximize the protective factors available to students through appropriate educational interventions and actions, and take timely action when their students show early signs of social or emotional disturbance. Schools can be "resilient communities" that provide support and guidance to all children and help facilitate their development and school adjustment (Doll et al., 2014; Hatzichristou et al., 2009; Hatzichristou et al., 2010; Henderson & Milstein, 2008; Jones & Lafreniere, 2014). An important role within these "mentally resilient communities" can also be played by informed sensitive educators, who understand the needs and capabilities of their students due to the daily contact they have with their students. Such educators can be an important external protective factor for their students, promoting their mental resilience, offering them care, support and emotional guidance, opportunities for meaningful participation, but also having high expectations of them. These teachers may be able to contribute to the reduction of risk factors by having clear and consistent boundaries, developing positive emotional bonds, and teach skills useful for life. Regarding students with learning difficulties, teachers need to be aware of the difficulties faced by their students, as well as the educational practices they could adopt, in order to be able to facilitate their learning process and adaptation. To achieve the above, it is considered necessary to train educators through relevant training.

REFERENCES

Aburn, G., Gott, M., & Hoare, K. (2016). What is resilience? An integrative review of the empirical literature. *Journal of Advanced Nursing*, 72(5), 980–1000. 10.1111/jan.1288826748456

Affi, T. O., & Macmillan, H. L. (2011). Resilience following child maltreatment: A review of protective factors. *Canadian Journal of Psychiatry*, 56(5), 266–272. 10.1177/070674371105600505 21586192

Alvord, M. K., & Grados, J. J. (2005). Enhancing resilience in children: A proactive approach. *Professional Psychology, Research and Practice*, 36(3), 238–245. 10.1037/0735-7028.36.3.238

Baird, G., Scott, W., Dearing, E., & Hamill, S. (2009). Cognitive self-regulation in youth with and without learning disabilities: Academic self-efficacy, theories of intelligence, learning versus performance goal preferences, and effort attributions. *Journal of Social and Clinical Psychology*, 28(7), 881–908. 10.1521/jscp.2009.28.7.881

Bandura, A. (1989). Human agency in social cognitive theory. *The American Psychologist*, 44(9), 1175–1184. 10.1037/0003-066X.44.9.11752782727

Bandura, A. (1997). Self-efficacy: The exercise of control. *The Freeman.*

Barnová, S., & Tamášová, V. (2018). Risk and protective factors in the life of youth in relation to resilience. *Psychology and Pathopsychology of Child*, 52(1), 50–59. 10.2478/papd-2018-0001

Bauminger, N., Edelsztein, H. S., & Morash, J. (2005). Social information processing and emotional understanding in children with LD. *Journal of Learning Disabilities*, 38(1), 45–61. 10.1177/00222194050380010401 15727328

Bempechat, J., & Shernoff, D. J. (2012). Parental Influences on Achievement Motivation and Student Engagement. In Christenson, S. L., Reschly, A. L., & Wylie, C. (Eds.), *Handbook of research on student engagement* (pp. 315–342). Springer. 10.1007/978-1-4614-2018-7_15

Benard, B. (1995). *Fostering resilience in children.* ERIC. https://files.eric.ed.gov/fulltext/ED386327.pdf

Bender, W. N. (1994). Social-emotional development: The task and the challenge. *Learning Disability Quarterly*, 17(4), 250–252. 10.2307/1511122

Benzies, K., & Mychasiuk, R. (2009). Fostering family resiliency: A review of the key protective factors. *Child & Family Social Work*, 14(1), 103–114. 10.1111/j.1365-2206.2008.00586.x

Bloom, L., Tinker, E., & Scholnick, E. K. (2001) The intentionality model and language acquisition: Engagement, effort, and the essential tension in development. *Monographs of the Society for Research in Child Development, 66*(4), Serial No. 267.

Boden, J. M., Sanders, J., Munford, R., & Liebenberg, L. (2018). The Same But Different? Applicability of a General Resilience Model to Understand a Population of Vulnerable Youth. *Child Indicators Research*, 11(1), 79–96. 10.1007/s12187-016-9422-y

Brooks, J. E. (2006). Strengthening resilience in children and youths: Maximizing opportunities in the schools. *Children & Schools*, 28(2), 69–76. 10.1093/cs/28.2.69

Brooks, R. (1994). Children at risk: Fostering resilience and hope. *The American Journal of Orthopsychiatry*, 64(4), 545–553. 10.1037/h00795657847570

Chapman, J. W., & Tunmer, W. E. (2003). Reading difficulties, reading-related self-perceptions, and strategies for overcoming negative self-beliefs. *Reading & Writing Quarterly*, 19(1), 5–24. 10.1080/10573560308205

Chen, G., Gully, S. M., & Eden, D. (2001). Validation of a new general self-efficacy scale. *Organizational Research Methods*, 4(1), 62–83. 10.1177/109442810141004

Christensen, A. J., Turner, C. W., Smith, T. W., Holman, J. M., & Gregory, M. C. (1991). Health locus of control and depression in end-stage renal disease. *Journal of Consulting and Clinical Psychology*, 59(3), 419–424. 10.1037/0022-006X.59.3.4192071727

Condly, S. J. (2006). Resilience in children: A review of literature with implications for education. *Urban Education*, 41(3), 211–236. 10.1177/0042085906287902

Davies, S. L., Thind, H. R., Chandler, S. D., & Tucker, J. A. (2011). Enhancing resilience among young people: The role of communities and asset-building approaches to intervention. *Adolescent Medicine: State of the Art Reviews*, 22, 402–440.22423458

Doll, B., Zucker, S., & Brehm, K. (2009). Σχολικές τάξεις που προάγουν την ψυχική ανθεκτικότητα (επιστ. επιμ. Χατζηχρήστου, Χ.). Τυπωθήτω, Einfeld, S. L., & Tonge, B. J. (1996). Population prevalence of psychopathology in children and adolescents with intellectual disability, II: Epidemiological findings. *Journal of Intellectual Disability Research*, 40(2), 99–109.

Everly, G. S., & Lating, J. M. (2013). Resilience: The Final Frontier. In Everly, G. S., & Lating, J. M. (Eds.), *A Clinical Guide to the Treatment of the Human Stress Response* (3rd ed., pp. 143–154). Springer. 10.1007/978-1-4614-5538-7_7

Everly, G. S., McCormack, D. K., & Strouse, D. A. (2012). Seven Characteristics of Highly Resilient People. *International Journal of Emergency Mental Health*, 14(2), 137–143.23350224

Everly, G. S., Smith, K. J., & Lobo, R. (2013). Resilient Leadership and the Organizational Culture of Resilience: Construct Validation International. *Journal of Emergency Mental Health and Human Resilience*, 15(2), 123–128.24558699

Feagans, L., Merriwether, A., & Haldane, D. (1991). Goodness of fit in the home: Its relationship to school behavior and achievement in children with learning disabilities. *Journal of Learning Disabilities*, 24(7), 413–420. 10.1177/0022219491 024007061895009

Fergus, S., & Zimmerman, M. A. (2005). Adolescent resilience: A framework for understanding healthy development in the face of risk. *Annual Review of Public Health*, 26(1), 399–419. 10.1146/annurev.publhealth.26.021304.14435715760295

Frances, D. A., Caruana, N., Hudson, J. L., & McArthur, G. M. (2019). The association between poor reading and internalizing problems: A systematic review and meta-analysis. *Clinical Psychology Review*, 67, 45–60. 10.1016/j.cpr.2018.09.00230528985

Fraser, M. W., Galinsky, M. J., & Richman, J. M. (1999). Risk, protection, and resilience: Towards a conceptual framework for social work practice. *Social Work Research*, 23(3), 131–144. 10.1093/swr/23.3.131

Gallagher, A. L., Galvin, R., Robinson, K., Murphy, C. A., Conway, P. F., & Perry, A. (2020). The characteristics, life circumstances and self-concept of 13 year-olds with and without disabilities in Ireland: A secondary analysis of the Growing Up in Ireland (GUI) study. *PLoS One*, 15(3), 135–156. 10.1371/journal.pone.022959932168358

Gans, A. M., Kenny, M. C., & Ghany, D. L. (2003). Comparing the self-concept of students with and without learning disabilities. *Journal of Learning Disabilities*, 36(3), 287–295. 10.1177/00222194030360030715515648

Garmezy, N. (1991). Resilience in children's adaptation to negative life events and stressed environments. *Pediatric Annals*, 20(9), 459–466. 10.3928/0090-448 1-19910901-051945543

Garmezy, N., Masten, A. S., & Tellegen, A. (1984). The study of stress and competence in children: A building block for developmental psychopathology. *Child Development*, 55(1), 97–111. 10.2307/11298376705637

Gerber, P. J., Ginsberg, R., & Reiff, H. B. (1992). Identifying alterable patterns in employment success for highly successful adults with learning disabilities. *Journal of Learning Disabilities*, 25(8), 475–487. 10.1177/002221949202500802146039l

Glennie, E. J. (2010). Coping and Resilience. In Rosen, J. A., Glennie, E. J., Dalton, B. Q., Lennon, J. M., & Bozwick, R. N. (Eds.), *Noncognitive skills in the classroom: New perspectives on educational research*. RTI International. 10.3768/rtipress.2010.bk.0004.1009.8

Goldstein, S., & Brooks, R. B. (2013). Why Study Resilience. In S. Goldstein & R. B. Brooks (Eds.), *Handbook of Resilience in Children* (2nd ed., pp. 3-14). Springer. 10.1007/978-1-4614-3661-4_1

Gorman-Smith, D., & Tolan, P. H. (2003). Positive adaptation among youth exposed to community violence. In *Resilience and vulnerability: Adaptation in the context of childhood adversities*. Cambridge University Press. 10.1017/CBO9780511615788.018

Grolnick, W. S., & Ryan, R. M. (1990). Self-perceptions, motivation, and adjustment in children with learning disabilities: A multiple group comparison study. *Journal of Learning Disabilities*, 23(3), 177–184. 10.1177/002221949002300308231319l

Gutman, L. M., Brown, J., Akerman, R., & Obolenskaya, P. (2010). *Change in wellbeing from childhood to a: risk and resilience*. Institute of Education.

Hadjichristou, C., Dimitripoulou, A., Lykitsakou, K., & Lambropoulou, A. (2009). Προαγωγή της ψυχικής ευεξίας στη σχολική κοινότητα: Εφαρμογή παρεμβατικού προγράμματος σε επίπεδο συστήματος. Ψυχολογία. *E (Norwalk, Conn.)*, 16(3), 381–401.

Haft, S. L., Chen, T., LeBlanc, C., Tencza, F., & Hoeft, F. (2019). Impact of mentoring on socio-emotional and mental health outcomes of youth with learning disabilities and attention-deficit hyperactivity disorder. *Child and Adolescent Mental Health*, 24(4), 318–328. 10.1111/camh.1233131649490

Haft, S. L., Myers, C. A., & Hoeft, F. (2016). Socio-emotional and cognitive resilience in children with reading disabilities. *Current Opinion in Behavioral Sciences*, 10, 133–141. 10.1016/j.cobeha.2016.06.00527747263

Hatzichristou, C., Lykitsakou, K., Lampropoulou, A., & Dimitropoulou, P. (2010). Promoting the well-being of school communities: A systemic approach. In B. Doll, W. Phohl, & J. Yoon (Eds.), *Handbook of Prevention Science* (pp. 255-274). Routledge.

Hen, M., & Goroshit, M. (2012). Academic procrastination, emotional intelligence, academic self-efficacy, and GPA: A comparison between students with and without learning disabilities. *Journal of Learning Disabilities*, 20, 1–9.22442254

Henderson, N., & Milstein, M. M. (2008). *Σχολεία που προάγουν την ψυχική ανθεκτικότητα - Πώς μπορεί να γίνει πραγματικότητα για τους μαθητές και τους εκπαιδευτικούς* (επιστ. επιμ. Χατζηχρήστου, X.). Τυπωθήτω.

Herrman, H., Stewart, D. E., Diaz-Granados, N., Berger, E. L., Jackson, B., & Yuen, T. (2011). What Is Resilience? *Canadian Journal of Psychiatry*, 56(5), 258–265. 10.1177/07067437110560050421586191

Hill, M., Stafford, A., Seaman, P., Ross, N., & Daniel, B. (2007). *Parenting and resilience*. Joseph Rowntree Foundation.

Hojati, M., & Abbasi, M. (2013). Comparisons of self-efficacy and hope among students with and without learning disabilities. *Journal of Special Education and Rehabilitation*, 14(1-2), 66–77. 10.2478/v10215-011-0034-2

Jacelon, C. S. (1997). The trait and process of resilience. *Journal of Advanced Nursing*, 25(1), 123–129. 10.1046/j.1365-2648.1997.1997025123.x9004020

Jones, G., & Lafreniere, K. (2014). Exploring the Role of School Engagement in Predicting Resilience Among Bahamian Youth. *The Journal of Black Psychology*, 40(1), 47–68. 10.1177/0095798412469230

Keogh, B. K., & Weisner, T. (1993). An ecocultural perspective on risk and protective factors in children's development: Implications for learning disabilities. *Learning Disabilities Research & Practice*, 8(l), 3–10.

King, L., Jolicouer-Martineau, A., Laplante, D. P., Szekely, E., Levitan, R., & Wazana, A. (2020). Measuring resilience in children: A review of recent literature and recommendations for future research. *Current Opinion in Psychiatry*, 34(1), 10–21. 10.1097/YCO.000000000000066333105167

Klassen, R. M., & Lynch, S. L. (2007). Self-efficacy from the perspective of adolescents with learning disabilities and their specialist teachers. *Journal of Learning Disabilities*, 40, 94–507. 10.1177/00222194070400060201

Lackaye, T. D., & Margalit, M. (2006). Comparisons of achievement, effort, and self-perceptions among students with learning disabilities and their peers from different achievement groups. *Journal of Learning Disabilities*, 39(5), 432–446. 10.1177/00222194060390050117004675

Leichtentritt, J., & Shechtman, Z. (2010). Children with and without learning disabilities: A comparison of processes and outcomes following group counseling. *Journal of Learning Disabilities*, 43(2), 169–17. 10.1177/0022219409345008198900 74

Leonard, S., Stiles, A. A., & Gudino, O. G. (2016). School engagement of youth investigated by child welfare services: Associations with academic achievement and mental health. *School Mental Health*, 8(3), 386–398. 10.1007/s12310-016-9186-z

Leondari, A. (1993). Comparability of self-concept among normal achievers, low achievers and children with learning difficulties. *Educational Studies*, 19(3), 357–371. 10.1080/0305569930190309

Luthar, S. S. (1991). Vulnerability and resilience: A study of high-risk adolescents. *Child Development*, 62(3), 600–616. 10.2307/11311341914628

Luthar, S. S., & Cicchetti, D. (2000). The construct of resilience: Implications for interventions and social policies. *Development and Psychopathology*, 12(4), 857–885. 10.1017/S095457940000415611202047

Luthar, S. S., Cicchetti, D., & Becker, B. (2000). The construct of resilience: A critical evaluation and guidelines for future work. *Child Development*, 71(3), 543–562. 10.1111/1467-8624.0016410953923

Luthar, S. S., & Zigler, E. (1991). Vulnerability and competence: A review of the research on resilience in childhood. *The American Journal of Orthopsychiatry*, 61(1), 6–22. 10.1037/h00792182006679

Margalit, M. (2004). Second-Generation Research on Resilience: Social Emotional Aspects of Children with Learning Disabilities. *Learning Disabilities Research & Practice*, 19(1), 45–48. 10.1111/j.1540-5826.2004.00088.x

Masten, A. S. (2001). Ordinary magic: Resilience processes in development. *The American Psychologist*, 56(3), 227–238. 10.1037/0003-066X.56.3.22711315249

Masten, A. S. (2007). Resilience in developing systems: Progress and promise as the fourth wave rises. *Development and Psychopathology*, 19(3), 921–930. 10.1017/S0954579407000442177059 08

Masten, A. S. (2011). Resilience in children threatened by extreme adversity: Frameworks for research, practice, and translational synergy. *Development and Psychopathology*, 23(2), 493–506. 10.1017/S095457941100019823786691

Masten, A. S. (2014a). Global perspectives on resilience in children and youth. *Child Development*, 85(1), 6–20. 10.1111/cdev.1220524341286

Masten, A. S., Best, K. M., & Garmezy, N. (1990). Resilience and development: Contributions from the study of children who overcome adversity. *Development and Psychopathology*, 2(4), 425–444. 10.1017/S0954579400005812

Masten, A. S., & Coatsworth, J. D. (1998). The development of competence in favorable and unfavorable environments: Lessons from research on successful children. *The American Psychologist*, 53(2), 205–220. 10.1037/0003-066X.53.2.2059491748

Masten, A. S., & Curtis, W. J. (2000). Integrating competence and psychopathology: Pathways toward a comprehensive science of adaptation in development. *Development and Psychopathology*, 12(3), 529–550. 10.1017/S095457940000314X11014751

Masten, A. S., & Gewirtz, A. H. (2008). Vulnerability and resilience in early child development. In McCartney, K., & Phillips, D. A. (Eds.), *Handbook of early childhood development* (pp. 22–43). Blackwell Publishing.

Miller, D., & Daniel, B. (2007). Competent to Cope, Worthy of Happiness? How the Duality of Self-Esteem Can Inform a Resilience-Based Classroom Environment. *School Psychology International*, 28(5), 605–622. 10.1177/0143034307085661

Miller, M. (1996). Relevance of resilience to individuals with learning disabilities. *International Journal of Disability Development and Education*, 43(3), 255–269. 10.1080/0156655960430306

Miller, M. (2002). Resilience elements in students with learning disabilities. *Journal of Clinical Psychology*, 58(3), 291–298. 10.1002/jclp.1001811836710

Morrison, G. M., & Cosden, M. A. (1997). Risk, resilience and adjustment of individuals with learning disabilities. *Learning Disability Quarterly*, 20(1), 43–60. 10.2307/1511092

Morrison, G. M., Robertson, L., Laurie, B., & Kelly, J. (2002). Proactive factors related to antisocial behavior. *Journal of Clinical Psychology*, 58(3), 277–290. 10.1002/jclp.1002211836709

Mukund, B., & Dehuri, B. K. (2016). Building Resilience in School Children: Need of The Hour. *Global Journal for Research Analysis*, 5(10), 279–282.

Naglieri, J. A., & LeBuffe, P. A. (2005). Measuring Resilience in Children, From Theory to Practice. In Goldstein, S., & Brooks, R. B. (Eds.), *Handbook of Resilience in Children* (pp. 241–259). Springer. 10.1007/0-306-48572-9_8

Oade-Sese, G. V., & Li, V. (2011). Attachment relationships as predictors of language skills for at risk bilingual preschool children. *Psychology in the Schools*, 48(7), 707–722. 10.1002/pits.20583

Olsson, C. A., Bond, L., Burns, J. M., Vella-Brodrick, D. A., & Sawyer, S. M. (2003). Adolescent resilience: A concept analysis. *Journal of Adolescence*, 26(1), 1–11. 10.1016/S0140-1971(02)00118-512550818

Pellegrini, D. S., Masten, A. S., Garmezy, N., & Ferrarese, M. J. (1987). Correlates of social and academic competence in middle childhood. *Journal of Child Psychology and Psychiatry, and Allied Disciplines*, 28(5), 699–714. 10.1111/j.1469-7610.1987.tb01553.x3667735

Pianta, R. C., & Walsh, D. J. (1998). Applying the construct of resilience in schools: Cautions from a developmental systems perspective. *School Psychology Review*, 27(3), 407–417. 10.1080/02796015.1998.12085925

Polk, L. V. (1997). Toward a middle-range theory of resilience. *Advances in Nursing Science*, 19(1), 1–13. 10.1097/00012272-199703000-000029055026

Prince-Embury, S., & Courville, T. (2008). Comparison of one-, two-, and three factor models of personal resiliency using the resiliency scales for children and adolescents. *Canadian Journal of School Psychology*, 23(1), 11–25. 10.1177/0829573508316589

Rak, C. F., & Patterson, L. E. (1996). Promoting resilience in at-risk children. *Journal of Counseling and Development*, 74(4), 368–373. 10.1002/j.1556-6676.1996.tb01881.x

Rutter, M. (1987). Psychosocial resilience and protective mechanisms. *The American Journal of Orthopsychiatry*, 57(3), 316–331. 10.1111/j.1939-0025.1987.tb03541.x3303954

Rutter, M. (2012). Resilience as a dynamic concept. *Development and Psychopathology*, 24(2), 335–344. 10.1017/S095457941200002822559117

Sabornie, E. J. (1994). Social-affective characteristics in early adolescents identified as learning disabled and nondisabled. *Learning Disability Quarterly*, 17(4), 268–279. 10.2307/1511124

Sameroff, A. J., & Rosenblum, K. L. (2006). Psychosocial Constraints on the Development of Resilience. *Annals of the New York Academy of Sciences*, 194(1), 116–124. 10.1196/annals.1376.01017347345

Singh, S. P. (2017). Educational differential among disabled children: A study in elementary schools in Uttar Pradesh. *International Education and Research Journal*, 3(10), 22–28.

Smokowski, P. R., Reynolds, A. J., & Bezruczko, N. (1999). Resilience and protective factors in adolescence: An autobiographical perspective from disadvantaged youth. *Journal of School Psychology*, 37(4), 425–448. 10.1016/S0022-4405(99)00028-X

Sparks, R. L., & Lovett, B. J. (2009). College students with learning disability diagnoses: Who are they and how do they perform? *Journal of Learning Disabilities*, 42(6), 494–510. 10.1177/002221940933874619704046

Spekman, N. J., Goldberg, R. J., & Herman, K. L. (1992). Learning disabled children grow up: A search for factors related to success in the young adult years. *Learning Disabilities Research & Practice*, 7(3), 161–170.

Turner, S., Norman, E., & Zunz, S. (1995). Enhancing Resiliency in Girls and Boys: A Case for Gender Specific Adolescent Prevention Programming. *The Journal of Primary Prevention*, 16(1), 25–37. 10.1007/BF0240723124254657

Vanderbilt-Adriance, E., & Shaw, D. S. (2008). Protective Factors and the Development of Resilience in the Context of Neighborhood Disadvantage. *Journal of Abnormal Child Psychology*, 36(6), 887–901. 10.1007/s10802-008-9220-118288604

Waaktaar, T., Christie, H. J., Borge, A. I., & Turgersen, S. (2004). How can young people's resilience be enhanced? Experiences from a clinical intervention project. *Clinical Child Psychology and Psychiatry*, 9(2), 167–183. 10.1177/1359104504041917

Werner, E. E. (1989). High risk children in young adulthood: A longitudinal study from birth to 32 years. *The American Journal of Orthopsychiatry*, 59(1), 72–81. 10.1111/j.1939-0025.1989.tb01636.x2467566

Werner, E. E. (2000). Protective factors and individual resilience. In Shonkoff, J. P., & Meisels, S. J. (Eds.), *Handbook of Early Childhood Intervention* (2nd ed., pp. 115–132). Cambridge University Press. 10.1017/CBO9780511529320.008

Werner, E. E., & Smith, R. (1982). *Vulnerable but invincible: A study of resilient children*. McGraw-Hill.

Werner, E. E., & Smith, R. S. (2001). *Journeys from childhood to midlife*. Cornell University Press.

Willcutt, E. G., & Pennington, B. F. (2000). Psychiatric comorbidity in children & adolescents with reading disability. *Journal of Child Psychology and Psychiatry, and Allied Disciplines*, 41(8), 1039–1048. 10.1111/1469-7610.0069111099120

William, N. R., Lindsey, E. W., Kurtz, P. D., & Jarvis, S. (2001). From trauma to resiliency: Lessons from runaway and homeless youth. *Journal of Youth Studies*, 4(2), 233–253. 10.1080/13676260123589

Windle, G., Bennett, K. M., & Noyes, J. (2011). A methodological review of resilience measurement scales. *Health and Quality of Life Outcomes*, 9(8), 1–18. 10.1186/1477-7525-9-821294858

Wright, M. O., & Masten, A. S. (2005). Resilience Processes in Development - Fostering Positive Adaptation in the Context of Adversity. In Goldstein, S., & Brooks, R. B. (Eds.), *Handbook of Resilience in Children* (pp. 17–37). Springer. 10.1007/0-306-48572-9_2

Zheng, C., Erickson, A. G., Kingston, N. M., & Noonan, P. M. (2012). Self-determination, self-concept, and academic achievement for students with learning disabilities. *Journal of Learning Disabilities*, 20(10), 1–13.23223201

Zimmerman, B. J. (2000). Self-efficacy: An essential motive to learn. *Contemporary Educational Psychology*, 25(1), 82–91. 10.1006/ceps.1999.101610620383

Zucker, R. A., Wong, M. M., Puttler, L. I., & Fitzgerald, H. E. (2003). Resilience and vulnerability among sons of alcoholics: Relationships to developmental outcomes between early childhood and adolescence. In Luthar, S. S. (Ed.), *Resilience and vulnerability: Adaptation in the context of childhood adversities* (pp. 76–103). Cambridge University Press. 10.1017/CBO9780511615788.006

Chapter 11
Nurturing Children's Mental Resilience Through Art, Play, and Creativity

Maria Athanasekou
https://orcid.org/0000-0002-2971-9452
University of Athens, Greece

ABSTRACT

Creativity constitutes the adaptive ability of the individual to face new realities and problems, as well as to produce original and innovative ideas, which is close to the idea of resilience, the capacity to withstand or to recover quickly from difficulties. Studies conducted on the effects of art, the cradle of creativity, on children, showed an increase in mental resilience. Visual creation, art in general, breaks isolation and helps children communicate, to give meaning/content to their experience, to their feelings and fosters harmony in their personality. Art helps children express unpleasant feelings constructively (stress, anger, sadness, frustration). The basic function of art is to objectify feelings so they can be observed and understood. Art as a therapeutic approach through its symbolic expression can help children externalize in the work they create part of their psyche and, thus, reconcile to understand and assimilate facts and experiences and work them out.

DOI: 10.4018/979-8-3693-8312-4.ch011

Copyright © 2024, IGI Global. Copying or distributing in print or electronic forms without written permission of IGI Global is prohibited.

INTRODUCTION

More than ever, creativity has been a fundamental tool for expressing the desire for freedom. Many children, encouraged by teachers and parents, use creative tools that allow them to fulfil themselves. This attitude has shown new ways of learning and generating dialogue to express one's personality. Art has always been enjoyed socially, as well as individually. «What play is for a child, is art for an adult» (Romano, 2000). This expression highlights how play represents the most pleasant and spontaneous activity for the child: it is not 'an activity' among others, but it is the 'activity' ante litteram, mainly, if not exclusive to childhood. Psychologists, neuropsychiatrists, and pedagogists of the modern and contemporary age agree in attributing enormous importance to play as a diagnostic, emotional, affective and social factor. Of fundamental importance for mental development, for the training of the future adult, and for the first social interaction with others, play contributes to peaceful and balanced growth (Ungar et al, 2020). In a playful context, the child can free their imagination, express their entire inner world, manipulate reality by adapting it to their specific universe and explore the external world in its physical and social aspects. Play allows the child to express their subconscious, preferences, and fears, it introduces them to life, guides their abilities towards a goal, educates their intelligence, and allows them to carry out fictional experiments, even risky ones, without encountering the possibility of failure. Play in the sense of free improvisation, uncontrolled imagination, movement and fun is similar to the Greek concept of *paideia* (Winner, 2018).

Creativity

Creativity as a concept describes the adaptive capacity of the individual to face new realities and problems, as well as to produce original and innovative ideas. In this way, the human psyche creates thoughts that break new ground and remove barriers, leading to an innate desire for discovery and progress (Bucci, 1990).

From infancy, creativity is evident and an inherent element of human development. Infancy is guided by the senses and the infant learns about the world through an intuitive approach to the environment. As a result, children make trial-and-error decisions about everything they touch, finding uses, textures, and reasons why something was made. Every human being has the capacity for creative processes. Creativity exists in thinking, dancing, singing, musical instruments, using and transforming materials (Schirrmancher, 1995). It is known that the human brain consists of two hemispheres, each of which performs different activities. The left hemisphere is responsible for the mental processes associated with logical thinking, reading, math, and writing, while the right hemisphere is associated with intuitive thinking and creative ways of analyzing information in problems. Therefore, both the family environment and the school must provide the appropriate stimuli for the equal strengthening of both (Bresky, 2008).

Preschoolers are at the peak of their creativity as their imagination is the driving force behind their discovery of the world. Approaches to creativity vary, depending on the context in which it is studied. For example, the theory of emotions suggests that children resolve their emotions by painting what troubles them, distorting and exaggerating forms etc. From the perspective of perception theory, children project an image of their personal view of the world as they experience it. New research highlights the importance of cooperation between the brain's hemispheres in producing and performing complex functions. Very often, people with brain damage can create works of art without their natural creativity being affected. This is because creativity is not located in a specific part of the cerebral hemisphere, but is a result of other brain activities. Indeed, through imagination and inspiration, an inner dialogue opens between the presented world and the self, as what the subject has mentally envisioned, emerges (Brown et al, 2009).

Winnicott (1971) argued that creativity is not only present in artistic activity but it is a fundamental property of being in the world. It involves subjective existence in the world and objective observation of the environment, both as part of the self and as something separate and detached from the external world. Winnicott refers to a 'truly autonomous state', where the creative individual is open to the stimulus of the outside world, but does not lose their centre by moving away from it.

Creativity as a concept is influenced by four factors: the creative situation, the creative process, the creative person and the result. Some theorists argue that creativity is difficult to observe or measure. Others argue that creativity is a characteristic of the human intellect, which lacks stability and is expressed in specific activities that derive from the individual's personality. Creativity arises when the individual needs to solve a problem and it is an unconscious process that dominates their psyche and personality. Therefore, it can be successfully combined with therapeutic processes to bring about personal change and healthy development (Wright, 2012).

Montessori (1950) argues that children are led to knowledge when they are allowed to be guided by their emotions and to freely choose how to work creatively. Childhood brings a creative mood and all elements of the environment are integrated into the child's existence through observation and experience.

Art

The benefits of art in children's development are well documented and the literature is endless. From developing brain function and fine motor skills to channelling emotional expression, art is fundamental to improving children's lives and self-actualization. It can boost their confidence and help build their emotional intelligence while instilling and strengthening the kind of problem-solving skills that will support development throughout adolescence and adulthood. By offering a safe space to explore creative and expressive possibilities, art can help children better understand the nature of limits and risk-taking, as well as beneficial ways to respond productively to their mistakes. Creativity requires emotional intelligence (Αθανασέκου, 2020)—the relationship with art, the understanding of the language of images and symbols, too.

Harvard Philosophy Professor, Nelson Goodman, writes, 'What we learn through art is felt in our bones, nerves, and muscles, just as well as it is conceived by our mind… All the sensitivity and responsiveness of the organization participate in the invention and interpretation of symbols' (Freeland, 2010). The language of art is symbolic, even when this is not intentionally planned by the artist. Visual expression involves the element of psychic connection with the creation as the subconscious part is activated, which manifests itself through the depicted feelings and experiences. Jung (1971) wrote that '…art represents a new synthesis between the inner subjective world of the artist and external reality. The artist/trainee-therapist, often unconsciously, selects materials from external and internal reality. The work incorporates a combination of both and this integration gives a sense of reconciliation and release'.

The interaction with visual arts brings the person in contact with their inner world. Thus, fear can be recognized, captured, processed, made more familiar and ultimately dealt with. The real world is made of borders and boundaries, on the contrary, the space of art is free, unsubdued to 'must do' and conditions (Rodari, 1973). A study conducted on the effects of visual art production showed an increase in resilience, a person's ability to adapt to circumstances and disadvantages (Shand, 2014). Visual creation, art in general, breaks isolation and helps man to communicate, to give meaning, and content to his experience, to his feelings and takes care of the unity of his personality. Making a brief reference to children with special educational needs 'art offers a unique means of understanding the world through the senses […], perception […] and action […]. Art helps children express unpleasant emotions in a creative way (e.g. stress, anger, sadness, frustration) that is not destructive to themselves or to those around them. The basic function of art is to objectify emotions so that we can observe and understand them' (Rodari, 1973).

Art and Play

Through art and play, the child can symbolically accomplish good wishes and bad impulses, without the fear of real consequences, and can symbolically experience various difficult and traumatic scenarios, finding a way out to become mentally empowered. Let's not forget that, as Winnicott has shown, art is also a process of play (Winnicott, 1971). The child can learn to control the real world by skillfully exploring the tools, media, ideas and feelings expressed in the process.

The brain, the hard drive of our existence, is responsible for our emotional reactions and for retaining or not the memory of events, while the traces of our experience, our experienced body, are imprinted there. 'It is a common observation that experience leaves a mark. This observation has been confirmed experimentally thanks to the recent discoveries of neurobiology, which demonstrate that the plasticity of neural networks allows the recording of experience' (Ζωγάκη, 2020). This plasticity is considered a key component of memory and learning mechanisms and is an important area of neurobiology. Beautiful feelings start with four neurotransmitters: dopamine, oxytocin, serotonin and endorphins. Art and aesthetic pleasure trigger feelings and sensations. The positive effect of art on humans is scientifically proven. During the recent quarantine, an ever-increasing number of people became even more creative using art as a mechanism to cope with the stress of the pandemic by creating art. Photography, music, painting and drawing kept people busy and distracted them from the anxiety of COVID-19 (Zarghami, 2021).

Art doesn't just bring us together - it also benefits us on a physical/physiological level. Studies show that spending just 45 minutes creating art/doing art activities can relieve stress, strengthen critical thinking skills, improve and maintain memory. A new Drexel University study has shown that creating art can significantly reduce stress-related hormones in our bodies. The results of the study were published in the scientific journal Art Therapy under the title Reduction in Cortisol Levels and Participants' Reactions After Art Production. 'Biomarkers' are biological indicators (such as hormones) that can be used to measure conditions in the body, such as stress. The benefits of exposure to art are immeasurable. According to a study conducted by the University of Westminster, participants who visited an art gallery during their lunch break reported feeling less stressed afterwards. They had lower concentrations of the stress hormone cortisol just 35 minutes after wandering through the gallery (Αθανασέκου, 2021).

Looking at art also makes people experience joy, similar to the feeling of being in love. Neurobiologist Semir Zeki scanned the brains of 28 volunteers as they looked at art and observed an immediate release of dopamine, the chemical associated with love and pleasure. Furthermore, visiting the gallery has relieved people of mental exhaustion, in the same way that the outdoors can (Αθανασέκου, 2021).

The relationship and interconnection between art and play has concerned Psychology. Freud's view was that our primal drive is to satisfy our sexual needs, and from childhood, sexual desire is a key element of our psychological makeup, while art and play are ways of releasing it. 'The creation of something new is achieved not by the intellect but by the instinct of play,' wrote the Swiss psychologist Carl Jung

(1971). Suttie believes our creativity came from play. According to him, 'Necessity is not the mother of invention. Playing is.' Play, according to Winnicott, can, together with art and religious practice, unify and integrate human personality. Through play, the child can complete the image of him/herself as a unified human being. Only through play can a child or an adult be creative and utilize their whole personality. He believes that 'the continuous evidence of creativity means vitality' (Ishizu, 2011).

Montessori claims that children are led to knowledge when, guided by their emotions, they are left free to choose how to work creatively. Childhood brings a creative mood where all elements of the environment are integrated through observation and experience into the child's being (Malaguti, 2005).

In 2015, research was carried out regarding the benefits that nature offers to children's developmental needs, while also highlighting what the disconnection from the natural environment causes to the child. By moving away from nature, creativity, growth and development are negatively affected (Petrella et al,1998). Today's fast-paced technological society constantly demands functions that include problem-solving, selective attention, and multitasking. The Attention Restoration Theory states that when the brain is exposed to images from nature, it restores its involuntary attention and reprograms itself.

Martensson in 2009, in a study he carried out with preschool children noticed that their concentration increased after play and activities in nature, where there was rich vegetation, bushes and soil. Taylor in 2001, conducted research with children diagnosed with ADHD and observed that the symptoms of the disorder were significantly reduced after activities in a natural environment (Moore, 1997). More specifically, they scored higher in concentration, task completion and following instructions. Research conducted on four hundred and twenty-one children in 2011, showed that playing daily in a natural environment is enough to limit the manifestation of symptoms of ADHD disorder. The researchers concluded that children who played in areas with vegetation over the long term appeared to be calmer and showed higher rates of concentration (Montalti, 2012). The surprise that is born in the soul of children when they play is a way of learning, a process of companionship, and coexistence with the real world. Boundaries cease to exist. There, they can discover, exorcise fears and anxieties, and grow in a safe framework guided and defined by them. In essence, the children's relationship with the world of adults is strengthened, it is like a union of the body with the mind.

Contemporary trends in society and education leave little room for valuable free play, even though recent research has highlighted its importance and influence in cultivating interests, discovering inclinations, and regulating the emotions that the child experiences. Researchers argue that, in the long run, this lack will lead to an increase in anxiety and depression in the young population. In Waldorf schools, play is a key stage for the child's psycho-emotional development and does not focus on achieving through it only cognitive goals (Longobardi et al, 2018).

Their effort is focused on using simple and natural materials to make toys and activities proposed by educators that allow children to use their imagination without restrictions. Social imperatives have limited what play means to specific actions, objects, and spaces. In these schools, play is so integrated into the daily routine that play itself along with knowledge is mixed like a mystagogy in which the children act independently and grow up in a quiet environment with an absolute connection to nature. Geometric shapes cease to be images on paper and become observational images in the physical world. Knowledge and assimilation happen at the same time. For example, ropes are hanging from the trees creating a design, which the students are then asked to walk and then draw, either in their notebooks or by taking natural materials (stones, wood, leaves, pine cones) to imprint, paint, and construct. From the awakening of the senses and these representations, the telling of stories can be born, sounds can be created from rustling or rubbing leaves, from wood in different sizes, from handicrafts that can play a central role in the flow of teaching. Art is the step to strengthen the child's self-image by creating motivation for learning. Art with materials that the earth can offer sharpens the senses, developing the child's cognitive skills.

So where does play end and knowledge begin? Could it be that by losing play, education was compromised and man was deprived of evolution, innovation, and creativity in favour of automation and everyday normality? Adults, the facilitators of this non-play culture, are trapped in their ambition of the successful future of the child through academic achievements and this unfairly leads them to violate the rights of children concerning play (Neil, 1960). It is as if adulthood sits opposite childhood and invites it to grow up quickly and always according to the dictates of the former. But childhood is equal to carefree play which has innumerable benefits when it exists and is found in various contexts and areas in a child's daily life, let alone when it exists and fits within the framework of the educational system.

Research carried out among kindergarten teachers regarding the importance of outdoor and free play and its role in psychosocial development, showed that educators are now aware of its importance as well as the positive impact it has on the all-round development of the psychosocial skills of children aged 4- 6 years old. Researchers, more specifically, noticed that free and outdoor play develops interaction, mutual help, the ability to negotiate, to have patience, to communicate more effectively and to manage negative feelings of failure and rejection. The same study highlighted the need to address difficulties arising in the integration of such approaches as educators need further training in educational methods and practices related to outdoor play (Taylor et al, 2011).

Another study to examine the views of educators on the value of play and the interaction it exerts on the development of social skills of children aged 5-6, was carried out in 2016, highlighting key milestones related to the role of the kindergarten teacher in the classroom, their beliefs regarding the correlation that play has with the child's social development and the types of play that are part of the daily routine in the classroom. The findings of this study, in summary, show that play is a ticket for the holistic learning and development of the child. It promotes the psycho-emotional, physical and social development of the child, creating fertile ground for cognitive success (Ντίνου, 2018).

Play, for toddlers, equates to situational learning, a term which suggests that learning is initially inherent in social processes and may not be aimed at formal or overt learning. The end in itself as defined by Piaget, must be clad with liberation, with a certain lack of organization, with pleasure and with hypermobility. Through play, the child takes the step to pass the level of behaviour that lies in his age context, what Vygotsky calls the zone of proximal development. (Ντίνου, 2018). Art is often understood in terms of play. The tradition began with Kant (1790) and Schiller (1793). It is continued by Herbert Spencer (1855) and many others while being renewed by important intellectual figures such as Huizinga (1938). From a different perspective, and with an entirely different - anti-imitative - motive, a new impetus is given by Gombrich (1963). In the same vein, but rather inspired by the theory of 'language games' in Wittgenstein's 'Philosophische Untersuchungen' (1953), Kendall L. Walton understands imitation as a special kind of 'game' in 'Mimesis as make-believe' (1990).

Learning through play, essentially, means using enjoyable, fun activities to engage and stimulate children's interest. Play enables us to think, create and interact in a very natural and cognitive way. One of the many benefits of play is that students develop social and emotional bonds from cooperative play with their peers (Efland, 2002). Play, enables us to communicate with each other more and understand each other more empathetically because teamwork is a big part of many games. Other key habits of mind developed through play include persistence (the greater the challenge, the sweeter the reward), impulse management (developing metacognitive strategies for effective goal setting and staying on track), and responsible risk-taking (play embraces uncertainty and allows for calculated judgments in the absence of rules). Play is so developmentally important because it allows children to design a world uniquely for them and carve out a place where they can feel independent and responsible for their outcomes.

Giuseppe Arcimboldo (1527 - 1593) was an Italian painter known for creating fantastical portraits made entirely of objects such as fruit, vegetables, flowers, fish and books. He painted representations of these objects on canvas, arranged in such a way that the whole of the objects formed a recognizable likeness of the subject of the portrait. His work has the potential to be used with children because of the potential it offers in education, because food, body parts, and animals can be discussed alongside getting to know the art.

Modern art embraces the element of play very effectively. Artists seek creative strategies to address aesthetic and conceptual issues to create engaging and entertaining artwork. Regardless of our age, the most wonderful thing about play is that it helps us express our inner child. This is evident in Nicolas Henry's photo series 'The Playhouses of Our

Grandparents', which allows participants (and viewers) to reflect on the joy of playful and dramatic storytelling. The artist travelled the world to meet older people from a variety of cultures and collaborated with them to construct intricate 'toys' that symbolize the spirit of imagination, innovation, independence and cultural identity. These constructions are reminiscent of the forts that children create imaginatively with a variety of materials. Similar to children's forts, these playhouses provided older participants with a sense of safety, protection, social and emotional expression. It is so important for all of us to have a special place where we can feel safe, take creative risks and express our autonomy from the confines of the physical and emotionally demanding world we live in.

Brain, Behaviour, and Aesthetics

The Central Nervous System (CNS) consists of the brain and spinal cord. The CNS is the basic structure that is responsible for behaviour. Behaviour consists of certain 'patterns' that occur over time. Some behaviours are innate (biologically inherited) and fixed, and others are learned (culturally inherited). When we look at something that we consider beautiful, a work of art for example, our concept of beauty is satisfied and the orbitofrontal cortex and other areas that make up the brain's so-called reward system are activated. A work of art that one finds beautiful will cause increased activity in the reward system. This system gives rise to the sensations of pleasure associated with eating and drinking (to survive) and sex (to reproduce). Reward is the pleasure derived from food, drink, drugs or behaviour such as performing an altruistic act. Reward is broken down into three psychological components: learning, emotion, and motivation. Learning is a necessary component of reward as a person must learn the relationships between stimuli and the consequences of their actions to know which stimuli and which actions can lead to the acquisition of a reward. The emotional component of the reward is liking, which is the hedonic effect that the reward has on the person who acquires it. Finally, motivation is the motivational component of the reward, which is expressed as a person's desire to obtain the reward (Ζωγάκη, 2020).

Also, recently, the official prescription and not just the admonition to engage in art has begun. The Department of Health of the United Kingdom is launching a program that started in 2023: The country's doctors will be able to prescribe 'artistic' treatments for patients suffering from dementia as well as mental health problems. Contact with art can also reduce the stress of death, of the impending transition to another state of consciousness. A volunteer-based non-profit organization in the Netherlands undertakes to fulfil the last wishes of terminally ill patients. There are many cases of people whose last wish is to be with their favourite work of art for the last time or to attend a concert or a theatre performance. Organizations of this purpose are now found in many countries of the world (Αθανασέκου, 2021).

Let us consider what the last visit to our favourite work of art, our favourite museum means. The works acquire another psycho-emotional meaning, they are transformed into a living entity, they are living organisms that return to the patient a feeling of pleasure, excitement, completion, and satisfaction, just as it is done with an association with a loved one. Art can even help in cases of mental illness, and addictions (drugs, alcohol, etc.). Not only the aesthetic enjoyment of a work, through the reward system, but also through creating art/engaging in artistic activities is important. A very central role is played by Art Therapy and the philosophy of releasing repressed emotions, consciously or unconsciously, through artistic action. Creating art is a healing process that brings a person closer to themselves. In the words of Mark Rothko: 'A painting is not a picture of an experience. It's an experience' (Αθανασέκου, 2020).

Resilience Through Art Therapy

When people engage in complex activities, the brain creates new connections between brain cells. It also stimulates communication between the right and left hemispheres of the brain. Consequently, a study conducted on the effects of visual art production showed an increase in mental resilience, a person's ability to adapt to circumstances and disadvantages. Creating art also reduces stress and negative emotions, creating an experience similar to meditation. Similar to meditation or prayer, art draws people's attention to details and surroundings that create a distraction from everyday thoughts (Κοτσαμπόπουλος et al, 2020).

Art Therapy also improves the quality of life for dementia patients and reduces the burden for those with chronic health conditions. For dementia patients, creating art enhances cognitive abilities and memory, in addition to helping symptoms of depression and anxiety. Dr. Arnold Bresky has used art therapy to help people with dementia and Alzheimer's, reporting a 70% success rate in improving his patients' memories (Αθανασέκου, 2021).

Many children these days are exposed to traumatic experiences. These are victims of domestic violence, natural disasters, pandemics, they may be victims of terrorist attacks, and racism. In various countries, regimes of violence, abuse and situations of hostile climate prevail, due to political developments or war. The result of this exposure is that they are psychologically hurt, experience post-traumatic stress disorder, difficulties in developing interpersonal relationships and managing situations. Children deal with trauma differently than adults, depending on their resilience, flexibility and stage of development. Positive results in dealing with childhood trauma have been achieved with creative therapies, including art therapy, music therapy, dance therapy, poetry therapy and psychodrama. This is because they provide therapists with the right tools to deal with unlocking hidden aspects of the self (Garista, 2022).

In 2018 Cohen-Yatziv and Regev conducted a review of research (2000-2017) that has been carried out concerning the effect and contribution of art therapy in children (Αθανασέκου, 2020). They focused on thirteen case studies. Four of them involved children who had traumatic experiences and concluded that art therapy has a positive effect on dealing with trauma. The second category included four studies and evaluated the effect of art on children with special needs and difficulties. The researchers observed that there is a positive influence on the children's self-esteem but also in various areas related to behavioural and social issues. The third category included three studies of children without difficulties who attended art therapy. By completing appropriate questionnaires about their psychosocial level, it was found that through art they could be helped to face the various challenges of life. Finally, the last category concerned four studies with children facing medical difficulties, one of which involved children with asthma. The children underwent seven weeks of art therapy sessions and then completed questionnaires related to quality of life. It has been found that art therapy can have a positive effect even in this situation (Αθανασέκου, 2020).

McDonald and Drey in 2017 focused on four studies published between 1993-2013 and were conducted in Israel, Iran and America. Their purpose was to concentrate on the influence of art on primary school children. The first study evaluated how art therapy works in children with behavioural problems. The sample consisted of 36 children between 8-11 years of age. The second was related to the effect of art on the psycho-emotional level of children with learning difficulties. The sample consisted of 109 students between 8-11 years of age. The third studied whether art therapy reduces the symptoms of oppositional defiant disorder as manifested in thirty boys between 7-12 years of age. The fourth researched whether there would be a reduction in symptoms in thirty boys between 7-12 years of age, who had been diagnosed with an anxiety disorder. The study of the above revealed that art brought about positive changes in all cases and had absolutely no negative influence (Αθανασέκου, 2020).

In 2019, Mcdonald, Holttum and Drey, conducted research with the ultimate aim of studying whether the school community observes changes in the psycho-emotional and social difficulties faced by children after the art therapy sessions they attended. Art therapists gave questionnaires to the teachers before and after the sessions. In addition, the children were asked through interviews whether they noticed differences and were asked to focus on the level up to which they felt they were helped. Overall, students and teachers noted positive changes in both social and emotional areas. The children emphasized that creating and thinking about art helped them express themselves, think and learn about feelings and thoughts and all this included the element of fun (Kaimal et al, 2016).

Art as a therapeutic approach can, through its symbolic expression, help the child externalize in the work they create, part of their psyche and in this way reconcile, understand and assimilate elements, experiences and images from which they were previously separated. The benefits of interaction with art are oceanic. Mental resilience is steeled through art and the children have the outlet and the opportunity to express themselves creatively by regaining and maintaining their psycho-emotional balance (Kolb et al, 2009).

Art and Imagination

Art expresses the function of the soul, of our inner life. Without imagination, without symbolic life, we are downgraded as personalities and deprived of an important gift for our evolution (Αθανασέκου, 2020).

Art has been recognized as one of the first forms through which people communicate and societies have transmitted their knowledge, culture and history to future generations (Dissanayake, 1992). Through the use of 'symbols that manipulate images and concepts' (Wright, 2012) the arts act as vehicles not only for our ability to make sense of the world around us (McArdle, 2012) but also for our ability to understand abstract concepts and express them ourselves to others (Eisner, 2002). Furthermore, engagement with the arts can activate our senses and affective cognition by subsequently exposing us to aesthetic experiences (Eisner, 2002).

Through art, man can externalize their experiences, feelings, desires and needs, either consciously or unconsciously. All kinds of creative or artistic expression are a way to bring to light the innermost aspects of the intrapsychic process (Αθανασέκου, 2020). Art allows the past, 'which is dead and gone', to 'still live ... through words, images or music, as a particle of dust dances in a ray of sunlight' (Αθανασέκου, 2020). Lighter or not, the past can be projected again and again into the present through art, until an emotional resonance and identification with the image is achieved, until its symbolic nature is recognized and its ability to work therapeutically by purifying and purging its traumatic dimension. 'The power of identification with the image accounts for much of its effectiveness. Children recognize and identify with pictures before they understand words, and like adults, they are fascinated by reflections in mirrors and shadows, which are visual. Look at the poem My Shadow by Robert Louis Stevenson: 'I have a little shadow that goes in and out with me.' The fascination with shadows and reflections inspired myths, which trace the origin of art to drawing a line around a reflection or shadow. Such myths derive from the fact that mirrors and shadows, like the one in the poem, are copies of ourselves (Schneider, 2006).

Art and creativity contribute to our cultivation and psycho-emotional development, something that becomes better understood as we grow older and retrieve from our memory images, words, music, and the art we knew from an early age and we can identify or recognize its emotional and psychological impact on us. The artist and the viewer create a two-way communication relationship through art and reveal elements of their personality.

Creativity requires emotional intelligence, a relationship with art, and an understanding of the language of images and symbols, too.

Art contributes to aesthetic cultivation as it helps, among other things, in visual literacy and the formation of visual perception. Also, it can offer a great deal to adults, as in addition to familiarizing and immersing them in it, it can be a serious and creative escape from everyday life, problems, and anxieties and offer significant advantages to their psycho-emotional balance (Dissanayake, 1992).

It contributes to the cultivation of visual sensitivity, observation, empathy, problem management, contact with emotion, 'imagination (Dewey, 1980), the development of multiple types of intelligence (Gardner&Hatch, 1999), and familiarity with the unconventional way of thinking. The fact that great works of art speak of important truths, and have a holistic dimension, requires mental and emotional alertness for their understanding, the cultivation of self-esteem, historical knowledge, aesthetic cultivation, and the assimilation and appreciation of cultural heritage. Mainly, beyond and above all this, the power of art lies in transforming those who know it or at least laying the foundations for a new view of oneself and life' (Αθανασέκου, 2020).

CONCLUSION

Our era is plagued by monotonous rhythms, lack of ideas, outdated systems and perceptions. So, in almost all areas of our daily life, the need for innovation and creativity is observed - concepts which are intertwined with Art and Education. These two paths create a way to guide the children's minds through the senses, cultivate and develop their intelligence and ultimately lead to creative, transformative thinking (Τσέργας, 2014).

Therefore, the collaboration of these two fields transforms conventional teaching by developing expression, artistic creation, and experience which help to consolidate the curriculum. They act as facilitators for a teacher-child connection, helping to define the educational function. The human brain is made up of two hemispheres, each performing different activities. Guidi (2013), argued that in children the function of the right hemisphere prevails (Schirrmacher, 1995). The meeting of art with the educational process strengthens young people to learn more effectively, assimilating and applying what they gain, strengthening their interest in knowledge, since they now experience their progress, and feel optimistic (Τσέργας, 2014).

'The creation of something new is not achieved by the intellect but by the instinct of play,' wrote Carl Jung in Psychological Types (1921). The well-being of children, to a large extent, depends on their cognitive development, being a companion for their future development. In the second phase comes the structured thought which soon, if a careful embrace of the imagination has been followed, will be clothed in improvisation. Free, outdoor and imaginative play is a primary educational tool through which children approach the world and create personal interpretations of how it works. Could it be that the attitude of adults towards children is completely arbitrary?

Perhaps we should ask ourselves if our attitude as adults interferes with the purpose of the child's existence, which is none other than to live their life - not through the world built by the significant others, who think they know better. Maybe we need to see their world, to escape the generation of mindless adults. In the end, the only thing that counts as an inviolable command is that 'you must always be on the side of the child' (Neill, 1960).

REFERENCES

Ντίνου, Β. (2018). Παιχνίδι και καταστασιακή μάθηση σε παιδιά προσχολικής ηλικίας. In Ι. Παπαδάτος & Α. Μπαστέα & Ι. Νικολόπουλος (Ed.), *Εκπαίδευση Χαρισματικών Ατόμων στην Ελλάδα Ιδεολογικές- Πολιτικές- Ψυχολογικές- Παιδαγωγικές Προϋποθέσεις Εκπαίδευσης Χαρισματικών Ατόμων, 8ο Πανελλήνιο Επιστημών Εκπαίδευσης.*

Αθανασέκου, Μ. (2020). *Γιατί με αφορά η τέχνη. Οι πολλές της διαστάσεις και πως αξιοποιούνται στη ζωή μας*. Ηδυέπεια.

Αθανασέκου, Μ. (2021). Η σχέση της τέχνης με την ψυχολογία - Η πρόσληψη της νοητικής υστέρησης και η απεικόνισή της στη ζωγραφική από τον 15ο έως τον 19ο αιώνα. In Αργυριάδης, Α. (Ed.), *Λόγος, αναπηρία, θεραπευτικές και εκπαιδευτικές παρεμβάσεις –Νέα δεδομένα και τάσεις στην Ειδική Αγωγή* (pp. 99–116). Ηδυέπεια.

Bresky, A. (2008). *The Secret for Caregiver Success (Dr. Bresky's 9 Pt. Brain Tune Up System, Book 1)*. SM publishing.

Brown, S., & Vaughan, C. (2009). *Play: How It Shapes the Brain, Opens the Imagination and Invigorates the Soul.* Avery Publishing Group.

Bucci, S. (1990). *Educazione dell'infanzia e pedagogia scientifica. Da Froebel a Montessori*. Bulzoni.

Dewey, J. (1980). *Art as Experience*. The Penguin Group.

Dissanayake, E. (1992). *Homo Aestheticus: Where Art comes From and Why*. University of Washington Press.

Efland, A. D. (2002). *Art and Cognition: Integrating the Visual Arts in the Curriculum*. Teachers College.

Eisner, E. (2002). *The Arts and the Creation of Mind*. Yale University Press.

Freeland, C. (2010). *Μα, είναι αυτό τέχνη*. Πλέθρον.

Garista, P. (2022). Resilience and coping styles for transformative teaching and learning. In Biswal, (Eds.), *Edureform Handbook for innovative pedagogy*. La Scuola Sei.

Gombrich, E. H. (1963). *Meditations on a Hobby Horse and other essays on the Theory of Art*. Phaidon Press.

Guidi, A. (2013). *La funzione del gioco dal bambino all' età adulta. L'orientamento psicoanalitico lacaniano sul gioco*. Edizioni Ets.

Huizinga, J. (1938). *Homo Ludens: Proeve Ener Bepaling Van Het Spelelement Der Cultuur*. Wolters-Noordhoff.

Ishizu, T., & Zeki, S. (2011). Toward a brain-based theory of beauty. *PLoS One*, 6.21755004

Jung, C. G. (1971). *Psychological Types*. Princeton University Press.

Κοτσαμπόπουλος, Π., & Γαλανάκη, Ε. (2020). Η προαγωγή της ψυχικής υγείας των μαθητών στα πλαίσια της παιδαγωγικής Waldorf. *Παιδαγωγική επιθεώρηση, 66*.

Kaimal, G., Ray, K., & Muniz, J. (2016). Reduction of Cortisol Levels and Participants' Responses Following Art Making. *Art Therapy Journal.*

Kant, I. (2006). *Kritik der Urteilskraft*. Felix Meiner Verlag.

Kendall, L. W. (1990). *Mimesis as make-believe*. Harvard University Press.

Kolb, B., & Whishaw, I. Q. (2009). Fundamentals of Human Neuropsychology. *Worth.*

Longobardi, S., Agasisti, T., Avvisati, F., & Borgonovi, F. (2018). Academic resilience. What schools and countries do to help disadvantaged students succeed. *In PISA*,10.1787/19939019

Malaguti, E. (2005). *Educarsi alla resilienza*. Centro Studi Erickson.

Montalti, M. (2012). Area problema. Le aree e le attrezzature per il gioco. In Laurìa, A. (Ed.), *I piani per l'accessibilità. Una sfida per promuovere l'autonomia dei cittadini e valorizzare i luoghi dell'abitare*. Gangemi.

Montessori, M. (1950). *La scoperta del bambino*. Garzanti.

Moore, R. C. (1997). The Need of Nature: A Childhood Right. *Social Justice (San Francisco, Calif.)*, 24(3), 203–220.

Neill, S. A. (1960). *Summerhill, A Radical Approach to Child Rearing*. Hart Publishing Co.

Petrella, F., & Romitti, I. (1998). *Gli spazi verdi per il gioco dei bambini*. Alinea Editrice.

Pontiggia, G. (2000). *Nati due volte*. Mondadori.

Rodari, G. (1973). *La grammatica della fantasia. Introduzione all'arte di inventare storie*. Collana PBE, Einaudi.

Romano, R. G. (2000). *L'arte del giocare. Storia, epistemologia e pedagogia del gioco*. Pensa Multimedia.

Schiller, F. (2019). *Über die Ästhetische Erziehung des Menschen in einer Reihe von Briefen*. Gideon Stiening.

Schirrmancher, R. (1995). *Τέχνη & Δημιουργική Ανάπτυξη των παιδιών*. Έλλην.

Schneider, A. L. (2006). *Τα μηνύματα της τέχνης*. Δίαυλος.

Shand, M. (2014). *Understanding and building resilience with art: A socio-ecological approach*. Edith Cowan University.

Spencer, H. (1855). *The Principles of Psychology*. Longman, Brown, Green and Longmans. 10.1037/14065-000

Τσέργας, Ν. (2014). *Θεραπευτικές Προσεγγίσεις μέσω της Τέχνης*. Τόπος.

Taylor, F. A., & Kuo, F. E. (2011). Could exposure to Everyday Green Spaces Help Treat ADHD? Evidence from Children's Play Settings. *Applied Psychology. Health and Well-Being*, 3(3), 281–303. 10.1111/j.1758-0854.2011.01052.x

Ungar, M., & Theron, L. (2020). Resilience and Mental Health: How Multisystemic Processes Contribute to Positive Outcomes. *The Lancet. Psychiatry*, 7(5), 441–448. 10.1016/S2215-0366(19)30434-131806473

Winner, H. (2018). *How art works*. Oxford University Press. 10.1093/oso/9780190863357.001.0001

Winnicott, D. W. (1971). *Playing and reality*. Tavistock.

Winnicott, D. W. (1988). *Human Nature*. Free Associations Books.

Wittgenstein, L. (1953). *'Preface'. Philosophical Investigations: The German Text, with a Revised English Translation*. Blackwell.

Wright, S. (2012). Ways of knowing in the arts. In Wright, S. (Ed.), *Children, Meaningmaking and the Arts* (pp. 1–29). Pearson Australia.

Ζωγάκη, Ε. (2020). Όψεις του πραγματικού: οι εικαστικές τέχνες και η ματιά του θεατή. Οπτική αντίληψη, αισθητικές θεωρίες και καλλιτεχνικές συμβάσεις. In Αθανασέκου (Ed.), *Γιατί με αφορά η τέχνη*. Ηδυέπεια.

Zarghami, M. (2021). Psychiatric aspects of coronavirus (2019-nCoV) infection. *Iranian Journal of Psychiatry and Behavioral Sciences*, 14(1). Advance online publication. 10.5812/ijpbs.102957

Chapter 12
Exploring Constructive Play:
Interactions Within Play-Based Pedagogy

Olga Drakopoulou
University of Patras, Greece

Maria Kampeza
https://orcid.org/0000-0003-2405-2334
University of Patras, Greece

ABSTRACT

Constructive play is a crucial aspect of kindergarten activities, influencing the pedagogy of preschoolers, and has been extensively studied in educational research. However, studies focusing on the relationship between constructive play and the interactions that develop during it are limited. The aim of this systematic review was to investigate the characteristics of interactions during constructive play in kindergarten and their impact on preschoolers' development. The method of this study was a systematic review of the current literature over the past 14 years. A literature search was conducted on Google Scholar, ERIC, Scopus, Elsevier, and PubMed from December 2023 to March 2024, resulting in 18,200 studies (N=18,200). The results indicate that through constructive play, children develop cognitive and thinking skills. The review highlights that constructive play serves as a conduit for initiating learning processes, facilitating language development, aiding in knowledge acquisition, and cultivating essential interactive problem-solving and conflict-resolution skills.

DOI: 10.4018/979-8-3693-8312-4.ch012

Copyright © 2024, IGI Global. Copying or distributing in print or electronic forms without written permission of IGI Global is prohibited.

INTRODUCTION

A significant portion of the literature discusses the overall impact of play on the holistic development of children. According to this perspective, play is one of the fundamental components in preschool education, used as a means of learning and exploration (Mardell et al., 2023; LEGO Learning Institute, 2013). The literature suggests that play promotes learning (Bateson & Martin, 2013; Frost et al., 2012; Hale & Bocknek, 2015; Hirsh-Pasek et al., 2009; Honeyford & Boyd, 2015; Plenty, 2015; Sullivan, 2011), can provide joy and pleasure, is repetitive, socially engaging, substantive, and active (Zosh et al., 2017). In recent years, efforts have been made to integrate play more substantially into schools, as it enhances learning (Mardell et al., 2023). Play-based learning is gaining ground as an educational approach, as children encounter various challenges and opportunities for exploration (Kampeza & Sfyroera, 2016; Pyle & Danniels, 2017). The concept of play-based learning is influenced by earlier research and is based on a socio-constructivist approach to human development and learning (Cavanaugh et al., 2017; Hirsh-Pasek et al., 2009; Mraz, Porcelli, & Tyler, 2016; Pyle & Danniels, 2017; Taylor & Boyer, 2020; Vogt et al., 2018; Zosh et al., 2017).

The Pedagogical Value of Constructive Play

Constructive play constitutes a dimension of childhood activities encountered in the daily life of children in kindergarten. It serves as a critical pillar in the pedagogical process of young children, and thus, educational research has increasingly focused on it in recent years. Already from the works of Piaget and Vygotsky, the importance of constructive play has been highlighted. Through the lens of Piaget's theory of cognitive development, play with building materials can be seen as a period during which young children actively create their worldview. Constructive play provides a platform for expressing this cognitive transition, emphasized by the sensorimotor and preoperational phases. Vygotsky's sociocultural theory underscores the nature of social symbolic play. Constructive play is used as a tool for exploring a child's Zone of Proximal Development, highlighting the impact of social interactions on the formation of symbolic representations and the promotion of cognitive development (Alharbi, 2022).

Therefore, constructive play is not merely a series of activities, nor does it only concern the development of specific skills in the field of mathematics, but it is a way for children to express themselves and understand the world. Overall, constructive play in kindergarten promotes a holistic approach to their education (Weber & Leuchter, 2022). During these activities, children do not simply use materials (e.g. blocks) to create constructions; they experience an engagement that activates their emotional, social, cognitive, and intellectual domains of development (Cankaya et al., 2023; Zhang et al., 2022). In this symbolic dimension, children use building materials to represent ideas and perceive the real world in which they are called to integrate (Cunningham, 2022; Zosh, 2022). A simple piece of wood, for example, can become a ship sailing the ocean, while markers and paper can compose an entire imaginary city. Thus, constructive play is more than what is often referred to as "block play". It carries the concept of symbolic representation of the objects used, which may not only be blocks but also other materials such as figurines, drawings, and more (Papandreou, 2020).

Through this process, children develop their mental and cognitive skills and are introduced to the world of learning, language development, knowledge acquisition, and interaction skills, as well as conflict and problem-solving abilities (Zong et al., 2022). The symbolic dimension not only enhances language skills as children describe their constructions but also develops their ability to think symbolically and creatively (Cunningham, 2022). This aspect of symbolic expression also positively impacts the formation of appropriate ways of interacting within the social context, the expression of ideas, and effective communication (Fleer & Li, 2023; Lee & Hong, 2023; Suleiman & Abdulkareem, 2023).

However, contemporary literature examines constructive play primarily concerning the integration of new technologies into education and the cultivation of technological thinking (Fislake, 2022; Kodsi, 2022; Spektor-Levy & Shechter, 2022), the role educators play in its technological dimension (Cheung et al., 2022; Jahreie, 2023; Zhang et al., 2022), as well as its role in children's communication skill acquisition (Andayani & Wijayanti, 2022; Ekeh et al., 2022; Papandreou & Dragouni, 2022). The development of engineering behavior and the establishment of foundations for STEM (Science, Technology, Engineering, and Mathematics) skills during early childhood are also studied (Tunnicliffe, 2022). There is particular research interest in constructive play as a creative activity wherein children engage in a type of constructive design problem, simulating the work processes of adult engineers (Gold & Elicker, 2020).

Research specifically focusing on constructive play in preschool education is limited. While there is relative emphasis on learning through play and the benefits of play in the learning process, the focus on constructive play is lacking. At this juncture, it is crucial to highlight the pivotal role of preschool educators in shaping the quality of these play experiences. They maintain a delicate balance between supervision and children's autonomy, structured activities, and freedom, while fostering an environment that stimulates children's interests (Ivrendi, 2020; Park, 2019). Additionally, it is important to examine the interactions not only between teachers and students but also peers, as the socio-constructivist approach to human development and learning (Cavanaugh et al., 2017; Hirsh-Pasek et al., 2009; Mraz,

Porcelli, & Tyler, 2016; Pyle & Danniels, 2017; Taylor & Boyer, 2020; Vogt et al., 2018; Zosh et al., 2017) considers constructive play an integral part.

The Importance of Interactions in Children's Play

Interactions during children's play are crucial for early childhood development, offering essential opportunities for social, cognitive, and emotional growth. Constructive play, in particular, provides a rich environment for these interactions, involving both peer-to-peer and teacher-student engagements that significantly contribute to the holistic development of preschoolers.

Peer interactions during play are vital for fostering social skills, language development, and collaborative problem-solving abilities. When children engage in play with their peers, they practice communication, negotiate roles, and develop empathy. These interactions are fundamental for social competence and emotional regulation. Research indicates that peer interactions in play contexts help children learn to cooperate, share, and resolve conflicts, which are essential skills for future academic and social success. Play with peers offers a unique opportunity for children to engage in complex social scenarios that require negotiation, turn-taking, and perspective-taking (Zosh et al., 2017; Hirsh-Pasek et al., 2009).

The role of the teacher in facilitating constructive play is also significant. Teachers guide, scaffold, and enhance children's play experiences, providing the necessary support for cognitive and language development. Effective teacher-student interactions during play include modeling behaviors, introducing new vocabulary, and posing open-ended questions that stimulate thinking and exploration. High-quality teacher-student interactions are linked to greater gains in children's language, literacy, and social-emotional development (Cavanaugh et al., 2017; Pyle & Danniels, 2017). Teachers play a crucial role in balancing structure and freedom within play, allowing children to explore creatively while providing the necessary scaffolding to deepen their learning. Research supports that well-organized classrooms and high-quality instructional support positively influence children's language development and overall academic performance (Dobbs-Oates et al., 2011; Dickinson et al., 2014).

The socio-constructivist approach to human development and learning, as proposed by Vygotsky, emphasizes the importance of social interactions in cognitive development. Constructive play is an integral part of this approach, offering a dynamic environment where children construct knowledge through interactions with their peers and teachers. This framework suggests that learning is inherently a social process, and through play, children internalize new concepts and skills. Play-based learning environments that incorporate social interactions are essential for developing higher-order thinking skills (Mraz, Porcelli, & Tyler, 2016). These interactions facilitate cognitive development and help children learn the norms and rules of social engagement, preparing them for future academic and social challenges.

Additionally, the aspect of symbolic expression enhances children's engagement in the learning process at three levels of interaction: a) with the pedagogical material, b) with their peers, and c) with the classroom educator (Argyriadis et al., 2023; Putri, 2022). At this point, it is worth mentioning that the role of the preschool educator seems to be crucial in determining the quality of these play experiences (Loizou & Olymbiou, 2023), as they manage the delicate balance between supervision and children's autonomy, structured activity and freedom, while simultaneously cultivating an environment that stimulates children's interest (Ivrendi, 2020; Park, 2019).

A comprehensive understanding of the impact of interactions during constructive play on preschoolers' development requires a systematic review of the literature. This review should analyze studies focusing on both peer-to-peer and teacher-student interactions, examining their roles in enhancing various developmental domains. Such a review can highlight best practices and inform educational strategies that optimize the benefits of constructive play. Play-based pedagogies that emphasize interaction are significantly more effective in promoting cognitive and social-emotional outcomes compared to more traditional instructional methods (Taylor & Boyer, 2020). The integration of guided play with peer and teacher interactions leads to substantial improvements in early childhood mathematics learning (Vogt et al., 2018). High-quality teacher-child interactions are closely linked to the development of children's receptive vocabulary, underscoring the importance of instructional support and classroom organization (Hu et al., 2016).

The observation of children's behavior during constructive play and the study of the interactions they engage in have not been adequately explored, indicating a significant research gap. Thus, this systematic review embarked on a meticulous examination of interaction qualities during constructive play and their impact on preschoolers' development. As there are significantly fewer studies on constructive play in comparison to other kinds of children's play (e.g. symbolic play) the current study aimed to review the literature which pertain to the interactions that occur during constructive play in kindergarten and their influence on the developmental progress of preschoolers.

METHODOLOGICAL FRAMEWORK

Methods

This systematic review aimed to investigate the characteristics of interactions during constructive play in kindergarten and their impact on preschoolers' development. Especially, peer reviewed journal articles (written in English), examining interactions within constructive play in the early years setting from 2009 to date, were included. The period of 15 years was considered safe for a first overview of the trends in research on the issue of our interest. The method used for successful and comprehensive data review and utilization involved searching the relevant English literature in databases such Google Scholar, ERIC, Scopus, Elsevier, and PubMed (US National Library of Medicine). The systematic review was conducted between December 2023 and March 2024 as part of a postgraduate thesis. Studies and research related to the topic of interactions during the preschooler's constructive play were sought.

Criteria for Article Inclusion

- Publications in reputable databases.
- Languages of publication limited to English.
- Access to the full text of the study.
- Inclusion of articles from the last fourteen years, between 2009 and 2024.
- Inclusion of quantitative or qualitative studies.

Criteria for Article Exclusion

- Articles written in languages other than English.
- Articles published beyond the last fourteen years.
- Articles without access to the full text.
- Systematic reviews or bibliographic reviews.
- Publications in non-reputable databases.
- Not educational research
- Interactions between parents and children
- Other age group of participants

Keywords used during the simple and advanced data search included: "constructive play", "block play", "blocks", "preschool children", "preschoolers", "interactions", "peer interactions", "teacher interactions" along with the use of operators such as AND, OR, NOT.

The search stages followed the PRISMA 2020 flowchart, where the exact number of studies examined against the selection criteria was determined, and then they were distributed into specific categories. Finally, the characteristics of the selected studies in the systematic review were analyzed. The screening and selection process is presented in Figure 1.

Figure 1. PRISMA 2020 flow chart outlining the screening and selection process of articles included in this systematic review

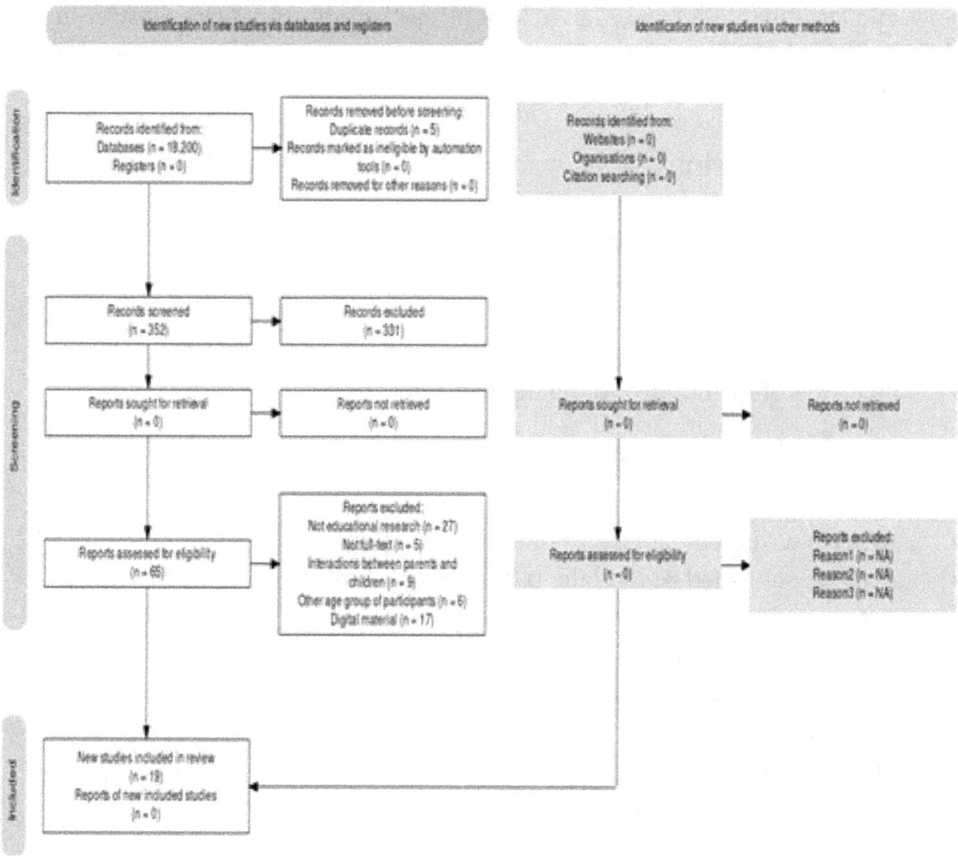

RESULTS

The selected studies, ranging from January 2009 to March 2023, were categorized into two main thematic areas, each with subcategories, illuminating distinctive aspects:

1. Conceptual Understanding in Constructive Play (13 studies)
2. Constructive Play and Pedagogical Practices (6 studies):
    2.1 Interventions (4 studies)
    2.2 Teachers' Role (2 studies)

Completed in March 2023, a total of 18,200 studies underwent scrutiny, with 17,848 excluded for failing to meet the specified acceptance criteria. Following the initial screening, 352 studies persisted after title reading, out of which 287 were excluded after abstract reading. Noteworthy among the excluded studies, only two were found to lack access to the full text. Additionally, a meticulous examination revealed 5 duplicate sources. Ultimately, a thorough evaluation culminated in the selection of 19 sources for inclusion in the review. Consequently, the final cohort for review consisted of these 19 sources.

The selected studies were categorized into the two main thematic areas:

1. Conceptual Understanding in Constructive Play: This category aimed to analyze the cognitive aspects involved in constructive play interactions. It delves into the thought processes and intellectual engagement of preschoolers as they participate in constructive play activities, aiming to discern how these interactions stimulate cognitive development and problem-solving skills.
2. Constructive Play and Pedagogical Practices
    2.1 Interventions: This subcategory explores various programs and interventions designed to enhance constructive play, assessing their effectiveness and impact on children's development.
    2.2 Teachers' Role: This subcategory examines the interactions between teachers and preschoolers during constructive play. The objective is to gain insights into how these interactions influence the holistic development of the child, encompassing emotional, social, cognitive, and intellectual domains.

By scrutinizing these categories, the systematic review sought to provide a comprehensive understanding of the qualitative aspects of interactions during constructive play in kindergarten and their nuanced effects on preschoolers' developmental facets. The synthesis of findings aimed to contribute valuable insights for educators, researchers, and policymakers in optimizing the educational benefits derived from constructive play in early childhood settings. These 19 studies are delineated in Table 1, providing a comprehensive overview of the research landscape within the specified timeframe. The specific characteristics of the studies included in the systematic review, categorized by thematic area and subcategory are represented in Table 2.

Table 1. Table of the results of systematic review

	Author, Year, Country	Title	Number of participants	Aim	Method	Results
1	(Gold, 2014)	Purdue e-Pubs Preschoolers' Physical, Social, and Engineering Play Behaviors: Differences in Gender and Play Environment	N= 66 preschoolers' (ages 3-to-5; 29 girls, 37 boys)	Preschoolers' physical activity, social behaviors, and "engineering thinking play" were studied through observations of their engagement with Imagination PlaygroundTM blocks, a new and engaging play material that promotes imaginative and creative play.		The study identified no gender differences in early engineering thinking play, pointing to the need for more research into early cognitive processes and girls' disinterest in STEM fields. Large, manipulable play with loose pieces resulted in three times more engineering thinking play than standard outdoor playgrounds.
2	(Gold et al., 2021)	Engineering play with blocks as an informal learning context for executive function and planning	*N= 66 preschool children*	The study investigated engineering play and gender differences in three play settings: standard playground, dramatic play area, and giant blocks.		The results revealed no gender differences, but considerable context variations in the frequency of engineering play, with larger blocks appearing to provide more chances. More study is needed to understand the impact of big, loose elements in early STEM play behavior.
3	(Schmitt et al., 2023)	First Insights into Preschool Teachers' Instructional Quality in Block Play and Its Associations with Children's Knowledge, Interest, Academic Self-Concept and Cognitive Aspects	N = 73 preschool teachers and N = 431 children (207 boys and 224 girls).	The study sought to provide preliminary insights into the relationships between children's cognitive and self-related aspects, as well as the relationships between preschool teachers' instructional quality in block play and children's self-concept, stability knowledge, spatial language, and math knowledge.		Preschool teachers' instructional quality, including spatial, math, and cognitive scaffolding, positively impacts children's stability knowledge and self-concept in block play, while general language use and sensitivity also contribute.
4	(Tavassoli et al., 2023)	Preschoolers' responses to prosocial opportunities during naturalistic interactions with peers: A cross-cultural comparison	*N* = 306; 48% female, 3-6 years old children.	This study aimed to identify similarities and variations in preschool children's prosocial responses to peers' needs in two culturally distinct contexts.		The findings shed light on how cultural traditions may influence the presentation of needs and prosocial responsiveness in peer relationships.

continued on following page

Table 1. Continued

	Author, Year, Country	Title	Number of participants	Aim	Method	Results
5	**(Sillanpää et al., 2022)**	**Froebel Box: A Tool for Participatory and Creative Learning**	**N=7 teachers.**	**The aim is to expand the tool based on Froebel's concepts and encourage creative, collaborative, and constructive play, as well as comprehensive bodily and verbal expression.**	**Interview**	**Froebelian applications improve children's interaction and learning in a holistic manner. Children's social and motor abilities, as well as their mathematics and spatial comprehension, are enhanced when they play with giant-sized blocks. Giant blocks allow toddlers to express themselves physically.**
6	(Loizou & Olymbiou, 2023)	Constructive play: Exploring pre-service early childhood teachers' play involvement	N= 4 early childhood pre-service students (PSSs) and N=17 children (5–6 years)	This study aimed to investigate the role of early childhood pre-service students (PSSs) on children's constructive play and their impact on advanced play behaviors, in line with prior research.		The study investigated how PSSs participated in children's play, including direct and indirect engagement.
7	(Henschen et al., 2022)	Peer interactions and their role in early mathematical learning in kindergarten discourses	N= 4 preschool children (two girls 6;0 and 5;3 years old and two boys 4;10 and 4;8 years old)	The study focuses on peer relations in the context of block play settings.		The text emphasizes the significance of mathematical content in children's interactive building activities. It highlights the ongoing negotiation of meaning and experiences gained through actions with the material, with both children actively participating in interpretations and clarifications. This process results in new interpretative perspectives, including mathematical experiences in topology, sizes, and geometric relations.
8	(Fleer, 2020)	Engineering PlayWorld—a Model of Practice to Support Children to Collectively Design, Imagine and Think Using Engineering Concepts	N= 2 teachers and N= 13 childen (4.7–6.4 years)	This article studied how teachers and preschoolers used engineering principles over a 12-month period.		Despite prior research that focused on engineering affordances during free play, this study identifies new play pedagogies that promote meaningful engineering learning for preschool children. New Engineering PlayWorld techniques involve youngsters seeing themselves as engineers and solving engineering challenges in groups.

continued on following page

Table 1. Continued

	Author, Year, Country	Title	Number of participants	Aim	Method	Results
9	(Tian et al., 2018)	The impact of individual differences, types of model and social settings on block building performance among Chinese preschoolers	N= 180 preschoolers	Participants engaged in a natural block building exercise and were scored using several measures to determine particular skills. Three dependent variables were investigated using the scores obtained from these measures: block building abilities, structural balance, and structural characteristics.		The study found that gender and grade level significantly influenced children's block construction skills, with boys outperforming girls. Block building skills improved significantly from the first to second year of preschool, but not from second to third. Preschoolers developed more representational constructs when given a wooden model, and performed better in small groups compared to large groups.
	(Sylla et al., 2018)	Blocks as symbolic tools for children's playful collaboration	N= 22 children (5 years old)	A study in two Danish kindergartens examined the impact of a Digital Manipulative (DM) on children's interactions, experiences, and play.		Research shows that children's involvement with physical blocks fosters democratic collaboration among peers, leading to prolonged engagement and attention span. Children's play with the blocks revealed two levels of articulation: one where they utilized the blocks to build visual tales, and another where they used the blocks as construction material.
	(Hu et al., 2018)	Using Peer-Mediated LEGO® Play Intervention to Improve Social Interactions for Chinese Children with Autism in an Inclusive Setting	N= 16 (3 boys with ASD and 13 typically developing children).	This study aimed to examine the impact of a peer-mediated LEGO® play intervention on social skills in children with Autism spectrum disorder (ASD) at an inclusive preschool in China.		The intervention resulted in greater social initiations and reactions among all three children with ASD. Social validity was also established.

continued on following page

Table 1. Continued

	Author, Year, Country	Title	Number of participants	Aim	Method	Results
	(Park, 2019)	The Qualities Criteria of Constructive Play and the Teacher's Role	N= 97 (5-year-old children, 53 boys and 44 girls)	This study aimed to identify the qualities of constructive play and the role of teachers in enhancing them.		Constructive play requirements included length, diversity (number of constructions), organization, elaboration, imagination, concentration, and variety (number and form of blocks). Teachers should foster and strengthen the features of constructive play. Encourage children to engage in constructive play by providing ample time, open-ended materials, various stories, fairy tales, and a safe setting. Effective direction, planning, support, and encouragement from teachers fosters children's constructive play skills. Constructive play may enhance young children's learning and development.
	(Barton et al., 2018)	Increasing the engagement and complexity of block play in young children	N= 8 (36 and 72 months, 4 pairs of children, each pair included a target child with or at-risk for a disability and a peer without an identified disability or risk status).	This study examined the impact of imitation and play expansions in small group teaching on the involvement and complexity of block play in young children with or at-risk for impairments and their peers.		The intervention package resulted in higher levels of engagement among target children. Adding visual and verbal suggestions to the intervention package improved the complexity of block play.
		Block play and mathematics learning in preschool: The effects of building complexity, peer and teacher interactions in the block area, and replica play materials	N= 41 preschool children	The aim of the study was to examine the relationship of block play variables to both the complexity of block structures and math learning in naturalistic free play settings.		The results indicated that the level of social interaction and the percentage of structures made without toys predicted the complexity of children's buildings. This increased architectural complexity was connected with improved math learning, as evaluated by Tools for Early Assessment in Mathematics. Based on these findings, a route model was developed to test the causal links between block play characteristics, structure complexity, and math learning.

continued on following page

Table 1. Continued

	Author, Year, Country	Title	Number of participants	Aim	Method	Results
	(Otsuka & Jay, 2016)	Understanding and supporting block play: video observation research on preschoolers' block play to identify features associated with the development of abstract thinking Video Observation Research on Preschoolers' Block Play: Identifying Features Associated with the Development of Abstract Thinking	N= 30 preschool children	The aim was to identify behaviors associated with aspects of the functional dependence relationship, a cognitive function that connects symbolic representations to abstract thinking. The essay uses three episodes to highlight three dominant features: i) child/child and adult/child sharing of thinking; ii) pause for reflection; and iii) satisfaction as a result of self-directed play.		i) child/child and adult/child thinking sharing; ii) pause for reflection; and iii) satisfaction as a result of self-directed play were identified as signs of learning, and were highlighted as phenomena that can assist practitioners in understanding the value of quality play and thus providing adequate time and space for young children and planning for a meaningful learning environment. The study also found that block play is important for developing abstract thinking skills.
	(Gold et al., 2015)	Preschoolers' Engineering Play Behaviors: Differences in Gender and Play Context	N= 66 preschool children	The study examined constructive play and gender differences in three play settings: regular playgrounds, dramatic play areas, and huge blocks.		The results revealed no gender differences, but considerable context variations in the frequency of constructive play, with larger blocks appearing to provide more chances.
	(Ramani et al., 2014)	Preschool children's joint block building during a guided play activity	N= 38 prescholers (4- and 5-year-old same-age, same-sex dyads)	The research aimed to examine children's communication and building behaviors, as well as the role of their coordinated behavior in the structures that they built		Children's spatial language correlates with home aspects in buildings, whereas their constructing behavior correlates with structure complexity. Children's coordinated conduct during interactions controlled the relationship between spatial talking and the structures they constructed.
	(Heisner, 2005)	Telling Stories with Blocks: Encouraging Language in the Block Center	N=? A small preschool classroom	This study aimed to explore a shared book-reading and modeling technique designed to promote sociodramatic play in the block center		Changes observed in pretend play as a result of reading and modeling varied from more play with the plastic animals in the block center to an extensive dramatic play episode utilizing a book in the block center as a reference point.
	(Nicole, 2015).	Building Curriculum during Block Play	N= 3 preschool boys	The study aimed to explore how the children's behaviors revealed their ability to use spoken language communication, cooperative play, sharing, and problem solving while building a vehicle ramp.		Block building projects offer numerous benefits, including assigning projects to the class or individuals, allowing exploration of indoor and outdoor activities, relating tasks to specific math skills, and assessing student abilities, promoting a child-centered curriculum that encourages student participation and sparks ideas.

Table 2. Characteristics of the studies included in the systematic review, categorized by thematic area and subcategory

Main Category		Description	Title	Author(s) and Year
Conceptual Understanding in Constructive Play		**Includes all aspects related to the development of children's concepts through constructive play, encompassing cognitive processes, language development, and problem-solving skills.**		
Constructive Play and Pedagogical Practices		Covers interventions, programs, and structured activities designed to enhance constructive play.		
Constructive Play and Pedagogical Practices	Teachers' Role	Focuses on the role of teachers in facilitating and guiding constructive play, including their interactions with children and the educational strategies they employ.		
Conceptual Understanding in Constructive Play			Purdue e-Pubs Preschoolers' Physical, Social, and Engineering Play Behaviors: Differences in Gender and Play Environment	Gold (2014)
Conceptual Understanding in Constructive Play			Engineering play with blocks as an informal learning context for executive function and planning	Gold et al. (2021)
Conceptual Understanding in Constructive Play			First Insights into Preschool Teachers' Instructional Quality in Block Play and Its Associations with Children's Knowledge, Interest, Academic Self-Concept and Cognitive Aspects	Schmitt et al. (2023)
Conceptual Understanding in Constructive Play			Preschoolers' responses to prosocial opportunities during naturalistic interactions with peers: A cross-cultural comparison	Tavassoli et al. (2023)
Conceptual Understanding in Constructive Play			Froebel Box: A Tool for Participatory and Creative Learning	Sillanpää et al. (2022)
Conceptual Understanding in Constructive Play			Engineering PlayWorld—a Model of Practice to Support Children to Collectively Design, Imagine and Think Using Engineering Concepts	Fleer (2020)
Conceptual Understanding in Constructive Play			The impact of individual differences, types of model and social settings on block building performance among Chinese preschoolers	Tian et al. (2018)
Conceptual Understanding in Constructive Play			Block play and mathematics learning in preschool: The effects of building complexity, peer and teacher interactions in the block area, and replica play materials	Trawick-Smith et al. (2017)
Constructive Play and Pedagogical Practices			Peer interactions and their role in early mathematical learning in kindergarten discourses	Henschen et al. (2022)

continued on following page

Table 2. Continued

Main Category		Description	Title	Author(s) and Year
Conceptual Understanding in Constructive Play		**Includes all aspects related to the development of children's concepts through constructive play, encompassing cognitive processes, language development, and problem-solving skills.**		
Constructive Play and Pedagogical Practices			Using Peer-Mediated LEGO® Play Intervention to Improve Social Interactions for Chinese Children with Autism in an Inclusive Setting	(Hu et al., 2018)
Constructive Play and Pedagogical Practices			Increasing the engagement and complexity of block play in young children	Barton et al. (2018)
Conceptual Understanding in Constructive Play			Blocks as symbolic tools for children's playful collaboration	(Sylla et al., 2018)
Constructive Play and Pedagogical Practices	Teachers' Role		The Qualities Criteria of Constructive Play and the Teacher's Role	Park (2019)
Constructive Play and Pedagogical Practices	Teachers' Role		Constructive play: Exploring pre-service early childhood teachers' play involvement	(Loizou & Olymbiou, 2023)
Conceptual Understanding in Constructive Play			Understanding and supporting block play: video observation research on preschoolers' block play to identify features associated with the development of abstract thinking Video Observation Research on Preschoolers' Block Play: Identifying Features Associated with the Development of Abstract Thinking	Otsuka & Jay (2016)
Conceptual Understanding in Constructive Play			Preschoolers' Engineering Play Behaviors: Differences in Gender and Play Context	Gold et al. (2015)
Conceptual Understanding in Constructive Play			Preschool children's joint block building during a guided play activity	Ramani et al. (2014)
Constructive Play and Pedagogical Practices			Telling Stories with Blocks: Encouraging Language in the Block Center	Heisner (2005)
Conceptual Understanding in Constructive Play			Building Curriculum during Block Play	Nicole (2015)

1. Conceptual Understanding in Constructive Play

Constructive play, especially block play, serves as a crucial medium for young children's cognitive development. The studies reviewed emphasize the multifaceted nature of these activities, revealing that they significantly contribute to children's conceptual understanding, language development, and problem-solving skills (Gold, 2014; Gold et al., 2021; Schmitt et al., 2023; Tavassoli et al., 2023). This type of play allows children to experiment with different ideas, engage in abstract thinking, and enhance their cognitive flexibility.

The reviewed literature underscores that constructive play is more than a mere pastime; it is a foundational element of early childhood education that fosters significant cognitive growth. For instance, the studies collectively suggest that through activities such as block building, children develop their executive functions, including planning, spatial awareness, and logical reasoning (Schmitt et al., 2023; Fleer, 2020; Tian et al., 2018). These activities encourage children to visualize different outcomes, test their hypotheses, and adjust their strategies based on the results, thereby enhancing their problem-solving abilities.

Furthermore, constructive play is instrumental in language development. As children engage in constructive play, they often describe their creations, negotiate roles, and collaborate on building projects, which enhances their vocabulary and communication skills (Sylla et al., 2018; Heisner, 2005). This interactive aspect of play helps children develop their narrative abilities and understand the use of language in social contexts. The studies reviewed highlight that the richness of language used during play correlates with improvements in children's expressive and receptive language skills, indicating that constructive play is a powerful tool for language acquisition (Hu et al., 2018; Ramani et al., 2014).

Additionally, the social interactions that occur during constructive play are pivotal for emotional and social development. Children learn to navigate social dynamics, resolve conflicts, and cooperate with peers. These interactions provide a context for children to develop empathy, understand different perspectives, and build social competence (Sillanpää et al., 2022; Otsuka & Jay, 2016). The synthesis of the studies reveals that the collaborative nature of constructive play fosters a sense of community and belonging among children, which is crucial for their overall well-being and development (Nicole, 2015).

2. Constructive Play and Pedagogical Practices

The role of educators in facilitating constructive play cannot be overstated. The studies reviewed highlight the importance of teacher involvement in optimizing the educational benefits of play (Park, 2019; Barton et al., 2018; Trawick-Smith et al.,

2017). Teachers who actively engage with children during play, provide scaffolding, and introduce new concepts enhance the learning outcomes associated with constructive play. The pedagogical practices of teachers, including their ability to create a stimulating and supportive play environment, are critical for fostering children's cognitive, social, and emotional development (Loizou & Olymbiou, 2023; Henschen et al., 2022).

The reviewed literature points to several effective interventions and strategies that teachers can employ to maximize the benefits of constructive play. For example, structured interventions that integrate educational content into play activities have been shown to enhance children's engagement and learning (Loizou & Olymbiou, 2023). Teachers can use block play to introduce mathematical concepts, encourage scientific thinking, and promote literacy skills. By guiding children's play experiences, teachers can help children make connections between play and real-world concepts, thereby deepening their understanding and retention of knowledge (Henschen et al., 2022).

Moreover, the studies emphasize the importance of teacher-child interactions in facilitating constructive play. High-quality interactions, characterized by warmth, responsiveness, and instructional support, are associated with better developmental outcomes for children (Park, 2019; Barton et al., 2018). Teachers who model problem-solving strategies, ask open-ended questions, and encourage children to explore different possibilities help children develop critical thinking skills and curiosity for learning. The synthesis of the studies indicates that teachers play a pivotal role in creating a learning-rich environment where constructive play can thrive (Sylla et al., 2018; Hu et al., 2018).

The findings also highlight the need for professional development and training for teachers to effectively incorporate constructive play into their pedagogical practices. Educators who are well-versed in the principles of play-based learning are better equipped to design meaningful play experiences that support children's holistic development. The studies suggest that ongoing training and support for teachers are essential for sustaining high-quality play-based education in early childhood settings (Gold et al., 2015; Fleer, 2020).

The synthesis of the reviewed studies underscores the significant role of constructive play in early childhood education. Constructive play activities, particularly those involving blocks, are crucial for promoting cognitive, social, and language development among preschoolers. The reviewed literature highlights the multifaceted benefits of constructive play, including the development of executive functions, language skills, and social competence (Schmitt et al., 2023; Gold et al., 2021; Sylla et al., 2018). Furthermore, the role of teachers in facilitating constructive play is critical for optimizing its educational benefits. High-quality teacher-child interactions, structured interventions, and professional development for educators are essential components of effective play-based learning (Park, 2019; Barton et al., 2018; Loizou & Olymbiou, 2023). This body of research provides compelling evidence for the inclusion of constructive play as a central element of early childhood education, emphasizing its importance for fostering children's holistic development.

DISCUSSION

The systematic review of the literature on constructive play in early childhood education reveals several key points that underscore its significance for preschoolers' development. The discussion is organized around three main axes are 1) the direct connection of constructive play with specific content areas, 2) the importance of quality interactions facilitated by educators, and 3) the relationship between constructive play and cultural context and everyday life.

1. Constructive Play and Specific Content Areas

The literature consistently demonstrates that constructive play is directly linked to the development of specific academic and cognitive skills. For instance, several studies highlight the role of constructive play in fostering language development. During constructive play, children engage in rich verbal interactions, negotiating roles, and describing their constructions, which enhances their vocabulary and narrative skills (Hu et al., 2018; Ramani et al., 2014; Heisner, 2005). This type of play provides a natural context for children to practice and expand their language abilities, making it a powerful tool for language acquisition.

In addition to language development, constructive play also supports mathematical learning. Studies have shown that activities such as building with blocks help children develop spatial awareness, understand geometric concepts, and engage in problem-solving (Trawick-Smith et al., 2017; Schmitt et al., 2023; Fleer, 2020). These cognitive processes are crucial for early mathematical understanding and lay the foundation for more advanced mathematical skills. Furthermore, the manipulation of blocks and other materials during constructive play helps children grasp basic physics concepts, such as balance and symmetry, further enriching their cognitive development (Gold et al., 2021; Tian et al., 2018).

2. Quality Interactions and the Role of Educators

The quality of interactions during constructive play is a critical factor influencing its educational benefits. High-quality interactions, characterized by warmth, responsiveness, and instructional support, are essential for maximizing the developmental outcomes of play. The literature emphasizes the pivotal role of teachers in facilitating these interactions (Park, 2019; Barton et al., 2018). Teachers who actively engage with children during play, provide scaffolding, and introduce new concepts enhance the learning experiences associated with constructive play (Loizou & Olymbiou, 2023; Henschen et al., 2022).

Effective teacher-child interactions during constructive play include modeling problem-solving strategies, asking open-ended questions, and encouraging children to explore different possibilities. These interactions help children develop critical thinking skills, creativity, and a love for learning (Sylla et al., 2018; Hu et al., 2018). The studies reviewed highlight that teachers play a crucial role in creating a supportive and stimulating play environment, which is essential for fostering children's cognitive, social, and emotional development (Schmitt et al., 2023; Fleer, 2020).

Furthermore, professional development and training for teachers are crucial for effectively incorporating constructive play into their pedagogical practices. Educators who are well-versed in the principles of play-based learning can design meaningful play experiences that support holistic development (Gold et al., 2015; Fleer, 2020). Ongoing training and support for teachers are essential for sustaining high-quality play-based education in early childhood settings.

3. Cultural Context and Everyday Life

Constructive play is deeply influenced by the cultural context and everyday life experiences of children. The literature indicates that cultural factors play a significant role in shaping children's play behaviors and interactions. For instance, the study by Tavassoli et al. (2023) highlights how cultural context affects prosocial behaviors during play, suggesting that children from different cultural backgrounds may exhibit distinct interaction patterns and social norms.

Moreover, the materials used in constructive play often reflect the cultural and social environment of the children. For example, studies have shown that children use building materials to represent real-world objects and scenarios, which helps them make sense of their environment and develop a deeper understanding of their cultural context (Cankaya et al., 2023; Zhang et al., 2022). This symbolic representation during play allows children to explore and internalize cultural values, practices, and knowledge (Sillanpää et al., 2022; Otsuka & Jay, 2016).

The relationship between constructive play and everyday life is also evident in the way children incorporate elements of their daily experiences into their play activities. For instance, children often recreate familiar settings, such as homes, schools, and communities, during constructive play, which helps them process and understand their everyday experiences (Cunningham, 2022; Zosh, 2022). This connection between play and real life enhances the relevance and meaningfulness of constructive play, making it a powerful tool for learning and development.

CONCLUSION

The systematic review underscores the pivotal role of constructive play in early childhood education, highlighting its extensive benefits for cognitive, social, and language development. The literature reveals that constructive play, particularly block play, significantly enhances children's conceptual understanding, language skills, and problem-solving abilities. This type of play provides a dynamic context for children to engage in rich verbal interactions, develop spatial awareness, and practice cognitive flexibility, making it a fundamental element of early education.

Moreover, the review emphasizes the critical importance of quality interactions facilitated by educators. High-quality teacher-child interactions, characterized by warmth, responsiveness, and instructional support, are essential for optimizing the educational outcomes of constructive play. Teachers play a crucial role in scaffolding children's play experiences, introducing new concepts, and encouraging exploration and creativity. Effective teacher involvement not only enhances cognitive and language development but also fosters social-emotional growth, preparing children for future academic and social success.

The review also highlights the influence of cultural context on children's play behaviors and interactions. Constructive play reflects the cultural and social environment of children, allowing them to explore and internalize cultural values, practices, and knowledge. This connection between play and everyday life enhances the relevance and meaningfulness of constructive play, making it a powerful tool for learning and development.

The synthesis of the reviewed studies provides compelling evidence for the inclusion of constructive play as a central element of early childhood education. Constructive play activities, supported by high-quality teacher interactions and mindful of cultural context, are crucial for fostering holistic development in preschoolers. This body of research underscores the need for ongoing professional development for educators to sustain high-quality play-based education and optimize the educational benefits of constructive play. As such, constructive play should be recognized and integrated as a fundamental component of early childhood curricula, given its profound impact on children's cognitive, social, and emotional development.

IMPLICATIONS

The findings of this systematic review highlight the critical role of educators in fostering a positive educational environment that promotes mental health in schools. Constructive play, as emphasized in the review, is essential for cognitive, social, and emotional development in early childhood education. Educators contribute significantly by providing diverse materials that stimulate creativity and engagement, ensuring that children are supported in their explorations. This active involvement not only enhances cognitive and language development but also helps children develop social skills and emotional resilience.

Furthermore, creating a supportive and stimulating learning environment requires quality interactions between educators and children, as well as among the children themselves. Encouraging collaborative play allows children to engage in shared problem-solving and creative thinking, which enhances learning outcomes and fosters a sense of community and belonging. Finally, constructive play should be integrated into innovative curricula and teaching approaches, as it supports holistic development and promotes mental health in schools, creating an inclusive and supportive environment for all children.

REFERENCES

Bagiati, A., & Evangelou, D. (2015). Engineering curriculum in the preschool classroom: The teacher's experience. *European Early Childhood Education Research Journal*, 23(1), 112–128. 10.1080/1350293X.2014.991099

Barton, E. E., Ledford, J. R., Zimmerman, K. N., & Pokorski, E. A. (2018). Increasing the engagement and complexity of block play in young children. *Education & Treatment of Children*, 41(2), 169–196. 10.1353/etc.2018.0007

Brooker, L., Blaise, M., & Edwards, S. (2014). Contexts for play and learning. *The SAGE handbook of play and learning in early childhood*, 277-282.

Clements, D. H., & Sarama, J. (2007). *Early childhood mathematics learning. Second handbook of research on mathematics teaching and learning, 1, 461-555.*

Dickinson, D. K., & Porche, M. V. (2014). Relation between language experiences in preschool classrooms and children's kindergarten and fourth-grade language and reading abilities. *Child Development*, 82(3), 870–886. 10.1111/j.1467-8624.2011.01576.x21413936

Dobbs-Oates, J., Kaderavek, J. N., Guo, Y., & Justice, L. M. (2011). Effective classroom practices: Preschool teachers' literacy instruction and children's print awareness. *Journal of Research in Childhood Education*, 25(3), 252–275.

Fisher, K. R., Hirsh-Pasek, K., Golinkoff, R. M., & Gryfe, S. G. (2008). Conceptual split? Parents' and experts' perceptions of play in the 21st century. *Journal of Applied Developmental Psychology*, 29(4), 305–316. 10.1016/j.appdev.2008.04.006

Fleer, M. (2022). Engineering PlayWorld—A Model of Practice to Support Children to Collectively Design, Imagine and Think Using Engineering Concepts. *Research in Science Education*, 52(2), 583–598. 10.1007/s11165-020-09970-6

Gold, Z. S. (2014). *Purdue e-Pubs Preschoolers' Physical, Social, and Engineering Play Behaviors: Differences in Gender and Play Environment.*

Gold, Z. S., Elicker, J., Choi, J. Y., Anderson, T., & Brophy, S. P. (2015). Preschoolers' engineering play behaviors: Differences in gender and play context. *Children, Youth and Environments*, 25(3), 1–21. 10.1353/cye.2015.0046

Gold, Z. S., Elicker, J., Evich, C. D., Mishra, A. A., Howe, N., & Weil, A. E. (2021). Engineering play with blocks as an informal learning context for executive function and planning. *Journal of Engineering Education*, 110(4), 803–818. 10.1002/jee.20421

Hamre, B. K., & Pianta, R. C. (2005). Can instructional and emotional support in the first-grade classroom make a difference for children at risk of school failure? *Child Development*, 76(5), 949–967. 10.1111/j.1467-8624.2005.00889.x16149994

Heisner, J. (2005). Telling Stories with Blocks: Encouraging Language in the Block Center. *Early Childhood Research & Practice*, 7(2), n2.

Henrich, J., Heine, S. J., & Norenzayan, A. (2010). The weirdest people in the world? *Behavioral and Brain Sciences*, 33(2-3), 61–83. 10.1017/S0140525X0999152X20550733

Henschen, E., Teschner, M., & Vogler, A.-M. (2022). Peer interactions and their role in early mathematical learning in kindergarten discourses. *International Electronic Journal of Mathematics Education*, 17(4), em0709. Advance online publication. 10.29333/iejme/12362

Hu, B. Y., Fan, X., Gu, C., & Yang, N. (2016). Teacher-child interaction quality, regulatory focus, and children's school readiness skills in China. *Learning and Instruction*, 41, 1–10.

Hu, X., Zheng, Q., & Lee, G. T. (2018). Using Peer-Mediated LEGO® Play Intervention to Improve Social Interactions for Chinese Children with Autism in an Inclusive Setting. *Journal of Autism and Developmental Disorders*, 48(7), 2444–2457. 10.1007/s10803-018-3502-429453705

Kampeza, M., & Sfyroera, M. (2016). Enhancing children's learning: Meaning-making and play. In Avgitidou, S., Tzekaki, M., & Tsafos, V. (Eds.), *Prospective educators observe, intervene, and reflect: Supporting their practicum* (Vol. 3, pp. 90–118). Gutenberg.

Loizou, E. (2021). Small blocks and building materials. *The Ultimate Handbook of Developmentally Appropriate Toys,* 49-60.

Loizou, E., & Loizou, E. K. (2022). Creative play and the role of the teacher through the cultural-historical activity theory framework. *International Journal of Early Years Education*, 30(3), 527–541. 10.1080/09669760.2022.2065248

Loizou, E., & Olymbiou, M. (2023). Constructive play: Exploring pre-service early childhood teachers' play involvement. *Journal of Early Childhood Research*, 1476718X231210642. Advance online publication. 10.1177/1476718X231210642

Loizou, E., & Olymbiou, M. (2023). Constructive play: Exploring pre-service early childhood teachers' play involvement. *Journal of Early Childhood Research*, 1476718X231210642. 10.1177/1476718X231210642

Mardell, B., Ryan, J., Krechevsky, M., Baker, M., Schulz, T. S., & Liu-Constant, Y. (2023). *A pedagogy of play: Supporting playful learning in classrooms and schools. Cambridge*. Project Zero.

Mashburn, A. J., Pianta, R. C., Hamre, B. K., Downer, J. T., Barbarin, O. A., Bryant, D., Burchinal, M., Early, D. M., & Howes, C. (2008). Measures of classroom quality in prekindergarten and children's development of academic, language, and social skills. *Child Development*, 79(3), 732–749. 10.1111/j.1467-8624.2008.01154.x18489424

Newcombe, N. (2010). Picture This: Increasing Math and Science Learning by Improving Spatial Thinking. *American Educator*, 34(2), 29.

Otsuka, K., & Jay, T. (n.d.). *Understanding and supporting block play: video observation research on preschoolers' block play to identify features associated with the development of abstract thinking Video Observation Research on Preschoolers' Block Play: Identifying Features Associated with the Development of Abstract Thinking*. http://shura.shu.ac.uk/13380/

Papandreou, M. (2020). *Participatory Learning in Preschool and Early Primary Education: Understanding Children's Languages and Enhancing Their Participation in Learning and Research Processes*. Sofia Publications.

Park, J. (2019). The Qualities Criteria of Constructive Play and the Teacher's Role. *The Turkish Online Journal of Educational Technology*, 18(1).

Ramani, G. B., Zippert, E., Schweitzer, S., & Pan, S. (2014). Preschool children's joint block building during a guided play activity. *Journal of Applied Developmental Psychology*, 35(4), 326–336. 10.1016/j.appdev.2014.05.005

Schmitt, L., Weber, A., Weber, D., & Leuchter, M. (2023). First Insights into Preschool Teachers' Instructional Quality in Block Play and Its Associations with Children's Knowledge, Interest, Academic Self-Concept and Cognitive Aspects. *Early Education and Development*, 1–23. Advance online publication. 10.1080/10409289.2023.2233879

Sillanpää, T., Visuri, F., & Ruokonen, I. (n.d.). *Froebel Box: A Tool for Participatory and Creative Learning*. Academic Press.

Sylla, C., Brooks, E., & Tümmler, L. (2018). Blocks as symbolic tools for children's playful collaboration. *Lecture Notes of the Institute for Computer Sciences. Social-Informatics and Telecommunications Engineering, LNICST*, 229, 413–423. 10.1007/978-3-319-76908-0_40

Tavassoli, N., Dunfield, K., Kleis, A., Recchia, H., & Conto, L. P. (2023). Preschoolers' responses to prosocial opportunities during naturalistic interactions with peers: A cross-cultural comparison. *Social Development*, 32(1), 204–222. 10.1111/sode.12620

Tian, M., Deng, Z., Meng, Z., Li, R., Zhang, Z., Qi, W., Wang, R., Yin, T., & Ji, M. (2018). The impact of individual differences, types of model and social settings on block building performance among Chinese preschoolers. *Frontiers in Psychology*, 9(JAN), 27. Advance online publication. 10.3389/fpsyg.2018.0002729441031

Trawick-Smith, J., Swaminathan, S., Baton, B., Danieluk, C., Marsh, S., & Szarwacki, M. (2017). Block play and mathematics learning in preschool: The effects of building complexity, peer and teacher interactions in the block area, and replica play materials. *Journal of Early Childhood Research*, 15(4), 433–448. 10.1177/1476718X16664557

Zippert, E. L., Eason, S. H., Marshall, S., & Ramani, G. B. (2019). Preschool children's math exploration during play with peers. *Journal of Applied Developmental Psychology*, 65, 101072. 10.1016/j.appdev.2019.101072

Zosh, Hopkins, Jensen, Liu, Neale, Hirsh-Pasek, Solis, & Whitebread. (2017). *Learning through Play: A Review of the Evidence. Billund: LEGO Foundation.* akcesedukacja.pl/images/dokumenty-pdf/Insight_and_Research/LEGO-Foundation---Learning-through-play---review-of-evidence-2017.pdf.

APPENDIX

Table 3.

	Author, Year, Country	Title	Number of participants	Aim	Method	Results
1	(Gold, 2014)	Purdue e-Pubs Preschoolers' Physical, Social, and Engineering Play Behaviors: Differences in Gender and Play Environment	N= 66 preschoolers' (ages 3-to-5; 29 girls, 37 boys)	Preschoolers' physical activity, social behaviors, and "engineering thinking play" were studied through observations of their engagement with Imagination PlaygroundTM blocks, a new and engaging play material that promotes imaginative and creative play.		The study identified no gender differences in early engineering thinking play, pointing to the need for more research into early cognitive processes and girls' disinterest in STEM fields. Large, manipulable play with loose pieces resulted in three times more engineering thinking play than standard outdoor playgrounds.
2	(Gold et al., 2021)	Engineering play with blocks as an informal learning context for executive function and planning	*N= 66 preschool children*	The study investigated engineering play and gender differences in three play settings: standard playground, dramatic play area, and giant blocks.		The results revealed no gender differences, but considerable context variations in the frequency of engineering play, with larger blocks appearing to provide more chances. More study is needed to understand the impact of big, loose elements in early STEM play behavior.
3	(Schmitt et al., 2023)	First Insights into Preschool Teachers' Instructional Quality in Block Play and Its Associations with Children's Knowledge, Interest, Academic Self-Concept and Cognitive Aspects	N = 73 preschool teachers and N = 431 children (207 boys and 224 girls).	The study sought to provide preliminary insights into the relationships between children's cognitive and self-related aspects, as well as the relationships between preschool teachers' instructional quality in block play and children's self-concept, stability knowledge, spatial language, and math knowledge.		Preschool teachers' instructional quality, including spatial, math, and cognitive scaffolding, positively impacts children's stability knowledge and self-concept in block play, while general language use and sensitivity also contribute.
4	(Tavassoli et al., 2023)	Preschoolers' responses to prosocial opportunities during naturalistic interactions with peers: A cross-cultural comparison	*N* = 306; 48% female, 3-6 years old children.	This study aimed to identify similarities and variations in preschool children's prosocial responses to peers' needs in two culturally distinct contexts.		The findings shed light on how cultural traditions may influence the presentation of needs and prosocial responsiveness in peer relationships.

continued on following page

Table 3. Continued

	Author, Year, Country	Title	Number of participants	Aim	Method	Results
5	**(Sillanpää et al., 2022)**	**Froebel Box: A Tool for Participatory and Creative Learning**	**N=7 teachers.**	**The aim is to expand the tool based on Froebel's concepts and encourage creative, collaborative, and constructive play, as well as comprehensive bodily and verbal expression.**	**Interview**	**Froebelian applications improve children's interaction and learning in a holistic manner. Children's social and motor abilities, as well as their mathematics and spatial comprehension, are enhanced when they play with giant-sized blocks. Giant blocks allow toddlers to express themselves physically.**
6	(Loizou & Olymbiou, 2023)	Constructive play: Exploring pre-service early childhood teachers' play involvement	N= 4 early childhood pre-service students (PSSs) and N=17 children (5–6 years)	This study aimed to investigate the role of early childhood pre-service students (PSSs) on children's constructive play and their impact on advanced play behaviors, in line with prior research.		The study investigated how PSSs participated in children's play, including direct and indirect engagement.
7	(Henschen et al., 2022)	Peer interactions and their role in early mathematical learning in kindergarten discourses	N= 4 preschool children (two girls 6;0 and 5;3 years old and two boys 4;10 and 4;8 years old)	The study focuses on peer relations in the context of block play settings.		The text emphasizes the significance of mathematical content in children's interactive building activities. It highlights the ongoing negotiation of meaning and experiences gained through actions with the material, with both children actively participating in interpretations and clarifications. This process results in new interpretative perspectives, including mathematical experiences in topology, sizes, and geometric relations.
8	(Fleer, 2020)	Engineering PlayWorld—a Model of Practice to Support Children to Collectively Design, Imagine and Think Using Engineering Concepts	N= 2 teachers and N= 13 childen (4.7–6.4 years)	This article studied how teachers and preschoolers used engineering principles over a 12-month period.		Despite prior research that focused on engineering affordances during free play, this study identifies new play pedagogies that promote meaningful engineering learning for preschool children. New Engineering PlayWorld techniques involve youngsters seeing themselves as engineers and solving engineering challenges in groups.

continued on following page

Table 3. Continued

	Author, Year, Country	Title	Number of participants	Aim	Method	Results
9	(Tian et al., 2018)	The impact of individual differences, types of model and social settings on block building performance among Chinese preschoolers	N= 180 preschoolers	Participants engaged in a natural block building exercise and were scored using several measures to determine particular skills. Three dependent variables were investigated using the scores obtained from these measures: block building abilities, structural balance, and structural characteristics.		The study found that gender and grade level significantly influenced children's block construction skills, with boys outperforming girls. Block building skills improved significantly from the first to second year of preschool, but not from second to third. Preschoolers developed more representational constructs when given a wooden model, and performed better in small groups compared to large groups.
	(Sylla et al., 2018)	Blocks as symbolic tools for children's playful collaboration	N= 22 children (5 years old)	A study in two Danish kindergartens examined the impact of a Digital Manipulative (DM) on children's interactions, experiences, and play.		Research shows that children's involvement with physical blocks fosters democratic collaboration among peers, leading to prolonged engagement and attention span. Children's play with the blocks revealed two levels of articulation: one where they utilized the blocks to build visual tales, and another where they used the blocks as construction material.
	(Hu et al., 2018)	Using Peer-Mediated LEGO® Play Intervention to Improve Social Interactions for Chinese Children with Autism in an Inclusive Setting	N= 16 (3 boys with ASD and 13 typically developing children).	This study aimed to examine the impact of a peer-mediated LEGO® play intervention on social skills in children with Autism spectrum disorder (ASD) at an inclusive preschool in China.		The intervention resulted in greater social initiations and reactions among all three children with ASD. Social validity was also established.

continued on following page

Table 3. Continued

	Author, Year, Country	Title	Number of participants	Aim	Method	Results
	(Park, 2019)	The Qualities Criteria of Constructive Play and the Teacher's Role	N= 97 (5-year-old children, 53 boys and 44 girls)	This study aimed to identify the qualities of constructive play and the role of teachers in enhancing them.		Constructive play requirements included length, diversity (number of constructions), organization, elaboration, imagination, concentration, and variety (number and form of blocks). Teachers should foster and strengthen the features of constructive play. Encourage children to engage in constructive play by providing ample time, open-ended materials, various stories, fairy tales, and a safe setting. Effective direction, planning, support, and encouragement from teachers fosters children's constructive play skills. Constructive play may enhance young children's learning and development.
	(Barton et al., 2018)	Increasing the engagement and complexity of block play in young children	N= 8 (36 and 72 months, 4 pairs of children, each pair included a target child with or at-risk for a disability and a peer without an identified disability or risk status).	This study examined the impact of imitation and play expansions in small group teaching on the involvement and complexity of block play in young children with or at-risk for impairments and their peers.		The intervention package resulted in higher levels of engagement among target children. Adding visual and verbal suggestions to the intervention package improved the complexity of block play.
		Block play and mathematics learning in preschool: The effects of building complexity, peer and teacher interactions in the block area, and replica play materials	N= 41 preschool children	The aim of the study was to examine the relationship of block play variables to both the complexity of block structures and math learning in naturalistic free play settings.		The results indicated that the level of social interaction and the percentage of structures made without toys predicted the complexity of children's buildings. This increased architectural complexity was connected with improved math learning, as evaluated by Tools for Early Assessment in Mathematics. Based on these findings, a route model was developed to test the causal links between block play characteristics, structure complexity, and math learning.

continued on following page

Table 3. Continued

	Author, Year, Country	Title	Number of participants	Aim	Method	Results
	(Otsuka & Jay, 2016)	Understanding and supporting block play: video observation research on preschoolers' block play to identify features associated with the development of abstract thinking Video Observation Research on Preschoolers' Block Play: Identifying Features Associated with the Development of Abstract Thinking	N= 30 preschool children	The aim was to identify behaviors associated with aspects of the functional dependence relationship, a cognitive function that connects symbolic representations to abstract thinking. The essay uses three episodes to highlight three dominant features: i) child/child and adult/child sharing of thinking; ii) pause for reflection; and iii) satisfaction as a result of self-directed play.		i) child/child and adult/child thinking sharing; ii) pause for reflection; and iii) satisfaction as a result of self-directed play were identified as signs of learning, and were highlighted as phenomena that can assist practitioners in understanding the value of quality play and thus providing adequate time and space for young children and planning for a meaningful learning environment. The study also found that block play is important for developing abstract thinking skills.
	(Gold et al., 2015)	Preschoolers' Engineering Play Behaviors: Differences in Gender and Play Context	N= 66 preschool children	The study examined constructive play and gender differences in three play settings: regular playgrounds, dramatic play areas, and huge blocks.		The results revealed no gender differences, but considerable context variations in the frequency of constructive play, with larger blocks appearing to provide more chances.
	(Ramani et al., 2014)	Preschool children's joint block building during a guided play activity	N= 38 prescholers (4- and 5-year-old same-age, same-sex dyads)	The research aimed to examine children's communication and building behaviors, as well as the role of their coordinated behavior in the structures that they built		Children's spatial language correlates with home aspects in buildings, whereas their constructing behavior correlates with structure complexity. Children's coordinated conduct during interactions controlled the relationship between spatial talking and the structures they constructed.
	(Heisner, 2005)	Telling Stories with Blocks: Encouraging Language in the Block Center	N=? A small preschool classroom	This study aimed to explore a shared book-reading and modeling technique designed to promote sociodramatic play in the block center		Changes observed in pretend play as a result of reading and modeling varied from more play with the plastic animals in the block center to an extensive dramatic play episode utilizing a book in the block center as a reference point.
	(Nicole, 2015).	Building Curriculum during Block Play	N= 3 preschool boys	The study aimed to explore how the children's behaviors revealed their ability to use spoken language communication, cooperative play, sharing, and problem solving while building a vehicle ramp.		Block building projects offer numerous benefits, including assigning projects to the class or individuals, allowing exploration of indoor and outdoor activities, relating tasks to specific math skills, and assessing student abilities, promoting a child-centered curriculum that encourages student participation and sparks ideas.

Chapter 13
The Play as a Mediator of Learning and Psychosocial Empowerment of Children With Learning Difficulties

Dimitra V. Katsarou
https://orcid.org/0000-0001-8690-0314
University of the Aegean, Greece

ABSTRACT

Play and playful forms of development and imitation are placed at the center of the child's early developmental years. Regarding the learning support of children with special learning difficulties in reading, play, and especially the social type of play, contributes to the strengthening of phonological and phonemic processing, but to the practice of phonological awareness, through the phonological decoding of words, into phonemic and syllabic level, through the improvement of vocabulary and through the repetition of words. As a result, there is the restoration of any phonological deficits that make it difficult to process the reading ability, and by extension, the strengthening of reading fluency and accuracy. At the same time, through the play, the above-mentioned skills directly related to reading ability are supported, keeping children's interest in the classroom and minimizing the fatigue caused by frequent repetitions. The purpose of this chapter is to highlight the key role of play in the processes of learning and psychosocial empowerment of children with learning difficulties.

DOI: 10.4018/979-8-3693-8312-4.ch013

Copyright © 2024, IGI Global. Copying or distributing in print or electronic forms without written permission of IGI Global is prohibited.

INTRODUCTION

Extensive research has been carried out, for several decades, regarding the game and the beneficial effects it causes both in the learning, emotional and psychosocial fields. Through research, different types of play have been described, each serving different developmental, cognitive, and psychoemotional purposes (Ginsburg, 2007). It has therefore been observed that "kinetic/physical" play, which basically includes children's physical activity, has been found to contribute to children's muscle strengthening, as well as to the coordination of muscles, nerves and brain functions (Piaget, 2013). Then, in "social" play, through which children interact with peers and adults, children internalize social norms and values and are pushed to form a moral reasoning about the world around them (Santrock, 2020). "Constructive" play has also been observed, which refers to the manipulation of objects and the environment by children during their play and through this the sense of control is formed in children, the finding of alternative forms of behavior, the combination of symbols, forms and objects and a more general sense of completion and adequacy (Abdul Rauf & Abu Bakar, 2019). Through "imagination" play, children then learn to try on new roles and new situations, experiment with language and feelings, use new words, word combinations and numbers to express ideas, dreams and stories (Yogman et al., 2018). Finally, games "with rules" are observed, through which children internalize the value of laws and rules for the orderly functioning of any social system (Schacter et al.,, 2012).

More generally, research on play has repeatedly demonstrated its value both for developmental and learning and cognitive areas in children, while a strong correlation has been shown between various forms of play and linguistic, cognitive, physical, social, mental and emotional development of children. However, the contribution of the game to the learning and psychosocial development of children with special learning difficulties, who face special difficulties in the above-mentioned areas, is judged to be special (Djamnezhad et al., 2021). Therefore, given that students with special learning difficulties face special problems in internalizing, understanding and processing linguistic and lexical information, in terms of symbols, numbers and concepts, in terms of social and communication skills, as well as in terms of their psycho-emotional adaptability, play as an educational tool, strengthens each of these areas that are affected in children who face specific learning difficulties (Cortiella & Horowitz, 2014).

The Role of Play in Children's Learning and Development

With reference to the form of physical/physical play, as mentioned above, it has been found by recent research that there is a strong connection between children's activity that includes stimuli, and their brain development (Chuang et al., 2021). In other words, this type of play provides the vital opportunity for children to develop and evolve brain structures and functions, develop their psychomotor skills and coordinate movement with the cognitive processing of stimuli in their environment. Brain researchers have advocated the value of motor play in enhancing the creation and development of brain synapses related to language, movement, social and emotional experiences, through the stimulation of sensory systems and the intake of a multitude of environmental stimuli (Howard, 2007).

In relation, then, to social play, this contributes to the development in children of social skills, social reciprocity, socially desirable ways of interacting, social values, but also to the internalization of a moral code and the development of the values of cooperation and sharing (Elliott, et al., 2010). Recent research has shown that the social type of play encourages the development of children's imagination, the development of their ability to use speech and language correctly, promotes the development of empathy in children and a fuller understanding of those around them, while contributing to the reducing their levels of aggressive and disruptive behaviors. Furthermore, this type of play contributes to the development of trusting relationships between children and the adults around them and to learning the appropriate management and expression of their emotional experiences (Whitebread, et al., 2017).

Through constructive play, it has been found by research that children develop a sense of control of the environment around them and self-confidence and self-sufficiency, the development of problem-solving strategies is promoted, as well as the formation of concepts and ideas (Howard, 2007). Research on the role of fantasy play in children's development has proven that through this type of play, children develop critical, abstract and flexible thinking, their language and communication skills develop, their ability to combine and understand the time, space, quantity, symbols, words, numbers as well as concepts, while also developing a sense of security and control in the environment around them. Finally, through games with rules, children move beyond self-centered thinking and develop an understanding of the value of rules and conventions (Singer et al., 2006; Terpstra et al., 2002).

Play is a flexible and adaptable classroom tool, providing personalized learning experiences that address the specific needs and challenges of children with learning disabilities. It specifically provides a tailored approach that meets the special needs of children, who often struggle in conventional educational settings (Parker et al., 2022). By incorporating the physical involvement of play into the educational process, educators can create inclusive learning environments that enhance these children's talents, facilitate their academic progress, and enhance their overall development in a way that matches their individual abilities (Tlili et al., 2022).

First and foremost, engaging in play offers a comprehensive and interactive learning experience, which is proven to be beneficial for children with special learning challenges such as dyslexia, dyscalculia, dysgraphia or attention deficit hyperactivity disorder (ADHD). Play enables children to engage in learning using multiple methods to suit their different learning styles and talents.

For example, engaging in hands-on activities such as using physical objects or materials that stimulate the senses, puzzles, or counting games can help children with dyscalculia understand math concepts by providing a concrete illustration of intangible concepts (Reeve & Waldecker, 2017). These visual and tactile aids empower individuals to visualize and manipulate numbers, thereby improving understanding of mathematical concepts. Participating in problem-solving games also promotes critical thinking and builds self-confidence in students with dyscalculia (Castaldi et al., 2020). These games create an environment in which children can engage in the practical application of mathematical principles, thereby promoting a deeper understanding of number relationships.

Then, engaging in play fosters a relaxed atmosphere that reduces anxiety and fosters a favorable attitude toward education. Children afflicted with specific learning difficulties often experience anxiety or dissatisfaction within conventional educational settings. Playful approaches to learning provide a safe environment where mistakes are embraced as a natural part of the learning journey, reducing the stress of making mistakes and enabling children to develop confidence and self-esteem (Hess & Gunter, 2013).

Play and Children With Learning Difficulties

Regarding the learning support of children with special learning difficulties in reading, play, and especially the social type of play, contributes to the strengthening of phonological and phonemic processing, but to the practice of phonological awareness, through the phonological decoding of words, into phonemic and syllabic level, through vocabulary improvement and word repetition. As a result, there is the restoration of any phonological deficits that make it difficult to process the reading ability, and by extension, the strengthening of reading fluency and accuracy (Slavin, 2007). At the same time, through the game, the above-mentioned skills directly related to reading ability are supported, keeping children's interest in the classroom and minimizing the fatigue caused by frequent repetitions. In addition, through the game as an educational tool to support the specific learning difficulty in reading, children's language skills are strengthened, as it has been found that oral language is directly related to reading comprehension (Polychroni, 2023). Also, through the game, the learning of the appropriate handling of the phonemes of the language is enhanced, the visual vocabulary is significantly enriched, the use of cognitive strategies is promoted, while the drawing of conclusions is promoted, which is related to reading comprehension and the extraction of meaning from the written text, skills in which students with special learning disabilities in reading also show deficits (Smith & Tyler, 2019).

As for the learning support of children with special learning difficulties in the written word, it has been found that the game contributes to the strengthening of complex psychomotor skills, which play a key role in the process of writing and spelling (Malekian & Askari, 2013). Also, the game promotes memory skills, and since it has been established that during the writing process the forms of the words stored in the memory and the possibility of retrieving them are a key source of retrieving the requested information, through the game spelling and writing are significantly enhanced student expression (Santrock, 2020). At the same time, the game contributes to the practice of visual memory, the creation of mental images and stories, the visualization and classification of information into conceptual categories, as well as the practice of the visual sequence of objects, symbols and events, processes crucial to the processing of the written word (Swanson & Siegel, 2009).

Many studies, having recognized the above difficulties in the learning field, have investigated the special needs of students with Learning Difficulties and Dyslexia. Among other things in her research, Exley (2003) found that the majority of students with Dyslexia desire learning methods related to visuospatial and kinesthetic abilities, as these are what contribute to improving their school performance. Accordingly, Reid & Kirk (2001) reported that for students with dyslexia, the use of the multisensory method, combined with gradual and clear teaching (visual, auditory and kinesthetic), is preferable because it utilizes their potential and meets their needs (Manna, 2013). In this way they can use many of their senses to transform learning information into visual or other representations and thus better understand it. So we must not forget that students with Dyslexia are distinguished for their ingenuity, creativity, combinatory thinking, the ability to be led to logical conclusions, provided they have been properly approached (Pavlidis, 2015).

Since textbooks alone are not able to utilize their abilities and meet their specialized needs, it becomes necessary to take effective emotional and educational approaches, using alternative pedagogical and learning media, such as games (Yong & McIntyre, 2015). The game meets the requirements of teaching children with Dyslexia, as it can be adapted and differentiated in a way that responds to their learning level, their interests and in combination with their existing knowledge to encourage their motivation to learn. Also, the game can be differentiated based on the learning profile of the students, as the way the material is presented is adaptable in terms of format (visual, auditory or oral, individual or group), the assessment or the type of intelligence it examines (e.g. .eg linguistic, interpersonal) (Panteliadou & Antoniou, 2008; Reeve & Waldecker, 2017). In particular, it has the advantage of offering multidimensional education, as the combination of image, movement and sound enhances understanding and memory. This helps children with dyslexia associate words with visual and auditory stimuli so they can recall them at any time and also understand them more easily. But in addition to understanding, the game promotes language skills, which through activities reinforce vocabulary and grammar, encouraging their gradual progress (Valente, 2017). Finally, it supports self-confidence in the learning area, as it creates environments where children with LD can, without the pressure and fear of possible failure, achieve through individualized exercises and feedback, the expected skills and the intended goals. Thus, they improve their weaknesses while at the same time gaining positive experiences

In the learning support of children who face special learning difficulties in mathematics, it has been found that the game promotes the formation of the perception of relationships in space, such as direction, distance and the understanding of right and left, as well as the visual discrimination of shapes, characters and details of objects, which are related to the understanding of mathematical relationships, concepts and operations (Johnson et al., 2011). Also, through the game, the processing of mathematical activities is promoted, through the exploration of patterns and spatial forms, through the understanding of sizes, the comparison of elements, the enumeration, the quantification and the internalization of mathematical judgments (Sutton-Smith, 2008). Numerous studies have shown the strengthening of mathematical abilities and mathematical performance through the game in the classroom, as the central point of the game is the creation of relationships between things and objects, the understanding of space, time, sizes, colors, quantities and pattern recognition, as well as classifying objects, which are considered vital for the development of mathematical thinking in children (Castaldi et al., 2020; Wajiuhullah et al., 2018). Furthermore, through the promotion of abstract thinking, through the strengthening of visual perception and spatio-temporal organization, the understanding of mathematical problems is also strengthened, for students with special learning difficulties in mathematics (Pehlivan, 2016).

More generally, the game, with the functions it contains, has been shown to strengthen every learning area, as it promotes expressive speech, the development of critical thinking, children's motivation to learn, selective attention and concentration, but also the stimulation of simultaneous processing of multiple information and stimuli, which are critical functions for the learning process (Elliott et al., 2010). In addition, the game promotes the use of internal self-questioning aimed at self-regulating behavior when conducting cognitive learning projects, as well as monitoring, controlling and regulating the learning process, as well as self-regulated learning (Hess & Gunter, 2013). Finally, through neurological studies that investigated the correlation between play and learning, it was found that since a wide range of the human brain is connected to the processing of stimuli from the extremities, the practical skills required by playing games activate the appropriate brain areas that appear to have difficulties in dealing with specific learning difficulties in various learning projects (Howard & Wood, 2010).

Continuing, the game facilitates the cultivation of fundamental skills. Children diagnosed with ADHD may have difficulty maintaining focus and regulating impulsive behaviors. Engaging in play activities that involve physical movement or sensory stimulation can help these children control their attention, enhance concentration, and better manage their impulses (Vargianniti & Karpouzis, 2019).

Another important feature and offer of the game is the adaptation of its activities to address the special challenges of students with learning disabilities. For example, using word games or telling stories can help students with dyslexia improve their reading and language proficiency (Valente, 2017). By modifying games and activities to suit their specific requirements, educators can develop approaches that directly target the difficulties faced by these children, thus enhancing the accessibility and enjoyment of the learning process (Polychroni, 2011).

Additionally, in the case of dyslexia, which is a learning disorder characterized by difficulty in reading, spelling, and writing, phonemic awareness can be improved through the use of games that focus on rhyming, sound discrimination, and word play (Adipat et al., 2021). These activities specifically target the individual sounds in words, helping to improve comprehension and pronunciation. Additionally, multisensory approaches that include the use of games that incorporate visual, auditory, and tactile elements play a critical role in enhancing the connection between letters and their corresponding sounds (Javed et al., 2023). These approaches enhance dyslexic students' understanding of the association between letters and sounds, thereby enhancing their ability to decode words.

Then, structured play is essential to provide vital help to dyslexic children. Engaging in storytelling, participating in word-building games, or using color-coded systems helps these students better organize knowledge (Christiansen et al., 2019). Systematic methods facilitate improved understanding and long-term memory of language-related ideas (Penderi et al., 2021).

In the case of dysgraphia, which is a condition characterized by difficulties in writing, often resulting from reduced motor skills or problems with the ability to organize thoughts and ideas, engaging in play-based activities that focus on fine motor skills, such as sketching, tracing or using tools such as clay or building blocks, can help improve and refine motor skills (Chung et al., 2020). In addition, engaging in visual-spatial activities such as puzzles, mazes, or pattern-based games helps build spatial thinking skills needed to address problems in written communication

(Crouch & Jakubecy, 2007). Finally, writing projects that include storytelling, creating comics, or participating in interactive writing games can help people with dysgraphia develop a positive attitude toward writing and promote self-expression (Ronimus et al., 2019).

In summary, by incorporating a variety of recreational activities specifically tailored to address these specific learning disabilities, educators can create conducive learning environments that enhance talents and normalize the challenges faced by their students (Pandeliadou, 2011).

Along with the learning support of children with special learning difficulties through the game, the game also supports the specific group of students psychosocially, through the reduction of anxiety, by stimulating the children's self-esteem, through the development of an internal base of behavioral control, but also through dealing with the school anxiety that it has been found that students with learning difficulties very often face (Smith & Tyler, 2019). Also, through the game, cooperation with the teacher and classmates is promoted, the interpersonal relationships of students with learning difficulties are improved and they develop both social and emotional competence (Denham et al., 2016). They learn to negotiate, take turns and manage both themselves and others, and the anxiety, disruptive behaviors and aggression that have been found to be more often exhibited by students with learning disabilities, compared to students without, are largely addressed. face similar difficulties (Pellegrini, 2009). It develops behavioral adjustment, empathy, social altruism and interpersonal skills, in which students with learning disabilities also show deficits. In conclusion, research shows that the emotional and behavioral adaptability of children and the developed social and interpersonal skills, areas in which the functions of the game contribute decisively and in which students with learning problems present difficulties, are necessary structural elements for school and academic children's success (Polychroni, 2011).

Students with Special Learning Difficulties, mainly with dyslexia, in addition to difficulties in the learning field, also present behavioral difficulties, such as emotional immaturity, inability to determine space-time, memory retention, which deprives them of self-confidence, creates anxiety, frustration, insecurity and isolation tendency (Polychroni et al., 2023). For this reason, the game also plays a crucial role in the psychosocial support of these students, as it promotes integration, self-confidence and social skills (Dafermou et al., 2006). In particular, the game ensures a safe environment, in which children with Dyslexia, through pleasant, interesting challenges, can develop their communication skills. Especially participating in group games, where many children participate, encourages interaction and cooperation, facilitating the development of relationships with their classmates. Through shared activities, such as role play, children take the opportunity to cultivate strong friendships and thus feel socially accepted members of the school environment. In addition, it is worth mentioning that the game offers opportunities for understanding and accepting differences e.g. multicultural, promoting mutual respect (Alharbi, & Alzahrani, 2020) Finally, group or individual games boost self-confidence, as through contact with people and objects they discover and develop their skills in a fun way. Of course, successes in play bring self-confidence, they are not limited only to this interpersonal-emotional space, but are transferred to the teacher and later to the wider society, encouraging the child's effort and active participation in every activity that will arise in his life (Backenson et al., 2015) .

Moreover, play provides a safe and non-intimidating outlet for students with learning disabilities to express their feelings (Bakar et al., 2022). Engaging in imaginative play scenarios, creative activities, or role-playing allows individuals to analyze and express complex emotions, thereby enhancing emotional resilience and improving their ability to effectively manage their emotions (Chuang et al., 2021; Rose et al., 2013).

Participating in playful activities helps foster sociability among individuals with learning challenges. By participating in cooperative games, group activities, and shared play experiences, individuals acquire basic social skills, including the ability to take turns, cooperate, empathize, and resolve conflict (Abdul Rauf & Abu Bakar, 2019). These interactions offer an opportunity to improve communication skills, strengthen peer connections, and foster a sense of belonging to a supportive social network (Djamnezhad et al., 2021).

Moving forward, engaging in play fosters a sense of curiosity and a willingness to take risks in a relaxed environment, allowing students to build confidence as they dare to test their abilities and discover talents they didn't know they possessed. Success in activities involving play enhances the sense of achievement, positively influencing their self-esteem (Djamnezhad et al., 2021). Additionally, the lack of criticism in play situations reduces the fear of making mistakes, allowing children to tackle problems with increased confidence (Sorrenti et al., 2019). Finally, engaging in play acts as an intrinsic method of stress reduction, helping to alleviate the anxiety and tension that children with learning disabilities often experience (Hess & Gunter, 2013). Thus, engaging in enjoyable and refreshing activities can reduce stress levels, enhancing calmness and psychological well-being.

CONCLUSION

A lot of research over decades has proven the importance of play both in learning and in general in the development of children, as analyzed above. Over the last decades, there has been an increase in research that studies the positive effects of the game on the learning, but also on the psychosocial development of students who face learning difficulties, through the cognitive, emotional and psychosocial functions that are employed during the realization of the game (Macintyre, 2016).

In more detail, on the one hand, through the game, specific cognitive areas related to specific learning difficulties and the specific learning objects that affect them are strengthened, while in general, the game strengthens the students' motivation to learn, their sense of competence with regard to the various cognitive objects and removes the stress that accompanies educational processes. On the other hand, the game also contributes to the psychosocial development of students who face learning difficulties, through strengthening the development of social and interpersonal skills, as well as through the promotion of social and emotional adaptability, areas in which it has also been found that the students with learning disabilities show significant deficits (Lin & Bratton, 2015).

Therefore, it is considered necessary to design and implement educational and teaching programs that will include play activities, in order to create learning environments that will promote both cognitive, emotional and psychosocial development of children, and to move teaching away from a sterile transmission of information, which students with learning difficulties are unable to process within the grade-centered and competitive nature of the modern education system (Kieff & Casbergue, 2015).

REFERENCES

Abdul Rauf, A. L., & Abu Bakar, K. (2019). Effects of Play on the Social Development of Preschool Children. *Creative Education*, 10(12), 2640–2648. 10.4236/ce.2019.1012191

Adipat, S., Laksana, K., Busayanon, K., Ausawasowan, A., & Adipat, B. (2021). Engaging Students in the Learning Process with Game-Based Learning: The Fundamental Concepts. *International Journal of Technology in Education*, 4(3), 542–552. 10.46328/ijte.169

Alharbi, M. O., & Alzahrani, M. M. (2020). The importance of learning through play in early childhood education: Reflection on the Bold Beginnings Report. *International Journal of the Whole Child*, 5(2), 9–17.

Backenson, E. M., Holland, S. C., Kubas, H. A., Fitzer, K. R., Wilcox, G., Carmichael, J. A., Fraccaro, R. L., Smith, A. D., Macoun, S. J., Harrison, G. L., & Hale, J. B. (2015). Psychosocial and Adaptive Deficits Associated with Learning Disability Subtypes. *Journal of Learning Disabilities*, 48(5), 511–522. 10.1177/002221941351186124300589

Bakar, S. N. S. A., Mahamarowi, N. H., & Mustapha, S. (2022, December). *Game Based Learning as a Teaching and Learning Tool for Dyslexic Children* [Conference session]. 2022 IEEE 10th Conference on Systems, Process & Control (ICSPC), Melaka, Malaysia.

Castaldi, E., Piazza, M., & Iuculano, T. (2020). Learning disabilities: Developmental dyscalculia. *Neurocognitive Development: Disorders and Disabilities, 174*, 61 75

Christiansen, L., Beck, M. M., Bilenberg, N., Wienecke, J., Astrup, A., & Lundbye Jensen, J. (2019). Effects of Exercise on Cognitive Performance in Children and Adolescents with ADHD: Potential Mechanisms and Evidence-based Recommendations. *Journal of Clinical Medicine*, 8(6), 841. 10.3390/jcm806084131212854

Chuang, T.-Y., Yeh, M. K.-C., & Lin, Y.-L. (2021). The Impact of Game Playing on Students' Reasoning Ability, Varying According to Their Cognitive Style. *Journal of Educational Technology & Society*, 24(3), 29–43.

Chung, P. J., Patel, D. R., & Nizami, I. (2020). Disorder of written expression and dysgraphia: Definition, diagnosis, and management. *Translational Pediatrics*, 9(S1), S46–S54. 10.21037/tp.2019.11.0132206583

Cortiella, C., & Horowitz, S. H. (2014). The state of learning disabilities: Facts, trends and emerging issues. *National Center for Learning Disabilities*, 3, 182–189.

Crouch, A., & Jakubecy, J. (2007). Dysgraphia: How It Affects A Student's Performance and What Can Be Done About It. *Teaching Exceptional Children Plus, 3*(3). https://files.eric.ed.gov/fulltext/EJ967123.pdf

Denham, A. R., Mayben, R., & Boman, T. (2016). Integrating Game-Based Learning Initiative: Increasing the Usage of Game-Based Learning Within K-12 Classrooms Through Professional Learning Groups. *TechTrends*, 60(1), 70–76. 10.1007/s11528-015-0019-y

Djamnezhad, D., Koltcheva, N., Dizdarevic, A., Mujezinovic, A., Peixoto, C., Coelho, V., Achten, M., Kolumbán, E., Machado, F., & Hofvander, B. (2021). Social and Emotional Learning in Preschool Settings: A Systematic Map of Systematic Reviews. *Frontiers in Education*, 6, 181–189. 10.3389/feduc.2021.691670

Elliott, N. S., Kratochwill, R. T., Littlefield, C. J., & Travers, F. J. (2010). *Educational psychology: effective teaching – effective learning*. Gutenberg.

Ginsburg, K. R. (2007). The Importance of Play in Promoting Healthy Child Development and Maintaining Strong Parent-Child Bonds. *Pediatrics*, 119(1), 182–191. 10.1542/peds.2006-269717200287

Hess, T., & Gunter, G. (2013). Serious game-based and nongame-based online courses: Learning experiences and outcomes. *British Journal of Educational Technology*, 44(3), 372–385. 10.1111/bjet.12024

Howard, J., & Wood, E. (2010). *Play and learning: From research to practice.* Sage Publications.

Howard, S. (2007). *The developing child. The Getaway Series.* Waldorf Early Childhood Association of North America.

Javed, S., Manoranjitham, M., Chen, K. L., & Husniza, H. (2023). Enhancing teaching and learning for pupils with dyslexia: A comprehensive review of technological and non-technological interventions. *Education and Information Technologies*, 11, 754–768.

Johnson, E. S., Humphrey, M., & Swanson, H. L. (2011). Cognitive processing deficits and students with specific learning disabilities: A selective meta – analysis of the literature. *Learning Disability Quarterly*, 33(1), 206–223.

Kieff, J., & Casbergue, R. (2017). *Playful learning & teaching: The integration of play in kindergarten and primary school.* Gutenberg.

Lin, Y. W., & Bratton, S. C. (2015). A meta-analytic review of child-centered play therapy approaches. *Journal of Counseling & Development, 93*(1), 45-58.

Malekian, F., & Askari, B. (2013). Investigating the effect of multi-sensory games on decrease of male students' dyslexia (Based on Goodman Theory) specified for elementary school second grade in Aligudarz city. *Procedia: Social and Behavioral Sciences*, 82, 796–802. 10.1016/j.sbspro.2013.06.351

Manna, S. (2013). *Play and its role in child development*. Unpublished Thesis. Faculty of Humanities and Social Sciences. Department of Preschool Education. University of Patras

Pandeliadou, S. (2011). *Learning disabilities and educational practice: what & why*. Topos.

Parker, R., Thomsen, B. S., & Berry, A. (2022). Learning Through Play at School – A Framework for Policy and Practice. *Frontiers in Education*, 7(1), 1014. 10.3389/feduc.2022.751801

Pehlivan, H. (2016). The role of play on development and learning. *International Journal of Human Sciences*, 13(2), 123–142. 10.14687/jhs.v13i2.3767

Pellegrini, A. D. (2009). *The role of play in human development*. Oxford University Press, Inc. 10.1093/acprof:oso/9780195367324.001.0001

Penderi, E., Hlapana, E., Melliou, K., Filippidi, A., & Marinatou, T. (2021). Kindergarten Preschool Education Curriculum. In the framework of the Action *"Upgrading the Study Programs and Creating Educational Materials for Primary and Secondary Education*" of the IEP with MIS 5035542. https://ean.auth.gr/wp content/uploads/2021/11/programma_spoudwn_2021.pdf

Piaget, J. (2013). *Play, dreams and imitation in childhood* (Vol. 25). Routledge. 10.4324/9781315009698

Plass, J. L., Homer, B. D., & Kinzer, C. K. (2015). Foundations of Game-Based Learning. *Educational Psychologist, 50*(4), 258-283.

Polychroni, F. (2011). *Special learning difficulties*. Pedio.

Polychroni, F. (2023). *Teaching Strategies to Children with Learning Difficulties*. Gutenberg.

Reeve, R. A., & Waldecker, C. (2017). Evidence-Based Assessment and Intervention for Dyscalculia and Maths Disabilities in School Psychology. In M. Thielking & M. Terjesen (Eds.), *Handbook of Australian School Psychology* (pp. 197 213). Springer. 10.1007/978-3-319-45166-4_10

Ronimus, M., Eklund, K., Pesu, L., & Lyytinen, H. (2019). Supporting Struggling Readers with Digital Game-Based Learning. *Educational Technology Research and Development*, 67(3), 639–663. 10.1007/s11423-019-09658-3

Rose, C. A., Forber-Pratt, A. J., Espelage, D. L., & Aragon, S. R. (2013). The influence of psychosocial factors on bullying involvement of students with disabilities. *Theory into Practice*, 52(4), 272–279. 10.1080/00405841.2013.829730

Santrock, J. W. (2020). *Educational psychology*. Tziola.

Schacter, D. L., Gilbert, D. M., & Wegner, D. M. (2012). *Psychology*. Gutenberg.

Singer, D. G., Golinkof, R. M., & Pasek, K. H. (2006). *Play = learning. How play motivates and enhances children' s cognitive and social – emotional growth*. Oxford University Press. 10.1093/acprof:oso/9780195304381.001.0001

Slavin, R. E. (2007). *Educational psychology: theory and practice*. Gutenberg.

Smith, D. D., & Tyler, N. C. (2019). *Introduction to special education and training bringing about change*. Gutenberg.

Sorrenti, L., Spadaro, L., Mafodda, A. V., Scopelliti, G., Orecchio, S., & Filippello, P. (2019). The predicting role of school learned helplessness in internalizing and externalizing problems. An exploratory study in students with Specific Learning Disorder. *Mediterranean Journal of Clinical Psychology*, 7(2), 437–478.

Sutton-Smith, B. (2008). The role of play in cognitive development. *Reading in Human Development,* 83-95.

Swanson, H. L., & Siegel, L. (2009). Learning disabilities and working memory deficit. *Issues in Education*, 7(1), 48–60.

Terpstra, J. E., Higgins, K., & Pierce, T. (2002). Can I play? Classroom-based interventions for teaching play skills to children with autism. *Focus on Autism and Other Developmental Disabilities*, 17(2), 119–127. 10.1177/10883576020170020701

Tlili, A., Denden, M., Duan, A., Padilla-Zea, N., Huang, R., Sun, T., & Burgos, D. (2022). Game-Based Learning for Learners With Disabilities—What Is Next? A Systematic Literature Review From the Activity Theory Perspective. *Frontiers in Psychology*, 12, 1–12. 10.3389/fpsyg.2021.81469135211058

Valente, D. (2017). *Using stories to "reach and teach" primary learners with dyslexia*. World of Better Learning I Cambridge University Press.

Vargianniti, I., & Karpouzis, K. (2019). Effects of Game-Based Learning on Academic Performance and Student Interest. In Liapis, A., Yannakakis, G. G., Gentile, M., & Ninaus, M. (Eds.), Lecture Notes in Computer Science. Springer. 10.1007/978-3-030-34350-7_32

Wajiuhullah, A., Ashraf, S., & Majad, S. (2018). Development of Number Concepts in Students with Intellectual Disability by Using Digital Game Based Learning. *The Journal of Educational Research*, 21(1), 122.

Whitebread, D., Neale, D., Jensen, H., Hopkins, E., Hirsh-Pasek, K., & Zosh, J. (2017). *The role of play in children's development: a review of the evidence*. Oxford University Press.

Yogman, M., Garner, A., Hutchinson, J., Hirsh-Pasek, K., Golinkoff, R. M., Baum, R., Gambon, T., Lavin, A., Mattson, G., Wissow, L., Hill, D. L., Ameenuddin, N., Chassiakos, Y. L. R., Cross, C., Boyd, R., Mendelson, R., Moreno, M. A., Radesky, J., Swanson, W. S., & Smith, J. (2018). The power of play: A pediatric role in enhancing development in young children. *Pediatrics*, 142(3), 1–16. 10.1542/peds.2018-205830126932

Compilation of References

Abdul Rauf, A. L., & Abu Bakar, K. (2019). Effects of Play on the Social Development of Preschool Children. *Creative Education*, 10(12), 2640–2648. 10.4236/ce.2019.1012191

Abou Assali, M., & Al Abdouli, K. (2024). Unleashing the power of teacher's wellbeing and selfcare. Research Journal in Advanced Humanities, 5(1).

Aburn, G., Gott, M., & Hoare, K. (2016). What is resilience? An integrative review of the empirical literature. *Journal of Advanced Nursing*, 72(5), 980–1000. 10.1111/jan.1288826748456

Adalsteinsson, R. I., Frímannsdóttir, I. B., & Konrádsson, S. (2014). Teachers' self-esteem and self-efficacy. *Scandinavian Journal of Educational Research*, 58(5), 540–550. 10.1080/00313831.2013.773559

Adipat, S., Laksana, K., Busayanon, K., Ausawasowan, A., & Adipat, B. (2021). Engaging Students in the Learning Process with Game-Based Learning: The Fundamental Concepts. *International Journal of Technology in Education*, 4(3), 542–552. 10.46328/ijte.169

Adi, Y., Killoran, A., Janmohamed, K., & Stewart-Brown, S. (2007). *Systematic review of the effectiveness of interventions to promote mental wellbeing in children in primary education. Report 1: Universal approaches: non-violence related outcomes. Database of Abstracts of Reviews of Effects (DARE).* Quality-assessed Reviews.

Affi, T. O., & Macmillan, H. L. (2011). Resilience following child maltreatment: A review of protective factors. *Canadian Journal of Psychiatry*, 56(5), 266–272. 10.1177/07067437110560050521586192

Ahmed, N., & Malik, B. (2019). Impact of psychological empowerment on job performance of teachers: Mediating role of psychological well-being. *Review of Economics and Development Studies*, 5(3), 451–460. 10.26710/reads.v5i3.693

Ahuja, S. (2012). Research Results for Quality Schooling: Bridging the Gap between Research and Practice. *MIER Journal of Educational Studies. Trends and Practices*, 2(2), 206–214. 10.52634/mier/2012/v2/i2/1570

Akbarovna, A. S. (2022). Inclusive education and its essence. International journal of social science & interdisciplinary research, 11(1), 248-254.

Alba, V., & Marc, C. (2023). Conceptualizing teacher resilience: A comprehensive framework to articulate the research field. *Teachers and Teaching*, 29(1), 105–117. 10.1080/13540602.2022.2149483

Aldridge, J. M., & Blackstock, M. J. (2024). Assessing students' perceptions of school climate in primary schools. *Learning Environments Research*, 1–24. 10.1007/s10984-024-09492-2

Aldridge, J. M., & Fraser, B. J. (2016). Teachers' views of their school climate and its relationship with teacher self-efficacy and job satisfaction. *Learning Environments Research*, 19(2), 291–307. 10.1007/s10984-015-9198-x

Aldridge, J. M., Fraser, B. J., Fozdar, F., Ala'i, K., Earnest, J., & Afari, E. (2016). Students' Perceptions of School Climate as Determinants of Wellbeing, Resilience and Identity. *Improving Schools*, 19(1), 5–26. 10.1177/1365480215612616

Aldridge, J. M., & McChesney, K. (2018). The Relationships between School Climate and Adolescent Mental Health and Wellbeing: A Systematic Literature Review. *International Journal of Educational Research*, 88, 121–145. 10.1016/j.ijer.2018.01.012

Aldridge, J. M., & McLure, F. I. (2023). Preparing Schools for Educational Change: Barriers and Supports – A Systematic Literature Review. *Leadership and Policy in Schools*, 1–26. 10.1080/15700763.2023.2171439

Alex Linley, P., Joseph, S., Harrington, S., & Wood, A. M. (2006). Positive Psychology: Past, present, and (possible) future. *The Journal of Positive Psychology*, 1(1), 3–16. 10.1080/17439760500372796

Algozzine, B., Browder, D., Karvonen, M., Test, D. W., & Wood, W. M. (2001). Effects of interventions to promote self-determination for individuals with disabilities. *Review of Educational Research*, 71(2), 219–277. 10.3102/00346543071002219

Alharbi, M. O., & Alzahrani, M. M. (2020). The importance of learning through play in early childhood education: Reflection on the Bold Beginnings Report. *International Journal of the Whole Child*, 5(2), 9–17.

Ali, H. H., Bashir, R., Raza, A. A., Ejaz, H., Shabir, R., & Aftab, M. J. (2024). Role of Inclusive Education in Promoting Equity in Education: Teacher's Perspectives. *Qualitative Research*, 24(1), 133–151.

Allen, J., & Cohen, J. (2014). Emotional intelligence in classrooms and in schools: What we see in the educational setting. In *A Critique of Emotional Intelligence* (pp. 125–139). Psychology Press.

Allen, K. A., Jamshidi, N., Berger, E., Reupert, A., Wurf, G., & May, F. (2021). Impact of school-based interventions for building school belonging in adolescence: A systematic review. *Educational Psychology Review*, 1–29. 10.1007/s10648-021-09621-w

Allen, K.-A., Kern, M. L., Vella-Brodrick, D., & Waters, L. (2018). Understanding the Priorities of Australian Secondary Schools Through an Analysis of Their Mission and Vision Statements. *Educational Administration Quarterly*, 54(2), 249–274. 10.1177/0013161X18758655

Allen, K.-A., & Kern, P. (2019). *Boosting school belonging in adolescents: Interventions for teachers and mental health professionals*. Routledge. 10.4324/9780203729632

Allen, K.-A., Slaten, C. D., Arslan, G., Roffey, S., Craig, H., & Vella-Brodrick, D. A. (2021). School belonging: The importance of student and teacher relationships. In Kern, M. L., & Wehmeyer, M. L. (Eds.), *The Palgrave Handbook of Positive Education* (1st ed., pp. 525–550). Palgrave Macmillan. 10.1007/978-3-030-64537-3_21

Allison, S., Roeger, L., & Reinfeld–Kirkman, N. (2009). Does school bullying affect adult health? Population survey of health–related quality of life and past victimization. *The Australian and New Zealand Journal of Psychiatry*, 43(12), 1163–1170. 10.3109/00048670903270399200001416

Allix, N. (2000). The theory of multiple intelligences: A case of missing cognitive matter. *Australian Journal of Education*, 44(3), 272–293. 10.1177/000494410004400306

Al-Muslimawi, I., & Hamid, A. (2019). External and internal factors affecting student's academic performance. *Soc Sci*, 14(4), 155–168. 10.36478/sscience.2019.155.168

Aloe, A. M., Shisler, S. M., Norris, B. D., Nickerson, A. B., & Rinker, T. W. (2014). A Multivariate Meta-analysis of Student Misbehavior and Teacher Burnout. *Educational Research Review*, 12(1), 30–44. 10.1016/j.edurev.2014.05.003

Alonso-Tapia, J., Ruiz, M. & Huertas, J. A. (2020). Differences in classroom motivational climate: Causes, effects and implications for teacher education. A multilevel study. Anales De Psicología/ Annals of Psychology, 36(1), 122-133.

Altaleb, A. (2021). Using Growth Mindset Strategies in the Classroom. Taboo. *The Journal of Culture and Education*, 20(2), 207–212. https://digitalscholarship.unlv.edu/taboo/vol20/iss2/16

Alva, S. A. (1991). Academic invulnerability among Mexican-American students: The importance of protective resources and appraisals. *Hispanic Journal of Behavioral Sciences*, 13(1), 18–34. 10.1177/07399863910131002

Alvord, M. K., & Grados, J. J. (2005). Enhancing resilience in children: A proactive approach. *Professional Psychology, Research and Practice*, 36(3), 238–245. 10.1037/0735-7028.36.3.238

Anagnostopoulou, T., Triliva, S., & Hatjinikolou, S. (2007). *Development of Social Skills: Health Education Program*. Address P.E. Eastern Thessaloniki.

Anderson, A. R., Christenson, S. L., Sinclair, M. F., & Lehr, C. A. (2004). Check & Connect: The importance of relationships for promoting engagement with school. *Journal of School Psychology*, 42(2), 95–113. 10.1016/j.jsp.2004.01.002

Archibald, S., Coggshall, J., Croft, A., & Goe, L. (2011). High-quality professional development for all teachers: Effectively allocating resources. Eric. https://eric.ed.gov/?id=ED520732

Armstrong, L. L., Desson, S., St. John, E., & Watt, E. (2019). The DREAM program: Developing resilience through emotions, attitudes, & meaning (gifted edition)–a second wave positive psychology approach. *Counselling Psychology Quarterly*, 32(3-4), 307–332. 10.1080/09515070.2018.1559798

Artiles, A. J., Kozleski, E. B., Dorn, S., & Christensen, C. (2009). Learning in Inclusive Education Research: Re-mediating Theory and Methods With a Transformative Agenda. Inclusion in diversity and education, 2, 1-13.

Aspinwall, L. G., & Staudinger, U. M. (2003). *A psychology of human strengths: Fundamental questions and future directions for a positive psychology*. American Psychological Association. 10.1037/10566-000

Atkinson, M. (2016). Ethnography. In *Routledge handbook of qualitative research in sport and exercise* (pp. 71–83). Routledge.

Au, W. C. C., & Kennedy, K. J. (2018). A Positive Education Program to Promote Wellbeing in Schools: A Case Study from a Hong Kong School. *Higher Education Studies, 8*(4), 9-22. https://eric.ed.gov/?id=EJ1189599

Austin, E. J., Saklofske, D. H., & Egan, V. (2005). Personality, well-being and health correlates of trait emotional intelligence. *Personality and Individual Differences*, 38(3), 547–558. 10.1016/j.paid.2004.05.009

Au, W. C. C., & Kennedy, K. J. (2018). A Positive Education Program to Promote Wellbeing in Schools: A Case Study from a Hong Kong School. *Higher Education Studies*, 8(4), 9. 10.5539/hes.v8n4p9

Azorín, C., & Ainscow, M. (2020). Guiding schools on their journey towards inclusion. *International Journal of Inclusive Education*, 24(1), 58–76. 10.1080/13603116.2018.1450900

Αθανασέκου, Μ. (2020). *Γιατί με αφορά η τέχνη. Οι πολλές της διαστάσεις και πως αξιοποιούνται στη ζωή μας*. Ηδυέπεια.

Αθανασέκου, Μ. (2021). Η σχέση της τέχνης με την ψυχολογία - Η πρόσληψη της νοητικής υστέρησης και η απεικόνισή της στη ζωγραφική από τον 15ο έως τον 19ο αιώνα. In Αργυριάδης, A. (Ed.), *Λόγος, αναπηρία, θεραπευτικές και εκπαιδευτικές παρεμβάσεις –Νέα δεδομένα και τάσεις στην Ειδική Αγωγή* (pp. 99–116). Ηδυέπεια.

Backenson, E. M., Holland, S. C., Kubas, H. A., Fitzer, K. R., Wilcox, G., Carmichael, J. A., Fraccaro, R. L., Smith, A. D., Macoun, S. J., Harrison, G. L., & Hale, J. B. (2015). Psychosocial and Adaptive Deficits Associated with Learning Disability Subtypes. *Journal of Learning Disabilities*, 48(5), 511–522. 10.1177/002221941351186124300589

Bagdžiūnienė, D., Kazlauskienė, A., Nasvytienė, D., & Sakadolskis, E. (2022). Linking supportive school leadership and teacher resilience: The mediating role of job resources. *Frontiers in Education*, 7.

Bagiati, A., & Evangelou, D. (2015). Engineering curriculum in the preschool classroom: The teacher's experience. *European Early Childhood Education Research Journal*, 23(1), 112–128. 10.1080/1350293X.2014.991099

Baird, G., Scott, W., Dearing, E., & Hamill, S. (2009). Cognitive self-regulation in youth with and without learning disabilities: Academic self-efficacy, theories of intelligence, learning versus performance goal preferences, and effort attributions. *Journal of Social and Clinical Psychology*, 28(7), 881–908. 10.1521/jscp.2009.28.7.881

Bakadorova, O., & Raufelder, D. (2014). The mediating role of socio-motivational support in the association between individual school self-concept and achievement motivation amongst adolescent students. *European Journal of Psychology of Education*, 29(3), 347–366. 10.1007/s10212-013-0202-5

Bakar, S. N. S. A., Mahamarowi, N. H., & Mustapha, S. (2022, December). *Game Based Learning as a Teaching and Learning Tool for Dyslexic Children* [Conference session]. 2022 IEEE 10th Conference on Systems, Process & Control (ICSPC), Melaka, Malaysia.

Baker-Henningham, H., & Walker, S. (2009). A qualitative study of teacher's perceptions of an intervention to prevent conduct problems in Jamaican pre-schools. *Child: Care, Health and Development*, 35(5), 632–642. 10.1111/j.1365-2214.2009.00996.x19689568

Baker, L., Green, S., & Falecki, D. (2017). Positive early childhood education: Expanding the reach of Positive Psychology into early childhood. *European Journal of Applied Positive Psychology*, 1(8), 1–12.

Bales, S., & Gilliam, F. (2007). Lessons from the story of early child development: Domain decisions and framing youth development. *New Directions for Youth Development*, 124, 119–134.20082431

Ball, S. J. (2012). *Politics and policy making in education: Explorations in sociology*. Routledge. 10.4324/9780203808726

Bandura, A. (1989). Human agency in social cognitive theory. *The American Psychologist*, 44(9), 1175–1184. 10.1037/0003-066X.44.9.11752782727

Bandura, A. (1997). Self-efficacy: The exercise of control. *The Freeman.*

Banks, J. A. (2017). *An Introduction to Multicultural Education*. Pearson Education.

Barnová, S., & Tamášová, V. (2018). Risk and protective factors in the life of youth in relation to resilience. *Psychology and Pathopsychology of Child*, 52(1), 50–59. 10.2478/papd-2018-0001

Bar-On, R. 2007. The Bar-On model of emotional intelligence: a valid, robust and applicable EI model. *Organisations and People, 14*(2), 27–34. https://amed.org.uk/wp-content/uploads/2022/08/OPMay2007.pdf#page=29

Bar-On, R. (1997). *The emotional quotient inventory (EQ-i): A test of emotional intelligence*. Multi-Health Systems.

Bar-On, R. (2000). Emotional and social intelligence: Insights from the Emotional Intelligence Quotient Inventory. In Bar-On, R., & Parker, D. A. (Eds.), *The handbook of emotional intelligence* (pp. 363–388). John Wiley & Sons.

Bar-On, R. (2006). The Bar-On model of emotional-social intelligence (ESI). *Psicothema*, 18, 13–25. https://reunido.uniovi.es/index.php/PST/article/view/841517295953

Baroody, A. E., Rimm-Kaufman, S. E., Larsen, R. A., & Curby, T. W. (2014). The link between responsive classroom training and student–teacher relationship quality in the fifth grade: A study of fidelity of implementation. *School Psychology Review*, 43(1), 69–85. 10.1080/02796015.2014.12087455

Barouma, C., & Kougioumtzis, G. A. (2016). Emotional Intelligence, Consulting & Education. *Journal of Regional Socio-Economic Issues, 6*(2), 10-18.

Barrett, P. M., Farrell, L. I., Ollendick, T. H., & Dadds, M. (2006). Long- term outcomes of an Australian universal prevention trial of anxiety and depression symptoms in children and youth: An evaluation of the FRIENDS program. *Journal of Clinical Child and Adolescent Psychology, 35*(3), 403– 411. doi: 510.1207/s15374424jccp3503_

Barrett, P. M., Lowry-Webster, H., & Turner, C. M. (1999). *FRIENDS for children group leader manual.* Brisbane: Australian Academic Press.

Barron, B., & Darling-Hammond, L. (2008). *Teaching for Meaningful Learning: A Review of Research on Inquiry-Based and Cooperative Learning*. Book Excerpt. George Lucas Educational Foundation.

Barton, E. E., Ledford, J. R., Zimmerman, K. N., & Pokorski, E. A. (2018). Increasing the engagement and complexity of block play in young children. *Education & Treatment of Children*, 41(2), 169–196. 10.1353/etc.2018.0007

Bastian, V. A., Burns, N. R., & Nettelbeck, T. (2005). Emotional intelligence predicts life skills, but not as well as personality and cognitive abilities. *Personality and Individual Differences*, 39(6), 1135–1145. 10.1016/j.paid.2005.04.006

Batool, S., & Khalid, R. (2009). Low emotional intelligence: A risk factor for depression. *Journal of Pakistan Psychiatric Society*, 6(2), 65–72.

Battistich, V., Solomon, D., Watson, M., & Shaps, E. (1997). Caring school communities. *Educational Psychologist*, 32(3), 137–151. 10.1207/s15326985ep3203_1

Baumeister, R. F., Campbell, J. D., Krueger, J. I., & Vohs, K. D. (2003). Does High Self-Esteem Cause Better Performance, Interpersonal Success, Happiness, or Healthier Lifestyles? *Psychological Science in the Public Interest: A Journal of the American Psychological Society, 4*(1), 1–44. 10.1111/1529-1006.01431

Baumeister, R. F., Gailliot, M., DeWall, C. N., & Oaten, M. (2006). Self-Regulation and Personality: How Interventions Increase Regulatory Success, and How Depletion Moderates the Effects of Traits on Behavior. *Journal of Personality*, 74(6), 1773–1802. 10.1111/j.1467-6494.2006.00428.x17083666

Baumeister, R. F., & Leary, M. R. (1995). The need to belong: Desire for interpersonal attachments as a fundamental human motivation. *Psychological Bulletin*, 117(3), 497–529. 10.1037/0033-2909.117.3.4977777651

Bauminger, N., Edelsztein, H. S., & Morash, J. (2005). Social information processing and emotional understanding in children with LD. *Journal of Learning Disabilities*, 38(1), 45–61. 10.1177/00222194050380010401115727328

Bear, G. G. (2020). *Improving school climate: Practical strategies to reduce behavior problems and promote social and emotional learning*. Routledge. 10.4324/9781351170482

Beauchemin, J., Hutchins, T. L., & Patterson, F. (2008). Mindfulness Meditation May Lessen Anxiety, Promote Social Skills, and Improve Academic Performance Among Adolescents With Learning Disabilities. *Complementary Health Practice Review*, 13(1), 34–45. 10.1177/1533210107311624

Becker, B. D., Gallagher, K. C., & Whitaker, R. C. (2017). Teachers' dispositional mindfulness and the quality of their relationships with children in head start classrooms. *Journal of School Psychology*, 65, 40–53. 10.1016/j.jsp.2017.06.00429145942

Becker, D., & Marecek, J. (2008). Dreaming the American Dream: Individualism and Positive Psychology. *Social and Personality Psychology Compass*, 2(5), 1767–1780. 10.1111/j.1751-9004.2008.00139.x

Benard, B. (1995). *Fostering resilience in children*. ERIC. https://files.eric.ed.gov/fulltext/ED386327.pdf

Benard, B. (1993). Fostering resiliency in kids. *Educational Leadership*, 51, 44–48. https://kaching.socialwork.hku.hk/Workshop%20Notes/Resiliency/Foster%20Resiliency.pdf

Bender, W. N. (1994). Social-emotional development: The task and the challenge. *Learning Disability Quarterly*, 17(4), 250–252. 10.2307/1511122

Benzies, K., & Mychasiuk, R. (2009). Fostering family resiliency: A review of the key protective factors. *Child & Family Social Work*, 14(1), 103–114. 10.1111/j.1365-2206.2008.00586.x

Berger, E., Reupert, A., Campbell, T. C. H., Morris, Z., Hammer, M., Diamond, Z., Hine, R., Patrick, P., & Fathers, C. (2022). A systematic review of evidence-based wellbeing initiatives for schoolteachers and early childhood educators. *Educational Psychology Review*, 34(4), 2919–2969. 10.1007/s10648-022-09690-5

Bergin, C., & Bergin, D. (2009). Attachment in the classroom. *Educational Psychology Review*, 21(2), 141–170. 10.1007/s10648-009-9104-0

Bernard, B. (2004). *Resiliency: What we have learned*. WestEd.

Bernstein, B. (2000). *Pedagogy, symbolic control, and identity: Theory, research, critique* (Vol. 5). Rowman & Littlefield.

Bernstein, B. (2003). *Theoretical Studies Towards a Sociology of Language* (1st ed.). Routledge., 10.4324/9780203014035

Bernstein, G. A., Layne, A. E., Egan, E. A., & Tennison, D. M. (2005). School- based interventions for anxious children. *Journal of the American Academy of Child and Adolescent Psychiatry*, 44(11), 1118–1127. 10.1097/01.chi.0000177323.40005.a116239860

Biegel, G. M., Brown, K. W., Shapiro, S. L., & Schubert, C. M. (2009). Mindfulness-based stress reduction for the treatment of adolescent psychiatric outpatients: A randomized clinical trial. *Journal of Consulting and Clinical Psychology*, 77(5), 855–866. 10.1037/a001624119803566

Bishop, S. R., Lau, M., Shapiro, S., Carlson, L., Anderson, N. D., Carmody, J., Segal, Z. V., Abbey, S., Speca, M., Velting, D., & Devins, G. (2004). Mindfulness: A proposed operational definition. *Clinical Psychology : a Publication of the Division of Clinical Psychology of the American Psychological Association*, 11(3), 230–241. 10.1093/clipsy.bph077

Bisquerra, R. (2003). Educación emocional y competencias básicas para la vida. *Revista de Investigación Educacional*, 21, 7–43.

Black, P., & Wiliam, D. (2018). Classroom assessment and pedagogy. *Assessment in Education: Principles, Policy & Practice*, 25(6), 551–575. 10.1080/0969594X.2018.1441807

Bleak, K. W., & Abernathy, T. (2022). *Individuals with Disabilities Education Act (IDEA)*. Routledge., 10.4324/9780367198459-REPRW196-1

Bloom, L., Tinker, E., & Scholnick, E. K. (2001) The intentionality model and language acquisition: Engagement, effort, and the essential tension in development. *Monographs of the Society for Research in Child Development, 66*(4), Serial No. 267.

Blum, R. W. (2005). A case for school connectedness. *The Adolescent Learner*, 62(7), 16–20.

Boaler, J. (2022). *Mathematical mindsets: Unleashing students' potential through creative mathematics, inspiring messages and innovative teaching*. John Wiley & Sons.

Boden, J. M., Sanders, J., Munford, R., & Liebenberg, L. (2018). The Same But Different? Applicability of a General Resilience Model to Understand a Population of Vulnerable Youth. *Child Indicators Research*, 11(1), 79–96. 10.1007/s12187-016-9422-y

Bögels, S., Hoogstad, B., van Dun, L., de Schutter, S., & Restifo, K. (2008). Mindfulness training for adolescents with externalizing disorders and their parents. *Behavioural and Cognitive Psychotherapy*, 36(2), 193–209. 10.1017/S1352465808004190

Bonell, C., Parry, W., Wells, H., Jamal, F., Fletcher, A., Harden, A., Thomas, J., Campbell, R., Petticrew, M., Murphy, S., Whitehead, M., & Moore, L. (2013). The effects of the school environment on student health: A systematic review of multi-level studies. *Health & Place*, 21, 180–191. 10.1016/j.healthplace.2012.12.00123501377

Boniwell, I., & Tunariu, A. D. (2019). *Positive psychology: Theory, research and applications*. Open University Press.

Borgonovi, F., & Pál, J. (2016). A Framework for the Analysis of Student Well-Being in the PISA 2015 Study: Being 15 In 2015. OECD Education Working Papers, No. 140, OECD Publishing. 10.1787/19939019

Borrelli, B. (2011). The Assessment, Monitoring, and Enhancement of Treatment Fidelity In Public Health Clinical Trials. *Journal of Public Health Dentistry*, 71(1), 52–63. 10.1111/j.1752-7325.2011.00233.x21499543

Bothe, D. A., Grignon, J. B., & Olness, K. N. (2014). The Effects of a Stress Management Intervention in Elementary School Children. *Journal of Developmental and Behavioral Pediatrics*, 35(1), 62–67. 10.1097/DBP.000000000000001624336090

Bowlby, J. (1958). The nature of the child's tie to his mother. *The International Journal of Psycho-Analysis*, 39, 350–373.13610508

Bowlby, J. (1982). Attachment and loss: Retrospect and prospect. *The American Journal of Orthopsychiatry*, 52(4), 664–678. 10.1111/j.1939-0025.1982.tb01456.x7148988

Brackett, M., & Katulak, N. (2007). Emotional Intelligence in the Classroom: Skill Based Training for teachers and students In J. Chiarrochi & L. Marziyah (Eds), *7 Successful Strategies to Promote Emotional Intelligence in the Classroom* (pp 227-56). MPG Books Ltd.

Brackett, M. A., Rivers, S. E., Reyes, M. R., & Salovey, P. (2012). Enhancing academic performance and social and emotional competence with the RULER feeling words curriculum. *Learning and Individual Differences*, 22(2), 218–224. 10.1016/j.lindif.2010.10.002

Brackett, M. A., Rivers, S. E., & Salovey, P. (2011). Emotional intelligence: Implications for personal, social, academic, and workplace success. *Social and Personality Psychology Compass*, 5(1), 88–103. 10.1111/j.1751-9004.2010.00334.x

Bradshaw, C. P., Koth, C. W., Thornton, L. A., & Leaf, P. J. (2009). Altering school climate through school-wide Positive Behavioral Interventions and Supports: findings from a group-randomized effectiveness trial. *Prevention Science: The Official Journal of the Society for Prevention Research, 10*(2), 100–115. 10.1007/s11121-008-0114-9

Bradshaw, C. P., Cohen, J., Espelage, D. L., & Nation, M. (2021). Addressing school safety through comprehensive school climate approaches. *School Psychology Review*, 50(2-3), 221–236. 10.1080/2372966X.2021.1926321

Brandsma, R. (2017). *The Mindfulness Teaching Guide: Essential Skills and Competencies for Teaching Mindfulness-Based Interventions*. New Harbinger Publications.

Braun, S. S., Roeser, R. W., Mashburn, A. J., & Skinner, E. (2019). Middle school teachmindfulness, occupational health and well-being, and the quality of teacher-student Interactions. *Mindfulness*, 10(2), 245–255. 10.1007/s12671-018-0968-2

Brayfield, A. H., & Roth, H. F. (1951). An index of job satisfaction. *The Journal of Applied Psychology*, 35(5), 307–311. 10.1037/h0055617

Brdar, I., & Kashdan, T. B. (2010). Character strengths and well-being in Croatia: An empirical investigation of structure and correlates. *Journal of Research in Personality*, 44(1), 151–154. 10.1016/j.jrp.2009.12.001

Brensilver, M., Hardy, J., & Sofer, O. J. (2020). *The mindful schools curriculum and teacher's guide*. W.W. Norton and Company.

Bresky, A. (2008). *The Secret for Caregiver Success (Dr. Bresky's 9 Pt. Brain Tune Up System, Book 1)*. SM publishing.

Brinia, V. (2008). *Management and Emotional Intelligence*. Stamoulis.

Broderick, P. (2013). *Learning to BREATHE: A Mindfulness Curriculum for Adolescents to Cultivate Emotion Regulation, attention, and Performance*. New Harbinger.

Bronfenbrenner, U. (1979). *The ecology of human development*. Harvard University Press. 10.4159/9780674028845

Brooker, L., Blaise, M., & Edwards, S. (2014). Contexts for play and learning. *The SAGE handbook of play and learning in early childhood*, 277-282.

Brooks, J. E. (2006). Strengthening resilience in children and youths: Maximizing opportunities through the schools. *Children & Schools*, 28(2), 69–76. 10.1093/cs/28.2.69

Brooks, R. (1994). Children at risk: Fostering resilience and hope. *The American Journal of Orthopsychiatry*, 64(4), 545–553. 10.1037/h00795657847570

Brophy, J. (1998). Classroom Management As Socializing Students Into Clearly Articulated Roles. *Journal of Classroom Interaction*, 33(1), 1–4. https://www.jstor.org/stable/23870337

Brown, K. W., & Ryan, R. M. (2003). The benefits of being present: Mindfulness and its role in psychological well-being. *Journal of Personality and Social Psychology*, 84(4), 822–848. 10.1037/0022-3514.84.4.82212703651

Brown, S., & Vaughan, C. (2009). *Play: How It Shapes the Brain, Opens the Imagination and Invigorates the Soul*. Avery Publishing Group.

Brunwasser, S. M., Gillham, J. E., & Kim, E. S. (2009). A meta-analytic review of the Penn Resiliency Program's effect on depressive symptoms. *Journal of Consulting and Clinical Psychology*, 77(6), 1042–1054. 10.1037/a001767119968381

Bucci, S. (1990). *Educazione dell'infanzia e pedagogia scientifica. Da Froebel a Montessori*. Bulzoni.

Buckman, D. G., Hand, N. W., & Johnson, A. (2021). Improving high school graduation through school climate. *NASSP Bulletin*, 105(1), 5–24. 10.1177/0192636521993212

Buecker, S., Luhmann, M., Haehner, P., Bühler, J. L., Dapp, L. C., Luciano, E. C., & Orth, U. (2022). The Development of Subjective Well-Being Across the Life Span: A Meta-Analytic Review of Longitudinal Studies. *Psychological Bulletin*, 149(7-8), 418–446. 10.1037/bul0000401

Bull, A., Brooking, K., & Campbell, R. (2008). *Successful Home–School Partnerships*. Ministry of Education.

Buss, D. M. (2000). The evolution of happiness. *The American Psychologist*, 55(1), 15–23. 10.1037/0003-066X.55.1.1511392858

Byrne, A., & Byrne, D. G. (1993). The effect of exercise on depression, anxiety and other mood states-A review. *Journal of Psychosomatic Research*, 37(6), 565–574. 10.1016/0022-3999(93)90050-P8410742

Cahill, H., Shaw, G., Wyn, J., & Smith, G. (2004). *Translating Caring Into Action: An Evaluation of the Victorian Catholic Education Student Welfare Professional Development Initiative*. Youth Research Centre, The University of Melbourne.

Calear, A. L., & Christensen, H. (2010). Systematic review of school-based prevention and early intervention programs for depression. *Journal of Adolescence*, 33(3), 429–438. 10.1016/j.adolescence.2009.07.00419647310

Caleon, I. S., & King, R. B. (2020). Examining the phenomenon of resilience in schools. *European Journal of Psychological Assessment*, 37(1), 52–64. Advance online publication. 10.1027/1015-5759/a000572

Camodeca, M., & Coppola, G. (2019). Participant roles in preschool bullying: The impact of emotion regulation, social preference, and quality of the teacher–child relationship. *Social Development*, 28(1), 3–21. 10.1111/sode.12320

Cann, R., Sinnema, C., Daly, A. J., & Rodway, J. (2024a). A contextual approach to designing, implementing, and adapting a wellbeing program: A case study of the MARKERS wellbeing program for educators. *International Journal of Applied Positive Psychology*, 9(1), 301–325. 10.1007/s41042-023-00123-4

Cann, R., Sinnema, C., Daly, A. J., & Rodway, J. (2024b). Swimming against the tide: A mixed-methods study of how the markers educator wellbeing program changed educators' relational space. *International Journal of Applied Positive Psychology*, 1–28. 10.1007/s41042-024-00153-6

Carvalho, L., & Yeoman, P. (2018). Framing learning entanglement in innovative learning spaces: Connecting theory, design and practice. *British Educational Research Journal*, 44(6), 1120–1137. 10.1002/berj.3483

CASEL. (2013). *What Is Social and Emotional Learning?* Retrieved from http://www. casel.org/social–and–emotional–learning/

Castaldi, E., Piazza, M., & Iuculano, T. (2020). Learning disabilities: Developmental dyscalculia. *Neurocognitive Development: Disorders and Disabilities, 174*, 61 75

Castro-Villarreal, F., Rodriguez, B. J., & Moore, S. (2014). Teachers' perceptions and attitudes about Response to Intervention (RTI) in their schools: A qualitative analysis. *Teaching and Teacher Education*, 40(1), 104–112. 10.1016/j.tate.2014.02.004

Catalano, R. F., Haggerty, K. P., Oesterle, S., Fleming, C. B., & Hawkins, J. D. (2004). The Importance of Bonding to School for Healthy Development: Findings from the Social Development Research Group. *The Journal of School Health*, 74(7), 252–261. 10.1111/j.1746-1561.2004.tb08281.x15493702

Cavioni, V., Grazzani, I., Ornaghi, V., Agliati, A., Gandellinia, S., Cefai, C., Camilleri, L., Bartolo, P., Tatalović Vorkapić, S., Golob, L., Poulou, M., Martinsone, B., Supe, I., Simões, C. S., Lebre, P., Colomeischi, A., Rusu, P. R., Acostoaie, L., Vintur, T., & Conte, E. (2023). A multi-component curriculum to promote teachers' mental health: Findings from the PROMEHS program. *The International Journal of Emotional Education*, 15(1), 34–52. 10.56300/KFNZ2526

Cefai, C., & Cavioni, V. (2015). Mental Health Promotion in School: An Integrated, School-Based, Whole School. In Kirkcaldy, B. (Ed.), *Promoting Psychological Wellbeing in Children and Families* (pp. 52–67). Palgrave McMillan. 10.1057/9781137479969.0007

Çelik, N. D. (2018). Happiness in high school students: Autonomy, relatedness, competence and meaning in life. *Kıbrıslı Eğitim Bilimleri Dergisi*, 13(3), 422–430. 10.18844/cjes.v13i3.3561

Celma-Pastor, L., & Rodríguez-Ledo, C. (2017). Educación Socioemocional Para Jóvenes. In *El Aula: Programa SEA*. TEA Ediciones., 10.1016/j.chb.2013.05.009

Chambers, R., Gullone, E., & Allen, N. B. (2009). Mindful emotion regulation: An integrative review. *Clinical Psychology Review*, 29(6), 560–572. 10.1016/j.cpr.2009.06.00519632752

Chamizo-Nieto, M. T., Arrivillaga, C., Rey, L., & Extremera, N. (2021). The role of emotional intelligence, the teacher-student relationship, and flourishing on academic performance in adolescents: A moderated mediation study. *Frontiers in Psychology*, 12, 695067. 10.3389/fpsyg.2021.69506734335411

Chan, Y. H., Nadler, S. S., & Hargis, M. B. (2015). Attitudinal and behavioral outcomes of employees' psychological empowerment: A structural equation modeling approach. Journal of Organizational Culture. *Communications and Conflict*, 19(1), 24–41.

Chapman, J. W., & Tunmer, W. E. (2003). Reading difficulties, reading-related self-perceptions, and strategies for overcoming negative self-beliefs. *Reading & Writing Quarterly*, 19(1), 5–24. 10.1080/10573560308205

Chen, G., Gully, S. M., & Eden, D. (2001). Validation of a new general self-efficacy scale. *Organizational Research Methods*, 4(1), 62–83. 10.1177/109442810141004

Cheung, C. S. (2019). Parents' involvement and adolescents' school adjustment: Teacher–student relationships as a mechanism of change. *School Psychology*, 34(4), 350–362. 10.1037/spq000028831294593

Chiarrochi, J., & Panju, M. (2008). *7 Successful Strategies to Promote Emotional Intelligence in the Classroom*. MPG Books Ltd.

Chiriac, E. H., Forsberg, C., & Thornberg, R. (2023). Teachers' perspectives on factors influencing the school climate: A constructivist grounded theory case study. *Cogent Education*, 10(2).

Chodkiewicz, A. R., & Boyle, C. (2017). Positive Psychology school-based interventions: A reflection on current success and future directions. *Review of Education*, 5(1), 60–86. 10.1002/rev3.3080

Chodkiewicz, A., & Boyle, C. (2015). *Believing you can is the first step to achieving: A CBT and Attribution Retraining Programme to improve self-belief in students aged 8-12*. Jessica Kingsley Publishers.

Christens, B. D., Winn, L. T., & Duke, A. M. (2016). Empowerment and critical consciousness: A conceptual cross-fertilization. *Adolescent Research Review*, 1(1), 15–27. 10.1007/s40894-015-0019-3

Christensen, A. J., Turner, C. W., Smith, T. W., Holman, J. M., & Gregory, M. C. (1991). Health locus of control and depression in end-stage renal disease. *Journal of Consulting and Clinical Psychology*, 59(3), 419–424. 10.1037/0022-006X.59.3.4192071727

Christiansen, L., Beck, M. M., Bilenberg, N., Wienecke, J., Astrup, A., & Lundbye Jensen, J. (2019). Effects of Exercise on Cognitive Performance in Children and Adolescents with ADHD: Potential Mechanisms and Evidence-based Recommendations. *Journal of Clinical Medicine*, 8(6), 841. 10.3390/jcm806084131212854

Chuang, T.-Y., Yeh, M. K.-C., & Lin, Y.-L. (2021). The Impact of Game Playing on Students' Reasoning Ability, Varying According to Their Cognitive Style. *Journal of Educational Technology & Society*, 24(3), 29–43.

Chung, P. J., Patel, D. R., & Nizami, I. (2020). Disorder of written expression and dysgraphia: Definition, diagnosis, and management. *Translational Pediatrics*, 9(S1), S46–S54. 10.21037/tp.2019.11.0132206583

Ciarrochi, J., & Deane, F. P. (2001). Emotional competence and willingness to seek help from professional and nonprofessional sources. *British Journal of Guidance & Counselling*, 29(2), 233–246. 10.1080/03069880124843

Cicchetti, D. (1984). The emergence of developmental psychopathology. *Child Development*, 55(1), 1–7. 10.2307/11298306705613

Cicchetti, D., & Garmezy, N. (1993). Prospects and promises in the study of resilience. *Development and Psychopathology*, 5(4), 497–502. 10.1017/S0954579400006118

Clements, D. H., & Sarama, J. (2007). *Early childhood mathematics learning. Second handbook of research on mathematics teaching and learning, 1, 461-555.*

Cohen, J., McCabe, E. M., Michelli, N. M., & Pickeral, T. (2009). School climate: Research, policy, practice, and teacher education. *Teachers College Record*, 111(1), 180–213. 10.1177/016146810911100108

Collaborative for Academic Social and Emotional Learning. (2015). *Casel Guide: effective social and emotional learning programs, middle and high school edition.* CASEL.

Collaborative for Academic, *Social and Emotional Learning.* (2003). *Safe and sound: An education leader's guide to evidence-based social and emotional learning (SEL) programs*. Chicago, IL: Collaborative for Academic, Social and Emotional Learning.

Colley, H., James, D., Diment, K., & Tedder, M. (2003). Learning as becoming in vocational education and training: Class, gender and the role of vocational habitus. *Journal of Vocational Education and Training*, 55(4), 471–498. 10.1080/13636820300200240

Collie, R. J. (2023). Teacher well-being and turnover intentions: Investigating the roles of job resources and job demands. *The British Journal of Educational Psychology*, 93(3), 712–726. 10.1111/bjep.1258736720462

Comer, J. P. (1987). New Haven's school community connection. *Educational Leadership*, 44, 13–16. https://eric.ed.gov/?id=EJ353781

Condly, S. J. (2006). Resilience in children: A review of literature with implications for education. *Urban Education*, 41(3), 211–236. 10.1177/0042085906287902

Conesa, P. J., Onandia-Hinchado, I., Duñabeitia, J. A., & Moreno, M. Á. (2022). Basic psychological needs in the classroom: A literature review in elementary and middle school students. *Learning and Motivation*, 79, 101819. Advance online publication. 10.1016/j.lmot.2022.101819

Cook, C. R., Fiat, A., Larson, M., Daikos, C., Slemrod, T., Holland, E. A., Thayer, A. J., & Renshaw, T. (2018). Positive Greetings at the Door: Evaluation of a Low-Cost, High-Yield Proactive Classroom Management Strategy. *Journal of Positive Behavior Interventions*, 20(3), 149–159. 10.1177/1098300717753831

Cook, J. W. (2019). *Sustainability, human well-being, and the future of education.* Springer Nature. 10.1007/978-3-319-78580-6

Cooper, R. K. (1996/1997). *E.Q Map.* AIT and Essi Systems.

Corbin, C. M., Alamos, P., Lowenstein, A. E., Downer, J. T., & Brown, J. L. (2019). The role of teacher-student relationships in predicting teachers' personal accomplishment and emotional exhaustion. *Journal of School Psychology*, 77, 1–12. 10.1016/j.jsp.2019.10.00131837719

Corcoran, R. P., & Tormey, R. (2013). Does emotional intelligence predict student teachers' performance? *Teaching and Teacher Education*, 35, 34–42. 10.1016/j.tate.2013.04.008

Cornelius-White, J. (2007). Learner-centered teacher-student relationships are effective: A meta-analysis. *Review of Educational Research*, 77(1), 113–143. 10.3102/003465430298563

Cortiella, C., & Horowitz, S. H. (2014). The state of learning disabilities: Facts, trends and emerging issues. *National Center for Learning Disabilities*, 3, 182–189.

Costarelli, V., Demertzi, M., & Stamou, D. (2009). Disordered eating attitudes in relation to body image and emotional intelligence in young women. *Journal of Human Nutrition and Dietetics*, 22(3), 239–245. 10.1111/j.1365-277X.2009.00949.x19344378

Coulter, R. W., Birkett, M., Corliss, H. L., Hatzenbuehler, M. L., Mustanski, B., & Stall, R. D. (2016). Associations between LGBTQ-affirmative school climate and adolescent drinking behaviors. *Drug and Alcohol Dependence*, 161, 340–347. 10.1016/j.drugalcdep.2016.02.02226946989

Critchley, H., & Gibbs, S. (2012). The effects of positive psychology on the efficacy beliefs of school staff. *Educational and Child Psychology*, 29(4), 64–76. 10.53841/bpsecp.2012.29.4.64

Crooks, C. V., Hoover, S., & Smith, A. C. G. (2020). Feasibility trial of the school-based STRONG intervention to promote resilience among newcomer youth. *Psychology in the Schools*, 57(12), 1815–1829. 10.1002/pits.22366

Crouch, A., & Jakubecy, J. (2007). Dysgraphia: How It Affects A Student's Performance and What Can Be Done About It. *Teaching Exceptional Children Plus, 3*(3). https://files.eric.ed.gov/fulltext/EJ967123.pdf

Csikszentmihalyi, M. (1990). *Flow: The psychology of optimal experience.* Harper and Row.

Cui, L. (2022). The Role of Teacher-Student Relationships in Predicting Teachers' Occupational Wellbeing, Emotional Exhaustion, and Enthusiasm. *Frontiers in Psychology*, 13, 896813. 10.3389/fpsyg.2022.89681335664194

Cumming, T. M., & Rodriguez, C. D. (2018). *School success for at-risk students: A culturally responsive tiered approach.* Routledge. 10.4324/9781315101996

Daily, S. M., Mann, M. J., Kristjansson, A. L., Smith, M. L., & Zullig, K. J. (2019). School climate and academic achievement in middle and high school students. *The Journal of School Health*, 89(3), 173–180. 10.1111/josh.1272630680750

Daily, S. M., Mann, M. J., Lilly, C. L., Bias, T. K., Smith, M. L., & Kristjansson, A. L. (2020). School climate as a universal intervention to prevent substance use initiation in early adolescence: A longitudinal study. *Health Education & Behavior*, 47(3), 402–411. 10.1177/109019812091425032281413

Dake, J. A., Price, J. H., & Telljohann, S. K. (2003). The Nature and Extent of Bullying at School. *The Journal of School Health*, 73(5), 173–180. 10.1111/j.1746-1561.2003.tb03599.x12793102

Dane, E. (2011). Paying attention to mindfulness and its effects on task performance in the workplace. *Journal of Management*, 37(4), 997–1018. 10.1177/0149206310367948

Darling-Hammond, L., & Cook-Harvey, C. M. (2018). Educating the Whole Child: Improving School Climate to Support Student Success. Learning Policy Institute. https://files.eric.ed.gov/fulltext/ED606462.pdf

Darling-Hammond, L., Hyler, M. E., & Gardner, M. (2017). Effective teacher professional development. Available at: https://bibliotecadigital.mineduc.cl/bitstream/handle/20.500.12365/17357/46%20Effective_Teacher_Professional_Development_REPORT.pdf?sequence=1

Davidson, R. J. (2012). *El Perfil Emocional De Tu Cerebro, Claves Para Modificar Nuestras Actitudes Y Reacciones*. Destino. 10.1093/ije/30.5.1042

Davies, S. L., Thind, H. R., Chandler, S. D., & Tucker, J. A. (2011). Enhancing resilience among young people: The role of communities and asset-building approaches to intervention. *Adolescent Medicine: State of the Art Reviews*, 22, 402–440.22423458

Davis, D. M., & Hayes, J. A. (2011). What are the benefits of mindfulness? A practice review of psychotherapy-related research. *Psychotherapy (Chicago, Ill.)*, 48(2), 198–208. 10.1037/a002206221639664

Davis, K. Y., & Newstrom, J. W. (1999). *Comportamiento humano en el trabajo: Comportamiento Organicional*. McGraw- Hill.

Dawood, R. (2013). Positive Psychology in School-Based Psychological Intervention: A Study of the Evidence-Base. *The European Journal of Social & Behavioural Sciences*, 5(2), 281–306. 10.15405/ejsbs.70

De La Fuente, J., Salvador, M., & Franco, C. (2010). Efectos de un programa de entrenamiento en conciencia plena (mindfulness) en la autoestima y la inteligencia emocional percibidas. *Psicología Conductual*, 18, 297–315.

de Romilly, J. (2007). *Gentleness in ancient Greek thought*. Livanis.

de Ruiter, J. A., Poorthuis, A. M., & Koomen, H. M. (2021). Teachers' emotional labor in response to daily events with individual students: The role of teacher–student relationship quality. *Teaching and Teacher Education*, 107, 103467. 10.1016/j.tate.2021.103467

Dearing, J. (2020). The Effect of School Climate on Teacher Burnout, Perceived Health and Wellbeing (Publication No. 28258625) [Doctoral Dissertation, Oklahoma State University]. ProQuest Dissertations and Theses Global.

Debarbieux, E., Anton, N., Astor, R. A., Benbenishty, R., Bisson-Vaivre, C., Cohen, J., Giordan, A., Hugonnier, B., Neulat, N., Ortega Ruiz, R., Saltet, J., Veltcheff, C., & Vrand, R. (2012). Le «Climat scolaire»: définition, effets et conditions d'amélioration. Prisme-asso.https://www.prisme-asso.org/wp-content/uploads/save/pdf/climat-scolaire2012.pdf

Deci, E. L., & Ryan, R. M. (2012). Self-determination theory. Handbook of theories of social psychology, 1(20), 416-436.

Deci, E. L., & Ryan, R. M. (2008). Self-determination theory: A macrotheory of human motivation, development, and health. *Canadian Psychology*, 49(3), 182–185. 10.1037/a0012801

Demir, M., Burton, S., & Dunbar, N. (2019). Professor–student rapport and perceived autonomy support as predictors of course and student outcomes. *Teaching of Psychology*, 46(1), 22–33. 10.1177/0098628318816132

Demirtas-Zorbaz, S., Akin-Arikan, C., & Terzi, R. (2021). Does school climate that includes students' views deliver academic achievement? A multilevel meta-analysis. *School Effectiveness and School Improvement*, 32(4), 543–563. 10.1080/09243453.2021.1920432

Denham, A. R., Mayben, R., & Boman, T. (2016). Integrating Game-Based Learning Initiative: Increasing the Usage of Game-Based Learning Within K-12 Classrooms Through Professional Learning Groups. *TechTrends*, 60(1), 70–76. 10.1007/s11528-015-0019-y

Dernowska, U. (2017). Teacher and student perceptions of school climate. Some conclusions from school culture and climate research. Journal of Modern science, 32(1), 63-82.

Dewey, J. (1980). *Art as Experience*. The Penguin Group.

Dewey, J. (1986, September). Experience and education. *The Educational Forum*, 50(3), 241–252. 10.1080/00131728609335764

DeWitt, P. M. (2017). *School climate: Leading with collective efficacy*. Corwin Press.

DeWitt, P., & Slade, S. (2014). *School Climate Change: How do I build a positive environment for learning? (ASCD Arias)*. ASCD.

Di Fabio, A. (2012). *Emotional Intelligence- New Perspectives and Applications*. Intech Open Access Publisher. 10.5772/1188

Dickinson, D. K., & Porche, M. V. (2014). Relation between language experiences in preschool classrooms and children's kindergarten and fourth-grade language and reading abilities. *Child Development*, 82(3), 870–886. 10.1111/j.1467-8624.2011.01576.x21413936

Dickman, M.H. & Stanford-Blair, N. (2002). *Connecting leadership to the brain*. Sage.

Dissanayake, E. (1992). *Homo Aestheticus: Where Art comes From and Why*. University of Washington Press.

Djamnezhad, D., Koltcheva, N., Dizdarevic, A., Mujezinovic, A., Peixoto, C., Coelho, V., Achten, M., Kolumbán, E., Machado, F., & Hofvander, B. (2021). Social and Emotional Learning in Preschool Settings: A Systematic Map of Systematic Reviews. *Frontiers in Education*, 6, 181–189. 10.3389/feduc.2021.691670

Dobbs-Oates, J., Kaderavek, J. N., Guo, Y., & Justice, L. M. (2011). Effective classroom practices: Preschool teachers' literacy instruction and children's print awareness. *Journal of Research in Childhood Education*, 25(3), 252–275.

Doll, B., Zucker, S., & Brehm, K. (2009). *Classrooms that promote mental resilience: How to create a favorable learning environment*. Typothito.

Doll, B., Zucker, S., & Brehm, K. (2009). Σχολικές τάξεις που προάγουν την ψυχική ανθεκτικότητα (επιστ. επιμ. Χατζηχρήστου, Χ.). Τυπωθήτω, Einfeld, S. L., & Tonge, B. J. (1996). Population prevalence of psychopathology in children and adolescents with intellectual disability, II: Epidemiological findings. *Journal of Intellectual Disability Research*, 40(2), 99–109.

Drake, S. M., & Reid, J. L. (2018). Integrated curriculum as an effective way to teach 21st century capabilities. Asia Pacific Journal of Educational Research, 1(1), 31-50.

Dray, J., Bowman, J., Campbell, E., Freund, M., Wolfenden, L., Hodder, R. K., McElwaine, K., Tremain, D., Bartlem, K., Bailey, J., Small, T., Palazzi, K., Oldmeadow, C., & Wiggers, J. (2017). Systematic Review of Universal Resilience-Focused Interventions Targeting Child and Adolescent Mental Health in the School Setting. *Journal of the American Academy of Child and Adolescent Psychiatry*, 56(10), 813–824. 10.1016/j.jaac.2017.07.78028942803

Dray, J., Bowman, J., Wolfenden, L., Campbell, E., Freund, M., Hodder, R., & Wiggers, J. (2015). Systematic review of universal resilience interventions targeting child and adolescent mental health in the school setting: Review protocol. *Systematic Reviews*, 4(1), 186. 10.1186/s13643-015-0172-626715359

Dreer, B. (2020). Positive Psychological Interventions for Teachers: A Randomised Placebo-Controlled Field Experiment Investigating the Effects of Workplace-Related Positive Activities. *International Journal of Applied Positive Psychology*, 5(1-2), 77–97. 10.1007/s41042-020-00027-7

Dreer, B. (2022). Teacher well-being: Investigating the contributions of school climate and job crafting. *Cogent Education*, 9(1), 2044583. 10.1080/2331186X.2022.2044583

Duda, R. O., Hart, P. E., & Stork, D. G. (2000). *Pattern Classification* (2nd ed.). Wiley-Interscience.

DuFour, R., DuFour, R., Eaker, R., & Karhanek, G. (2010). *Raising the bar and closing the gap: Whatever it takes*. Bloomington, IN: Solution Tree.

Durlak J. A. (2015). Studying Program Implementation Is Not Easy but It Is Essential. *Prevention Science: The Official Journal of the Society for Prevention Research, 16*(8), 1123–1127. https://doi.org/10.1007/s11121-015-0606-3

Durlak, J. A., & DuPre, E. P. (2008). Implementation matters: A review of research on the influence of implementation on program outcomes and the factors affecting implementation. *American Journal of Community Psychology*, 41(3-4), 327–350. 10.1007/s10464-008-9165-018322790

Durlak, J. A., Mahoney, J. L., & Boyle, A. E. (2022). What we know, and what we need to find out about universal, school-based social and emotional learning programs for children and adolescents: A review of meta-analyses and directions for future research. *Psychological Bulletin*, 148(11-12), 765–782. 10.1037/bul0000383

Durlak, J. A., Weissberg, R. P., Dymnicki, A. B., Taylor, R. D., & Schellinger, K. B. (2011). The impact of enhancing students' social and emotional learning: A meta-analysis of school-based universal interventions. *Child Development*, 82(1), 405–432. 10.1111/j.1467-8624.2010.01564.x21291449

Dweck, C. S. (1999). *Self-theories: Their role in motivation, personality, and development*. Psychology Press.

Dweck, C. S. (2006). *Mindset: The New Psychology of Success*. Random House.

Dweck, C. S. (2008). *Mindset: The new psychology of success*. Random House Digital, Inc.

Dweck, C. S., & Leggett, E. L. (1988). A social-cognitive approach to motivation and personality. *Psychological Review*, 95(2), 256–273. 10.1037/0033-295X.95.2.256

Dye, L., Burke, M. G., & Wolf, C. (2020). Teaching mindfulness for the self-care and well-being of counselors-in-training. *Journal of Creativity in Mental Health*, 15(2), 140–153. 10.1080/15401383.2019.1642171

Dymond, D. S. (2018). Promoting student empowerment through autonomy supportive practices: Examining the Influence of professional development for primary grade teachers. (Publication No. 10814745) [Doctoral Dissertation, University of Missouri-Saint Louis]. ProQuest Dissertations and Theses Global.

Ecclestone, K., & Lewis, L. (2014). Interventions for resilience in educational settings: Challenging policy discourses of risk and vulnerability. *Journal of Education Policy*, 29(2), 195–216. 10.1080/02680939.2013.806678

Efland, A. D. (2002). *Art and Cognition: Integrating the Visual Arts in the Curriculum*. Teachers College.

Eiser, C., Eiser, J. R., & Stride, C. B. (2005). Quality of life in children newly diagnosed with cancer and their mothers. *Health and Quality of Life Outcomes*, 3(1), 1–5. 10.1186/1477-7525-3-2915860126

Eisner, E. (2002). *The Arts and the Creation of Mind*. Yale University Press.

Elias, M. J. (2003). *Academic and Social- Emotional learning*, The International Academy of Education – IAE, The International Academy of Education, France: SADAG. Διαθέσιμο: https://www.ibe.unesco.org/publications/EducationalPracticesSeriesPdf/prac1 e.pdf

Elias, M. J., Zins, J., Weissberg, R. P., Frey, K., Greenberg, M., Haynes, N., Kessler, R., Schwab-Stone, M., & Shriver, T. (1997). *Promoting Social and Emotional Learning: Guidelines for Educators*. Association for Supervision and Curriculum Development.

Eliot, M., Cornell, D., Gregory, A., & Fan, X. (2010). Supportive school climate and student willingness to seek help for bullying and threats of violence. *Journal of School Psychology*, 48(6), 533–553. 10.1016/j.jsp.2010.07.00121094397

Elliott, N. S., Kratochwill, R. T., Littlefield, C. J., & Travers, F. J. (2010). *Educational psychology: effective teaching – effective learning*. Gutenberg.

Elrod, B. G., Rice, K. G., & Meyers, J. (2022). PBIS fidelity, school climate, and student discipline: A longitudinal study of secondary schools. *Psychology in the Schools*, 59(2), 376–397. 10.1002/pits.22614

Emerson, L. M., Leyland, A., Hudson, K., Rowse, G., Hanley, P., & Hugh-Jones, S. (2017). Teaching Mindfulness to Teachers: A Systematic Review and Narrative Synthesis. *Mindfulness*, 8(5), 1136–1149. 10.1007/s12671-017-0691-428989547

Emmons, R. A., & McCullough, M. E. (2003). Counting blessings versus burdens: An experimental investigation of gratitude and subjective well-being in daily life. *Journal of Personality and Social Psychology*, 84(2), 377–389. 10.1037/0022-3514.84.2.37712585811

Engelbrecht, P., Savolainen, H., Nel, M., Koskela, T., & Okkolin, M. A. (2017). Making Meaning of Inclusive Education: Classroom Practices in Finnish and South African Classrooms. *Compare: A Journal of Comparative Education*, 47(5), 684–702. 10.1080/03057925.2016.1266927

Epstein, J. L., Sanders, M. G., Sheldon, S. B., Simon, B. S., Salinas, K. C., Jansorn, N. R., & Williams, K. J. (2018). *School, family, and community partnerships: Your handbook for action.* Corwin Press.

Erikson, E. H. (1994). *Identity: Youth and crisis* (No. 7). WW Norton & Company.

Espelage, D. L., Low, S., Polanin, J. R., & Brown, E. C. (2013). The impact of a middle school program to reduce aggression, victimization, and sexual violence. *The Journal of Adolescent Health*, 53(2), 180–186. 10.1016/j.jadohealth.2013.02.02123643338

Espelage, D. L., Polanin, J. R., & Low, S. K. (2014). Teacher and staff perceptions of school environment as predictors of student aggression, victimization, and willingness to intervene in bullying situations. *School Psychology Quarterly*, 29(3), 287–305. 10.1037/spq000007225089334

Evans, R., Murphy, S., & Scourfield, J. (2015). Implementation of a school-based social and emotional learning intervention: understanding diffusion processes within complex systems. *Prevention Science: The Official Journal of the Society for Prevention Research, 16*(5), 754–764. 10.1007/s11121-015-0552-0

Everly, G. S., & Lating, J. M. (2013). Resilience: The Final Frontier. In Everly, G. S., & Lating, J. M. (Eds.), *A Clinical Guide to the Treatment of the Human Stress Response* (3rd ed., pp. 143–154). Springer. 10.1007/978-1-4614-5538-7_7

Everly, G. S., McCormack, D. K., & Strouse, D. A. (2012). Seven Characteristics of Highly Resilient People. *International Journal of Emergency Mental Health*, 14(2), 137–143.23350224

Everly, G. S., Smith, K. J., & Lobo, R. (2013). Resilient Leadership and the Organizational Culture of Resilience: Construct Validation International. *Journal of Emergency Mental Health and Human Resilience*, 15(2), 123–128.24558699

Extremera, N., Fernadez-Berrocal, P. & Salovey, P. (2006). Spanish version of the Mayer- Salovey-Caruso Emotional Intelligence Test- Version 2.0: Reliabilities, age, and gender differences. *Psicothema*, 18, 42–48.17295956

Eysenck, H. (1985). *A model for intelligence*. Springer-Verlag.

Fabiano, G. A., Chafouleas, S. M., Weist, M. D., Sumi, W. C., & Humphrey, N. (2014). Methodology considerations in school mental health research. *School Mental Health: A Multidisciplinary Research and Practice Journal, 6*(2), 68–83. 10.1007/s12310-013-9117-1

Fabris, M. A., Lin, S., & Longobardi, C. (2023). A cross-cultural comparison of teacher-student relationship quality in Chinese and Italian teachers and students. *Journal of School Psychology*, 99, 101227. 10.1016/j.jsp.2023.10122737507185

Fang, J., & Qi, Z. (2023). The influence of school climate on teachers' job satisfaction: The mediating role of teachers' self-efficacy. *PLoS One*, 18(10), e0287555. 10.1371/journal.pone.028755537796911

Fan, W., Williams, C. M., & Corkin, D. M. (2011). A multilevel analysis of student perceptions of school climate: The effect of social and academic risk factors. *Psychology in the Schools*, 48(6), 632–647. 10.1002/pits.20579

Farina, K. A. (2019). Promoting a culture of bullying: Understanding the role of school climate and school sector. *Journal of School Choice*, 13(1), 94–120. 10.1080/15582159.2018.1526615

Fariselli, L., Ghini, M., & Freedman, J. (2006). *Age and emotional intelligence.* Six Seconds. www.6seconds.org

Farrington, D. P., & Ttofi, M. M. (2011). Effectiveness of school-based programs to reduce bullying: A systematic and meta-analytic review. *Journal of Experimental Criminology*, 7(1), 27–56. 10.1007/s11292-010-9109-1

Fasano, C., & Pellittery, J. (2006). Infusing Emotional Learning into the school environment. In *Emotionally intelligent school counseling* (pp. 65–78). Lawrence Erlbaum Associates, Inc.

Fathi, J., Pawlak, M., Kruk, M., & Naderi, M. (2023). Modelling boredom in the EFL context: An investigation of the role of coping self-efficacy, mindfulness, and foreign language enjoyment. *Language Teaching Research*, 13621688231182176. Advance online publication. 10.1177/13621688231182176

Fatou, N., & Kubiszewski, V. (2018). Are perceived school climate dimensions predictive of students' engagement? *Social Psychology of Education*, 21(2), 427–446. 10.1007/s11218-017-9422-x

Fazel, M., Hoagwood, K., Stephan, S., & Ford, T. (2014). Mental health interventions in schools in high-income countries. *The Lancet. Psychiatry*, 1(5), 377–387. 10.1016/S2215-0366(14)70312-826114092

Feagans, L., Merriwether, A., & Haldane, D. (1991). Goodness of fit in the home: Its relationship to school behavior and achievement in children with learning disabilities. *Journal of Learning Disabilities*, 24(7), 413–420. 10.1177/0022219491024007061895009

Fearon, R. P., & Roisman, G. I. (2017). Attachment theory: Progress and future directions. *Current Opinion in Psychology*, 15, 131–136. 10.1016/j.copsyc.2017.03.00228813253

Ferguson, C. (2008). *The School–Family Connection: Looking at the Larger Picture: A Review of Current Literature*. National Center for Family and Community Connections with Schools.

Fergus, S., & Zimmerman, M. A. (2005). Adolescent resilience: A framework for understanding healthy development in the face of risk. *Annual Review of Public Health*, 26(1), 399–419. 10.1146/annurev.publhealth.26.021304.14435715760295

Fisher, K. R., Hirsh-Pasek, K., Golinkoff, R. M., & Gryfe, S. G. (2008). Conceptual split? Parents' and experts' perceptions of play in the 21st century. *Journal of Applied Developmental Psychology*, 29(4), 305–316. 10.1016/j.appdev.2008.04.006

Fitton, V. A. (2013). Attachment theory: History, research, and practice. *Psychoanalytic Social Work*, 19(1-2), 121–143. 10.1080/15228878.2012.666491

Fleer, M. (2022). Engineering PlayWorld—A Model of Practice to Support Children to Collectively Design, Imagine and Think Using Engineering Concepts. *Research in Science Education*, 52(2), 583–598. 10.1007/s11165-020-09970-6

Fletcher, D., & Sarkar, M. (2013). Psychological resilience: A review and critique of definitions, concepts and theory. *European Psychologist*, 18(1), 12–17. 10.1027/1016-9040/a000124

Florian, L., & Black-Hawkins, K. (2011). Exploring inclusive pedagogy. *British Educational Research Journal*, 37(5), 813–828. 10.1080/01411926.2010.501096

Florian, L., Black-Hawkins, K., & Rouse, M. (2016). *Achievement and inclusion in schools*. Routledge. 10.4324/9781315750279

Florian, L., & Camedda, D. (2020). Enhancing teacher education for inclusion. *European Journal of Teacher Education*, 43(1), 4–8. 10.1080/02619768.2020.1707579

Flowers, A. A., Jr. (2019). The Impact of Declining Teacher Retention on a School System. Eric. https://eric.ed.gov/?id=ED601980

Forman, S. G., Olin, S. S., Hoagwood, K. E., Crowe, M., & Saka, N. (2009). Evidence-based intervention in schools: Developers' views of implementation barriers and facilitators. *School Mental Health: A Multidisciplinary Research and Practice Journal, 1*(1), 26–36. https://doi.org/10.1007/s12310-008-9002-5

Forsberg, C., Chiriac, E. H., & Thornberg, R. (2021). Exploring pupils' perspectives on school climate. *Educational Research*, 63(4), 379–395. 10.1080/00131881.2021.1956988

Forsberg, C., Sjögren, B., Thornberg, R., Hong, J. S., & Longobardi, C. (2023). Longitudinal reciprocal associations between student–teacher relationship quality and verbal and relational bullying victimization. *Social Psychology of Education*, •••, 1–23. 10.1007/s11218-023-09821-y

Forslund Frykedal, K., & Hammar Chiriac, E. (2018). Student collaboration in group work: Inclusion as participation. *International Journal of Disability Development and Education*, 65(2), 183–198. 10.1080/1034912X.2017.1363381

Fox, S., & Spector, P. E. (2000). Relations of emotional intelligence, practical intelligence, general intelligence and trait affectivity with interview outcomes: It's not all just "G". *Journal of Organizational Behavior*, 21(2), 203–220. 10.1002/(SICI)1099-1379(200003)21:2<203::AID-JOB38>3.0.CO;2-Z

Frances, D. A., Caruana, N., Hudson, J. L., & McArthur, G. M. (2019). The association between poor reading and internalizing problems: A systematic review and meta-analysis. *Clinical Psychology Review*, 67, 45–60. 10.1016/j.cpr.2018.09.00230528985

Franco, K., Baumler, E., Torres, E. D., Lu, Y., Wood, L., & Temple, J. R. (2022). The link between school climate and mental health among an ethnically diverse sample of middle school youth. *Current Psychology (New Brunswick, N.J.)*, 42(22), 18488–18498. 10.1007/s12144-022-03016-y35370383

Frank, J. L., Jennings, P. A., & Greenberg, M. T. (2016). Validation of the mindfulness in teaching scale. *Mindfulness*, 7(1), 155–163. 10.1007/s12671-015-0461-0

Frankl, V. E. (2006). *Man's search for meaning*. Beacon Press.

Fraser, M. W., Galinsky, M. J., & Richman, J. M. (1999). Risk, protection, and resilience: Towards a conceptual framework for social work practice. *Social Work Research*, 23(3), 131–144. 10.1093/swr/23.3.131

Frawley, A. (2015). Happiness Research: A Review of Critiques. *Sociology Compass*, 9(1), 62–77. 10.1111/soc4.12236

Frazier, T., & Doyle Fosco, S. L. (2024). Nurturing positive mental health and wellbeing in educational settings–the PRICES model. *Frontiers in Public Health*, 11, 11. 10.3389/fpubh.2023.128753238312141

Fredrickson, B. L. (2000). Cultivating positive emotions to optimize health and well being. *Prevention & Treatment*, 2(1), 21–29. 10.1037/1522-3736.3.1.31a

Fredrickson, B. L. (2001). The role of positive emotions in positive psychology: The broaden-and-build theory of positive emotions. *The American Psychologist*, 56(3), 218–226. 10.1037/0003-066X.56.3.21811315248

Fredrickson, B. L. (2004). The broaden–and–build theory of positive emotions. *Philosophical Transactions of the Royal Society of London. Series B, Biological Sciences*, 359(1449), 1367–1377. 10.1098/rstb.2004.151215347528

Free, J. L., & Križ, K. (2022). The not-so-hidden curriculum: How a public school system in the United States minoritizes migrant students. *Equity & Excellence in Education*, 55(1-2), 50–72. 10.1080/10665684.2022.2047409

Freeland, C. (2010). *Μα, είναι αυτό τέχνη*. Πλέθρον.

Freeman, R. (2016). Is student voice necessarily empowering? Problematisingstudent voice as a form of higher education governance. *Higher Education Research & Development*, 35(4), 859–862. 10.1080/07294360.2016.1172764

Freiberg, H. J. (2005). *School climate: Measuring, improving and sustaining healthy learning environments*. Routledge. 10.4324/9780203983980

Frisby, B. N., & Martin, M. M. (2010). Instructor–student and student–student rapport in the classroom. *Communication Education*, 59(2), 146–164. 10.1080/03634520903564362

Froh, J. J., Kashdan, T. B., Ozimkowski, K. M., & Miller, N. (2009). Who benefits the most from a gratitude intervention in children and adolescents? Examining positive affect as a moderator. *The Journal of Positive Psychology*, 4(5), 408–422. 10.1080/17439760902992464

Froh, J. J., Sefick, W. J., & Emmons, R. A. (2008). Counting blessings in early adolescents: An experimental study of gratitude and subjective well-being. *Journal of School Psychology*, 46(2), 213–233. 10.1016/j.jsp.2007.03.00519083358

Froiland, J. M., Worrell, F. C., & Oh, H. (2019). Teacher–student relationships, psychological need satisfaction, and happiness among diverse students. *Psychology in the Schools*, 56(5), 856–870. 10.1002/pits.22245

Frydenberg, E. (2010). *Think positively! A course for developing coping skills in adolescents*. Continuum International Publishing Group.

Frymier, A. B., & Houser, M. L. (2000). The teacher-student relationship as an interpersonal relationship. *Communication Education*, 49(3), 207–219. 10.1080/03634520009379209

Gable, S. L., & Haidt, J. (2005). What (and why) is positive psychology? *Review of General Psychology*, 9(2), 103–110. 10.1037/1089-2680.9.2.103

Galassi, J. P., & Akos, P. (2004). Developmental advocacy: Twenty-first century school counseling. *Journal of Counseling and Development*, 82(2), 146–157. 10.1002/j.1556-6678.2004.tb00296.x

Galassi, J. P., & Akos, P. (2007). *Strength-based school: Promoting student development and achievement*. Earlbaum.

Gallagher, A. L., Galvin, R., Robinson, K., Murphy, C. A., Conway, P. F., & Perry, A. (2020). The characteristics, life circumstances and self-concept of 13 year-olds with and without disabilities in Ireland: A secondary analysis of the Growing Up in Ireland (GUI) study. *PLoS One*, 15(3), 135–156. 10.1371/journal.pone.022959932168358

Galloway, N., Foulstone, A., & Lurie, J. (2022). Yoga and couple relationship satisfaction: The synergy between mindfulness and emotional intelligence. *International Journal of Yoga Therapy*, 32(2022), 16. 10.17761/2022-D-21-0004936602865

Gallup. (2014). *State of America's schools: The path to winning again in education*. Washington, DC: Author. Retrieved from www.gallup.com/services/178709/state-america-schools-report.aspx

Gans, A. M., Kenny, M. C., & Ghany, D. L. (2003). Comparing the self-concept of students with and without learning disabilities. *Journal of Learning Disabilities*, 36(3), 287–295. 10.1177/002221940303600307155515648

Gardner, H. (1983). *Frames of mind: The theory of multiples intelligences*. Basic Books.

Gardner, J. (1999). *Intelligence reframed: Multiple intelligence for the 21st century*. Basic Books.

Garista, P. (2022). Resilience and coping styles for transformative teaching and learning. In Biswal, (Eds.), *Edureform Handbook for innovative pedagogy*. La Scuola Sei.

Garmezy, N. (1991). Resilience in children's adaptation to negative life events and stressed environments. *Pediatric Annals*, 20(9), 459–466. 10.3928/0090-4481-19910901-051945543

Garmezy, N., Masten, A. S., & Tellegen, A. (1984). The study of stress and competence in children: A building block for developmental psychopathology. *Child Development*, 55(1), 97–111. 10.2307/11298376705637

Garmezy, N., & Streitman, S. (1974). Children at risk: the search for the antecedents to schizophrenia: Part 1. Conceptual models and research methods. *Schizophrenia Bulletin*, 8(8), 14–90. 10.1093/schbul/1.8.144619494

Garro, A., Janal, M., Kondroski, K., Stillo, G., & Vega, V. (2023). Mindfulness Initiatives for Students, Teachers, and Parents: A Review of Literature and Implications for Practice During COVID-19 and Beyond. *Contemporary School Psychology*, 27(1), 152–169. 10.1007/s40688-022-00446-036741424

Garzia, V., & Molinari, L. (2021). School climate multidimensionality and measurement: A Systematic literature review. *Research Papers in Education*, 36(5), 561–587. 10.1080/02671522.2019.1697735

Gase, L. N., Gomez, L. M., Kuo, T., Glenn, B. A., Inkelas, M., & Ponce, N. A. (2017). Relationships among student, staff, and administrative measures of school climate and student health and academic outcomes. *The Journal of School Health*, 87(5), 319–328. 10.1111/josh.1250128382671

Geraci, A., Di Domenico, L., Inguglia, C., & D'Amico, A. (2023). Teachers' emotional intelligence, burnout, work engagement, and self-efficacy during COVID-19 lockdown. *Behavioral Sciences (Basel, Switzerland)*, 13(4), 296. 10.3390/bs1304029637102810

Gerber, P. J., Ginsberg, R., & Reiff, H. B. (1992). Identifying alterable patterns in employment success for highly successful adults with learning disabilities. *Journal of Learning Disabilities*, 25(8), 475–487. 10.1177/002221949202500802146039l

Gerhardt, S. (2015). *Why love matters: How affection shapes a baby's brain* (2nd ed.). Routledge.

Ghaith, G. (2003). The relationship between forms of instruction, achievement and perceptions of classroom climate. *Educational Research*, 45(1), 83–93. 10.1080/0013188032000086145

Gheihman, G., Cooper, C., & Simpkin, A. (2018). Everyday resilience: Practical tools to promote resilience among medical students. *Journal of General Internal Medicine*, 34(4), 498–501. 10.1007/s11606-018-4728-830535748

Gibbs, N. (1995). The EQ factor. *Time*, 146, 60–68.

Gibbs, S., & Miller, A. (2014). Teachers' resilience and well-being: A role for educational psychology. *Teachers and Teaching*, 20(5), 609–621. 10.1080/13540602.2013.844408

Gilio, B., & Dorsey, T. (2016). The reflective principal: Principals' emotional intelligence Outweighs IQ. *Principal.*

Gill, S. (2009, July). Monitoring and promoting well-being in education principles and possible approaches to child wellbeing indicators (Working paper, Education for Well-Being Europe Consortium).

Gillespie, M. (2005). Student–teacher connection: A place of possibility. *Journal of Advanced Nursing*, 52(2), 211–219. 10.1111/j.1365-2648.2005.03581.x16164482

Ginsburg, K. R. (2007). The Importance of Play in Promoting Healthy Child Development and Maintaining Strong Parent-Child Bonds. *Pediatrics*, 119(1), 182–191. 10.1542/peds.2006-269717200287

Giroux, H. A., & Penna, A. N. (1979). Social education in the classroom: The dynamics of the hidden curriculum. *Theory and Research in Social Education*, 7(1), 21–42. 10.1080/00933104.1979.10506048

Gkolia, A., Belias, D., & Koustelios, A. (2014). The impact of principals' transformational leadership on teachers' satisfaction: Evidence from Greece. *European Journal of Business and Social Sciences*, 3, 69–80.

Glaso, L., & Einarsen, S. (2008). Emotion regulation in leader–follower relationships. *European Journal of Work and Organizational Psychology*, 17(4), 482–500. 10.1080/13594320801994960

Glennie, E. J. (2010). Coping and Resilience. In Rosen, J. A., Glennie, E. J., Dalton, B. Q., Lennon, J. M., & Bozwick, R. N. (Eds.), *Noncognitive skills in the classroom: New perspectives on educational research.* RTI International. 10.3768/rtipress.2010.bk.0004.1009.8

Gold, Z. S. (2014). *Purdue e-Pubs Preschoolers' Physical, Social, and Engineering Play Behaviors: Differences in Gender and Play Environment.*

Goldberg, J. M., Sklad, M., Elfrink, T. R., Schreurs, K. M. G., Bohlmeijer, E. T., & Clarke, A. M. (2019). Effectiveness of interventions adopting a whole school approach to enhancing social and emotional development: A meta-analysis. *European Journal of Psychology of Education*, 34(4), 755–782. 10.1007/s10212-018-0406-9

Goldenberg, J., & Klavir, R. (2017). School Climate, Classroom Climate, and Teaching Quality: Can Excellent Students Unravel This Connection? *International Journal for Talent Development and Creativity*, 5(1-2), 137–148.

Goldstein, S., & Brooks, R. B. (2013). Why Study Resilience. In S. Goldstein & R. B. Brooks (Eds.), *Handbook of Resilience in Children* (2nd ed., pp. 3-14). Springer. 10.1007/978-1-4614-3661-4_1

Gold, Z. S., Elicker, J., Choi, J. Y., Anderson, T., & Brophy, S. P. (2015). Preschoolers' engineering play behaviors: Differences in gender and play context. *Children, Youth and Environments*, 25(3), 1–21. 10.1353/cye.2015.0046

Gold, Z. S., Elicker, J., Evich, C. D., Mishra, A. A., Howe, N., & Weil, A. E. (2021). Engineering play with blocks as an informal learning context for executive function and planning. *Journal of Engineering Education*, 110(4), 803–818. 10.1002/jee.20421

Goleman, D. (1995). *Emotional intelligence*. Bantam Books.

Goleman, D. (2000). *Emotional Intelligence at work*. Ellinika Grammata.

Gombrich, E. H. (1963). *Meditations on a Hobby Horse and other essays on the Theory of Art*. Phaidon Press.

Gonzales, M. (2022). *Emotional Intelligence for students, parents, teachers and school leaders. A Handbook for the Whole School Community*. Springer. 10.1007/978-981-19-0324-3

Gonzalez, R., & Padilla, A. M. (1997). The academic resilience of Mexican American high school students. *Hispanic Journal of Behavioral Sciences*, 19(3), 301–317. 10.1177/07399863970193004

Goodall, J. (2013). Parental engagement to support children's learning: A six-point model. *School Leadership & Management*, 33(2), 133–150. 10.1080/13632434.2012.724668

Gorman-Smith, D., & Tolan, P. H. (2003). Positive adaptation among youth exposed to community violence. In *Resilience and vulnerability: Adaptation in the context of childhood adversities*. Cambridge University Press. 10.1017/CBO9780511615788.018

Gorski, P. C. (2017). *Reaching and teaching students in poverty: Strategies for erasing the opportunity gap*. Teachers College Press.

Government of Wales. (2021). *Framework on embedding a wole- school approach to emotional and mental well – being*. Llywodraeth Cymru Welsh Government, ADDYSG, Education Wales.

Graber, R., Pichon, F., & Carabine, E. (2015). *Psychological resilience: State of knowledge and future research agendas*. Psychology Press.

Grabovac, A. D., Lau, M. A., & Willett, B. R. (2011). Mechanisms of mindfulness: A Buddhist psychological model. *Mindfulness*, 2(3), 154–166. 10.1007/s12671-011-0054-5

Gray, C., Wilcox, G., & Nordstokke, D. (2017). Teacher mental health, school climate, inclusive education and student learning: A review. *Canadian Psychology*, 58(3), 203–210. 10.1037/cap0000117

Grayson, J. L., & Alvarez, H. K. (2008). School climate factors relating to teacherburnout: A mediator model. *Teaching and Teacher Education*, 24(5), 1349–1363. 10.1016/j.tate.2007.06.005

Greenberg, M. T., Domitrovich, C., & Bumbarger, B. (2001). The prevention of mental disorders in school-aged children: Current state of the field. *Prevention & Treatment*, 4(1), 1a–1a. 10.1037/1522-3736.4.1.41a

Greenberg, M. T., Weissberg, R. P., O'Brien, M. U., Zins, J. E., Fredericks, L., Resnik, H., & Elias, M. J. (2003). Enhancing school-based prevention and youth development through coordinated social, emotional, and academic learning. *The American Psychologist*, 58(6-7), 466–474. 10.1037/0003-066X.58.6-7.46612971193

Greenier, V., Derakhshan, A., & Fathi, J. (2021). Emotion regulation and psychological well-being in teacher work engagement: A case of British and Iranian English language teachers. *System*, 97, 102446. 10.1016/j.system.2020.102446

Greenockle, K. M. (2010). The new face in leadership: Emotional intelligence. *Quest*, 62(3), 260–267. 10.1080/00336297.2010.10483647

Green, S., Oades, L., & Robinson, P. (2011). Positive education: Creating flourishing students, staff and schools. *InPsych*, 33(2), 37–43.

Gregory, A., Clawson, K., Davis, A., & Gerewitz, J. (2016). The promise of restorative practices to transform teacher-student relationships and achieve equity in school discipline. *Journal of Educational & Psychological Consultation*, 26(4), 325–353. 10.1080/10474412.2014.929950

Gregory, A., & Cornell, D. (2009). "Tolerating" adolescent needs: Moving beyond zero tolerance policies in high school. *Theory into Practice*, 48(2), 106–113. 10.1080/00405840902776327

Grolnick, W. S., & Ryan, R. M. (1987). Autonomy in children's learning: An experimental and individual difference investigation. *Journal of Personality and Social Psychology*, 52(5), 890–898. 10.1037/0022-3514.52.5.8903585701

Grolnick, W. S., & Ryan, R. M. (1990). Self-perceptions, motivation, and adjustment in children with learning disabilities: A multiple group comparison study. *Journal of Learning Disabilities*, 23(3), 177–184. 10.1177/00222194900230030823131 91

Gross, J. J., & John, O. P. (2003). Individual differences in two emotion regulation processes: Implications for affect, relationships, and well-being. *Journal of Personality and Social Psychology*, 85(2), 348–362. 10.1037/0022-3514.85.2.34812916575

Grossman, P., Niemann, L., Schmidt, S., & Walach, H. (2004). Mindfulness-based stress reduction and health benefits: A meta-analysis. *Journal of Psychosomatic Research*, 57(1), 35–43. 10.1016/S0022-3999(03)00573-715256293

Guðjónsdóttir, H., & Karlsdóttir, J. (2009). Látum þúsund blóm blómstra. Uppeldi og menntun, 18(1), 61-77.

Guðjónsdóttir, H., & Óskarsdóttir, E. (2016). Inclusive education, pedagogy and practice. In Markic, S., & Abels, S. (Eds.), *Science education towards inclusion* (pp. 7–22). Nova Science Publishers.

Guendelman, S., Medeiros, S., & Rampes, H. (2017). Mindfulness and emotion regulation: Insights from neurobiological, psychological, and clinical studies. *Frontiers in Psychology*, 8, 220. 10.3389/fpsyg.2017.0022028321194

Guidi, A. (2013). *La funzione del gioco dal bambino all' età adulta. L'orientamento psicoanalitico lacaniano sul gioco*. Edizioni Ets.

Guilford, J. (1967). *The Nature of Human Intelligence*. McGraw-Hill.

Guo, P., Choe, J., & Higgins-D'Alessandro, A. (2011). Report of construct validity and internal consistency findings for the comprehensive school climate inventory. Unpublished manuscript Fordham University, Bronx, NY.

Gu, Q. (2014). The role of relational resilience in teachers' career-long commitment and effectiveness. *Teachers and Teaching*, 20(5), 502–529. 10.1080/13540602.2014.937961

Gutiérrez, K. D., & Rogoff, B. (2003). Cultural ways of learning: Individual traits or repertoires of practice. *Educational Researcher*, 32(5), 19–25. 10.3102/0013189X032005019

Gutman, L. M., Brown, J., Akerman, R., & Obolenskaya, P. (2010). *Change in wellbeing from childhood to a: risk and resilience*. Institute of Education.

Hadjichristou, C., Dimitripoulou, A., Lykitsakou, K., & Lambropoulou, A. (2009). Προαγωγή της ψυχικής ευεξίας στη σχολική κοινότητα: Εφαρμογή παρεμβατικού προγράμματος σε επίπεδο συστήματος. Ψυχολογία. *E (Norwalk, Conn.)*, 16(3), 381–401.

Haft, S. L., Chen, T., LeBlanc, C., Tencza, F., & Hoeft, F. (2019). Impact of mentoring on socio-emotional and mental health outcomes of youth with learning disabilities and attention-deficit hyperactivity disorder. *Child and Adolescent Mental Health*, 24(4), 318–328. 10.1111/camh.1233131649490

Haft, S. L., Myers, C. A., & Hoeft, F. (2016). Socio-emotional and cognitive resilience in children with reading disabilities. *Current Opinion in Behavioral Sciences*, 10, 133–141. 10.1016/j.cobeha.2016.06.00527747263

Hagelskamp, C., Brackett, M. A., Rivers, S. E., & Salovey, P. (2013). Improving Classroom Quality with The RULER Approach to Social and Emotional Learning: Proximal and Distal Outcomes. *American Journal of Community Psychology*, 51(3–4), 530–543. 10.1007/s10464-013-9570-x23444004

Halliday, A. J., Kern, M. L., Garrett, D. K., & Turnbull, D. A. (2019). The student voice in well-being: A case study of participatory action research in positive education. *Educational Action Research*, 27(2), 173–196. 10.1080/09650792.2018.1436079

Hamilton, N. A., Kitzman, H., & Guyotte, S. (2006). Enhancing health and emotion: Mindfulness as a missing link between cognitive therapy and positive psychology. *Journal of Cognitive Psychotherapy*, 20(2), 123–134. 10.1891/jcop.20.2.123

Hammill, J., Nguyen, T., & Henderson, F. (2022). Student engagement: The impact of positive psychology interventions on students. *Sage Journals, 23*(2).

Hamre, B. K., & Pianta, R. C. (2001). Early teacher–child relationships and the trajectory of children's school outcomes through eighth grade. *Child Development*, 72(2), 625–638. 10.1111/1467-8624.0030111333089

Hamre, B. K., & Pianta, R. C. (2005). Can instructional and emotional support in the first-grade classroom make a difference for children at risk of school failure? *Child Development*, 76(5), 949–967. 10.1111/j.1467-8624.2005.00889.x16149994

Hamre, B. K., Pianta, R. C., Downer, J. T., DeCoster, J., Mashburn, A. J., Jones, S. M., Brown, J. L., Cappella, E., Atkins, M., Rivers, S. E., Brackett, M. A., & Hamagami, A. (2013). Teaching through interactions: Testing a developmental framework of teacher effectiveness in over 4,000 classrooms. *The Elementary School Journal*, 113(4), 461–487. 10.1086/66961634497425

Hansen, N. K., & Vogel, R. (2011). Organizational routines: A review and outlook on practice-based micro-foundations. *Economics, Management & Financial Markets, 6*(3), 86–111. https://www.ceeol.com/search/article-detail?id=87415

Hanuliaková, J., & Barnová, S. (2015). Positive school climate (A theoretical empirical conspectus). *Acta Educationis Generalis*, 5(1), 68–73.

Hargreaves, A., & Goodson, I. (2006). Educational change over time? The sustainability and nonsustainability of three decades of secondary school change and continuity. *Educational Administration Quarterly*, 42(3), 3–41. 10.1177/0013161X05277975

Hart, A., Blincow, D., & Thomas, H. (2007). *Resilient therapy: Working with children and families*. Routledge/Taylor & Francis Group.

Hart, A., & Heaver, B. (2013). Evaluating resilience-based programs for schools using a systematic consultative review. *Journal of Child and Youth Development*, 1, 27–53.

Hart, A., & Heaver, B. (2015). *Resilience approaches to supporting young people's mental health appraising the evidence base for schools and communities*. University of Brighton/ Boingboing.

Harter, S. (1982). The Perceived Competence Scale for Children. *Child Development*, 53(1), 87–97. 10.2307/11296406525886

Hartley, M. T. (2011). Examining the relationships between resilience, mental health, and academic persistence in undergraduate college students. *Journal of American College Health*, 59(7), 596–604. 10.1080/07448481.2010.51563221823954

Hattie, J. (2008). *Visible learning: A synthesis of over 800 meta-analyses relating to achievement*. Routledge. 10.4324/9780203887332

Hattie, J., & Timperley, H. (2007). The power of feedback. *Review of Educational Research*, 77(1), 81–112. 10.3102/003465430298487

Hatzichristou, C., Lykitsakou, K., Lampropoulou, A., & Dimitropoulou, P. (2010). Promoting the well-being of school communities: A systemic approach. In B. Doll, W. Phohl, & J. Yoon (Eds.), *Handbook of Prevention Science* (pp. 255-274). Routledge.

Hatzichristou, S., Dimitropoulou, P., Lampropoulou, A., & Lykitsakou, K. (2009). Intervention programs in the school community: The experience of the Center for Research and Applications of School Psychology of the University of Athens. In D. Nikolopoulos (Ed.), *School Psychology: Applications in the School Environment* (pp. 283-306). Athens: Place.

Heine, S. J., Kitayama, S., Lehman, D. R., Takata, T., Ide, E., Leung, C., & Matsumoto, H. (2001). Divergent consequences of success and failure in Japan and North America: An investigation of self-improving motivations and malleable selves. *Journal of Personality and Social Psychology*, 81(4), 599–615. 10.1037/0022-3514.81.4.59911642348

Heisner, J. (2005). Telling Stories with Blocks: Encouraging Language in the Block Center. *Early Childhood Research & Practice*, 7(2), n2.

Henderson, N., & Milstein, M. M. (2008). *Resiliency in schools: Making it happen for students and educators*. Corwin Press.

Henderson, N., & Milstein, M. M. (2008). *Σχολεία που προάγουν την ψυχική ανθεκτικότητα - Πώς μπορεί να γίνει πραγματικότητα για τους μαθητές και τους εκπαιδευτικούς* (επιστ. επιμ. Χατζηχρήστου, Χ.). Τυπωθήτω.

Hen, M., & Goroshit, M. (2012). Academic procrastination, emotional intelligence, academic self-efficacy, and GPA: A comparison between students with and without learning disabilities. *Journal of Learning Disabilities*, 20, 1–9.22442254

Henrich, J., Heine, S. J., & Norenzayan, A. (2010). The weirdest people in the world? *Behavioral and Brain Sciences*, 33(2-3), 61–83. 10.1017/S0140525X0999152X20550733

Henry, A., & Thorsen, C. (2018). Teacher–student relationships and L2 motivation. *Modern Language Journal*, 102(1), 218–241. 10.1111/modl.12446

Henschen, E., Teschner, M., & Vogler, A.-M. (2022). Peer interactions and their role in early mathematical learning in kindergarten discourses. *International Electronic Journal of Mathematics Education*, 17(4), em0709. Advance online publication. 10.29333/iejme/12362

Herrman, H., Stewart, D. E., Diaz-Granados, N., Berger, E. L., Jackson, B., & Yuen, T. (2011). What Is Resilience? *Canadian Journal of Psychiatry*, 56(5), 258–265. 10.1177/070674371105 60050421586191

Hess, T., & Gunter, G. (2013). Serious game-based and nongame-based online courses: Learning experiences and outcomes. *British Journal of Educational Technology*, 44(3), 372–385. 10.1111/bjet.12024

Higgins, E., & O'Sullivan, S. (2015). "What Works": Systematic review of the "FRIENDS for Life" programme as a universal school-based intervention programme for the prevention of child and youth anxiety. *Educational Psychology in Practice*, 31(4), 424–438. 10.1080/02667363.2015.1086977

Hill, M., Stafford, A., Seaman, P., Ross, N., & Daniel, B. (2007). *Parenting and resilience*. Joseph Rowntree Foundation.

Hodder, R. K., Freund, M., Wolfenden, L., Bowman, J., Nepal, S., Dray, J., Kingsland, M., Yoong, S. L., & Wiggers, J. (2017). Systematic review of universal school-based 'resilience' interventions targeting adolescent tobacco, alcohol or illicit substance use: A meta-analysis. *Preventive Medicine*, 100, 248–268. 10.1016/j.ypmed.2017.04.00328390835

Hojati, M., & Abbasi, M. (2013). Comparisons of self-efficacy and hope among students with and without learning disabilities. *Journal of Special Education and Rehabilitation*, 14(1-2), 66–77. 10.2478/v10215-011-0034-2

Holfve–Sabel, M. (2014, January). Learning, Interaction and Relationships as Components of Student Well– being: Differences Between Classes from Student and Teacher Perspective. *Social Indicators Research*, 119(3), 1535–1555. Advance online publication. 10.1007/s11205-013-0557-7

Holt, M. K., Vivolo-Kantor, A. M., Polanin, J. R., Holland, K. M., DeGue, S., Matjasko, J. L., Wolfe, M., & Reid, G. (2015). Bullying and suicidal ideation and behaviors: A Meta-Analysis. *Pediatrics*, 135(2), 496–509. 10.1542/peds.2014-186425560447

Hoover–Dempsey, K. V., Walker, J. M. T., Sandler, H. M., Whetsel, D., Green, C. L., Wilkins, A. S., & Closson, K. (2005). Why Do Parents Become Involved? Research Findings and Implications. *The Elementary School Journal*, 106(2), 105–130. 10.1086/499194

Hopkins, J. (2001). *Cultivating compassion*. Broadway Books.

Horn, A. B., Pössel, P., & Hautzinger, M. (2011). Promoting Adaptive Emotion Regulation and Coping in Adolescence: A School-based Programme. *Journal of Health Psychology*, 16(2), 258–273. 10.1177/135910531037281420733014

Hornby, G. (2015). Inclusive special education: Development of a new theory for the education of children with special educational needs and disabilities. *British Journal of Special Education*, 42(3), 213–229. 10.1111/1467-8578.12101

Horner, R. H., Sugai, G., & Anderson, C. M. (2010). Examining the evidence base for school-wide positive behavior support. *Focus on Exceptional Children*, 42(8). Advance online publication. 10.17161/foec.v42i8.6906

Hosford, S., & O'Sullivan, S. (2016). A climate for self-efficacy: The relationship between school climate and teacher efficacy for inclusion. *International Journal of Inclusive Education*, 20(6), 604–621. 10.1080/13603116.2015.1102339

Howard, J., & Wood, E. (2010). *Play and learning: From research to practice*. Sage Publications.

Howard, S. (2007). *The developing child. The Getaway Series*. Waldorf Early Childhood Association of North America.

Howell, A. J. (2009). Flourishing: Achievement-related correlates of students' well-being. *The Journal of Positive Psychology*, 4(1), 1–13. 10.1080/17439760802043459

Hoy, A. W., Hoy, W. K., & Davis, H. A. (2009). Teachers' self-efficacy beliefs. In K. R. Wenzel & A. Wigfield (Eds.), *Handbook of motivation at school* (pp. 627–653). Routledge/Taylor & Francis Group.

Hoyert, M. S., O'Dell, C. D., & Hendrickson, K. A. (2012). Using Goal Orientation to Enhance College Retention and Graduation Rates. *Psychology Learning & Teaching*, 11(2), 171–179. 10.2304/plat.2012.11.2.171

Hoyt, L. T., Chase-Lansdale, P. L., McDade, T. W., & Adam, E. K. (2012). Positive Youth, Healthy Adults: Does Positive Well-being in Adolescence Predict Better Perceived Health and Fewer Risky Health Behaviors in Young Adulthood? *The Journal of Adolescent Health*, 50(1), 66–73. 10.1016/j.jadohealth.2011.05.00222188836

Hoy, W. K., Hannum, J., & Tschannen-Moran, M. (1998). Organizational climate and student achievement: A parsimonious and longitudinal view. *Journal of School Leadership*, 8(4), 336–359. 10.1177/105268469800800401

Hoy, W. K., & Sweetland, S. R. (2001). Designing better schools: The meaning and measure of enabling school structures. *Educational Administration Quarterly*, 37(3), 296–321. 10.1177/00131610121969334

Hoy, W. K., Tarter, C. J., & Hoy, A. W. (2006). Academic optimism of schools: A force for student achievement. *American Educational Research Journal*, 43(3), 425–446. 10.3102/00028312043003425

Huang, S., Yin, H., & Lv, L. (2019). Job characteristics and teacher well-being: The mediation of teacher self-monitoring and teacher self-efficacy. *Educational Psychology*, 39(3), 313–331. 10.1080/01443410.2018.1543855

Hu, B. Y., Fan, X., Gu, C., & Yang, N. (2016). Teacher-child interaction quality, regulatory focus, and children's school readiness skills in China. *Learning and Instruction*, 41, 1–10.

Huebner, E. S., Gilman, R., Reschly, A., & Hall, R. (2009). Positive schools. In Lopez, S. J., & Snyder, C. R. (Eds.), *Oxford handbook of positive psychology* (2nd ed., pp. 561–569). Oxford University Press. 10.1093/oxfordhb/9780195187243.013.0053

Hughes, J. N., Wu, J. Y., Kwok, O. M., Villarreal, V., & Johnson, A. Y. (2012). Indirect effects of child reports of teacher–student relationship on achievement. *Journal of Educational Psychology*, 104(2), 350–365. 10.1037/a002633923226873

Huizinga, J. (1938). *Homo Ludens: Proeve Ener Bepaling Van Het Spelelement Der Cultuur*. Wolters-Noordhoff.

Humphrey, R. (2002). The many faces of emotional leadership. *The Leadership Quarterly*, 13(5), 493–504. 10.1016/S1048-9843(02)00140-6

Hu, X., Zheng, Q., & Lee, G. T. (2018). Using Peer-Mediated LEGO® Play Intervention to Improve Social Interactions for Chinese Children with Autism in an Inclusive Setting. *Journal of Autism and Developmental Disorders*, 48(7), 2444–2457. 10.1007/s10803-018-3502-429453705

Hwang, Y.-S., Bartlett, B., Greben, M., & Hand, K. (2017). A systematic review of mindfulness interventions for in-service teachers: A tool to enhance teacher wellbeing and performance. *Teaching and Teacher Education*, 64, 26–42. 10.1016/j.tate.2017.01.015

Ingersoll, R. M., & Strong, M. (2011). The impact of induction and mentoring programs for beginning teachers: A critical review of the research. *Review of Educational Research*, 81(2), 201–233. 10.3102/0034654311403323

Ishizu, T., & Zeki, S. (2011). Toward a brain-based theory of beauty. *PLoS One*, 6.21755004

J. (2021). Burned or engaged teachers? The role of mindfulness, self-efficacy, teacher and students' relationships, and the mediating role of intrapersonal and interpersonal mindfulness. *Curr. Psychol.* 42, 11719–11732. 10.1007/s12144-021-02433-9

Jacelon, C. S. (1997). The trait and process of resilience. *Journal of Advanced Nursing*, 25(1), 123–129. 10.1046/j.1365-2648.1997.1997025123.x9004020

Jackson, P. W. (1990). Life in classrooms. Teachers College Press.

Jackson, C. K., & Bruegmann, E. (2009). Teaching students and teaching each other: The importance of peer learning for teachers. *American Economic Journal. Applied Economics*, 1(4), 85–108. 10.1257/app.1.4.85

Jacobson, D. A. (2016). Causes and effects of teacher burnout. (Publication No. 10162782) [Doctoral Dissertation, Walden University]. ProQuest Dissertations and Theses Global.

Jain, S., Shapiro, S. L., Swanick, S., Roesch, S. C., Mills, P. J., Bell, I., & Schwartz, G. E. (2007). A randomized controlled trial of mindfulness meditation versus relaxation training: effects on distress, positive states of mind, rumination, and distraction. *Annals of behavioral medicine: a publication of the Society of Behavioral Medicine, 33*(1), 11–21. https://doi.org/10.1207/s15324796abm3301_2

Javed, S., Manoranjitham, M., Chen, K. L., & Husniza, H. (2023). Enhancing teaching and learning for pupils with dyslexia: A comprehensive review of technological and non-technological interventions. *Education and Information Technologies*, 11, 754–768.

Jaycox, L. H., Reivich, K. J., Gillham, J., & Seligman, M. (1994). Prevention of depressive symptoms in school children. *Behaviour Research and Therapy*, 32(8), 801–816. 10.1016/0005-7967(94)90160-07993324

Jennings, P. A., & Greenberg, M. T. (2009). The prosocial classroom: Teacher social and emotional competence in relation to student and classroom outcomes. *Review of Educational Research*, 79(1), 491–525. 10.3102/0034654308325693

Jeynes, W. (2012). A Meta–Analysis of the Efficacy of Different Types of Parental Involvement Programs for Urban Students. *Urban Education*, 47(4), 706–742. 10.1177/0042085912445643

Johnson, B., Down, B., Le Cornu, R., Peters, J., Sullivan, A., Pearce, J., & Hunter, J. (2010). Conditions that support early career teacher resilience. Refereed paper presented at 'Teacher education for a sustainable future', the annual conference of the Australian Teacher Education Association (ATEA), Townsville. https://atea.edu.au/wp-content/uploads/2010_johnson_et_al.pdf

Johnson, B. (2008). Teacher–student relationships which promote resilience at school: A micro–level analysis of students' views. *British Journal of Guidance & Counselling*, 36(4), 385–398. 10.1080/03069880802364528

Johnson, B., & Lazarus, S. (2008). The role of schools in building the resilience of youth faced with adversity. *Journal of Psychology in Africa*, 18(1), 19–30. 10.1080/14330237.2008.10820168

Johnson, E. S., Humphrey, M., & Swanson, H. L. (2011). Cognitive processing deficits and students with specific learning disabilities: A selective meta – analysis of the literature. *Learning Disability Quarterly*, 33(1), 206–223.

Johnson, S. M., Kraft, M. A., & Papay, J. P. (2012). How context matters in high-need schools: The effects of teachers' working conditions on their professional satisfaction and their students' achievement. *Teachers College Record*, 114(10), 1–39. 10.1177/016146811211401004

Jones, J. S. (2012). The external and internal educational factors that contribute to student achievement and self-perceptions of urban middle school Title I students [Doctoral Dissertation, Rowan University]. Rowan Digital Works. https://rdw.rowan.edu/etd/240/

Jones, G., & Lafreniere, K. (2014). Exploring the Role of School Engagement in Predicting Resilience Among Bahamian Youth. *The Journal of Black Psychology*, 40(1), 47–68. 10.1177/0095798412469230

Jones, S. M., & Kahn, J. (2017). *The Evidence Base for How We Learn: Supporting Students' Social, Emotional, and Academic Development. Consensus Statements of Evidence from the Council of Distinguished Scientists*. Aspen Institute.

Jones, T. M., Fleming, C., & Williford, A. (2020). Racial equity in academic success: The role of school climate and social emotional learning. *Children and Youth Services Review*, 119, 119. 10.1016/j.childyouth.2020.10562333311826

Jordan, P. J., & Troth, A. C. (2006). Emotions and coping with conflict: An introduction. *Journal of Management & Organization*, 12(2), 98–100. 10.5172/jmo.2006.12.2.98

Judge, T. A. (1992). The dispositional perspective in human resources research. In Ferris, G. R., & Rowland, K. M. (Eds.), *Research in personnel and human resources management* (pp. 145–156). Jai Press.

Jung, C. G. (1971). *Psychological Types*. Princeton University Press.

Kabat-Zinn, J. (1994, September). Catalyzing movement towards a more contemplative/sacred-appreciating/non-dualistic society. *Meeting of the working group.*

Kabat-Zinn, J. (1990). *Full Catastrophe Living: Using the Wisdom of Your Body and Mind to Face Stress, Pain and Illness*. Delacourt.

Kabat-Zinn, J. (1994). *Wherever you go, there you are: Mindfulness meditation in everyday life*. Hyperion.

Kabat-Zinn, J. (1994). *Wherever You Go, There You Are: Mindfulness Meditation in Everyday Life*. Hyperion.

Kabat-Zinn, J. (2003). Mindfulness-based interventions in context: Past, present, and future. *Clinical Psychology : a Publication of the Division of Clinical Psychology of the American Psychological Association*, 10(2), 144–156. 10.1093/clipsy.bpg016

Kafetsios, K. (2003). Attachment, emotion regulation and psychological well being: Review and clinical applications. *Encephalos*, 40, 30–45.

Kafetsios, K. (2004). Attachment and emotional intelligence abilities across the life course. *Personality and Individual Differences*, 37(1), 129–145. 10.1016/j.paid.2003.08.006

Kaimal, G., Ray, K., & Muniz, J. (2016). Reduction of Cortisol Levels and Participants' Responses Following Art Making. *Art Therapy Journal.*

Kakavoulis, K. A. (1997). *Emotional development and education.* Self publishing.

Kamins, M. L., & Dweck, C. S. (1999). Person versus process praise and criticism: Implications for contingent self-worth and coping. *Developmental Psychology*, 35(3), 835–847. 10.1037/0012-1649.35.3.83510380873

Kampeza, M., & Sfyroera, M. (2016). Enhancing children's learning: Meaning-making and play. In Avgitidou, S., Tzekaki, M., & Tsafos, V. (Eds.), *Prospective educators observe, intervene, and reflect: Supporting their practicum* (Vol. 3, pp. 90–118). Gutenberg.

Kangas-Dick, K., & O'Shaughnessy, E. (2020). Interventions that promote resilience among teachers: A systematic review of the literature. *International Journal of School & Educational Psychology*, 8(2), 131–146. 10.1080/21683603.2020.1734125

Kant, I. (2006). *Kritik der Urteilskraft*. Felix Meiner Verlag.

Karcher, M. J. (2005). The effects of developmental mentoring and high school mentors' attendance on their younger mentees' self-esteem, social skills, and connectedness. *Psychology in the Schools*, 42(1), 65–77. 10.1002/pits.20025

Katsantonis, I. G. (2019). Investigation of the impact of school climate and teachers' self-efficacy on job satisfaction: A cross-cultural approach. *European Journal of Investigation in Health, Psychology and Education*, 10(1), 119–133. 10.3390/ejihpe10010011134542474

Katsarou, D. (2019). Emotional Intelligence of adult educators of second chance schools: A pilot study on job satisfaction. *Proceedings of 2nd International Congress on Management of Educational Units*, 60-66.

Katsarou, D., Panda, D., Konstantinidou, E., & Zisi, B. (2015). The Emotional Intelligence of Teachers of Second Chance Schools. *Educational Circle*, 3(2), 69–81.

Keefer, K., Parker, J., & Saklofske, D. H. (2018). *Emotional Intelligence in Education: Integrating Research with Practice*. Springer. 10.1007/978-3-319-90633-1

Kefallinou, A., Symeonidou, S., & Meijer, C. J. (2020). Understanding the value of inclusive education and its implementation: A review of the literature. *Prospects*, 49(3), 135–152. 10.1007/s11125-020-09500-2

Kehoe, M., Bourke-Taylor, H., & Broderick, D. (2018). Developing student social skills using restorative practices: A new framework called HEART. *Social Psychology of Education*, 21(1), 189–207. 10.1007/s11218-017-9402-1

Kelley, T. R., Knowles, J. G., Holland, J. D., & Han, J. (2020). Increasing high school teachers' self-efficacy for integrated STEM instruction through a collaborative community of practice. *International Journal of STEM Education*, 7(14), 14. Advance online publication. 10.1186/s40594-020-00211-w

Kendall, L. W. (1990). *Mimesis as make-believe*. Harvard University Press.

Keng, S. L., Smoski, M. J., & Robins, C. J. (2011). Effects of mindfulness on psychological health: A review of empirical studies. *Clinical Psychology Review*, 31(6), 1041–1056. 10.1016/j.cpr.2011.04.00621802619

Kentucky Department of Education. (2022). School Climate and Educator Well-Being in Kentucky. Retrieved May 22, 2024 from https://files.eric.ed.gov/fulltext/ED618565.pdf

Keogh, B. K., & Weisner, T. (1993). An ecocultural perspective on risk and protective factors in children's development: Implications for learning disabilities. *Learning Disabilities Research & Practice*, 8(l), 3–10.

Kern, M. L., Adler, A., Waters, L. E., & White, M. A. (2015). Measuring whole-school well-being in students and staff. *Evidence-based approaches in positive education: Implementing a strategic framework for well-being in schools*, 65-91. 10.1007/978-94-017-9667-5_4

Kern, M. L., Waters, L. E., Adler, A., & White, M. A. (2015). A multidimensional approach to measuring well-being in students: Application of the PERMA framework. *The Journal of Positive Psychology*, 10(3), 262–271. 10.1080/17439760.2014.93696225745508

Kern, M. L., Williams, P., Spong, C., Colla, R., Sharma, K., Downie, A., Taylor, J. A., Sharp, S., Siokou, C., & Oades, L. G. (2020). Systems informed positive psychology. *The Journal of Positive Psychology*, 15(6), 705–715. 10.1080/17439760.2019.1639799

Keyes, C. L. (2002). The mental health continuum: From languishing to flourishing in life. *Journal of Health and Social Behavior*, 43(2), 207–222. 10.2307/309019712096700

Keyes, C. L. (2006). Mental health in adolescence: Is America's youth flourishing? *The American Journal of Orthopsychiatry*, 76(3), 395–402. 10.1037/0002-9432.76.3.39516981819

Keyes, C. L., & Haidt, J. (2003). *Flourishing: Positive psychology and the life well-lived.* American Psychological Association. 10.1037/10594-000

Khany, R., & Tazik, K. (2016). On the relationship between psychological empowerment, trust, and Iranian EFL teachers' job satisfaction: The case of secondary school teachers. *Journal of Career Assessment*, 24(1), 112–129. 10.1177/1069072714565362

Khaw, D., & Kern, M. (2014). A cross-cultural comparison of the PERMA model of well-being. *Undergraduate Journal of Psychology at Berkeley. University of California., 8*(1), 10–23.

Kidger, J., Araya, R., Donovan, J., & Gunnell, D. (2012). The effect of the school environment on the emotional health of adolescents: A systematic review. *Pediatrics*, 129(5), 925–949. 10.1542/peds.2011-224822473374

Kieff, J., & Casbergue, R. (2017). *Playful learning & teaching: The integration of play in kindergarten and primary school.* Gutenberg.

Kielblock, S., & Woodcock, S. (2023). Who's included and Who's not? An analysis of instruments that measure teachers' attitudes towards inclusive education. *Teaching and Teacher Education*, 122(2), 103922. 10.1016/j.tate.2022.103922

King, L., Jolicouer-Martineau, A., Laplante, D. P., Szekely, E., Levitan, R., & Wazana, A. (2020). Measuring resilience in children: A review of recent literature and recommendations for future research. *Current Opinion in Psychiatry*, 34(1), 10–21. 10.1097/YCO.000000000000066333105167

Klassen, R. M., & Lynch, S. L. (2007). Self-efficacy from the perspective of adolescents with learning disabilities and their specialist teachers. *Journal of Learning Disabilities*, 40, 94–507. 10.1177/00222194070400060201

Klassen, R., & Tze, V. M. C. (2014). Teachers' self-efficacy, personality, and teaching effectiveness: A meta-analysis. *Educational Research Review*, 12, 59–76. 10.1016/j.edurev.2014.06.001

Knight, C., & Crick, T. (2022). Inclusive Education in Wales: Interpreting discourses of values and practice using critical policy analysis. *ECNU Review of Education*, 5(2), 258–283. 10.1177/20965311211039858

Knight, D. S., & Duncheon, J. C. (2019). Broadening conceptions of a "college-going culture": The role of high school climate factors in college enrollment and persistence. *Policy Futures in Education*, 18(2), 314–340. 10.1177/1478210319860987

Kõiv, K., Liik, K., & Heidmets, M. (2019). School leadership, teacher's psychological empowerment and work-related outcomes. *International Journal of Educational Management*, 33(7), 1501–1514. 10.1108/IJEM-08-2018-0232

Kolb, B., & Whishaw, I. Q. (2009). Fundamentals of Human Neuropsychology. *Worth.*

Konold, T., Cornell, D., Jia, Y., & Malone, M. (2018). School climate, student engagement, and academic achievement: A latent variable, multilevel multi-informant examination. *AERA Open*, 4(4). 10.1177/2332858418815661

Kougioumtzis, G. A., & Louka, D. (2021). Advocacy and Teacher Mentoring. In Khosrow-Pour, M. (Ed.), *Research Anthology on Instilling Social Justice in the Classroom* (pp. 138–160). IGI Global. 10.4018/978-1-7998-7706-6.ch010

Kougioumtzis, G. A., Sofologi, M., Fella, A., Kaliotsou, I., Koundourou, C., Bonti, E., & Papantoniou, G. (2021a). Specific Learning Disabilities-Implementation of an Intervention Program: An Analysis of a Case Study. In AuCoin, D. (Ed.), *Building Integrated Collaborative Relationships for Inclusive Learning Settings* (pp. 161–180). IGI Global. 10.4018/978-1-7998-6816-3.ch007

Kougioumtzis, G. A., Verykiou, J., & Mallouchou, A. (2021b). Bullying and Advocacy. In Khosrow-Pour, M. (Ed.), *Research Anthology on School Shootings, Peer Victimization, and Solutions for Building Safer Educational Institutions* (pp. 1–33). IGI Global. 10.4018/978-1-7998-5360-2.ch001

Kovich, M. K., Simpson, V. L., Foli, K. J., Hass, Z., & Phillips, R. G. (2023). Application of the PERMA Model of Well-being in Undergraduate Students. *International Journal of Community Well-being*, 6(1), 1–20. 10.1007/s42413-022-00184-436320595

Koziori, K. B., & Alexandropoulos, G. (2020). The impact of the school climate on professional satisfaction of primary education teachers. *Research in Education*, 9(1), 35–57.

Kraft, M. A., & Falken, G. T. (2020). Why School Climate Matters for Teachers and Students. *State Education Standard*, 20(2), 33–35.

Kristjánsson, K. (2012). Positive psychology and positive education: Old wine in new bottles? *Educational Psychologist*, 47(2), 86–105. 10.1080/00461520.2011.610678

Kruschke, J. K. (2003). Attention in learning. *Current Directions in Psychological Science*, 12(5), 171–175. 10.1111/1467-8721.01254

Kun, Á., Balogh, P., & Krasz, K. G. (2016). Development of the Work-Related Well-Being Questionnaire Based on Seligman's PERMA Model. *Periodica Polytechnica Social and Management Sciences*, 25(1), 56. 10.3311/PPso.9326

Kun, A., & Gadanecz, P. (2022). Workplace happiness, well-being and their relationship with psychological capital: A study of Hungarian teachers. *Current Psychology (New Brunswick, N.J.)*, 41(1), 185–199. 10.1007/s12144-019-00550-0

Kundu, S. C., & Kumar, S. (2017). Effects of psychological empowerment on firm's performance: Mediation of affective commitment. *Journal of Organisation and Human Behaviour*, 6(1-2), 41–53.

Kuperminc, G. P., Thomason, J., DiMeo, M., & Broomfield-Massey, K. (2011). Cool Girls, Inc.: Promoting the positive development of urban preadolescent and early adolescent girls. *The Journal of Primary Prevention*, 32(3-4), 171–183. 10.1007/s10935-011-0243-y21800162

Kutsyuruba, B., Klinger, D. A., & Hussain, A. (2015). Relationships among school climate, school safety, and student achievement and well-being: A review of the literature. *Review of Education*, 3(2), 103–135. 10.1002/rev3.3043

Κοτσαμπόπουλος, Π., & Γαλανάκη, Ε. (2020). Η προαγωγή της ψυχικής υγείας των μαθητών στα πλαίσια της παιδαγωγικής Waldorf. *Παιδαγωγική επιθεώρηση, 66.*

La Paro, K. M., Hamre, B. K., Locasale-Crouch, J., Pianta, R. C., Bryant, D., Early, D., & Burchinal, M. (2009). Quality in kindergarten classrooms: Observational evidence for the need to increase children's learning opportunities in early education classrooms. *Early Education and Development*, 20(4), 657–692. 10.1080/10409280802541965

La Salle, T. P., Rocha-Neves, J., Jimerson, S., Di Sano, S., Martinsone, B., Majercakova Albertova, S., Gajdošová, E., Baye, A., Deltour, C., Martinelli, V., Raykov, M., Hatzichristou, C., Palikara, O., Szabó, É., Arlauskaite, Z., Athanasiou, D., Brown-Earle, O., Casale, G., Lampropoulou, A., & Zvyagintsev, R. (2021). A multinational study exploring adolescent perception of school climate and mental health. *School Psychology*, 36(3), 155–166. 10.1037/spq000043034014698

La Velle, L. (2020). Teacher education approaching crisis: External and internal factors. *Journal of Education for Teaching*, 46(3), 259–262. 10.1080/02607476.2020.1768692

Lackaye, T. D., & Margalit, M. (2006). Comparisons of achievement, effort, and self-perceptions among students with learning disabilities and their peers from different achievement groups. *Journal of Learning Disabilities*, 39(5), 432–446. 10.1177/0022219406039005050117004675

Lai, M. K., Leung, C., Kwok, S. Y., Hui, A. N., Lo, H. H., Leung, J. T., & Tam, C. H. (2018). A multidimensional PERMA-H positive education model, general satisfaction of school life, and character strengths use in Hong Kong senior primary school students: Confirmatory factor analysis and path analysis using the APASO-II. *Frontiers in Psychology*, 9, 1090. 10.3389/fpsyg.2018.0109030008690

Laininen, E. (2019). Transforming our worldview towards a sustainable future. In J. Cook (Ed.), Sustainability, human well-being, and the future of education (pp.161-200). Palgrave Macmillan. 10.1007/978-3-319-78580-6_5

Lakioti, A. (2011). The concept of mental resilience. In Stalikas, A., & Mitskidou, P. (Eds.), *Introduction to Positive Psychology* (pp. 61–70). Topos.

Lambert D'raven, L., & Pasha-Zaidi, N. (2016). Using the PERMA Model in the United Arab Emirates. *Social Indicators Research*, 125(3), 905–933. 10.1007/s11205-015-0866-0

Langer, E. J. (1989). *Mindfulness: choice and control in everyday life*. Harper Collins.

Lantieri, L. (2009). *Inteligencia Emocional Infantil Y Juvenil*. Aguilar. 10.1037/a0034755

LaRusso, M., & Selman, R. (2011). Early adolescent health risk behaviors, conflict resolution strategies, and school climate. *Journal of Applied Developmental Psychology*, 32(6), 354–362. 10.1016/j.appdev.2011.05.003

Lavy, V. (2015). Do differences in schools' instruction time explain international achievement gaps? Evidence from developed and developing countries. *Economic Journal (London)*, 125(588), F397–F424. 10.1111/ecoj.12233

Law, K. S., Wong, C. S., Huang, G. H., & Li, X. (2008). The effects of emotional intelligence on job performance and life satisfaction for the research and development scientists in China. *Asia Pacific Journal of Management*, 25(1), 51–69. 10.1007/s10490-007-9062-3

Lazarus, R. S. (1999). *Stress and emotion: A new synthesis*. Springer.

Le Cornu, R. (2013). Building Early Career Teacher Resilience: The Role of Relationships. *The Australian Journal of Teacher Education*, 38(4), 1–16. 10.14221/ajte.2013v38n4.4

Lee, J. H., Nam, S. K., Kim, A. R., Young, M. L., & Lee, S. M. (2013). Resilience: A meta-analytic approach. *Journal of Counseling and Development*, 91(3), 269–279. 10.1002/j.1556-6676.2013.00095.x

Lee, J., Krause, A. E., & Davidson, J. W. (2017). The PERMA well-being model and music facilitation practice: Preliminary documentation for well-being through music provision in Australian schools. *Research Studies in Music Education*, 39(1), 73–89. 10.1177/1321103X17703131

Lee, M., & Louis, K. S. (2019). Mapping a strong school culture and linking it to sustainable school improvement. *Teaching and Teacher Education*, 81, 84–96. 10.1016/j.tate.2019.02.001

Lee, P. C., & Stewart, D. E. (2013). Does a Socio-Ecological School Model Promote Resilience in Primary Schools? *The Journal of School Health*, 83(11), 795–804. 10.1111/josh.1209624138350

Leichtentritt, J., & Shechtman, Z. (2010). Children with and without learning disabilities: A comparison of processes and outcomes following group counseling. *Journal of Learning Disabilities*, 43(2), 169–17. 10.1177/002221940934500819890074

Lei, H., Cui, Y., & Zhou, W. (2018). Relationships between student engagement and academic achievement: A meta-analysis. *Social Behavior and Personality*, 46(3), 517–528. 10.2224/sbp.7054

Lemberger-Truelove, M. E., Carbonneau, K. J., Atencio, D. J., Zieher, A. K., & Palacios, A. F. (2018). Self-regulatory growth effects for young children participating in a combined social and emotional learning and mindfulness-based intervention. *Journal of Counseling and Development*, 96(3), 289–302. 10.1002/jcad.12203

Leonard, S., Stiles, A. A., & Gudino, O. G. (2016). School engagement of youth investigated by child welfare services: Associations with academic achievement and mental health. *School Mental Health*, 8(3), 386–398. 10.1007/s12310-016-9186-z

Leondari, A. (1993). Comparability of self-concept among normal achievers, low achievers and children with learning difficulties. *Educational Studies*, 19(3), 357–371. 10.1080/0305569930190309

Lerner, R. M., Von Eye, A., Lerner, J. V., Lewin-Bizan, S., & Bowers, E. P. (2010). Special Issue Introduction: The Meaning and Measurement of Thriving: A View of the Issues. *Journal of Youth and Adolescence*, 39(7), 707–719. 10.1007/s10964-010-9531-820387108

Lester, L., & Cross, D. (2015). The relationship between school climate and mental and emotional wellbeing over the transition from primary to secondary school. *Psychology of Well-Being*, 5(9), 1–15. 10.1186/s13612-015-0037-826516619

Leuner, B. (1966). Emotional intelligence and emancipation. A psychodynamic study on women. *Praxis der Kinderpsychologie und Kinderpsychiatrie*, 1, 12–15.5975008

Leuner, H. (1966). Emotional Intelligence and Emancipation. A Psychodynamic Study on Women. *Prax Kinder Psychology*, 15, 196–203.5975008

Liebowitz, D. D., & Porter, L. (2019). The effect of principal behaviors on student, teacher, and school outcomes: A systematic review and meta-analysis of the empirical literature. *Review of Educational Research*, 89(5), 785–827. 10.3102/0034654319866133

Lin, Y. W., & Bratton, S. C. (2015). A meta-analytic review of child-centered play therapy approaches. *Journal of Counseling & Development, 93*(1), 45-58.

Linh, N. T. N. (2024). Strategies for developing emotional intelligence in Generation Z students in higher education in Ho Chi Minh City. *Educational Administration: Theory and Practice*, 30(5), 2517–2522.

Liu, R., & Chiang, Y. L. (2019). Who is more motivated to learn? The roles of family background and teacher-student interaction in motivating student learning. *The Journal of Chinese Sociology*, 6(1), 1–17. 10.1186/s40711-019-0095-z

Li, Z. (2016). Psychological empowerment on social media: Who are the empowered users? *Public Relations Review*, 42(1), 49–59. 10.1016/j.pubrev.2015.09.001

Lloyd, M. (2018). Domestic violence and education: Examining the impact of domestic violence on young children, children, and young people and the potential role of schools. *Frontiers in Psychology*, 9, 396402. 10.3389/fpsyg.2018.0209430483170

Loizou, E. (2021). Small blocks and building materials. *The Ultimate Handbook of Developmentally Appropriate Toys,* 49-60.

Loizou, E., & Loizou, E. K. (2022). Creative play and the role of the teacher through the cultural-historical activity theory framework. *International Journal of Early Years Education*, 30(3), 527–541. 10.1080/09669760.2022.2065248

Loizou, E., & Olymbiou, M. (2023). Constructive play: Exploring pre-service early childhood teachers' play involvement. *Journal of Early Childhood Research*, 1476718X231210642. Advance online publication. 10.1177/1476718X231210642

Lomas, T. (2015). Positive social psychology: A multilevel inquiry into sociocultural well-being initiatives. *Psychology, Public Policy, and Law*, 21(3), 338–347. 10.1037/law0000051

Lomas, T., Waters, L., Williams, P., Oades, L. G., & Kern, M. L. (2021). Third wave positive psychology: Broadening towards complexity. *The Journal of Positive Psychology*, 16(5), 660–674. 10.1080/17439760.2020.1805501

Lombardi, E., Traficante, D., Bettoni, R., Offredi, I., Giorgetti, M., & Vernice, M. (2019). The impact of school climate on well-being experience and school engagement: A study with high-school students. *Frontiers in Psychology*, 10, 10. 10.3389/fpsyg.2019.0248231749747

Longaretti, L. (2011). *Re−conceptualising Educational Resilience: Giving Voice to Young People's Perspectives* (Doctor of Philosophy PhD). University of Melbourne.

Longobardi, C., Prino, L. E., Marengo, D., & Settanni, M. (2016). Student-teacher relationships as a protective factor for school adjustment during the transition from middle to high school. *Frontiers in Psychology*, 7, 1988. 10.3389/fpsyg.2016.0198828066305

Longobardi, C., Settanni, M., Berchiatti, M., Mastrokoukou, S., & Marengo, D. (2023). Teachers' sentiment about physical appearance of primary school students: Associations with student–teacher relationship quality and student popularity among classroom peers. *Social Psychology of Education*, 26(2), 383–403. 10.1007/s11218-022-09749-9

Longobardi, C., Settanni, M., Lin, S., & Fabris, M. A. (2021). Student–teacher relationship quality and prosocial behaviour: The mediating role of academic achievement and a positive attitude towards school. *The British Journal of Educational Psychology*, 91(2), 547–562. 10.1111/bjep.1237832920835

Lopes, P. N., Brackett, M. A., Nezlek, J. B., Schütz, A., Sellin, I., & Salovey, P. (2004). Emotional intelligence and social Interaction. *Personality and Social Psychology Bulletin*, 30(8), 1018–1034. 10.1177/014616720426476215257786

Lopes, P. N., Grewal, D., Kadis, J., Gall, M., & Salovey, P. (2006). Evidence that emotional intelligence is related to job performance and affect and attitudes at work. *Psicothema*, 18, 132–138.17295970

Lopes, P. N., Salovey, P., & Straus, R. (2003). Emotional intelligence personality and the perceived quality of social relationships. *Personality and Individual Differences*, 35(3), 641–658. 10.1016/S0191-8869(02)00242-8

Lopez, S. J., & Louis, M. C. (2009). The Principles of Strengths-Based Education. *Journal of College and Character*, 10(4), 1–8. 10.2202/1940-1639.1041

Low, G., & Nelson, D. (2005). Emotional Intelligence: The Role of Transformative Learning in Academic Excellence. *Texas Study Magazine*.http://www.unic.ac.cy/media/Research/Photos/parispapergreek.pdf

Lowry-Webster, H. M., Barrett, P. M., & Dadds, M. R. (2001). A universal prevention trial of anxiety and depressive symptomatology in childhood: Preliminary data from an Australian study. *Behaviour Change*, 18(1), 36–50. 10.1375/bech.18.1.36

Lundqvist, C., & Kenttä, G. (2010). Positive Emotions Are Not Simply the Absence of the Negative Ones: Development and Validation of the Emotional Recovery Questionnaire (EmRecQ). *The Sport Psychologist*, 24(4), 468–488. 10.1123/tsp.24.4.468

Luthar, S. S. (1991). Vulnerability and resilience: A study of high-risk adolescents. *Child Development*, 62(3), 600–616. 10.2307/11311341914628

Luthar, S. S. (2006). Resilience in development: A synthesis of research across five decades. In Cicchetti, D., & Cohen, D. J. (Eds.), Developmental psychopathology: Vol. 3. *Risk, disorder, and adaptation* (2nd ed., pp. 739–795). Wiley.

Luthar, S. S., & Cicchetti, D. (2001). The construct of resilience: Implications for interventions and social policies. *Development and Psychopathology*, 12(4), 857–885. 10.1017/S0954579400004156 11202047

Luthar, S. S., Cicchetti, D., & Becker, B. (2000). The construct of resilience: A critical evaluation and guidelines for future work. *Child Development*, 71(3), 543–562. 10.1111/1467-8624.00164 10953923

Luthar, S. S., & Zigler, E. (1991). Vulnerability and competence: A review of the research on resilience in childhood. *The American Journal of Orthopsychiatry*, 61(1), 6–22. 10.1037/h0079218 2006679

MacCann, C., Jiang, Y., Brown, L. E., Double, K. S., Bucich, M., & Minbashian, A. (2020). Emotional intelligence predicts academic performance: A meta-analysis. *Psychological Bulletin*, 146(2), 150–186. 10.1037/bul0000219 31829667

MacDonald, E., & Shirley, D. (2009). *The Mindful Teacher*. Teachers College Press.

Mackintosh, N. J. (1988). Approaches to the study of animal intelligence. *British Journal of Psychology*, 79(4), 509–525. 10.1111/j.2044-8295.1988.tb02749.x

MacSuga-Gage, A. S., Simonsen, B., & Briere, D. E. (2012). Effective teaching practices: Effective teaching practices that promote a positive classroom environment. *Beyond Behavior*, 22(1), 14–22. 10.1177/107429561202200104

Madaus, G., & Russell, M. (2010). Paradoxes of high-stakes testing. *Journal of Education*, 190(1-2), 21–30. 10.1177/0022057410190001-205

Madden, W., Green, S., & Grant, A. M. (2011). A pilot study evaluating strengths-based coaching for primary school students: Enhancing engagement and hope. *International Coaching Psychology Review*, 6(1), 71–83. 10.53841/bpsicpr.2011.6.1.71

Mahomed, N. J. B., Johari, K. S. K., & Mahmud, M. I. (2019). Coping strategies and psychological well-being of guidance and counselling teachers in schools. *Creative Education*, 10(12), 3028–3040. 10.4236/ce.2019.1012227

Main, P. (2022, February 9). Growth Mindset: A teacher's guide. Retrieved from https://www.structural-learning.com/post/growth-mindset-a-teachers-guide

Malaguti, E. (2005). *Educarsi alla resilienza*. Centro Studi Erickson.

Malekian, F., & Askari, B. (2013). Investigating the effect of multi-sensory games on decrease of male students' dyslexia (Based on Goodman Theory) specified for elementary school second grade in Aligudarz city. *Procedia: Social and Behavioral Sciences*, 82, 796–802. 10.1016/j.sbspro.2013.06.351

Malinen, O. P., & Savolainen, H. (2016). The Effect of Perceived School Climate and Teacher Efficacy in Behavior Management on Job Satisfaction and Burnout: A Longitudinal Study. *Teaching and Teacher Education*, 60(1), 144–152. 10.1016/j.tate.2016.08.012

Malisiova, A., Kougioumtzis, G. A., Tsitsas, G., Koundourou, C., & Mitraras, A. (2023). Implementing Inclusive Education in Mixed-Ability Classrooms by Employing Differentiated Instruction. In Sofologi, M., Kougioumtzis, G., & Koundourou, C. (Eds.), *Perspectives of Cognitive, Psychosocial, and Learning Difficulties From Childhood to Adulthood: Practical Counseling Strategies* (pp. 155–178). IGI Global. 10.4018/978-1-6684-8203-2.ch009

Mandelli, L., Petrelli, C., & Serretti, A. (2015). The role of specific early trauma in adult depression: A meta-analysis of published literature. Childhood trauma and adult depression. *European psychiatry: the journal of the Association of European Psychiatrists, 30*(6), 665–680. https://doi.org/10.1016/j.eurpsy.2015.04.007

Manla, V. H. (2021). School climate: Its impact on teachers' commitment and school performance. *Journal of World Englishes and Educational Practices*, 3(2), 21–35. 10.32996/jweep.2021.3.2.3

Manna, S. (2013*). Play and its role in child development.* Unpublished Thesis. Faculty of Humanities and Social Sciences. Department of Preschool Education. University of Patras

Mann, M. J., Kristjansson, A. L., Smith, M. L., & Sigfusdottir, I. D. (2016). The Influence of negative life events and problem behavior on grades in early adolescence: Pathways to academic risk in the middle grades. *RMLE Online: Research in Middle Level Education*, 39(10), 1–13. 10.1080/19404476.2016.1244402

Mardell, B., Ryan, J., Krechevsky, M., Baker, M., Schulz, T. S., & Liu-Constant, Y. (2023). *A pedagogy of play: Supporting playful learning in classrooms and schools. Cambridge*. Project Zero.

Margalit, M. (2004). Second-Generation Research on Resilience: Social Emotional Aspects of Children with Learning Disabilities. *Learning Disabilities Research & Practice*, 19(1), 45–48. 10.1111/j.1540-5826.2004.00088.x

Margolis, E. (2001). *The Hidden Curriculum in Higher Education* (1st ed.). Routledge., 10.4324/9780203901854

Mariani, M., Webb, L., Villares, E., & Brigman, G. (2015). Effect of Participation in Student Success Skills on Prosocial and Bullying Behavior. *The Professional Counselor*, 5(3), 341–353. 10.15241/mm.5.3.341

Marinette, B., & Hui, X. (2021). School environment and teachers job satisfaction. *European Journal of Education Studies*, 8(7), 16–43.

Martin, A. J., & Dowson, M. (2009). Interpersonal relationships, motivation, engagement, and achievement: Yields for theory, current issues, and educational practice. *Review of Educational Research*, 79(1), 327–365. 10.3102/0034654308325583

Martin, A. J., Ginns, P., Brackett, M. A., Malmberg, L. E., & Hall, J. (2013). Academic buoyancy and psychological risk: Exploring reciprocal relationships. *Learning and Individual Differences*, 27, 128–133. 10.1016/j.lindif.2013.06.006

Martinsone, B., DiSano, S., D'Elia, P., & LaSalle-Finley, T. (2023). A conceptual framework for sustainable promotion of a positive school climate: Context, challenges, and solutions. *Journal of Teacher Education for Sustainability*, 25(1), 64–85. 10.2478/jtes-2023-0005

Mas-Expósito, L., Krieger, V., Amador-Campos, J. A., Casañas, R., & Lalucat-Jo, L. (2022). Pocket restorative practice approaches to foster peer-based relationships and positive development in schools. *Education Sciences*, 12(12), 880. 10.3390/educsci12120880

Mashburn, A. J., Pianta, R. C., Hamre, B. K., Downer, J. T., Barbarin, O. A., Bryant, D., Burchinal, M., Early, D. M., & Howes, C. (2008). Measures of classroom quality in prekindergarten and children's development of academic, language, and social skills. *Child Development*, 79(3), 732–749. 10.1111/j.1467-8624.2008.01154.x18489424

Masten, A. S., & Wright, M. (2009). Resilience over the lifespan: Developmental perspectives on resistance, recovery, and transformation. In J. W. Reich, A. J. Zautra, & J. S. Hall (Eds.), *Handbook of adult resilience* (pp. 213– 237). New York: Guilford Press.

Masten, A. S. (2001). Ordinary magic: Resilience processes in development. *The American Psychologist*, 56(3), 227–238. 10.1037/0003-066X.56.3.22711315249

Masten, A. S. (2006a). Developmental psychopathology: Pathways to the future. *International Journal of Behavioral Development*, 31(1), 47–54. 10.1177/0165025406059974

Masten, A. S. (2006b). Promoting resilience in development: A general framework for systems of care. In Flynn, R. J., Dudding, P., & Barber, J. G. (Eds.), *Promoting resilience in child welfare* (pp. 3–17). University of Ottawa Press.

Masten, A. S. (2007). Resilience in developing systems: Progress and promise as the fourth wave rises. *Development and Psychopathology*, 19(3), 921–930. 10.1017/S0954579407000442177059 08

Masten, A. S. (2011 in press). Risk and resilience in development. In Zelazo, P. D. (Ed.), *Oxford handbook of developmental psychology*. Oxford University Press.

Masten, A. S. (2011). Resilience in children threatened by extreme adversity: Frameworks for research, practice, and translational synergy. *Development and Psychopathology*, 23(2), 493–506. 10.1017/S0954579411000198237866 91

Masten, A. S. (2014a). Global perspectives on resilience in children and youth. *Child Development*, 85(1), 6–20. 10.1111/cdev.1220524341286

Masten, A. S., Best, K. M., & Garmezy, N. (1990). Resilience and development: Contributions from the study of children who overcome adversity. *Development and Psychopathology*, 2(4), 425–444. 10.1017/S0954579400005812

Masten, A. S., & Coatsworth, J. D. (1998). The development of competence in favorable and unfavorable environments: Lessons from successful children. *The American Psychologist*, 53(2), 205–220. 10.1037/0003-066X.53.2.2059491748

Masten, A. S., & Curtis, W. J. (2000). Integrating competence and psychopathology: Pathways toward a comprehensive science of adaptation in development. *Development and Psychopathology*, 12(3), 529–550. 10.1017/S095457940000314X11014751

Masten, A. S., & Gewirtz, A. H. (2008). Vulnerability and resilience in early child development. In McCartney, K., & Phillips, D. A. (Eds.), *Handbook of early childhood development* (pp. 22–43). Blackwell Publishing.

Masten, A. S., Hubbard, J. J., Gest, S. D., Tellegen, A., Garmezy, N., & Ramirez, M. (1999). Competence in the context of adversity: Pathways to resilience and maladaptation from childhood to late adolescence. *Development and Psychopathology*, 11(1), 143–169. 10.1017/S095457949900199610208360

Masten, A. S., Monn, A. R., & Supkoff, L. M. (2011). *Resilience in children and adolescents*. Published by Cambridge University Press. 10.1017/CBO9780511994791.009

Masten, A. S., & Osofsky, J. (2010). Disasters and the impact on child development: Introduction to the special section. *Child Development*, 81(4), 1029–1039. 10.1111/j.1467-8624.2010.01452.x20636680

Masten, A. S., & Shafer, A. (2006). How families matter in child development: Reflections from research on risk and resilience. In Clarke-Stewart, A., & Dunn, J. (Eds.), *Families count: Effects on child and adolescent development* (pp. 5–25). Cambridge University Press. 10.1017/CBO9780511616259.002

Matiz, A., Fabbro, F., Paschetto, A., Cantone, D., Paolone, A. R., & Crescentini, C. (2020). Positive Impact of Mindfulness Meditation on Mental Health of Female Teachers during the COVID-19 Outbreak in Italy. *International Journal of Environmental Research and Public Health*, 17(18), 6450. 10.3390/ijerph1718645032899739

Matthews, G., Zeidner, M., & Roberts, R. (2002). *Emotional Intelligence: Science and myth*. The MIT Press. 10.7551/mitpress/2704.001.0001

Mattison, E., & Aber, M. S. (2007). Closing the achievement gap: The association of racial climate with achievement and behavioral outcomes. *American Journal of Community Psychology*, 40(1-2), 1–12. 10.1007/s10464-007-9128-x17587175

Mavroveli, S., Petrides, K. V., Sangareau, Y., & Furnham, A. (2009). Exploring the relationships between trait emotional intelligence and objective socio-emotional outcomes in childhood. *The British Journal of Educational Psychology*, 79(2), 259–272. 10.1348/000709908X36884818950549

Maxwell, S., Reynolds, K. J., Lee, E., Subasic, E., & Bromhead, D. (2017). The impact of school climate and school identification on academic achievement: Multilevel modeling with student and teacher data. *Frontiers in Psychology*, 8, 8. 10.3389/fpsyg.2017.0206929259564

Mayer, J. D., & Salovey, P. (1997). What is emotional intelligence? In Salovey, P., & Sluyter, D. (Eds.), *Emotional Development and Emotional Intelligence: Implications for Educators* (pp. 3–31). Basic Books.

Mayer, J. D., Salovey, P., & Caruso, D. R. (2002). Mayor- Salovey- Caruso Emotional Intelligence Test (MSCEIT): User's manual. *Personality and Social Psychology Bulletin*, 30, 1018–1034.

Mayer, J. D., Salovey, P., & Caruso, D. R. (2007). *Mayer-Salovey-Caruso Emotional Intelligence Test (MSCEIT) Item Booklet*. MHS Publishers.

McColl-Kennedy, J. R., & Anderson, R. D. (2002). Impact of leadership style and emotions on subordinate performance. *The Leadership Quarterly*, 13(5), 545–559. 10.1016/S1048-9843(02)00143-1

McCubbin, M. A., & McCubbin, H. I. (1996). Resiliency in families: A conceptual model of family adjustment and adaptation in response to stress and crises. In McCubbin, H. I., Thompson, A. I., & McCubbin, M. A. (Eds.), *Family assessment: Resiliency, coping and adaptation: Inventories for research and practice* (pp. 1–64). University of Wisconsin.

McGiboney, G. W. (2023). *The psychology of school climate*. Cambridge Scholars Publishing.

McGrath, H. (2009). An evidence-based positive psychology approach to student well-being. *Paper presented at theFirst Australia Positive Psychology in Education Symposium*. University of Sydney.

McInerney, D. M., Ganotice, F. A.Jr, King, R. B., Marsh, H. W., & Morin, A. J. (2015). Exploring commitment and turnover intentions among teachers: What we can learn from Hong Kong teachers. *Teaching and Teacher Education*, 52, 11–23. 10.1016/j.tate.2015.08.004

McLeskey, J., Waldron, N. L., & Redd, L. (2014). A case study of a highly effective, inclusive elementary school. *The Journal of Special Education*, 48(1), 59–70. 10.1177/0022466912440455

McMillan, J. H., & Reed, D. F. (1994). At-risk students and resiliency: Factors contributing to academic success. *The Clearing House: A Journal of Educational Strategies, Issues and Ideas*, 67(3), 137–140. 10.1080/00098655.1994.9956043

McNeely, C. A., Nonnemaker, J. M., & Blum, R. W. (2002). Promoting School Connectedness: Evidence from the National Longitudinal Study of Adolescent Health. *The Journal of School Health*, 72(4), 138–146. 10.1111/j.1746-1561.2002.tb06533.x12029810

Megari, K., Sofologi, M., Kougioumtzis, G. A., Thomaidou, E., Thomaidis, G., Katsarou, D., Yotsidi, V., & Theodoratou, M. (2024). Neurocognitive and psycho-emotional profile of children with disabilities. *Applied Neuropsychology. Child*, 1–6. 10.1080/21622965.2024.230478138574392

Meiklejohn, J., Phillips, C., Freedman, M. L., Griffin, M. L., Biegel, G., Roach, A., Frank, J., Burke, C., Pinger, L., Soloway, G., Isberg, R., Sibinga, E., Grossman, L., & Saltzman, A. (2012). Integrating mindfulness training into K-12 education: Fostering the resilience of teachers and students. *Mindfulness*, 3(4), 291–307. 10.1007/s12671-012-0094-5

Memedovic, S., Grisham, J. R., Denson, T. F., & Moulds, M. L. (2010). The effects of trait reappraisal and suppression on anger and blood pressure in response to provocation. *Journal of Research in Personality*, 44(4), 540–543. 10.1016/j.jrp.2010.05.002

Mendelson, T., Greenberg, M. T., Dariotis, J. K., Gould, L. F., Rhoades, B. L., & Leaf, P. J. (2010). Feasibility and preliminary outcomes of a school-based mindfulness intervention for urban youth. *Journal of Abnormal Child Psychology*, 38(7), 985–994. 10.1007/s10802-010-9418-x20440550

Méndez, I., Martínez-Ramón, J. P., Ruiz-Esteban, C., & García-Fernández, J. M. (2020). Latent Profiles of Burnout, Self-Esteem and Depressive Symptomatology among Teachers. *International Journal of Environmental Research and Public Health*, 17(18), 6760. 10.3390/ijerph1718676032948075

Meng, Y. (2021). Fostering EFL/ESL students' state motivation: The role of teacher-student rapport. *Frontiers in Psychology*, 12, 754797. 10.3389/fpsyg.2021.75479734589039

Mergendoller, J. R., Maxwell, N. L., & Bellisimo, Y. (2006). The effectiveness of problem-based instruction: A comparative study of instructional methods and student characteristics. *The Interdisciplinary Journal of Problem-Based Learning*, 1(2), 49–69. 10.7771/1541-5015.1026

Mérida-López, S., & Extremera, N. (2017). Emotional intelligence and teacher burnout: A systematic review. *International Journal of Educational Research*, 85, 121–130. 10.1016/j.ijer.2017.07.006

Messiou, K. (2017). Research in the field of inclusive education: Time for a rethink? *International Journal of Inclusive Education*, 21(2), 146–159. 10.1080/13603116.2016.1223184

Mestre, J. M., Turanzas, J., García-Gómez, M., Guerra, J., Cordon, J. R., De LaTorre, G. G., & Lopez-Ramos, V. M. (2019). Do trait emotional intelligence and dispositional mindfulness have a complementary effect on the children's and adolescents' emotional states? *Frontiers in Psychology*, 10, 2817. 10.3389/fpsyg.2019.0281731920855

Meyer, A., Rose, D. H., & Gordon, D. (2014). *Universal design for learning: Theory and Practice*. CAST Professional Publishing.

Miao, C., Humphrey, R. H., & Qian, S. (2018). The relationship between emotional intelligence and trait mindfulness: A meta-analytic review. *Personality and Individual Differences*, 135, 101–107. 10.1016/j.paid.2018.06.051

Michalec, B., Keyes, C. L. M., & Nalkur, S. (2009). Flourishing. In Lopez, S. J. (Ed.), *The encyclopedia of positive psychology* (Vol. I, pp. 391–394). Wiley-Blackwell.

Mikolajczak, M. (2009). Going beyond the ability-trait debate: The three-level model of emotional intelligence. *E-Journal of Applied Psychology : Clinical and Social Issues*, 5(2), 25–31.

Milam, L., Butler, A. J., & Vanderhaar, J. (2022). School Climate and Emotional Wellbeing. OSF. https://osf.io/dcgax

Miller, D., & Daniel, B. (2007). Competent to Cope, Worthy of Happiness? How the Duality of Self-Esteem Can Inform a Resilience-Based Classroom Environment. *School Psychology International*, 28(5), 605–622. 10.1177/0143034307085661

Miller, G. E., Brehm, K., & Whitehouse, S. (1998). Reconceptualizing school-based prevention for antisocial behavior within a resiliency framework. *School Psychology Review*, 27(3), 364–379. 10.1080/02796015.1998.12085922

Miller, L. D., Short, C., Garland, E. J., & Clark, S. (2010). The ABCs of CBT (Cognitive Behavior Therapy): Evidence-Based Approaches to Child Anxiety in Public School Settings. *Journal of Counseling and Development*, 88(4), 432–439. 10.1002/j.1556-6678.2010.tb00043.x

Miller, M. (1996). Relevance of resilience to individuals with learning disabilities. *International Journal of Disability Development and Education*, 43(3), 255–269. 10.1080/0156655960430306

Miller, M. (2002). Resilience elements in students with learning disabilities. *Journal of Clinical Psychology*, 58(3), 291–298. 10.1002/jclp.1001811836710

Milner, H. R. (2021). *Start where you are, but don't stay there: Understanding diversity, opportunity gaps, and teaching in today's classrooms*. Harvard Education Press.

Mitchell, D., & Sutherland, D. (2020). *What really works in special and inclusive education: Using evidence-based teaching strategies*. Routledge. 10.4324/9780429401923

Mitra, D. L. (2014). *Student voice in school reform: Building youth-adult partnerships that strengthen schools and empower youth*. State University of New York Press. 10.1515/9780791478943

Mlinac, M. E., & Schwabenbauer, A. (2018). *Psychological resilience. In the Handbook of developmental psychopathology*. Springer. 10.1007/978-3-030-04555-5_5

Mohammadi, N. K., Rowling, L., & Nutbeam, D. (2010). Acknowledging educational perspectives on health promoting schools. *Health Education*, 110(4), 240–251. 10.1108/09654281011052619

Montalti, M. (2012). Area problema. Le aree e le attrezzature per il gioco. In Laurìa, A. (Ed.), *I piani per l'accessibilità. Una sfida per promuovere l'autonomia dei cittadini e valorizzare i luoghi dell'abitare*. Gangemi.

Montessori, M. (1950). *La scoperta del bambino*. Garzanti.

Moore, R. C. (1997). The Need of Nature: A Childhood Right. *Social Justice (San Francisco, Calif.)*, 24(3), 203–220.

Mor Barak, M. E., Luria, G., & Brimhall, K. C. (2022). What leaders say versus what they do: Inclusive leadership, policy-practice decoupling, and the anomaly of climate for inclusion. *Group & Organization Management*, 47(4), 840–871. 10.1177/10596011211005916

Morais, A., & Neves, I. P. (2010). Basil Bernstein as an inspiration for educational research: Specific methodological approaches. ToolKits, translation devices and conceptual accounts: Essays on Basil Bernstein's sociology of knowledge, 11-32.

Moreira, P. A. S., Inman, R. A., Cloninger, K., & Cloninger, C. R. (2021). Student engagement with school and personality: A biopsychosocial and person-centred approach. *The British Journal of Educational Psychology*, 91(2), 691–713. 10.1111/bjep.1238833247604

Morote, R., Las Hayas, C., Izco-Basurko, I., Anyan, F., Fullaondo, A., Donisi, V., Zwiefka, A., Gudmundsdottir, D. G., Ledertoug, M. M., Olafsdottir, A. S., Gabrielli, S., Carbone, S., Mazur, I., Królicka-Deręgowska, A., Knoop, H. H., Tange, N., Kaldalóns, I. V., Jónsdóttir, B. J., González Pinto, A., & Hjemdal, O. (2022). Co-creation and regional adaptation of a resilience-based universal whole-school program in five European regions. *European Educational Research Journal*, 21(1), 138–164. 10.1177/1474904120947890

Morrison, G. M., & Allen, M. R. (2007). Promoting Student Resilience in School Contexts. *Theory into Practice*, 46(2), 162–169. 10.1080/00405840701233172

Morrison, G. M., & Cosden, M. A. (1997). Risk, resilience and adjustment of individuals with learning disabilities. *Learning Disability Quarterly*, 20(1), 43–60. 10.2307/1511092

Morrison, G. M., Robertson, L., Laurie, B., & Kelly, J. (2002). Proactive factors related to antisocial behavior. *Journal of Clinical Psychology*, 58(3), 277–290. 10.1002/jclp.1002211836709

Mostafa, T., & Pál, J. (2018). Science Teachers' Satisfaction: Evidence from the PISA 2015 Teacher Survey. In *OECD Education Working Papers, No. 168*. OECD Publishing. https://www.oecd-ilibrary.org/education/science-teachers-satisfaction_1ecdb4e3-

Mousena, E., & Raptis, N. (2020). Beyond teaching: School climate and communication in the educational context. In Waller, S., Waller, L., Mpofu, V., & Kurebwa, M. (Eds.), *Education at the Intersection of Globalization and Technology* (pp. 153–170). IntechOpen.

Mueller, C. M., & Dweck, C. S. (1998). Praise for intelligence can undermine children's motivation and performance. *Journal of Personality and Social Psychology*, 75(1), 33–52. 10.1037/0022-3514.75.1.339686450

Muhati-Nyakundi, L. I. (2023). Teachers' Agency and Wellbeing in Inclusive Education: Challenges and Opportunities. *Journal of Educational Studies*, 2023(si1), 365–379. 10.59915/jes.2023.special.1.19

Mukund, B., & Dehuri, B. K. (2016). Building Resilience in School Children: Need of The Hour. *Global Journal for Research Analysis*, 5(10), 279–282.

Naglieri, J. A., & LeBuffe, P. A. (2005). Measuring Resilience in Children, From Theory to Practice. In Goldstein, S., & Brooks, R. B. (Eds.), *Handbook of Resilience in Children* (pp. 241–259). Springer. 10.1007/0-306-48572-9_8

Nash, R. (2006). Bernstein and the explanation of social disparities in education: A realist critique of the socio-linguistic thesis. British Journal of Sociology of Education, 27(5), 539-553.

Nataria, Y. (2016). *Goal setting and perseverance*. Psychology Forum UMM.

National Association of School Psychologists in the USA, Institute for Educational Leaderships. (2019). *Nine Elements of Effective School Community Partnerships to Address Student Mental Health*. Physical Health and Overall Wellness.

National Research Council and Institute of Medicine. (2004). *Engaging schools: Fostering high school students' motivation to learn*. The National Academies Press.

National School Climate Center. (2023). The 14 Dimensions of School Climate Measured by the CSCI. Retrieved May 20, 2024 from https://schoolclimate.org/wp-content/uploads/2022/01/CSCI-14-Dimensions-Chart.pdf

Neff, K. D. (2003). Self-compassion: An alternative conceptualization of a healthy attitude toward oneself. *Self and Identity*, 2(2), 85–101. 10.1080/15298860309032

Neil, A. L., & Christensen, H. (2009). Efficacy and effectiveness of school-based prevention and early intervention programs for anxiety. *Clinical Psychology Review*, 29(3), 208–215. 10.1016/j.cpr.2009.01.00219232805

Neill, S. A. (1960). *Summerhill, A Radical Approach to Child Rearing*. Hart Publishing Co.

Nelsen, J., Lott, L., & Glenn, H. S. (2011). Positive Discipline in the Classroom, *Revised 3rd Edition: Developing Mutual Respect, Cooperation, and Responsibility in Your Classroom*. Three Rivers Press.

Nelson, G., Westhues, A., & MacLeod, J. (2003). A meta–analysis of longitudinal research on preschool prevention programs for children. *Prevention & Treatment*, 6(31), 1–35. 10.1037/1522-3736.6.1.631a

Nettles, S. M., Mucherach, W., & Jones, D. S. (2000). Understanding resilience: The role of social resources. *Journal of Education for Students Placed at Risk*, 5(1), 47–60. 10.1207/s15327671espr0501&2_4

Newcombe, M. J., & Ashkanasy, N. M. (2002). The role of affect and affective congruence in perceptions of leaders: An experimental study. *The Leadership Quarterly*, 13(5), 601–614. 10.1016/S1048-9843(02)00146-7

Newcombe, N. (2010). Picture This: Increasing Math and Science Learning by Improving Spatial Thinking. *American Educator*, 34(2), 29.

Nicolescu, B. (2002). *Manifesto of transdisciplinarity*. SUNY Press.

Niehaus, K., Rudasill, K. M., & Rakes, C. R. (2012). A longitudinal study of school connectedness and academic outcomes across sixth grade. *Journal of School Psychology*, 50(4), 443–460. 10.1016/j.jsp.2012.03.00222710015

Nielsen, L., Meilstrup, C., Nelausen, M. K., Koushede, V., Holstein, B. E., Weare, K., & Weare, K. (2015). Promotion of social and emotional competence: Experiences from a mental health intervention applying a whole school approach. *Health Education*, 115(3/4), 339–356. 10.1108/HE-03-2014-0039

Noble, T., & McGrath, H. (2015). PROSPER: A New Framework for Positive Education. *Psychology of Well-Being*, 5(1), 2. 10.1186/s13612-015-0030-2

Noddings, N. (2003). *Happiness and education.* Cambridge University Press. 10.1017/CBO9780511499920

Norrish, J. M. (2015). *Positive Education: The Geelong Grammar School Journey.* Oxford University Press. 10.1093/acprof:oso/9780198702580.001.0001

Norrish, J. M., Williams, P., O'Connor, M., & Robinson, J. (2013). An applied framework for positive education. *International Journal of Wellbeing*, 3(2), 157–161. 10.5502/ijw.v3i2.2

NSCC-National School Climate Council. (2021). What Is School Climate and Why Is It Important? Retrieved May 20, 2024 from https://schoolclimate.org/school-climate/

Nwoko, J. C., Emeto, T. I., Malau-Aduli, A. E., & Malau-Aduli, B. S. (2023). A systematic review of the factors that influence teachers' occupational wellbeing. *International Journal of Environmental Research and Public Health*, 20(12), 6070. 10.3390/ijerph2012607037372657

O'Sullivan, C., Ryan, S., O'Sullivan, L., Masterson, M., Murphy, T., Twomey, K., Brennan, S., Kearney, L., O'Sullivan, M., & Corry, J. (2019). Teacher well-being and diversity: a manual for teachers in diverse educational settings. University of Limerick. https://hdl.handle.net/10344/9327

Oade-Sese, G. V., & Li, V. (2011). Attachment relationships as predictors of language skills for at risk bilingual preschool children. *Psychology in the Schools*, 48(7), 707–722. 10.1002/pits.20583

Oberle, E., & Schonert-Reichl, K. A. (2017). Social and emotional learning: recent research and practical strategies for promoting children's social and emotional competence in schools. Handbook of social behavior and skills in children, 175-197.

Oberle, E., Domitrovich, C. E., Meyers, D. C., & Weissberg, R. P. (2020). Establishing systemic social and emotional learning approaches in schools: A framework for schoolwide implementation. In *Social and Emotional Learning* (pp. 6–26). Routledge. 10.4324/9780429444692-2

Obradović, J., Shafer, A., & Masten, A. S. (2011). Risk in developmental psychopathology: Progress and future directions. In Mayes, L. C., & Lewis, M. (Eds.), *The environment of human development: A handbook of theory and measurement.* Cambridge University Press.

OECD. (2019). PISA 2018 Results (Volume III): What School Life Means for Students' Lives A framework for the analysis of school climate and students well-being. OECD Publishing. https://www.oecd-ilibrary.org/education/pisa-2018-results-volume-iii_3b42acd8-en

Olsson, C. A., Bond, L., Burns, J. M., Vella-Brodrick, D. A., & Sawyer, S. M. (2003). Adolescent resilience: A concept analysis. *Journal of Adolescence*, 26(1), 1–11. 10.1016/S0140-1971(02)00118-512550818

Ortan, F., Simut, C., & Simut, R. (2021). Self-efficacy, job satisfaction and teacher well-being in the K-12 educational system. *International Journal of Environmental Research and Public Health*, 18(23), 12763. 10.3390/ijerph18231276334886493

Ortega, R., Sanchez, V., & Ortega Rivera Viejo, C. (2011). La violencia sexual en las relaciones interpersonales de adolescents. In Lameiras, M., & Iglesias, I. (Eds.), *Violencia de género:la violencia sexual a debate* (pp. 99–126). Tirant Lo Blanch.

Osborne, E. L., & Atkinson, M. J. (2022). Effects of decentering and non-judgement on body dissatisfaction and negative affect among young adult women. *Mindfulness*, 13(3), 615–626. 10.1007/s12671-021-01817-z

Osher, D., Sprague, J., Weissberg, R. P., Axelrod, J., Keenan, S., & Kendziora, K. T. (2007). A comprehensive approach to promoting social, emotional, and academic growth in contemporary schools. In Thomas, A., & Grimes, J. (Eds.), *Best practices in school psychology* (5th ed., pp. 1263–1278). National Association of School Psychologists.

Otsuka, K., & Jay, T. (n.d.). *Understanding and supporting block play: video observation research on preschoolers' block play to identify features associated with the development of abstract thinking Video Observation Research on Preschoolers' Block Play: Identifying Features Associated with the Development of Abstract Thinking*. http://shura.shu.ac.uk/13380/

Owens, R. L., & Patterson, M. M. (2013). Positive psychological interventions for children: A comparison of gratitude and best possible selves approaches. *The Journal of Genetic Psychology*, 174(4), 403–428. 10.1080/00221325.2012.69749623991613

Pagès, B. E., & Reñé, T. A. (2008). Cómo Ser Docente Y No Morir. In *El Intento, Técnicas De Concentración Y Relajación En El Aula*. GRAO.

Pahl, K. M., & Barrett, P. M. (2010). Preventing Anxiety and Promoting Social and Emotional Strength in Preschool Children: A Universal Evaluation of the Fun FRIENDS Program. *Advances in School Mental Health Promotion*, 3(3), 14–25. 10.1080/1754730X.2010.9715683

Pajares, F. (1996). Self-efficacy beliefs in academic settings. *Review of Educational Research*, 66(4), 543–578. 10.3102/00346543066004543

Pandeliadou, S. (2011). *Learning disabilities and educational practice: what & why*. Topos.

Pandia, W. S. S., & Purwanti, M. (2019). Teachers' perceptions of school climate in inclusive schools. Psikohumaniora. *Jurnal Penelitian Psikologi*, 4(1), 27–42. 10.21580/pjpp.v4i1.3357

Panesi, S., Bocconi, S., & Ferlino, L. (2020). Promoting students' well-being and inclusion in schools through digital technologies: Perceptions of students, teachers, and school leaders in Italy expressed through SELFIE piloting activities. *Frontiers in Psychology*, 11, 11. 10.3389/fpsyg.2020.0156332848988

Papandreou, M. (2020). *Participatory Learning in Preschool and Early Primary Education: Understanding Children's Languages and Enhancing Their Participation in Learning and Research Processes*. Sofia Publications.

Papanelopoulou, E. (2002). *Multiple intelligences: Theory- application and perspectives in primary education*. Unpublished PhD thesis. Volos: University of Thessaly.

Papapetrou, K. (1968). Theology and emotion. Theology L.Th., 241-245.

Papay, J. P., & Kraft, M. A. (2017). Developing workplaces where teachers stay, improve, and succeed. In Quintero, E. (Ed.), *Teaching in context: How social aspects of school and school systems shape teachers' development & effectiveness* (pp. 15–35). Harvard Education Press.

Parker, R., Thomsen, B. S., & Berry, A. (2022). Learning Through Play at School – A Framework for Policy and Practice. *Frontiers in Education*, 7(1), 1014. 10.3389/feduc.2022.751801

Park, J. (2019). The Qualities Criteria of Constructive Play and the Teacher's Role. *The Turkish Online Journal of Educational Technology*, 18(1).

Park, N., & Peterson, C. (2006). Character strengths and happiness among young children: Content analysis of parental descriptions. *Journal of Happiness Studies*, 7(3), 323–341. 10.1007/s10902-005-3648-6

Park, N., & Peterson, C. (2006). Moral competence and character strengths among adolescents: The development and validation of the Values in Action Inventory of Strengths for Youth. *Journal of Adolescence*, 29(6), 891–909. 10.1016/j.adolescence.2006.04.01116766025

Patrikakou, A., & Kougioumtzis, G. A. (2016). Art, Emotional Intelligence & Counseling: Detection of the effect of making art and its applications in Career Counseling. *Journal of Regional SocioEconomic Issues, 6*(2), 206-219.

Patterson, G. R., DeGarmo, D. S., & Forgatch, M. S. (2004). Systematic changes in families following prevention trials. *Journal of Abnormal Child Psychology*, 32(6), 621–633. 10.1023/B:JACP.0000047211.11826.5415648529

Pattison, C., & Lynd-Stevenson, R. M. (2001). The prevention of depressive symptoms in children: The immediate and long-term outcomes of a school based program. *Behaviour Change*, 18(2), 92–102. 10.1375/bech.18.2.92

Payne, W. L. (1983/86). A study of emotion: Developing emotional intelligence, self integration, relating to fear, pain and desire. Unpublished PhD. University of Cincinnati: Ohio.

Payton, J. W., Weissberg, R. P., Durlak, J. A., Dymnicki, A. B., Taylor, R. D., & Schellinger, K. B. (2008). *The positive impact of social and emotional learning for kindergarten to eighth-grade students: Findings from three scientific reviews*. Collaborative for Academic, Social, and Emotional Learning.

Pedlar, M. (2018). Teachers play a key role in helping students feel they 'belong' at school. *The Conversation.* Https://Theconversation.Com/Teachers-Play-A-Key-Role-In-Helping-Students -Feel-They-Belong-At-School-99641

Pehlivan, H. (2016). The role of play on development and learning. *International Journal of Human Sciences*, 13(2), 123–142. 10.14687/jhs.v13i2.3767

Pellegrini, A. D. (2009). *The role of play in human development.* Oxford University Press, Inc. 10.1093/acprof:oso/9780195367324.001.0001

Pellegrini, D. S., Masten, A. S., Garmezy, N., & Ferrarese, M. J. (1987). Correlates of social and academic competence in middle childhood. *Journal of Child Psychology and Psychiatry, and Allied Disciplines*, 28(5), 699–714. 10.1111/j.1469-7610.1987.tb01553.x3667735

Penderi, E., Hlapana, E., Melliou, K., Filippidi, A., & Marinatou, T. (2021). Kindergarten Pre-school Education Curriculum. In the framework of the Action *"Upgrading the Study Programs and Creating Educational Materials for Primary and Secondary Education*" of the IEP with MIS 5035542. https://ean.auth.gr/wp content/uploads/2021/11/programma_spoudwn_2021.pdf

Pereira, H., Gonçalves, V. O., & Assis, R. M. (2021). Burnout, Organizational Self-Efficacy and Self-Esteem among Brazilian Teachers during the COVID-19 Pandemic. *European Journal of Investigation in Health, Psychology and Education*, 11(3), 795–803. 10.3390/ejihpe1103005734563070

Pescolido, A. T. (2002). Emergent leaders as managers of group emotion. *The Leadership Quarterly*, 13(5), 583–599. 10.1016/S1048-9843(02)00145-5

Peterson, A. J., Allen, E., Viner, R., & Bonell, C. (2020). Effects of the school environment on early sexual risk behavior: A longitudinal analysis of students in English secondary schools. *Journal of Adolescence*, 85(9), 106–114. 10.1016/j.adolescence.2020.10.00433130414

Peterson, C., Ruch, W., Beermann, U., Park, N., & Seligman, M. E. P. (2007). Strengths of character, orientations to happiness, and life satisfaction. *The Journal of Positive Psychology*, 2(3), 149–156. 10.1080/17439760701228938

Peterson, C., & Seligman, M. E. (2004). *Character strengths and virtues: A handbook and classification* (Vol. 1). Oxford University Press.

Peterson, C., & Seligman, M. E. P. (2004). *Character Strengths and Virtues: A Handbook and Classification.* Oxford University Press.

Petrella, F., & Romitti, I. (1998). *Gli spazi verdi per il gioco dei bambini.* Alinea Editrice.

Petrides, K. V., Sanchez-Ruiz, M. J., Siegling, A. B., Saklofske, D. H., & Mavroveli, S. (2018). Emotional intelligence as personality: Measurement and role of trait emotional intelligence in educational contexts. *Emotional intelligence in education: Integrating research with practice*, 49-81.

Petrides, K. V., & Furnham, A. (2003). Trait emotional intelligence: Behavioral validation in two studies of emotion recognition and reactivity to mood induction. *European Journal of Personality*, 17(1), 39–57. 10.1002/per.466

Petrides, K. V., Furnham, A., & Mavroveli, S. (2007a). Trait emotional intelligence: moving forward in the field of EI. In Matthews, G., Zeidner, M., & Roberts, R. D. (Eds.), *Series in Affective Science. The Science of Emotional Intelligence: Knowns and Unknowns* (pp. 151–166). Oxford University Press. 10.1080/08959280903120295

Petrides, K. V., Pérez-González, J. C., & Furnham, A. (2007b). On the criterion and incremental validity of trait emotional intelligence. *Cognition and Emotion*, 21(1), 26–55. 10.1080/02699930601038912

Petrou, A., Angelides, P., & Leigh, J. (2009). Beyond the difference: From the margins to inclusion. *International Journal of Inclusive Education*, 13(5), 439–448. 10.1080/13603110701776024

Pfeifer, S. I. (2001). Emotional intelligence: Popular but elusive construct. *Roeper Review*, 23(3), 138–142. 10.1080/02783190109554085

Phan, M. L., Renshaw, T. L., Caramanico, J., Greeson, J. M., MacKenzie, E., Atkinson-Diaz, Z., Doppelt, N., Tai, H., Mandell, D. S., & Nuske, H. J. (2022). Mindfulness-based school interventions: A systematic review of outcome evidence quality by study design. *Mindfulness*, 13(7), 1591–1613. 10.1007/s12671-022-01885-936186722

Piaget, J. (2013). *Play, dreams and imitation in childhood* (Vol. 25). Routledge. 10.4324/9781315009698

Pianta, R. C., Hamre, B. K., & Allen, J. P. (2012). Teacher-student relationships and engagement: conceptualizing, measuring, and improving the capacity of classroom interactions. In *Handbook of Research on Student Engagement*. Springer Nature.

Pianta, R. C., Hamre, B. K., & Allen, J. P. (2012). Teacher-student relationships and engagement: Conceptualizing, measuring, and improving the capacity of classroom interactions. In Christenson, S. L., Reschly, A. L., & Wylie, C. (Eds.), *Handbook of research on student engagement* (pp. 365–386). Springer. 10.1007/978-1-4614-2018-7_17

Pianta, R. C., & Steinberg, M. (1992). Teacher-child relationships and the process of adjusting to school. *New Directions for Child and Adolescent Development*, 1992(57), 61–80. 10.1002/cd.23219925706

Pianta, R. C., & Walsh, D. J. (1998). Applying the construct of resilience in schools: Cautions from a developmental systems perspective. *School Psychology Review*, 27(3), 407–417. 10.1080/02796015.1998.12085925

Piechurska-Kuciel, E. (2011). Perceived teacher support and language anxiety in polish secondary school EFL learners. *Studies in Second Language Learning and Teaching*, 1(1), 83–100. 10.14746/ssllt.2011.1.1.5

Pine, D. S., Costello, J., & Masten, A. S. (2005). Trauma, proximity, and developmental psychopathology: The effects of war and terrorism on children. *Neuropsychopharmacology*, 30(10), 1781–1792. 10.1038/sj.npp.130081416012537

Pinheiro, M. D. R. (2015). *A Parental Program for the Prevention of Depression in Adolescents*. 10.15405/epsbs.2015.08.9

Pinker, S. (2007). *The Stuff of Thought: Language as a Window into Human Nature*. Viking.

Pinkus, L. M. (2009). Moving beyond AYP: High school performance indicators. Alliance for Excellent Education. Eric. https://eric.ed.gov/?id=ED506873

Pirola-Merlo, A., Hartel, C., Mann, L., & Hirst, G. (2002). How leaders influence the impact of affective events on team climate and performance in R&D teams. *The Leadership Quarterly*, 13(5), 561–581. 10.1016/S1048-9843(02)00144-3

Plass, J. L., Homer, B. D., & Kinzer, C. K. (2015). Foundations of Game-Based Learning. *Educational Psychologist, 50*(4), 258-283.

Platsidou, M. (2005). Emotional intelligence: Modern approaches to an old concept. *Education in Science*, 1, 27–39.

Platsidou, M. (2010). *Emotional Intelligence, Theoretical Models, Methods of Measurement and Applications in Education and Work*. Gutenberg.

Platt, I. A., Hochard, K. D., Tytherleigh, M., Kannangara, C., Carson, J., McFaul, C., & North, C. (2024). The Hummingbird Project year 2: Decreasing distress and fostering flourishing in a pragmatic pre-post study. *Frontiers in Psychology*, 15, 1257446. 10.3389/fpsyg.2024.125744638596339

Platt, I. A., Kannangara, C., Tytherleigh, M., & Carson, J. (2020). The Hummingbird Project: A Positive Psychology Intervention for Secondary School Students. *Frontiers in Psychology*, 11, 2012. 10.3389/fpsyg.2020.0201232849165

Plomaritou, B. (2004). *Emotional Intelligence Development Program*. Grigoris Publications.

Pluess, M., Boniwell, I., Hefferon, K., & Tunariu, A. (2017). Preliminary evaluation of a school-based resilience-promoting intervention in a high-risk population: Application of an exploratory two-cohort treatment/control design. *PLoS One*, 12(5), e0177191. 10.1371/journal.pone.017719128481905

Pluskota, A. (2014). The application of Positive Psychology in the practice of education. *SpringerPlus*, 3(1), 147. 10.1186/2193-1801-3-14724790805

Polk, L. V. (1997). Toward a middle-range theory of resilience. *Advances in Nursing Science*, 19(1), 1–13. 10.1097/00012272-199703000-000029055026

Polychroni, F. (2011). *Special learning difficulties*. Pedio.

Polychroni, F. (2023). *Teaching Strategies to Children with Learning Difficulties*. Gutenberg.

Pontiggia, G. (2000). *Nati due volte*. Mondadori.

Post, S. G. (2005). Altruism, happiness, and health: It's good to be good. *International Journal of Behavioral Medicine*, 12(2), 66–77. 10.1207/s15327558ijbm1202_415901215

Poulou, M. S. (2017). Social and emotional learning and teacher–student relationships: Preschool teachers' and students' perceptions. *Early Childhood Education Journal*, 45(3), 427–435. 10.1007/s10643-016-0800-3

Pozo-Rico, T., & Sandoval, I. (2020). Can academic achievement in primary school students be improved through teacher training on emotional intelligence as a key academic competency? *Frontiers in Psychology*, 10, 2976. 10.3389/fpsyg.2019.0297631998203

Preventing Mental, Emotional, and Behavioral Disorders Among Young People: Progress and Possibilities. (2009). National Academies Press. 10.17226/12480

Prewett, S. L., Bergin, D. A., & Huang, F. L. (2019). Student and teacher perceptions on student-teacher relationship quality: A middle school perspective. *School Psychology International*, 40(1), 66–87. 10.1177/0143034318807743

Prince-Embury, S., & Courville, T. (2008). Comparison of one-, two-, and three factor models of personal resiliency using the resiliency scales for children and adolescents. *Canadian Journal of School Psychology*, 23(1), 11–25. 10.1177/0829573508316589

Psyllou, A. (2014). Phd Dissertation: *Construction, implementation and Evaluation of emotional resilience: a CBT programme in primary schools in Greece*, University of Thessaly, Greece, Department of Pre-School Education.

Psyllou, R. & Zafiropoulou, M. (2012). *Friends.... how can we deal with our negative feelings*, Pedion Publications (republication), Athens, 2012.

Psyllou, R., & Zafiropoulou, M. (2023). *Child anxiety. What is it?* Topos Publications.

Quin, D. (2017). Longitudinal and contextual associations between teacher–student relationships and student engagement: A systematic review. *Review of Educational Research*, 87(2), 345–387. 10.3102/0034654316669434

Rak, C. F., & Patterson, L. E. (1996). Promoting resilience in at-risk children. *Journal of Counseling and Development*, 74(4), 368–373. 10.1002/j.1556-6676.1996.tb01881.x

Ramani, G. B., Zippert, E., Schweitzer, S., & Pan, S. (2014). Preschool children's joint block building during a guided play activity. *Journal of Applied Developmental Psychology*, 35(4), 326–336. 10.1016/j.appdev.2014.05.005

Ramelow, D., Currie, D., & Felder-Puig, R. (2015). The assessment of school climate: Review and appraisal of published student-report measures. *Journal of Psychoeducational Assessment*, 33(8), 731–743. 10.1177/0734282915584852

Ramos, N. S., Hernández, S. M., & Blanca, M. J. (2009). Efecto de un programa integrado de mindfulness e inteligencia emocional sobre las estrategias cognitivas de regulación emocional. *Ansiedad y Estrés*, 15, 207–216. 10.1016/j.jrp.2015.09.001

Reaves, S., McMahon, S. D., Duffy, S. N., & Ruiz, L. (2018). The test of time: A meta-analytic review of the relation between school climate and problem behavior. *Aggression and Violent Behavior*, 39(3), 100–108. 10.1016/j.avb.2018.01.006

Reeve, R. A., & Waldecker, C. (2017). Evidence-Based Assessment and Intervention for Dyscalculia and Maths Disabilities in School Psychology. In M. Thielking & M. Terjesen (Eds.), *Handbook of Australian School Psychology* (pp. 197 213). Springer. 10.1007/978-3-319-45166-4_10

Reeve, J. (2016). Autonomy-supportive teaching: What it is, how to do it. In *Building autonomous learners: Perspectives from research and practice using self-determination theory* (pp. 129–152). Springer Singapore. 10.1007/978-981-287-630-0_7

Reinke, W. M., Stormont, M., Herman, K. C., Puri, R., & Goel, N. (2011). Supporting children's mental health in schools: Teacher perceptions of needs, roles, and barriers. *School Psychology Quarterly*, 26(1), 1–13. 10.1037/a0022714

Reiter, A. B., & Davis, S. N. (2011). Factors Influencing Pre-Service Teachers' Beliefs about Student Achievement: Evaluation of a Pre-Service Teacher Diversity Awareness Program. *Multicultural Education*, 19(3), 41–46.

Resnick, B., Gwyther, L. P., & Roberto, K. A. (2011). *Resilience in aging*. Springer. 10.1007/978-1-4419-0232-0

Ressa, T., Daniels, D., & Wells-Jensen, S. (2021). Time as a hidden curriculum: Qualitative study of challenges faced by students with mobility, speech, and visual disabilities in P-12 settings. *International Journal of Educational Research Review*, 6(3), 250–263. 10.24331/ijere.927574

Reynolds, C. F.III. (2019). Building resilience through psychotherapy. *World Psychiatry; Official Journal of the World Psychiatric Association (WPA)*, 18(3), 289–291. 10.1002/wps.2066331496086

Rigby, K. (2013). Bullying in schools and its relation to parenting and family life. *Family Matters (Melbourne, Vic.)*, 92, 61–67.

Rimm–Kaufman, S. E., Larsen, R. A. A., Baroody, A. E., Curby, T. W., Ko, M., Thomas, J. B., Merritt, E. G., Abry, T., & DeCoster, J. (2014). Efficacy of the Responsive Classroom Approach: Results From a 3–Year, Longitudinal Randomized Controlled Trial. *American Educational Research Journal*, 52(3), 567–603. 10.3102/0002831214523821

Ritter, A., & Alvarez, I. (2020). Mindfulness and Executive Functions: Making the Case for Elementary School Practice. *European Journal of Investigation in Health, Psychology and Education*, 10(1), 544–553. 10.3390/ejihpe1001003934542502

Rodari, G. (1973). *La grammatica della fantasia. Introduzione all'arte di inventare storie*. Collana PBE, Einaudi.

Rodríguez-Ledo, C., & Orejudo-Hernández, S. (2017). La educación de la inteligencia emocional. In García-Campayo, J., Demarzo, M., & Modrego, M. (Eds.), *Bienestar Emocional Y Mindfulness En Educación* (pp. 51–82). Alianza Editorial. 10.1016/j.jesp.2009.03.009

Roeser, R. W., Skinner, E., Beers, J., & Jennings, P. A. (2012). Mindfulness training and teachers' professional development: An emerging area of research and practice. *Child Development Perspectives*, 6(2), 167–173. 10.1111/j.1750-8606.2012.00238.x

Roffey, S. (2012). Positive relationships: Evidence-based practice across the world. *Educational and Child Psychology*, 29(1), 15–30.

Romano, R. G. (2000). *L'arte del giocare. Storia, epistemologia e pedagogia del gioco*. Pensa Multimedia.

Ronaldson, A., Poole, L., Kidd, T., Leigh, E., Jahangiri, M., & Steptoe, A. (2014). Optimism measured pre-operatively is associated with reduced pain intensity and physical symptom reporting after coronary artery bypass graft surgery. *Journal of Psychosomatic Research*, 77(4), 278–282. 10.1016/j.jpsychores.2014.07.01825129850

Ronimus, M., Eklund, K., Pesu, L., & Lyytinen, H. (2019). Supporting Struggling Readers with Digital Game-Based Learning. *Educational Technology Research and Development*, 67(3), 639–663. 10.1007/s11423-019-09658-3

Rønning, J. A., Sourander, A., Kumpulainen, K., Tamminen, T., Niemelä, S., Moilanen, I., Helenius, H., Piha, J., & Almqvist, F. (2009). Cross−informant agreement about bullying and victimization among eight−year−olds: Whose information best predicts psychiatric caseness 10−15 years later? *Social Psychiatry and Psychiatric Epidemiology*, 44(1), 15–22. 10.1007/s00127-008-0395-018604618

Roorda, D. L., Jak, S., Zee, M., Oort, F. J., & Koomen, H. M. Y. (2017). Affective teacher–student relationships and students' engagement and achievement: A meta-analytic update and test of the mediating role of engagement. *School Psychology Review*, 46(3), 239–261. 10.17105/SPR-2017-0035.V46-3

Roorda, D., Koomen, H., Spilt, J., & Oort, F. (2011). The Influence of Affective Teacher- Student Relationships on Students' School Engagement and Achievement: A Meta- Analytic Approach. *Review of Educational Research*, 81(4), 493–529. 10.3102/0034654311421793

Rose, C. A., Forber-Pratt, A. J., Espelage, D. L., & Aragon, S. R. (2013). The influence of psychosocial factors on bullying involvement of students with disabilities. *Theory into Practice*, 52(4), 272–279. 10.1080/00405841.2013.829730

Rowe, F., & Stewart, D. E. (2009). Promoting Connectedness through Whole−School Approaches: A Qualitative Study. *Health Education*, 109(5), 396–413. 10.1108/09654280910984816

Ruch, W., Weber, M., Park, N., & and Peterson, C. (2014). Character Strengths in Children and Adolescents: Reliability and Initial Validity of the German Values in Action Inventory of Strengths for Youth (German VIA-Youth). *European Journal of Psychological Assessment*, 30(1), 57–64. 10.1027/1015-5759/a000169

Rucinski, C. L., Brown, J. L., & Downer, J. T. (2018). Teacher–child relationships, classroom climate, and children's social-emotional and academic development. *Journal of Educational Psychology*, 110(7), 992–1004. 10.1037/edu0000240

Rudasill, K. M., Snyder, K. E., Levinson, H., & Adelson, J. (2018). Systems view of school climate: A theoretical framework for research. *Educational Psychology Review*, 30(1), 35–60. 10.1007/s10648-017-9401-y

Russel, J. A. (1991). Culture and the categorization of emotions. *Psychological Bulletin*, 110(3), 426–450. 10.1037/0033-2909.110.3.4261758918

Rutter, M. (1987). Psychosocial resilience and protective mechanisms. *The American Journal of Orthopsychiatry*, 57(3), 316–331. 10.1111/j.1939-0025.1987.tb03541.x3303954

Rutter, M. (1998). Developmental catch-up, and deficit, following adoption after severe global early privation. English and Romanian Adoptees (ERA) Study Team. *Journal of Child Psychology and Psychiatry, and Allied Disciplines*, 39(4), 465–476.9599775

Rutter, M. (2012). Resilience as a dynamic concept. *Development and Psychopathology*, 24(2), 335–344. 10.1017/S095457941200002822559117

Ryan, R. M., & Deci, E. L. (2017). *Self-determination theory: Basic psychological needs in motivation, development, and wellness*. Guilford publications. 10.1521/978.14625/28806

Ryan, R. M., & Deci, E. L. (2021). Self-determination theory: Basic psychological needs in motivation, development, and wellness. *Rajagiri Management Journal*, 15(1), 88–90.

Saarni, C. (2011). Emotional competence and effective negotiation: The integration of emotion understanding, regulation, and communication. In F. Aquilar & M. Galluccio (Eds.), *Psychological and political strategies for peace negotiation: A cognitive approach* (pp. 55–74). Springer Science + Business Media.

Sabornie, E. J. (1994). Social-affective characteristics in early adolescents identified as learning disabled and nondisabled. *Learning Disability Quarterly*, 17(4), 268–279. 10.2307/1511124

Sadeghi, K., & Esmaeili, F. (2022). English teachers' perception of school climate and effective teaching. *Interdisciplinary Studies in English Language Teaching*, 1(1), 1–21.

Sadovnik, A. R. (1991). Basil Bernstein's theory of pedagogic practice: A structuralist approach. *Sociology of Education*, 64(1), 48–63. 10.2307/2112891

Saeed, S., & Zyngier, D. (2012). How motivation influences student engagement: A qualitative case study. *J. Educ. Learn.*, 1(2), 252–267. 10.5539/jel.v1n2p252

Sakiz, G., Pape, S. J., & Hoy, A. W. (2012). Does perceived teacher affective support matter for middle school students in mathematics classrooms? *Journal of School Psychology*, 50(2), 235–255. 10.1016/j.jsp.2011.10.00522386122

Salami, S. O. (2011). Personality and psychological well-being of adolescents: The moderating role of emotional intelligence. *Social Behavior and Personality*, 39(6), 785–794. 10.2224/sbp.2011.39.6.785

Salovey, P., & Mayer, J. D. (1990). 1997). Emotional intelligence. *Imagination, Cognition and Personality*, 9(3), 185–211. 10.2190/DUGG-P24E-52WK-6CDG

Saltzman, A. (2010). *Amy, Author at Still Quiet Place. Still Quiet Place.* https://stillquietplace.com/author/amy/

Saltzman, A. (2014). *A still quiet place: A mindfulness program for teaching children and adolescents to ease stress and difficult emotions.* New Harbinger Publications.

Sameroff, A. J., & Rosenblum, K. L. (2006). Psychosocial Constraints on the Development of Resilience. *Annals of the New York Academy of Sciences*, 194(1), 116–124. 10.1196/annals.1376.01017347345

Sánchez-Álvarez, N., Berrios Martos, M. P., & Extremera, N. (2020). A meta-analysis of the relationship between emotional intelligence and academic performance in secondary education: A multi-stream comparison. *Frontiers in Psychology*, 11, 1517. 10.3389/fpsyg.2020.0151732793030

Sandstrom, G. M., & Dunn, E. W. (2014). Social Interactions and Well-Being: The Surprising Power of Weak Ties. *Personality and Social Psychology Bulletin*, 40(7), 910–922. 10.1177/0146167214529799 24769739

Sanetti, L. M. H., Kratochwill, T. R., & Long, A. C. J. (2013). Applying adult behavior change theory to support mediator-based intervention implementation. *School Psychology Quarterly: The Official Journal of the Division of School Psychology, American Psychological Association, 28*(1), 47–62. https://doi.org/10.1037/spq0000007

Sanetti, L. M. H., Dobey, L. M., & Gallucci, J. (2014). Treatment integrity of interventions with children in School Psychology International from 1995–2010. *School Psychology International*, 35(4), 370–383. 10.1177/0143034313476399

Santhosh, J. S., & Flower, F. L. L. (2023). School Climate and its Determinant Factors of Well-Being in a Residential School Community. *Indian Journal of Social Psychiatry*, 39(2), 147–152. 10.4103/ijsp.ijsp_11_21

Santrock, J. W. (2020). *Educational psychology*. Tziola.

Sarker, N. I. (2024). Promoting community resilience through disaster education: Review of community-based interventions with a focus on teacher resilience and well-being. *PLoS One*, 19(1), e0296393. 10.1371/journal.pone.029639338166092

Scales, P. C. (1999). Reducing risks and building developmental assets: Essential actions for promoting adolescent health. *The Journal of School Health*, 69(3), 113–119. 10.1111/j.1746-1561.1999.tb07219.x10332647

Schacter, D. L., Gilbert, D. M., & Wegner, D. M. (2012). *Psychology*. Gutenberg.

Schaufeli, W. B., Bakker, A. B., & Salanova, M. (2006). The Measurement of Work Engagement With a Short Questionnaire: A Cross-National Study. *Educational and Psychological Measurement*, 66(4), 701–716. 10.1177/0013164405282471

Scheier, M. F., & Carver, C. S. (1985). Optimism, coping, and health: Assessment and implications of generalized outcome expectancies. *Health Psychology*, 4(3), 219–247. 10.1037/0278-6133.4.3.2194029106

Scheier, M. F., & Carver, C. S. (1993). On the power of positive thinking: The benefits of being optimistic. *Current Directions in Psychological Science*, 2(1), 26–30. 10.1111/1467-8721.ep10770572

Scheier, M. F., Carver, C. S., & Bridges, M. W. (1994). Distinguishing optimism from neuroticism (and trait anxiety, self-mastery, and self-esteem): A reevaluation of the Life Orientation Test. *Journal of Personality and Social Psychology*, 67(6), 1063–1078. 10.1037/0022-3514.67.6.10637815302

Schiller, F. (2019). *Über die Ästhetische Erziehung des Menschen in einer Reihe von Briefen.* Gideon Stiening.

Schirrmancher, R. (1995). *Τέχνη & Δημιουργική Ανάπτυξη των παιδιών*. Έλλην.

Schmitt, L., Weber, A., Weber, D., & Leuchter, M. (2023). First Insights into Preschool Teachers' Instructional Quality in Block Play and Its Associations with Children's Knowledge, Interest, Academic Self-Concept and Cognitive Aspects. *Early Education and Development*, 1–23. Advance online publication. 10.1080/10409289.2023.2233879

Schneider, A. L. (2006). *Τα μηνύματα της τέχνης*. Δίαυλος.

Schoeberlein, D. (2012). *Mindfulness Para Enseñar Y Aprender.* Louisville, CO. *Gaia (Heidelberg)*. Advance online publication. 10.1080/08959280802541039

Schonert-Reichl, K. A., Oberle, E., Lawlor, M. S., Abbott, D., Thomson, K., Oberlander, T. F., & Diamond, A. (2015). Enhancing cognitive and social–emotional development through a simple-to-administer mindfulness-based school program for elementary school children: A randomized controlled trial. *Developmental Psychology*, 51(1), 52–66. 10.1037/a003845425546595

Schonert-Reichl, K. A., & Roeser, R. W. (Eds.). (2016). *Handbook of mindfulness in education: Integrating theory and research into practice.* Springer-Verlag Publishing/Springer Nature., 10.1007/978-1-4939-3506-2

Schonfeld, I. S. (2001). Stress in first-year women teachers: The context of social support and coping. *Genetic, Social, and General Psychology Monographs*, 127, 7547–8756. https://academicworks.cuny.edu/cc_pubs/315/11471976

Schreiner, L. A. (2013). Strengths-based advising. In J. K. Drake, P. Jordan, and M. A. Miller Eds.), *Academic advising approaches: Strategies that teach students to make the most of college* (pp. 105-120). Jossey Bass.

Schriver, J. L., & Harr Kulynych, R. (2021). Do professor–student rapport and mattering predict college student outcomes? *Teaching of Psychology*, 50(4), 342–349. 10.1177/00986283211037987

Schutte, N. S., Malouff, J. M., Bobik, C., Coston, T. D., Greeson, C., Jedlicka, C., Rhodes, E., & Wendorf, G. (2001). Emotional intelligence and interpersonal relations. *The Journal of Social Psychology*, 141(4), 523–536. 10.1080/0022454010960056911577850

Schutte, N. S., Malouff, J. M., Hall, L. E., Hagerty, D. J., Cooper, J. T., Golden, C. J., & Dornheim, L. (1998). Development and validation of emotional intelligence. *Personality and Individual Differences*, 25(2), 167–177. 10.1016/S0191-8869(98)00001-4

Schwab, S. (2018). *Attitudes towards inclusive schooling: A study on students', teachers' and parents' attitudes*. Waxmann Verlag.

Scorsolini-Comin, F., Fontaine, A. M. G. V., Koller, S. H., & Santos, M. A. D. (2013). From authentic happiness to well-being: The flourishing of Positive Psychology. *Psicologia: Reflexão e Crítica*, 26(4), 663–670. 10.1590/S0102-79722013000400006

Scott-Ladd, B., & Chan, C. C. A. (2004). Emotional intelligence and participation in decision-making: Strategies for promoting organizational learning and change. *Strategic Change*, 13(2), 95–105. 10.1002/jsc.668

See, B., Morris, R., Gorard, S., Kokotsaki, D., & Abdi, S. (2020). Teacher recruitment and retention: A critical review of international evidence of most promising interventions. *Education Sciences*, 10(10), 262. 10.3390/educsci10100262

Seligman, M. E. (2002). Positive Psychology, positive prevention, and positive therapy. In *Handbook of Positive Psychology 2* (pp. 3–12). Academic Press.

Seligman, M. E. P. (2002). *Authentic happiness: Using the new Positive Psychology to realize your potential for lasting fulfillment*. Free Press.

Seligman, M. E. P. (2002). Positive psychology, positive prevention, and positive therapy. In Snyder, C. R., & Lopez, S. J. (Eds.), *Handbook of positive psychology* (pp. 3–9). Oxford University Press.

Seligman, M. E. P. (2011). *Flourish: A visionary new understanding of happiness and well-being*. Free Press.

Seligman, M. E. P., & Csikszentmihalyi, M. (2000). Positive psychology: An introduction. *The American Psychologist*, 55(1), 5–14. 10.1037/0003-066X.55.1.511392865

Seligman, M. E. P., & Csikszentmihalyi, M. (Eds.). (2000a). Happiness, excellence, and optimal human functioning [special issue]. *The American Psychologist*, 55(1).11392865

Seligman, M. E. P., Ernst, R. M., Gillham, J., Reivich, K., & Linkins, M. (2009). Positive education: Positive psychology and classroom interventions. *Oxford Review of Education*, 35(3), 293–311. 10.1080/03054980902934563

Seligman, M. E. P., Schulman, P., & Tryon, A. M. (2007). Group prevention of depression and anxiety symptoms. *Behaviour Research and Therapy*, 45(6), 1111–1126. 10.1016/j.brat.2006.09.01017074301

Seligman, M. E. P., Steen, T. A., Park, N., & Peterson, C. (2005). Positive Psychology Progress: Empirical Validation of Interventions. *The American Psychologist*, 60(5), 410–421. 10.1037/0003-066X.60.5.41016045394

Semple, R. J., Droutman, V., & Reid, B. A. (2017). Mindfulness goes to school: Things learned (so far) from research and real-world experiences. *Psychology in the Schools*, 54(1), 29–52. 10.1002/pits.2198128458403

Serrat, O. (2009). Understanding and developing emotional intelligence. *Knowledge Solutions*, 49, 34–61.

Seville, E. (2008). *Resilience: Great concept…but what does it mean*? Wilmington.

Shae-Leigh, V., & Nagesh, P. (2019). A theoretical review of psychological resilience. Defining resilience and resilience research over the decades. *Archives of Medicine and Health Sciences*, 7(2), 233–239. 10.4103/amhs.amhs_119_19

Shahriari Shaghaghi, Z., Ghanbaripanah, A., & Tajalli, P. (2021). The Role of Affective Family Atmosphere, School Atmosphere and Perceived Social Support in Predicting Aggressive Behavior and Addiction Readiness among Students. *International Journal of Behavioral Sciences*, 15(1), 20–26.

Shakki, F. (2022). Iranian EFL students' L2 engagement: The effects of teacher-student rapport and teacher support. *Lang. Relat. Res.*, 13, 175–198. 10.52547/LRR.13.3.8

Shand, M. (2014). *Understanding and building resilience with art: A socio-ecological approach*. Edith Cowan University.

Shankland, R., & Rosset, E. (2017). Review of brief school-based positive psychological interventions: A taster for teachers and educators. *Educational Psychology Review*, 29(2), 363–392. 10.1007/s10648-016-9357-3

Shapiro, S. L., Carlson, L. E., Astin, J. A., & Freeman, B. (2006). Mechanisms of mindfulness. *Journal of Clinical Psychology*, 62(3), 373–386. 10.1002/jclp.2023716385481

Sharot, T. (2011, June 6). The optimism bias. *Time*, 177(23), 40–45. 10.1016/j.cub.2011.10.03021682073

Sheldon, K. M., Corcoran, C., & Prentice, M. (2019). Pursuing eudaimonic functioning versus pursuing hedonic well-being: The first goal succeeds in its aim, whereas the second does not. *Journal of Happiness Studies*, 20(3), 919–933. 10.1007/s10902-018-9980-4

Sheldon, K. M., & King, L. (2001). Positive psychology [special issue]. *The American Psychologist*, 56(3), 216–263. 10.1037/0003-066X.56.3.21611315247

Sherer, J. Z., & Spillane, J. P. (2011). Constancy and change in work practice in schools: The role of organizational routines. *Teachers College Record*, 113(3), 611–657. 10.1177/016146811111300302

Shirley, E. L., & Cornell, D. G. (2012). The contribution of student perceptions of school climate to understanding the disproportionate punishment of African American students in a middle school. *School Psychology International*, 33(2), 115–134. 10.1177/0143034311406815

Sibinga, E. M., Kerrigan, D., Stewart, M., Johnson, K., Magyari, T., & Ellen, J. M. (2011). Mindfulness-based stress reduction for urban youth. *Journal of Alternative and Complementary Medicine (New York, N.Y.)*, 17(3), 213–218. 10.1089/acm.2009.060521348798

Siegel, D. (1999). *The developing mind: Toward a neurobiology of interpersonal experience*. Guilford.

Sillanpää, T., Visuri, F., & Ruokonen, I. (n.d.). *Froebel Box: A Tool for Participatory and Creative Learning*. Academic Press.

Simion, A. (2021). Children's Emotional Health In The Context Of E-Learning. Parents' And Teachers' Perspective. In I. Albulescu & C. Stan (Eds.), Education, Reflection, Development -ERD 2021, vol.2 European Proceedings of Educational Sciences (pp. 204-214). European Publisher. 10.15405/epes.22032.20

Singer, D. G., Golinkof, R. M., & Pasek, K. H. (2006). *Play = learning. How play motivates and enhances children' s cognitive and social – emotional growth*. Oxford University Press. 10.1093/acprof:oso/9780195304381.001.0001

Singh, K., & Kaur, S. (2019). Psychological empowerment of teachers: Development and validation of multi-dimensional scale. *International Journal of Recent Technology and Engineering*, 7(655), 340–347.

Singh, S. P. (2017). Educational differential among disabled children: A study in elementary schools in Uttar Pradesh. *International Education and Research Journal*, 3(10), 22–28.

Sin, N. L., & Lyubomirsky, S. (2009). Enhancing well-being and alleviating depressive symptoms with positive psychology interventions: A practice-friendly meta-analysis. *Journal of Clinical Psychology*, 65(5), 467–487. 10.1002/jclp.2059319301241

Sisto, A., Ricci, G., Vicinanza, F., & Campanozzi, L. L. (2019). Towards a transversal definition of psychological resilience: A literature review. *Medicina*, 55(11), 745. 10.3390/medicina5511074531744109

Skaalvik, E. M., & Skaalvik, S. (2011). Teacher job satisfaction and motivation to leave the teaching profession: Relations with school context, feeling of belonging, and emotional exhaustion. *Teaching and Teacher Education*, 27(6), 1029–1038. 10.1016/j.tate.2011.04.001

Skovdal, M., & Campbell, C. (2015). Beyond education: What role can schools play in the support and protection of children in extreme settings? *International Journal of Educational Development*, 41, 175–183. Advance online publication. 10.1016/j.ijedudev.2015.02.005

Slaski, M., & Cartwright, S. (2002). Health, performance and emotional intelligence: An exploratory study of retail managers. *Stress and Health*, 18(2), 63–68. 10.1002/smi.926

Slavin, R. E. (2007). *Educational psychology: theory and practice*. Gutenberg.

Slee, R. (2018). *Inclusive education isn't dead, it just smells funny*. Routledge. 10.4324/9780429486869

Sleeter, C. E., & Grant, C. A. (2008). *Making choices for multicultural education: Five approaches to race, class and gender*. John Wiley & Sons.

Slemp, G. R., Chin, T.-C., Kern, M. L., Siokou, C., Loton, D., Oades, L. G., Vella-Brodrick, D., & Waters, L. (2017). Positive Education in Australia: Practice, Measurement, and Future Directions. In Frydenberg, E., Martin, A. J., & Collie, R. J. (Eds.), *Social and Emotional Learning in Australia and the Asia-Pacific* (pp. 101–122). Springer Singapore. 10.1007/978-981-10-3394-0_6

Smiley, P. A., Buttitta, K. V., Chung, S. Y., Dubon, V. X., & Chang, L. K. (2016). Mediation models of implicit theories and achievement goals predict planning and withdrawal after failure. *Motivation and Emotion*, 40(6), 878–894. 10.1007/s11031-016-9575-5

Smith, D. D., & Tyler, N. C. (2019). *Introduction to special education and training bringing about change*. Gutenberg.

Smokowski, P. R., Reynolds, A. J., & Bezruczko, N. (1999). Resilience and protective factors in adolescence: An autobiographical perspective from disadvantaged youth. *Journal of School Psychology*, 37(4), 425–448. 10.1016/S0022-4405(99)00028-X

Snyder, C. R., Harris, C., Anderson, J. R., Holleran, S. A., Irving, L. M., Sigmon, S. T., Yoshinobu, L., Gibb, J., Langelle, C., & Harney, P. (1991). The will and the ways: Development and validation of an individual-differences measure of hope. *Journal of Personality and Social Psychology*, 60(4), 570–585. 10.1037/0022-3514.60.4.5702037968

Snyder, C. R., Irving, L. M., & Anderson, J. R. (2002). Hope and health: Measuring the will and the ways. In Snyder, C. R. (Ed.), *Handbook of hope: Theory, measures, and applications* (pp. 201–210). Academic Press.

Sofologi, M., Kamari, A., Kougioumtzis, G. A., Tatsiopoulou, P., Bonti, E., Papadimitropoulou, P., & Sarris, D. (2023). Emphasizing the Developmental Trajectory of Executive Functions in Preschool, School Children, Adolescence, and Its Relations with School Performance: The Development of Executive Functions. In D. Katsarou (Ed.), *Developmental Language Disorders in Childhood and Adolescence* (pp. 224-238). IGI Global. 10.4018/979-8-3693-0644-4.ch017

Sofologi, M., Markou, E., Kougioumtzis, G. A., Kamari, A., & Tsanidou, A. (2020). Polymorphous Heterogeneity and Episodes of Violence in School Community: Educational Implications for Building a Democratic School. *Dual Diagnosis Open Access, 5*(1:4). doi: 10.36648/2472-5043.5.1.4

Sofologi, M., Kougioumtzis, G. A., Efstratopoulou, M., Skoura, E., Sagia, S., Karvela, S., Salli, P.-M., Makri, E., & Bonti, E. (2022). Specific Learning Disabilities and Psychosocial Difficulties in Children. In *Advising Preservice Teachers Through Narratives from Students With Disabilities* (pp. 31–54). IGI Global. 10.4018/978-1-7998-7359-4.ch002

Sokou, K. (2004). *The promotion of mental health in the school community of the Southeastern Cyclades: The effect of the intervention with the words of teachers and students.* Scale-Tributes, 14-17.

Soloway, G. B. (2016). Preparing teacher candidates for the present: Investigating the value of mindfulness-training in teacher education. *Handbook of mindfulness in education: Integrating theory and research into practice* (pp. 191-205). https://doi.org/10.1007/978-1-4939-3506-2_12

Song, K. (2022). Well-Being of Teachers: The Role of Efficacy of Teachers and Academic Optimism. *Frontiers in Psychology*, 12, 831972. 10.3389/fpsyg.2021.83197235153944

Sorkos, G., & Hajisoteriou, C. (2021). Sustainable intercultural and inclusive education: Teachers' efforts on promoting a combining paradigm. *Pedagogy, Culture & Society*, 29(4), 517–536. 10.1080/14681366.2020.1765193

Sorrenti, L., Spadaro, L., Mafodda, A. V., Scopelliti, G., Orecchio, S., & Filippello, P. (2019). The predicting role of school learned helplessness in internalizing and externalizing problems. An exploratory study in students with Specific Learning Disorder. *Mediterranean Journal of Clinical Psychology*, 7(2), 437–478.

Sparks, R. L., & Lovett, B. J. (2009). College students with learning disability diagnoses: Who are they and how do they perform? *Journal of Learning Disabilities*, 42(6), 494–510. 10.1177/0022219409338746l9704046

Spekman, N. J., Goldberg, R. J., & Herman, K. L. (1992). Learning disabled children grow up: A search for factors related to success in the young adult years. *Learning Disabilities Research & Practice*, 7(3), 161–170.

Spektor-Levy, O., & Yifrach, M. (2019). If science teachers are positively inclined toward inclusive education, why is it so difficult? *Research in Science Education*, 49(3), 737–766. 10.1007/s11165-017-9636-0

Spencer, H. (1855). *The Principles of Psychology*. Longman, Brown, Green and Longmans. 10.1037/14065-000

Spillane, J. P., Parise, L. M., & Sherer, J. Z. (2011). Organizational routines as coupling mechanisms: Policy, school administration, and the technical core. *American Educational Research Journal*, 48(3), 586–619. 10.3102/0002831210385102

Spiteri, D. (2016). *Multiculturalism, higher education and intercultural communication: developing strengths-based narratives for teaching and learning*. Springer.

Stalikas, A., Triliva, S., & Roussi, P. (2011). *Positive psychology applications*. Klidarithmos Publications.

Stallard, P., Simpson, N., Anderson, S., Carter, T., Osborn, C., & Bush, S. (2005). An evaluation of the FRIENDS programme: A cognitive behaviour therapy intervention to promote emotional resilience. *Archives of Disease in Childhood*, 90(10), 1016–1019. 10.1136/adc.2004.06816316049062

Stallard, P., Simpson, N., Anderson, S., Hibbert, S., & Osborn, C. (2007). The FRIENDS emotional health programme: Initial findings from a school- based project. *Child and Adolescent Mental Health*, 12(1), 32–37. 10.1111/j.1475-3588.2006.00421.x32811032

Stallard, P., Skryabina, E., Taylor, G., Phillips, R., Daniels, H., Anderson, R., & Simpson, N. (2014). Classroom-based cognitive behaviour therapy (FRIENDS): A cluster randomised controlled trial to Prevent Anxiety in Children through Education in Schools (PACES). *The Lancet. Psychiatry*, 1(3), 185–192. 10.1016/S2215-0366(14)70244-526360730

Stasinós, D. (2016). Towards Inclusive or Total Education in the New-Digital School with Digital Champions. Papazisis publications.

State of Victoria (Department of Education and Training). (2021). *Empowering Students and Building School Pride Implementation Guide*, How schools promote and sustain student empowerment.

Staw, B. M., Sutton, R. I., & Pelled, L. H. (1994). Employee positive emotion and favorable outcomes at the workplace. *Organization Science*, 5(1), 51–71. 10.1287/orsc.5.1.51

Sternberg, R. J. (1997). *Successful intelligence: How practical and creative intelligence determine success in life*. Simon and Shuster.

Sternberg, R. J. (2013). Intelligence. In Handbook of Psychology. John Wiley. 10.18637/jss.v048.i02

Stockings, E. A., Degenhardt, L., Dobbins, T., Lee, Y. Y., Erskine, H. E., Whiteford, H. A., & Patton, G. (2016). Preventing depression and anxiety in young people: A review of the joint efficacy of universal, selective and indicated prevention. *Psychological Medicine*, 46(1), 11–26. 10.1017/S003329171500172526315536

Stronge, J. H., Ward, T. J., & Grant, L. W. (2011). What makes good teachers good? A cross-case analysis of the connection between teacher effectiveness and student achievement. *Journal of Teacher Education*, 62(4), 339–355. 10.1177/0022487111404241

Styss, Y., & Brown, S. (2004). *A review of Emotional Intelligence literature and implications for corrections*. Research Report, Research Branch Correctional Service of Canada.

Suldo, S. M., McMahan, M. M., Chappel, A. M., & Loker, T. (2012). Relationships between perceived school climate and adolescent mental health across genders. School Mental Health: A Multidisciplinary Research and Practice Journal, 4(2), 69-80.

Suldo, S. M., Savage, J. A., & Mercer, S. H. (2014). Increasing middle school students' life satisfaction: Efficacy of a positive psychology group intervention. *Journal of Happiness Studies*, 15(1), 19–42. 10.1007/s10902-013-9414-2

Sutton-Smith, B. (2008). The role of play in cognitive development. *Reading in Human Development,* 83-95.

Swanson, H. L., & Siegel, L. (2009). Learning disabilities and working memory deficit. *Issues in Education*, 7(1), 48–60.

Sylla, C., Brooks, E., & Tümmler, L. (2018). Blocks as symbolic tools for children's playful collaboration. *Lecture Notes of the Institute for Computer Sciences. Social-Informatics and Telecommunications Engineering, LNICST*, 229, 413–423. 10.1007/978-3-319-76908-0_40

Tafuri, F., & Latino, F. (2024). School medical service: Strategies to promote psycho-physiological well-being. *Pediatric Reports*, 16(1), 214–231. 10.3390/pediatric1601001938535515

Tavassoli, N., Dunfield, K., Kleis, A., Recchia, H., & Conto, L. P. (2023). Preschoolers' responses to prosocial opportunities during naturalistic interactions with peers: A cross-cultural comparison. *Social Development*, 32(1), 204–222. 10.1111/sode.12620

Taylor, F. A., & Kuo, F. E. (2011). Could exposure to Everyday Green Spaces Help Treat ADHD? Evidence from Children's Play Settings. *Applied Psychology. Health and Well-Being*, 3(3), 281–303. 10.1111/j.1758-0854.2011.01052.x

Taylor, G. J. (2001). Low Emotional Intelligence and mental illness. In Ciarrochi, J., Forgas, J. P., & Mayer, J. D. (Eds.), *Emotional intelligence in everyday life: a scientific inquiry* (pp. 76–81). Psychology Press.

Taylor, I. M., & Ntoumanis, N. (2007). Teacher Motivational Strategies and Student Self-Determination in Physical Education. *Journal of Educational Psychology*, 99(4), 747–760. 10.1037/0022-0663.99.4.747

Taylor, R. D., Oberle, E., Durlak, J. A., & Weissberg, R. P. (2017). Promoting positive youth development through school-based social and emotional learning interventions: A meta-analysis of follow-up effects. *Child Development*, 88(4), 1156–1171. 10.1111/cdev.1286428685826

Terpstra, J. E., Higgins, K., & Pierce, T. (2002). Can I play? Classroom-based interventions for teaching play skills to children with autism. *Focus on Autism and Other Developmental Disabilities*, 17(2), 119–127. 10.1177/10883576020170020701

Thapa, A., Cohen, J., Guffey, S., & Higgins-D'Alessandro, A. (2013). A review of school climate research. *Review of Educational Research*, 83(3), 357–385. 10.3102/0034654313483907

Theodoratou, M., Farmakopoulou, I., Kougioumtzis, G. A., Kaltsouda, A., Siouti, Z., Sofologi, M., Gkintoni, E., & Tsitsas, G. (2023). Emotion-focused coping, social support, and active coping among university students: Gender differences. *Journal of Psychology & Clinical Psychiatry.*, 14(1), 5–9. 10.15406/jpcpy.2023.14.00720

Thornberg, R., Forsberg, C., Chiriac, E. H., & Bjereld, Y. (2020). Teacher–student relationship quality and student engagement: A sequential explanatory mixed-methods study. *Research Papers in Education*, 37(6), 840–859. 10.1080/02671522.2020.1864772

Thorndike, E. L. (1920). A constant error in psychological ratings. *The Journal of Applied Psychology*, 4(1), 25–29. 10.1037/h0071663

Tian, M., Deng, Z., Meng, Z., Li, R., Zhang, Z., Qi, W., Wang, R., Yin, T., & Ji, M. (2018). The impact of individual differences, types of model and social settings on block building performance among Chinese preschoolers. *Frontiers in Psychology*, 9(JAN), 27. Advance online publication. 10.3389/fpsyg.2018.0002729441031

Tlili, A., Denden, M., Duan, A., Padilla-Zea, N., Huang, R., Sun, T., & Burgos, D. (2022). Game-Based Learning for Learners With Disabilities—What Is Next? A Systematic Literature Review From the Activity Theory Perspective. *Frontiers in Psychology*, 12, 1–12. 10.3389/fpsyg.2021.81469135211058

Toland, J., & Carrigan, D. (2011). Educational Psychology and Resilience: New Concept, New Opportunities. *School Psychology International*, 32(1), 95–106. 10.1177/0143034310397284

Tomlinson, C. A. (2017). *How to differentiate instruction in academically diverse classrooms*. ASCD.

Tomlinson, E. R., Yousaf, O., Vittersø, A. D., & Jones, L. (2018). Dispositional mindfulness and psychological health: A systematic review. *Mindfulness*, 9(1), 23–43. 10.1007/s12671-017-0762-629387263

Tonegawa, Y. (2022). Contextualization of inclusive education: Education for children with disabilities in Myanmar. *International Journal of Instruction*, 15(1), 365–380. 10.29333/iji.2022.15121a

Toriello, H. V., Van de Ridder, J. M., Brewer, P., Mavis, B., Allen, R., Arvidson, C., Kovar-Gough, I., Novak, E., O'Donnell, J., Osuch, J., & Ulrich, B. (2022). Emotional intelligence in undergraduate medical students: A scoping review. *Advances in Health Sciences Education : Theory and Practice*, 27(1), 1–21. 10.1007/s10459-021-10079-234709484

Tosto, M. G., Asbury, K., Mazzocco, M. M., Petrill, S. A., & Kovas, Y. (2016). From classroom environment to mathematics achievement: The mediating role of self-perceived ability and subject interest. *Learning and Individual Differences*, 50, 260–269. 10.1016/j.lindif.2016.07.00927766018

Trawick-Smith, J., Swaminathan, S., Baton, B., Danieluk, C., Marsh, S., & Szarwacki, M. (2017). Block play and mathematics learning in preschool: The effects of building complexity, peer and teacher interactions in the block area, and replica play materials. *Journal of Early Childhood Research*, 15(4), 433–448. 10.1177/1476718X16664557

Triliva, S., & Chimienti, G. (1998). *You and I Become We - Conflict Control Program*. Greek Letters.

Trinidad, D. R., & Johnson, C. A. (2002). The association of emotional intelligence and early adolescent tobacco and alcohol use. *Personality and Individual Differences*, 32(1), 95–105. 10.1016/S0191-8869(01)00008-3

Triviño-Amigo, N., Mendoza-Muñoz, D. M., Mayordomo-Pinilla, N., Barrios-Fernández, S., Contreras-Barraza, N., Gil-Marín, M., Castilio, D., Gallan-Arroyo, C., & Rojo-Ramos, J. (2022). Inclusive education in primary and secondary school: Perception of teacher training. *International Journal of Environmental Research and Public Health*, 19(23), 15451. 10.3390/ijerph192315451 36497523

Tsang, K. K. Y., Shum, K. K., Chan, W. W. L., Li, S. X., Kwan, H. W., Su, M. R., Wong, B. P. H., & Lam, S. F. (2021). Effectiveness and Mechanisms of Mindfulness Training for School Teachers in Difficult Times: A Randomized Controlled Trial. *Mindfulness*, 12(11), 2820–2831. 10.1007/s12671-021-01750-1 34545293

Tsaousis, I., & Nikolaou, I. (2005). Exploring the relationship of emotional intelligence with physical and psychological health functioning. *Stress and Health*, 21(2), 77–86. 10.1002/smi.1042

Tschannen-Moran, M., & Hoy, A. W. (2007). The differential antecedents of self-efficacy beliefs of novice and experienced teachers. *Teaching and Teacher Education*, 23(6), 944–956. 10.1016/j.tate.2006.05.003

Turner, I., Reynolds, K. J., Lee, E., Subasic, E., & Bromhead, D. (2014). Well-being, school climate, and the social identity process: A latent growth model study of bullying perpetration and peer victimization. *School Psychology Quarterly*, 29(3), 320–335. 10.1037/spq0000074 24933217

Turner, S., Norman, E., & Zunz, S. (1995). Enhancing Resiliency in Girls and Boys: A Case for Gender Specific Adolescent Prevention Programming. *The Journal of Primary Prevention*, 16(1), 25–37. 10.1007/BF02407231 24254657

Tyack, D., & Tobin, W. (1994). The "grammar" of schooling: Why has it been so hard to change? *American Educational Research Journal*, 31(3), 453–479. 10.3102/00028312031003453

Τσέργας, Ν. (2014). *Θεραπευτικές Προσεγγίσεις μέσω της Τέχνης*. Τόπος.

U.S. Department of Education. (2023). Guiding Principles for Creating Safe, Inclusive, Supportive, and Fair School Climates. Retrieved May 20, 2024 from https://www2.ed.gov/policy/gen/guid/school-discipline/guiding-principles.pdf

Ullman, J. (2022). Trans/gender-diverse students' perceptions of positive school climate and teacher concern as factors in school belonging: Results from an Australian National Study. *Teachers College Record*, 124(8), 145–167. 10.1177/01614681221121710

UNESCO International Bureau of Education. (2013). Glossary of Curriculum Terminology. UNESCO.

UNESCO. (1994). The Salamanca Statement and Framework for Action on Special Needs Education. Organized by the World Conference on Special Needs Education: Access and Equity. Paris: UNESCO.

UNESCO. (2017). *MoE-Alberta*. Training Tools for Curriculum Development.

Ungar, M. (2004). A constructionist discourse on resilience: Multiple contexts, multiple realities among at-risk children and youth. *Youth & Society*, 35(3), 341–365. 10.1177/0044118X03257030

Ungar, M. (2005). A thicker description of resilience. *International Journal of Narrative Therapy and Community Work*, 3, 89–96.

Ungar, M. (2008). Resilience across cultures. *British Journal of Social Work*, 38(2), 218–235. 10.1093/bjsw/bcl343

Ungar, M. (2018). Systemic resilience: Principles and processes for a science of change in contexts of adversity. *Ecology and Society*, 23(4), art34. Advance online publication. 10.5751/ES-10385-230434

Ungar, M., Connelly, G., Liebenberg, L., & Theron, L. (2019). How schools enhance the development of young people's resilience. *Social Indicators Research*, 145(2), 615–627. 10.1007/s11205-017-1728-8

Ungar, M., Russell, P., & Connelly, G. (2014). School-Based Interventions to Enhance the Resilience of Students. *Journal of Educational and Developmental Psychology*, 4(1), 66. 10.5539/jedp.v4n1p66

Ungar, M., & Theron, L. (2020). Resilience and Mental Health: How Multisystemic Processes Contribute to Positive Outcomes. *The Lancet. Psychiatry*, 7(5), 441–448. 10.1016/S2215-0366(19)30434-131806473

United Nations Educational Scientific and Cultural Organization, Institute for Lifelong Learning. (1994). The Salamanca Statement and Framework for Action on Special Needs Education. https://unesdoc.unesco.org/images/0009/000984/098427eo.pdf

United Nations Educational Scientific and Cultural Organization, Institute for Lifelong Learning. (2020). Inclusive teaching: preparing all teachers to teach all students. https://unesdoc.unesco.org/ark:/48223/pf0000374447

United Nations Educational Scientific and Cultural Organization, Institute for Lifelong Learning. (2021). Reimagining our futures together: A new social contract for education. https://unesdoc.unesco.org/ark:/48223/pf0000379707

United Nations Educational Scientific and Cultural Organization, Institute for Lifelong Learning. (2022). Welcoming Diversity in the Learning Environment. Teacher's Handbook for Inclusive Education. https://www.minedu.gov.gr/publications/docs2023/eidiki-agogi/C.%20Welcoming%20Diversity%20.pdf

United Nations. (1966). International covenant on economic, social and cultural rights. Retrieved May 20, 2024 from https://www.ohchr.org/en/instruments-mechanisms/instruments/international-covenant-economic-social-and-cultural-rights

Valente, D. (2017). *Using stories to "reach and teach" primary learners with dyslexia.* World of Better Learning | Cambridge University Press.

Valente, S., & Lourenço, A. A. (2020). Conflict in the classroom: How teachers' emotional intelligence influences conflict management. *Frontiers in Education*, 5, 5. 10.3389/feduc.2020.00005

Valiente, C., Lemery-Chalfant, K., Swanson, J., & Reiser, M. (2008). Prediction of children's academic competence from their effortful control, relationships, and classroom participation. *Journal of Educational Psychology*, 100(1), 67–77. 10.1037/0022-0663.100.1.6721212831

Vallejo, M. A. (2006). Mindfulness (Presencia reflexiva y atenta). *Psicología Conductual*, 14, 433–451. 10.1037/0021-9010.82.1.30

Van Beurden, J., Van Veldhoven, M., Nijendijk, K., & Van De Voorde, K. (2017). Teachers' remaining career opportunities: The role of value fit and school climate. *Teaching and Teacher Education*, 68(1), 143–150. 10.1016/j.tate.2017.09.002

van Driel, M.L., De Sutter, A. I., Habraken, H., Thorning, S., & Christiaens, T. (2016). Different antibiotic treatments for group A streptococcal pharyngitis. *Cochrane Database Syst Rev., 11*(9). .10.1002/14651858.CD004406.pub4

Van Eck, K., Johnson, S. R., Bettencourt, A., & Johnson, S. L. (2017). How school climate relates to chronic absence: A multi–level latent profile analysis. *Journal of School Psychology*, 61, 89–102. 10.1016/j.jsp.2016.10.00128259246

van Uden, J. M., Ritzen, H., & Pieters, J. M. (2014). Engaging students: The role of teacher beliefs and interpersonal teacher behavior in fostering student engagement in vocational education. *Teaching and Teacher Education*, 37, 21–32. 10.1016/j.tate.2013.08.005

VanBreda, A. D. P. (2001). *Resilience Theory: A literature review*. South Africa Military Health Service.

Vandenbroucke, L., Spilt, J., Verschueren, K., Piccinin, C., & Baeyens, D. (2018). The classroom as a developmental context for cognitive development: A meta-analysis on the importance of teacher–student interactions for children's executive functions. *Review of Educational Research*, 88(1), 125–164. 10.3102/0034654317743200

Vanderbilt-Adriance, E., & Shaw, D. S. (2008). Protective Factors and the Development of Resilience in the Context of Neighborhood Disadvantage. *Journal of Abnormal Child Psychology*, 36(6), 887–901. 10.1007/s10802-008-9220-118288604

Vargianniti, I., & Karpouzis, K. (2019). Effects of Game-Based Learning on Academic Performance and Student Interest. In Liapis, A., Yannakakis, G. G., Gentile, M., & Ninaus, M. (Eds.), Lecture Notes in Computer Science. Springer. 10.1007/978-3-030-34350-7_32

Veldman, I., Van Tartwijk, J., Brekelmans, M., & Wubbels, T. (2013). Job satisfaction and teacher–student relationships across the teaching career: Four case studies. *Teaching and Teacher Education*, 32, 55–65. 10.1016/j.tate.2013.01.005

Vella-Broderick, D. (2011). Positive psychology: Reflecting on the past and projecting into the future. *InPsych*, 33(2), 10–13. https://www.psychology.org.au/publications/inpsych/2011/april/vella-brodrick

Vesely Maillefer, A., Udayar, S., & Fiori, M. (2018). Enhancing the prediction of emotionally intelligent behavior: The PAT integrated framework involving trait EI, ability EI, and emotion information processing. *Frontiers in Psychology*, 9, 1078. 10.3389/fpsyg.2018.0107830013496

Vesely-Maillefer, A. K., & Saklofske, D. H. (2018). Emotional intelligence and the next generation of teachers. In Keefer, K. V., Parker, J. D. A., & Saklofske, D. H. (Eds.), *Emotional Intelligence in Education: Integrating Research with Practice* (pp. 377–402). Springer International Publishing/ Springer Nature. 10.1007/978-3-319-90633-1_14

Victoria and State Government, Department of Education and Training. (2021). *Empowering Students and Building School Pride Implementation Guide.* Author.

Virat, M. (2022). Teachers' compassionate love for students: A possible determinant of teacher-student relationships with adolescents and a mediator between teachers' perceived support from coworkers and teacher-student relationships. *Educational Studies*, 48(3), 291–309. 10.1080/03055698.2020.1751083

Virtanen, M., Kivimäki, M., Luopa, P., Vahtera, J., Elovainio, M., Jokela, J., & Pietikäinen, M. (2009). Staff reports of psychosocial climate at school and adolescents' health, truancy and health education in Finland. *European Journal of Public Health*, 19(5), 554–560. 10.1093/ eurpub/ckp03219321716

Vlahaki, E. X. (2006). *Eating disorders and their relation to Emotional intelligence in 18-20 year olds.* Master Thesis. Athens: Harokopio University.

Volk, D. T. (2020). An Examination of the Relationship Between School Climate, Self-Determined Academic Motivation, and Academic Outcomes Among Middle and High School Students [Doctoral Dissertation, University of Connecticut]. UCONN. https://opencommons.uconn.edu/ dissertations/2435

Vygotsky, L. S., & Cole, M. (1978). *Mind in society: Development of higher psychological processes.* Harvard University Press.

Waaktaar, T., Christie, H. J., Borge, A. I., & Turgersen, S. (2004). How can young people's resilience be enhanced? Experiences from a clinical intervention project. *Clinical Child Psychology and Psychiatry*, 9(2), 167–183. 10.1177/1359104504041917

Wächter, T., Gorges, J., Apresjan, S., & Lütje-Klose, B. (2024). How can inclusion succeed for all? Children's well-being in inclusive schools and the role of teachers' inclusion-related attitudes and self-efficacy. *Teaching and Teacher Education*, 139, 139. 10.1016/j.tate.2023.104411

Wajiuhullah, A., Ashraf, S., & Majad, S. (2018). Development of Number Concepts in Students with Intellectual Disability by Using Digital Game Based Learning. *The Journal of Educational Research*, 21(1), 122.

Walls, J., Ryu, J., Fairchild, L., & Johnson, J. (2021). Contexts of belonging: Toward a multilevel understanding of caring and engagement in schools. *Educational Policy*, 35(5), 748–780. 10.1177/0895904819843590

Walton, G. M., Cohen, G. L., Cwir, D., & Spencer, S. J. (2012). Mere belonging: The power of social connections. *Journal of Personality and Social Psychology*, 102(3), 513–532. 10.1037/a002573122023711

Wang Y., Pan B., Yu Z., & Song Z. (2023). The relationship between preschool teacher trait mindfulness and teacher-child relationship quality: the chain mediating role of emotional intelligence and empathy. *Curr. Psychol.*, 1–12. 10.1007/s12144-023-04512-5

Wang, C. H., Ke, Y. T., Wu, J. T., & Hsu, W. H. (2012). Collaborative action research on technology integration for science learning. *Journal of Science Education and Technology*, 21(1), 125–132. 10.1007/s10956-011-9289-0

Wang, M. C., Haertel, G. D., & Walberg, H. J. (1994). Educational resilience in inner cities. In Wang, M. C., & Gordon, E. W. (Eds.), *Educational resilience in inner-city America: Challenges and prospects* (pp. 45–72). Lawrence Erlbaum.

Wang, M. T., & Degol, J. L. (2016). School climate: A review of the construct, measurement, and impact on student outcomes. *Educational Psychology Review*, 28(2), 315–352. 10.1007/s10648-015-9319-1

Wang, M. T., Degol, J. L., Amemiya, J., Parr, A., & Guo, J. (2020). Classroom climate and children's academic and psychological wellbeing: A systematic review and meta-analysis. *Developmental Review*, 57, 100912. 10.1016/j.dr.2020.100912

Wang, M. T., & Eccles, J. S. (2013). School context, achievement motivation, and academic engagement: A longitudinal study of school engagement using a multidimensional perspective. *Learning and Instruction*, 28, 12–23. 10.1016/j.learninstruc.2013.04.002

Wang, M. T., & Fredricks, J. A. (2014). The reciprocal links between school engagement, youth problem behaviors, and school dropout during adolescence. *Child Development*, 85(2), 722–737. 10.1111/cdev.1213823895361

Wang, M. T., & Huguley, J. P. (2012). Parental racial socialization as a moderator of the effects of racial discrimination on educational success among African American adolescents. *Child Development*, 83(5), 1716–1731. 10.1111/j.1467-8624.2012.01808.x22717004

Wang, Y., & Derakhshan, A. (2023). Teacher confirmation and caring as predictors of Chinese and Iranian EFL students' willingness to attend EFL classes. *Porta Linguarum Rev. Int.Didáctica Lenguas Extranjeras*, 39(39), 165–192. 10.30827/portalin.vi39.23625

Warunwutthi, N., Wattananonsakul, S., & Ekpansyaskul, C. (2022). The effectiveness of growth mindset counseling program to enhance students resilience in a public autonomous university in Thailand. *Journal of Research and Curriculum Development, 12*(1). https://so03.tci-thaijo.org/index.php/jrcd/article/view/260705

Waterman, A. S. (2013). Eudaimonia: Contrasting two conceptions of happiness: Hedonia and eudaimonia. In Froh, J. J., & Parks, A. C. (Eds.), *Activities for teaching Positive Psychology: A guide for instructors* (pp. 29–34). American Psychological Association. 10.1037/14042-005

Waters, L. (2011). A review of school-based positive psychology interventions. *The Australian Educational and Developmental Psychologist*, 28(2), 75–90. 10.1375/aedp.28.2.75

Waters, L. (2015). The Relationship between Strength-Based Parenting with Children's Stress Levels and Strength-Based Coping Approaches. *Psychology (Irvine, Calif.)*, 6(6), 689–699. 10.4236/psych.2015.66067

Waters, L., & Loton, D. (2019). SEARCH: A meta-framework and review of the field of positive education. *International Journal of Applied Positive Psychology*, 4(1–2), 1–46. 10.1007/s41042-019-00017-4

Watt, N. F., Anthony, E. J., Wynne, L. C., & Rolf, J. E. (Eds.). (1984). *Children at risk for schizophrenia: A longitudinal perspective*. Cambridge University Press.

Waxman, H. C., Huang, S. L., & Wang, M. C. (1997). Investigating the multilevel classroom learning environment of resilient and nonresilient students from inner-city elementary schools. *International Journal of Educational Research*, 27(4), 343–353. 10.1016/S0883-0355(97)90016-1

Weare, K., & Gray, G. (2000). *Promoting Mental and Emotional Health at School, A Handbook for Educators*. Greek Letters.

Weare, K., & Nind, M. (2011). Mental health promotion and problem prevention in schools: What does the evidence say? *Health Promotion International*, 26(suppl_1), i29–i69. 10.1093/heapro/dar07522079935

Weekes, D. P. (1991). Application of the life-span developmental perspective to nursing research with adolescents. *Journal of Pediatric Nursing*, 6(1), 38–48. https://europepmc.org/article/med/19901251990125

Weinstein, C. S., Mignano, A. J., & Romano, M. E. (2007). Elementary classroom management: Lessons from research and practice. Academic Press.

Weinstein, N., Brown, K. W., & Ryan, R. M. (2009). A multi-method examination of the effects of mindfulness on stress attribution, coping and emotional well-being. *Journal of Research in Personality*, 43(3), 374–385. 10.1016/j.jrp.2008.12.008

Weissberg, R. P., & Greenberg, M. T. (1998). School and community competence enhancement and prevention programs. In *Handbook of child psychology: Child psychology in practice* (pp. 877-954). New York: John Wiley & Sons.

Weissberg, R. P., & O'Brien, M. U. (2004). What works in school-based social and em otional learning programs for youth development. *The Annals of the American Academy of Political and Social Science*, 591(1), 86–97. 10.1177/0002716203260093

Weiss, H., & Cropanzano, R. (1996). Affective events theory: A theoretical discussion of the structure, causes and consequences of affective experiences at work. *Research in Organizational Behavior*, 18, 1–74.

Werner, E. E. (1989). High risk children in young adulthood: A longitudinal study from birth to 32 years. *The American Journal of Orthopsychiatry*, 59(1), 72–81. 10.1111/j.1939-0025.1989.tb01636.x2467566

Werner, E. E. (2000). Protective factors and individual resilience. In Shonkoff, J. P., & Meisels, S. J. (Eds.), *Handbook of Early Childhood Intervention* (2nd ed., pp. 115–132). Cambridge University Press. 10.1017/CBO9780511529320.008

Werner, E. E., & Smith, R. (1982). *Vulnerable but invincible: A study of resilient children.* McGraw-Hill.

Werner, E. E., & Smith, R. S. (1992). *Overcoming the odds: High risk children from birth to adulthood.* Cornell University Press. 10.7591/9781501711992

Werner, E. E., & Smith, R. S. (2001). *Journeys from childhood to midlife.* Cornell University Press.

Werner, K., & Gross, J. J. (2009). Emotion regulation and pathology: A conceptual framework. In Gross, J. J. (Ed.), *Handbook of emotion regulation* (pp. 13–37). Guilford Press.

Werner-Seidler, A., Perry, Y., Calear, A. L., Newby, J. M., & Christensen, H.Werner- Seidler. (2017). School- based depression and anxiety prevention programs for young people: A systematic review and meta- analysis. *Clinical Psychology Review*, 51, 30–47. 10.1016/j.cpr.2016.10.00527821267

Whitebread, D., Neale, D., Jensen, H., Hopkins, E., Hirsh-Pasek, K., & Zosh, J. (2017). *The role of play in children's development: a review of the evidence.* Oxford University Press.

White, J. (2005). Howard Gardner: The myth of multiple intelligences. *Viewpoint*, 16, 1–11.

White, M. A. (2016). Why won't it Stick? Positive Psychology and Positive Education. *Psychology of Well-Being*, 6(1), 2. 10.1186/s13612-016-0039-126900547

White, M. A., & Murray, A. S. (Eds.). (2015). *Evidence-Based Approaches in Positive Education: Implementing a Strategic Framework for Well-being in Schools.* Springer Netherlands. 10.1007/978-94-017-9667-5

White, M. A., & Waters, L. E. (2015). A case study of 'The Good School:' Examples of the use of Peterson's strengths-based approach with students. *The Journal of Positive Psychology*, 10(1), 69–76. 10.1080/17439760.2014.92040825431614

WHO. (2014). What is a health promoting school? School and youth health. Retrieved 24 February, 2014, from https://www.who.int/school_youth_health/gshi/hps/en/

Wiedermann, C. J., Barbieri, V., Plagg, B., Marino, P., Piccoliori, G., & Engl, A. (2023). Fortifying the Foundations: A Comprehensive Approach to Enhancing Mental Health Support in Educational Policies Amidst Crises. *Healthcare (Basel)*, 11(10), 1423. 10.3390/healthcare1110142337239709

Wierzbicka, A. (1992). Defining emotion concepts. *Cognitive Science,* 16(4), 539-581.

Wigod, R. (1998). EQ versus IQ: Scientists see value in emotional intelligence. *Psychology in Africa*, 1, 58–61.

Willcutt, E. G., & Pennington, B. F. (2000). Psychiatric comorbidity in children & adolescents with reading disability. *Journal of Child Psychology and Psychiatry, and Allied Disciplines*, 41(8), 1039–1048. 10.1111/1469-7610.0069111099120

Willemse, T. M., Goei, S. L., Boei, F. B., & Erica, J. (2023). School-wide positive behavior interventions and support in Dutch schools for special education. *European Journal of Special Needs Education*, 38(3), 424–439. 10.1080/08856257.2022.2120331

William, N. R., Lindsey, E. W., Kurtz, P. D., & Jarvis, S. (2001). From trauma to resiliency: Lessons from runaway and homeless youth. *Journal of Youth Studies*, 4(2), 233–253. 10.1080/13676260123589

Windle, G., Bennett, K. M., & Noyes, J. (2011). A methodological review of resilience measurement scales. *Health and Quality of Life Outcomes*, 9(8), 1–18. 10.1186/1477-7525-9-821294858

Winner, H. (2018). *How art works*. Oxford University Press. 10.1093/oso/9780190863357.001.0001

Winnicott, D. W. (1971). *Playing and reality*. Tavistock.

Winnicott, D. W. (1988). *Human Nature*. Free Associations Books.

Wittgenstein, L. (1953). *'Preface'. Philosophical Investigations: The German Text, with a Revised English Translation*. Blackwell.

Woltjer, R., Trnka, J., Lundberg, J., & Johansson, B. (2006, September). Role-playing exercises to strengthen the resilience of command and control systems. In *Proceedings of the 13th Eurpoean conference on Cognitive ergonomics: trust and control in complex socio-technical systems* (pp. 71-78). DOI: 10.1145/1274892.1274904

Wong, M. D., Dosanjh, K. K., Jackson, N. J., Rünger, D., & Dudovitz, R. N. (2021). The longitudinal relationship of school climate with adolescent social and emotional health. *BMC Public Health*, 21(207), 1–8. 10.1186/s12889-021-10245-633485308

Wood, A. (2005). The Importance of Principals: Site Administrators' Roles in Novice Teacher Induction. *American Secondary Education*, 33(2), 39–62. https://www.jstor.org/stable/41064612

Wood, W., & Neal, D. T. (2007). A new look at habits and the habit-goal interface. *Psychological Review*, 114(4), 843–863. 10.1037/0033-295X.114.4.84317907866

World Health Organization. (2013). Mental health action plan 2013–2020. https://www.who.int/publications/i/item/9789241506021

World Health Organization. (Ed.). (2008). *World health statistics 2008*. World Health Organization.

Wright, S. (2012). Ways of knowing in the arts. In Wright, S. (Ed.), *Children, Meaningmaking and the Arts* (pp. 1–29). Pearson Australia.

Wubbels, T., Brekelmans, M., Mainhard, T., den Brok, P., & van Tartwijk, J. (2016). Teacher–student relationships and student achievement. In *Handbook of Social Influences in School Contexts*. Routledge.

Wu, G., Feder, A., Cohen, H., Kim, J. J., Calderon, S., Charney, D. S., & Mathe, A. A. (2013). Understanding resilience. *Frontiers in Behavioral Neuroscience*, 7. Advance online publication. 10.3389/fnbeh.2013.0001023422934

Wyn, J., Cahill, H., Holdsworth, R., Rowling, L., & Carson, S. (2000). MindMatters, a whole–school approach promoting mental health and wellbeing. *The Australian and New Zealand Journal of Psychiatry*, 34(4), 594–601. 10.1080/j.1440-1614.2000.00748.x10954390

Xiong, X. (2022). The role of EFL/ESL teachers' psychological empowerment and optimism on their job commitment. *Frontiers in Psychology*, 13, 13. 10.3389/fpsyg.2022.94136135814068

Yang, C., Chan, M. K., Nickerson, A. B., Jenkins, L., Xie, J. S., & Fredrick, S. S. (2022). Teacher victimization and teachers' subjective well-being: Does school climate matter? *Aggressive Behavior*, 48(4), 379–392. 10.1002/ab.2203035383978

Yeager, D. S., & Dweck, C. S. (2012). Mindsets that promote resilience: When students believe that personal characteristics can be developed. *Educational Psychologist*, 47(4), 302–314. 10.1080/00461520.2012.722805

Yeh, C. S. H., & Barrington, R. (2023). Sustainable positive psychology interventions enhance primary teachers' wellbeing and beyond–A qualitative case study in England. *Teaching and Teacher Education*, 125, 104072. 10.1016/j.tate.2023.104072

Yen, J. (2014). Positive Psychology. In *Encyclopedia of Critical Psychology* (pp. 1431–1437). New York: Springer. 10.1007/978-1-4614-5583-7_225

Yeung, R. (1996). The acute effects of exercise on mood state. *Journal of Psychosomatic Research*, 40(2), 123–141. 10.1016/0022-3999(95)00554-48778396

Yogman, M., Garner, A., Hutchinson, J., Hirsh-Pasek, K., Golinkoff, R. M., Baum, R., Gambon, T., Lavin, A., Mattson, G., Wissow, L., Hill, D. L., Ameenuddin, N., Chassiakos, Y. L. R., Cross, C., Boyd, R., Mendelson, R., Moreno, M. A., Radesky, J., Swanson, W. S., & Smith, J. (2018). The power of play: A pediatric role in enhancing development in young children. *Pediatrics*, 142(3), 1–16. 10.1542/peds.2018-205830126932

Young, M. (2007). Bringing Knowledge Back. In *From Social Constructivism to Social Realism in the Sociology of Education* (1st ed.). Routledge., 10.4324/9780203073667

Young, M., & Muller, J. (2010). Three educational scenarios for the future: Lessons from the sociology of knowledge. *European Journal of Education*, 45(1), 11–27. 10.1111/j.1465-3435.2009.01413.x

Zacarian, D., & Silverstone, M. (2020). *Teaching to empower: Taking action to foster student agency, self-confidence, and collaboration.* ASCD.

Zajonc, A. (2006). Love and knowledge: Recovering the heart of teaching through contemplation. *Teachers College Record*, 108(9), 1742–1759. 10.1111/j.1467-9620.2006.00758.x

Zakariya, Y. F. (2020). Effects of school climate and teacher self-efficacy on job satisfaction of mostly STEM teachers: A structural multigroup invariance approach. *International Journal of STEM Education*, 7(10), 1–12. 10.1186/s40594-020-00209-4

Zampetakis, L. A., & Kafetsios, K. (2010). Group entrepreneurial behavior in established organizations: The role of middle managers' emotion regulation and groups' diversity. *Research on Emotion in Organizations*, 6, 33–61. 10.1108/S1746-9791(2010)0000006006

Zarghami, M. (2021). Psychiatric aspects of coronavirus (2019-nCoV) infection. *Iranian Journal of Psychiatry and Behavioral Sciences*, 14(1). Advance online publication. 10.5812/ijpbs.102957

Zhang, L. J., Fathi, J., & Mohammaddokht, F. (2023). Predicting teaching enjoyment from teachers' perceived school climate, self-efficacy, and psychological wellbeing at work: EFL teachers. *Perceptual and Motor Skills*, 130(5), 2269–2299. 10.1177/0031512523118226937395156

Zheng, C., Erickson, A. G., Kingston, N. M., & Noonan, P. M. (2012). Self-determination, self-concept, and academic achievement for students with learning disabilities. *Journal of Learning Disabilities*, 20(10), 1–13.23223201

Žic Ralić, A. (2023). Differences in Emotional Well-Being, Social Inclusion and Academic Self-Concept Between Students With and Without Disabilities in Bosnia and Herzegovina. HSS. https://hss.ruh.ac.lk/ruichss/ruichss2023/

Zimmer-Gembeck, M. J., & Skinner, E. A. (2016). The development of coping: Implications for psychopathology and resilience. In Cicchetti, D. (Ed.), Developmental psychopathology. John Wiley & Sons. 10.1002/9781119125556.devpsy410

Zimmerman, B. J. (2000). Self-efficacy: An essential motive to learn. *Contemporary Educational Psychology*, 25(1), 82–91. 10.1006/ceps.1999.101610620383

Zippert, E. L., Eason, S. H., Marshall, S., & Ramani, G. B. (2019). Preschool children's math exploration during play with peers. *Journal of Applied Developmental Psychology*, 65, 101072. 10.1016/j.appdev.2019.101072

Zosh, Hopkins, Jensen, Liu, Neale, Hirsh-Pasek, Solis, & Whitebread. (2017). *Learning through Play: A Review of the Evidence. Billund: LEGO Foundation.* akcesedukacja.pl/images/dokumenty-pdf/Insight_and_Research/LEGO-Foundation---Learning-through-play---review-of-evidence-2017.pdf.

Zucker, R. A., Wong, M. M., Puttler, L. I., & Fitzgerald, H. E. (2003). Resilience and vulnerability among sons of alcoholics: Relationships to developmental outcomes between early childhood and adolescence. In Luthar, S. S. (Ed.), *Resilience and vulnerability: Adaptation in the context of childhood adversities* (pp. 76–103). Cambridge University Press. 10.1017/CBO9780511615788.006

Zullig, K. J., Koopman, T. M., Patton, J. M., & Ubbes, V. A. (2010). School climate: Historical review, instrument development, and school assessment. *Journal of Psychoeducational Assessment*, 28(2), 139–152. 10.1177/0734282909344205

Zylowska, L., Ackerman, D. L., Yang, M. H., Futrell, J. L., Horton, N. L., Hale, T. S., Pataki, C., & Smalley, S. L. (2008). Mindfulness meditation training in adults and adolescents with ADHD: A feasibility study. *Journal of Attention Disorders*, 11(6), 737–746. 10.1177/108705470730850218025249

Zysberg, L., & Schwabsky, N. (2021). School climate, academic self-efficacy and student achievement. *Educational Psychology*, 41(4), 467–482. 10.1080/01443410.2020.1813690

Ζωγάκη, Ε. (2020). Όψεις του πραγματικού: οι εικαστικές τέχνες και η ματιά του θεατή. Οπτική αντίληψη, αισθητικές θεωρίες και καλλιτεχνικές συμβάσεις. In Αθανασέκου (Ed.), *Γιατί με αφορά η τέχνη*. Ηδυέπεια.

Ντίνου, Β. (2018). Παιχνίδι και καταστασιακή μάθηση σε παιδιά προσχολικής ηλικίας. In Ι. Παπαδάτος & Α. Μπαστέα & Ι. Νικολόπουλος (Ed.), *Εκπαίδευση Χαρισματικών Ατόμων στην Ελλάδα Ιδεολογικές- Πολιτικές- Ψυχολογικές- Παιδαγωγικές Προϋποθέσεις Εκπαίδευσης Χαρισματικών Ατόμων, 8ο Πανελλήνιο Επιστημών Εκπαίδευσης*.

About the Contributors

Louiza Ioannidou has been a Lecturer and member of the Department of Psychology and Social Sciences of Frederick University since 2015. She has also been an accredited School Psychologist since 2009. She has obtained her PhD degree in Psychology (2019), her Master's degree in School Psychology (2009) (duration of 3 years, including 1600 hours of supervised clinical practice), and her BA degree in Psychology (2005) from the University of Cyprus. In the context of continuing education, she has also trained in the field of Cognitive - Behavioural Therapy for children and adults. She has also a diploma in the Treatment and Management of Eating Disorders and Obesity, based on the Cognitive Behavioural model (Master Practitioner in Eating Disorders and Obesity). In addition to the above specializations, she has been awarded certificates in the areas of Positive Psychology, Mindfulness, Solution Focused Therapy, and Business - Team Coaching. Her research interests include bullying, psychopathology, children's mental health and well-being, and the development, implementation, and evaluation of psychoeducational preventive programs to promote children's mental health and resilience, a safe school climate and, parental involvement. Her research findings are published in scientific journals and presented in scientific conferences.

Agathi Argyriadi is a Psychologist with specialization on Cognitive – Behavioral Psychotherapy and Developmental Psychology. Her PhD thesis is entitled "The effects of "Aesthetic flow experiences" in school's environment of first graders. A psycho-educational approach". She also holds a M.Ed. on Special Education. She is a Lecturer in the Department of Education at Frederick University, teaching developmental and cognitive psychology. In the past she has also taught at Cyprus University of Technology (Therapeutic communication), at the East London University (Research Methods and Statistics) and at the Technological Educational Institute of Peloponnese at the department of Speech Pathology (teaching Developmental Psychology and Clinical Neuropsychology), for 3 years. She has acted as a self- employed Psychologist and for a 3-year project against violence at the Ministry of Internal Affairs of the Hellenic Republic. She has also acted for two years, as an external associate at a private school in Greece, with the aim of monitoring and supporting students with learning difficulties, psychological problems and counseling of parents. Agathi Argyriadi was also a professor at the Foundation for Youth and Lifelong Learning and specifically at the Institute for Vocational Training of the Ministry of Education. She has published articles in international journals and she has participated in numerous of training seminars. She is the writer of 10 scientific books in the field of psychology. Her research interests focus on optimizing learning environments using positive psychology and aesthetic theories, developmental psychological issues, special education field, social inclusion issues. She teaches in the Distance Learning Program of Special Education.

* * *

About the Contributors

Alexandros Argyriadis is an Assistant Professor at Frederick University, in the domain of Mental Health and Learning Disabilities. At Frederick University, he coordinates the Distance Learning Master's Program in Community Health Care and the Practicum of the MEd in Special Education. He has authored numerous scholarly books and high impact factor articles; Administratively, he is a member of several committees at Frederick University but also in other international organizations such as the European Union Commission, the Assessors team of the Latvian Ministry of Education Academic Information Center (AIC) / Quality Agency for Higher Education (AIKA), a member of the Electors register of Hellenic Mediterranean University and others. His research interests focus on diversity and inclusion, people with disabilities, special education, health promotion and education and community health.

Effie Efthymiou is an accomplished professional in the field of special education, currently serving as an Assistant Professor at Zayed University in the United Arab Emirates (UAE). With a strong background in special education, her research focuses on inclusive teaching practices, classroom discourse, and creating educational environments that support the inclusion of all students, including those with special needs. Her work centers on understanding the perspectives of various stakeholders, such as teachers and children with special needs, to develop more inclusive educational systems. She explores the role of both physical and psychological environments in shaping attitudes, positioning, and inclusion. Her research aims to identify and overcome barriers to inclusive education, with particular emphasis on leveraging technology-based teaching practices to address digital exclusion and promote inclusive teaching methods. In addition to her research efforts, Dr. Efthymia actively contributes to the advancement of inclusive education through her workshops and seminars conducted for teachers and principals in federal schools within the UAE.

Eirini Karakasidou serves as an Assistant Professor of Counselling Psychology at the Department of Psychology within Panteion University of Social and Political Sciences. With a strong academic background, she completed her postgraduate studies with a specialization in Sport Psychology. Concurrently, she dedicated four years to training in Existential Psychotherapy and an additional two years in mastering Behavioral Therapy for Anxiety Disorders. Her multifaceted research interests encompass Counselling Psychology, Positive Psychology, Sport Psychology, Psychometrics, and Psychotherapy. Eirini has actively contributed as a principal investigator and coordinator in various European funded projects, showcasing her commitment to advancing the field. Eirini Karakasidou is a prolific author, with publications including articles in peer-reviewed journals and insightful book chapters. Her expertise extends beyond academia, as she has delivered numerous presentations and experiential workshops at Greek and international conferences, NGOs, schools, businesses, and hospitals. In addition to her academic pursuits, Eirini practices as a psychologist and psychotherapist in both individual and group settings in private practice. She shares her knowledge and experience by teaching at various educational institutions in Greece and abroad. Furthermore, she serves as a lecturer in specialized seminars tailored for diverse audiences, contributing to the broader dissemination of psychological insights.

Konstantinos Karampas holds a PhD in Counselling-Positive Psychology at the Panteion University. His research interests include studies on psychological resilience, mindsets, and the implementation of Positive Psychology interventions.

Dimitra Katsarou is an Assistant Professor of Developmental Psychopathology and Language Disorders at the Department of Preschool Education Sciences and Educational Design of the University of the Aegean. She has authored, co autored and edited several books and participated in more than 25 chapters so far in other scientific publications. Her research interests focus on the special education and psychological problems of children with intellectual disabilities, neurolinguistics, cognitive processes, autism, developmental psychopathology, speech development, genetic syndromes and intergenerational activities.

Fotini Kyriakides Kranou is a Lecturer in the Department of Psychology and Social Sciences at Frederick University. She completed her Ph.D in Psychology at the University of Cyprus (2014), her Master's Degree in Counseling (2000) and her BA in Psychology (1997) at the University of Louisiana. She is a lecturer at Frederick University Cyprus since 2017 teaching undergraduate courses in the B.A in Psychology program and graduate courses in the Distance program of Masters in Special Education. She has worked at the Cyprus University of Technology as Head of Counseling and Student Development Center (2008-2017), at the University of Cyprus as Head of Counseling (2004-2008) and at the Cyprus Social Welfare Services (2001-2004) in the Family/child protective services as a therapist. She has worked for the Louisiana Correctional Services Department as a therapist in a correctional facility detention center and for the USA Veteran Affairs working with Vietnam veteran soldiers. She has designed and developed the Counseling and Student Development Center of the Cyprus University of Technology with the Student Personal Counseling Center, Student Disability Center, Substance Abuse Information Center and Learning Center. She published a monograph textbook with the title "Psychosocial and Cognitive Development of Undergraduate University Students in Greek Cypriot Universities", a book chapter titled "Counseling Couples and Families in Cyprus" in the book "On Multicultural Counseling" and various articles in international scientific journals. Her research interests focus on mental health counseling and psychotherapy issues and developmental subjects in children and adults. As of 2021 she holds a position in the Board of Directors of the International Association of Psychology and Counseling (IAPC) and is the Chair of IAPC for Greece and Cyprus. She has been appointed as Editor in Chief of the Journal of the International Association of Psychology and Counseling.

Nataly Loizidou Ieridou is an Assistant Professor in the Department of Psychology and Social Sciences at Frederick University where she has been a faculty member since 2006, teaching undergraduate and postgraduate students of the School of Education and Social Sciences. As from February 2024 she is the head of the Department of Psychology and Social Sciences. She completed her Ph.D. in Psychology, at the University of Essex, her Master Degree at the Institute of Education, University of London (Master in Child Development) and her undergraduate studies at the University of Nottingham (BA in Psychology). Her research activity that is published in scientific journals and presented in scientific conferences covers several areas of her scientific domain. Her research interests lie in the areas of developmental and school psychology, specifically in the development of literacy skills and the psychological perspective of special education, as well as factors affecting school life (both academic and socioemotional and the interaction between them).

Olga Lyra is an Assistant Professor at the School of Education and Human Sciences at Frederick University in the field of Special and Inclusive Education. She is the coordinator of the Distance Learning Postgraduate Program of Special Education (Frederick University). She holds a doctorate in Special and Inclusive Education from the University of Cologne (Germany) and a Bachelor degree in Elementary Education from the University of Ioannina (Greece). She has many years of teaching experience in both conventional and distance learning programmes at undergraduate and postgraduate level in the field of Special and Inclusive Education. She has served as an invited assistant professor at the University of Madeira, where she pursued her research interests in the educational and social dimension of inclusion. Her doctoral dissertation focused on the initiation and management of change processes towards inclusive education, where she co-ordinated a two-year research project with a team of educational stakeholders in formal and informal leadership positions. She has numerous years of experience in organizing and coordinating team processes for managing change and professional development in education, as well as writing research proposals both at national (Portugal) and European level (H2020, Erasmus +). Her research interests focus on special and inclusive education, managing diversity in education, changing the way disability is understood and addressed, on self-improvement processes for school units and inclusive school climate, and managing change for inclusive education.

About the Contributors

Anna Papadimitriou is a PhD candidate in the Department of Psychology at Panteion University of Social and Political Sciences in Athens. She holds a Master's degree in Organizational Psychology and Positive Psychology. She is a certified psychotherapist and has been trained in Cognitive Behavioral Therapy, Acceptance and Commitment Therapy and Compassion-Focused Therapy, working with adolescents and adults. Additionally, she has worked as a course instructor in various settings teaching CBT, Positive Psychology and Academic Writing, as supervisor in bachelor and masters' theses, as an adult, child, and adolescent educator in various contexts and as a year tutor. She has participated in European and panhellenic research projects and has publications on positive psychology, counseling, CBT and the three waves of CBT in scientific journals and book chapters.

Dimitrios Sarris is Associate Professor of Special Education and Developmental Disorders at the Pedagogical Department of Kindergarten Teachers of the University of Ioannina, Clinical Psychologist and Director of the Laboratory of Special and Therapeutic Education (LAB.E.SPE.C.).

Maria Sofologi is an Adjunct Ass. Professor at the Department of Early Childhood and Education at the University of Ioannina in Greece. She delivers the courses "Cognitive Psychology", and "Developmental Psychology". She is also a postdoctoral researcher at the University of Ioannina in Greece. She holds a Ph.D. in Cognitive Psychology from the Aristotle University of Thessaloniki. She also holds a Master of Science degree in Cognitive Psychology from the Aristotle University of Thessaloniki. During her master's degree years she trained and practiced different assessment cognitive tools to evaluate all cognitive functions like memory, attention, language, executive functions both in adults and children. She is the key speaker in many European and Hellenic conferences concerning cognitive psychology, educational psychology, special education in children and adults, as well. Her academic work includes a series of many scientific publications, books, and book chapters concerning Cognitive Psychology, Special Education, Educational Psychology, and Cognitive impairments in children and adults as well.

Dimitra Tasiouli is a PhD candidate in the Department of School of Education and Social Sciences at Frederick University in Cyprus in the field of Special and Inclusive Education. As part of her PhD, she attended courses in special and inclusive education. Additionally, she holds a Master's degree in Educational Sciences in the field of development of the child in the social environment from the Hellenic Open University in Greece. During her master's degree years she trained and practiced in schools with special and bilingual students in France (Erasmus +). Her undergraduate studies were at the University of Cyprus in the department of Classics in Faculty of Letters. Moreover, she was an Erasmus student at Université Paris Nanterre in Paris. She has participated in conferences, she has attended a numerous of seminars in general and special education and also she has been awarded certificates in Braille Code and in Greek Sign Language. In addition, she is working as a teacher in secondary education and also as a teaching assistant at Frederick University. Her research interests lie in special and inclusive education, managing diversity in education, inclusive school climate, developmental and school psychology.

Maria Zafiropoulou is Emeritus Professor of Clinical Psychology, Department of Early Childhood Education, School of Humanities and Social Sciences, University of Thessaly.

Index

A

Adaptive Coping Strategies 69, 183
Anxiety 4, 6, 13, 32, 51, 52, 53, 56, 59, 61, 62, 63, 64, 65, 70, 82, 102, 104, 105, 108, 111, 113, 124, 125, 130, 132, 141, 146, 150, 155, 158, 162, 179, 181, 183, 184, 186, 187, 191, 192, 219, 228, 229, 231, 233, 237, 239, 241, 242, 245, 246, 247, 254, 266, 269, 272, 289, 290, 294, 296, 335, 339, 340
Art 95, 167, 227, 276, 285, 286, 287, 288, 289, 290, 291, 292, 293, 294, 295, 296, 297, 298, 299, 300, 301

B

Bernstein 84, 85, 86, 87, 88, 89, 90, 91, 92, 93, 94, 96, 97, 102, 106, 107, 108, 109, 110, 111, 112, 113, 114, 117, 118, 228, 233

C

Constructive Play 302, 303, 304, 305, 306, 307, 308, 309, 310, 311, 313, 314, 315, 316, 317, 318, 319, 320, 321, 322, 324, 325, 328, 330, 331, 334
Creativity 8, 17, 41, 50, 68, 87, 102, 107, 196, 198, 232, 268, 285, 286, 287, 288, 290, 291, 297, 320, 321, 322, 336

D

Developmental Psychology 29, 64, 65, 142, 201, 237, 323, 325, 326

E

Emotional Intelligence 5, 7, 17, 40, 45, 46, 50, 120, 121, 122, 123, 124, 125, 126, 127, 129, 130, 131, 132, 133, 135, 136, 137, 139, 140, 141, 142, 143, 144, 145, 146, 147, 148, 149, 151, 152, 153, 154, 155, 156, 157, 158, 159, 161, 162, 163, 164, 165, 166, 167, 168, 169, 170, 190, 191, 202, 245, 247, 251, 259, 260, 262, 263, 279, 288, 297
Emotional Skills 3, 5, 13, 45, 53, 56, 89, 91, 105, 121, 130, 154, 155, 157, 218, 225, 228, 229
Empathy 13, 17, 18, 98, 105, 106, 124, 127, 128, 129, 131, 132, 133, 134, 144, 152, 154, 156, 157, 158, 159, 213, 222, 254, 297, 305, 317, 334, 339

F

Flourishing 1, 2, 4, 5, 6, 28, 29, 31, 33, 39, 41, 42, 46, 48, 64, 67, 69, 81, 82, 136, 179
Framing 84, 85, 86, 87, 88, 89, 90, 91, 92, 94, 95, 96, 97, 101, 102, 103, 106, 107, 108, 109, 110, 111, 112, 113, 114, 161

H

Hope 5, 8, 9, 18, 19, 30, 39, 41, 42, 50, 66, 67, 68, 70, 71, 72, 74, 75, 76, 77, 78, 83, 221, 276, 279

I

Inclusive Education 85, 88, 90, 92, 93, 96, 98, 99, 109, 110, 112, 114, 117, 166, 173, 174, 177, 178, 179, 189, 193, 194, 196, 198, 199, 200, 203, 205, 206, 207, 208
Intervention Programs 7, 32, 56, 60, 125, 132, 164, 211, 217, 219, 220, 223, 229, 239

J

Job Satisfaction 20, 66, 70, 71, 72, 74, 75, 76, 77, 78, 79, 130, 149, 156, 162, 164, 173, 181, 185, 186, 187, 193, 197, 200, 202, 204, 206, 208, 209

L

Learning Difficulties 70, 166, 223, 224, 230, 265, 269, 270, 271, 272, 273, 280, 295, 332, 333, 335, 336, 337, 338, 339, 341, 344

M

Mental Health 2, 3, 4, 13, 16, 18, 19, 20, 21, 23, 25, 27, 29, 31, 32, 44, 45, 52, 54, 55, 56, 58, 60, 63, 69, 80, 84, 85, 86, 88, 89, 90, 91, 92, 93, 101, 102, 103, 104, 105, 106, 107, 110, 111, 113, 118, 119, 128, 147, 158, 159, 169, 171, 174, 179, 180, 181, 183, 184, 185, 187, 191, 193, 196, 197, 198, 201, 207, 209, 211, 214, 215, 220, 223, 225, 226, 227, 228, 229, 234, 236, 238, 241, 242, 260, 266, 273, 277, 278, 280, 294, 301, 322

Mental Resilience 80, 81, 189, 211, 212, 213, 214, 218, 219, 220, 221, 222, 223, 224, 228, 231, 232, 266, 267, 271, 273, 285, 294, 296

O

Optimism 17, 20, 21, 33, 34, 36, 39, 41, 42, 66, 68, 70, 71, 72, 74, 75, 76, 77, 78, 81, 82, 153, 154, 156, 159, 209, 211, 213, 221, 228, 232, 240, 268

P

Pedagogic Practices 85, 86, 87, 88, 97, 101, 102, 103, 104, 105, 106, 108, 113

Positive Education 4, 5, 6, 7, 8, 21, 22, 23, 28, 29, 30, 35, 36, 38, 39, 40, 44, 45, 46, 47, 54, 55, 57, 58, 59, 61, 62, 63, 64, 65, 81, 199

Positive Psychology 1, 2, 3, 4, 5, 6, 7, 8, 16, 17, 18, 19, 20, 21, 22, 24, 25, 26, 27, 28, 29, 30, 31, 32, 33, 34, 35, 36, 37, 38, 39, 40, 41, 42, 43, 44, 45, 46, 47, 52, 54, 55, 56, 57, 59, 60, 61, 62, 63, 64, 65, 66, 67, 68, 69, 70, 71, 72, 77, 78, 79, 80, 81, 82, 83, 138, 255, 257, 258, 259

Protective Factors 21, 56, 181, 213, 214, 215, 217, 219, 220, 248, 265, 266, 267, 268, 269, 270, 271, 272, 273, 275, 276, 279, 283

Psycho-Emotional Empowerment 171, 174, 188, 189

Psychological Resilience 44, 70, 235, 236, 238, 240, 243, 265, 266, 267, 268, 269, 271, 273

Psychosocial Empowerment 174, 332

Q

Quality Education 112, 171, 177, 178

R

Risk Factors 197, 213, 216, 217, 220, 224, 266, 269, 270, 272, 273

S

school Environment 4, 7, 8, 21, 90, 91, 99, 100, 106, 145, 155, 157, 163, 164, 171, 174, 175, 177, 182, 183, 184, 185, 191, 192, 194, 197, 200, 202, 205, 211, 219, 220, 221, 228, 244, 246, 247, 254, 255, 258, 265, 271, 339

School Interventions 7, 13, 33, 52, 231, 232

Self-Awareness 13, 45, 120, 131, 151, 153, 154, 158, 159, 160, 190, 191, 252, 253, 254, 268

Sociolinguistic Theory 84, 85, 86, 97, 106, 108, 109, 111, 113

Special Education 66, 70, 71, 72, 77, 78, 79, 83, 116, 117, 279, 345

students' well-being 194

Student-Teacher Relationships 10, 12, 48, 66, 75, 76, 77, 139

Symbolic Expression 285, 296, 304, 306

T

Teacher-Student Relationship 72, 120, 121, 123, 124, 126, 127, 128, 129, 130, 131,

133, 136, 137, 186, 211
Teacher Well-Being 16, 28, 174, 196, 204, 253
Therapy 18, 34, 53, 55, 56, 62, 64, 65, 137, 138, 225, 226, 228, 229, 236, 241, 289, 294, 295, 296, 300, 343
Trauma 3, 31, 69, 91, 213, 239, 284, 295

W

Well-Being 1, 2, 4, 5, 6, 7, 9, 10, 12, 13, 16, 18, 19, 20, 21, 27, 28, 29, 30, 31, 34, 35, 36, 38, 39, 41, 42, 43, 44, 45, 46, 47, 48, 50, 51, 52, 55, 56, 57, 58, 59, 61, 62, 63, 64, 65, 66, 67, 69, 70, 71, 72, 77, 78, 80, 82, 84, 85, 86, 88, 89, 90, 91, 92, 93, 101, 102, 103, 104, 105, 106, 107, 110, 111, 112, 113, 121, 123, 124, 125, 126, 127, 129, 130, 132, 135, 138, 142, 154, 156, 161, 164, 171, 173, 174, 175, 176, 177, 179, 180, 181, 182, 183, 184, 185, 187, 188, 189, 191, 192, 193, 194, 195, 196, 199, 200, 201, 202, 204, 205, 207, 208, 210, 213, 214, 218, 219, 228, 230, 233, 240, 243, 244, 245, 247, 253, 260, 262, 263, 265, 268, 271, 279, 298, 301, 317, 340
Whole School Approach 32, 211, 221, 228, 236

IGI Global
Publishing Tomorrow's Research Today
www.igi-global.com

Publishing Tomorrow's Research Today

Uncover Current Insights and Future Trends in

Education

with IGI Global's Cutting-Edge Recommended Books

Print Only, E-Book Only, or Print + E-Book.

Order direct through IGI Global's Online Bookstore at **www.igi-global.com** or through your preferred provider.

ISBN: 9781668493007
© 2023; 234 pp.
List Price: US$ **215**

ISBN: 9798369300749
© 2024; 383 pp.
List Price: US$ **230**

ISBN: 9781668486467
© 2023; 471 pp.
List Price: US$ **215**

ISBN: 9781668465387
© 2024; 389 pp.
List Price: US$ **215**

ISBN: 9781668475836
© 2024; 359 pp.
List Price: US$ **215**

ISBN: 9781668444238
© 2023; 334 pp.
List Price: US$ **240**

Do you want to stay current on the latest research trends, product announcements, news, and special offers?
Join IGI Global's mailing list to receive customized recommendations, exclusive discounts, and more.
Sign up at: www.igi-global.com/newsletters.

Scan the QR Code here to view more related titles in Education.

www.igi-global.com | Sign up at www.igi-global.com/newsletters | facebook.com/igiglobal | twitter.com/igiglobal | linkedin.com/igiglobal

Ensure Quality Research is Introduced to the Academic Community

Become a Reviewer for IGI Global Authored Book Projects

The overall success of an authored book project is dependent on quality and timely manuscript evaluations.

Applications and Inquiries may be sent to:
development@igi-global.com

Applicants must have a doctorate (or equivalent degree) as well as publishing, research, and reviewing experience. Authored Book Evaluators are appointed for one-year terms and are expected to complete at least three evaluations per term. Upon successful completion of this term, evaluators can be considered for an additional term.

If you have a colleague that may be interested in this opportunity, we encourage you to share this information with them.

IGI Global
Publishing Tomorrow's Research Today
www.igi-global.com

IGI Global Open Access Journal Program

Publishing Tomorrow's Research Today

IGI Global's Open Access Journal Program

Including Nearly 200 Peer-Reviewed, Gold (Full) Open Access Journals across IGI Global's Three Academic Subject Areas: Business & Management; Scientific, Technical, and Medical (STM); and Education

Consider Submitting Your Manuscript to One of These Nearly 200 Open Access Journals for to Increase Their Discoverability & Citation Impact

Web of Science Impact Factor 6.5 — Journal of Organizational and End User Computing

Web of Science Impact Factor 4.7 — Journal of Global Information Management

Web of Science Impact Factor 3.2 — International Journal on Semantic Web and Information Systems

Web of Science Impact Factor 2.6 — Journal of Database Management

Choosing IGI Global's Open Access Journal Program Can Greatly Increase the Reach of Your Research

Higher Usage
Open access papers are 2-3 times more likely to be read than non-open access papers.

Higher Download Rates
Open access papers benefit from 89% higher download rates than non-open access papers.

Higher Citation Rates
Open access papers are 47% more likely to be cited than non-open access papers.

Submitting an article to a journal offers an invaluable opportunity for you to share your work with the broader academic community, fostering knowledge dissemination and constructive feedback.

Submit an Article and Browse the IGI Global Call for Papers Pages

We can work with you to find the journal most well-suited for your next research manuscript.
For open access publishing support, contact: journaleditor@igi-global.com

Publishing Tomorrow's Research Today

IGI Global

e-Book Collection

Including Essential Reference Books Within Three Fundamental Academic Areas

Business & Management
Scientific, Technical, & Medical (STM)
Education

- Acquisition options include Perpetual, Subscription, and Read & Publish
- No Additional Charge for Multi-User Licensing
- No Maintenance, Hosting, or Archiving Fees
- Continually Enhanced Accessibility Compliance Features (WCAG)

Over **150,000+** Chapters	Contributions From **200,000+** Scholars Worldwide	More Than **1,000,000+** Citations	Majority of e-Books Indexed in Web of Science & Scopus	Consists of Tomorrow's Research Available Today!

Recommended Titles from our e-Book Collection

Innovation Capabilities and Entrepreneurial Opportunities of Smart Working
ISBN: 9781799887973

Advanced Applications of Generative AI and Natural Language Processing Models
ISBN: 9798369305027

Using Influencer Marketing as a Digital Business Strategy
ISBN: 9798369305515

Human-Centered Approaches in Industry 5.0
ISBN: 9798369326473

Modeling and Monitoring Extreme Hydrometeorological Events
ISBN: 9781668487716

Data-Driven Intelligent Business Sustainability
ISBN: 9798369300497

Information Logistics for Organizational Empowerment and Effective Supply Chain Management
ISBN: 9798369301593

Data Envelopment Analysis (DEA) Methods for Maximizing Efficiency
ISBN: 9798369302552

Request More Information, or Recommend the IGI Global e-Book Collection to Your Institution's Librarian

For More Information or to Request a Free Trial, Contact IGI Global's e-Collections Team: eresources@igi-global.com | 1-866-342-6657 ext. 100 | 717-533-8845 ext. 100

Are You Ready to Publish Your Research?

IGI Global
Publishing Tomorrow's Research Today

IGI Global offers book authorship and editorship opportunities across three major subject areas, including Business, STM, and Education.

Benefits of Publishing with IGI Global:

- Free one-on-one editorial and promotional support.
- Expedited publishing timelines that can take your book from start to finish in less than one (1) year.
- Choose from a variety of formats, including Edited and Authored References, Handbooks of Research, Encyclopedias, and Research Insights.
- Utilize IGI Global's eEditorial Discovery® submission system in support of conducting the submission and double-blind peer review process.
- IGI Global maintains a strict adherence to ethical practices due in part to our full membership with the Committee on Publication Ethics (COPE).
- Indexing potential in prestigious indices such as Scopus®, Web of Science™, PsycINFO®, and ERIC – Education Resources Information Center.
- Ability to connect your ORCID iD to your IGI Global publications.
- Earn honorariums and royalties on your full book publications as well as complimentary content and exclusive discounts.

Join Your Colleagues from Prestigious Institutions, Including:

Australian National University

Massachusetts Institute of Technology

Johns Hopkins University

Harvard University

Tsinghua University

Columbia University in the City of New York

Learn More at: www.igi-global.com/publish

or by Contacting the Acquisitions Department at: acquisition@igi-global.com

www.ingramcontent.com/pod-product-compliance
Lightning Source LLC
LaVergne TN
LVHW080610300926
849162LV00005B/1107
* 9 7 9 8 3 6 9 3 8 3 1 2 4 *